tulsa
LIBRARY TRUST

BY LYNNE OLSON

Empress of the Nile:
The Daredevil Archaeologist Who Saved Egypt's Ancient Temples from Destruction

Madame Fourcade's Secret War:
The Daring Young Woman Who Led France's Largest Spy Network Against Hitler

Last Hope Island:
Britain, Occupied Europe, and the Brotherhood That Helped Turn the Tide of War

Those Angry Days:
Roosevelt, Lindbergh, and America's Fight over World War II, 1939–1941

Citizens of London:
The Americans Who Stood with Britain in Its Darkest, Finest Hour

Troublesome Young Men:
The Rebels Who Brought Churchill to Power and Helped Save England

A Question of Honor:
The Kosciuszko Squadron; Forgotten Heroes of World War II (with Stanley Cloud)

Freedom's Daughters:
The Unsung Heroines of the Civil Rights Movement from 1830 to 1970

The Murrow Boys:
Pioneers on the Front Lines of Broadcast Journalism (with Stanley Cloud)

EMPRESS OF THE NILE

EMPRESS OF THE NILE

THE DAREDEVIL ARCHAEOLOGIST WHO SAVED EGYPT'S ANCIENT TEMPLES FROM DESTRUCTION

LYNNE OLSON

RANDOM HOUSE • NEW YORK

Published in the United States by Random House,
an imprint and division of Penguin Random House LLC, New York.

RANDOM HOUSE and the HOUSE colophon are registered
trademarks of Penguin Random House LLC.

Photo credits and permissions begin on page 407.

LIBRARY OF CONGRESS CATALOGING-IN-PUBLICATION DATA
Names: Olson, Lynne, author.
Title: Empress of the Nile : the daredevil archaeologist who saved
Egypt's ancient temples from destruction / Lynne Olson.
Description: New York : Random House, [2022] |
Includes bibliographical references and index.
Identifiers: LCCN 2022012856 (print) | LCCN 2022012857 (ebook) |
ISBN 9780525509479 (hardcover) | ISBN 9780525509493 (ebook)
Subjects: LCSH: Desroches-Noblecourt, Christiane, 1913–2011. | Egyptologists—
France—Biography. | Egypt—Antiquities.
Classification: LCC PJ1064.D47 O47 2022 (print) | LCC PJ1064.D47 (ebook) |
DDC 932/.0090909--dc23/eng/20221019
LC record available at https://lccn.loc.gov/2022012856
LC ebook record available at https://lccn.loc.gov/2022012857

Printed in the United States of America on acid-free paper

randomhousebooks.com

2 4 6 8 9 7 5 3 1

FIRST EDITION

Book design by Barbara M. Bachman

For Stan and Carly,
as always

CONTENTS

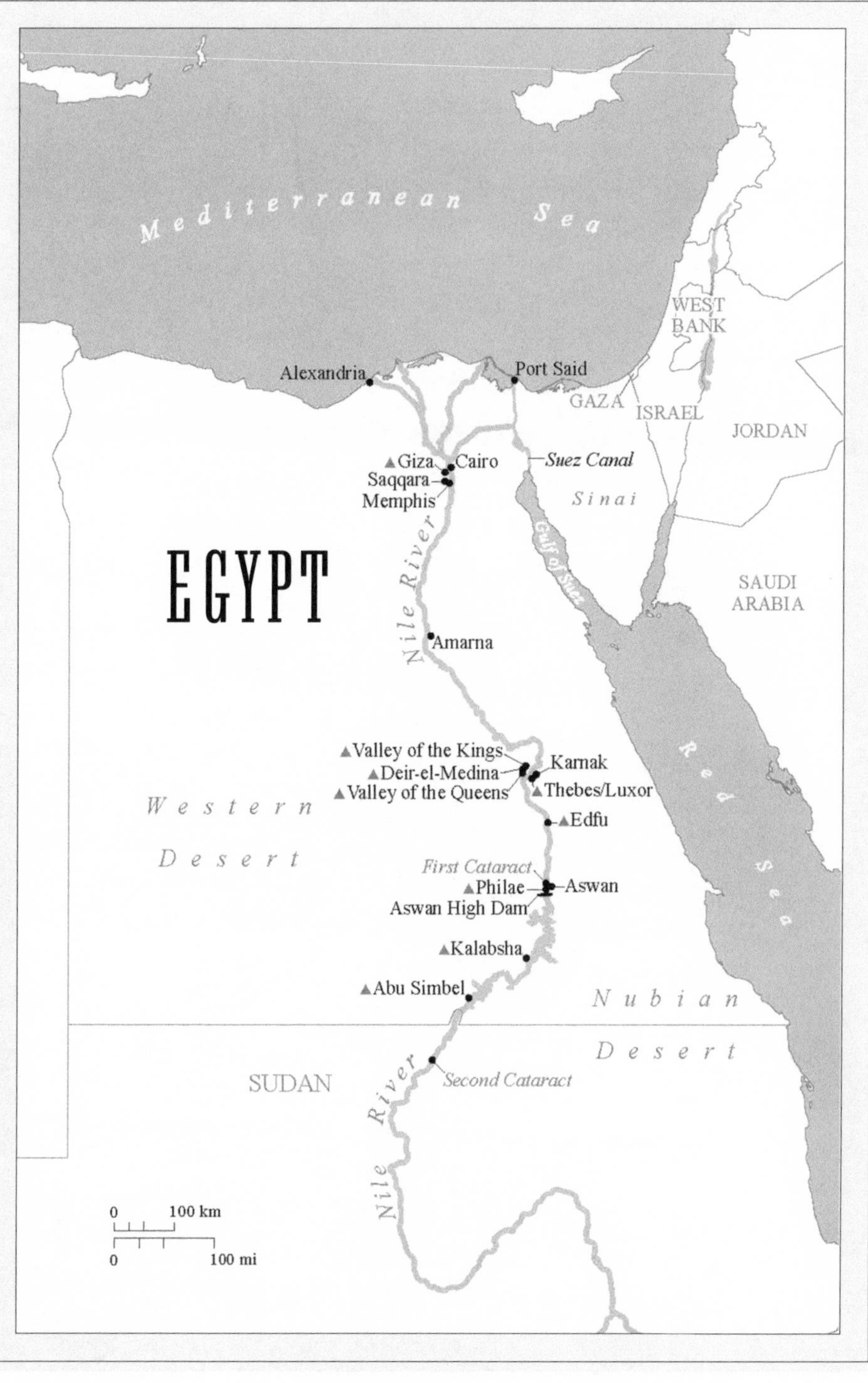

Mediterranean Sea
WEST BANK
Alexandria
Port Said
GAZA
ISRAEL
JORDAN
Giza
Cairo
Suez Canal
Saqqara
Memphis
Sinai
Gulf of Suez
EGYPT
SAUDI ARABIA
Nile River
Amarna
Valley of the Kings
Karnak
Deir-el-Medina
Valley of the Queens
Thebes/Luxor
Red Sea
Western Desert
Edfu
First Cataract
Philae
Aswan
Aswan High Dam
Kalabsha
Abu Simbel
Nubian Desert
SUDAN
Second Cataract
Nile River
0
100 km
0
100 mi

INTRODUCTION

THE TRAIN HAD JUST PULLED INTO THE STATION AT MOULINS, A town in central France, when a German in a black SS uniform burst into the compartment in which Christiane Desroches was sitting and demanded to see her papers. Her German-issued identity card, which named her as the Louvre's acting curator of Egyptian antiquities, was in perfect order, but the SS man thought otherwise. He stared at it, then at her, and shouted, "Get off!" Pulling the twenty-seven-year-old Desroches to her feet, he hustled her off the train.

It was December 12, 1940—a freezing cold day. Desroches spent the next several hours huddled in an icy cell at the Gestapo headquarters in Moulins. At last she was escorted to a large room containing several Germans in SS uniforms, who were leaning back in their chairs, their boots on a desk, smoking cigars.

One of them asked her in French if she spoke German. Although she did, she replied, "Not only do I not speak it, I don't understand a word of it." Right from the start of this interrogation, "I was not willing to be amiable," she later said. The men began peppering her with a volley of questions, to which she responded, "Why do you want to know this?" One of her interrogators snapped, "You weren't asked for your opinion," and she snapped back, "Tell me first why I am here." He snarled, "If you don't know, you'll find out soon enough."

The Germans refused to believe her claim of being an Egyptologist; to them, she was a spy for the Allies. In reality, she was both. But she kept pushing back against their allegations, insisting that they go through the address book they had just confiscated and call her contacts in Paris to prove that, despite her youth, she was indeed one of the Louvre's curators and blameless of the charges they were lodging against her.

As the questioning proceeded, Desroches's temper grew shorter and shorter. She'd already had plenty of experience dealing with arrogant men like these. In the macho, rough-and-tumble world of French archaeology, women were an extreme rarity, and she'd been shunned and harassed since her earliest days in the field.

"I had encountered a certain amount of misogyny at the Louvre," she recalled, "but nothing like at the French Institute of Oriental Archaeology"—France's elite Cairo-based research center for the study of ancient Egypt. When she was named its first female fellow in 1938, her male colleagues rose up in revolt, refusing to "share the library or even the dining room with me. They said I would collapse and die in the field."

But neither that revolt nor the myriad other acts of discrimination she faced in her career were enough to stop Desroches from establishing herself as one of the world's foremost experts on ancient Egypt. She was well along that path at the time of her arrest by the Gestapo, and, even at a moment when her life was clearly in danger, the young archaeologist, who stood just five feet tall, could not abide the idea of men refusing to take her seriously.

At one point, she scolded her interrogators for their bad manners: "I can't believe how poorly you were raised. Is this any way to receive a woman, with your feet on the table?" For a moment, they were speechless. "Then they tried to silence me," she remembered, "but I kept going. I couldn't stop cursing at them, and they ended up sending me back to my cell. Unbelievably, the next day, they summoned me again, to tell me that for the time being I was free. They kept my address book and said I'd hear from them soon."

As the Gestapo had learned, Desroches refused to be intimidated by anyone. A willful real-life female version of Indiana Jones, she told an interviewer many years after the war, "You don't get anywhere without a fight, you know. I never looked for the fight. If I became a brawler, it was out of necessity."

WHEN CHRISTIANE DESROCHES WAS little more than a toddler, her paternal grandfather had hoisted her on his shoulders and taken her to see the Obelisk of Luxor, the pink granite monolith that looms over the vast Place de la Concorde in Paris. At that moment, her lifelong love affair with ancient Egypt began.

In later visits to the obelisk, her grandfather told her a bit about its history. It was more than three thousand years old, he said—created during the reign of Rameses II, one of Egypt's most powerful pharaohs, to stand guard outside a temple in the royal city of Thebes (now Luxor). In 1833, Egypt's viceroy had presented it to the king of France to mark France's close attachment to Egypt and its fabled ancient history—an association dating back to a military expedition led by Napoleon Bonaparte in 1798.

The primary purpose of Napoleon's mission had been to annex Egypt to France, establishing his country as the dominant military power in the Mediterranean and in the process undermining the interests of its archrival, Britain. But several dozen members of Napoleon's party had embarked on a very different quest. Experts in various fields, they included artists, engineers, linguists, cartographers, historians, mineralogists, botanists, and other scholars—all there to study Egypt and its people, both past and present.

The military campaign was an almost immediate disaster: One month after the French arrived in Egypt, the British fleet, under the command of Admiral Horatio Nelson, defeated the French navy at the Battle of the Nile. The scholarly expedition, however, proved to be a success beyond anyone's imagination. Its greatest triumph was to introduce France and the rest of the West to a complex, vibrant civilization that predated both the Romans and Greeks.

After their return to France, the scholars wrote more than a dozen

OBELISK OF LUXOR,
PLACE DE LA CONCORDE, PARIS

books overflowing with engravings of the pyramids, obelisks, temples, sphinxes, colossal statues, and a multitude of other antiquities they had encountered during their stay in Egypt. In doing so, they revealed an exotic, mysterious land rarely before glimpsed by the outside world.

The oldest nation-state in history, Egypt had been welded into a single country more than 3,200 years before the birth of Christ. Despite extended periods of internal strife and foreign attacks, it remained under the rule of a series of pharaohs, encompassing thirty-two dynasties, until its conquest by the Romans in 30 B.C.

The Egyptians' invention of the concept of a unified nation, whose population shared a common identity, was remarkable not only for its impact on the world but also for its longevity. "The pharaonic state as originally conceived lasted for three millennia," the Cambridge Egyptologist Toby Wilkinson observed. "By comparison, Rome barely managed one millennium, while western culture has yet to survive two."

As a child, Christiane Desroches had no interest in the arcane details of the history of ancient Egypt—or, for that matter, of the Obelisk of Luxor. What fascinated her were the mysterious hieroglyphs engraved on the obelisk's four sides, particularly the representations of birds and animals. "Those images spoke to me," she said decades later. So did the Egyptian antiquities on display at the Louvre, also one of her favorite childhood haunts. There, she studied brightly colored papyrus scrolls of Egyptians working in the fields—"these funny men with their faces and feet in profile."

The sticklike figures were strange-looking, to be sure, yet the scenes seemed familiar to her. Every summer, she and her older brother spent several weeks with a great-uncle and -aunt who lived in the countryside near Grenoble, in the French Alps. The two spent much of their time playing with the children of local peasants and learning how to milk cows and harvest wheat and grapes. To her, the Egyptian laborers depicted in the scrolls resembled the workers with whom she happily spent her summer days.

During their visits to the museum, Christiane's grandfather tried to interest her in the *Venus de Milo* and other Greek and Roman antiquities, but to no avail. "Look at her eyes," she would later say of the famed marble statue. "They are empty, totally empty." To her, the Greek and Roman artifacts were cold and lifeless, with no personality at all. Not so Egyptian antiquities like the famous *Seated Scribe,* a painted limestone figure chiseled more than 2,500 years before the *Venus de Milo* but which seemed to Desroches to resemble a living, breathing human being. "Every time I walk past him in the Louvre, his gaze petrifies me, after all these years," she said late in her life. "There is, in that one look, a whole civilization expressing itself. . . . The Egyptians had guts and a heart. You could see it in everything."

Because of the abundance of pyramids, funerary temples, and tombs that dot Egypt's landscape, most people today think of the ancient

THE *SEATED SCRIBE*, CREATED IN ROUGHLY 2500 B.C. AND CURRENTLY IN THE LOUVRE IN PARIS

Egyptians as being interested only in death. In reality, they were a convivial, tolerant, generous people who greatly relished life—so much so that they did everything they could to ensure that the pleasures they enjoyed in what they considered their first phase of existence would be available to them in the next. Death was not regarded as a finality but rather an obstacle to be overcome. As one American archaeologist put it, the Egyptians believed that "their paradise would be like the Nile Valley."

When one visits Egypt's temples and other antiquities today, these relics of the past seem bleached-out, ghostly, and austere. But when they were built, their columns, colossal statues, and wall paintings were painted in brilliant hues of red, blue, green, and orange—an explosion of color that dazzled the eye. Just as breathtaking were the glittering tops of obelisks, which were sheathed in gold.

During the Eighteenth and Nineteenth dynasties, which lasted from roughly 1550 B.C. to 1190 B.C., the use of gold was particularly ubiquitous—in jewelry, ceremonial weapons, statues of gods and goddesses, funerary masks, coffins, and countless other items related to the activities of both life and death. The high-water mark of ancient Egypt's wealth and influence, this period was truly the country's golden age. It was then that the nation emerged as a great imperial power, acquiring territory that stretched for more than two thousand miles and included parts of what are now Sudan, Lebanon, Syria, and Israel, as well as the island of Cyprus.

Among the pharaohs of the time were several of the country's most celebrated rulers. They included Thutmose III, Egypt's greatest warrior king; the heretic Akhenaten, who tried to end the nation's worship of its many gods; and Rameses II, the flamboyant, long-lived monarch who built more monuments to himself than any other pharaoh. But in 1922, the fame of these titans was eclipsed—and remains overshadowed to this day—by the finding of the tomb of King Tutankhamun, an obscure pharaoh of the period who did nothing of note during his short reign and who died before he was out of his teens.

What prompted the deluge of international attention was not Tutankhamun himself but the fact that his burial place, unlike those of his predecessors, had not been plundered. The greatest archaeological feat of the twentieth century, the discovery by the English explorer Howard Carter and his patron, Lord Carnarvon, yielded a vast cornucopia of treasures from the burial chamber, including the solid gold coffin containing Tutankhamun's linen-wrapped mummified body and the gold mask covering his face. There was also a myriad of life-size statues, along with gilded chariots, large model boats, a gold throne, paintings, clothing, and exquisite jewelry—more than five thousand objects in all. It took Carter and his team more than five years to record, conserve, and clear the tomb of all its artifacts.

Like countless other people around the world, nine-year-old Christiane Desroches was mesmerized by news of the find. Over the next several years, she devoured the frequent stories and photos about Tutankhamun's treasures that appeared in *L'Illustration*, an early French pictorial magazine. At one point, she made crepe paper replicas of the robes worn by Egyptian women depicted on some of the Tutankhamun artifacts, for her friends to wear at Mardi Gras.

"For me it was like a fairy tale," she recalled. "At the time no one understood why this pharaoh was buried with all these beautiful objects. We were talking about the treasures without trying to go further. But I was asking myself a lot of questions, trying to figure out the reason for them."

Desroches's quest to know more about the boy king's riches would lead to a lifetime of work to unlock the secrets of ancient Egypt. In the 1950s and 1960s, her passion for the country, both past and present, would culminate in a crusade to save some of its most priceless antiquities. Initially derided as quixotic and hopelessly delusional, that effort would end up producing the greatest single example of international cultural cooperation the world has ever known.

Through it all, Christiane Desroches's behavior, like her response to the Gestapo, resembled nothing so much as that of a female action hero come to life. A woman who swaggered. A woman who talked and fought back. A woman who owned her power.

EMPRESS OF THE NILE

CHAPTER I

A CHILDHOOD PASSION

CHRISTIANE'S EARLY FASCINATION WITH ANCIENT EGYPT WAS an unusual preoccupation for a little girl from the French upper middle class, which tended to have fairly rigid, conservative ideas about girls' proper interests and behavior. But her parents had no desire to limit her horizons or encourage her to conform to the prevalent view in French society that women's roles should be restricted to those of wife and mother.

That opinion was particularly strong in the aftermath of World War I, when Christiane was growing up. With more than 1.3 million of France's young men killed in the war, the country's birthrate had dropped dramatically. As a result, young women faced considerable pressure to marry and have children as soon as possible; contraception was illegal, and refusing motherhood was considered an unpatriotic act.

Christiane's father, Louis, paid no attention to such ideas. He was unusual in other ways as well. A literature major in college, he was a lawyer by profession, but his true passions lay outside his work. He was a talented violinist, and Christiane recalled frequent impromptu evening duets in which he played the violin and her mother, Madeleine, who had an operatic voice, sang arias. On Sunday mornings in winter, her father would often lock himself in his office at home and study sheet music. When Christiane asked him what he was doing, he replied,

"I am listening to an opera." Indeed, she added, he could read the notes on paper and hear the music in his head, an ability that left her awestruck.

Somewhat surprisingly for someone of his social class, he was also a staunch man of the left, a lifelong advocate of individual freedom, tolerance, social equality, and economic justice. Madeleine Desroches, meanwhile, was one of the rare Frenchwomen of that time to have graduated from college, collecting a classics degree. Although she never worked outside the home, she was a powerful role model for her daughter—"living proof," as Christiane said, "that a woman, no less than a man, could have access to the world of knowledge." Her father, "already a feminist," supported that principle as much for his daughter as he had for his wife.

"My parents were humanists," Desroches later told an interviewer. "They taught me humanist values such as respect for one another, for your neighbors, for people in general, respect for civilization. My brother and I grew up in an environment very open to culture, music, and foreign languages." For both Desroches children, curiosity about the world outside France was highly encouraged.

Unlike many of their more insular compatriots, Louis and Madeleine Desroches had an eclectic group of friends, some of them intellectuals, who came from a wide variety of countries and cultures. Once, Desroches remembered, her father told her that "we were considered to be strange people because we received strangers." She added, "Believe me, there were very few Parisians at that time who felt the same way." Among the Desroches family's closest friends were Sir Norman Angell, the Nobel Prize–winning British economist, and his family. The two families often spent several weeks together in the summer.

From her earliest days, the petite, dark-haired Christiane was talkative, opinionated, curious, and self-confident—all qualities that her parents encouraged. From the time they were small, she and her older brother were included in mealtime conversations about a wide variety of subjects, from current events in France and the rest of the world to literature and music. "It was a sacred ritual," she remembered. "My parents were constantly bringing up subjects that would open our minds, and they wanted us to talk about them." Baptized as Catholics, the Desroches siblings went to catechism classes, but their father encouraged them to maintain a certain skepticism about what they were taught, instructing them not to take literally everything they were told.

CHRISTIANE'S QUESTIONING ATTITUDE AND budding determination to think for herself were reinforced at the Lycée Molière, the public high school for girls she attended not far from her home in Paris's affluent 16th arrondissement. In France, girls were not allowed to study at public high schools until 1880; even then the sexes were segregated. The Lycée Molière, which was established in 1888, was only the third girls' high school to open in Paris.

The idea of public secondary schools for girls touched off a fierce controversy in France when it was first introduced. For some, the thought of girls focusing on their studies rather than on their domestic future was shocking. In the case of the Lycée Molière, the decision to name the school after the famed seventeenth-century playwright was considered even more of a scandal. Some critics on the right pointed out that Molière's sophisticated satirical comedies contained more than their fair share of racy dialogue, not considered fit for the ears of innocent young women. Naysayers on the left noted that Molière was hardly an advocate of education as a tool for the advancement of women. His plays, like *Les Femmes Savantes* (*Learned Ladies*), made savage fun of women who flaunted their learning. Education, in his view, had its place but should never be allowed to interfere with a woman's natural destiny as a wife and mother.

As it happened, the Lycée Molière did indeed prove to be a seedbed for women's emancipation. It was, one student said, "a nursery for our aspirations. Our teachers encouraged us not to stop our intellectual activity after we graduated but instead to continue our studies."

After leaving the lycée, a number of its graduates received university degrees and went on to become trailblazers in a variety of previously all-male professions. Among them was Jeanne Debat-Ponsan, who after acquiring her medical degree became, in 1906, one of the first women doctors in France. Another was Louise Weiss, who graduated from Oxford in 1914 and later became the founder and editor of a noted French political review, *L'Europe Nouvelle.*

In 1930, the lycée produced two particularly stellar graduates. One was Christiane Desroches. The other was Jacqueline David, who as Jacqueline de Romilly (her married name) became one of France's leading scholars of Greek culture and language. Like Desroches with ancient Egypt, de Romilly "embraced the culture of ancient Athens with an almost romantic fervor," *The New York Times* wrote. She was only the second woman to be elected to the Académie Française, the elite group of political and scholarly figures charged with maintaining high standards of literary taste in the country.

Six years after Desroches and David graduated from the lycée, another woman scholar, who would become internationally known herself, was hired there as a philosophy teacher. But Simone de Beauvoir lasted only three years. While the school considered itself broad-minded, its tolerance did not extend to a teacher's having an affair with a student—or in this case, students. Beauvoir was fired for seducing at least three of them.

IN THE DESROCHES HOUSEHOLD, it was a given that Christiane would go to college; the only question was what she would study. At that point, neither she nor her parents entertained the idea of turning her obsession with ancient Egypt into an academic pursuit. "At the time, we never considered a career for me as an Egyptologist," she said. "It was considered a fad, a madness, not a profession."

Shortly before she graduated from the lycée, her father encouraged her to think about studying art history, perhaps focusing on sixteenth-century French drawings. She could combine studies at the Sorbonne, he said, with classes at the École du Louvre, a small institution of higher learning located on the museum grounds that specialized in art history. The idea of sixteenth-century drawings, however, "bored me stiff," she recalled. So Louis Desroches made an appointment with Henri Verne—who, as the director of France's national museums, was in charge of the Louvre—to explore what other avenues his bright, lively sixteen-year-old daughter might follow in her studies.

In retrospect, it might seem a little surprising that the head of the Louvre would have the time or interest to offer advice to Desroches about Christiane's educational future. He was, after all, the chief of one of the most august public institutions in France, which also happened to be the oldest, largest, and most highly regarded public museum in the world.

At the center of Paris, both literally and figuratively, the Louvre had long been considered an emblem of the power and majesty of France. Dating back to the fifteenth century, it first served as a fortress, then was rebuilt as a royal palace, and finally became a museum, opening in 1793. Housed in a magnificent baroque complex shaped like a horseshoe, it was overwhelming in every way. One of the largest man-made structures in the world, it stretched nearly half a mile from end to end and housed nearly two hundred thousand objects from fifty centuries and two hundred generations of human culture. Its collection of European paintings, with works by Leonardo da Vinci, Rembrandt, Michelangelo, Titian, Vermeer, and countless other masters, was widely considered the finest in the world.

The grandeur of the Louvre's honey-colored stone was matched by the impressiveness of its interior, featuring marble and parquet floors, richly ornamented Corinthian columns and pilasters, soaring barrel-vaulted ceilings, and majestic stairways. La Grande Galerie, an immense corridor that displayed some of the Louvre's greatest masterpieces, was more than a quarter of a mile long, thirty feet high, and one hundred feet wide.

As the man who presided over the Louvre, Henri Verne was the steward of all this splendor. But he also wore another hat—that of the head of the École du Louvre. In that role, he often met with prospective students and their parents to discuss possible courses of study. During his session with Louis Desroches, Verne discussed the various areas of art history in which the school specialized, none of which involved ancient Egypt. Nonetheless, in a casual aside just before he left, Christiane's father mentioned her "very strong taste for Egypt." Un-

THE LOUVRE MUSEUM, C. 1900

fortunately, despite the Louvre's dominance in Egyptology, its school did not have a full-fledged curriculum in the subject, Verne said. But it did offer a class in Egyptian archaeology, as well as a course in deciphering hieroglyphs. Verne suggested that Christiane come see him the following day to discuss her options.

When she did, he "listed all the possibilities that were open to me: the general history of art and the study of painting, sculpture, and other works of art from various periods, but none of the ones he mentioned were before the Middle Ages," she recalled.

"What about before then?" she asked. "Well, there's Greece and Rome," Verne responded.

"And even before that?" she asked, to which Verne replied, "Mesopotamia."

"Wasn't Egypt even before that?" she pressed. At that, he surrendered, describing in detail the class in Egyptian archaeology, taught by the head curator of the museum's Egyptian artifacts department, and the course in hieroglyphics, whose instructor, he said, was "a very interesting abbot, Father Drioton."

Christiane immediately signed up for three classes: general art history, archaeology, and—in what would turn out to be her most consequential choice of all—hieroglyphics. Her subsequent encounter with the "very interesting" Étienne Drioton would end up changing her life.

CHAPTER 2

COMING OF AGE AT THE LOUVRE

WHEN SEVENTEEN-YEAR-OLD CHRISTIANE DESROCHES STARTED her classes at the École du Louvre, she quickly learned how important the museum had been in the creation and development of modern archaeology and the study of ancient Egypt. The Louvre's Egyptian artifacts were—and are—considered one of its most prized collections. Among the largest and most diverse in the world, the collection boasts masterpieces from every period of ancient Egyptian history. Jean-François Champollion, the scholar who at thirty-one years old first decoded Egyptian hieroglyphs, was the Louvre's initial curator of Egyptian art; the artifacts he helped amass formed the nucleus of its collection.

But what's left unmentioned by the Louvre, as well as by the British Museum and other prominent repositories of Egyptian antiquities in the West, is the cutthroat way in which many if not most of those treasures ended up in their collections. The nineteenth and early twentieth centuries—the heyday of such acquisitions—were a buccaneering era, marked by fierce and bitter competition between the French and collectors from other countries, especially Britain.

Not coincidentally, the French and British were the largest and most active colonial powers during that period. Their no-holds-barred struggles to acquire such artifacts as mummies, sarcophagi, and papyrus scrolls—which on occasion involved bribery, fistfights, and gun battles—reflected the larger rivalry between the two nations for power and influence in Egypt and the rest of the Middle East. "From its very inception," noted the Cambridge historian Toby Wilkinson, "Egyptology was . . . the handmaid of imperialism."

The Anglo-French rivalry for Egyptian antiquities dated back to Napoleon's ill-fated expedition. When the British navy defeated the French at the Battle of the Nile, the result was not only a military humiliation for France but also the loss of all the Egyptian artifacts collected by the French scholars accompanying Napoleon during their lengthy stay there. Included in those spoils of war was the now famed Rosetta Stone (named for the town near which it was discovered), a massive slab of black granite bearing a lengthy inscription in ancient Egyptian and Greek. A French officer had found the slab embedded in the walls of a fortress, and it was being stored in an Alexandria warehouse awaiting shipment to the Louvre when the British nabbed it. It ended up at the British Museum in London—one of the first Egyptian artifacts claimed by the museum and the prized centerpiece of its growing collection.

Two decades later, however, the French were able to get a bit of their own back by using the Rosetta Stone as a tool to unlock one of ancient Egypt's greatest mysteries: its language. From the time the British acquired the stone, lithographic copies of the inscriptions on it had been circulating in European academic circles. In 1822, the young French linguist and philologist Jean-François Champollion rushed into his brother's office in Paris. "I've got it!" he shouted, then fell to the floor in a dead faint. After two years of painstaking study of the Rosetta Stone's hieroglyphs, Champollion had finally deciphered them, thus making intelligible a written language that had stymied other scholars for centuries. "For over forty generations, no living soul had been able accurately to read an ancient Egyptian text," Toby Wilkinson wrote. "[Champollion's] achievement allowed ancient Egyptian culture to emerge out of the fog of classical myth and esoteric legend into the spotlight of serious scientific enquiry, to be studied and appreciated as a sophisticated culture in its own right and on its own terms." In effect, the Frenchman's accomplishment marked the beginning of the science of Egyptology, laying the groundwork for ferreting out the secrets of thousands of years of pharaonic civilization.

In addition, it gave new impetus to the already relentless efforts of treasure seekers to find and acquire as many antiquities as possible, resulting in an orgy of looting of many of Egypt's most sacred sites. Champollion, as it happened, inserted himself squarely into the middle of that scrum. A brilliant scholar who cared deeply about advancing the understanding of this long-vanished civilization, he also had a fervent interest in furthering his own career. He knew that if the Louvre acquired a major collection of Egyptian antiquities, it would have to appoint a curator to take charge of them. He was determined to be its choice.

In 1825, he succeeded in persuading the French king, Charles X, to purchase three large private collections that had come up for sale that year, including one assembled by the Italian antiquities collector Bernardino Drovetti. In all, more than five thousand items, among them the pink granite sarcophagus of the pharaoh Rameses III, found their way to the Louvre, thanks to Champollion. That enormous cache was followed two years later by four thousand items from another private collection, making the museum the greatest repository of Egyptian artifacts outside Egypt itself. As Champollion had foreseen, the Louvre created a new department to house the treasures and appointed him the curator to oversee them.

At the time, there was little or no pushback from Egyptian officials over the widespread ransacking of their country's antiquities. Indeed, Muhammad Ali, the Ottoman governor of Egypt and its de facto ruler for the first half of the nineteenth century, was only too happy to swap them for money and political favors from Britain, France, and other European countries. For their part, Western museum officials defended their stream of acquisitions by claiming that these treasures deserved to be exhibited in "civilized countries" (i.e., their own), where they could be properly cared for and appreciated. In the words of one French official, "Antiquity is a garden that belongs by natural right to those who cultivate and harvest its fruits."

A generation later, another French Egyptologist and budding treasure hunter followed in Champollion's footsteps. He was Auguste Mariette, a low-level employee in the Louvre's Egyptian department, who in 1851 was sent to Egypt to obtain ancient manuscripts for the collection. When the Egyptian owners of the manuscripts refused to sell them, Mariette decided to launch a search instead for the long-lost Serapeum, a sprawling temple complex dedicated to the Greek-Egyptian deity Serapis.

Mariette began his excavation work at Saqqara, a huge ancient burial ground located twenty miles south of Cairo that dated back more than three thousand years. At first glance, Mariette said, the site seemed "a spectacle of desolation," with vast sand dunes everywhere. But then one day, he spotted the head of a small sphinx peeking up from a dune. Recalling that the Serapeum was famous for its avenue of sphinxes, he hastily recruited thirty native workmen and began to dig in earnest.

Within weeks, he and his team had unearthed the avenue—comprising 135 sphinxes in all—and eventually the tomb-temple complex itself. Among Mariette's most spectacular finds were twenty-four massive stone sarcophagi—the burial places of the famous Apis bulls, sacred animals that were supposedly incarnations of the Egyptian god Ptah, the lord of darkness. He also found thousands of other priceless artifacts, including the *Seated Scribe,* the exquisite, perfectly preserved limestone statue that so fascinated Christiane as a girl and continues to be one of the Louvre's most valued treasures.

Next to the Rosetta Stone, the discovery of the Serapeum at Saqqara was considered the greatest Egyptian find of the nineteenth century, as well as a bonanza for the Louvre. Over the next two years, Mariette sent 230 crates of antiquities—almost six thousand works in all—to the museum. In doing so, he blatantly violated an agreement he had made with the Egyptian government.

After Muhammad Ali fell from power in 1848, Egypt had finally begun to impose some controls on the antiquities trade. Under the new regulations, Mariette was allowed to keep one hundred items for the Louvre, but the rest of his Serapeum discoveries were to stay in Egypt. Unwilling to accept that edict, the wily Mariette found a variety of extraordinarily inventive ways to get around it. Excavating at night, he hid his finds in deep underground shafts and smuggled them out in grain sacks to ship them to France. To placate Egyptian inspectors, he produced fake copies of some of the objects he had commandeered.

But then, having succeeded in making the Louvre the West's preeminent museum of Egyptian antiquities, Mariette, like Saint Paul on the road to Tarsus, found religion. He became a staunch opponent of the wholesale pillaging of Egyptian monuments by foreigners like himself. In 1858, he founded the Egyptian Antiquities Service to protect the country's ancient heritage. Although it was an agency of the Egyptian government, the Antiquities Service was supported by the French, and for the next ninety-four years, a Frenchman would head it. As a result, France's already significant cultural influence in Egypt would continue to far exceed that of Britain, Germany, or any other Western country.

As head of the service, Mariette did indeed fulfill his pledge to crack down on heedless ransacking by, among other things, sending inspectors out into the field to find and put an end to clandestine excavations. The Antiquities Service had exclusive control over excavation rights throughout Egypt, and in 1860 alone, Mariette authorized thirty-five new dig sites, while attempting to conserve already explored locations. He helped create an Egyptian antiquities museum in Cairo, then filled it with a dazzling array of treasures from the many excavations he had approved. Noting his accomplishments, Desroches wrote, "Every time you stop in front of a masterpiece on display at the Egyptian Museum, you can be virtually assured that it was Mariette who found it."

In Giza, Mariette ordered the clearing of sand that had built up around the great sphinx, and in doing so, he uncovered a temple that had been built in front of the creature's legs. He also cleared the sand from several other noted temple complexes, including those at Dendera and Edfu.

When he died in 1881 at the age of fifty-nine, "Mariette Pasha," as he was known in Egypt, was buried in a sarcophagus in the garden of Cairo's Egyptian Museum. In the encomiums paid to him at the time of his death, there was little or no talk of his plundering past. Nor was there mention of reports that he had actively resisted the promotion of

Egyptian employees within the Antiquities Service, reflecting his determination that Egypt's ancient heritage should remain under the purview of Frenchmen like himself.

COINCIDENTALLY, THE LAST FRENCHMAN to direct the Egyptian Antiquities Service would be Father Étienne Drioton, the Catholic priest who in the early 1930s served as Desroches's mentor at the École du Louvre and whom she credited for jump-starting her extraordinary career.

In addition to his duties as professor of hieroglyphics, the rotund Drioton was deputy curator of the Louvre's Egyptian antiquities department. The author of several books, he was regarded as one of the country's most eminent Egyptologists. Desroches recalled him as a tolerant, open-minded man overflowing with joie de vivre. He loved good food and wine, was warm and witty, and, in her words, "was even more talkative than me."

In his hieroglyphics class as well as in his conversation, Drioton made ancient Egypt come alive, she remembered, adding that he "could have awakened a dead man and turned any idiot into a scholar." He quickly realized that his young student's intelligence and passion for the subject matched his own and took her on as his protégée.

During her time at the school, Desroches acted as Drioton's unofficial assistant at the Louvre. In her behind-the-scenes work there, she witnessed the stark difference between the public museum, with its high-ceilinged, marble-floored galleries, and the ramshackle warren of employees' offices. The Louvre displayed no works of art created after the mid-nineteenth century, and its physical structure, too, had a Dickensian air about it. Many of the Louvre's guards—middle-aged men who had been wounded in World War I—were missing a limb or an eye. When Desroches began assisting Drioton, the museum still did not have electric lighting; it would not be installed until 1936. As a result, the galleries and offices were chilly, drafty, and perpetually dim. During winter, oil lamps were distributed in midafternoon to allow the curators and other staffers to continue with their work.

Yet for all the Louvre's anachronistic qualities, Desroches loved her time there. She especially enjoyed the ambiance of Drioton's huge, dim office, which was, she remembered, "a museum within a museum." It boasted two high windows overlooking the Louvre's courtyard, but they were cleaned only twice a year, the insides in the winter and the outsides in the summer; as a result, "we never risked being dazzled with sunlight," she remarked dryly. The smoke from Drioton's cigarettes added to the constant haze in the air.

A row of dark green display cases lining the walls contained some of the sarcophagi and stelae—upright stone slabs covered with reliefs and hieroglyphs—brought back by Mariette from the Serapeum. In the middle of the room was a large table that served as Drioton's desk. On it sat a rose quartz statue of Neferrenpet, a high official in the reign of Rameses II, that also bore a lengthy inscription. Drioton, who was in the process of copying and deciphering it, explained to Desroches that thanks to the inscriptions on these artifacts and others like it, he and his fellow Egyptologists had been able to establish a more precise chronology of the history of the period in which they were created.

Much of what Desroches learned about Egyptology during her three years at the École du Louvre came from her frequent conversations with Drioton, she later said: "There were no manuals yet on the subject. He was the one who taught me how to interpret these objects, these witnesses to history."

He also advised her on her studies, helping her choose a topic for the thesis she was required to write in order to graduate. She settled on an exploration of domestic Egyptian life, with an emphasis on how housing styles had changed over the millennia. It was an unusual subject for archaeological study in the early decades of the twentieth century, when detailed knowledge about how ancient Egyptian society actually functioned was still relatively rare. The focus of archaeology was still more on the finds themselves rather than a more comprehensive understanding of the ancient civilization that produced them.

In the fall of her third year, Desroches was summoned to a meeting with the École du Louvre's academic director. The school, the director said, had just begun a series of evening lectures for the public on various subjects related to the Louvre's collections. The first speaker, a curator in the paintings department, had been an abysmal failure, she said, and it was vital that the next lecture, which was scheduled for three days later, be more engaging. She had asked a number of other curators for names of possible speakers, and Father Drioton had mentioned Desroches, suggesting that she make a presentation on the discovery of King Tutankhamun's treasures.

The twenty-year-old Desroches was appalled by the idea. She was just a student, she pointed out. She had never spoken in public before, had not yet been to Egypt, had not made an academic study of the Tutankhamun discovery, and had no slides of the treasures to show an audience.

The director was unperturbed. She told Desroches that Drioton had offered to help her with the presentation and that she shouldn't refuse until she had talked to him. When she went to see him, he calmly insisted that it was important she accept the assignment, adding that he would lend her slides he had acquired of the Tutankhamun artifacts, along with the three books Howard Carter had written about his discovery.

Desroches went home in a panic that night, determined to tell Drioton the following day that she was not up to what she considered an overwhelming task. She was sure her father would agree with her. But when she described what had happened, he said that Drioton had offered her a challenge that she shouldn't try to evade. "On the contrary," he said, "this is a wonderful opportunity to teach you to speak in public and without notes. I'll help you. We will start after dinner and stay up all night if necessary."

Drawing on his own expertise as a lawyer in presenting oral arguments, Louis Desroches taught Christiane how to synthesize the main points she wanted to get across, as well as how to write an introduction, transitions between subjects ("If you don't have good transitions, you're ruined"), and a memorable conclusion. "I sweated blood and water that night," she recalled. "It was a painful session for me, but ever since then, whenever I've given a lecture, I've used the method my father taught me. And ever since then, I've spoken without notes."

Over the next two days, Desroches spent hours refining and practicing her speech. On the night of the lecture, she arrived at the École du Louvre in a daze. But her stage fright lasted less than five minutes. With the help of Drioton's slides, she lost herself in her presentation, bringing to vivid life the wonder and excitement that Howard Carter had felt when he first made his discovery of the young pharaoh's mummified body and the unimaginable riches heaped up in the tomb. Her lecture, delivered with passion and verve, was a hit with the audience, and she discovered she loved the experience. Thanks to Drioton, she had been given a taste of the spotlight, and she would never shy away from it again.

IN ADDITION TO HER courses at the École du Louvre, Desroches took classes at other elite schools in Paris, including classical Egyptian grammar at the Sorbonne and Egyptian history at the Collège de France. She excelled in all of them. But while most of her professors thought highly of her, she was treated like a pariah by several of her fellow Egyptology students, all of whom were male.

At the time, archaeology in general—and Egyptology in particular—was still very much the exclusive domain of men. There had been no women among the scholars who accompanied Napoleon on his expedition to Egypt, nor on subsequent expeditions led by Champollion, Mariette, and later explorers and archaeologists. "Over the course of the last 150 years, a rigid power structure has been established in archaeology," the American anthropologist and archaeologist Mary Ann Levine wrote in 1994. "Men have controlled this power structure throughout the history of the discipline." Even as late as the mid-twentieth century, a substantial percentage of those in the profession considered women unsuitable, in both mind and body, to take on the dirty, exhausting, sometimes dangerous labor involved in an archaeological dig.

As it happened, however, a handful of women Egyptologists had been working in the field as early as the mid-1800s. But since their existence and achievements were basically ignored by their male colleagues, most have slipped into the cracks of history. Virtually all of these female trailblazers were British. Some were the wives of prominent Egyptologists: Hilda Petrie, for one, shared the work of her husband, William Flinders Petrie, who is regarded as one of the giants in the field. But she never published anything in her own name, and her contributions were never formally acknowledged. Her husband wrote the reports, headed the excavation teams, and garnered all the credit for their finds.

A few other British women struck out on their own. Unlike in France, Egyptology in Britain had a long tradition of attracting well-heeled amateurs with no academic or professional background in the subject. The women who became involved—like Margaret Benson, the daughter of the archbishop of Canterbury and one of the first female scholars at Oxford—had independent financial means. In 1894, Benson, then in her late twenties, traveled to Egypt for health reasons and, during her stay there, became obsessed with Egyptology. The first woman to be granted an excavation permit from the Egyptian government, she headed a dig for three years at the temple of the goddess Mut, the consort of Amun, king of the gods, in the ancient city of Thebes. Benson's excavations uncovered a number of statues of the lion-headed goddess, as well as an array of other valuable artifacts, some of which are still displayed at the temple.

Of the dozen or so female pioneers in the study of ancient Egypt, only one—Amelia B. Edwards—is relatively well known today. Although not an archaeologist herself, Edwards would end up having an extraordinary influence on the field. In Britain, she is called the godmother of Egyptology.

A British journalist and bestselling novelist, Edwards was a peripatetic traveler who wrote a series of books about her experiences. In 1873, she traveled to Egypt, where she spent five months aboard a houseboat sailing up the Nile. Captivated by the climate, scenery, and, above all, the remnants of the country's pharaonic past, the forty-two-year-old Edwards toured every temple and tomb she could find along the Nile's banks, ferreting out information about each from leading archaeologists. Carrying a parasol in one hand and a sketchpad in the other, she strode across acres of ruins, ventured down into ink-black burial chambers, and, at the temples at Abu Simbel in Nubia, made an archaeological discovery of her own—a small, square underground chamber whose walls were covered with brightly colored painted friezes and bas-relief sculptures.

Edwards's account of her trip, illustrated with dozens of her sketches, was published in 1877 to huge acclaim; it became a runaway bestseller. "A unique, intoxicating blend of romance and scholarship," as Toby Wilkinson described it, *A Thousand Miles up the Nile* is widely regarded today as one of the best travel books ever written about Egypt. Still in print, it's filled with vivid writing that brings Edwards's experiences to life for the reader, including this evocative description of the vast expanses of sand she encountered everywhere: "The beauty of sand more than repays the fatigue of climbing it. Smooth, sheeny, satiny; fine as diamond dust . . . like a snowdrift turned to gold."

In her book, Edwards was one of the first to express worry about the effects of rampant tourism and modern development on the ancient treasures scattered throughout Egypt. She reported how tourists from America and Europe, including some in her own party, were buying artifacts from pillagers of ancient ruins, looting graves themselves, and defacing antiquities with graffiti. Echoing Edwards, the French philosopher Joseph Ernest Renan wrote snappishly in the late 1800s: "The worst enemy of Egyptian antiquity is the English or American traveler. The name of these idiots will go down in posterity, since they were careful to inscribe their names on famous monuments across the most delicate drawings."

Edwards's concern about the growing threats to Egypt's cultural patrimony led her to spend the rest of her life championing its preservation and conservation. In 1882, she, together with several financial backers, founded the Egypt Exploration Fund, later renamed the Egypt Exploration Society, to fund scientifically conducted excavations there. The organization helped pay for several of the digs of William Flinders Petrie, whose sixty years in the field produced an enormous amount of archaeological evidence for all periods of Egyptian history, from prehistoric times through the medieval era.

"Almost singlehandedly by her actions in life and her generosity in death, Edwards established Egyptian archaeology as a serious discipline in Britain," one historian wrote. When she died in 1892, she left money in her will to endow the first academic chair of Egyptology in the country, to be established at University College London. UCL was the first British institution of higher learning to award degrees to women on an equal basis with men, and Edwards wanted young women to have the opportunity to study Egyptology as a science. Of the first eight students who enrolled in the program, seven were women. The first professor to hold the Edwards Chair of Egyptology was William Flinders Petrie.

One of the standouts among Petrie's early students was Gertrude Caton-Thompson, a young woman from a wealthy British family whose fiancé had been killed in fighting in the western desert of Egypt during World War I. During a trip to Paris, Caton-Thompson had become mesmerized by the Egyptian antiquities at the Louvre—so much so that when she returned to London, she began studying Arabic and took a class in prehistoric archaeology at UCL. A year later, she was invited to join one of Petrie's expeditions.

In the early 1920s, Caton-Thompson embarked on her own dig, blithely disregarding warnings about the dangers she would face as a woman alone in the Egyptian desert. She assured those who worried about her safety that she carried a pistol everywhere and slept with it under her pillow at night.

Caton-Thompson's chief interest was the Neolithic period, an era from roughly 8000 to 3000 B.C., during which prehistoric peoples switched from hunting and gathering to agriculture and food production. In 1924, at an excavation site near the region of Fayum in Upper Egypt, Caton-Thompson and her team discovered Neolithic pottery, flint tools, grinding stones, and cereal remains—evidence of the earliest settled agricultural community ever found in the country. The artifacts dated back to 5000 B.C., almost two thousand years before the pharaohs began their reigns. It was an extremely important find, but with everyone's attention still riveted by the discovery of King Tutankhamun's tomb two years earlier, her achievement, and Caton-Thompson herself, never received the public attention they deserved.

IN BRITAIN, IT MIGHT have been acceptable—if considered eccentric—for a woman to launch a career in Egyptology on her own. In France, the idea was anathema. For the French, dominance in the study of ancient Egypt had been an important element of their national self-image since the days of Napoleon's expedition. As a result, Egyptology remained firmly under the control of state institutions like the Louvre.

Although there were many women students at the École du Louvre, the Sorbonne, and the other higher education institutions Desroches attended, she was the only one intent on pursuing a career in Egyptology. What's more, she was the star of all her courses. The more she shone, the less her fellow students in the field liked it.

Until then, Egyptology, a small and highly competitive world, had been an exclusive men's club in France, and most of those in the club clearly wanted it to remain that way. As was true elsewhere, it was—and is—"a very restricted community, within which love of neighbor is not always the dominant feeling," the French Egyptian writer Robert Solé has sardonically noted. "The most prestigious positions are too rare not to arouse jealousy and sometimes real loathing."

In 2016, the French Egyptologist Amandine Marshall noted that "the fear of intellectual domination by a woman is not new and is still relevant in France today. . . . But at a time when women Egyptologists were still pioneers, and even more so in France where there had never been a woman to shake the already elitist and very fixed palm tree of French Egyptology, a personality with the character of Christiane Desroches-Noblecourt was bound to disturb and make waves."

At first, Desroches was bewildered by the hostility toward her. Growing up with an older brother to whom she was close, she had always felt comfortable around boys. From the time she was little, her brother had included her in his circle. When she was a teenager, she recalled, "I would spend every Sunday with my brother and his friends," both boys and girls. "We'd dance the Charleston outside, then run inside our house and play ping-pong on the dining room table. It was fantastic. I learned how to be with other young people without having to flirt. The boys were my friends. It taught me that relations between men and women could be on a much higher level than just flirting."

Accustomed to being treated as an equal by the opposite sex, she never thought to hide her abundant energy, outspokenness, or intellect—character traits that sparked animosity on the part of a good many male colleagues, both during her college years and afterward. When she was a student, anonymous letters questioning her morals were sent to fellow students, professors, and even her parents. She later said that the letter writers "were trying to destroy me." While she never disclosed the exact contents of the letters, she called them "despicable" and added, "I know who sent them. I won't name names, but I'll never forget it."

Much later in life, Desroches-Noblecourt made equally scathing comments about the attitude of some of the male Egyptologists with whom she had dealt throughout her career: "They thought the fact that they devoted their life to piercing some of the secrets of this brilliant and mysterious civilization made them superior beings. They might be mediocrities in real life, but if they were Egyptologists, they considered themselves geniuses." Interestingly, though, while she often had a difficult time with men who were her contemporaries, some of France's most esteemed veteran Egyptologists were more than happy to act as her mentors.

Étienne Drioton was the first. Shortly before her graduation from the École du Louvre in 1933, Drioton approached her with an intriguing proposition. Thanks to her brilliant academic record, she had proved herself good enough to join the Louvre curatorial staff, he said. But to have a shot, she would have to write and defend a second thesis, which she agreed to do—in this case, a study of the evolution of the Egyptian language between the country's occupation by the Persians and the arrival of Alexander the Great in the fourth century B.C.

In 1934, thanks to Drioton's influence, Desroches became, at the age of twenty-one, a project manager in the department of Egyptian antiquities—the only woman at the time to hold a professional position in the department. She was put in charge of cataloging the tens of thousands of Egyptian objects in storage. Only a tiny percentage of the museum's holdings were on display in the Egyptian galleries, while the rest—many of which were antiquities gathered by Champollion and Mariette in the early and mid-nineteenth century—were still in their original crates in the Louvre's basement. Indeed, Desroches discovered that most of the crates had never been opened since their arrival at the museum.

"Can you imagine," she later told an interviewer, "that when I started to work in the Louvre, almost nothing had changed since the time of Mariette? No one had updated the catalog since then." Assigned that mission, she spent the next three years opening crates, carefully evaluating the objects she found, then cataloging and properly storing them. Her examination of these antiquities was dusty and time-consuming, but it proved to be invaluable preparation for her future work in the field: "I got to handle everyday objects that were nothing special, but they taught you everything about daily life in ancient Egypt. . . . So, by the time I went to work on excavations, I was way ahead of my colleagues."

CHAPTER 3

"A DANGEROUS BLACK SHEEP"

AS CLOISTERED AS DESROCHES'S LIFE WAS AT THE MUSEUM, IT was impossible for her, or any other French citizen, to be oblivious to the wrenching political, economic, and social turmoil tearing the country apart during the 1930s. Little more than a decade before, France and its capital had seemed well on their way to recovery from the destruction and chaos of World War I. "We were emerging from a nightmare, but at the same time we were sure that this nightmare would be the last one," recalled the poet and writer Jean Cassou, a future colleague of Desroches at the Louvre and in France's resistance movement in World War II. "Despite everything it cost, we wanted to forget it."

Within months of the 1918 armistice, Paris had reemerged as the cultural capital of the Western world, becoming the hub of modernity in literature, the fine arts, architecture, design, and fashion. The city's creative ferment proved to be a magnet for trendsetting writers, artists, dancers, composers, and intellectuals, as well as seekers of excitement and adventure, from all over the globe.

And then, on a late October day in 1929, everything changed. The crash on Wall Street brought an end to the fizz and fun of 1920s Paris, as it did to so much else. The Great Depression that followed, along with the growing threat to peace by the dictators Hitler and Mussolini, hit France hard. The 1930s were marked by skyrocketing unemployment, businesses going under, political and economic scandals, and civil unrest. France had long been known for what one historian called its "people's ineradicable love of political squabbles," but as the 1930s progressed, its traditional divisiveness metastasized into intolerance, bitterness, and outright strife between the right and the left.

In the nineteenth and early twentieth centuries, French governments had come and gone at frequent intervals, but ever since the end of World War I, such instability had grown considerably worse. During that period, there were more than forty governments, an average of one every six months. None lasted long enough to come to grips with the country's increasingly severe economic and social problems, heightened exponentially by the Depression and resulting in tens of thousands of businesses collapsing and the unemployment rate shooting to more than 20 percent. Racked by infighting and claims of corruption, the various governments in power failed to cope with these challenges, leaving a vacuum that was filled by the actions of extremist groups from both ends of the political spectrum.

On the left, workers, increasingly alienated by the government's refusal to respond to their calls for higher wages and better working conditions, launched a massive wave of wildcat strikes across the country that caused significant disruption to factory production. Those on the right, who included members of the aristocracy and haute bourgeoisie, business and legal communities, the military, and the hierarchy of the Catholic Church, opposed any attempts to institute economic and social reforms. Some of the more extreme rightists formed nationalist groups, several of which were fascist and anti-Semitic; a few went so far as to call for the overthrow of France's democratic parliamentary system.

When French voters elected a leftist government in 1932, the extreme right's anger exploded into violence. After a series of riots throughout 1933 and early 1934, rightists launched an all-out effort to oust the government and install an authoritarian regime. On the night of February 6, 1934, tens of thousands of members belonging to ultra-right-wing organizations converged on the Place de la Concorde, across the Seine from the seat of the Chamber of Deputies, the lower house of France's parliament. Their aim was to storm the Assembly, throw out the legislators, and occupy the building. Also in the massive crowd that night were leftist students demonstrating against the coup attempt, among them Christiane Desroches and a group of her friends.

After setting fire to two ministry buildings, the rioters pelted Paris police and Republican Guards, who were mounted on horses, with stones and bricks as they rushed toward the bridge that led to the Chamber of Deputies. Desroches saw young toughs, wielding sticks topped with razor blades, slashing the legs of guardsmen's horses to bring them down. Some of the attempts were successful, and several guardsmen were trampled in the melee. As the riot reached its height, both sides began firing, and several people around Desroches were hit by stray bullets. Late that night, the mob began a fierce assault on the bridge. It was finally repulsed, and after eight hours of chaos, the authorities gained control of the situation, but not before sixteen people had been killed and more than six thousand injured.

The February 6 riot provoked a major political crisis in France. In response, the country's leading leftist parties formed a coalition, which in 1936 came to power under the leadership of Léon Blum, the country's first Socialist—and Jewish—prime minister. Called the Popular Front, the coalition was strongly antifascist and supported a series of reforms that were a French version of President Franklin Roosevelt's New Deal. Although the French Communist Party backed Blum's new government, its members held no positions in it.

Within weeks of taking office, the Popular Front began implementing the social and economic programs it had promised, including a forty-hour workweek, paid vacations, wage increases, the right to strike, collective bargaining, and social insurance. Such reforms were hugely popular among workers and some in the country's middle class, who saw them as the beginning of a much-needed overhaul of the antiquated, inadequate social and economic structure of the country. But for French conservatives, these kinds of measures amounted to nothing less than harbingers of a Communist revolution that would destroy the political and financial underpinnings of France. The nation seemed irrevocably split. As Desroches discovered, those deep divisions existed at the Louvre as well.

Another of the Popular Front's objectives was to make culture more accessible to the general public—an aim that dovetailed with the determination of Henri Verne, who was in charge of the Louvre, to haul the hidebound institution, ready or not, into the modern world. Determined to attract more people to the museum, Verne created a department of public education, renovated and modernized a number of galleries, and, most important, installed electric lighting throughout the vast building.

After all these improvements were made, he reintroduced the Louvre to France by inaugurating a plan to keep it open until midnight two nights a week. A spectacular success, the Louvre at Night program drew throngs of Parisians eager to see this grand institution, dim and dark for centuries, illuminated for the first time. It was regarded as one of the Popular Front's greatest triumphs.

Verne's efforts to modernize the museum, however, were met with considerable hostility from some of the Louvre's top curators, who had tremendous power of their own. Until the early twenty-first century, the chief curators ran their various departments like separate fiefdoms and "had a hard time tolerating any authority from above," noted Henri Loyrette, the director of the Louvre from 2001 to 2013. "Each acted as though [his department] was a small museum in its own right."

A number of the Louvre's curators strongly opposed Verne's reforms; one referred to them as "pure insanity." Conservative to the core, they were content with the museum's nineteenth-century atmosphere, and, according to Desroches, they hated what they viewed as "this invasion by the public." They also heartily disliked the leftist government that had encouraged such programs.

Soon after the Louvre opened its doors at night, Henri Verne invited Jean Zay, the Popular Front minister responsible for cultural affairs, to come and see the renovated galleries. As word of the invitation circulated among curators and staffers, "a wave of panic and disapproval blew throughout the Louvre," Desroches recalled.

One of the most vociferous critics of the visit was Charles Boreux, head of the Egyptian antiquities department, who summoned Desroches to his office. Her support of the Popular Front was no secret among her colleagues, and Boreux, an archconservative, "obviously considered me a revolutionary," she said. Indeed, anyone who sympathized with the current government was looked upon as a "dangerous black sheep, a bloodthirsty communist."

Boreux told Desroches that he had no intention of greeting Zay and showing him around the Egyptian galleries. "Mademoiselle," he said, "it is you who will represent the department." Desroches was stunned. She recognized Boreux's order as the gratuitous insult it was meant to be—relegating a senior government minister to the care of a young, inexperienced junior staffer, who, adding to the insult, happened to be a woman.

When Zay arrived at the gallery with two aides, an embarrassed Desroches was there to meet him and give him a tour. "Although the minister listened to me attentively, he looked at me without hiding his surprise," she wrote. "He probably was expecting an old bearded Egyptologist, and instead he found a young girl."

At the end of the tour, Zay asked her how old she was. "Twenty-two," she said. "And you're already the chief curator?" he asked with a smile. "No, sir, I'm just a project manager," she replied, explaining that she was substituting for Boreux, who had suddenly taken ill. After thanking her for her time, he asked her to come see him the next day at his government office.

When she did, he asked if Boreux had really been sick. Stammering, she said that she wasn't sure, that it might have been his wife who was ill. Shaking his head, Zay told her he hadn't been fooled. He knew exactly what was going on, and he appreciated her stepping in and giving him a tour that he found both enlightening and entertaining.

Desroches later heard that word of her visit to Zay's office had gotten back to the Louvre, with some of the curators laughingly speculating that the minister had taken more than a professional interest in her, which certainly would help advance her career. Outraged by the salacious gossip, she found herself newly unsure about what to do with her life and her future. Étienne Drioton was no longer around to give her counsel. In 1934, he had gone to Egypt to work on several excavation projects, and two years later, he had been named director general of the Egyptian Antiquities Service. There was no one else at the Louvre to help her navigate the thicket of infighting and rivalries that beset the museum staff.

Was she destined to be stuck in the Louvre's basement forever? That situation wasn't helped by the fact that she had spent the last three years working there without pay. When Desroches first got the job, it was made clear that she would receive no remuneration. She was able to get by because she lived with her parents, but she didn't want to be dependent on them indefinitely. At one point, she approached Henri Verne to see about a possible salary. As enlightened as he was about other matters, the museum's head showed no sympathy or understanding in this case. He replied that it was honor enough to occupy the post Desroches held and she should realize how fortunate she was.

But just as she was beginning to despair, Father Drioton came to her rescue once again. In 1937, thanks to his intercession, she was awarded a three-month government-sponsored study mission in Egypt. Her childhood dream was about to become reality at last.

CHAPTER 4

A SPLENDID ADVENTURE

SHE STOOD ON THE DECK OF THE OCEAN LINER AS IT SLOWLY began to edge away from the pier in Marseille. On either side of her, passengers waved goodbye to the people who had come to see them off. As the ship's whistle sounded, Christiane Desroches began to cry. Her tears had nothing to do with homesickness or apprehension about what lay ahead; they were a reflection of the pure joy she felt at that moment. For the first time in her life, she was on her own. She felt gloriously free.

She knew how lucky she was to have parents who let her think for herself and follow her dreams. But their liberated attitude did not extend to allowing her to live as she wanted, with no restrictions. They were as intensely protective of her as were the more conservative parents of her friends; even in her twenties, she was expected to be home by midnight when she went out in the evening. When she was awarded the study grant in Egypt, her mother and father at first adamantly opposed her going. A girl her age traveling alone to a non-Western country? Unthinkable!

She finally got them to agree by promising that she would wear a pith helmet at all times in the field to ward off sunstroke and that she would travel first class by ship to avoid the "wrong kind of men." To ensure her safety, her parents enlisted her brother, a junior naval officer, to travel to Marseille and hand her over personally to the captain of the ship, entrusting her to his care.

But she put all that out of her mind during her three days aboard the S.S. *Champollion*. It was a good omen, she thought, that the passenger ship taking her to Egypt for the first time was named for the founding father of Egyptology. Launched in 1924 for service between Marseille and ports in the Middle East, the *Champollion* and her sister ship, the *Mariette Pasha*, set new standards for opulence and comfort, and the twenty-two-year-old Desroches loved every minute of the experience.

More than fifty years later, she remembered the wonder she'd felt when she first stepped into the ship's dining room for lunch and saw a huge three-level oval buffet piled high with "the most delectable dishes, like plucked pheasants, lobsters, and exotic fruits. I had never seen such luxury before." Even when the seas became rough and many of her fellow passengers were overcome with seasickness, Desroches never missed a meal. She followed the advice of a friend, who told her that if she ate a ham sandwich with mustard and took a shot of whiskey afterward, she would never be seasick. "She was absolutely right," Desroches said years later. "Thanks to this method, I've never felt sick while traveling."

At dinner each night, the captain of the *Champollion* seated her at his table. Among his other guests were the fabulously wealthy Aga Khan—a bon vivant and champion horse breeder who also happened to be the spiritual leader of more than twelve million Shiite Muslims spread across the Islamic world. Present as well was the Ethiopian emperor Haile Selassie, in exile after Mussolini's Italian army attacked and occupied his homeland in 1935. Desroches relished getting to know not only these two larger-than-life world figures but also their families. She spent several hours chatting with the Aga Khan's vivacious wife, Princess Andrée, a thirty-nine-year-old Frenchwoman who had owned a dress shop in Paris before her marriage. She also played with the couple's five-year-old son, Sadruddin, who, twenty-three years later as a young United Nations official, would play an important role in Desroches-Noblecourt's campaign to save the temples of Nubia.

When the *Champollion* docked at the Egyptian port of Alexandria,

Desroches traveled to Cairo by train, sharing a compartment with the Aga Khan's wife. She was met at the station by Étienne Drioton, who, Desroches was amused to observe, had gone slightly native. Clad in a Western suit, the head of the Egyptian Antiquities Service was wearing a red fez (also known as a tarbouche), its black tassel swaying as he enthusiastically greeted her. But when he took her to his home for lunch, she discovered that in at least one crucial area he remained French to the core. The meal, prepared by his Egyptian cook, consisted of French dishes of Cordon Bleu quality, thanks to Drioton's mother, who lived with her son in Cairo and had taught his cook the basics of fine French cuisine.

DESROCHES WOULD LATER DESCRIBE her experiences during the next three months as a splendid adventure. Her assignment was to observe one of the most remarkable excavation projects in the Valley of the Kings, itself the most prized archaeological site in all of Egypt, under the guidance of two legends in Egyptology.

Located across the Nile from the ancient city of Thebes, the Valley of the Kings was the burial ground for almost all the pharaohs of the Eighteenth, Nineteenth, and Twentieth dynasties—a period that spanned almost five centuries (c. 1539–1075 B.C.) and is regarded as the peak of pharaonic power and majesty. As the country's religious capital, Thebes, whose ruins lay in and around the modern city of Luxor, boasted the grandest temples in the country, including those of Karnak and of Luxor, the original location of the obelisk now in Paris's Place de la Concorde.

Pharaoh Thutmose I, who ruled from about 1494 to 1483 B.C., decided to establish a new royal cemetery in a long, narrow valley on the west side of the Nile, surrounded by barren fawn-colored hills and cliffs that resemble a lunar landscape. Over the centuries, more than sixty tombs were cut out of solid rock in this kingdom of the dead, their entrances pockmarking the hillsides. "No ancient site has yielded a greater harvest of antiquities than this famous stretch of rocky land," wrote Lord Carnarvon, who had ample personal justification for that claim. He was the wealthy patron of Howard Carter, who had discovered Tutankhamun's tomb in the Valley of the Kings.

Although just a short walk from the site of that famous tomb, the excavation project to which Desroches was assigned was a world apart from it or any other royal burial place. Rather than focusing on pharaohs and their deaths, it was devoted to the study of how ordinary people in the area had actually lived.

The site was the ruins of a village called Deir-el-Medina, home to the many artisans and other laborers involved in the digging and decoration of the pharaohs' tombs over a span of roughly four hundred years, from the reign of Thutmose I to the end of the Twentieth Dynasty (c. 1080 B.C.). Hidden away at the bottom of a small valley within easy walking distance of the royal necropolis, Deir-el-Medina was meant to be a secret place, shut off from the outside world: The pharaohs wanted no one else to know the locations of their final resting places and the magnificent treasures they held. A thick stone wall was built around the village to ensure that nobody went in or out without official permission.

The archaeologist in charge of the site was Bernard Bruyère, the

RUINS OF DEIR-EL-MEDINA, 2009

head of excavations for the French Institute of Oriental Archaeology (IFAO) in Cairo—France's prestigious center for research into the archaeology, history, and language of ancient Egypt. In 1937, when Desroches arrived at Deir-el-Medina, the fifty-nine-year-old Bruyère had been working there for sixteen years.

A former art instructor at the École des Beaux-Arts in Paris, Bruyère had fallen in love with Egyptology and spent four years in Egypt before World War I. When war broke out, he returned to France to enlist. Badly wounded, he was captured by the Germans but managed to escape several times, only to be caught after each attempt. At one POW camp, his fellow prisoners included an extraordinarily tall captain named Charles de Gaulle, who joined him and others in yet another unsuccessful escape. Decorated after the war with the Legion of Honor and Croix de Guerre, Bruyère returned to Egypt as a scholar at the IFAO and was sent to oversee the Deir-el-Medina site. He would remain there for the rest of his career.

The Egyptian Antiquities Service severely limited the number of excavations in the Valley of the Kings, and in the early 1920s, only a few archaeologists were given the prized authorization, including Bruyère and Howard Carter, who knew each other well. One morning in the summer of 1922, a melancholy Carter arrived at the Deir-el-Medina site to seek Bruyère's advice.

The English explorer had been working for years to find the tomb of the little-known boy pharaoh Tutankhamun, but with scant success. Lord Carnarvon, weary of subsidizing Carter's excavations with nothing to show for them, had informed him he was ending their collaboration and would stop making payments to him the following January.

Bruyère urged Carter not to give up. He reminded him of all the years Carter had spent clearing massive amounts of rubble and sand from the area where he thought Tutankhamun's tomb was located. He was getting close, Bruyère believed. Only one spot remained to be explored: the ruins of the mud huts where the workers digging the tomb of the pharaoh Rameses VI had stored their chisels and other tools at night. Carter had feared that digging there might undermine Rameses's tomb, but Bruyère insisted he go ahead: "Your duty is not to overlook any clue, no matter how tiny."

At first Carter said no, then changed his mind and followed Bruyère's advice. A few weeks after his workers began to dig, he arrived at the site one morning and, for the first time since the excavations had resumed, heard nothing but silence. His workers were awaiting him, eager to show him what they had just uncovered. It was the first step of a stone staircase, one that they would discover led down to Tutankhamun's tomb. Although Carter later invited Bruyère to be present at the opening of the pharaoh's sarcophagus, he never publicly mentioned the Frenchman's role in one of the greatest archaeological finds in history, and it would go unrecognized until the late 1960s.

From her childhood, Desroches had revered Howard Carter and his work. "His find was of paramount importance to our understanding of Egypt," she said years later. "We owe to him the discovery of the one virtually complete royal treasure known today, and if only for this reason, we must pay him homage."

But as she learned more about Egyptology and its practitioners, she concluded that, in many ways, Bernard Bruyère's contributions to the profession were far more important and far-reaching than those of Carter. In the early 1960s, when Desroches-Noblecourt was doing research for her bestselling book on Tutankhamun and the discovery of his tomb, she was amazed to find that Carter, who had never been trained in Egyptology, had done little to shed light on the teenage pharaoh and the extraordinary objects found around his mummified body. In his reports, he offered scant descriptive details of the items, nor much explanation of what they meant or why they were there. "When we compare his files with those of Bernard Bruyère," she said, "we are stunned by their poverty."

During the years that Carter was acquiring international fame, Bruyère and his team had been painstakingly clearing the ruins of Deir-el-Medina of the enormous mass of rubble and sand burying them—tedious, frustrating, often dangerous work that offered no guarantee of eventual success. Quiet and unassuming, Bruyère never

CHRISTIANE DESROCHES AT DEIR-EL-MEDINA, 1937

sought the public spotlight, then or later, and as a result, according to Desroches-Noblecourt, "his memory almost disappeared from the circle of eminent Egyptologists at a time when vanity and publicity were sovereign."

In 1925, when Bruyère finally uncovered the remains at the bottom of the valley and began more detailed excavation work, he acquired a partner—another remarkable Egyptologist who is also little known today. "Czech by birth but French at heart," as Desroches-Noblecourt described him, Jaroslav Černý was as quiet and gentlemanly as the Frenchman with whom he would work for the next twenty-five years.

The bespectacled Černý, who received his doctorate from Charles University in Prague, was only twenty-seven when he first arrived at Deir-el-Medina. But he was already an expert at something Bruyère had little experience in—deciphering hieratic writing, the cursive form of hieroglyphs that was commonly used during this period. And as it turned out, there was an enormous amount of deciphering to be done. Scattered throughout the ruins of the village were thousands of pieces of pottery and shards of limestone left over from work on the tombs. Some were smaller than a postcard; others were more than two feet long. Many of these fragments, known as ostraca, were covered with

FRENCH ARCHAEOLOGISTS AT DEIR-EL-MEDINA IN THE EARLY 1930S. BERNARD BRUYÈRE IS SECOND FROM LEFT, ÉTIENNE DRIOTON THIRD FROM LEFT, AND JAROSLAV ČERNÝ FAR RIGHT.

hieratic writing; by decoding them, Černý was able to reconstitute in detail the daily lives of the craftsmen and their families over four centuries.

Working on the tombs had been a prestigious position, and the jobs were often handed down from father to son. Successive generations of stonemasons, artists, sculptors, quarrymen, plasterers, scribes, and other craftsmen were born, lived with their wives and children, and died in the village. Unusually for ancient Egypt, some of the residents of Deir-el-Medina, including women, could read and write; in the rest of the country, scribes were generally the only ones who were literate. The remarkable bounty of ostraca recovered from the ruins revealed how varied and prolific its inhabitants were in their writing, which included letters, laundry lists, gossip, bills, wills, prayers, wedding and death announcements, poems, love songs, hymns, contracts, medical diagnoses and prescriptions, and lists of household tips, among other minutiae of daily life.

Thanks to this bonanza, today's Egyptologists have a far better understanding of the lives of ordinary Egyptian citizens than they do of the lives of the pharaohs. As the American Egyptologist David O'Connor noted, "It is these ostraca, and not the better known and better studied monumental inscriptions of tombs and temples, which contain the wealth of detail needed to reconstruct the social, economic, and religious activities that made up the fabric of life for most Egyptians." No other archaeological site has come close to producing such an extraordinary amount of information about an ancient community's organization, social interactions, and working and living conditions.

The work of Černý and Bruyère was particularly valuable because of the great care they took in documenting every detail and sharing it. Both of them, Desroches said, were extremely generous in imparting their knowledge and explaining the material they'd collected to younger scholars like her. At the end of every workday, Bruyère would meticulously notate in his excavation diary the work done by his team that day, including any items they had found and where in the ruins they had been located. His written notes, supplemented by drawings and photographs, were compiled into voluminous yearly reports that he made public.

As Bruyère grew older, the war wounds he suffered in World War I, caused by grenade fragments in his right hand and other parts of his body, gave him considerable pain. Desroches remembered watching him struggle to write in his diary, pushing his right hand with his left. But the pain, she said, never stopped him from recording the progress of the work on the site.

Černý's reports were just as thorough. Over the years of his decryption of the ostraca, he had become intimately acquainted with many of the village's inhabitants, learning their names, where they lived, and how good they were at their jobs, not to mention their loves, hates, quarrels, and rivalries, and how they were affected by great outside events, like war and devastating floods. Of Černý, the British archaeologist and historian John Romer wrote, "He learned to sift through the very dust of their lives like no one else; this experience, perhaps, helped to give the sensitivity and humanity to his writings that still fires young scholars today."

As Bruyère had done, Černý set down all his findings in great detail, providing future researchers with invaluable source material for their own work. Indeed, several later archaeological discoveries, including the finding of a small temple near Deir-el-Medina, were sparked by the study of Bruyère's and Černý's archives.

ALTHOUGH DESROCHES'S STUDY GRANT did not allow her to take an active part in the excavations at the village, from the outset Bruyère and his fellow archaeologists treated her like a full-fledged member of the team, including the sharing of their exceedingly primitive living conditions. Like all the others on the dig, Desroches lived in one of a series of small chambers in an empty tomb carved into a limestone cliff, which was reached by climbing a steep ramp. At night, wild hyenas,

CHRISTIANE DESROCHES COPYING HIEROGLYPHS CARVED ON THE WALL OF A TOMB NEAR DEIR-EL-MEDINA, 1937

"looking like great wolves of the desert," galloped across the roofs of the cells. There was no running water or electricity.

During the day, Desroches carefully observed Bruyère and his team as they continued their excavation of the remains of the village's mud brick homes. It was a remarkable learning experience, she later said, one that continued even after the workday was over. In the evening, as the sun set behind the steep cliff towering over Deir-el-Medina, Desroches sat enthralled as Bruyère and Černý told stories about the ancient residents of the village and their lives, bringing them to life and allowing her to see them as real people rather than shadowy figures of myth and legend.

The two men talked about how, at the beginning of each shift, the workers would leave the village, walk up a hillside and along a path at the edge of the cliff, then descend into the Valley of the Kings. From the cliff, they could see in the distance a long row of enormous and elaborate mortuary temples, all of them brightly painted, built by various pharaohs to serve as their permanent public memorials. Each temple was surrounded by a hive of buildings—a ceremonial palace to accommodate the current pharaoh when he came to honor his predecessors, as well as homes and offices for the high priests, scribes, and other officials who administered the temples' estates.

Farther in the distance were dazzlingly green fields, farmed by peasants and watered by the nearby Nile; across the river was the bustling city of Thebes. From the cliff, the valley below appeared to be a narrow emerald belt stretching for miles and surrounded by a vast expanse of desert.

The longest river on earth, rising in sub-Saharan Africa and flowing more than four thousand miles north to the Mediterranean, the Nile, with its annual floods, was the lifeblood of this arid, searingly hot land. As Toby Wilkinson noted, it "shaped Egypt's geography, controlled its economy, molded its civilization, and determined its destiny." Every summer, tropical rains drenched the African highlands and caused the Nile's tributaries to swell, sending torrents of water downstream. When the deluge reached the borders of Egypt, it overflowed the river's banks from south to north, flooding the entire length of the Nile

Valley. For several weeks, all the valley's cultivated fields lay underwater. But when the water finally receded, it left behind a layer of fertile silt, replenishing the soil and making it ready for that year's sowing of crops.

During most years, the Nile fulfilled its essential life-giving role. But when it didn't, the results could be catastrophic. When the floods were excessive, water rampaged through the valley, washing away the primitive dikes and mud brick villages perched precariously above the floodplain. When rains were scarce and the Nile's water level was low, the result often was a paucity of crops, causing widespread hunger and even starvation.

"The Egyptians have always been acutely aware of their unique environment; its harmonies and contrasts have shaped their society and world view," Wilkinson wrote. "The sharp divide between the green strip of floodplain and the yellow-brown desert on either side only emphasizes the precariousness of existence and the delicate balance between feast and famine, life and death." For the Egyptians, the concept of *maat*—the maintenance of order and harmony in life—was all-important.

Through the stories told by Bruyère and Černý, Desroches learned a great deal about the daily activities of the Deir-el-Medina craftsmen, whose lives were almost exclusively devoted to honoring the dead. Černý talked about finding ostraca on which scribes kept track of the progress of the work done on the royal tombs, whose construction began as soon as a new pharaoh took power and usually lasted several years. The tombs were meant not only as a final resting place but as the pharaoh's passport to the next world, where he hoped for a rebirth. The precious objects left in the tomb were meant to provide him with every necessity for the hereafter.

On the ostraca, the scribes carefully recorded the tasks, work schedules, and pay of each worker, along with evaluations of the quality of their efforts. They also noted details of the men's supplies and equipment, down to the exact number of wicks and amount of oil used in the small pottery lamps that illuminated the pitch-black darkness of the burial chambers. The oil, delivered from the storerooms of the royal temples, had to be of the highest quality to prevent the lamps from smoking and depositing soot on the walls and paintings. That close attention to detail accounts for the fact that so many of the wall paintings in Egyptian tombs and temples have retained their original glowing, richly pigmented colors.

The workers received six days off each month, although they often wangled more by pleading illness, family problems, or, in at least one case, a bad hangover. The six holidays were supplemented by frequent feast days devoted to celebrations of the ancient Egyptians' vast array of gods. As Desroches noted, "If we put together all the feast days of the various gods, there would not be a single working day left." Even though Deir-el-Medina had to assign priorities to which gods its residents would honor, a full third of the year was taken up by celebrations.

The two most important annual festivals for the village—and for Thebes as a whole—were both in honor of the deity Amun, who was revered as king of the gods. During the first, held during the annual flooding of the Nile, a statue of Amun was taken from his temple at Karnak by shaven-headed priests and carried along a ceremonial road leading to the temple of Luxor, about one and a half miles away. During the second, Amun's statue was placed on a cedar barge and transported across the Nile to pay calls on the various temples on the west side of the river.

The second holiday, usually held in May, was an occasion for wild, carnivalesque rejoicing by the area's entire population. A dazzling procession of partiers paraded along the riverbank, including African drummers bedecked with feathers, naked dancing girls turning backflips, demurely clothed girls playing lutes, wrestlers, harpists, jugglers, army officers, and royal charioteers.

The ancient Egyptians liked to party, and the inhabitants of Deir-el-Medina were no exception. After taking part in the day's festivities, they returned home for a lavish communal feast. Along with abundant food, beer, and wine, there was music and dancing that lasted until early the next morning. To this exuberant celebration, both men and women wore heavy dark wigs and billowing, elaborately pleated white linen robes. The women's faces were heavily made up, their eyes lined with kohl and their eyelids tinted with colored powder.

Other festival days involved smaller, quieter celebrations, sometimes observed only by part of the community or single families who would visit the tombs of their ancestors, light lamps, and feast in the chapels above the tombs, where family members would present offerings to their ancestors' statues. On their days off, the men of Deir-el-Medina often worked on their own tombs and funeral chapels, which—not surprisingly, since their creators were among ancient Egypt's best artists and artisans—are considered some of the most beautiful burial places in the area.

While the men were at work, the women of the village tended to their children and homes. They were helped by servants provided by the government who assisted with laundry; with the baking of bread, the village's prime food source; and with the brewing of beer, made from barley, which was also an important part of the ancient Egyptians' diet. Families received rations of fish, lamb, eggs, and vegetables like eggplant and beans. They also enjoyed hunting and consuming the wild ducks and other aquatic birds that flocked to the area during the annual flooding of the Nile, when water covered all the fields below the Valley of the Kings and came close to the village. Considered a delicacy, the birds were smoked or grilled on a spit and usually eaten on the great festival days.

Although relatively simple, the lifestyle of these villagers was considerably privileged, especially compared with that of the vast majority of their countrymen, who eked out a far less substantial living. As employees of the pharaoh, the men of Deir-el-Medina reported directly to the vizier, the pharaoh's top minister, who was in charge of the government's bureaucracy. He supplied them with their wages and other provisions, all of which came from the warehouses of royal temples or were transported by the servants working for the village. Since there was no water in the desolate hills and valleys surrounding Deir-el-Medina, it had to be carried in earthenware jars on the backs of donkeys from the fertile valley below. The same was true for the village's grains, vegetables, meat, and fish.

Like other communities in the country, Deir-el-Medina had its own law court that was authorized to deal with all civil and some criminal cases. In principle, any Egyptian could demand a trial by his peers. Such trials were held in a small clearing at the edge of Deir-el-Medina, where members of the tribunal gathered to judge the alleged wrongdoings of their fellow villagers. The plaintiffs and defendants represented themselves, and cases could sometimes drag on for years.

Under Egyptian law, the women of Deir-el-Medina had most of the same rights as the men. Both women and men were considered independent citizens, equally responsible to the community. Women were entitled to own property, including a third of all the property acquired during their marriage, which would revert to them in the case of divorce or the death of their husband. If they died first, the goods would go to their heirs rather than to their spouse.

The Egyptians were hardly puritanical in their daily lives. There was no moral prohibition against sexual relations between unmarried persons, nor was there a stigma attached to children born out of wedlock. Divorce was not uncommon, and many people married several times, usually after amicable property settlements had been arranged by members of the village tribunal.*

On occasion, girls were apparently allowed to attend the village school with boys, where they learned to read and write, with emphasis on folk tales and prayers. One evening during Desroches's stay at Deir-el-Medina, Jaroslav Černý arrived at dinner brimming with excitement. He had just decrypted writing on a shard of limestone that turned out to be a letter from a woman to her neighbor, asking her to prevent her son from bothering the woman's daughter. "Every morning," Černý said, "this boy was waiting for the little girl to throw stones at her, and she no longer dared to go to school on her own." Unfortunately, he was unable to find any evidence of an answer.

As the centuries passed, the prosperity and stability of Egypt gave

* Unlike ordinary Egyptians, who tended to be monogamous, their pharaohs customarily had several wives at a time, as well as a large number of concubines. Also unlike their subjects, ancient Egypt's rulers were frequently incestuous, often contracting marriages with their sisters and daughters.

way to mounting civil strife, including internecine fighting among members of pharaonic families over who would rule next, as well as outside threats from neighboring nations, which were growing increasingly powerful. Even in previously stable villages like Deir-el-Medina, life became considerably more difficult.

About 1170 B.C., the workmen of the village complained to the vizier that they had not received their full pay for several weeks. When nothing was done to correct the situation, they laid down their tools and walked off the job in what was arguably the first strike action in recorded history. Despite pleas from the village elders and court officials, they refused to go back to work until their demands were met. The vizier finally gave in.

In later years, as the stability of Egyptian society continued to crumble, a sizable number of the villagers went so far as to break into and plunder pharaohs' tombs, several of which they and their forebears had helped build and decorate. Virtually every royal tomb was robbed in ancient times, with the thieves stripping the burial vaults and even the kings' mummies of the treasures that surrounded them. One of the robbers turned out to be the foreman of a work crew at Deir-el-Medina, a man named Paneb.

Throughout most of his life, Paneb took center stage at the village as the most notorious character in its history. Although a highly skilled stone carver, he was better known for his frequent drunkenness, hot-tempered rages, and seduction of other men's wives. Étienne Drioton, whose love of gossip extended to the affairs of ancient Egypt, told Desroches that Paneb was also known for procuring sex partners for the sons of the pharaoh during the major festivals. But the most serious accusation against him charged that he had taken part in the looting of a royal tomb. During his trial, Paneb swore an oath to the gods that he was innocent, and, with no concrete evidence connecting him to the robbery, he was acquitted.

When Desroches came to Deir-el-Medina, Bruyère and his team were in the middle of excavating the ruins of Paneb's house, which he had shared with his wife and eight children. Having cleared two large family rooms, they were now working on a smaller space, which they assumed to be the kitchen. Desroches watched closely as Bruyère and another archaeologist dug down to find the hearthstone and then began excavating under it. After several minutes of digging, they found a small hiding place. Concealed inside was a fragment of a wooden sarcophagus, plated with gold and bearing an inscription dedicated to the pharaoh whose tomb Paneb had allegedly robbed. More than three thousand years after the fact, Bruyère and his team had uncovered concrete evidence that Paneb was indeed guilty as charged.

DESROCHES'S TIME AT DEIR-EL-MEDINA was brief, but her experience there, particularly her tutelage by Bruyère, would have a powerful effect on her life and career. His interest in the ordinary people of ancient Egypt, his devotion to teaching, and his assiduous attention to detail were all traits that she, too, would exhibit. But his influence on her extended far beyond his skills as an Egyptologist. She was also guided by his interactions with other people, particularly the Egyptian workmen who did most of the hard labor on the dig. Unlike a good number of his fellow archaeologists, who tended to be arrogant and condescending to their Egyptian employees, Bruyère took an interest in his workers and treated them with dignity and respect. So did his wife, Françoise.

Twenty-five-plus years younger than her husband, Françoise Bruyère was the niece of Pierre Jouguet, the director of Cairo's French Institute of Oriental Archaeology. In 1931, she had traveled from Paris to Egypt to escape the aftershocks of her parents' nasty divorce. Jouguet and his wife were concerned about their twenty-five-year-old niece, who had sunk into a deep depression, and invited her to accompany them on an inspection trip to Luxor and Deir-el-Medina, thinking that the jaunt would provide a distraction. Although she was reluctant at first, she finally agreed to go.

To her surprise, she was seduced by the quiet, barren majesty of this land of vanished palaces, ruined temples, and rock-cut tombs. Its allure for her was heightened by her instant attraction to the man in charge of the excavation, who in turn became besotted by her. She and Bruyère were married in Paris in 1932, astonishing Bruyère's friends and acquaintances, who believed him to be a confirmed bachelor interested in nothing but his work.

Although his lively, intelligent wife became heavily involved in the Deir-el-Medina project, she did not follow the example of other archaeologists' wives, who served as assistants or partners in their spouses' work. Instead, she set up a makeshift dispensary near the empty tombs that served as the lodging for the project's team. There she provided care for the injuries and sicknesses of both the French archaeologists and Egyptian workmen on the dig.

Although she had no formal medical training, she quickly became adept at treating everything from dysentery to cobra bites—so much so that she agreed to care for residents of the nearby village of Gourna when they started coming to her for help. Since virtually none of them understood a word of French, she embarked on a crash course to learn Arabic, eventually speaking the language far more fluently than her husband or his fellow archaeologists.

At first, Françoise Bruyère's ad hoc medical practice was confined to the archaeological site. But she finally succumbed to pleas from the villagers to come to Gourna to treat them. There she focused on the care of women and children, which included providing prenatal care, delivering babies, and helping new mothers to care for their infants. "Nothing frightened her," noted the French writer Claudine Le Tourneur d'Ison. "Nothing repelled her. Her only concern was to help, in one way or another, those who were in pain, no matter who they were."

As she spent more time with the villagers, she began adapting her behavior to theirs. She wore a burnoose—a long, hooded cloak favored by Arabs—over her clothes, and a scarf to cover her hair whenever she went to Gourna. She also began to study the Koran.

Faced with a growing influx of patients, she lacked sufficient money for the drugs, snake venom serum, and other medical supplies she needed, so she made the rounds of pharmacies and doctors in Luxor to ask them for any unused medicine they might have. When word of her work and appeals reached Cairo, a wealthy Egyptian princess, a first cousin of King Fuad, summoned Bruyère to announce that she would give her the financial resources she needed to continue her work.

During her three months in Deir-el-Medina, Christiane Desroches became a good friend of Françoise Bruyère and frequently accompanied her on her visits to Gourna. She was greatly impressed by Bruyère's closeness to the Arabs she was treating and particularly by an extraordinary encounter that began early one morning, when a swarthy stranger, clearly a Bedouin tribesman, showed up at Bruyère's dispensary with a wound on his arm that was badly infected. He didn't say a word, and, after unsuccessfully trying to find out who he was, neither did Bruyère. She cleaned and disinfected the wound, then, after extracting a bullet, dressed it and gave the man some medicine. For several days afterward, the stranger came back to have the wound dressed again; each time, neither he nor Bruyère spoke. Once his injury began healing, he vanished and never returned.

A few weeks later, Bruyère, accompanied by an Arab helper, traveled by donkey to Luxor to buy food supplies for the camp and to get money to pay the dig's Egyptian workers. Returning at dusk, she and her companion were passing the Colossi of Memnon, two massive stone statues of the pharaoh Amenhotep III, when their donkeys stumbled over a heavy rope stretched across the road. When Bruyère and her assistant fell to the ground, three men in Bedouin robes emerged from the shadows and surrounded them, demanding money. Their demand enraged the usually calm Bruyère, who showered her attackers with Arabic curses.

Hearing her voice, one of the bandits raised his arms to the sky and sharply issued orders to the others. As Bruyère and her assistant were helped to their feet, she recognized the man who had spoken: He was the Bedouin whose arm she had treated. "You are sacred to us," he declared. "We will never touch a hair on your head." With that, he and the others left. She never saw him again.

AT THE END OF her stint at Deir-el-Medina, Desroches bade a reluctant farewell to the Bruyères and Jaroslav Černý, to whom she would remain close for the rest of their lives. She went home to Paris exhilarated by her three months of freedom, only to be jolted back to reality. Soon after her return, she went out to dinner at a restaurant with a group of friends. As they caught up with one another's lives, they lost track of time, and when they finally ended their evening, they discovered it was early morning. The Métro had stopped running, so several of her friends walked Desroches back to her parents' apartment building. As it came within view, she saw that all the lights were still on in her family's apartment and her father was standing on the balcony. When he saw her, he snapped, "Get up here quickly! If you could only see the anguish of your mother . . ."

"I had to ask her for forgiveness on my knees," Desroches-Noblecourt remembered. "I was then twenty-three years old."

CHAPTER 5

UPHEAVAL IN CAIRO

TO HER GREAT RELIEF, DESROCHES'S RETURN TO HER SEMIMONASTIC life at the Louvre and her parents' apartment proved to be short-lived. The glowing reviews she had received from Étienne Drioton, Bernard Bruyère, and Jaroslav Černý helped burnish her credentials as a promising Egyptologist, and in 1938 the French government awarded her a salaried fellowship at the elite French Institute of Oriental Archaeology in Cairo—a plum assignment reserved for those considered France's top young archaeologists. She was the first woman to win the three-year fellowship, which would allow her to live in Egypt for nine months each year and take part in various excavation projects sponsored by the institute.

The IFAO was housed in a cavernous former royal palace in the Arab quarter of Cairo, a city Desroches would come to know well. The capital of Egypt since A.D. 969, Cairo was the one major settlement in the country that did not spring from Egypt's ancient civilization. It was established by the country's Arab conquerors, and the influence of Islam, the religion of most Arabs, was evident throughout the city. Mosques dating back to medieval days dotted many of its neighborhoods, and the haunting calls of the muezzin, summoning the faithful to prayer five times a day from the mosques' minarets, echoed in its streets.

In the neighborhood where the IFAO was based, most women who went out in public wore veils covering their faces, with only their eyes showing. The wife of Pierre Jouguet, IFAO's head, warned Desroches that to avoid upsetting the sensibilities of the institute's neighbors, she should never go for a walk alone in the Arab section. If she took the tram to the center of Cairo, she must travel in what was called the harem coach—the car reserved exclusively for women.

But once Desroches ventured beyond the Arab quarter, she discovered that the rest of Cairo was extraordinarily cosmopolitan—and had been from its creation. Since medieval times, the city had served as one of the Middle East's most important political and economic centers, and its wharves had bustled for centuries with trade from all corners of the Mediterranean.

In the nineteenth century, Muhammad Ali, the Ottoman governor of Egypt, added throngs of Europeans to Cairo's polyglot, multiracial mix. An Albanian soldier in the employ of the Turkish sultan, he had engineered the fall of Egypt's previous governor and succeeded to the post in 1805. Establishing himself as an absolute ruler, he founded a dynasty that ruled Egypt for the next century and a half.

Determined to force Egypt's feudal society into the modern era, Muhammad Ali and his successors opened the door to European investment, primarily by the British and French. Their growing influence in the country contributed to the transformation of the physical appearance of much of Cairo, with the French having a particularly significant impact. Khedive Ismail, Muhammad Ali's grandson, had studied in Paris and had been impressed by the recent renovation of that city by Baron Georges-Eugène Haussmann. Haussmann's improvements included an array of new parks and squares, grand wide boulevards, and elegant stone apartment blocks featuring wrought iron balconies and tall shuttered windows. Ismail ordered the creation of a new district in Cairo that followed the Parisian style of urban planning, featuring wide avenues and graceful Haussmann-like apartment buildings set back on streets lined with oleander and jacaranda trees.

But although the French and British were the dominant Westerners in Cairo, trading and business opportunities had brought many other

Europeans as well—Italians, Greeks, and Maltese among them. Substantial numbers of Syrians, Lebanese, and Turks also lived there, adding to the frenetic busyness of daily life.

Downtown Cairo was particularly overwhelming. Dense crowds packed the streets. Trams overloaded with passengers shouldered their way through throngs of bicycles, horse-drawn carriages, donkey carts, wagons piled high with vegetables and other foodstuffs, and, not infrequently, processions of camels and flocks of sheep. The noise was cacophonous, with at least a dozen different languages assaulting one's ear, accompanied by a variety of distinctive odors, including kerosene, spices, fried fish, incense, and animal dung. "These were not unpleasant smells," recalled the British novelist Penelope Lively, who grew up in Egypt in the 1930s. "They were rich and organic, an inescapable element of Cairo, like the heat and the noise of invisible insects."

Disconcerted at first by Cairo's clamor and disorder, Desroches came to love the vibrancy and exoticism of its wonderfully varied street life—conjurers performing magic tricks; organ grinders and their monkeys; sidewalk vendors selling oranges, dates, kebabs, and roasted melon seeds; even the child pickpockets who threaded their way through crowds, looking for unwary marks. Yet at the same time she became increasingly aware of the huge disparity between the city's haves and have-nots. The "haves" comprised an extremely thin slice of Egyptian society—intellectuals and the wealthy, and foreigners like herself. The "have-nots" were most of the rest of Cairo's residents. Desroches saw signs of poverty everywhere, from the emaciated men, their backs bowed, herding their animals down the streets, to the haggard, sad-eyed women begging for money on street corners, to the small children and babies in ragged clothes with sores on their faces and flies crawling around their mouths and eyes.

In some ways, the modernization of Egypt and its capital city had been a triumph. Cash crops, like cotton, had been introduced to boost exports, factories and mills built to cut down on imports, and roads, bridges, and dams constructed to improve transport and communication. All this had been done, however, on the backs of the fellahin, the country's peasants, who had been conscripted by the government to

DOWNTOWN CAIRO IN THE 1930S

work on these massive projects under extremely harsh conditions. Lucie Duff-Gordon, an Englishwoman who settled in Luxor in the late 1800s, wrote that "whole towns and villages were raided for able-bodied men who were taken away, often for years, to dig canals, build bridges, dams and railways, and work like slaves." In return for their labor, the fellahin had received little or nothing. Indeed, in most cases, they were worse off than before.

As well as contributing to the growing deprivation and oppression of the vast majority of Egyptians, the modernization campaign had exacted another crushing cost: the loss of national sovereignty. In effect, Egypt's rulers, in exchange for foreign protection and investment, had handed over to Europeans the running of their country. Such domination became particularly pronounced in the late 1800s, after the French diplomat Ferdinand de Lesseps persuaded Sa'id Pasha, Muhammad Ali's son and successor, to give French business interests permission to build the Suez Canal. The canal, which was opened in 1869, connected the Mediterranean to the Red Sea, allowing ships heading from Western Europe to India and other points in the Near and Far East to proceed directly there rather than having to make a lengthy journey around Africa.

The canal deal proved far more beneficial for the French than for the Egyptians. In addition to helping to underwrite it and providing forced labor for construction (an estimated 120,000 workers died in the venture), Egypt was pressured into giving costly concessions to the Suez Canal Company. Egypt's revenue from the canal's operation proved insufficient, and Sa'id began borrowing heavily to try to steady his country's economy and pay for the country's many modernization projects. His successor, Isma'il Pasha, accumulated even more government debt, which by 1875 had soared to $443 million.

Unable to meet the increasingly steep interest payments, Egyptian leaders were forced in 1875 to sell the country's 44 percent holdings in the canal to raise cash. The buyers were none other than the British prime minister Benjamin Disraeli and his government. Before construction began on the canal, Britain, believing the project to be too expensive and almost impossible to achieve, played no part in the deal. But when it proved to be an outstanding technological and economic success, British leaders, whose country now accounted for more than half the canal traffic, quickly changed their minds. With their 44 percent share, they gained a firm foothold in its operations.

The year after the sale, Britain and France cracked down hard on the debt-ridden Egyptian government. Under pressure from the bondholders and governments of the two countries, Egypt was forced to accept British and French control of its economy until its staggering loans were paid. Evelyn Baring, a British statesman and diplomat, was named controller general of the country—that is, the man in charge of collecting the debt. In time, Baring and his administrators, most of them British, would become the de facto rulers of Egypt, dominating its political affairs as well as its economy.

The British and Egyptians lived in totally separate worlds—a situation that the British vigorously encouraged. They had arrived in Egypt "with all the racial baggage of their native land," the British historian Alan Allport wrote. "Most of them had a firm and unchallengeable belief in their own superiority as white people. The result was an attitude toward non-Europeans which was patronizing at its best, ugly and vindictive at its worst, a crude intolerance which degraded the persecutors as much as it did the persecuted." In Cairo, the British barred most Egyptians, whom they called "wogs," from the clubs and other social gathering places that they had established and where they spent much of their abundant free time—places like the Gezira Sporting Club, the Turf Club, and Shepheard's Hotel.

Convinced that the Egyptians were incapable of self-government, Baring was determined to keep them in their place. Rather than expand their educational opportunities by subsidizing the country's small number of primary schools, he ordered that the schools' tuition be raised to reduce enrollment, thereby ensuring that only a limited number of students could go on to secondary schools and institutions of higher learning. When Egyptians complained about the lack of good jobs available to them, owing in large part to their limited access to education, the controller general, who feared that an educated working class might rise up against British rule, ignored their protests. He was particularly adamant that Egyptian women not be given any chance for independence and upward mobility.

Baring's fears proved to be well founded. Not long after the de facto British takeover of the country, a spirit of rebellion began to simmer within the Egyptian military. It boiled over in the spring of 1882 when an Egyptian army colonel led an uprising of thousands of fellow officers and enlisted men who sought to depose Tewfik Pasha, the then current Egyptian ruler and great-grandson of Muhammad Ali, and end British and French influence in the country.

Tewfik appealed to Abdul Hamid II, the sultan ruling the Ottoman Empire, to quell the revolt. But the sultan, reluctant to use his troops against fellow Muslims who were opposing foreign colonial rule, turned him down, opening the door for British intervention. After violent riots broke out in the streets of Alexandria, the British fleet bombarded the seaside city and British troops occupied it after stamping out fierce resistance. Several thousand Egyptians were killed or wounded in the fighting. In a show of force, British troops then paraded through the streets of Alexandria, Cairo, and other major population centers in Egypt before retiring to their barracks.

In the aftermath of the violence in Alexandria, the British created what came to be called a veiled protectorate, pretending to give limited independence to the Egyptians but in reality keeping a tight rein on the country. Under the arrangement, Egypt supposedly had control over its domestic affairs while Britain retained control of defense, foreign policy, and the security of communications. The Egyptians were well aware, however, that, even in the areas where they supposedly had power, any conflicts with the British would invariably end in defeat.

When World War I began in 1914, Britain found itself at war with the Ottoman Empire, of which Egypt was still technically a part. It used that fact as an excuse to drop the pretense of limited independence and declared Egypt a formal British protectorate. But once the war was over, Egyptian nationalists in 1919 staged another revolt. Caught by surprise, British authorities resorted to a variation of their earlier ploy, replacing the protectorate with an Anglo-Egyptian treaty granting Egypt independence as a constitutional monarchy. Again, however, there was a major catch. Britain would retain the right to maintain troops in the country, as well as to appoint advisers and permanent officials to the various Egyptian government ministries. In other words, the country would have self-determination in name only.

Nonetheless, with great fanfare, Egyptian independence was declared on February 28, 1922. Two weeks later, Sultan Fuad, another great-grandson of Muhammad Ali and a brother of Tewfik Pasha, became King Fuad I, and a new prime minister was named. But the upper ranks of the government's civil service and military remained dominated by the British, who also continued to control the country's banking system and business community.

AS POWERFUL AS THE BRITISH were in Egypt, however, their control wasn't total. While they pulled the strings in the government and economy, the French still held sway in other areas, particularly culture, the press, medicine, and education. Although Napoleon's venture in Egypt had ended in military defeat, it had opened the door to a steady flow of immigrating French professionals. In addition to explorers and archaeologists, they included medical personnel, architects, lawyers, engineers, and educators. In the early 1800s, Muhammad Ali authorized a French doctor named Antoine Clot to reform the Egyptian medical system along French lines. In 1836, Clot was put in charge of medical care for the entire country.

French Catholic missionaries, for their part, founded a number of private schools that from 1844 onward were open to Egyptian students. French became the lingua franca of Egypt's intellectuals and its government, business, and cultural figures, as well as other members of the country's elite. As one Egyptian scholar put it, "To be French-speaking was to think of Cairo as home but to think of Paris as the [center] of the world." The Comédie Française and the Paris Opéra made frequent tours to Cairo, and well-off Egyptians much preferred the French style in clothing, furniture, and other household goods.

And of course the French, just as they had done for more than a century, remained in control of Egyptian archaeology, overseeing not only all excavations in the country but the treasures that resulted from them. The leaders and professional staff members of Egypt's two leading cultural institutions, the Antiquities Service and the Egyptian Museum, continued to be French—with one notable exception.

In 1886, at the request of the Egyptian government, Eugène Grébaut, the then current Antiquities Service director, had reluctantly agreed to hire a young Egyptian named Ahmad Kamal as an assistant curator at his agency. The French-speaking Kamal, who had previously worked as a translator at the museum, was the first Egyptian to win a professional position in this elite world.

But that was as far as Grébaut and his successors were prepared to go. During the twenty-eight years Kamal worked at the Antiquities Service, he was passed over repeatedly for promotion; despite his pleading, his French superiors also refused to consider training or appointing any more of his countrymen to professional jobs. In 1914, after one such appeal, Pierre Lacau, who then headed the Antiquities Service, retorted that no Egyptian other than Kamal had ever shown any interest. "Ah, Monsieur Lacau," Kamal sadly replied, "in the sixty-five years you French have directed the Service, what opportunities have you given us?"

Not until the 1920s would Egyptians finally be given the opportunity to train as professional Egyptologists.

IN 1880, THE FRENCH GOVERNMENT further tightened its control over Egyptian archaeology by creating the French Institute of Oriental Archaeology, the first European institution of its kind to be established in the country. The founding of the IFAO fulfilled the dream of the savants who had accompanied Napoleon on his 1798 expedition: a permanent outpost in Egypt of French scientists dedicated to studying the Nile Valley and, not incidentally, to acquiring more antiquities on behalf of the Louvre and the country's other museums.

During the institute's first few years, its fellows spent most of their time copying and publishing the texts of hieroglyphic inscriptions on tombs, temples, and other monuments in well-known sites like the Valley of the Kings. It was only during the winter of 1899 that its first excavations began.

IFAO's home base in Cairo was the Mounira Palace—named after Princess Mounira, the daughter of the Ottoman Empire's sultan, who was given the palace in 1854 after marrying the son of Egypt's then ruler. The mansion, with its majestic staircase, towering entrance hall, and lush gardens and lawns, provided a fitting backdrop for an institution that soon emerged as a leading center of culture in Cairo. At its glittering parties, the cultural and intellectual elite of the country mingled with visitors from throughout the world.

Not surprisingly, the IFAO was also a bastion of male privilege—a "jealously closed environment," as Desroches put it, "where only young men were welcome." It was noted, too, for its distinct lack of collegiality. In the late 1920s, there was so much tension and infighting among the ambitious young Egyptologists there that the French government decided to replace the Egyptologist who was its current director with Pierre Jouguet, a highly respected Hellenist whose specialty was the influence of Greek civilization on Egypt.

When he arrived in 1927, Jouguet was appalled by what he considered the pampered treatment of the archaeologists at the institute, particularly the young men on fellowships. In addition to their receiving a substantial stipend, almost all their expenses were covered, including their stay at Mounira Palace. Among the fellows, there was a sense of privilege and exclusivity that Jouguet found distasteful.

Eleven years later, the institute still retained its aura of arrogance and self-importance, as Desroches discovered when she became its first female fellow. Her selection "caused a huge scandal among my old and future colleagues," she recalled. Indeed, the other fellows at the institute had formed a cabal against her even before she arrived, appealing to Jouguet to have her appointment rescinded. They insisted, she said, that "a woman could never be a sacred Egyptologist. It was impossible for a woman to live on an excavation site—the work and living conditions would be too difficult for her. The truth was, they hated the idea of a woman becoming a member of their illustrious circle. They couldn't bear the idea of living near a skirt, either in Cairo or in the field." Years later, she came to the conclusion that their intense opposition to her presence at the institute was sparked by their fear that after her three years there, she would be in a position to capture one of the scarce available positions in Egyptology in France, for which they all were fiercely competing.

When Jouguet told them that Desroches's appointment had been made by the French government and that there was nothing he could—or would—do, they insisted that she not be allowed to share their residence at the palace. "What are you so afraid of, gentlemen?" an increasingly annoyed Jouguet snapped. "Mademoiselle Desroches is not going to rape you." One of them protested, "We won't be able to go down to the morning meal in our pajamas anymore. Her presence will be a constant annoyance. You have to install her at a hotel."

Rejecting that idea out of hand, Jouguet told the protesters that if anybody was going to a hotel, it would be they. When he informed Desroches about all this, "I immediately declared I would not stay a day more in the residents' wing," she recalled. Jouguet put her up in an apartment next to the institute's library, where, "since these gentlemen were indisposed to eating with me, I took all my meals."

Meanwhile, she informed Étienne Drioton, who loved gossip and "was as talkative as a magpie," of her male colleagues' uprising. "Of course," she said, "he was quick to tell everyone else," including the French director of the Egyptian Museum, who in turn passed the story along. "Soon the whole French colony knew what had happened, so that whenever these gentlemen were invited to a party or dinner from then on, there was always someone to ridicule them and ask them why I scared them so much. They ended up coming to see me in a delegation, to beg me to come down to the common dining room. But I stayed in my apartment, where I invited to lunch and dinner whomever I wanted."

Determined to give Desroches a chance to prove herself as the first Frenchwoman to be formally assigned to a dig, Jouguet decided to send her to a particularly arduous excavation project at Edfu, on the west bank of the Nile in Upper Egypt—a remote region about five hundred miles south of Cairo. The IFAO director warned her that the working and living conditions at Edfu were exceptionally difficult, but if she were able to surmount them and prove herself there, her success would be all the more significant. Desroches eagerly accepted the challenge.

At the same time that Desroches breached the formerly all-male sanctum of the IFAO, another young outsider penetrated a bastion of exclusivity in Egypt that until then had been closed to people like him. Twenty-year-old Gamal Abdel Nasser was reaping the benefits of one of the concessions the British had made in its granting of so-called independence to Egypt in 1922: a major expansion of the Egyptian armed forces. As part of that growth, the country's royal military academy, which until then had chosen its cadets from the Egyptian upper classes, opened its doors to young men from a far wider section of society. Among the new cadets were Nasser and his friend Anwar Sadat, both of whom came from relatively poor and uninfluential families.

Like Desroches, Nasser was determined to seize the moment and prove himself. Twenty years later, their paths would cross, with momentous consequences for both.

CHAPTER 6

"LUCK SMILED ON ME AGAIN"

TRAVELING FROM CAIRO TO EDFU WAS FAR FROM EASY: FIRST A NIGHT train from Cairo to Luxor, then continuing south on another train to the Edfu station, followed by a boat trip across the Nile to the left bank of the town. After more than twelve hours of travel, Desroches finally got her first glimpse of her new dig. It was an astonishing sight, unlike anything she had seen in the Valley of the Kings or, for that matter, any other archaeological site in Egypt.

An important market town for much of its existence, Edfu boasted a history of more than four thousand years, most of which was reflected in the gigantic mound towering high above her. More than seventy feet high, it was about a quarter of a mile long and five hundred feet wide—roughly the size of fifteen football fields.

The mound, known as a "tell" by archaeologists, was like a vast layer cake, each layer made up of ruins from an era in Edfu's history. The bottom layers were the remains of much of the pharaonic period, covering more than fifteen centuries, from about 2200 to 600 B.C. The next strata provided evidence of the decline and end of the Egyptian empire and the beginning of the next two thousand years of foreign occupation. The Persians were the first conquerors, ruling until the fourth century B.C. Then came Alexander the Great, who vanquished

Egypt in 332 B.C. and installed a Greek-dominated regime, whose members quickly assimilated with the Egyptians.

When Alexander died nine years later at the age of thirty-two, one of his Greek generals, a man named Ptolemy, claimed Egypt as his kingdom and established hereditary rule. Ptolemy and his descendants reigned for 275 years, from 305 to 30 B.C. The dynasty's final—and most famous—ruler was Cleopatra VII, lover of Julius Caesar and Mark Antony, who killed herself when the forces of the Roman emperor Octavian (also known as Caesar Augustus) crushed the Egyptian army in 30 B.C. and took control of the country.

The ruins of the Ptolemaic age were located near the summit of the Edfu tell, but there were even more layers—the remains of the Roman and Byzantine periods—above them. The Byzantine Empire, from its capital of Constantinople, took over from the Romans in the fourth century A.D. and ruled Egypt until Arabs conquered it in the seventh century.

FOR A TALENTED YOUNG archaeologist like Desroches, Edfu was a fascinating and challenging first dig, which is the main reason Pierre Jouguet sent her there. But there was another likely reason: The archaeologist in charge of the excavation was not French, and he had no hesitation at all about having a woman working under his supervision.

Beginning in 1938, IFAO had taken on a partner—the University of Warsaw in Poland—to work with it on the Edfu site. The collaboration marked the first archaeological partnership between France and Poland in the Mediterranean area. Leading the effort was Dr. Kazimierz Michałowski, who, at the age of thirty-seven, was already regarded as Poland's preeminent archaeologist. He is considered the founding father of Egyptology in his country.

Like Jouguet, who was a close friend, Michałowski had been trained as a Hellenist, specializing in the language and culture of ancient Greece. After studying at universities in Berlin, Heidelberg, Paris, Rome, and Athens, he took part in various French-led excavations at the ancient Greek sites of Delphi, Thasos, and Delos. Having established the University of Warsaw's classical archaeology department in 1931, he then began to concentrate on the centuries-old Greek presence in Egypt.

Desroches felt an instant kinship with the tall, dark-haired Michałowski, who sported a rakish mustache and spoke excellent French, although with a strong Polish accent. He was a perfect gentleman—a *"grand seigneur"*—who treated her with courtesy and respect, she recalled. At the same time, he had a wicked sense of humor and loved to play practical jokes on her and everyone else on the team.

For centuries, Polish men had prided themselves on their charm and chivalry to women, and Michałowski and the other Polish members of the Edfu team were no exception. Desroches was as taken with their verve and dash as she was with their archaeological skills. "They accepted me as one of them," she said. "We got along wonderfully."

She had arrived at the dig at the beginning of that year's excavation season, as had a barge piled high with the team's provisions and supplies, sent up the Nile from Cairo. After some forty workers unloaded the barge, the first order of business was to help pitch the small military canvas tents that would house individual members of the team at their camp near the excavation site. Desroches put up her own tent, then draped mosquito netting over her iron cot and carefully placed the feet of the cot in cups of water to prevent scorpions and other poisonous creatures and vermin from climbing up its legs. She was also warned to keep a close watch for cobras and other deadly snakes, which were wont to slip under the tents' canvas walls.

Her other furnishings consisted of a wooden chair, a small table that served as her desk, and a tripod stand that held a basin and pitcher. There was no electricity or running water in the camp. Water came from a nearby well, and at night she, like the others, used a gasoline lamp, which produced a smoky haze in her tent that made it difficult for her to read or write there.

Soon after her arrival, Desroches found herself working fifteen hours a day. As a junior member of the team, she was assigned several duties in addition to her excavation work; overseeing the kitchen was one of them. Besides ordering food and planning menus, she had to ride herd on the camp's recalcitrant Egyptian cook, whose culinary skills were less than adequate and who also had problems with his personal hygiene. "I kept begging him to take a shower," she wrote, "and when I saw the kinds of things he was preparing for us, I started teaching him his trade." Early every morning, before she left for the excavation, she laid out that day's food provisions. At lunch and dinner, she was so busy monitoring the cook's work that she was always the last one to eat. She showed him how to prepare various French dishes and was thrilled when he mastered a mousseline sauce (akin to hollandaise), which was served with fish caught in the Nile.

But even as his skills improved, Desroches was faced with another headache—planning the menus—which she called "a real Chinese puzzle." One member of the team "was a vegetarian, a second did not eat fish, a third refused to eat anything with salt in it, and a fourth hated cheese. Coming up with meals that pleased everyone, especially considering the shortage of ingredients when you're at the edge of the desert, was almost impossible."

While she was overseeing the kitchen, she also served as the team's nurse. Having been placed in charge of the camp's makeshift dispensary, she followed the example of Françoise Bruyère, treating colleagues and Egyptian workers who fell sick or were injured on the job. This, as she knew from her experience at Deir-el-Medina, was a vitally important assignment. Working in Egypt came with an array of health risks, ranging from mild gastrointestinal upsets to dysentery, hepatitis, typhoid, sand fly fever, and malaria, among other ailments. Any cut, bite, or scratch could easily become infected. Also common were sprains, broken bones, and other injuries from clambering up and down excavation sites.

Scorpion and snake bites were another major worry. Cobras, which were plentiful at Edfu, were particularly lethal, and Desroches kept large quantities of serum on hand to treat their bites, which happened relatively frequently. She became, as she recalled, "quite expert" at giving these lifesaving injections.

Also like Françoise Bruyère, Desroches was often approached for medical treatment by Egyptians not connected with the excavation—in this case, residents of a village just north of the Edfu tell. One afternoon, while working at the dig, she noticed that the Egyptian laborers under her supervision had stopped work and were staring at a procession of people rapidly approaching them from the north. As the column drew nearer, she saw that a man, who was clearly unconscious, was being carried by several of his fellow villagers, while another held high a dead cobra, almost five feet in length, whose head had been crushed.

The villager had been bitten, and after learning the details from the overwrought men who had brought him to her, Desroches figured she had only a few minutes before the victim succumbed to the poison. Motioning them to follow her, she raced toward the camp, about a quarter of a mile away, the procession following her at a frantic gallop.

When she reached the dispensary tent, she filled a syringe with cobra serum and injected the man in three different places on his body, but he remained unresponsive. Her desperation increasing, she remembered a story her father had told her about how his grandfather, a French officer during the Crimean War, revived a dying colleague by getting him to drink half a bottle of liquor and forcing him to run for several minutes. Why she thought that this singularly unconventional treatment might work with the dying villager is unclear, but her apparent conclusion was: What did she have to lose? So she poured half a bottle of Johnnie Walker whiskey down his throat and ordered two of his comrades to pick him up and run with him. He made it a couple of feet before collapsing.

Hearing about the furor at the camp, Michałowski left his section of the dig and hurried back to find out what was going on. When Desroches explained what had happened, the project head was incandescent with anger, "acting," she recalled, "as if I were totally insane." It was far too late to help the man, he shouted. She should have let him die in peace. Now, when he died, the people of his village would blame her and the rest of the team for his death. Not to mention the fact that the man was a Muslim and proscribed from drinking alcohol.

For the next two days, an exhausted, despondent Desroches kept watch over the man, who clung to life even as female members of his family surrounded the tent in which she was tending him and uttered piercing, nonstop ululations of grief. Just as she was giving up hope, he suddenly regained consciousness, "as if by a miracle," and within days had totally recovered. Before he left for home, he told Desroches he had been semiconscious during some of the ordeal, including the moment when she had given him the whiskey. Clasping her hands tightly in his, he exclaimed: "What a beautiful day! May Allah forgive me, but to drink whiskey again, I would willingly be bitten!" She burst out laughing, as did he and everyone surrounding them. With her patient's recovery, she went from pariah to heroine in the camp.

THROUGHOUT HER LIFE, DESROCHES-NOBLECOURT was always on the alert to the slings and arrows she received because of her gender. But her extracurricular assignments as kitchen supervisor and nurse at Edfu—stereotypically female roles, to be sure—never seemed to bother her. Indeed, she took great pride in how well she performed them. Perhaps her lack of resentment stemmed from the fact that Michałowski and his Polish colleagues seemed so grateful to her for taking care of them. "At first they treated me like I was their little sister, and then I was their mom," she recalled, adding that Michałowski repeatedly told her, "What would we do without you?" She expressed pride in the fact that during her five months at Edfu, she was never sick or injured herself but was repeatedly called on to "treat my male comrades, who obviously had weaker constitutions than I did."

It certainly helped that Michałowski made clear from the start that he took her seriously as an archaeologist. Shortly after she arrived, he told her he needed her help. As specialists in ancient Greece and Rome, he and the other Poles on the team worked on the upper layers of the tell containing the remains of the Greek, Roman, and Byzantine eras, while Desroches and her French colleagues conducted excavations close to the tell's base on ruins from the pharaonic period. Knowing little about antiquities from that age, Michałowski realized that, thanks to Desroches's work at the Louvre, she had a far better understanding of the objects than anybody else on the dig. He ended up putting her in charge of all the expedition's finds.

As she acknowledged, it was the perfect job for her: "Unlike some Egyptologists whose knowledge about antiquities came primarily from books, I had already taken an inventory of the items brought back by Mariette and the others at the Louvre, which gave me a hands-on knowledge of everyday objects." Every evening after dinner, she devoted a couple of hours to carefully examining and photographing the items discovered that day, then cataloging them in her daily excavation diary, just as Bernard Bruyère had taught her to do in Deir-el-Medina.

At that point she had already been up since well before dawn, rising when it was still dark to make preparations for breakfast and then arriving at the excavation site assigned her before 5:30 A.M. to get ready for that day's work. Each member of the team had his or her own foreman and workers, who did the actual digging under the archaeologist's supervision. The work on Desroches's site, which was very near the bottom of the tell, was carried out in a particularly slow and careful fashion: She had been warned not to dig too deep for fear of destabilizing the entire tell.

That already delicate labor was greatly complicated by an omnipresent cloud of dust, more than six feet high, that was stirred up whenever there was any movement on the site. Caused by the decomposition of centuries-old rubbish and waste, the fine dust, called *sebakh,* created a thick grayish veil that enveloped everybody working on the dig. Coated with dust, Desroches and her colleagues left the site for lunch looking like zombies from a horror movie. Before eating, they took turns bathing in one of the camp's two large galvanized iron tubs. They did the same in the late afternoon after finishing their work for the day.

THROUGHOUT HER STINT AT EDFU, Desroches firmly kept in mind the lessons she had learned from the Bruyères and Jaroslav Černý. For her, one of the most important was getting to know the Egyptian laborers with whom she worked and treating them with courtesy and respect, unlike other French Egyptologists she knew, who "behaved in the most odious way with their Egyptian workers, acting as if they were lower than the earth." As a woman who had experienced the same kind of treatment from some of her colleagues, she was determined not to follow their example. At Edfu, she worked hard to learn enough Arabic so that she could communicate directly with the workers, although, as she acknowledged, some of her early efforts were spectacularly unsuccessful. In later years, she told the story of the time she asked her foreman to get her a penknife so she could cut a notch at the top of a wooden stake to insert a card noting the location of a new find. Or, at least, that's what she thought she said. The foreman looked at her quizzically. When she repeated her request more emphatically, he nodded and turned, issuing a sharp order to four workers, who immediately rushed toward the camp, nearly a quarter of a mile away. Her irritation growing by the second, she wondered whether he "had completely lost his mind, sending four men to look for such a small thing." When she remonstrated with him, he reassured her, "almost with compassion," that what she had requested would arrive as soon as possible.

Finally, urged on by his shouted demands to hurry, the four men raced back, carrying one of the camp's portable canvas toilets, and set it down carefully in front of her. After staring at it for a moment, she collapsed in laughter, as did the Egyptians, once they realized what had happened. In the dust, she drew a hieroglyph of a penknife. "Ah," said the foreman, "you meant a *sekkini*." On that day, Desroches said, "I enriched my Arab vocabulary by two words—toilet and penknife."

When the workers took a midmorning break each day, they often invited her to join them in sampling the snacks they passed around, usually consisting of onions, hard boiled eggs, cheese, and bread. "The Egyptian people are deeply generous," she later said. "Even among the poor, food and other resources are fairly shared, so that no one lacks the essentials." In her dealings with her work crews, as well as other Egyptians, she was drawn to their gregariousness, spontaneity, and robust sense of humor.

As her Arabic improved and she could better understand what the laborers were saying, she enjoyed listening to their conversations during their breaks and their chanting as they worked. The chants "helped them keep a rhythm in their digging," she said, "but they were also used as a means of communicating with each other. It was a way to spread news about what was going on in their village and on the dig. I once heard a workman chant to the others, 'Look, here comes the cook, heading straight for *la mademoiselle*. Did he forget what he was supposed to make for lunch?'"

Shortly before the excavation season was over, Desroches was invited to attend the wedding of one of the workers. As she watched the ceremony, which included a procession of relatives and friends presenting gifts to the newlyweds, she was struck by how closely this modern tableau of gift giving resembled scenes she had seen on the walls of funeral chapels outside Deir-el-Medina. "These same gestures, these same concerns had been passed down from millennium to millennium without major changes," she later wrote.

THE DAYS IN EDFU were long and grueling and the working and living conditions rudimentary, to put it mildly, but Desroches felt completely at home there. She had grown close to nearly everyone on the dig, with one major exception: a young French colleague who, like her, was a resident fellow at IFAO and who had been working at the Edfu site for two years.

She and he engaged in constant arguments, mainly over politics. He was a member of a far-right antidemocracy group in France, while she hotly defended the Popular Front. Their most heated confrontations, one of which came close to a physical altercation, erupted over the Dreyfus affair, a political and criminal justice scandal that rocked France in the late nineteenth century and continued to divide the country for decades afterward. It involved a Jewish army captain named Alfred Dreyfus who was falsely accused and convicted of passing military secrets to the Germans. Even after Dreyfus's innocence was conclusively proven, many in the military and other rightist groups argued otherwise, including Desroches's colleague, who kept insisting Dreyfus was a traitor.

But what bothered her most about him was his constant complaining about almost everything, including the fact that he had made no significant discoveries in his two years at Edfu. By contrast, Desroches, in her first few months, had made two. The first, found in a burial vault, was a collection of small statuettes of naked young women, adorned with extravagant hairstyles, who were labeled "concubines of the dead" by Egyptologists. According to Desroches, they were supposedly placed in men's graves "so that these gentlemen could have a little fun in the afterlife." As she discovered later, their purpose was a little more complex than that. They served as fertility figures, promising aid in the quest for rebirth and the survival of the next generation. Not long after that find, she and her workers uncovered an exquisite small bas-relief fragment showing the profile of a beautiful young goddess from the Ptolemaic era. Smiling enigmatically, the goddess was attired in an elaborate, finely carved wig, a jeweled necklace, and richly detailed embroidered robes.

Irritated not only by Desroches's success but also by her very presence at the dig, her French colleague asked Michałowski to allow him to switch excavation sites with her. When the Pole approached her with the request, he was clearly embarrassed. Appealing to her generosity, he said, "Christiane, have some pity on him. The poor man has been here for two years with nothing to show for it." Recalling the incident years later, she said, "I know many who would have refused, but Michałowski convinced me. The next morning, my colleague had my work site, and me, his. And then luck smiled on me again."

Near her new site was the tomb of Vizier Izi, the chief government minister in Egypt in 2200 B.C., who was revered as a "living god" after his death. Izi's tomb was an aboveground, flat-roofed rectangular structure made of mud bricks—a common style of burial chamber for eminent Egyptians in the early centuries of pharaonic rule. Egyptologists called the structures *mastabas* ("benches") because they resembled the benches that were commonly placed in front of houses in Arab villages.

Izi's tomb, which had been turned into a place of worship after his death, had already been thoroughly explored by previous French archaeologists, as had the area around it. The consensus was that there was nothing left to find. Nonetheless, Desroches continued to dig nearby, hoping that she could at least uncover a stele—an upright slab engraved with hieroglyphs—or, barring that, any other small item that might be of interest.

Early one afternoon, after several days of fruitless digging, her workers uncovered a stone step. Desroches held her breath as, over the course of an hour or so, they exposed several more steps that led down to a door. It was the dream of every Egyptologist to discover an untouched tomb, but the number who actually had done so was extraordinarily small. Most tombs of the pharaohs and other prominent ancient Egyptians had already been plundered, some just a few years after their deaths, which is why the discovery of Tutankhamun's unpillaged tomb was so remarkable. Desroches had scarcely hoped that she might join Howard Carter and the others in that exclusive group.

But in fact she had. The burial vault that she and her workers had uncovered was intact. When they forced the door open, they could see on the ground traces of the footprints of the worker or priest who had sealed it more than three thousand years before. Later, she said, "I'll never forget that moment as long as I live."

The tomb, it turned out, was that of Vizier Izi's wife, the Lady Sechséchet. Her sarcophagus was surrounded by a rich display of items made of pure gold as well as alabaster, copper, and calcite. There were vases, jewelry, oil lamps, perfume cups, glazed terra-cotta tableware, food and wine jars, and, of all things, razor blades, hardly bigger than modern ones. With the help of her workers, Desroches carefully photographed, drew, and measured the items before wrapping them and placing them in baskets.

Clearing much of the vault by sunset, she and her men headed back to camp with the treasures they had found. "I watched the workers passing by in single file, carrying these precious things," she recalled. "The euphoria I felt was indescribable." After being showered with praise by Michałowski and most of the rest of her colleagues, she hurried to the wooden hut where all the camp's finds were stored, eager to examine the antiquities more thoroughly and begin to catalog them.

On her way there, she saw two cars approaching the camp, coming from Edfu. Determined not to be waylaid by visitors, she rushed into the hut and closed the door.

Once inside, still covered with dust from her afternoon's labors, Desroches got down on her hands and knees to unwrap the items and inspect them. A few minutes later, she heard Michałowski say in a loud voice, "Sire, Your Majesty must come and see our latest findings." A moment later there was a knock at the door, and her boss asked her to come out. "Christiane," he said, "the king of Siam has come to visit us."

Absorbed in her work, she was furious at the interruption. How could Michałowski play another of his incessant practical jokes at a time like this? Edfu was so far off the beaten path that it hardly ever had ordinary tourists as visitors, much less royalty. She didn't answer, and a few seconds later, the door opened. "If it pleases, Sire, Your Majesty may enter," Michałowski said.

Scrambling to her feet, Desroches whirled around, a furious retort on her lips. Standing before her was a diminutive Asian man, not much taller than she, with a retinue of other Asians, Egyptian officials, and police standing behind him. He was indeed the king of Siam, who, accompanied by his family, had come to Edfu during a weeklong tour of Egypt. Blushing furiously, Desroches apologized, then gave the monarch and his party a short lecture on the items she had found that day.

SOON AFTER THE DISCOVERY of Lady Sechséchet's tomb and the king's visit, the excavation season at Edfu came to an end. For Desroches, this first dig of hers had been an unalloyed triumph. Not only had she proved her naysayers wrong about the ability of a woman to withstand the rigors of an excavation, she had done it in style, producing one of the team's most consequential finds that season. Equally important were the lifelong friendships she forged with Michałowski and several others on the team. Indeed, the group had become so close that its members decided to go on holiday together following their departure from Edfu, taking a paddle-wheel steamboat up the Nile to Sudan.

CHRISTIANE DESROCHES AND TWO OTHER MEMBERS OF THE EDFU TEAM ON A DESERT OUTING, 1938

It was on this trip that Desroches first saw the temples of Abu Simbel, cut directly into sandstone cliffs overlooking the Nile. She remembered being overcome by the sight of the four majestic colossal statues on the front of the largest temple, staring sightlessly out over the river. Seated on thrones, each was more than sixty feet high, all of them representations of Rameses II, the great pharaoh who had built the temples in the mid-thirteenth century B.C.

During their holiday, Desroches, Michałowski, and the others made plans to reunite the following year for a new dig in the ruins of Sesebi, an ancient town near the border of Egypt and Sudan and the site of a temple built by Pharaoh Akhenaten, arguably the most controversial ruler of ancient Egypt. The 1939 outbreak of World War II put an end to those plans, but before the conflict began, Michałowski, who had stayed in touch with Desroches, presented her with a welcome surprise.

According to Egyptian government regulations, all the finds from an excavation were required to be shipped to the Egyptian Museum in Cairo, where officials would decide which items would stay in Egypt and which would be divided among the archaeologists' national museums. Michałowski requested that the Louvre be the beneficiary of Desroches's finds. Accordingly, just before the start of the war, the museum received crates containing the little relief of the Ptolemaic goddess and several items from Lady Sechséchet's tomb.

After the war, Desroches-Noblecourt, by then a curator in the Louvre's Egyptian department, returned the favor. Michałowski, who had been named deputy chief of Poland's National Museum before the war, fought against the Germans when Hitler invaded his country in September 1939. He was captured and spent the next six years in a prisoner of war camp in Germany, where he whiled away the time by, among other things, giving lectures on Egyptology to other Allied prisoners. In 1945 he returned to Warsaw, which had been largely destroyed by its German occupiers after the city's uprising in 1944. The National Museum was one of the most prominent casualties; the building had been gutted and nearly all its contents destroyed. To help revive the museum's Egyptian department, Desroches-Noblecourt arranged to send Michałowski a large assortment of artifacts from the Louvre, on a ninety-nine-year lease.

CHAPTER 7

SAVING THE TREASURES OF THE LOUVRE

IN JUNE 1939, DESROCHES WENT ON SUMMER LEAVE, EXCHANGING the scorching heat of Egypt for the blue skies and soft, warm air of Paris. When she arrived, she found the city at its most beautiful, with the chestnut and plane trees in full leaf and the air redolent with the scent of lilacs and wisteria.

But even as she savored the lovely weather, she knew it was as ephemeral as the ebbing hope for peace in Europe. Half a continent away, hundreds of thousands of German troops were massing on the borders of Poland. In Warsaw, residents were digging zigzag trenches in their parks while loudspeakers boomed out practice air raid warnings. If Hitler invaded the country, as now seemed likely, both Britain and France had pledged to take up arms in defense of the Poles.

When Desroches visited her old colleagues at the Louvre, she found the place in turmoil. Although the worsening international situation accounted for some of the angst, its main cause was closer to home. Just a week before she had returned to France, a painting by the renowned French artist Antoine Watteau had been stolen, and a few days later, Henri Verne had been sacked as the Louvre's director. The loss of the painting revealed, in a particularly embarrassing way, serious deficiencies in the Louvre's security system, which hadn't been tightened much since the museum's last great heist there—that of the *Mona Lisa* in 1911. (It was recovered two years later.)

The theft of the Watteau—a small portrait of a young nobleman in a rose-colored cloak and sky-blue breeches—occurred in broad daylight, at a time when guards were on duty and visitors crowded the gallery in which it was hung. The steel wires suspending the portrait from the wall had been snipped, and the thief had apparently slipped the painting under his coat and walked out of the gallery without anyone noticing. Although the theft was discovered later that day and an investigation immediately launched, the Louvre tried to keep the news quiet. Within a week, however, a Paris newspaper had been tipped off about it and broke the story.

Verne's successor was his deputy, Jacques Jaujard, a dark-haired, elegant dresser with saturnine good looks who, unlike virtually every other senior administrator at the museum, had no art history training or experience before joining the staff. The varied career of the forty-three-year-old Jaujard had included stints as an insurance salesman and a journalist before he made a dramatic career change, becoming secretary general of the Louvre and France's other state museums in 1926 and deputy director in 1933.

Before succeeding Verne, Jaujard, who was known for his calm, diplomatic manner and attention to detail, had been charged with the task of preparing France's museums for war. He already had participated in a trial run, having supervised the evacuation of more than five hundred paintings and drawings from the Prado Museum in Madrid to keep them safe from aerial bombardment during the Spanish Civil War in the late 1930s. The Prado treasures, which included works by Goya, El Greco, Velázquez, Titian, and Rubens, were transported across France in February 1939 and stored near the League of Nations headquarters in Geneva.

From the mid-1930s on, Jaujard was convinced that the appeasement policy of France and Britain toward an increasingly aggressive Hitler would not succeed. By 1938, he was sure that war was inevitable and began preparing for the evacuation of the Louvre's major works of

JACQUES JAUJARD, 1945

art. Shortly before the Munich agreement in September of that year, he had ordered the packing of some of the museum's most valuable masterpieces, ready to be whisked away in wooden crates at a moment's notice.

When British prime minister Neville Chamberlain and French premier Édouard Daladier returned from Munich after agreeing to hand over much of Czechoslovakia to Hitler, Jaujard failed to share the general belief that peace had been preserved. Telling his staff not to unpack anything, he intensified the museum's efforts to ready itself for war: ordering hundreds more crates, updating priority lists and evacuation routes, figuring out how to pack and transport large paintings and pieces of sculpture, and staging practice drills.

In early August 1939, Desroches accompanied her parents on a holiday to Savoie, a region in eastern France near the Swiss border, where her mother's family lived. Late in the month, she received a telegram from Jaujard, urging her to return immediately to the Louvre. Germany had just signed a nonaggression pact with the Soviet Union, clearing the way for Hitler to launch an invasion of Poland at any moment.

On the afternoon of August 25, as Desroches bicycled into the Louvre's courtyard, she saw workers digging trenches in the Tuileries gardens adjacent to the museum to provide protection for the outdoor sculptures, while other men were piling sandbags in front of the museum's many windows. Once inside the building, she joined a small army of museum employees and recruits awaiting the signal to get to work.

With the military draft claiming most young men in Paris, Jaujard had had a difficult time assembling a large enough group of people for the huge operation he had in mind. Museum guards, even those with World War I injuries, were drafted, alongside curators, technicians, other staffers, art students, and civilians from outside the museum, including professional movers and dozens of employees on loan from some of Paris's largest department stores.

At five o'clock that afternoon, guards ushered the last of the day's visitors out of the Louvre and locked its giant doors. Moments later, Desroches and hundreds of others swept into action, removing thousands of paintings, sculptures, antiquities, and objets d'art from walls, pedestals, and cases. Because the operation was top secret, Jaujard had banned the use of electric lights that night, to avoid tipping off passersby that something unusual was happening inside. For the workers, the dim light of small portable lamps had to suffice.

Desroches was put in charge of the staff wrapping and packing the *Seated Scribe* and hundreds of other priceless antiquities in the Egyptian department, many of which had been on display at the Louvre since Jean-François Champollion had brought them from Egypt in the early 1800s. But the wooden boxes containing the Egyptian treasures—389 crates in all—also held newer acquisitions, including Desroches's finds from the tomb of Lady Sechséchet in Edfu.

Thanks to the meticulous planning of Jaujard and his staff, the massive three-day effort proceeded with scarcely a hitch. Even the Louvre's largest painting—Veronese's *Wedding Feast at Cana,* which measured twenty-three by thirty-two feet—was able to be transported by removing it from its frame and wrapping it around a giant oak cylinder. Some sculptures and other items, however, were judged to be too fragile or too heavy to be moved, including the pink granite sarcophagus of Pharaoh Rameses III.

At 6:00 A.M. on August 27, after two days and nights of nonstop packing, a convoy of eight trucks pulled into the Louvre's courtyard. They were carefully loaded with crates containing the *Mona Lisa, Seated Scribe,* and other artworks and antiquities. Each crate was marked with a circle denoting the importance of its contents. A yellow circle meant a valuable piece; a green circle, a major work; and a red circle, a world treasure. The crate containing the *Seated Scribe* bore one red circle, while the *Mona Lisa,* nestled in her own velvet-lined case, boasted three.

The trucks were the first in a flotilla of more than two hundred vehicles that, over the next week, would carry some two thousand cases of the Louvre's treasures to hiding places in various châteaux in the Loire Valley, roughly one hundred miles south of Paris. Each convoy was accompanied by two curators or other senior staff members in passenger vehicles, one preceding the convoy and the other behind it. Armed guards were aboard each truck.

On September 1, Hitler invaded Poland. By September 3, when Britain and France finally declared war against Germany, nearly 90 percent of the more than six thousand paintings and antiquities on display at the Louvre had vanished. The only traces of them were white chalk marks on the gallery walls and the empty pedestals, cases, and picture frames lying on the floor.

Initially, most of the artwork was sent to the Château de Chambord, the largest castle in the Loire, which had been built in the sixteenth century to serve as a hunting lodge for Francis I, the French king most closely associated with the Louvre. An ardent patron of the arts, Francis had lured many of Italy's most renowned artists to work for him,

THE LOUVRE'S GRANDE GALERIE STRIPPED BARE OF ITS TREASURES, SEPTEMBER 1939

including Leonardo da Vinci, from whom he had acquired the *Mona Lisa*. Francis I had been the ruler responsible for transforming the Louvre from a medieval fortress to a Renaissance palace, and many of its most precious treasures originally came from his private collection.

At Chambord, the items from each of the museum's departments were processed and cataloged, then dispatched to one of a number of châteaux nearby. The cache of Egyptian artifacts ended up at the Château de Courtalain, a fifteenth-century castle owned by the Marquis de Gontaut-Biron, one of whose ancestors had fought alongside the Marquis de Lafayette in the American Revolution. The marquis was a bridge-playing friend of Charles Boreux, the curator in charge of the Egyptian antiquities department, who was assigned to keep watch over the artifacts for the duration of their stay there. Boreux took up residence at the château, while eight museum guards, also there to protect the treasures, were housed in other buildings on the estate.

ONCE THE LOUVRE'S COLLECTIONS were safely tucked away, there was nothing to do but wait for the war to begin. For the French and British, the interlude turned out to be a long one. While Germany spent September 1939 bombing the Poles into submission, Poland's western allies, after declaring war against Germany, failed to actually wage it. France and Britain's response consisted of sending a few token patrols across the French-German border, and dropping propaganda leaflets and flying reconnaissance flights over German territory.

The French, who had as many soldiers in uniform as Germany and far more reservists, never even considered going on the offensive. French military leaders seemed to believe that all they had to do was to sit tight and wait for the Germans to commit the folly of attacking the allegedly impregnable Maginot Line, with its eighty-seven miles of underground forts, barbed wire, pillboxes, tank traps, and guns.

In October, Desroches received a telegram from Pierre Jouguet in Cairo asking her to return to the IFAO immediately. All the other archaeologists on fellowships at the institute had been mobilized for military service, and even with a war on, there was much work to be done there. It took her eighteen nerve-racking days to get back to the Middle East aboard a ship, crowded with hard-drinking young British and French soldiers, that zigzagged its way across the Mediterranean to avoid German submarines.

As the "phony war" continued with no sign of imminent combat, the IFAO decided to continue the work it had begun on an excavation at a temple north of the ancient complex of Karnak—a gigantic collection of decayed temples, chapels, and other structures on more than two hundred acres near Luxor. Built more than two thousand years before, the main temple of Karnak—dedicated to Amun, the king of the gods; his consort, Mut; and their son, Khonsu, god of the moon—was the largest religious building ever constructed. According to one expert, three of the most majestic cathedrals in Europe—St. Peter's in Rome, Notre Dame in Paris, and the Duomo in Milan—would have fit comfortably within its walls. Although it was now in ruins, the Temple of Karnak and its surroundings, as one historian put it, were "still capable of overshadowing many wonders of the modern world."

But while the site might have been awe-inspiring, working there turned out to be an exercise in misery. Acknowledging later in life how lucky she'd been to be given Deir-el-Medina and Edfu as her first archaeological assignments, Desroches believed that her luck had deserted her this time. To begin with, she was collaborating with just one other archaeologist—a Frenchman named Alexandre Varille, who had been a fellow at IFAO five years before and was none too keen about being paired with a woman.

He and she began their work in March 1940, just as the dreaded khamsin—violent, sand-filled windstorms, with gusts of up to 60 miles an hour—began savaging the site. The winds would continue to rage for much of the next seven weeks, and Desroches bore the brunt of them. Early in her collaboration with Varille, he announced that he was accustomed to working only at night. That meant that while he would be in charge of cataloging the finds and other paperwork, she would be responsible for the actual excavation, which was done only during daylight hours and which was hot and exhausting at the best of times. For more than a month, she and her Egyptian workers struggled to continue their work as the wind-whipped sand scoured their faces and stung their eyes.

In late April, she and Varille received word from Cairo that the war was finally heating up—Germany had invaded Norway and Denmark—and the French government was reducing funds for IFAO.

Without consulting Pierre Jouguet, Varille decided on his own to shut down the site immediately. When the workers arrived the following morning, he announced that they were dismissed as of that day and could pick up the wages for their past work the next morning.

Appalled by the summary firings, Desroches was not surprised when the workers, instead of meekly accepting the abrupt loss of their livelihood, began shouting, "We want work!" When Varille rejected their demands, several started hurling stones at him. He slipped away to summon the police from Luxor, leaving Desroches to try to calm the men. For the short time they had been working together, she had managed to establish a rapport with them, treating their illnesses and injuries as she had done at Edfu and administering cobra serum when needed. She and they were in the midst of a discussion about how to resolve the matter when Varille returned to the site with a policeman. Seeing the pair, the workers erupted again, showering both the policeman and Varille with stones. Finally, armed guards arrived, and the site was shut down.

Varille's shabby treatment of her and the workers had already put him high on Desroches's growing blacklist of obnoxious male colleagues. He soared to the top when she later discovered that all the notes and photographs from her work on the site, which she had turned over to him when she left Egypt, had been published under his name in an IFAO official report. He never once mentioned her name.

ON MAY 10, 1940, Desroches was in Cairo when news broke that German troops had invaded Belgium, the Netherlands, and Luxembourg. Having conquered Poland and Scandinavia, the Nazi blitzkrieg was now slicing through the very heart of Europe. When Desroches heard three days later that German forces had crossed the Meuse River into France, she insisted on returning to Paris. "I could not conceive of staying away from my country under these circumstances," she remembered. "It was a visceral reaction."

Anxious to be close to her parents and the Louvre, she managed to wangle passage on the last French cruise ship to cross the Mediterranean before civilian travel was halted. Antiaircraft guns, sheathed by canvas covers, had been installed on the ship, and after it left Alexandria, naval gunners removed the covers and kept constant watch next to the weapons, searching the sky for enemy planes. The ship, however, made it to Marseille without incident, and Desroches caught the first train to Paris. When she arrived at her parents' apartment, she put down her bags, kissed them hello, and hurried to the Louvre.

She hadn't been back since her frenzied two days and nights of packing up the Egyptian treasures eight months before, and her first sight of the museum's empty galleries took her breath away. It was like a ghost town, she thought, a haunted place of denuded walls and empty picture frames littering the floors. But that sense of otherworldliness dissipated as soon as she entered the reassuring normality of Jaujard's office.

Greeting her warmly, he was his usual calm, unruffled self, albeit with an edge of urgency in his voice. Her return, he said, was providential. With Charles Boreux at the Château de Courtalain and the other Egyptian antiquities curator recovering from surgery, she was the only staffer who could carry out the top priority assignment he was about to give her.

German troops had marched virtually unhindered through northeast France and were now approaching the Loire Valley, Jaujard told her. The treasures at most of the châteaux would have to be evacuated again. Courtalain, the château closest to the German advance, was in the most immediate danger. It was vital that Desroches proceed there at once and oversee the removal of the Egyptian antiquities.

According to Jaujard, the Marquis de Gontaut-Biron had offered the use of another of his châteaux, this one in southwest France, fifty miles from Toulouse and not far from the Spanish border. After removing the artifacts from Courtalain, Desroches was to accompany them more than five hundred miles south to their new hiding place. She would be given two trucks and a carful of guards to complete her mission.

After agreeing to do what he asked, Desroches discovered that the trucks in question were not large enough to handle the massive number of wooden crates involved in the move. As a result, she and her convoy would have to make the trek between the Loire Valley and the south of France three times, each time crossing more than half the length of the country. Just as before, the trucks were to be escorted by cars carrying the curators and other museum staffers who were overseeing the move. But in the chaos of the German invasion, the shortage of passenger vehicles and petrol had become acute, and Jaujard had to rely on staff members and their friends to make up the shortfall by volunteering the use of their own vehicles.

On her first trip to Courtalain, Desroches was accompanied by Paul Deschamps, the retired head of the Museum of French Monuments in Paris and a specialist in the Middle Ages. The grave, dignified Deschamps was to take charge of overseeing the Egyptian antiquities once they reached the Château de Saint-Blancard, their new home. His and Desroches's chauffeur for the journey was a friend of his secretary, a beautiful young woman in a low-cut dress who had offered the use of her sports car for the venture.

When the "pin-up," as Desroches referred to her, emerged from her car at Courtalain, the truck drivers ogled her, while the mistress of the château, the Marquise de Gontaut-Biron, starchily informed Desroches that the woman would not be welcome there. "Madame," Desroches replied, "I would advise you to be kind to her, because it is in her car that we will go to Saint-Blancard tomorrow." The marquise stiffened. "How dare you take her side against me!" she snapped. In the end, the pin-up was allowed to spend the night, but the next day, Desroches noticed that the marquise was still sulking as they left.

After depositing Deschamps and the young woman, along with the first load of artifacts, at Saint-Blancard, Desroches returned to Courtalain with the two empty trucks. The marquise was still angry at her, and the frostiness increased at dinner that night, when another guest, a French general, announced confidently that he was sure Paris would stand firm against the Germans. He added that in order to make sure this would happen, he had commissioned several Catholic masses to be said for the safety of the city. An amused Desroches couldn't resist entering the conversation. "Do you honestly believe," she asked the general, "that your masses will stop the Germans from coming?" The table fell silent, and no one spoke to the young archaeologist for the rest of the evening. "My reputation with the Gontaut-Birons was definitely destroyed," she recalled. "Not only had I supported a 'daughter of the streets,' but even worse, I was a nonbeliever."

By the time of her third trip to Courtalain, German forces were flooding into the Loire Valley, and many roads were either under their control or choked with refugees. Overall, more than six million French citizens, resembling "an anthill that had been knocked over," had poured south during May and June 1940—the largest single movement of people in Europe since the Dark Ages. The scene was pure chaos, filled with "all the ugliness of panic, defeat, and demoralization" of a disintegrating society, remarked the American diplomat George Kennan, who witnessed the flight. The driver of one of the two trucks in Desroches's convoy refused to drive any farther, so she headed to the château with just one.

On the way, she and her diminished convoy stopped at the Château de Valençay, where Jaujard and the Louvre's administrative staff were staying, for last-minute instructions on how to get to Courtalain and back. The route they had previously taken was reportedly impossible to navigate now, with a number of the roads blocked or hopelessly congested with fleeing refugees and French soldiers.

When the convoy entered the grounds of Jaujard's temporary headquarters, Desroches was bedazzled. The hundred-room château, built during the French Renaissance and once owned by Talleyrand, Napoleon's renowned foreign minister, was regarded as one of France's most magnificent noble residences. The writer George Sand called it "one of the most beautiful buildings on earth," adding that "no king has owned a more picturesque park."

But it wasn't the château itself that captivated Desroches. It was the extraordinary variety of exotic animals and birds that the current Duke of Valençay had collected and were now running and flying loose over the château's grounds. There were cockatoos and peacocks, kangaroos and llamas, monkeys and ibises, all sharing the park with its more indigenous inhabitants—squirrels, deer, and foxes.

In the midst of this open-air zoo, Desroches found Jaujard. He was meeting with a small crowd of Louvre curators and administrators, some of whom were not at all happy about being uprooted from Paris, along with the artwork and other items from their respective galleries. While a number of staffers, like Desroches, fully supported Jaujard's determination to resist the Germans as much as possible, others wanted to make peace with the invaders so that they could return to their prewar routines. "Why are we involved in all this?" one curator demanded of Jaujard. "We are scientists, not soldiers!" Jaujard replied, "That's true. But today, we are citizens of France above all."

During Desroches's brief stop at Valençay, Jaujard, who was also in charge of France's other state museums, asked the head curator of the museum in Compiègne to return there to retrieve some valuable pastel drawings by the nineteenth-century French painter Henri Latour. The curator refused, saying Compiègne, a city northeast of Paris, was too close to the front lines and he risked being captured or shot by the Germans. "If the sound of cannons frightens you so much," Jaujard coldly responded, "I'll go myself."

Just then, a man standing near Desroches stepped forward. She recognized him as one of the government officials who had accompanied Jean Zay, the Popular Front minister in charge of culture, when she gave Zay a tour of the Egyptian antiquities department in 1936. He was Jean Cassou, a highly regarded writer, magazine editor, and art critic who, after his stint with the Popular Front, had joined the national museums' administrative staff.

The forty-two-year-old Cassou, who was helping to oversee the paintings and other items stored at Valençay, volunteered to go to Compiègne in Jaujard's place, to allow him to continue supervising this second evacuation. A few days later, Cassou would bring the Latour drawings back intact, and not long after that, he and Desroches would meet again.

But at that particular moment, all that Desroches cared about was snatching a few moments of Jaujard's time to talk about the last, most dangerous part of her assignment. After discussing possible new routes to Courtalain, he told her that in addition to the artifacts, she must evacuate the museum guards at the château, along with their wives and children, to the Château de Saint-Blancard. She agreed, having no idea how she was going to manage escorting all these people, let alone the remaining crates of artifacts, to safety.

After a nightmarish journey north, Desroches finally arrived at Courtalain, where she again angered the marquis and his wife by asking them to provide food for her passengers on the return journey south. When they refused, she declared that the provisions had been requisitioned by Jaujard and there was nothing they could do about it. "Of course," she later said, "I didn't have any requisition orders, but they didn't know that. And after all, I had to feed my troops."

Her "troops"—the guards and their families—numbered more than twenty people, ranging in age from a three-week-old baby to an eighty-two-year-old grandmother. They, along with the remaining crates, were crammed into the truck and two cars for the trip. As difficult as it had been to reach Courtalain, the five-hundred-mile return to Saint-Blancard turned out to be even more of a nightmare. The roads were virtually impassable, crammed with thousands of refugees and their bicycles, baby carriages, and carts and wagons piled high with mattresses and other belongings. At times, Desroches jumped out of the car she was riding in and played traffic cop, motioning carts, wagons, and people to the side of the road so that her little convoy could get through. More than once, she and the others in the caravan had to take cover in ditches and fields when Stuka dive-bombers flew low over the roads and emptied their machine guns into the swarms of refugees below them. Drawing on the nursing skills she had acquired in Egypt, Desroches tended to the wounded. Yet, "by some inexplicable luck," all her own charges managed to make it through without being hit.

This seemingly endless journey, which normally would have taken one day, stretched into three. By the second day, most of the food and water Desroches had managed to cadge from the marquis and his wife were gone. The convoy stopped at several shops in villages along the way, but their owners insisted they had nothing left to sell. At her wit's end, Desroches suddenly spied several cows, their udders swollen with milk, mooing loudly in a field. She ordered the driver of her car to stop, the truck and car behind them following suit.

Retrieving a bucket from the truck, she approached the cows. As a child, she had learned the fundamentals of milking during the summer vacations she and her brother had spent in the countryside of Savoie. Now she was able to put that skill to good use, filling the bucket to the brim with milk, which she gave to the children and a few adults in her party.

The next day, the truck, the cars, and their bedraggled, hungry occupants finally arrived at the Château de Saint-Blancard. After spending a couple of days helping to unload the crates and organizing housing, meals, and clothing for the guards and their families, Desroches returned home to her parents and the Louvre. "I wasn't going to stay there stashed away for the rest of the war," she later said. "There were far more important things to do in Paris."

CHAPTER 8

RESISTING THE NAZIS

WHILE DESROCHES WAS SHEPHERDING THE EGYPTIAN TREASURES from the Loire Valley to the south of France, German troops had marched into Paris and occupied the city. When she returned, she was stunned by what she saw—and didn't see. The weather was glorious, but Paris displayed none of the bustle and gaiety that were its usual hallmarks on a beautiful summer day. Gone were the incessant blare of car horns, the laughter and buzz of the conversations of Parisians strolling along the boulevards or sipping their coffee at sidewalk cafés. The city was eerily quiet—a silence only occasionally broken by the screech and roar of large black Citroën and Mercedes sedans carrying high-level Nazi functionaries along the Champs Élysées and other major thoroughfares.

Like the rest of occupied France, Paris was under the command of the German military, which had been quick to requisition its best hotels for their headquarters. Enormous black-and-red swastikas flew over the Ritz, the Crillon, and other grand hotels; atop the Eiffel Tower and the Arc de Triomphe; and above public buildings like the Senate and Chamber of Deputies. Wehrmacht troops goose-stepped along the Champs Élysées each afternoon, and German cannons pointed menacingly down the four main boulevards radiating out from the Place de l'Étoile. Restaurants that once displayed English Spoken Here signs now made clear that *Hier Spricht Man Deutsch*.

As she bicycled to the Louvre on her first day back, Desroches noticed Nazi flags fluttering along her route down the rue de Rivoli from the Place de la Concorde to the museum. When she arrived, she reported to Jaujard on her harrowing but successful final trip to Saint-Blancard. He in turn presented her with the civilian equivalent of a battlefield promotion: Because both Charles Boreux and the other Egyptian antiquities curator were still away, he made her acting head of the department.

For the twenty-six-year-old Desroches, it was an honor—but one that didn't mean very much at the time. "I was a leader without an army, a queen without a kingdom," she noted. "Apart from some statues that remained on site, the exhibition rooms were empty." While she took the job seriously, she devoted much of her prodigious energy for the rest of the war to defying the Germans—an effort of which Jaujard was well aware.

Within days of returning to Paris, she, along with a handful of others in the city, began challenging the Nazis at a time when virtually no one else in the country was doing so. The suddenness and magnitude of the collapse of the French army and government had traumatized the vast majority of her compatriots, producing an array of emotions—shame, shock, anger, and despair, not to mention a sense of relief on the part of some that the war had come to an early end for France.

For Desroches, there was no such relief. She'd been horrified when the new French prime minister, Marshal Philippe Pétain, announced on June 17, 1940, that he had asked Hitler for an armistice. The following day, she and her parents listened to a BBC broadcast by General Charles de Gaulle from London calling on his compatriots to defy Pétain's government and rebel against the Germans. "We all had tears in our eyes," she remembered. "The general was right—a thousand times right. France could not make an alliance with a Nazi state."

A few days later, she ran into Jean Cassou at the Place du Carrousel, a square at the end of the Louvre's expansive courtyard. She hadn't seen him since the memorable day in Valençay when he had volunteered to collect the Latour artwork from Compiègne. He told her he had just been named head of the new Museum of Modern Art. After exchanging a few more pleasantries, Cassou suddenly grew quiet and shook his head. "My poor young friend," he said, "we are in a very bad way in this country."

She nodded, then mentioned de Gaulle's speech. "Ah, you heard it, too!" Cassou exclaimed. "What did you think of it?"

"The same as you, I think. It was magnificent!"

Pulling her aside, Cassou whispered that he and eight other friends had just formed a group to come up with ways to fight back against the Nazis. He asked her to join them. She thought for a moment, then asked for twenty-four hours to consider it. "This was a decision I couldn't take lightly," she later said. "If I agreed, it had to be a full and unconditional commitment. I was inclined to do it right from the start, but I was worried about my parents. Should I tell them? I finally came to the conclusion it was wiser to keep them in the dark."

She found Cassou the next day and announced, "I'm in."

THE REST OF THE group included writers, professors, and other intellectuals, all of them prominent figures in Paris's close-knit leftist cultural circles. Among them was Marcel Abraham, who'd been Jean Zay's chief of staff in the Popular Front government and who was the official who had accompanied Zay to the Louvre and was present for Desroches's tour.

Yet another was the art historian Agnès Humbert, whom Desroches had known since 1936, when both were involved in activities promoting the Popular Front. A divorced mother of two grown sons, the forty-three-year-old Humbert was a curator at the National Museum of Popular Arts and Culture. Fiery, passionate, impetuous, and irreverent, she had a razor-sharp intelligence and a wicked sense of humor. She shared Desroches's and Cassou's fierce sense of outrage about France's capitulation to Germany. "I will go mad, literally, if I don't do something," she exploded to Cassou after the armistice was announced.

With Desroches now in attendance, the group held its clandestine meetings at the office of two other members—brothers who were book publishers—on the rue de l'Abbaye, behind Saint-Germain-des-Prés church and across the street from the famed café and literary hangout Les Deux Magots. At one of their first sessions, Agnès Humbert announced to the others that she had heard that the Nazis had just banned nonbusiness gatherings of three or more people. To evade German scrutiny, she suggested they pose as a literary committee called the Society of the Friends of Alain Fournier, whose ostensible purpose was to publish a new edition of a classic World War I novel written by Fournier, a young French writer killed during that conflict.

The group's first mission was to create flyers, leaflets, and posters that denounced both the Nazis and their French collaborators, drawing material from BBC news broadcasts as well as from speeches by President Franklin D. Roosevelt and the new British prime minister, Winston Churchill. To run off copies, members of the society were allowed to use a mimeograph machine in the basement of the Musée de l'Homme (Museum of Man), France's national museum of anthropology. The posters and flyers were then plastered on walls, public urinals, and telephone booths, stuffed into mailboxes, and deposited on park benches. Desroches and Agnès Humbert also slipped them under stacks of clothing and fabric remnants in department stores.

In the fall of 1940, the Friends of Alain Fournier joined forces with another fledgling resistance organization, whose headquarters was at the Musée de l'Homme and which was already involved not only in propaganda work but escape line activities and the gathering of military intelligence. Like Desroches's comrades, the Musée de l'Homme network was an unlikely collection of rebels. Most of its members were scholars and other intellectuals, including anthropologists, art historians, museum curators and directors, linguists, writers, and librarians.

It was hardly a surprise that the museum whose name the group bore was at the center of these early resistance activities. Housed in a massive Art Deco building on the Left Bank overlooking a marble plaza with spectacular views of the Seine and the Eiffel Tower, the

Musée de l'Homme, under the leadership of its director, Paul Rivet, had been a hotbed of opposition to Nazi racist theories promoting the innate superiority of Aryan peoples.

With little experience in politics and none at all in insurgency, the network's members set out to encourage their countrymen not only to reject collaboration with the enemy but to actively defy them. "What we wanted to do in 1940 was to somehow wake up France, force it to become aware that we were not at Pétain's service and that he did not represent us," one of its leaders remembered. "It was," a British historian remarked, "as though the upper echelons of the British Museum had turned to new careers as urban guerrillas and saboteurs."

In the first weeks of the occupation, the network was already busy recruiting friends and colleagues, making new contacts, and bringing other small, recently organized resistance groups, including the Friends of Alain Fournier, into the Musée de l'Homme orbit. Within a few months, the organization had "transformed itself into a veritable spider's web covering the whole of France," according to the French historian Tatiana Benfoughal.

In addition to creating propaganda material, Desroches and the others from her original group now found themselves helping to hide British and French troops who had been captured by the Germans during the battle for France and who, with the network's help, had slipped out of temporary POW encampments throughout the country. After providing British soldiers with civilian clothes and false papers, the network smuggled them into the Vichy-governed "free" zone in the south of the country, starting them on their way back to freedom.

But the most significant achievement of Desroches's outfit in those early days was publishing, on behalf of the larger network, the first underground newspaper in France's occupied zone. Called *Résistance,* it gave a name to the mass movement that would follow, equating "resistance" with a rejection of the occupation and a resolution to work against it, not through individual initiatives but through structured groups that would link with other organizations to form networks. First published on December 15, 1940, the newspaper was initially distributed mainly in Paris and then throughout the country. Jean Cassou and Marcel Abraham were its main writers, while Agnès Humbert came up with ideas for articles, then edited and typed them. Desroches served as her assistant.

In *Résistance*'s first issue, a front page editorial proclaimed to its readers: "Resistance! That's the cry that bursts from your heart, in your distress at the disaster that has befallen our nation." The editorial continued: "Your immediate task is to get organized like us so that you can resume the struggle. Yesterday we in this group did not know each other; none of us were involved in the party squabbles that took place in the government or the Assembly. We are independent, simply French. . . . We have only one ambition, one passion, one desire: to recreate France, pure and free."

Under the leadership of Boris Vildé, a Musée de l'Homme anthropologist, the network soon shifted into higher gear, opening escape routes over the Pyrenees into Spain and collecting and transmitting military intelligence to London, including information on German military installations and airfields. In early 1941, the group would provide British authorities with drawings of the German submarine pens and huge dry dock at the Atlantic port of St. Nazaire—information that would result in arguably the greatest Allied commando raid of the war, a March 1942 assault on the St. Nazaire dock that would put it out of action for the rest of the conflict.

Throughout the network's brief existence, its members considered themselves a team of equals. There were none of the rivalries, feuds, or struggles for power that plagued many if not most of the resistance organizations that followed them. Members who survived the war described a deeply collegial atmosphere in which they and their comrades felt themselves part of the same family, united by love of country and outrage against the Germans. Another difference between this early network and those that came later was the major role played by women—a stark contrast to subsequent male-dominated resistance organizations in which women were relegated to supporting roles.

That feeling of equality helped contribute to a sense of joy that the group's members felt in one another's company. Although "joy" seems at first glance an inappropriate word to use when referring to such dark and dangerous times, several prominent members of the network noted the lighthearted, cheerful atmosphere that pervaded their work. In his memoirs, Jean Cassou recalled, "For me, there is one word for this time in my life: happiness."

"Although [the network's members] were serious people," the American journalist and historian David Schoenbrun wrote, "they looked upon what they were doing as a lark, a gay adventure for cultured men and women who had always led a cloistered life." Echoing that view, Cassou noted, "We did not slink about in cloaks and daggers, looking grim. We laughed a lot and felt younger than we had in years."

Increasingly, however, there was much to be grim about. In October 1940, both Jean Cassou and Agnès Humbert were fired from their museum jobs by Pétain's Vichy government. Their dismissals had nothing to do with their covert resistance activities, which the authorities did not yet know about; they were among hundreds of French civil servants targeted by Vichy for having leftist, antifascist views. At that point, Desroches apparently was not on Vichy's radar, because she was left untouched.

As the months passed, the dangers increased. Total novices in clandestine activity, the Musée de l'Homme agents were organizing on the fly and making things up as they went along, with little idea of how to operate in this dark new netherworld. The threats they faced were heightened by the network's explosive growth. Put simply, they were trying to do too many things—publish a newspaper and other propaganda material, run escape lines, and collect military intelligence—all the while failing to pay close attention to security. Some of its agents, including Desroches, were involved in all these actions, which turned out to be a prescription for disaster.

"I think that if our network had survived, we would certainly have separated the activities of escape and intelligence," one of its leaders, the anthropologist Germaine Tillion, said after the war. "But that was something we couldn't do in the beginning, when we were starting from scratch. We simply didn't have the resources or the experience."

DURING THE EARLY YEARS of the war, Desroches led a surreal life. At night and on weekends, she was enmeshed in the secret world of the French resistance. During the work week, she was at the museum, overseeing her depleted department and teaching a class on hieroglyphics at the École du Louvre.

Despite the fact that most of the collections were in storage, German authorities ordered Jacques Jaujard to open the Louvre and display what was left. On September 29, 1940, the Germans staged a reception at the museum celebrating its reopening. Among the high-ranking Nazi officers there was Field Marshal Gerd von Rundstedt, who had led Germany's Panzer divisions during the invasion of France. Jaujard and the Louvre's curators were also ordered to attend; most of them, including Desroches, wore black.

When the Louvre opened its doors to the public a few days later, German troops were given free admission, while the French had to pay one franc. They didn't get much for the fee. With no paintings on display, all those galleries were closed. A small number of rooms on the first floor exhibited the sculptures and antiquities that had been left behind because they were too fragile or heavy to be moved. To fill the cases in the Egyptian antiquities galleries, Desroches brought up some of the reserve items stashed in crates in the basement. Even though she bitterly resented the presence of Germans in the museum, she was following the lead of Jaujard, who had instructed his staffers to do their best to maintain the Louvre's high standards in its service to the public. "Every day, we heard the sound of German army boots," she recalled. "Those boots with nails in them that scratched the marble floors. It was unbearable. But we had to do it."

Even as he looked after the museum, Jaujard was leading a double life, too: He was playing a cat-and-mouse game to prevent the Louvre's stored treasures from falling into the hands of the Germans. Their hiding places were not a secret. Within days of the occupation of Paris,

German military authorities had acquired reports of the artworks' locations and immediately stationed soldiers to guard the châteaux where they were being stored.

On June 30, 1940, Hitler sent a message to German officials in Paris ordering them to "take into custody the French state-owned treasures." He knew that an outright theft of the Louvre collections would cause a major international outcry: The Hague Convention of 1907, one of the first multilateral treaties that addressed the conduct of warfare, forbade the looting or destruction of monuments and works of art by invading military forces. To justify his order to seize the collections and bring them back to Paris, Hitler declared that he simply wanted to "safeguard" them.

Jaujard knew he could not flatly refuse the Führer's demand. Instead, he resorted to a strategy he would use again and again during the war: delay. He replied that the risk of Allied bombing of Paris was still a major threat. Couldn't they wait awhile until things died down?

In this campaign, he had an unlikely ally—none other than the German officer Hitler had appointed to monitor France's art collections and to assist top Nazis, like Luftwaffe chief Hermann Goering and foreign secretary Joachim von Ribbentrop, in looting treasures for themselves. The officer was Count Franz Wolff-Metternich, a noted scholar of Renaissance art and architecture who before the war had been an art history professor at the University of Bonn. To Jaujard's great relief, the aristocratic forty-seven-year-old Wolff-Metternich was also strongly anti-Nazi.

When Wolff-Metternich was introduced to Jaujard on August 16, 1940, he gave the museum director a hearty handshake and said, "Sir, you are the first high-ranking French civil servant I have found at his post." The two got along well from that moment. In his diary, Jaujard recalled that Wolff-Metternich seemed almost relieved to find the Louvre's art gone, and he agreed with Jaujard's strategy of delay and postponement.

Fierce bureaucratic infighting among the various Nazi authorities in Paris played into their hands. Citing Hitler's directive, Otto Abetz, the German ambassador in Paris, had ordered more than fifteen hundred

COUNT FRANZ WOLFF-METTERNICH (RIGHT) AND HIS DEPUTY, BERNHARD VON TIESCHOWITZ, BOTH OF WHOM WORKED TO SAVE THE LOUVRE'S TREASURES FROM THE NAZIS, UNDATED

paintings and other items to be retrieved from the Château de Chambord. Learning of Abetz's order, Wolff-Metternich informed the German military high command in Paris, which had control of the city. The military responded with a new order forbidding any confiscations without Hitler's express permission for each item. Abetz then invented a new ploy, saying that the items at Chambord had been inadequately packed and stored and therefore must be brought back to Paris for their own protection. In response, Wolff-Metternich said that nothing could be done until he received a full inventory of the items from the director of the Louvre, as well as a written order from the commander in chief of the German army. The army command in Paris upheld him.

But while Wolff-Metternich and Jaujard scored early victories against Abetz, they faced another serious foe: the government in Vichy, whose collaborationist leaders were only too eager to hand over France's art treasures to its German occupiers. Goering, a rapacious art collector and plunderer, approached Vichy to acquire two items he was keen on having. One was *La Belle Allemande,* an exquisite sixteenth-century life-size wooden figure of a naked Mary Magdalene. The other was the stunning *Ghent Altarpiece*—a many-paneled medieval work by the Flemish painters Hubert and Jan van Eyck that measured a monumental eleven by fifteen feet. Jaujard did all he could to stop the transfer of the two pieces, but Pétain's deputy, Pierre Laval, overrode him. They were sent to Carinhall, Goering's lavish country estate northeast of Berlin. Yet as difficult as it was for the Louvre's director to surrender these treasures, his months of delaying tactics resulted in overall victory. Although Abetz and other Nazi officials in Paris kept trying, they would never succeed in their attempts to snatch the vast majority of the Louvre's masterpieces.

At the same time, though, Jaujard was powerless to do anything to stop the Germans' massive looting of priceless artwork owned by French Jews. Even though such plundering was also a violation of the Hague Convention, Hitler made it clear he didn't care. He authorized the seizure of all Jewish-owned paintings, sculpture, furniture, carpets, jewelry, and other valuables, and Goering provided the staff and trains to transport the treasures to Germany.

Before they were transferred, the items were stored in several rooms on the ground floor of the Louvre. When that space proved insufficient, the overflow was sent to the Jeu de Paume, a small museum then used by the Louvre to house temporary exhibitions. Although Jaujard agreed to provide the space, he insisted on a quid pro quo: Museum employees must be allowed to keep an inventory of all the items brought to both the Louvre and the Jeu de Paume.

The staffer put in charge of the inventory was Rose Valland, a quiet, unassuming middle-aged art historian who had worked at the Louvre as an unpaid volunteer for years. The Germans paid little attention to the bespectacled Valland, considering her to be a harmless, insignificant administrative flunkey. She was in fact a spy planted by Jaujard to keep close track of every item brought in as they were cataloged and prepared for shipment; her main job was to find out their destination in Germany. She turned over her meticulous records to Jaujard and his staff, several of whom had links to the French resistance, which in turn passed much of the information to London. On occasion, Valland also managed to sneak out negatives of photos taken by the Germans of particularly valuable pieces, which a friend of hers printed. After returning the negatives the next morning, she passed on the photos to Jaujard. They, too, would find their way to London. As a result, before the war was over, the Allies were already aware of where much of the looted art had been sent and avoided bombing those locations.

Meanwhile, in late 1942, Jaujard lost his German collaborator. Franz Wolff-Metternich's bosses in Germany apparently figured out what he'd been up to. They fired him from his position in Paris and forced him to return to Berlin. His replacement, however, proved to be as anti-Nazi as Wolff-Metternich and continued to support Jaujard's efforts to thwart the Nazis.

LIKE ROSE VALLAND, CHRISTIANE Desroches, with Jaujard's help, was able to use her work at the museum as a cover for espionage activity. One of her tasks for the Musée de l'Homme network was to act as a courier, carrying messages back and forth between Paris and network members in the so-called "free zone" of Vichy France. To travel between the Nazi-occupied north and the unoccupied zone in the south, French citizens needed an *ausweis,* a German-issued identity card that was exceedingly difficult to obtain and carefully examined each time its bearer approached the border. Desroches was able to get one by claiming she needed to travel to the south to check on the Louvre's Egyptian artifacts, which were being stored in the free zone near the border between France and Spain.

When she asked Jaujard to arrange one for her, he looked at her with a knowing smile. Both of them were aware that the Egyptian antiquities were being well taken care of by senior staff at Saint-Blancard and didn't need any help from her. "You're right, mademoiselle," Jaujard said, his eyes twinkling. "Your crates need you. What professional dedication you have!"

On the morning of December 12, 1940, she set out on a trip that would take her to Vichy and then to Toulouse, both in the unoccupied zone. When she arrived in Toulouse, she was to hand over a small piece of paper she had been given, which she suspected contained military intelligence that was to be transmitted to London.

Three hours after leaving Paris, her train pulled into the station at Moulins, a town in central France near the demarcation line between the occupied and free zones. A few moments after it stopped, she was arrested by an SS man who demanded to see her *ausweis*. As she was hustled off the train, its other passengers stood silently and at attention, as if, she thought, they were acting as a final guard of honor for her.

Two more Germans were waiting for her on the platform. They shoved her into the back of a car and took her to the Gestapo headquarters in Moulins. She spent the next several hours huddled in an icy cell, shivering with cold and fear and wondering what she should do with the incriminating piece of paper she was carrying. Should she tear it up? But if she did that, how would she get rid of the pieces? Should she swallow them? But then she thought—"stupidly," as she later acknowledged—that they might X-ray her and detect the paper. So she folded it up to make it even smaller, placed it between her fingers, and put on her gloves.

At last she was escorted to the room containing her Gestapo interrogators. After she refused to answer their questions, they began searching for incriminating material, emptying the contents of her purse, breaking her umbrella and the heels of her shoes, and ripping out the lining of her sheepskin coat. Finding nothing, they ordered her to take off her clothes. She refused, saying that she would submit to a strip search only if it was done in another room and performed by a woman. A female guard was called, and she, too, found nothing. Desroches removed all her clothing, but, unaccountably, she was allowed to keep her leather gloves on.

After the search's failure, her interrogation resumed. As it proceeded, her mounting anger at her questioners' arrogance erupted into a diatribe about their extraordinary insolence. Convinced that further interrogations lay in store, perhaps involving torture, she was astonished when, after several hours, she was suddenly released. Years after the war, she concluded that her freedom was the result of Franz Wolff-

Metternich's intercession. Having signed the *ausweis* permitting her to cross the demarcation line, he must have been contacted by the Gestapo and calmed their suspicions about her. "That's why I was released so quickly," she surmised. "I understood that I probably owed my life to him, because an arrest at that time usually meant a trip to a concentration camp."

After she was freed, Desroches continued to Vichy, where she collapsed, spending the next forty-eight hours in bed before proceeding to Toulouse and handing over the message that had almost cost her her freedom and perhaps her life. Back in Paris, she correctly surmised that the Gestapo would now be keeping a close watch on her. Its agents began making conspicuous monthly visits to her office at the Louvre and occasionally searching it. Because of the intense scrutiny, she decided to cut back her resistance activities for a while.

Desroches believed that someone had tipped off the Gestapo about her. The German security net was closing in on the Musée de l'Homme network, and Jean Cassou was warned that he would be its next target. He was as worried about his wife as he was about himself: She was Jewish, and her brother, a well-known philosopher, was also on the run from the Gestapo. Thanks to Jacques Jaujard, Cassou and his family, including his wife's parents, were given *ausweis* documents, which allowed them to escape to the unoccupied zone. They took up residence in Toulouse, where Cassou continued his resistance work. Several other key members of the group, including Marcel Abraham and Paul Rivet, director of the Musée de l'Homme, managed to flee to the south as well.

Others were not so fortunate. In February 1941, seven months after the network was launched, the mass arrests began. The group's leaders were betrayed by one of its own members, a man who served as a top lieutenant to Boris Vildé but was in fact a double agent working for the Gestapo. In the first of several Gestapo roundups, Vildé and the two other founders of the network—Anatole Lewitsky and Yvonne Oddon, both high-level staff members of the anthropology museum—were captured. Soon to follow were Agnès Humbert and a dozen others.

For almost a year, those under arrest were kept in prisons and jails in and around Paris while the Germans investigated their resistance activities. The painstaking inquiry was part of the preparations for an elaborate show trial, meant to underscore to the French public the perils of engaging in any kind of opposition to the Third Reich.

On January 8, 1942, eighteen network members—twelve men and six women—were put on trial by a German military court in Fresnes Prison near Paris. Ten were sentenced to death by firing squad—seven men, including Vildé and Lewitsky, and three women, among them Oddon. (The judge, however, would commute the women's sentences to deportation to German concentration camps.) Agnès Humbert and five others were sentenced to five years in German prisons. The three remaining defendants were found not guilty.

In the late afternoon of February 23, the seven condemned men were loaded into a bus and driven to Mont-Valérien, a snow-covered hill overlooking the Bois de Boulogne and the main site the Germans had chosen for the execution of members of the French resistance. When asked if they wanted blindfolds, they all said no. As they faced their executioners, they began singing "La Marseillaise," somewhat haltingly at the beginning, then louder and louder in unison. They didn't stop until the shots rang out. The German prosecutor at their trial, who witnessed the executions, later declared, "They all died as heroes."

Although the Musée de l'Homme network lasted less than a year, it had a significant impact on the resistance groups that followed it. It served as an inspiration—a ray of light—to would-be resisters, showing them that it was indeed possible to oppose the Nazis, in action as well as in spirit. It was their readiness to fight and die that lit a fire in others, noted the *New York Times* correspondent Alan Riding, who wrote a book about cultural life in Paris during the war. "At a time when most of the French were coming to terms with the occupation," Riding wrote, "they were almost alone in acting on their belief in the idea of resistance." According to the French historian Julien Blanc, the Musée de l'Homme group "fed and watered the Resistance to come."

Devastated by the destruction of her network and the deaths and deportations of so many of her friends, Desroches knew how lucky she was to have escaped. When she eventually resumed her resistance activities, she was much more careful, working mostly within the confines of the Louvre. Many of her efforts involved collaborating with Jaujard on the reports he regularly sent to the Allies providing them with the latest updates regarding shipments of Jewish-owned art and the status of the Louvre's stored collections.

A good many other Louvre curators were also active in underground work, both in Paris and at the various châteaux where the museum's artwork was stored. Several of those based in the countryside joined newly formed quasi-guerrilla groups called maquis, which lived off the land and became involved in sabotage and subversion. Indeed, René Huyghe, the highly respected chief curator of the museum's paintings department, took over leadership of one such group in southwest France, near the Château de Montal, where Huyghe was in charge of the treasures it contained.

With Jaujard's blessing, the museum housed a variety of other resistance activities. His deputy founded an underground journal that regularly published news of the wholesale German theft of Jewish property and the Vichy government's collaboration in those efforts. Copies of it, along with those of another underground newspaper, were printed on the museum's duplicating machine and stored in the basement before being distributed.

The Louvre's labyrinth of dusty underground rooms, stretching almost half a mile, also served as hiding places throughout the war for escaped Allied soldiers and airmen, Jews, and members of the resistance, all on the run from the Nazis. In addition, Jaujard allowed his own apartment, which was located on the Louvre grounds, to be used occasionally as a safe house. He sheltered Jean Cassou there before his escape to Toulouse; later in the war, the apartment would be used as a secret meeting place for the National Council of the Resistance, a body organized in 1943 to coordinate the movements of the French underground.

One of the unsung heroes of World War II, Jacques Jaujard was high on the list of the people Desroches most admired in her very long life. In 1942, he named her to a permanent paid position at the Louvre.

But in a letter to Vichy officials, her nemesis—Charles Boreux, head curator of the Egyptian department—reported that while she was extremely qualified in terms of her work, she should be rejected for this new job and in fact should be dismissed from the Louvre for refusing to sign an oath of loyalty to Pétain and Vichy. Louis Hautecoeur, Vichy's director of fine arts, who was responsible for allowing Nazi leaders to steal Jewish-owned art, agreed with Boreux. In his report on Desroches, Hautecoeur pointed out that she had been arrested once by the Gestapo and was suspected of being a supporter of General de Gaulle and the Free French.

At that point, Jaujard took up the matter with Hautecoueur's superior—Jérôme Carcopino, Vichy's minister of culture. It was a risky move, but Jaujard was betting that Carcopino was one of the few Vichy officials who supported Pétain but were secretly opposed to his collaboration with the Germans. He turned out to be right: Carcopino upheld Desroches's appointment. If Jaujard hadn't stood up for her at that crucial moment, her career as an Egyptologist would have been over.

BY MID-1943, THE ALLIES had finally halted Germany's seemingly unstoppable momentum. Their attention now turned to planning the long-awaited invasion of Western Europe the following year. On June 6, 1944, after months of intense preparation, Allied troops landed on the beaches of Normandy to launch their assault on France's German occupiers. After a long, bloody summer of slogging across Normandy's hedgerow country, they finally broke out in late July and began storming through the heart of France.

As the days ticked by, Paris became a tinderbox. While waiting impatiently for the city's liberation, its residents were eager to settle the score with the Germans. In early August, a series of Communist-inspired strikes was launched in the capital; railway men, police officers, and postal and telegraph workers, among others, walked off the job. The Communists called for an armed insurrection, to start on August 18. At seven o'clock that morning, small bands of resistance fighters throughout Paris opened fire on German patrols. Other groups burst into public buildings, ousting their occupants and taking over. Although the uprising caught the Germans by surprise, it didn't take long for them to respond. Troops and tanks charged into the center of the city, killing and wounding hundreds.

The Louvre, just yards from the epicenter of the German military command, found itself at ground zero, under fire from all sides. German troops had dug in throughout the Tuileries Gardens, which bordered the museum, as well as along the rue de Rivoli and at the Place de la Concorde. Heated skirmishes, involving extensive gunfire, broke out between the Germans and resistance fighters, some of whom were attempting to gain control of the 1st arrondissement's town hall, located across the street from the Louvre.

Having anticipated such a scenario, Jaujard had mobilized his staff at the Louvre beforehand, just as he had done in his planning for the evacuation of the museum's treasures prior to Germany's invasion of Poland in 1939. Just before the Paris uprising broke out, he summoned Desroches and dozens of other curators and staffers to camp out at the Louvre for an indefinite period of time to protect the building from the mayhem that he was sure would soon engulf it.

On the morning of August 18, Desroches braved heavy gunfire as she rode her bicycle through the streets of Paris. As she passed the Place de la Concorde, a German tank opened fire on a nearby government building occupied by resistance members. Arriving at the museum, she hurried inside just as another German tank began firing at the Louvre itself. The cavernous galleries echoed with the noise of shellfire from the street fighting outside.

When Desroches reached her office, she was taken aback to find Jaujard there, along with a young colleague who'd been hired during the war to work in the Egyptian department and who had shared her office for several months before being assigned one of his own. Desroches was even more surprised when she saw a gun in Jaujard's hand; when she learned where it had come from, she was speechless with rage.

In his summons to the Louvre employees, Jaujard had instructed them to retrieve any firearms they might have hidden there, to be available for use if needed for the museum's defense. Under German regulations, possession of a firearm was punishable by death, and, earlier in the war, Jaujard had ordered his staffers who were in the resistance and had acquired weapons to make sure they were well concealed.

As it turned out, the colleague sharing Desroches's office, without her permission or knowledge, had stashed a gun and a box of ammunition on one of her bookshelves, behind a twelve-volume set of books on ancient Egyptian inscriptions. "He knew I had been arrested and was being closely watched by the Germans," she later said. "He put me at incredible risk, because if the Gestapo had found those weapons during one of their searches, I would have been shot on the spot."

Yet as angry as she and Jaujard were, they and everyone else at the Louvre had more immediate concerns. The museum was now surrounded by German tanks, and throughout that day, stray shells and bullets pockmarked its stone exterior and blew out dozens of windows. Those in Desroches's office were shattered, and Jaujard was almost hit by a bullet that passed through one of his apartment windows.

The Louvre staffers manned their stations for more than a week. While Desroches and the other curators stood watch in the galleries, guards patrolled the museum's ancient wooden roof, keeping an eagle eye out for sparks from projectiles that could instantly set it ablaze. With their bird's-eye view of the courtyard and streets below, the guards also acted as spotters for resistance fighters, signaling tank movements to a sentry box below, which was linked by phone to the Paris fire department. The information was passed on to the firemen, who in turn passed it on to the resistance.

When not on guard duty, the staffers retreated to the basement to confer with one another, as well as to sleep and eat. Jaujard's wife had stockpiled so much food that, despite the length of their stay at the museum, none of them went hungry. According to Desroches, Madame Jaujard had performed "a veritable miracle."

As the insurrection raged, Jaujard paid close attention to radio news broadcasts from the BBC. On August 24, hearing that the liberation of Paris was near, he summoned his bleary-eyed staff at five in the morning. Keeping a wary eye out for German tanks, he led them to the museum's clock tower overlooking the vast courtyard. When everyone had gathered, he unfurled a French flag, announcing that "the time has come to restore what we've been deprived of for the past four years." With that, he ordered the flag hoisted to the top of the tower. "I can't tell you how emotional that moment was for all of us," Desroches recalled.

The following morning, Allied troops entered Paris, led by the French Second Armored Division, under the command of General Philippe Leclerc. Throngs of Parisians hugged and kissed the soldiers as they marched and rode by on tanks. Climbing on the tanks, bystanders handed the troops flowers and glasses of champagne, while the church bells of Paris—Notre Dame, Sacré-Coeur, and Sainte-Chapelle, among others—rocked the city with their joyous peals.

But there was no celebration yet in the streets around the Louvre, where the fighting had, if anything, intensified. The Germans were still fiercely defending their military command buildings nearby, firing from behind the metal shutters of the Jeu de Paume and sandbag-blanketed statues in the Louvre's garden. The museum was caught in the cross fire. Only later in the day, as Allied tanks joined the fray, did resistance fighters finally gain the upper hand.

By the end of the next day, more than six hundred German soldiers in the area around the Louvre had surrendered. There was no building large enough to hold them on such short notice, so they were brought into the courtyard of the museum, where they would stay, guarded by resistance members, until they could be moved to a more secure area.

Late that evening, some resistance snipers on the rooftops of buildings on the rue de Rivoli decided to amuse themselves by taking potshots at the German prisoners in the courtyard. The panicked Germans scattered like ants, some taking shelter in the courtyard's corners while others smashed the Louvre's ground-floor windows and dived inside. In the confusion, several members of the resistance who had heard the shooting and rushed into the courtyard grabbed Louvre staffers who had gone to the aid of wounded prisoners, claiming that they were collaborators. Among them was Jacques Jaujard, who was marched across the street, a gun pointed at his back, to the 1st arrondissement's town hall, where an unruly group of resistance fighters threatened to shoot him on the spot. He was saved by Robert Rey, the director of the École du Louvre, who, having witnessed what was happening, rushed to the town hall and finally managed to convince Jaujard's captors that he was in fact the head of the museum.

Meanwhile, the search was on for the dozens of Germans who had taken shelter in the Louvre. As Desroches approached the massive pink granite sarcophagus of Rameses III, accompanied by several museum guards, she was confronted by a frightening apparition: several figures, black as soot, rising from the sarcophagus, their arms raised high in the air. "Our two groups, face-to-face, shared the same surprise, tinged, I must admit, with a certain fright," she later recalled. In addition to the Germans in the sarcophagus, who were covered from head to toe with the thick grease and dust that had accumulated inside it, an additional dozen prisoners were discovered in the Egyptian antiquities department, hiding behind cases and statues.

SEVERAL DAYS AFTER THE street fighting had died down and Paris had been officially liberated, officers from the Allied forces' Monuments, Fine Arts, and Archives Division (informally known as the Monuments Men) arrived at the Louvre. The group, whose members included art scholars, museum curators, archivists, and historians, had been assigned the job of tracking down and recovering the colossal lode of art and artifacts looted by the Nazis. They had come to Paris to thank Jaujard for passing on information about the plundered art during the war and to seek help from him and Rose Valland in finding it. With Valland by their side, they would locate thousands of stolen masterpieces squirreled away across the Continent, hidden deep in salt mines, stored in abandoned buildings, and secreted inside hilltop castles.

During the waning months of the war, as more areas of France were liberated, other resistance members returned from the prisons and camps in which they'd been held. One was Jean Cassou, who had been arrested in Toulouse in December 1941 and sentenced to a year in a Vichy prison for his resistance activity. After his release in 1943, he resumed his resistance work. That same year, Charles de Gaulle's provisional government, based in Algeria, appointed him its representative in the south of France. When Toulouse was liberated, Cassou and several other resistance members were involved in a car crash with an armed German patrol that had been chasing them; he was critically injured and spent three weeks in a coma. According to Desroches-Noblecourt, de Gaulle came to Cassou's bedside to present him with the Ordre de la Libération and to offer him a high-ranking job in the provisional government. Cassou shook his head, saying "I just want to go back to my museum." He got his wish: He was reinstated as director of the National Museum of Modern Art, a post from which he had been fired by Vichy after only three months on the job and that he would hold until 1965.

Cassou would later be joined there by his friend and resistance collaborator Agnès Humbert, who survived three hellish wartime years working in several German slave labor factories that made synthetic fibers. From the toxic chemicals used in the work, she suffered repeated acid burns to her hands, arms, throat, face, and eyes. In late 1944, with the war drawing to a close, the forty-seven-year-old Humbert caught a quick glimpse of herself in a mirror. "I look like I'm seventy," she wrote in the diary she secretly kept. "I'm stooped, my skin is yellow, my eyes are hollow, and every day I look more and more skeletal."

Yet her constant excruciating pain and lack of adequate nourishment failed to extinguish her natural resilience, rebelliousness, and sense of humor. In the spring of 1945, the factory in which Humbert worked was bombed by the Allies, and she and the other female prisoners were evacuated to various small towns in western Germany. On April 3, 1945, the U.S. Third Army took control of the town in which she was held, and, once free, she metamorphosed again into a woman of action. American military authorities took full advantage of her fluent German and English, irrepressible energy, and impressive organizational skills. They put her in charge of running the town and providing shelter, food, and first aid to refugees. She also began collecting political intelligence and set up a local denazification program before finally returning to France in the fall of 1945.

Jean Cassou immediately hired her as a curator at the Museum of Modern Art, where, at various gala receptions held in postwar years, she outraged her socialite daughter-in-law by ostentatiously turning her back on guests who had fraternized with the Germans during the war. After one such reception, Humbert's grandson remembered his mother saying, "I suppose that gentleman's behavior during the war wasn't beyond reproach, but really! Fancy refusing to shake his hand!" Humbert's grandson added admiringly, "That's the way Agnès always was: uncompromising, defiant, impervious to whatever people might say."

CHAPTER 9

SHOCK WAVES IN EGYPT

ONE MONTH AFTER THE WAR ENDED IN EUROPE, CHRISTIANE Desroches was on the road again with a truckload of the Louvre's most valuable Egyptian antiquities. This time, she was bringing them home.

The following day, the *Mona Lisa* returned to the Louvre. So did the *Winged Victory of Samothrace,* which arrived in an oversized truck provided by the British army. Soon after its return, Desroches and the Louvre's other curators looked on as the enormous headless figure of the goddess Nike was slowly hoisted up a giant ramp and placed on its old perch atop a broad marble staircase.

It would take more than a year for all the museum's collections to come back. During the war, Jacques Jaujard, taking advantage of the bareness of the galleries, had embarked on a major renovation of some of them, and the Louvre's interior still looked as though a maelstrom had swept through it. Many paintings remained at their wartime storage locations until the work was completed. But Parisians, recovering from the rigors of the war and occupation, clamored for life to return to normal, which included the reopening of the museum, one of the main centers of cultural life in Paris. In response, the Louvre mounted a small exhibition in July 1945, displaying the *Venus de Milo* as well as the *Mona Lisa* and more than eighty other paintings. Less than a year later, it staged a larger exhibit at the Petit Palais, a smaller museum off the Champs Élysées, featuring more than three hundred paintings by French artists.

At long last, on October 7, 1947, the entire museum, including the refurbished Grande Galerie, opened its doors to the public, with virtually every one of the many thousands of paintings and antiquities evacuated during the war safely back in its place. Among them was the *Belle Allemande*, the wooden statue of Mary Magdalene looted by Hermann Goering, which he had stashed in a German bunker as the Allies approached. It was found there by the Monuments Men.

After the war, tribute was paid to Jaujard and his small army of curators and other staffers who had risked their jobs and lives to keep the Louvre's treasures safe. James Rorimer—one of the Monuments Men who worked closely with Jaujard after the liberation of Paris and who later served as head of New York's Metropolitan Museum of Art—said of the Louvre director, "He had repeatedly fought the German demands for France's national art treasures with no weapon but courage and no defense but integrity."

In late 1944, Jacques Jaujard stepped down as head of the Louvre. He was replaced by Georges Salles, a former Louvre curator and the director of a small museum devoted to Asian art. The grandson of Gustave Eiffel, who built the Eiffel Tower, Salles had been in the resistance during the war and, having been caught by the Germans, was sent to prison. Jaujard persuaded Franz Wolff-Metternich to step in and arrange Salles's release.

In 1945, Jaujard was named director general of fine arts in France, and in 1959, he became secretary general of the country's cultural affairs. In 1964, at Jaujard's behest, the French government honored Count Franz Wolff-Metternich for his role in saving the Louvre's art from the Nazis, presenting him with the Legion of Honor.

With its grand reopening in 1947, the Louvre had finally turned the page on World War II. So had Christiane Desroches. After five years of uncertainty and upheaval, she was finally able to focus her full attention on her work at the museum. Now a permanent curator, she was also teaching at the École du Louvre and beginning to put down on paper some of the conclusions she had reached about various aspects of ancient Egyptian life.

"The first ambition of an Egyptologist should be to free oneself from received ideas about Egyptian civilization," she later said. In her early scholarly writings, she noted, "I repeated what the masters had written but also tried to express my personal opinions. Why, for example, had scenes from everyday life been depicted on the walls of royal tombs?" Many if not most Egyptologists thought that wall paintings in the tombs showing scenes of hunting, fishing, and working in the fields were reflections of the deceased's earthly existence that he wished to continue in the afterlife. Desroches, however, believed that they and the objects found in the burial vaults also should be viewed as symbolic images of the challenges faced by the dead royals during their journey through the underworld as they sought to find eternal life. That thesis would become a major theme of her later prolific body of writing.

At the same time, Desroches, while juggling her various professional responsibilities, had taken on two new roles. At the age of thirty-two, she was now a wife and mother.

EARLY IN THE WAR, during one of her trips to Toulouse as part of her resistance work, she had encountered André Noblecourt, an old friend of her brother's whom she had known since childhood and who had patiently helped her with her homework in math, one of the few academic subjects she had had trouble mastering. Now an engineer, the thirty-year-old Noblecourt wooed Desroches during their several meetings in Toulouse and eventually won her by promising that marriage to him would not mean an end to her career. "He was too intelligent to try to prevent me from doing what I wanted to do," she said.

They married in 1942 but, at Desroches-Noblecourt's insistence, remained apart until the end of the war. "I was still in the resistance," she said. "It was too dangerous. You never knew where you'd be the next day, or who you'd be exposing yourself to. I had comrades who'd been deported. I didn't want to put him in danger. It would have been completely stupid."

Later in the war, Noblecourt joined the French Forces of the Interior (FFI), a body of resistance fighters under the command of General Charles de Gaulle's Free French. As Paris and other regions of France were liberated, the FFI were organized into light infantry units and served as a valuable manpower addition to regular Free French troops.

When the couple finally began living together toward the end of the conflict, Desroches-Noblecourt was as methodical about having children as she was about marriage. "I told him, 'I'm working,'" she recalled. "We'll see about having a family later on. . . . After the Armistice, I decided that I wanted a child, and we had a son." When the baby was born in 1946, she named him Alain to commemorate the Society of the Friends of Alain Fournier, and she chose as his honorary godparents her nine comrades from that faux literary group.

Quiet and unassuming, André Noblecourt took a back seat to his energetic, outgoing wife throughout their fifty-seven-year marriage, supporting her in everything she did. "He demonstrated a feminism very unusual for his time by encouraging her in all her undertakings and helping her overcome the obstacles that arose with her projects," said Guillemette Andreu-Lanoë, a later colleague of hers at the Louvre. Desroches-Noblecourt's decision to combine her own surname with that of her husband—a rare step for a French woman to take in the 1940s—signaled her determination from the first to retain her own identity.

According to Henri Loyrette, the former director of the Louvre, André Noblecourt acted as his wife's "prince consort." Eventually Noblecourt would become part of her world, developing an expertise in museum security and serving for a number of years as a technical security adviser to the Louvre and other state museums of France.

Her life overflowing with activity, both professional and personal, Desroches-Noblecourt had almost no time in the immediate postwar years for what had been her favorite prewar pursuit—working in the field in Egypt. She returned there only twice in the late 1940s, both times for brief personal research missions. Each time, when she arrived in Cairo, she felt a distinct sense of unease.

—

FOR EGYPT, THE WARTIME years had been both searing and chaotic. As always, Cairo had been at the center of the action, serving as the base for Britain's military headquarters in the Middle East. The North Africa campaigns had been planned there, as had the battles for Greece and Crete, the invasion of Syria, and the guerrilla war in Yugoslavia. Indeed, as the historian Alan Allport pointed out, Cairo for several years served as "the military capital of the British Empire."

Late in 1940, British forces had scored a series of early triumphs over Italian troops in neighboring Libya. But those victories turned to dust when German general Erwin Rommel and his Afrika Korps rushed to the Italians' rescue. In only ten days, German forces regained almost all the ground the British had captured in three months. Resuming his attack in early 1942, Rommel and his troops swept toward Egypt, advancing 350 miles in little more than ten days. His offensive, which Winston Churchill termed "a disaster of the first magnitude," was a looming strategic calamity for Britain, threatening its access to Middle East oil as well as its control of the Suez Canal.

Egyptian officials, meanwhile, had no say in the British conduct of the war from their country. In 1936, the two nations had signed an agreement terminating the British military occupation of Egypt, but, as usual, the British had inserted a huge loophole: If Britain went to war, King Farouk, who had succeeded his father, King Fuad, in 1936, was obliged to turn over control of Egyptian ports, airfields, and territory for the duration.

When Britain declared war against Germany in September 1939, the agreement went into effect. But the twenty-two-year-old Farouk and his government threw a monkey wrench into the process by resisting pressure from the British to declare war on Germany themselves. They insisted that the Egyptian people would rebel against such a step, pointing out that there was already considerable public unrest over skyrocketing prices and shortages of food, particularly staples like bread and sugar. As the war progressed, the shortages grew worse and the turmoil deepened. Workers at the port of Suez, blaming the British for the shortages, staged a brief strike, and students at Cairo University mounted several demonstrations, carrying placards declaring LONG LIVE ROMMEL and DOWN WITH THE ENGLISH.

British authorities suspected that Farouk and his prime minister shared the students' pro-Axis sympathies in the belief that a victory by Germany and Italy in the Middle East would end British control of Egypt. When Rommel's advance posed a threat to the country in early 1942, the British decided to act. In early February, they gave Farouk an ultimatum: Get rid of his current prime minister and appoint a pro-British official in his place by February 4 or be forced to abdicate.

Late in the evening of the fourth, having heard nothing from the king, British authorities, in what the British writer James Morris called "one of the last acts of imperial swashbuckle," stationed tanks in front of the royal palace, while some six hundred British troops armed with Sten guns surrounded it. An armored car and a Rolls Royce carrying the British ambassador, Sir Miles Lampson, forced their way through the palace's iron gates, and six British officers, their guns drawn, disarmed the guards. Once inside, Lampson, a six-foot-five, 250-pound behemoth, read a prepared statement to the young king accusing him and his advisers of assisting the enemy by refusing to appoint pro-British government officials. Declaring that "Your Majesty is no longer fit to occupy the throne," Lampson, who habitually referred to Farouk as "the boy," handed him a letter of abdication and ordered him to sign it. The shaken king gave in to Lampson's threats, pleading for another chance and promising that he would get rid of the current prime minister and appoint the man the British wanted. Later that night, Lampson wrote, "So much for the events of the evening, which I confess I could not have more enjoyed."

Western governments had been ordering Arab leaders around for decades, but Lampson's humiliation of Farouk was regarded by most Egyptians, together with the rest of the Arab world, as well beyond the pale. The king was hardly a paragon of virtue; he was indolent, venal, devoted only to pleasure, and notoriously corrupt. But although his popularity had dramatically declined among Egyptians in the half dozen years he had ruled, he was still their king, and the indignities heaped on him by the British sparked a paroxysm of national outrage.

No group was more upset than twenty-four-year-old Gamal Abdel Nasser and his fellow officers in the Egyptian army. The son of a rural postal clerk, Nasser had spent three years at Egypt's royal military academy, which one historian described as "an incubator of intense Egyptian nationalism, sharply spiced with resentment of the academy's British military advisers." Tall and broad-shouldered, the well-spoken, well-read captain, who spoke fluent English, was a rising star in the Egyptian military. After graduating from the academy, he had studied at the army's elite postgraduate staff college, then returned to the academy as an instructor.

To Nasser and his generation, Britain was behind all the problems that afflicted Egypt. "Oppose them with all the force you can muster," he wrote a friend in 1936. Devastated by Farouk's mortification, Nasser wanted the army to rise up against his country's occupiers, declaring he was ready to die to defend Egyptian honor and dignity. He was hardly alone; dozens of other officers were eager to join the cabal. Hearing of the plot, Farouk sent the would-be rebels a message, thanking them for their support but ordering them to return peacefully to their duties. They obeyed, but their anger remained unassuaged. Nasser responded by creating an underground group of his military colleagues called the Association of Free Officers. Among the fourteen members of the founding committee was a young captain named Anwar Sadat, who was even more of a firebrand than Nasser.

Meanwhile, the German threat that had spawned Britain's crackdown on Farouk ended in failure. In July 1942, Rommel's advance on Cairo was stopped by the British at El Alamein, about 150 miles west of the city. That was the closest the Afrika Korps ever came to the Egyptian capital.

A few months later, Rommel's forces were defeated by the British Eighth Army at the second battle of El Alamein, and Allied forces invaded French North Africa during Operation Torch. By the spring of 1943, the Allies had ousted Germany and Italy from the Middle East,

COLONEL GAMAL ABDEL NASSER, UNDATED

and the Axis forces were headed for defeat in the war's other military theaters.

When the conflict finally ended in 1945, public pressure mounted again in Egypt for freedom from British control. The clamor escalated in 1948 when Britain ended its mandate over Palestine but refused to do the same for Egypt. After Britain's withdrawal from Palestine, the newly formed United Nations partitioned the region into two states, one controlled by Arabs and the other by Jews. The new Jewish state of Israel promptly declared its independence, which was followed just as promptly by an attack on Jewish territory by troops from five Arab countries, including Egypt.

Hoping to acquire a share of the territorial spoils if Israel was defeated, Farouk and his government sent the Egyptian army into battle without adequate training and preparation and with defective and outdated arms and other equipment. The result was a disaster: The disorganized Egyptian forces were outmaneuvered and outfought by the Israelis. Among the few units that acquitted themselves well was the brigade commanded by Nasser, which was cut off and surrounded in the Faluja Pocket, an area near Gaza, but refused to surrender. Nasser and his men held out until a cease-fire was ordered.

Infuriated by what they considered Farouk's betrayal of the army, Nasser and his secret organization added the ouster of the king and his cronies to their short list of priorities for the uprising they had been planning since the war.

WHEN CHRISTIANE DESROCHES-NOBLECOURT ARRIVED in Cairo in early 1948, the war between Israel and the Arabs was still five months in the future. Even so, there was a disquieting atmosphere of tension and restlessness in the city that she was happy to escape.

She returned to the excavation site near the ancient complex of Karnak that she'd been working on in early 1940, before it was so unceremoniously shut down by her supercilious French colleague Alexandre Varille. After the war, Varille's frequent collaborator, the equally arrogant Clément Robichon, had taken charge of the dig.

Desroches-Noblecourt was there to finish one of the projects she'd started in 1940: copying lengthy hieroglyphic inscriptions on a sixty-foot-high door at the Temple of Montu, the falcon-headed god of war. She asked Robichon to set up scaffolding so she could access the entire height of the door. He did so, but it was a ramshackle effort—she had to clamber up several rickety ladders to get to the top. "The ascent every day was quite perilous," she recalled. "It was freezing cold, and the wind was howling. I had to be extremely careful because there were no guardrails on the scaffolding." Years later, when she described the scene to an interviewer, he asked her why Robichon had not been more concerned for her safety. Her answer was brief and loaded with innuendo: "One can imagine that he was a bit of an anti-feminist."

At night, one of the Egyptian workers would stand watch over the scaffolding to prevent the wood from being stolen by local scavengers. On her second morning at the site, Desroches-Noblecourt recalled, "I was getting ready to climb onto the scaffolding, praying that it would hold up, when I noticed a new face in place of the guard from the day before." When she asked the man where the other guard was, he took his right hand out of his pocket and showed it to her. It was missing a thumb.

She suddenly recognized him. He was one of the workers on the dig in 1940; he had been trying to move a heavy sandstone column when it fell and crushed his thumb. Just as at Edfu, she had been in charge of nursing the sick and injured on the site, and after giving first aid to the man, she had rushed him to the infirmary.

He told her now that the first guard was a thief and would have stolen the boards of the scaffolding himself if he hadn't been replaced. "You might have fallen," he added. "Do you think I would let you break your neck after what you did for me? Your care will always remain in my head and in my heart!" She later noted, "This kind of gesture is frequent among Egyptians. If you respect them, if you don't hurt their dignity, you will never have any reason to reproach them. They are the most faithful and loyal of friends."

Throughout her time in Egypt, Desroches-Noblecourt had come to care deeply for the local people she had gotten to know. When her latest stint there was over and she headed home to her family and the Louvre, she couldn't help feeling a deep concern about the future of her friends and their country.

BY 1951, THE PRESSURE cooker that Egypt had become was approaching its boiling point. Three years earlier, the British had withdrawn some of their troops but kept ten thousand soldiers there to guard the Suez Canal. In 1950, the two countries' governments had begun renegotiating the 1936 agreement that, among other things, had granted Britain the right to station its forces at the canal until 1956. The Egyptians wanted them gone immediately, but the British resisted, and the negotiations dragged on with no end in sight. Finally on October 11, 1951, the Egyptian government had had enough. The country's prime minister unilaterally abrogated the agreement.

The British declared that the termination was both unacceptable and illegal. World War II might be over, but the Cold War had taken its place as the British rationale for maintaining control of the canal, which they insisted was a critical lifeline for their country. It was vital, they said, to defend not only the canal but the entire Middle East from what they claimed was an imminent Soviet threat. To underscore that argument, they flooded the Canal Zone with eighty thousand more troops—eight times the number permitted under the 1936 agreement.

Egyptian public reaction was swift and violent. Thousands of workers went on strike in the Canal Zone and against British-owned companies, while hundreds of young men joined what were called "liberation squads"—paramilitary groups that conducted guerrilla operations against British troops stationed in the zone. As casualties mounted, the Egyptian government seemed powerless to control the rapidly metastasizing disorder.

On January 25, 1952, the commander of the British forces in the Canal Zone issued an ultimatum to the police in the town of Ismailia, some of whom had been involved in guerrilla actions against the British, to surrender their station and leave the town, which lay inside the zone. When the police refused, a British battalion, accompanied by six tanks and armored personnel carriers, attacked the station, killing forty Egyptians, most of them policemen, and wounding more than seventy.

The next day, tens of thousands of Egyptians took to the streets of Cairo. In one of the most violent urban rampages in modern Egyptian history, mobs roamed throughout the city, killing, looting, and setting fire to hundreds of office buildings, hotels, shops, clubs, and other places owned or frequented by Europeans, particularly the British. Shepheard's Hotel went up in flames, as did the Thomas Cook travel agency, Barclay's Bank, the Turf Club, the British airline office, the British Council, and the French Chamber of Commerce. Seen from afar, it appeared that all of Cairo was ablaze. The Egyptian government made no effort to control the mayhem, which claimed the lives of seventy-six people, nine of them British. Unable to come to grips with the growing crisis, the country's cabinet was reshuffled four times between January and July 1952.

Until July, Nasser and his Association of Free Officers, which had greatly expanded in size, had remained relatively quiet. They had urged Egyptians to join the struggle against the British, and some of them had helped train guerrilla fighters, but they had not actively participated in the actual fighting. Now, with the vacuum of power deepening in Cairo, Nasser came under tremendous pressure from inside and outside the organization to take action.

On July 22, 1952, he decided the time had come. He and the association's other leaders, calling for "the liquidation of colonialism and the Egyptian traitors who supported it," placed their members and the army units they commanded on immediate alert. Early the next morning, the units occupied the post office, radio station, army headquarters, and other strategic centers, as well as all the bridges leading into and out of the city. That night, they surrounded the royal palace.

In the months leading to the coup, Nasser had been urged by some of his colleagues to arrest King Farouk, put him on trial, and execute him. He refused. Instead, Farouk was presented with a demand that he abdicate, with which he readily complied. Within a few hours, the king, his wife, and more than two hundred pieces of luggage were on their way to exile in Italy aboard the royal yacht, sent off by a twenty-one-gun salute.

The coup had been almost completely bloodless, and Nasser was determined to keep it that way. The plotters had encountered almost no resistance, and once it became clear what had happened, joyous demonstrations erupted throughout Cairo, with crowds chanting support for the army insurgents who had vanquished the detested Farouk and his government. Finally, for the first time in 2,138 years, Egyptians were in control of their country.

As soon as the king was gone from the scene, Nasser and his men turned their attention to the many British and French civil servants who filled high-ranking slots in the government bureaucracy. All of them were summarily dismissed, including Father Étienne Drioton, Desroches-Noblecourt's mentor, who had headed the Egyptian Antiquities Service for sixteen years.

To further underscore his determination to obliterate the British-controlled past, Nasser changed the name of Cairo's largest public square from Ismailia Square to Liberation Square. A sprawling British army barracks had once overlooked the square but had been torn down shortly before the army officers' coup.

THE EXPULSION OF FRENCHMEN from the Antiquities Service sent shock waves through the Egyptology community in France. The French had been in charge of archaeological pursuits in Egypt for almost a hundred years, and coming to grips with the end of that influence was exceptionally difficult. French Egyptologists also worried about what this seismic shift would mean for their and other Westerners' involvement in future excavation projects.

For the Egyptians, assuming total control over their antiquities was a priority that was not open to debate or discussion. For generations, the plundering of precious artifacts by the French, British, Germans, and other Westerners had been a particularly painful symbol of the colonialism that those struggling for Egyptian independence had been determined to end.

As it happened, the first Egyptian to take charge of the Antiquities Service was not an Egyptologist by training. He was Mustafa Amer, a renowned geographer and prehistorian who was known as "the spiritual father of geographical studies in Egypt." Now in his late fifties, Amer had founded the geography department at Cairo University, which, under his direction, had become noted for its study of the relationship between the natural world and human activity—an expansive conception of geography that included the study of archaeology. It operated separately from the university's archaeology department.

Founded in 1908, Cairo University* had become a seedbed for upward mobility in Egypt, helping to produce a rapidly growing educated and professional class—archaeologists, teachers, engineers, lawyers, journalists, and other white-collar workers—a number of whom were appointed to positions in the new government. Because British authorities had opposed any kind of public higher education for Egyptians, the university had begun as a small private school. It became a public university in 1925, three years after Britain granted quasi-independence to Egypt.

Since there were so few Egyptians with advanced degrees who could serve as deans and professors, the university had to rely at first on French and other European scholars to fill the gap. Egyptian students were sent to European universities for further education and training, with the idea that some of them, having acquired advanced degrees abroad, would return to Egypt to teach at the university and other educational institutions.

Mustafa Amer was one of them. After graduating from a teachers' college in Cairo in 1917, he earned a master's degree in geography from the University of Liverpool in 1921. He loved his time in Britain, and while he considered the study of geography to be intrinsic to Egypt's sense of national identity, he also strongly believed in the importance of international teamwork, including the idea that geographers from various countries should take part in joint expeditions in Egypt and other parts of the Arab world.

The need for international cooperation was especially essential in the field of Egyptology, Amer believed. He and others in the government were keen on the idea of creating an Egyptian counterpart to the

* For the first forty-two years of its existence, the university was known as Egyptian University. Renamed King Fuad University in 1940, it became Cairo University after the 1952 coup.

French Institute of Oriental Archaeology in Cairo. The creation of such a center, to be run by Egyptians, was regarded as particularly important at a time when the country's ancient temples, tombs, and other monuments were under increasing threat from flooding, erosion, and modern industrialization.

Amer wanted to recruit an Egyptologist from the West to help establish the new center. But with the barring of non-Egyptians from government positions, how could he possibly pull that off? The answer came from UNESCO, an agency of the nine-year-old United Nations.

IN APRIL 1945, THE United Nations was founded in San Francisco with the goal of preventing future wars. Seven months later, representatives of forty-five nations gathered in London to create an offshoot of the new body, called the United Nations Educational, Scientific and Cultural Organization—UNESCO for short. Its chief objective was to contribute to international peace and security by "promoting collaboration among nations through education, science, culture and communication." It would be based in Paris.

Initially, UNESCO's first priority, which would be funded by contributions from its member countries, was to help restore and reconstruct the cathedrals, museums, historical sites, and other artistic and cultural treasures of Europe that had been damaged or destroyed in the war. But it soon broadened its focus to the conservation and protection of "books, works of art, and monuments of history and science" throughout the world, including sites in Africa, Asia, and the Middle East.

In 1954, the Egyptian government, urged on by Amer, asked UNESCO for its assistance in creating the new research and documentation center it had in mind. Specifically, government officials asked the body to name a Western archaeologist to act as chief of a special UNESCO mission that would oversee the center's founding.

When UNESCO asked the Egyptians which archaeologists would be acceptable to them, the name Christiane Desroches-Noblecourt headed the list. But when she was first approached, she said no, pleading family responsibilities. Her son was still young, just eight years old, and she didn't want to leave him and her husband for an extended length of time. Unwilling to take no for an answer, UNESCO asked her again, and again she refused.

At that point, she was summoned to a meeting with a high-level French government official, who turned out to be Marcel Abraham, an old comrade from the Musée de l'Homme network and one of her son's honorary godfathers. "You were full of enthusiasm and energy during the war," Abraham barked. "Why not now? I don't understand how you can refuse a scientific assignment to help our Egyptian friends, when in the past you've always been in favor of international cooperation. You simply can't refuse this mission. Your husband and mother will take good care of your son. He will not lack for attention."

Desroches-Noblecourt finally gave in, but she made clear she considered the post a temporary one: She would stay in Egypt only long enough to set up the center. As it turned out, however, her mission there would lead to an intimate involvement with the country and its threatened heritage that would last for more than thirty years and take her all over the world. Her quiet life as a scholar focusing primarily on curating, teaching, and writing had come to an end.

CHAPTER 10

"OZYMANDIAS, KING OF KINGS"

NEWS OF DESROCHES-NOBLECOURT'S APPOINTMENT LANDED LIKE a bombshell in the male-dominated world of Egyptian archaeology. The forty-year-old Frenchwoman was one of the first women of any nationality ever appointed to a leadership position in the field, but that was not why the shock was so intense. It had more to do with the fact that she and UNESCO intended to make Egypt a major player in Egyptology. For more than a century, Western Egyptologists had been telling Egyptians what to do, and now their supremacy was being undermined.

Desroches-Noblecourt's close relationships with the Egyptians with whom she had worked had long annoyed some of her male colleagues. Unlike most of them, she spoke Arabic and was known for her care of the laborers she oversaw, treating them with dignity and getting to know them as individuals. But her colleagues' irritation exploded into outrage and violent protest when word spread of her participation in the creation of the new research center. "You can't possibly be serious about teaching them our methods," she was told. "We will no longer be the masters of our excavation sites."

There was also astonishment that officials in Egypt—a patriarchal, heavily Muslim country—would reach out to a woman for the UNESCO post. "At the time, a woman seemed to have hardly any chance of success in Egypt," Desroches-Noblecourt wrote. "How would I get men to listen to me, many of whom were considerably older? Would they respect me?"

The answer was simple, she said. "I was able to do it because I treated these people with respect and friendship and never allowed myself to speak to them in overly familiar terms, as many of my colleagues did. For me, it was unthinkable to consider the Egyptians as people unlike ourselves, simply because they were different and belonged to a country apparently less developed than ours. With regard to the Third World, Westerners have often shown a lack of subtlety that shocks me deeply." Although she didn't mention it, it was also true that as a woman, she had much in common with Egyptians, having been condescended to and treated like an outsider by male Egyptologists.

It helped, too, that Egypt's new government was more forward-thinking in its views about the status of women than most of the rest of the country's society. When he came to power, Nasser had promised life with dignity for all Egyptians regardless of their gender, introducing sweeping reforms to make education, healthcare, and jobs possible for everyone. The new Egyptian constitution explicitly called for equality of opportunity between men and women. In coming years, women would be granted the right to vote, earn equal pay, and be eligible for pensions. Female students flocked to Egyptian universities, as did men. In the first parliamentary election after the coup, several women ran for seats and two were elected.

Still, the country's patriarchal culture remained largely unchanged: Men were considered the unquestioned authority figures, and most women accepted society's dictum to confine themselves to their homes and focus solely on the care of their families. Notwithstanding all the official support she had, Desroches-Noblecourt knew she would have to step carefully.

WHEN DESROCHES-NOBLECOURT RETURNED TO Cairo in late 1954, she was startled to find herself in a country she no longer recognized. She echoed the shock expressed by the Nobel Prize–winning Egyptian novelist Naguib Mahfouz about the profound and sudden changes that had swept through his nation after Nasser's coup: "One morning we woke up, and our entire past was gone."

The differences that Desroches-Noblecourt first noticed were in the small quotidian details. The harem coaches on trams, reserved solely for women, had disappeared, and the black veils covering women's faces were not as common as they'd been before. At one point, the Muslim Brotherhood, an Islamic revivalist group, had urged Nasser to require all women to wear a veil, but he adamantly refused.

She also no longer saw men on the street wearing tarbouches—the ubiquitous red brimless hats, usually adorned with a black tassel, that had been exceedingly popular in the pre-coup days. Considered a sign of good breeding, they'd been worn by government officials, military officers, clerics, wealthy businessmen, and other members of the elite for more than a century. To Nasser, the tarbouche symbolized oppression, and he immediately banned it.

Another common sight—Egyptian peasants walking barefoot in the streets—had vanished too. The new government had mandated the wearing of sandals or other footwear to prevent the serious foot infections that afflicted many Egyptians. Those who didn't comply were fined.

Other changes were far more sweeping in scope. Among them was land reform, one of the major centerpieces of the revolution. Before 1952, most of Egypt's fertile land had been owned by a small group of wealthy Egyptian families and was used mainly for growing cotton, the country's main export and the largest source of its income. Illiterate and landless, the majority of Egyptians worked the fields in "a state of barely human existence . . . a condition close to slavery, with no end in sight," in the words of one historian. Shortly after taking power, Nasser limited individual land ownership to no more than 208 acres and distributed surplus land taken from the rich to those who had been tilling the soil. His government also established farm cooperatives, limited the rental rate for land, and established an agrarian minimum wage.

But the project closest to Nasser's heart, which he saw as the crowning glory of his regime, was construction of a massive new dam just south of the city of Aswan, upstream from Luxor. It would replace an older structure built in 1902 to regulate flooding of the Nile but that, by 1952, had fallen woefully short in its mission to provide enough water and electricity for the country's pressing agricultural and industrial needs. As Nasser saw it, the new Aswan High Dam, which would be the largest embankment dam in the world, would not only regulate the Nile's flooding and boost agriculture but also provide electricity for half of Egypt's population. The reservoir created by the dam would stretch southward for almost three hundred miles, extending into neighboring Sudan.

The 1902 dam had done considerable harm to many antiquities in southern Egypt, including the famed temple complex dedicated to the goddess Isis on the island of Philae, located on the Nile just below Aswan. After the dam was built, Philae, whose main temple was built in the third century B.C. and which was known as the Pearl of the Nile, was flooded nine months a year, and its temple, with its brilliantly painted reliefs and wall paintings, had suffered heavy damage. In his book *The Death of Philae*, the well-known French novelist Pierre Loti had condemned what he called "this symbolic death of ancient Egypt" and called upon Egyptians to rally in defense of their heritage.

But the Aswan High Dam, which was still in the planning stage, would have even more catastrophic consequences. Once it was finished, Philae would be submerged entirely, as would scores of other antiquities in Nubia, an area encompassing southern Egypt and northern Sudan, much of which would be engulfed by waters from the dam's reservoir. The threatened monuments included temples, forts, churches, chapels, mosques, tombs, and prehistoric wall drawings. The most notable victims, however, would be the spectacular temples at Abu Simbel, built more than three thousand years before by Rameses II during one of the most celebrated periods of pharaonic history. While lamentable, the incipient loss of these ancient treasures was unavoidable, according to the Egyptian government. "What else is left to us," said one young engineer working on plans for the dam, "but to drown the past in order to save the future?"

—

AS NASSER WORKED TO find international funding for the dam, Desroches-Noblecourt was focused on implementing his government's ambitious plan to create the Egyptian counterpart to France's Institute of Oriental Archaeology, which officials hoped would one day take its place among the world's leading centers of Egyptology. It was to be called the Documentation and Study Center for the History of the Art and Civilization of Ancient Egypt (CEDAE).

She came up with an ambitious agenda: to launch a series of surveys of ancient Egyptian monuments, publish the surveys' findings as quickly as possible, and establish a national archive of Egyptology. The new center also would work closely with the Egyptian Antiquities Organization, the successor to the government's old Antiquities Service, to inspect and protect monuments as well as to advise on requests from non-Egyptian archeologists for excavation permits.

Although Desroches-Noblecourt was to head the venture, she was well aware how delicate her situation was. She realized she had to make it clear to her Egyptian colleagues that she regarded this as a collaborative effort and that she was there as a partner, not as a boss. Fortunately, she and the fifty-five-year-old Mustafa Amer established an immediate rapport. She was immediately seduced by his courtesy and intelligence, and they got along so well that after CEDAE was formally established, he resigned as head of the Antiquities Organization and became the chief Egyptian official at the new center, working in close cooperation with her.

Over the previous thirty years, several hundred young Egyptians had received training in archaeology at Cairo University. But because of the difficulties in circumventing the control of Western Egyptologists over fieldwork, many if not most of those who wanted to enter the profession found themselves limited to either an academic career or working for the Egyptian Museum or Antiquities Service.

The creation of CEDAE was meant to offer the latest generation of Egyptian Egyptologists an opportunity most of their predecessors never had—to engage in thorough surveys of their country's ancient monuments, sometimes involving excavations, in order to understand and help to preserve them. According to the plan devised by Desroches-Noblecourt and Amer, CEDAE would pair young Egyptians with veteran Western archaeologists to collaborate on three-month survey projects. UNESCO would provide the funding for the teams, which would have at their disposal the most modern scientific techniques available.

As planning for the center progressed, Desroches-Noblecourt and Amer held weekly meetings with the Egyptian minister of education, whose portfolio included administration of the country's antiquities. He was Kamal Eddin Hussein, a former army officer who was a close associate of Nasser and one of the leaders of the 1952 coup. Hussein did not know much about archaeology, and Desroches-Noblecourt and Amer worked hard to educate him about why the center was so important. "We made him accept, chapter by chapter, our ideas as we developed them," Desroches-Noblecourt recalled. "It obviously helped that UNESCO was providing the funds."

In January 1955, the two finished their report outlining the goals and operation of CEDAE. In May of that year, UNESCO and the Egyptian government signed an agreement formally establishing the center. But Amer and Desroches-Noblecourt had begun taking action even before its official creation. The construction of the new dam was now looming, and they couldn't afford to waste a moment.

Five months earlier, Amer had won permission from UNESCO to allow the center to focus its first surveys and research on the threatened treasures of Nubia. At the same time, he persuaded Hussein to authorize a fact-finding mission to the area to begin documenting the antiquities before they were destroyed. "It obviously seemed monstrous, in the eyes of art and history, that these majestic foundations of Nubia could be swallowed up," Desroches-Noblecourt later wrote. "But at the time, the only remedy available seemed to be a careful study of them before they disappeared. We were powerless to do anything else."

ONE OF PERCY BYSSHE Shelley's best-known poems contains the lines "My name is Ozymandias, king of kings: / Look on my works, ye Mighty, and despair!" Ozymandias was the name the Greeks gave to Rameses II, the third pharaoh of ancient Egypt's Nineteenth Dynasty, whose reign lasted from about 1279 to 1213 B.C.

Shelley had written "Ozymandias" in 1818, inspired by the British Museum's much-publicized acquisition of a fragment of a colossal granite statue of Rameses that once had stood guard outside the pharaoh's mortuary temple at Thebes. The fragment—Rameses's head—was gigantic in its own right, measuring eight by six feet and weighing more than seven tons. The rest of the statue and another just like it lay shattered on the ground surrounding the temple.

Written as a cautionary tale about the transience of fame and power, Shelley's poem noted that Ozymandias's mighty empire had long since vanished:

Nothing beside remains. Round the decay
Of that colossal Wreck, boundless and bare
The lone and level sands stretch far away.

Shelley's observation was unquestionably true. But it's doubtful that Rameses II, arguably Egypt's most celebrated pharaoh, had spent much time worrying about thousands of years in the future. He possessed enormous power in the present, and to him, that's clearly what mattered most. Shelley's poem accurately described Rameses's state of mind: He considered himself almighty and was determined to make everyone else acknowledge that view.

Rameses's sixty-seven-year reign was the longest of any Egyptian monarch, at a time when ancient Egypt was at the peak of its power and prosperity. During his rule, his lands stretched more than a thousand miles, from the Mediterranean to Nubia, much of which is part of modern-day Sudan.

Virtually everything about this handsome, lusty, red-haired king, who boasted an aquiline nose, high cheekbones, and strong jaw, seemed larger than life. He had more wives—eight—and sired more children—at least a hundred—than any other pharaoh in history. Many of his myriad offspring were produced by the concubines he kept in his harem.

Rameses's fertility and military prowess were equaled only by his zeal to build monuments to himself. Each of his military campaigns and victories was memorialized by a plethora of temples, statues, obelisks, and other structures throughout his realm, paying homage to him and various gods. (Like other pharaohs, he was regarded as a living deity.) This great building boom began as soon as he assumed the throne in his early twenties, and it continued for decades.

Today more monuments bear his name than that of any other pharaoh, continuing even as late as three thousand years after his death. In 1955, Nasser ordered an ancient statue of Rameses, found broken outside a temple in the ancient city of Memphis, to be restored to its original height of thirty-five feet and placed in the middle of the square in front of Cairo's main railway station, which was renamed Rameses Square. The monumental statue was the first object travelers saw when they exited the station—something that undoubtedly would have pleased the pharaoh.

"We know now that some of the pharaohs were greater conquerors than Rameses II," the Victorian travel writer Amelia Edwards wrote in her 1877 guidebook, *A Thousand Miles up the Nile*. "We suspect that some were better rulers. Yet next to him, the others seem like shadows. . . . We seem to know the man—to feel his presence—to hear his name in the air. His features are as familiar to us as those of Henry VIII or Louis XIV."

The monuments to Rameses were scattered throughout the country, but he had a particular preoccupation with Nubia, a region in the south that now straddles the border of Egypt and Sudan. Nubia was the border zone between the Mediterranean world, including Egypt, and the heart of Africa. Its name means "gold"—aptly so, since it was an

important source of this most precious of metals, as well as timber and a variety of other minerals.

The first and longest-lasting of the great African trading empires, Nubia also served as the gateway to the continent's interior, supplying Egypt with the many other riches it coveted, including ebony, copper, ivory, ostrich feathers, and slaves. For almost three thousand years, the corridor along the Nile between Egypt and Nubia provided the only safe trade route linking Africa with the Mediterranean coast.

THE GREAT TEMPLE AT ABU SIMBEL AFTER ITS RELOCATION

The Nubians were also known as fierce warriors, and conflicts between them and the Egyptians were not uncommon. During the Egyptian Middle Kingdom (c. 2040–1640 B.C.), the pharaohs began expanding into Nubian territory. In the process, they built a chain of forts along the Nile to defend the Egyptian border and protect the all-important trade routes. Rameses II and later rulers continued that practice.

During his lengthy reign, Rameses ordered shrines to be built at seven different sites in Nubia, all of them meant to impress upon its people the immensity of Egypt's power and might. None was more important to that mission than the temples of Abu Simbel, the ultimate ancient embodiment of shock and awe. Their setting was the sheer rock face of a sandstone cliff towering over the Nile just north of the river's second cataract—a stretch of splintered rocks and foaming whitewater rapids.

As ancient travelers made their way up the Nile, they spied the Great Temple first, its massive façade—more than one hundred feet high—cut into the rock and looming above them. Its entrance was flanked by four enormous seated statues, each one almost seventy feet tall, all representing Rameses. Grave and majestic, the colossi sat side by side, crowns on their heads, hands resting on their knees, their eyes staring eastward. At their feet, looking almost like toys, were chiseled images of the most important members of the pharaoh's family: his mother, several sons and daughters, and, most important, his first and favorite wife, Nefertari, her sculpted figure slender and elegant, her hips voluptuously curved.

Of the multitude of women in Rameses's life, his heart was said to belong only to her. They apparently married before he became pharaoh and had at least six children together. Known for her striking beauty, she was described in one excavated papyrus scroll as "looking like the rising morning star at the start of a happy year. Shining bright, fair of skin, lovely the look of her eyes, sweet the speech of her lips."

The second temple at Abu Simbel, which is much smaller, simpler, and more delicate than the Great Temple, was dedicated to Nefertari and Hathor, the goddess of love and beauty. One of only two temples built in ancient Egypt to honor a pharaoh's wife, its façade features six statues—three on each side of the entrance—which are standing erect and appear to be walking out of the heart of the cliff. They represent Rameses and Nefertari and, uniquely, are the same size. Traditionally, when a pharaoh was portrayed with his consort in statuary, the queen was never taller than her husband's knee. Once again their children are depicted with their parents, their daughters beside Nefertari and their sons beside Rameses. Also on the façade is the inscription NEFERTARI, FOR WHOSE SAKE THE SUN RISES.

"Although he was the incarnation of god on earth, Rameses was nonetheless a man," Desroches-Noblecourt wrote. "In the Small Temple one is aware of all the deep passion he felt for his beloved wife." Throughout the interior of the temple, she added, "there is an indefinable charm, as if one has been taken by the hand by all these gods and goddesses, and drawn into an atmosphere of elegance, femininity, and also of youth. The sovereigns are young and handsome; their slender figures are striking; most of the time they are shown offering flowers." On pillars, walls, even in the innermost sanctuary, the names of Rameses and Nefertari are "coupled and inseparable," Amelia Edwards pointed out. On an outer wall, a hieroglyph attributed to the great pharaoh himself declares: "Rameses, the Strong in Truth, the Beloved of Amun, made this divine abode for his royal wife, Nefertari, whom he loved."

By contrast, in the hall and fifteen interior chambers of the pharaoh's Great Temple, there are no such tender pledges of love. Instead, the overall impression is a resounding affirmation of virility. The lofty

THE TEMPLE OF HATHOR AND NEFERTARI AT ABU SIMBEL

GIANT STATUES OF RAMESES STAND WATCH INSIDE THE GREAT TEMPLE AFTER THEIR RELOCATION

pillared hall features eight huge figures of Rameses facing one another, each standing about thirty-five feet high. Most of the interior wall carvings, originally painted in brilliant colors, depict Rameses smiting the many and varied enemies of Egypt and presenting them to the gods, among them a deified version of himself.

The Abu Simbel temples were built in part to commemorate the titanic Battle of Kadesh, fought in 1275 B.C. between Egypt and its longtime archrivals, the Hittites, an ancient people who occupied the kingdom of Anatolia (present-day Turkey). For centuries, the city of Kadesh, located in what is now western Syria, had played the Egyptians and Hittites off each other. In 1275 B.C., Rameses, who had been on the throne only four years, was forced to raise an army and march there to confront a Hittite force nearly twice as big as his. The battle ended in a stalemate, and sixteen years later, after several more skirmishes, the two rivals agreed to a treaty to respect each other's territory and defend each other against attack. The treaty, which lasted for the rest of Rameses's reign, is believed to be the world's earliest peace agreement.

But that's not the way Rameses, a true master of spin, told the story. On the inner walls of his Abu Simbel temple, he is depicted as almost single-handedly winning a great victory at Kadesh after praying to the gods to make him stronger than other men. According to his version, they complied magnificently. In hieroglyphs accompanying the carvings, the pharaoh declared: "I found that my heart grew stout and my breast swelled with joy. Everything which I attempted I succeeded. . . . I found the enemy chariots scattering before my horses. Not one of them could fight me. Their hearts quaked with fear when they saw me and their arms went limp so they could not shoot."

On one wall of the Great Hall, carved bas-reliefs tell the story of the battle in extraordinary, movie-epic detail. More than a thousand figures are depicted on the wall, which covers a space of fifty-seven by twenty-five feet. There's the city of Kadesh, the march of Rameses's forces, the capture and torture of Hittite spies, chariots charging at full gallop, hand-to-hand combat, and towering above everybody and everything else, the heroic pharaoh himself, standing tall in his chariot and drawing his bow to attack a fortress, then pursuing fleeing Hittite troops and crushing some of them under his chariot's wheels.

THE ABU SIMBEL TEMPLES' richly decorated interiors were a stunning sight, but during Rameses's lifetime and for several centuries afterward, only a handful of people, mainly high priests and other religious authorities, were allowed to enter them. As time passed, the temples fell into disuse and eventually were almost completely swallowed up by sand. It wasn't until 1813 that a Swiss explorer, Johann Burckhardt, spied the frieze at the top of the Great Temple peeking out from under sand drifts. Five years later, excavation of the temples began.

But even after they finally emerged from their sandy shrouds, the temples did not attract many visitors. Unlike the pyramids, the Valley of the Kings, and the temples outside Luxor, all of which are accessible from Cairo, Abu Simbel and the other monuments in Nubia were more than five hundred miles from the capital. To get there was a long, difficult trip, and few tourists—or archaeologists—made the effort. But those who did, like Amelia Edwards, never forgot what they had seen.

During her trip up the Nile in 1873, Edwards spent sixteen days at Abu Simbel, studying the temples' façades for hours and exploring every inch of their intricately carved and ornamented interiors. She seemed even more in awe of the sculptors and other artisans who created the temples than of the pharaoh who had commissioned them. "They took a mountain and fell upon it like Titans, and hollowed and carved it as though it was a cherry stone, and left it for the feebler men of after-ages to marvel at forever," she rhapsodized. "Armed with barbaric tools, they were the Michelangelos of their age."

Edwards was particularly bewitched by the sight of the four huge statues outside the Great Temple at the first glimmer of dawn. Every morning on her houseboat, she woke in time to see what she called "the daily miracle." In the gray light before daybreak, the statues' giant faces wore what she called "a fixed and fatal look." But as the sky lightened, that look

> was succeeded by a flush that mounted and deepened like the rising flush of life. For a moment they seemed to glow—to smile—to be transfigured. Then came a flash of the risen sun. It lasted less than a second, and was gone almost before one could say it was there. The next moment, mountain, river, and sky were distinct in the steady light of day; and the colossi—mere colossi now—sat serene and stony in the open sunshine. Every morning, I saw those awful brethren pass from death to life, from life to sculptured stone. I brought myself almost to believe at last that there must sooner or later come some sunrise when the ancient charm would snap asunder, and the giants must arise and speak.

During a trip down the Nile more than twenty years earlier, Florence Nightingale was equally transfixed by the sight of the Abu Simbel colossi at sunrise. Nightingale, who would later became known as the founder of modern nursing, was at that point a wealthy young Englishwoman accompanying friends on a tour of Egypt. She, too, found the statues remarkable: "They will live in my memory as the sublimest expression of spiritual and intellectual repose that I have ever seen." There was an indefinable grace about these giant figures, a serenity she had never witnessed before. Her experience at Abu Simbel, she later said, was akin to a religious conversion. When she and her companions finally left the site, "our eyes were full of sand and tears."

As it turned out, the "daily miracle" of which Edwards spoke was no accident. To the ancient Egyptians, the sun was a god who returned each morning after another night's battle with the forces of darkness and chaos. Under orders from Rameses, his engineers and architects, with the help of royal astronomers, looked for a site where rays from the rising sun would flood the façade and its colossal statues representing Rameses with light, demonstrating the daily regeneration not only of the world but of the deified pharaoh.

As impressive as that sight was, the pharaoh's men accomplished something even more remarkable. They oriented the Great Temple so that twice a year, as the sun rose above the hilltops across the river, a single beam of light flashed through the temple's doorway, pierced its inner darkness, and penetrated to the sacred sanctuary at the back. In this holy of holies, four figures were seated on thrones—the deified Rameses and the three gods to whom the temple is dedicated: Ptah, god of darkness; Amun, king of the gods; and Ra-Horakhty, the sun god. As the sunbeam entered the sanctuary, it illuminated three of the figures—Rameses, Amun, and Ra-Horakhty—leaving Ptah in perpetual night.

LIKE AMELIA EDWARDS AND Florence Nightingale, Christiane Desroches-Noblecourt had fallen under the spell of the Abu Simbel temples. Just weeks after her arrival as adviser to the new center, she became obsessed with the idea that the Egyptians must be persuaded "not to resign themselves to their inevitable disappearance, their sandstone glories dissolved to nothingness." They must be rescued for posterity. But she had no idea how to transform that dream into reality.

In January 1955, she was still in Cairo, wrapping up her work on the report to create CEDAE, when she heard that Luther Evans, the director general of UNESCO, was coming to the city for a few days. Without consulting anyone, she impulsively sent a personal message to Evans asking him to set aside one day during his short trip to visit Abu Simbel. Then she paid a visit to Kamal Eddin Hussein, the minister of public education, asking him to arrange it.

At first Hussein treated her request as a joke, implying that her real reason for making it was not to show off the temples to the UNESCO director general but to see them for herself. Angered by his patronizing attitude, she shot back: "Mr. Minister, you have not, I believe, fully understood the nature of my request. I did not come here to have fun, and I don't need an excuse to visit a monument likely to interest me. I have already been to Abu Simbel in 1939 and at my own expense!" Backing down, Hussein responded in a placating tone, "*Malesh, malesh* ("There, there"). Don't take it wrong. I was just teasing you!" He agreed to arrange the visit, provided Desroches-Noblecourt actually managed to persuade Evans to go. Having issued the invitation on impulse, she found herself nervous about approaching "the almighty master of this major international organization."

An American, Evans was a highly complex—and controversial—man. Tall and burly, he had grown up on a farm in the hill country of Texas. Like his contemporary Lyndon B. Johnson, he was known for his folksy humor, which he used to defuse tense situations and build consensus. His background, however, was not in politics but in academia. A renowned political scientist, Evans had earned his PhD at Stanford, followed by stints as a professor at Dartmouth and Princeton and work for presidential aide Harry Hopkins in Franklin Roosevelt's White House. He was named head of the Library of Congress in 1945 and promptly launched a major expansion of its collections.

A staunch internationalist, Evans was a member of the U.S. delegation to the London conference that established UNESCO, and he involved the Library of Congress in its activities, particularly in the drafting of a 1952 convention establishing universal copyright regulations. He was elected director general of UNESCO that same year.

Yet although he was highly regarded as an administrator, Evans had a dark side. An ardent anticommunist, he was an enthusiastic proponent of Senator Joseph McCarthy's witch hunt in Washington in the late 1940s and early 1950s. At the Library of Congress, he created a loyalty board to investigate current and potential employees regarding their views on Communism and homosexuality; several were fired or resigned because of their political or sexual history. He also prevented the appointment of William Carlos Williams to the post of U.S. poet laureate because of Williams's leftist political beliefs. When Evans arrived at UNESCO headquarters in Paris, he caused a firestorm by firing seven American employees of the organization because they refused to submit to a U.S. government loyalty investigation.

It's unlikely that Desroches-Noblecourt, a staunch leftist herself, was aware of the less savory aspects of Evans's background. In any case, she never mentioned it when she later wrote about her passionate presentation to him during a meeting in Hussein's office, describing the threats facing the Abu Simbel temples and urging him to come and see them for himself. She was overjoyed when he enthusiastically agreed to do so.

Accompanying Evans and Egyptian officials on the trip, she persuaded the pilot of the small plane carrying the party to fly as low as possible over the Nile in front of the temples so that Evans could clearly see the faces of the colossal statues. During the tour, she could see that the UNESCO chief "was in the grip of these shrines," just as she was, and in awe of the "giants who had created them, who were like the anonymous builders of our cathedrals." When he emerged from the temples, Evans declared, "These works are imperishable and must be protected. We must take action to do so."

Desroches-Noblecourt was thrilled by the director general's response, but UNESCO took no action to back up his words. It soon became clear that despite the many items high on Evans's agenda, saving the temples was not one of them. Writing many years later, Desroches-Noblecourt acknowledged that "I had not yet realized what a David-and-Goliath project this was going to be, or the almost insurmountable difficulties that I was to encounter."

CHAPTER II

DISASTER AT SUEZ

AFTER LUTHER EVANS'S VISIT TO ABU SIMBEL, DESROCHES-Noblecourt returned to her work at the Louvre, her mind churning with ideas about how to proceed with her quixotic campaign. In May 1955, just days after the signing of the formal agreement creating the Cairo research center, she decided to take her mission public.

The venue she chose was an international conference of museum directors and antiquities experts in Paris sponsored by the International Council of Museums, an organization closely allied with UNESCO. She urged Mustafa Amer to attend, and together, the two outlined to their audience the dire threat facing the Nubian monuments and the urgency of coming up with a plan to save them. In her remarks, Desroches-Noblecourt argued that the ancient temples should not be viewed simply as the property of Egypt but as part of the cultural heritage of all humanity.

She thought she and Amer had made a good case, but many in the audience clearly didn't agree. Overall, the reaction was sympathetic but negative. Although a wonderful idea in the abstract, such a rescue effort would be technologically impossible, some said. Others declared that their institutions had more important things to focus on at the moment and that she and Amer must accept the reality of the temples' disappearance.

Surprised and appalled, Desroches-Noblecourt made her indignation clear. "What use are the grand words you've spoken here about international cooperation, especially between East and West?" she asked the gathering. "You talk about these high ideals but don't do anything to put them into effect. That's all you seem interested in—pleasant talk that goes nowhere!"

Her outspokenness stunned the group into silence. Finally, Julien Cain, the sixty-eight-year-old head of the French National Library, rose to speak. One of France's most respected intellectuals, Cain, who was Jewish, had been fired from the library by the Vichy government during the war and sent by the Nazis to Buchenwald, which he barely survived. Now he turned to those sitting around him and calmly declared, "She's the one who is right. We should wake up and follow her example, or at least help her by our words, then follow them with actions that are within our reach."

Desroches-Noblecourt was grateful for Cain's support, and in later years he would turn out to be extremely helpful to her campaign. But at that point another, even more important ally appeared on the scene. Soon after the conference, UNESCO's chief lawyer, an Egyptian named Hanna Sabba, told Desroches-Noblecourt about "someone I know who I think can be convinced by your argument and be prompted to act. He's idealistic, intellectual, and above all has a genius for action. He is capable of carrying out the most audacious project if it's justified." The attributes of the man Sabba was describing—René Maheu, the undersecretary of UNESCO—sounded remarkably like those of Desroches-Noblecourt herself. A rebel all his life, Maheu was known for flouting convention and stirring up controversy wherever he went, just like his two good friends Simone de Beauvoir and Jean-Paul Sartre.

IN 1929, BEAUVOIR, THEN a twenty-one-year-old student at the École Normale Supérieure, fell passionately in love with the twenty-four-year-old Maheu, who, like Beauvoir, was studying philosophy at the École, one of Paris's most prestigious and selective schools of higher education. She was charmed by Maheu's blond good looks, his "rather awkward grace," his ironic wit, and his enjoyment of life, not to mention his irresistible laugh: "When he gave vent to his laughter, it was as if he had just unexpectedly dropped in on a strange planet and was making a rapturous discovery of its prodigious comicality."

As it happened, Maheu was equally infatuated with her, and the two spent almost all their free time together. When Sartre, another philosophy student at the school who happened to be a good friend of Maheu's, asked him to introduce Beauvoir to him, Maheu adamantly refused to do so.

Like Sartre, Maheu was a dedicated rationalist and nonconformist, opposed to most of the things much of French society held dear, like the church and the military. But to Beauvoir's chagrin, in one area of life he stuck to the rules, at least at that time. He was already married—to an aristocrat five years older than he—and, although he was devoted to the brilliant and beautiful Beauvoir, he wouldn't sleep with her. "My greatest happiness is Maheu," she wrote in her journal, but in the end, Sartre stole her away from him. "I need Sartre and I love Maheu," she later wrote. "I love Sartre for what he brings me, and Maheu for what he is." Despite this early romantic Sturm und Drang, the three remained on friendly terms for the rest of their lives.

After leaving the École, Maheu taught philosophy at the University of Cologne, where he observed the rise of Nazism in the early 1930s. He later taught at the French Institute in London and spent the war years in North Africa, teaching at a secondary school in Morocco before becoming an information officer with Charles de Gaulle's Free French administration in Algeria. Maheu's stays in Morocco and Algeria, both French colonies, turned him into a firm anticolonialist and a proponent of independence for both countries.

In 1945, he returned to Paris and joined the staff of UNESCO. His personal life, meanwhile, continued to be the stuff of soap operas. During the war, he had fallen in love with a student of his in Morocco named Nadine Chaveau, and, although he had no intention of divorcing his wife, he invited Chaveau to come to Paris after the conflict. "He was a very exciting teacher," she recalled years later in an interview with a biographer of Sartre and Beauvoir. "All the girls fell in love with him." Chaveau would become Maheu's lifelong mistress and bear his second son; his days of fidelity to anyone were now clearly over. "He always had affairs," Chaveau said. "It was like a game with him."

IF DESROCHES-NOBLECOURT WAS AWARE of Maheu's complicated, colorful private life, she never made public mention of it. The two, along with their spouses, first met at a luncheon hosted by Hanna Sabba at his home shortly after he suggested that she seek Maheu's help. She was immediately impressed by the UNESCO official's charm, seriousness, dynamism, and, above all, intense interest in the plight of the Nubian temples.

"Tell me your story," he said to her after they'd been introduced. With great passion, she complied. When she finished, he asked her several searching questions, then said, "I am your man, but, unfortunately, I can't do anything right now. I've just been appointed UNESCO's delegate to the U.N. in New York. When I get back, get in touch with me. I promise you I won't forget."

Before his transfer, Maheu had been Luther Evans's deputy, but the two had never gotten along, either politically or personally. The loquacious, homespun American, who was a conservative on most issues, was offended by what he considered the social and political radicalism of the sophisticated, energetic Frenchman, and he appointed him to the U.N. job to get him out of Paris. Maheu told his friends he was being sent into exile but assured them he would return.

But when would that be? Although heartened by Maheu's full-throated support, Desroches-Noblecourt worried that he would not come back before the beginning of construction of the Aswan High Dam, making it almost impossible to organize any serious effort to rescue the temples. She stayed in Paris for most of the spring and summer of 1955, spending time with her husband and son and giving a series of lectures, including to her students at the École du Louvre, about the importance of preserving the monuments. "At the time," she later said, "I was regarded as a naïf, devoid of a sense of reality. People would say, 'She wants to lift mountains! How foolish is that?'"

Toward the end of the summer, Desroches-Noblecourt returned to Cairo to launch the first survey expedition of the threatened monuments by the new documentation and research center. Over the previous seventeen years, she had met and worked with a wide array of archaeologists from different countries, several of whom she now asked to come to Egypt to supervise the work of the young Egyptians selected for the initial survey team. All those she contacted agreed.

She also reached out to John Wilson, the director of the Oriental Institute at the University of Chicago, to ask if she could borrow one of the institute's photographers. Widely considered America's most prestigious research institution in Middle and Near East studies and archaeology, the Oriental Institute was best known for its work in Egypt, operating out of its own center in Luxor called Chicago House.

Desroches-Noblecourt's insistence on having a photographer on the survey team was an example of her determination to use the most modern techniques available to document the details of the monuments the team would study. In the past, she and other Egyptologists would copy or trace hieroglyphic inscriptions, wall paintings, and carvings by hand, holding a pencil in one hand and a sketchbook in the other while trying to keep their balance on rickety scaffolding or at the top of a ladder. It was slow, difficult, and painstaking work, which would often take several months—or even years—to complete.

In this latest effort, Desroches-Noblecourt didn't have the luxury of years: The center had to complete its documentation of the Nubian antiquities before dam construction began. During the first expedition, which documented the interior rooms of the Great Temple at Abu Simbel, the Oriental Institute's photographer took hundreds of photos of the massive wall telling the story of the Battle of Kadesh. "His work was flawless," Desroches-Noblecourt said. "The photos made it possible for us to later produce a drawing in which the smallest details are faithfully reproduced."

The photographs were developed in a small makeshift darkroom aboard a boat anchored on the Nile that the center had borrowed from the Antiquities Organization to use as a base for the team's work. In the meantime, UNESCO had commissioned the building of a large air-conditioned barge, to be completed two years later, that would not only house later survey teams but also technical equipment and state-of-the-art laboratories, including a sophisticated photo lab.

Over the next year, Desroches-Noblecourt commuted between Paris and Cairo, splitting her time between her curatorial and teaching duties at the Louvre and her work overseeing the center. In October 1956, a new expedition—composed of Italian, French, and Polish archaeologists and another group of young Egyptians—was set to depart for three months of documentation work at the Temple of Kalabsha, the largest freestanding temple in Nubia.

After accompanying the team to the temple, Desroches-Noblecourt returned to Cairo. Over the previous few months, she had grown increasingly worried about the political situation there and what it meant for the center's work. Egypt's relations with Britain and France had deteriorated to the verge of total rupture. Protectively, the foreign archaeologists on her team had been granted a laissez-passer from the United Nations, a document that guaranteed them the freedom to travel back to their home countries in case of conflict. Having already been through one war and seen the havoc it caused, Desroches-Noblecourt fervently hoped that history was not about to repeat itself.

SINCE HIS RISE TO power, Gamal Abdel Nasser had become enemy number one for three countries—Britain, France, and Israel—all of which at various times had seriously considered assassinating him. Yet during this period, the Egyptian leader had neither attempted nor committed an aggressive act against any of them. In fact, where Britain and Israel were concerned, he had actively tried to pursue a path to peace.

In Britain's case, instead of immediately ejecting its forces from the Suez Canal following the officers' coup in 1952, Nasser had agreed to resume negotiations with the British government over withdrawal of its troops. An agreement was reached in October 1954 calling for total evacuation of British forces by June 1956 but leaving behind several hundred British civilian contractors to maintain the canal.

As for Israel, even though Nasser had opposed its creation, he had tried hard to avoid open conflict, even approving the establishment of secret channels of communication between Egypt and the Israelis. In the early years of his regime, "Nasser never closed the door on peace with Israel," said one of his closest associates. "In fact, he kept it wide open."

But neither of those efforts—or others like them—were enough to appease his antagonists. For them, and increasingly for the United States, the problem with Nasser was twofold: his determination not to kowtow to their demands and his extraordinary popularity in the Arab world. Fiercely independent, he had long rejected the idea of alliances with any non-Arab nation, whether Communist or Western.

France and Britain, for their part, were appalled by what they saw as his effrontery. Neither colonial power had come to grips with the fact that with many of their former colonies and protectorates now demanding independence, their empires were on the verge of extinction. France had lost Vietnam in May 1954 after Vietnamese nationalist forces led by Ho Chi Minh defeated the French army at the Battle of Dien Bien Phu, and in November of that year, Algerian nationalists launched an armed uprising against their colonial masters, who had controlled that North African country since 1830.

The rebellion had been organized by a group called the Algerian National Liberation Front (FLN), whose leader, Ahmed Ben Bella, demanded independence from France. The French government, which was determined to keep Algeria, was outraged that Nasser supported the insurgents' cause. Not only did he allow Ben Bella to live in exile in Egypt and his guerrilla fighters to train there, but he also tried to persuade the United Nations to condemn France and support the FLN. For more than a year, the French prime minister, Guy Mollet, and his administration had been considering ways to punish the Egyptian leader for his Algerian policies. According to the U.S. ambassador in Paris, Mollet "had developed almost a fixation about Nasser."

But Mollet's preoccupation was mild compared to the full-blown obsession with Nasser on the part of the British prime minister, Anthony Eden, and some in his government. After Egypt and Britain had agreed in 1954 on a date for withdrawal of British troops, Nasser was hopeful that relations between the two countries would become more friendly and cooperative. Not so Eden and the men around him, who were furious about losing military control of the canal, which they considered their country's lifeline, especially where oil was concerned. The Persian Gulf supplied most of Britain's oil, which was transported by pipeline and then by ship through the canal. Even though Britain remained the Canal Zone Company's major stockholder, the removal of British troops from the area meant that, according to Eden, Nasser now had "a thumb on our windpipe."

Although the canal was the immediate cause of Eden's fury, it was fueled by a larger, more overarching grievance: Britain's fast-slipping grasp on global power. Just fifty years before, the British Empire had been the largest in world history, controlling a quarter of the world's land surface. The empire began its downward slide in 1948, when the British gave up control of India, the most important jewel in its imperial crown. By the mid-1950s, it was being challenged all over the globe by colonies demanding independence, among them Cyprus, Malaya, and Kenya.

Unable to accept that Britain's days as a world power were over, its government took out its anger and frustration on Nasser and Egypt. The common feeling seemed to be: How dare these people—these *wogs*!—stand up to us? For Eden especially, the humiliation was deeply personal. He had finally become prime minister in April 1955 after acting as Winston Churchill's deputy during World War II and for most of the next decade. But for him, there was no political honeymoon. Soon after he took office, the British economy turned sour; wages and prices rose, as did inflation, sending the country into recession. Eden's government came under intense criticism for its handling of the crisis, and his popularity plummeted.

The beleaguered prime minister fixed on Nasser as the main reason for this cascading flood of problems: the dwindling empire, the sluggish economy, the collapse of his reputation. In a discussion of anti-British riots throughout the Arab world, Eden, according to one witness, "painted a haunting picture of what would happen if our oil supplies were cut off. We were obliged to suffer constant humiliations, sucking up to Egypt's President Nasser, all for the sake of 'oil, oil, oil.'"

At one point, the prime minister reacted to a subordinate's mention of Nasser's name by shouting, "I want him destroyed!" When the subordinate said Nasser could not be replaced without having an acceptable alternative ready to take over, Eden barked, "But I don't want an alternative! And I don't give a damn if there's anarchy and chaos in Egypt!"

ISRAEL, MEANWHILE, HAD ITS own reasons for wanting to get rid of Nasser and keep Egypt weak. With Nasser so hugely popular throughout the Arab world, Israeli leaders feared he could bring its people together in a united force, posing an existential threat to the new Jewish state. As was true of Mollet and Eden, the Israeli prime minister David Ben-Gurion's hatred of Nasser was personal. "Ben-Gurion could not stand Nasser from the beginning," said one Israeli journalist. "Here for the first time was a young Arab leader . . . inspiring a new generation of Arabs. . . . This was a new style of pan-Arab nationalism, and Ben-Gurion wanted to destroy it."

The chief founding father of Israel and its leading political force for the first fifteen years of its existence, Ben-Gurion was a staunch military hard-liner. To survive, he believed, his fledgling country had to remain on a war footing with the Arab states surrounding it, and he kept open the option of taking more territory from them to expand Israel's borders. He strongly opposed any idea of peace negotiations with Arab leaders, especially Nasser, believing such talks would be the first step toward weakening Israel and ensuring its destruction.

From the time Nasser took power in Egypt, Ben-Gurion was determined to provoke him into war, knowing that the Egyptian army would be no match for the Israelis. The setting for the Israeli incitements was the Gaza Strip, a barren no-man's-land between Egypt and Israel, whose boundaries had been set by an armistice agreement between the two countries in 1949.

Gaza, which was under Egyptian military control, was mainly populated by Palestinian refugees, who were housed in squalid camps. Having been refused the right to settle in either Israel or Egypt, many of the younger refugees became fedayeen, Arab guerrillas who took part in occasional small-scale raids against Israeli targets. In retaliation, Israeli forces attacked the refugee camps at a level far greater than the original assaults, often resulting in dozens of casualties. Although Nasser protested to the United Nations, no action was taken, and the quid pro quo raids continued.

In 1955, Israel upped the ante. On February 23, several fedayeen made it to the outskirts of Tel Aviv and killed an Israeli civilian. Five days later, the Israeli government unleashed Operation Black Arrow, a massive raid on an Egyptian military camp in Gaza that killed thirty-six Egyptian and Palestinian soldiers and wounded twenty-nine. A U.S. embassy official in Cairo called the Israeli raid "an atrocity by anyone's definition," and the United Nations Security Council unanimously condemned it.

The raid had been ordered by Ben-Gurion, who was then serving as Israeli defense minister. In early 1954, he had stepped down from the premiership and been replaced by Moshe Sharett, a longtime associate of his who spoke fluent Arabic and was far more open to the idea of peace negotiations with the Arabs. Until Operation Black Arrow, Nasser had been amenable to the idea too. Knowing that his army could never defeat the Israelis, he had rejected armed responses to the Israeli raids and declared he was opposed to turning borderlands like Gaza into battlegrounds. In early 1955, he went even further, authorizing the opening of secret peace talks with Sharett's government.

But thanks to Operation Black Arrow, along with the discovery of a covert Israeli intelligence operation in Cairo, the flickers of peace were extinguished before they could catch fire. In 1954, Israeli military intelligence had activated a sleeper cell of Egyptian Jewish agents tasked with setting off bombs in post offices, theaters, libraries, and other public buildings and pinning the blame on Egyptian opponents of Nasser. The goal was to undermine his regime by creating a climate of violence and instability. After the first bombing, however, the Egyptian government found out about the plot and rolled up the cell, executing several of its leaders.

The bombing plot, followed by the Gaza raid, marked a turning point in Middle East history. Sharett resigned, and Ben-Gurion again became prime minister, remaining in that post until 1963. Israeli raids on Gaza resumed: By March 1956, there had been four major assaults against Egypt and one against Syria.

Having tried hard to avoid open conflict, Nasser decided that was no longer an option; Israel, flaunting its military superiority, had left him little room to maneuver. He concluded he had to defend his country against Israeli incursions, but to do that he needed outside help. The Egyptian army was not much stronger than it had been at the end of the 1948 Arab-Israeli war; it still lacked adequate training and was in desperate need of modern weapons and equipment.

Ever since he came to power, Nasser had sought to buy arms from the West, but with little success. He had explored the possibility with the French but was told that in exchange for weapons, he would have to end his support for Ben Bella and the Algerian rebels, something he refused to do. In 1954, he learned that France had just signed a secret deal with the Israelis, which involved selling to them the most modern French fighter-bomber aircraft, the Mystère.

As aggravating as that was, Nasser's greatest frustration was his failure to persuade the United States to sell him arms. Although a staunch nationalist, he had always been an admirer of America for, among other things, winning its independence from British rule and opposing French and British colonialism. As a child, he had loved American films—a predilection that continued as an adult. His favorite was Frank Capra's *It's a Wonderful Life*.

In the years before the coup, he had won admirers in the U.S. embassy in Cairo for his opposition to British control and to King Farouk. Among them was a contingent of CIA agents who, after meeting regularly with him, decided he would be an acceptable alternative to the current Egyptian regime. The United States apparently had no direct involvement in the Egyptian officers' rebellion, but two days before it occurred, Nasser notified the U.S. embassy that it was about to take place. "If you are not Communists, then go for it," an American military attaché reportedly said.

Ever since, Nasser had been covertly seeking an arms deal with the Americans, an effort that greatly intensified after Israel's February 1955 raid on the military camp in Gaza. The CIA group in Cairo favored selling Egypt the weapons, but the State Department—led by the fervently anticommunist secretary of state John Foster Dulles—was much less accommodating. Like France, Dulles proposed a quid pro quo for providing arms to Nasser. In exchange, Egypt would have to join a military alliance of countries in the region whose purpose was to combat Soviet and other Communist influence in the Middle and Near East.

Although Nasser was avowedly anticommunist, he was determined to remain independent and not take part in alliances involving non-Arab countries, including the United States. In any event, he asked, why should Egypt concern itself with an imaginary Communist threat when it was faced with the real danger of continued Israeli attacks on Egyptian-controlled territory?

"The Americans . . . could have done something about assuaging Nasser's fears, but they did nothing," wrote Saïd K. Aburish, a Nasser biographer. Meanwhile, "the Israelis dealt him one humiliating blow after another. . . . They pushed him so hard that he had no option but to respond or lose the things most precious to him—his standing with his people [and] his dignity."

Nasser came to believe that the U.S. government, like those of Britain and France, didn't really care about the well-being of Egypt and its people. In his view, America's approval or rejection of his regime depended solely on whether it was subservient to U.S. plans and interests in the Middle East. Since Nasser wouldn't bow, it was in America's interest, he felt, to keep Egypt weak.

When the United States turned down his arms request, he decided to look elsewhere and informed the U.S. ambassador in Cairo that he was thinking about approaching the Soviet Union. There was little doubt about Nasser's anticommunist bona fides: Egypt's Communist

Party was illegal, and Nasser had rejected earlier Soviet attempts to expand its relationship with his country. But he told the ambassador he now had no choice.

In September 1955, Nasser and the Communist government of Czechoslovakia announced a major arms deal. In reality, the Czechs were acting as a front for the Soviets, who controlled that country as well as much of the rest of Eastern Europe. Unsurprisingly, the announcement served as a neon-red flag to the West, and the U.S. government sent emissaries to Nasser to beg him to cancel the agreement. He refused to budge.

For Western governments, Nasser's action was a seismic event. As leader of the first non-Communist nation to buy arms from the Communist bloc, he had broken the West's monopoly on weapons sales to the Arab world, and in doing so he had greatly undermined its plans for an Arab anticommunist alliance. In their eyes, he had gone too far, and now even the United States, which had been far more tolerant toward him than had Britain and France, began preparing to take action against him.

Although John Foster Dulles and the State Department had never been as enthusiastic about Nasser as the CIA and other U.S. government agencies, the secretary of state had been willing until now, because of Nasser's strong anticommunist record, to overlook his neutrality, socialism, and support of the Algerian rebels.

More than any other figure in the Eisenhower administration, Dulles was obsessed by Communism and the need to root it out wherever it was found. Other potential threats to the Middle East and elsewhere, like Islamic fundamentalism, were not seen as harmful to U.S. interests because these movements were considered bulwarks against Communism. As Dulles saw it, Nasser was no longer in the anticommunist camp.

When the Czech deal was announced, Dulles angrily declared that Egypt was "jeopardizing its ability to remain a fully independent member of the free world." It soon became clear that the U.S. government saw the arms deal as threatening its position in all of the Middle East, especially in regard to its and other Western countries' oil interests.

At the same time, though, U.S. and other Western officials were determined to keep Nasser from getting further involved with the Soviets. Shortly after the arms deal was made public, the Soviet Union hinted that it might finance construction of the new Aswan dam. To prevent that from happening, the U.S. and British governments in December 1955 offered to provide $70 million in aid for the project, along with a $200 million loan from the World Bank. The dam's overall cost was estimated to be about $1.3 billion.

Although they had agreed to the venture, neither the Americans nor the British were happy about it. During the first half of 1956, as relations worsened between Egypt and the West, the two countries began having serious second thoughts. Dulles had already taken steps to rein Nasser in, threatening to stop the U.S. food aid program and end most-favored-nation trade status for Egypt unless Nasser stopped his balancing act between the West and the Communist bloc. Those actions were endorsed by pro-Israel and anticommunist lobbies in the United States, both of which fiercely opposed aiding Egypt in any way. In May 1956, Nasser inflamed the already tense situation by recognizing the regime of the Communist leader Mao Tse-tung as the rightful government of China. "For Dulles, [Egypt's] recognition of China had come to assume almost religious significance," wrote a State Department official. "It was just short of devil worship."

The U.S. secretary of state had had enough. On July 19, 1956, he announced that the United States was withdrawing its offer to help finance the Aswan dam, citing the sizable debt that Egypt had assumed in order to buy Czech arms, which, Dulles said, had led to "weakness in the Egyptian economy." Although he said he was speaking for President Eisenhower, he had made the decision on his own, without consulting the president, who was in the hospital following major abdominal surgery.

Dulles's announcement came as a surprise to virtually everybody: his administration colleagues, America's allies, and above all Nasser himself, who was caught totally off guard. Although he was aware of the U.S. government's unhappiness with his overtures to Communist countries, he believed that his reliance on the West for their help with the dam balanced the military aid he was receiving from the Communist bloc and proved that he was completely neutral. He never thought America would cancel its commitment. The day after Dulles's announcement, the British government followed his lead. Nasser begged the World Bank to do the deal on its own, but its chairman, too, pulled out.

Building the dam meant everything to Nasser. He considered it essential for the modernization and industrialization of Egypt, and it remained the most important goal of his regime. His shock over Dulles's decision was quickly followed by rage. "He regarded it as a deliberate snub, a political challenge to Egypt's dignity as well as to her aspirations," the historian Alex von Tunzelmann wrote. Nasser told the American ambassador, "You fellows are out to kill me. And all I can do is protect myself. I tell you this. I am not going to be killed."

Nasser concluded he had no choice but to retaliate—to avenge the damage done to his and his country's honor and, in the process, to find a way to help pay for the dam. To him, there was only one possible solution: nationalizing the Suez Canal, the ultimate symbol of Western control of Egyptian resources and the source of huge amounts of revenue that ended up in Western pockets.

On July 26, one week after Dulles's announcement, Nasser went on the radio to announce he was reclaiming the canal "in the name of the people." As he spoke, Egyptian troops stormed into the headquarters of the Canal Zone Company, guns drawn, and took control. The last British troops had been withdrawn from the Canal Zone the month before, and the seizure was carried out without opposition or casualties.

Although Britain and France would argue otherwise, Nasser's nationalization of the Canal Zone Company was not illegal. As a privately owned and run firm, it was subject to Egyptian law and could be taken over by the government as long as Egypt offered financial compensation to its shareholders. Other nations, including Britain after World War II, had done the same in their own countries with railroads and other companies that provided public services. Nasser made it clear that in claiming ownership of the Canal Zone Company, he was not planning to limit the canal's operation or use. Determined not to give his foes any excuse to attack him, he issued instructions to allow international shipping to continue to operate freely through the canal.

To Anthony Eden and others in his government, however, the legality of Nasser's action was immaterial. They regarded themselves as the guardians of Western interests in the Middle East, and as such they viewed the canal's nationalization, which had sparked rejoicing throughout the Arab world, as a clear defiance of their and other Western countries' hold on the region. "For the first time in the twentieth century, an Arab leader had openly challenged all of the West," noted Saïd Aburish. Even worse in the eyes of Western officials, he seemed to be winning the fight.

Initially, Britain, along with France, the other major stockholder in the company, tried to make it as difficult as possible for Egypt to operate the canal. Their ploys included an attempt to paralyze traffic by pulling out all the European pilots responsible for guiding ships through its narrow boundaries. They hoped to prove that the Egyptians did not have the expertise to run the canal on their own, but the gamble failed. Egypt was more than up to the job, and traffic on the canal actually increased.

For British and French leaders, there remained only one solution: invading Egypt, taking back the canal, and getting rid of Nasser. As Miles Copeland, a CIA agent in Cairo at the time, put it, they were determined to prove to the world "that an upstart like him couldn't get away with so ostentatiously twisting the lion's tail."

The year 1956 was the twentieth anniversary of Hitler's remilitarization of the Rhineland, and Eden was quick to compare the Rhineland with Suez and Hitler with Nasser. "We all know this is how fascist governments behave," he declared, and "we all remember, only too well, what the cost can be in giving in to fascism." Not for the first time, and certainly not for the last, the lessons of Munich and appeasement were wrongly applied to a later international crisis. Hitler had been a real threat to Britain's security and survival. Nasser was not.

The day after the canal's seizure, Eden had sought and obtained his cabinet's approval for a show of force against Nasser. Four days later, the prime minister told President Eisenhower he was considering immediate military action against Egypt. Eisenhower was appalled and made it clear he opposed such a drastic step, especially since Nasser had signaled to the United Nations that he was willing to discuss the possibility of having the canal operated jointly by representatives of Egypt and the countries that used it.

The French, for their part, had been holding secret meetings with Israeli officials since June 1955 to discuss possible ways of removing Nasser, including assassination. Israel had also been considering a preemptive war against Egypt, with the aim of seizing the Gaza Strip and the Straits of Tiran, the narrow sea passage between Egypt and Saudi Arabia. The French had encouraged them to do so.

On October 22, 1956, Britain joined the cabal, agreeing to partner with Israel and France in launching a war against Egypt. According to the top-secret plan, Israel would invade Egypt, claiming it was doing so to eliminate fedayeen terrorist bases in the Egyptian-controlled Sinai Peninsula. (There were no such bases, as the Israelis themselves would later admit.) Britain and France would then issue a public condemnation of the Israeli attack, followed by an announcement that British and French forces, acting as peacekeepers, would intervene in the fight to separate the combatants and protect the Suez Canal. According to the scenario, the canal would be placed under international control, Nasser would be toppled, and a more cooperative Egyptian government would take his place.

Eden, who seemed to be living in an alternate reality, was convinced that the United States would back this extraordinary venture, even though Eisenhower had specifically warned him against military action. The U.S. president was willing to take Dulles's advice on many aspects of foreign policy, but where war was concerned, he made it clear he was in charge. And there was no way he would support an attack on Nasser.

Following Eisenhower's lead, Dulles warned Eden that any such assault would be forcefully opposed by the U.S. government. Eden's claims that the Suez Canal was in danger were clearly untrue, the secretary of state added. The Egyptians had not interfered with navigation of the canal, and there were no threats to the safety of British, French, or other foreign nationals in Egypt.

Paying no heed to such warnings, the British, French, and Israelis launched their attack on October 29. Israeli paratroopers were dropped into the middle of the Sinai Peninsula while Israeli warplanes bombed dozens of Egyptian targets, including army bases, airfields, and other military facilities. French planes, meanwhile, protected Israeli skies from a possible counterattack. In the hours and days to come, British and French aircraft would join the assault, zooming low over Port Said and Port Fuad, two towns in the Canal Zone, and dropping incendiary bombs that damaged or destroyed factories, shops, schools, and houses. Hundreds of civilians, clutching their children, leaped into the water of the canal to escape the bombing.

Taking personal command of Egypt's defense, Nasser ordered his army into combat against the Israelis in the Sinai Peninsula. When the leaders of Syria and Jordan offered to send troops, Nasser declined, telling Jordan's King Hussein that Jordan must conserve its forces. On November 2, he ordered the sinking of more than forty ships in the Suez Canal, thus blocking it and cutting off Europe's main route for oil supplies and shipping to the Near East and Asia.

If the three aggressors against Egypt truly believed that international opinion would accept their rationale for the attack, they were quickly disabused of that notion. The blowback was swift and massive. "In the eyes of the whole world, the British and French Governments have acted, not as policemen, but as gangsters," declared the *Observer*, a British newspaper. "It is no longer possible to bomb countries because you fear that your trading interests will be harmed." The United States, meanwhile, publicly condemned the three nations and demanded that they withdraw immediately from Egyptian territory.

The Suez crisis was on the verge of spiraling into a far more major conflict, and U.S. officials were desperate to get it resolved as soon as possible. Among other things, the attack on Egypt had ratcheted up Cold War tensions to their highest level since the end of World War II. The Soviet Union, which supported Egypt, had sent a threatening message to Britain and France implying that it might intervene with force unless they ended their incursion. Some officials—including Charles Bohlen, the U.S. ambassador to Moscow—read the message as a threat to use nuclear weapons. With the United States, Britain, and the Soviet Union all possessing nuclear arsenals, the world had clearly entered a period of unprecedented danger.

Using America's economic clout as a weapon, Eisenhower finally strong-armed Britain into giving up. As a result of the attack, the British were in desperate financial trouble. There was a run on the pound, and the country, facing bankruptcy, needed a loan from the International Monetary Fund to bail it out. But Eisenhower wouldn't permit authorization of the loan unless the invasion of Egypt was called off. Eden had no choice but to comply. On November 7, he accepted a U.N. cease-fire resolution. France and Israel followed suit.

Under U.N. supervision, the last of the British and French forces in Egypt were finally withdrawn by the end of 1956, but Israeli troops remained in the Sinai Peninsula until they were forced to leave in March 1957. The Suez Canal reopened to shipping a month later.

The Suez conflict had lasted less than two weeks, but its consequences were significant and long-lasting. It had claimed an estimated three thousand to four thousand lives, more than 75 percent of them Egyptians, many of them civilians. It had also done huge economic damage—not only to Egypt, which lost large amounts of its infrastructure, housing, and other property—but to Britain, France, and much of the rest of Europe, which suffered considerable financial losses as a result of the canal's blockage.

Thanks to the Suez debacle, the prestige and international standing of France and Britain suffered an enormous blow, from which Britain in particular would never fully recover. "Port Said, shattered and appalled, stood as a bitter memorial to the last display of British imperial machismo; and beyond the quays, the funnels and masts of sunken ships, blocking all passage through the lifeline of the Empire, ironically illustrated the point," the British journalist James Morris, who covered the Suez war, wrote at the time. "Future historians may well say the British Empire ended at Suez, for there it was finally made plain that Britain's imperial potency was lost."

Two weeks after agreeing to the cease-fire, Anthony Eden, emotionally and physically broken, left for a long stay in Jamaica. In January 1957, after only twenty-one months in office, he resigned from the post for which he had hungered most of his political life. Guy Mollet remained as prime minister of France for five more months until he, too, resigned. His government's handling of the Suez crisis had intensified an internal conflict between it and the French army—a discontent that led in 1958 to an even greater crisis over the question of Algeria and eventually to the collapse of the French Fourth Republic.

Israel, for its part, emerged from Suez with no regrets about deepening the rift between it and Egypt and other Arab states. It had abandoned the land its forces had taken in the Sinai only under duress. But while there, Israelis had mapped and photographed its territory in anticipation of future conflicts with Egypt, which seemed more and more likely as the years progressed.

Nasser, meanwhile, was celebrated as a hero in his own and other Arab countries and much of the rest of the Third World. Not only had he secured the Suez Canal for Egypt, he had inflicted a black eye on the Western colonialists who had dominated Egyptian citizens' lives for more than a century.

The Suez fiasco resulted in another clear winner: the United States. The decline in British and French influence in the Middle East and North Africa had left a vacuum, and U.S. officials were quick to fill it. Within months of the Suez crisis, America had begun to displace the European colonial powers as the main economic and military force in those regions, as it was doing also in Southeast Asia and the Pacific. Intent on preventing Communism from spreading in the Middle East, the Eisenhower administration sought to encourage the leaders of other Arab states, especially Saudi Arabia, to challenge Nasser, continuing to insist that he was in thrall to the Soviets.

In the midst of these geopolitical complications, Christiane Desroches-Noblecourt's quest to save the temples of Nubia seemed more and more impossible. How could she hope to accomplish anything, especially after she was placed under house arrest in Cairo during the Suez crisis and then thrown out of the country?

CHAPTER 12

"THESE MONUMENTS BELONG TO ALL OF US"

IN THE BLINK OF AN EYE, CHRISTIANE DESROCHES-NOBLECOURT had become persona non grata in the nation whose ancient history and culture had been at the center of her life since childhood. She was in Cairo when the Suez conflict began, taking shelter in her hotel room as British and French planes screamed overhead on their way to drop bombs on fuel storage tanks outside the capital. She couldn't believe her own country was waging war against Egypt—in her mind, a breathtakingly foolish and wrong thing to do.

The Egyptians, usually so warm and welcoming, had now turned hostile to Westerners. For Desroches-Noblecourt, the sudden shift in mood was devastating. She had spent years establishing close relationships with the Egyptians with whom she worked and socialized, from the workmen on her digs to government officials and members of Cairo's intelligentsia. Now everything had turned to ash. "This futile aggression," she wrote, "had destroyed in a few hours every beneficial gain from the French presence in Egypt for more than 150 years."

Immediately after the attack, the Egyptian government had severed diplomatic relations with Britain and France. British and French citizens in residence there were confined to their hotels and homes, and Egyptians were forbidden to have any contact with them. Desroches-Noblecourt was elated when a few of her closest Egyptian friends, among them Mustafa Amer, defied the order and came to see her off when she and the rest of the French and British communities were expelled from the country in early November.

Before she boarded one of the buses that would take her and the others to the port of Alexandria, she bade a poignant farewell to the friends clustered around her, not knowing when, if ever, she would see them again. As the buses pulled out, French and British warplanes roared over on another bombing mission. Desroches-Noblecourt remembered how the Egyptian driver of the bus, his jaw clenched with anger, looked up at the sky but continued on without saying a word. At dawn the next morning, she and hundreds of other Western evacuees boarded small launches at the port and were shuttled out to a warship from the U.S. Navy's Sixth Fleet as bombs from French and British aircraft fell nearby. Two days later, they were in Naples.

When Desroches-Noblecourt finally reached Paris, she found herself ostracized again—this time by her own countrymen. Most of French public opinion supported what she termed "this illegal intervention" and assigned blame for the conflict to Nasser and the Egyptians. "I told people about the great kindness of the Egyptians, about their dignity and their legendary friendship for the French, and about how we had wronged them," she said. "But I had difficulty being understood or believed, even by friends who were usually well informed." At that moment, she didn't seem to belong anywhere.

Yet, a little more than a month later, she learned otherwise. At the end of December 1956, UNESCO received a telegram from the Egyptian Antiquities Organization informing the U.N. agency that while it would no longer welcome experts from countries with which Egypt had cut diplomatic relations, it would make an exception for Desroches-Noblecourt. In fact, the Antiquities Organization wanted her to come back, still under the auspices of UNESCO, to continue her work with the documentation and study center.

She was touched—and tempted—by the offer. Although the challenges would be considerably greater than before, she desperately wanted the fledgling center to succeed, as well as to demonstrate, by her acceptance, her disagreement with the British-French-Israeli incursion. But, she told UNESCO, she couldn't return to Egypt without the authorization of the French government. When she approached the ministry of foreign affairs, she discovered she was not as alone in her views as she thought. "Don't hesitate," an official told her. "In fact, we want you to do it."

FOR THE NEXT TWO years, Desroches-Noblecourt was one of only a handful of Westerners allowed to enter Egypt, which seemed to have turned its back almost entirely on the West. When she returned to Cairo, she discovered that in the two months she had been gone, it had lost its usual bustling, cosmopolitan ambiance. There were far fewer cars in Egypt now, and the incessant honking of horns had largely vanished from Cairo's streets, as had the babel of a dozen or more foreign languages spoken by passersby.

Along with the British and French, the majority of the other Western residents of Cairo—Greeks, Italians, and Belgians among them—had also left. Western tourists, too, were no longer welcome. Instead of newsstands featuring publications in a variety of languages, street vendors now offered only Arabic reading material. "The country appeared to be dozing," Desroches-Noblecourt observed, "seemingly slipping back into its slow, thousand-year-old rhythm."

The Egyptian government had seized most of the British-, French-, and Jewish-owned companies operating in the country, including banks, restaurants, and an Anglo-Egyptian oilfield, as well as gas, tobacco, cement, pharmaceutical, and phosphate businesses. Most of them were transferred to the Egyptian public sector. Commercial contacts and transactions with the West were now a rarity, and the activities of the few foreign nationals allowed to work in Egypt were greatly constrained.

As much as Desroches-Noblecourt had always welcomed challenges, the difficulties she faced in this period were especially daunting. The restrictions on her life in Egypt were coupled with the problems of juggling a multitude of responsibilities, which gave her little time to spend with her family. In addition to her work at the Cairo documentation center, she was acting chief curator of the Egyptian department at the Louvre and a professor of archaeology at the École du Louvre. Every few weeks, she would fly from Paris to Cairo for a couple of days to monitor the missions surveying the threatened Nubian antiquities. During her summer holidays, she spent several weeks at the survey sites.

Meanwhile, the starting date for construction of the Aswan High Dam—early 1960—was drawing nearer and nearer. The Soviet Union, having provided Egypt with a substantial loan to build the dam, had dispatched hundreds of engineers to help design it, as well as technicians and heavy machinery for the actual work.

With the dangers to the Nubian antiquities creeping ever closer, the pressure on Desroches-Noblecourt and the center grew increasingly intense. Because of the Egyptian blacklist, she could no longer recruit French and British archaeologists to supervise the survey missions. But her list of foreign colleagues, many of whom were her friends, was long enough to allow her to fill the ranks with top-flight archaeologists from other Western countries. Answering the call, among others, was the legendary Jaroslav Černý, who had become her good friend when she worked with him at Deir-el-Medina. Although Černý was a professor at the University of Oxford, he was Czech by birth and thus eligible to work in Egypt.

As she focused on getting more missions into the field, she was confronted with yet another problem: a threat to the survival of the French Institute of Oriental Archaeology. After the expulsion of its French staff, IFAO and its headquarters, the Mounira Palace, were placed under United Nations protection. Once the cease-fire went into effect, however, that guardianship was no longer valid. Soon after she returned to Cairo, Desroches-Noblecourt was warned by an Egyptian friend that the government planned to dismantle the institute and install a school or military hospital in the palace.

She was horrified: Losing the institute would be a catastrophe for international Egyptology. "I went two nights without sleep," she recalled. "This decision meant that the institute's library, which is unique in the world, would vanish. The books would end up scattered, bought by unscrupulous resellers. As for our printing press, which allowed us to print thousands of hieroglyphic and other characters—they had already started to unbolt it from the floor." Because she represented UNESCO, she couldn't take a public role in trying to stop the plan, but she persuaded the French government to hire a lawyer to try to block it. She also approached several Western ambassadors to help in the cause. The only one who agreed was the Canadian ambassador, who, together with the lawyer hired by the French, was able to work out an agreement allowing IFAO to continue to function and to retain the palace as its headquarters.

But even as Desroches-Noblecourt was helping to save the institute, the misogyny she had encountered innumerable times from her French colleagues resurfaced—this time on the part of the current head of IFAO, who, having been expelled from Egypt after Suez, was back in Paris. She heard from friends there that he had approached various French and UNESCO authorities in an attempt to undermine her and her work. He reportedly expressed to the UNESCO director general "his surprise to see, in the present circumstances, that the responsibility of an archeological mission in Egypt had been entrusted to a Frenchwoman." Soon afterward, she received a message from Georges Salles, the director of the Louvre, who said that the IFAO head had asked him to order her to come back to Paris and "confine me to my post at the museum to avoid the shame of having a French citizen collaborating with the enemy"—i.e., Nasser and the Egyptian government. Salles assured Desroches-Noblecourt that he had ejected the man from his office and demanded he stop spreading his slander. Whether he did so is unknown, but regardless of how long the slander campaign lasted, it apparently had no effect on the French officials at whom it was aimed.

In the midst of dealing with this and all her other problems, Desroches-Noblecourt had not given up hope that an effort might still be made to save the temples of Nubia. Since her return to Egypt, she had made repeated appeals to Egyptian and UNESCO officials to consider taking action. That hope, however, was as yet unfulfilled. "It was like preaching in the desert," she recalled. "I was constantly told, 'You're wasting your time. Why are you even doing this? These are not even French monuments.' I heard that argument so many times. How stupid to think that one cannot take care of Egyptian monuments because one is not Egyptian! I was fighting for something that belonged to me as a citizen of the world, and also for the honor of humanity."

And then, suddenly, a powerful new ally appeared on the scene.

IN 1958, NASSER'S GOVERNMENT created a ministry to oversee Egyptian cultural affairs, which included protection of the country's antiquities. The man chosen to head the new Ministry of Culture was Dr. Sarwat Okasha, the son of a general and a former army officer himself who had been a member of the Nasser-led group responsible for the 1952 coup. He still was one of the president's closest advisers.

The thirty-seven-year-old Okasha, however, had always been an anomaly among his military colleagues. The scion of an aristocratic Egyptian family, he also was a scholar who was passionate about Western culture, particularly the music of Beethoven, Mozart, and other classical composers. After the coup, he had been appointed military attaché at the Egyptian embassy in Paris, where he studied for a doctorate at the Sorbonne, writing his dissertation on the Lebanese poet Khalil Gibran. Desroches-Noblecourt had met him there. She didn't learn until later that during his tenure in Paris, he had been heavily involved in secret talks in the early 1950s about possible peace negotiations between Egypt and Israel.

Okasha, who spoke fluent French, was as upset as Desroches-Noblecourt about the rupture of diplomatic relations between their two countries. "Nothing," he told her, "should tarnish the essential links so firmly established between our two cultures and maintained for so many years." He was also greatly worried about the impending destruction of the Nubian temples, but when she raised the possibility of saving them, he repeatedly rejected her arguments as impractical, pointing out that the Nasser regime was looking toward the future, not the past. The preservation of Egypt's national heritage was not high on its agenda.

However, in late 1958, just a little more than a year before construc-

GAMAL ABDEL NASSER AND
SARWAT OKASHA, UNDATED

tion on the dam was set to begin, Okasha underwent a sudden epiphany. The catalyst was a visit from Raymond A. Hare, the U.S. ambassador to Egypt, and James Rorimer, the director of the Metropolitan Museum of Art in New York. Rorimer, the former Monuments Man who had worked with the Louvre's Jacques Jaujard to track down Jewish-owned art stolen by the Nazis, had spent his entire museum career at the Met, joining its staff soon after his graduation from Harvard in 1927. While still in his twenties, he had presided over a huge expansion of the museum's medieval collection, helping to persuade John D. Rockefeller, Jr., to fund and build the Cloisters, the collection's new home overlooking the Hudson River in upper Manhattan. Once it was completed, Rorimer became its curator.

Described by the writer Robert M. Edsel as "a bulldog: short, squarely built, and not afraid of a challenge," the hard-charging, ambitious Rorimer was accustomed to getting what he wanted. And what he wanted from the Egyptian government, he made clear in his meeting with Okasha, was permission to buy one or two of the temples threatened with drowning by the dam. Since Egypt wasn't able to protect its own monuments, he suggested, it might be better to sell them off to countries that could.

"Think, Christiane, of the insult we have received!" Okasha, still in a state of shock, exploded to Desroches-Noblecourt the day after his meeting with Rorimer and Hare. "To sell off our temples! Better let them sink into the water forever!" In response, she repeated the plea she had used so often before: "These monuments belong to all of us. They constitute the very essence of your civilization, but also all our roots. We can't let this immense legacy disappear. We don't have it fully decrypted, and we cannot deprive our contemporaries and, more important, our heirs of this universal heritage."

When Okasha asked how they could possibly accomplish such a rescue, she replied that there was only one solution: to join forces and approach UNESCO about launching a campaign to save the temples. "With UNESCO, it will be Egypt working with all the rest of us," she said. "Here's a unique opportunity to put an end to these kinds of tragedies, to create a cultural crusade that no one has ever seen before." Okasha immediately agreed. Years later, he remembered being "haunted by the threat of appalling loss. I deemed it the duty of the Ministry of Culture to plan the salvation of the threatened monuments. Preserving our treasures for posterity became the imperative, and I determined then that the impossible should be made possible."

In Okasha, Desroches-Noblecourt had finally found someone whose enthusiasm, energy, and sense of urgency matched hers. Christiane Ziegler, a later head of the Louvre's Egyptian department, remembered Desroches-Noblecourt as "very dynamic, but also very tiring: she wanted everything done in a minute." Okasha was the same, Desroches-Noblecourt said. "When he made a decision, he stuck to it until the end, sweeping away the most stubborn resistance."

Such drive and determination were rare qualities indeed among officials in the Egyptian government. Virtually all government bureaucracies are known for their inertia, but the Egyptian bureaucracy was particularly notable for its glacial slowness. "Egyptians note with a mixture of conceit and bemusement that their bureaucracy is the oldest in the world, having begun to spin red tape three or four thousand years before the Arabs arrived in the seventh century with the sword and the Koran," *The New Yorker* reported.

HAVING RECRUITED AND INSPIRED OKASHA, Desroches-Noblecourt now enlisted the third major player in her nascent crusade. Serendipitously, René Maheu, the UNESCO official who had assured her of his support three years before, had just returned to Paris after his exile in New York. In early 1958, Maheu had successfully lobbied UNESCO's executive council to choose an Italian lawyer named Vittorino Veronese as the organization's new director general, succeeding Luther Evans, Maheu's nemesis. Later that year, Veronese, a prominent antifascist activist during World War II and an ardent proponent of social and economic justice, named Maheu as deputy director general.

In early January 1959, Desroches-Noblecourt suggested to Okasha that he call Maheu to discuss the possibility of a partnership. As it happened, Maheu was in the Ethiopian capital of Addis Ababa for several days, and he agreed to make a stop in Cairo on his way back to Paris. Okasha picked him up at the airport and drove him to his office for a three-hour meeting. There was an immediate rapport between the two men, and when Maheu got up to leave, Okasha, "convinced that I had found an ally," pressed into his hands a copy of Pierre Loti's book *The Death of Philae*, saying he hoped that "together we might write an epilogue, *The Resurrection of Philae*."

Twelve hours after departing for Paris, Maheu called Okasha and put Vittorino Veronese on the phone. The UNESCO secretary general expressed full support for the campaign and promised to present it to his agency's executive council once he received an official request from the Egyptian government with detailed information about the scope of the salvage project.

With Desroches-Noblecourt's dream finally moving a bit closer to the realm of possibility, she and Okasha had to clear an important first hurdle: gaining Nasser's consent. After ridding his country of non-Arab influence, how would he react to the idea of cooperating with

RENÉ MAHEU (RIGHT) BEING INTERVIEWED IN FRONT OF THE GREAT TEMPLE AT ABU SIMBEL, 1968

non-Arab countries on this project? And would he take umbrage at the idea of a campaign to mitigate the damage that his dam—the centerpiece of his regime—was about to cause?

In planning their strategy, however, she and Okasha had a trump card to play. Although Nasser's government had not placed much importance on the country's national heritage as a whole, it did pride itself on what it saw as its link to ancient Egypt, pointing out that the revolution marked the first time since the pharaonic period that Egypt was actually ruled by Egyptians. Nasser also noted the authority and power of Egypt in the ancient world, drawing parallels between that and modern Egypt's influence within the Arab sphere. His decision to install the colossal statue of Rameses II in front of Cairo's main railway station had been a reflection of his identification with his bygone predecessors.

Nonetheless, it took several months for Okasha to win Nasser's approval. The president responded favorably to Okasha's arguments about the importance of saving these priceless relics of pharaonic Egypt. But he was skeptical that international cooperation for such a proposal was possible during a time of sharply rising Cold War tensions and fierce opposition by Western powers to the growth of nationalism in Egypt and other developing countries. Okasha pledged that the cooperation he and Desroches-Noblecourt were seeking would be strictly cultural in nature—they intended to stay as far away as possible from political issues.

He outlined for Nasser the details of the plan they had in mind. The rescue operation would be overseen by UNESCO and the Egyptian Ministry of Culture, with Egypt covering a third of the costs. In return for donations to finance the temples' relocation, Egypt would also give other countries access to archaeological digs in the Nubian region and allow them to keep half of all finds from those digs. Finally, the Egyptian government would present to the nations making the largest financial contributions an array of antiquities from its own reserves, including four small Nubian temples on the list of those to be saved. That list, compiled by the Egyptians and UNESCO experts, would number more than twenty monuments.

If Nasser agreed to them, the inducements suggested by Okasha and Desroches-Noblecourt would signal an extraordinary about-face by Egypt, which for more than thirty years had been reluctant to allow foreign archaeologists to share in the fruits of their excavation work there. In effect, Nasser would be indicating his willingness to start inviting the outside world back into his country. Finally, in early April 1959, the president signed off on the plan.

Okasha and Desroches-Noblecourt, who was then in Egypt, wasted no time in putting the plan down on paper. The day after Nasser gave his approval, Desroches-Noblecourt was scheduled to leave for Paris, and Okasha wanted her to hand-deliver their letter to UNESCO outlining Egypt's offer. He was in a frenzy: He and she could draft the letter, but it had to be written in French. Whom could they get to type it? His ministry had no secretary who could speak or write French, and the ministry's typewriters had only Arabic characters.

"I'll do it," she told him. Okasha looked at her in amazement. "You?" he said. "You would do this for me? Do you know how to use a typewriter?" She laughed. In Egypt, as she knew from experience with the young native Egyptologists at the documentation center, men did not type. It was considered beneath them, so they never learned how. "Don't worry, Sarwat," she said. "Everyone types at home. It doesn't bother me at all."

But where would she find a typewriter with Roman letters rather than Arabic characters? As it happened, Okasha had a little Olivetti portable that he had brought back from Italy after a short stint as the Egyptian ambassador there. Taking it out of a closet in his office and placing it on a large table, he said, "I'll leave you alone to write the terms of our request in the beautiful language of Voltaire. I'll be in the sitting room outside. Call me if you need anything."

The letter, addressed to Vittorino Veronese, formally requested that UNESCO join the Egyptian cultural ministry in developing an international campaign to raise funds and obtain scientific and technical assistance for large-scale surveys and exploration of the threatened sites and for relocation of the temples and other antiquities. In the letter, Desroches-Noblecourt listed in detail the inducements the Egyptians were offering potential benefactors and suggested that a UNESCO committee of international experts manage the collection and dispersal of the revenue generated by the campaign.

As she worked, she heard the soft, beautiful strains of a piece of classical music coming from a phonograph in the sitting room. A few minutes later, Okasha opened the door and peeked in. "I hope you don't mind," he said with a bashful smile, "but I decided to play this music that I love so much. I hope it inspires you and makes your work easier." Desroches-Noblecourt smiled back. "Thus," she wrote later, "the first positive step in saving the monuments of Nubia was taken to the sound of Vivaldi's *Four Seasons*." When she finished the letter, Okasha dashed to Nasser's office to get it signed. A couple of hours later, the letter and Desroches-Noblecourt were on their way to Paris. The date was April 4, 1959.

In June, UNESCO's executive board authorized Veronese, in consultation with the Egyptian government, to draw up a formal plan for the campaign and to dispatch experts to Nubia to assess the situation and to decide whether the rescue of the antiquities was feasible. Their findings would be submitted to UNESCO in time for the organization's annual conference in November, when the final decision would be made.

With her customary verve, Desroches-Noblecourt embarked on the daunting tasks facing her and the documentation center in helping to plan the venture. Under her auspices, a team of engineers from France's National Geographical Institute—the state agency responsible for collecting geographical information about France—conducted an aerial survey of the Nubian antiquities, taking photographs from planes provided by the Egyptian air force. Meanwhile, the center had several teams already on the ground in Nubia examining and documenting the hundreds of temples, tombs, churches, fortresses, inscriptions, and carvings—the fruit of half a dozen cultures and civilizations—that were under threat.

That summer, Desroches-Noblecourt was also in charge of organizing a UNESCO-funded tour of the region by an international committee of experts that would ultimately decide the fate of the campaign.

She knew how critically important it was that its members be convinced of the value of the antiquities and the gravity of their loss.

Armed with working papers and preliminary technical reports that she and her team provided, the committee gathered in Cairo in October to begin its ten-day journey through Nubia. Its members included archaeologists, geologists, museum officials, art historians, architects, and other experts in related fields from a wide variety of countries. Leading the group was John O. Brew, a world-renowned American archaeologist who headed Harvard's Peabody Museum of Archaeology and Ethnology. Although Brew was not an Egyptologist (his specialty was Native American prehistory in the American Southwest), he'd been chosen because of his expertise in what was called "salvage archaeology"—the rescue and preservation of endangered sites.

As the group soon discovered, their trip up the Nile was hardly a pleasure jaunt. The days were steamy, with temperatures well over 90 degrees Fahrenheit. The river's annual flooding had not yet subsided, and the ground in and around the temples and other monuments was often waterlogged, forcing the committee's members to slog through glutinous mud to reach their destinations.

Acting as their tour guide, Desroches-Noblecourt wanted to make them forget the discomforts of the moment and lose themselves in the amazing history of these ancient places and the people who built them. A master storyteller, she had "a magnificent sense of popularization," said Guillemette Andreu-Lanoë. "She knew how to bring Rameses II back to life as if she had just had a drink with him the day before."

At the little rock temple of Beit el-Ouali, she described how it was built by a young Rameses II at the beginning of his reign—the first in a long string of such monuments. In the temple's open-air forecourt, there were bas-reliefs of the pharaoh fighting his enemies, bow in hand, the reins of the horses pulling his chariot tied around his waist. In the sanctuary, she pointed out a carving of an infant Rameses being suckled by Anuket, goddess of the Nile, and Isis, the goddess of healing and magic.

At the freestanding temple of Ouadi es Sebou, another Rameses-era monument, which centuries later had been turned into a Christian church, Desroches-Noblecourt showed how carvings of several of Rameses's wives and children had been plastered over and decorated with frescoes depicting the Nativity and Last Supper. She also took them to temples built more than a thousand years later, like the majestic Temple of Kalabsha, constructed during the last days of the Ptolemies and completed during the reign of Roman emperor Augustus. And then, in sharp contrast, she walked them through the little jewel-like temple of Dendur, built in Augustus's reign and dedicated to Isis and the god Osiris.

Last on the tour were the two pièces de résistance—the temples at Abu Simbel. Desroches-Noblecourt and the Egyptians had planned these final days of the visit especially carefully. Flying in by military helicopter, Okasha joined the group to make clear that of all the antiquities they were considering for preservation, Abu Simbel had the highest priority.

Desroches-Noblecourt was greatly relieved to see that from the moment the visitors arrived, Abu Simbel had them in thrall. The wild mimosas surrounding the temples were in full bloom, and, as if on cue, a family of crocodiles sunbathing on the sandy bank of the Nile in front of Abu Simbel slid into the water as they approached. Inside the Great Temple, she took the group from room to room, explaining in detail the carvings on the walls and inviting them to admire in particular "the stunning virtuosity with which the sculptors with their chisels told the story of the Battle of Kadesh" in the sweeping panorama on the back wall. She was relieved to see that "the splendor of this great stone testament had completely conquered them."

And of course she made sure that the visitors saw the Great Temple's façade at dawn. From their boat tied up in front of the temples, they watched as the rising sun suddenly emerged from a notch in the cliff on the other side of the river and shot its first rays at the four colossi keeping watch. She recalled how, "springing out of the twilight, the statues seemed to come to life, if only for a few seconds, as the birds began their morning song."

For many if not most members of the committee, it was a transcendent experience, and it underscored what Desroches-Noblecourt had long insisted: that the temples of Abu Simbel were an integral part of their environment. Rameses II and his builders had deliberately placed them in a spot where the sun would daily and dramatically revivify these enormous statues in his image, suggesting both the diurnal rejuvenation of the world and of the god-king himself.

It was unthinkable to consider the destruction of Abu Simbel, Desroches-Noblecourt said. If the decision was made to preserve them, she went on, they couldn't be uprooted and taken away to another location, like most of the other antiquities the committee had seen. They must be relocated in the same setting, albeit on much higher ground.

The committee agreed with both her points. It drew up a list of twenty-four temples and other antiquities to be saved, putting Abu Simbel at the top. It also discussed possible solutions for its rescue, including the construction of a rock-and-earth dam to protect it from the new reservoir's encroaching waters. In the committee's report to UNESCO's director general, it declared that the disappearance of the monuments would be "an irreparable loss for the world" and urged UNESCO to make an international appeal to save "Nubia's historical, archaeological, and artistic heritage which forms part of the human cultural patrimony."

The report, which was countersigned by the Egyptian government, was accepted by the UNESCO executive council in November, followed by unanimous approval by the organization's general conference in January 1960—the same month that construction was due to begin on the Aswan High Dam. In less than a year, Desroches-Noblecourt's one-woman campaign had morphed into the beginning of a massive international effort.

To prepare public opinion for the appeal, UNESCO and the Egyptian government staged a ten-day tour of the threatened antiquities for a large contingent of journalists from the United States and other countries whose support was considered essential to the success of the upcoming campaign. The press junket proved a success, with scores of stories appearing in the international press, particularly in the United States and Europe, about the imminent danger facing the Nubian temples.

Yet, while they generally approved of the idea of saving them, some of the pieces voiced skepticism about the chances of achieving that goal. Even if it were possible, could enough money be raised to make the attempt? In a story headlined DEATH BY DROWNING, *Time* magazine noted that the estimated cost of the venture might run as high as a heart-stopping $100 million. The story quoted an unnamed UNESCO spokesman as being "dubious" about the effort, "because, as he put it, the only recompense would be 'a few priceless treasures of history, perhaps not enough to attract the necessary funds.'"

Even John Wilson, the director of the University of Chicago's Oriental Institute, who would prove to be one of the effort's most ardent American supporters, had significant doubts. Decades later, Wilson would write in his memoirs that "although we would never have admitted it publicly, the full program of the Nubian campaign had seemed impossible at the start."

CHAPTER 13

THE GREATEST DIG IN HISTORY

ON JANUARY 9, 1960, GAMAL ABDEL NASSER STOOD ATOP A CLIFF overlooking the Nile and pushed a button. Seconds later, the deafening roar of an explosion rocked the stony wilderness surrounding the site. The Egyptian leader's detonation of ten tons of dynamite that had been cached half a mile away marked the ceremonial beginning of the construction of the Aswan High Dam. The blast, witnessed by a large crowd of Egyptian officials and foreign dignitaries, was followed by the cacophonous sound of giant bulldozers clearing the huge mounds of granite rubble left behind. With this thunderous starting gun, the race to save the Nubian antiquities from the waters of the dam had officially begun.

Two months later, on March 8, 1960, André Malraux, France's minister of culture and the nation's most renowned writer and intellectual, appeared before a large audience at UNESCO's headquarters in Paris to announce the start of a massive global effort to win that race and preserve the temples. "For the first time," Malraux declared, "all nations, some of which are pursuing secret or proclaimed wars against one another, are being called upon to band together to save the works of a civilization that does not belong to any of them."

Malraux's speech—a crucial element of the formal opening of

UNESCO's crusade—was particularly significant. Four years after the Suez crisis, France was still diplomatically estranged from Egypt, but during that period, there had been a dramatic shift in the French political situation. In 1958, the Algerian war had brought down the previous French regime, and with it the Fourth Republic, the country's form of government since 1946. The Fifth Republic, under the leadership of France's new president Charles de Gaulle, was then created. In 1959, de Gaulle set up a separate ministry of culture and put Malraux in charge.

Weeks before the launch of the UNESCO appeal, René Maheu had asked Desroches-Noblecourt to approach Malraux to see if he would appear at the event. At the time, it seemed an audacious idea: asking a high-ranking French official to engage in an effort involving cooperation with Egypt. But as it turned out, de Gaulle was looking for ways to improve relations between the two countries, and Malraux was eager to support the idea of an international cultural fraternity. He agreed not only to speak but to preside over the session.

Calling the Nubia rescue effort "a plan of magnificent and precise boldness," Malraux said that thanks to it, "the world for the first time is publicly claiming art as indivisible." He continued, "Of the force that brought Egypt into being out of prehistoric night, nothing now remains. But the impulse that engendered these giants which are threatened today still speaks to us as clearly as the genius of the master craftsmen of Chartres or the brilliance of Rembrandt."

Echoing Malraux's emphasis on the universality of artistic and cultural achievement, Nasser, in a letter read to the gathering, declared:

> We know deep in our hearts that if humanity has been able to progress, it is because it has been able to protect from oblivion the heritage accumulated by successive generations. . . . Humanity forms an indivisible whole. The parts that constitute it cannot do without each other or be isolated. That is why we appealed to UNESCO and all the nations of the world to save this part of civilization which belongs to all mankind.

For the first time, the Egyptian president publicly acknowledged that while his government's top priority was economic development, it also recognized the importance of saving Egypt's cultural heritage. He was now signaling his willingness to work with other nations, non-Arab as well as Arab, to do so.

AS EXPECTED, THE UNESCO appeal made front-page headlines around the world, and donations began flooding in from ordinary people in dozens of countries. Students at a high school in New York City held a rummage sale to raise money for the temples. A charwoman in the French city of Bordeaux also sent money, explaining in a letter: "I have made sacrifices all my life so that my daughter would be educated and cultivated. She is happily married, has a job and children. And so I am sending you what three of my dinners a week would cost, for if I cannot hope to see these Nubian temples myself, I want my grandchildren to see them."

Also from France, a twelve-year-old schoolgirl named Yvette Sauvage sent the contents of her piggy bank to UNESCO "so that the beautiful temples of Nubia do not disappear." Sarwat Okasha was so touched by her gesture that he invited Yvette and her mother to Egypt to show them the temples she wanted to save—a story that, not surprisingly, brought the project an additional dose of valuable publicity. "Egypt and Nubia seemed to be on every tongue," the Egyptian cultural minister proudly recalled.

In Paris, Desroches-Noblecourt was the beneficiary of yet another impromptu donation. Scheduled to appear on a British television program to promote the save-the-temples campaign, she was heading to the airport in a taxi, chatting with her secretary about the effort. When the taxi arrived at the airport, the driver refused to take her fare, telling her to contribute the amount to preserving the temples.

From the beginning of the campaign, Desroches-Noblecourt, Okasha, and René Maheu were its driving forces. The three were heavily involved in virtually every aspect of the mission, including reaching out to governments, private and public organizations, and individual citizens around the globe. In the early days, Okasha was particularly active.

To publicize the effort, he arranged for tours of collections of Egyptian antiquities to Europe, the United States, and Japan—the first time any artifacts belonging to Egypt had left the country in almost a century. Okasha had faced considerable opposition from other officials within the Egyptian government, a number of whom opposed the idea of any cooperation with the West. "It was an extremely difficult time," he said, but in the end, Nasser supported him.

The first tour—*5,000 Years of Egyptian Art*—was sent to Belgium, which had promised substantial financial support for the temples' preservation. The exhibit opened in Brussels soon after the official launch of the UNESCO campaign and was such a resounding success that other countries clamored to be included. Later exhibitions featuring masterpieces of Islamic and Coptic art, followed by a selection of small treasures from King Tutankhamun's tomb, were displayed in Washington, New York, Paris, London, and other major cities around the world. As part of his lobbying campaign, Okasha enlisted the support of several crowned heads of Europe, in particular King Baudouin of Belgium, King Gustav of Sweden, and King Frederick of Denmark, among others. He also met with foreign ambassadors to Egypt to enlist their countries' support, while Egyptian ambassadors to various nations around the world did the same in the countries in which they were based.

René Maheu, too, was engaged in intensive lobbying efforts directed at officials in the governments of the eighty-three countries that then belonged to UNESCO. Aiding him were several other UNESCO staffers, including twenty-eight-year-old Prince Sadruddin Aga Khan, the head of the agency's international action committee. The son of the third Aga Khan, Sadruddin, at the age of five, had met Christiane Desroches-Noblecourt when she played with him aboard the passenger liner taking her to her first assignment in Egypt in 1937. He went on to graduate from Harvard, where his roommates included the American writer and magazine editor George Plimpton. The two worked together on *The Harvard Lampoon,* and Sadruddin provided the initial funding for Plimpton's famed literary magazine, *The Paris Review.*

Unlike his playboy half brother, Aly Aga Khan, who was known for his womanizing and horse breeding, the handsome, urbane Sadruddin devoted himself to a lifelong career in international public service. Describing himself as "having a foot in the East and a foot in the West," he held French, Iranian, and Swiss citizenship and was fluent in French, English, German, and Italian, also speaking some Persian and Arabic. His first international job was the Nubia campaign, and he quickly became known as one of its most effective lobbyists and fundraisers. In 1965, the United Nations named him its high commissioner for refugees, a post he held for the next twelve years.

While Sadruddin Aga Khan spent much of his time trying to raise money in the United States, Maheu and other UNESCO officials focused their efforts on Western Europe. Two countries—West Germany and Italy—were particularly quick to volunteer substantial help. Not coincidentally, both had been Axis powers during World War II and, having become democracies since then, were trying to burnish their postwar reputations as responsible members of a global society. West Germany offered the boldest proposal: Rather than pledge funds to the Nubia campaign as a whole, its government said it would pay for the relocation of an entire monument—the Temple of Kalabsha—and handle all the work itself. Hochtief, Germany's largest construction company, would be in charge of the venture.

During World War II, Hochtief had been closely associated with Hitler and the Nazis. It had helped build the Nuremberg stadium where the Führer held party rallies, as well as his mountaintop home in the Bavarian Alps, the Berlin bunker where he killed himself, and the Siegfried Line, Germany's defensive chain of fortifications running from the Netherlands to Switzerland. Hochtief had also built a number of Germany's wartime armaments factories, employing thousands of forced laborers, many of whom died from starvation and physical abuse.

Years after the war, the company acknowledged its moral guilt and joined a countrywide business initiative to compensate forced workers and their descendants. It also erected a number of social centers, retirement homes, and other structures for Jewish organizations in Germany and the United States. In its official postwar work, it focused on projects in developing countries like Egypt.

Italy's participation in the UNESCO campaign followed a similar scenario. The company most intimately involved was the car manufacturer Fiat, whose founder, Giovanni Agnelli, had joined forces with Benito Mussolini before World War I. Fiat money helped fund Mussolini's fascist party, and in return, Fiat was awarded huge government contracts to produce military vehicles and other equipment. When Italy formed an alliance with Nazi Germany, Fiat also supplied war matériel to the Germans. Meanwhile, Agnelli's grandson and heir, Gianni, fought for Mussolini on the Russian and African fronts as a tank commander. When Italy switched sides and joined the Allies in 1943, Gianni Agnelli did the same, enlisting in an Italian unit under the command of U.S. general Mark Clark.

In 1958, Aurelio Peccei, the head of Fiat, left the company and founded Italconsult, an engineering consulting firm with a focus on social and economic development projects in Third World countries. The firm was underwritten by Fiat and three other major Italian companies. When Egypt ended its involvement with most of the West after the Suez Canal crisis, Peccei saw an opening for Italconsult, convinced that its experience trying to improve conditions in the poor and backward regions of southern Italy would prove valuable to the Egyptian government. His hunch proved correct. Nasser welcomed the assistance of Peccei's firm, whose first mission was to help Egypt regain the Italian market for Egyptian cotton. Italconsult also prepared a project to develop more than 150,000 acres of desert that would be transformed into farmland, thanks to the release of water from the new Aswan High Dam.

In the summer of 1960, as engineers from Hochtief minutely examined the Temple of Kalabsha, trying to figure out the best way to move a structure as big as Paris's Notre Dame Cathedral, the engineers from Italconsult were surveying the temples of Abu Simbel to determine how they could remove these delicate sandstone structures from the cliff without seriously damaging them. During that blazingly hot summer, the Italians were hardly alone at Abu Simbel. Also present were representatives of engineering firms from France and several other countries, all of them vying for the chance to pull off the greatest archaeological salvage operation in history.

WHILE THE UNESCO CAMPAIGN's most important goal was saving the threatened monuments, it had a secondary aim as well—to conduct archaeological surveys and excavations of the huge swath of land in Nubia that would eventually be engulfed by the dam's floodwaters. The actual rescues would take several years. But work on UNESCO's other objective began almost immediately. From the start, it proved to be an enormous success.

For more than twenty years, as the atmosphere in Egypt had grown increasingly hostile to Western exploitation, archaeological work had come to a virtual standstill in southern Egypt and northern Sudan, despite the abundance of antiquities in that sun-parched region. One of the few exceptions was the work of the survey teams of the Cairo documentation and survey center, which, under Desroches-Noblecourt's supervision, had been in various places in the area—day and night, winter and summer—to acquire as many details about the endangered monuments as they could.

With the launch of UNESCO's appeal, however, more than forty expeditions—representing universities, museums, and other organizations from nearly twenty countries—began pouring into the region. There were several reasons for the remarkable response, including the fact that if a foreign archaeologist wanted to work in Egypt during the early 1960s, Nubia was the only game in town. The Egyptian Antiquities Organization had suspended excavation work elsewhere in order to focus solely on exploration of the soon-to-be-submerged area. Even more compelling for archaeologists were the inducements offered by Egypt and Sudan: at least 50 percent of their finds plus preferential treatment for excavations in other parts of Egypt once the work in

Nubia had been completed, not to mention the gifts of four small temples and other antiquities to countries that made large contributions to the salvage effort. "Never before had such generous terms been offered to excavators," noted the University of Chicago's John Wilson, who was gratified by the magnitude of the response from archaeologists around the world.

"It was truly unprecedented, especially since it arose in a field without much of a tradition of cooperation," Wilson later wrote.

> Archaeologists have traditionally been insular individuals. . . . They are not accustomed to shift their leisurely pace and accept a rush project with a deadline. Furthermore, the financing for such emergency work was not in the budgets of nations, universities, or museums. And yet they showed up, with no trace of the earlier tradition of parochial jealousy. They visited one another and traded information about problems and techniques to achieve a common success.

He added, "Field archaeology has never seen such a unified and successful joining of forces."

Although John Wilson made no mention of it, Desroches-Noblecourt, with her pioneering work in bringing Egyptian and Western archaeologists together to conduct surveys for CEDAE, had already laid the foundation for greater international collaboration in Egypt; with the Nubia campaign, it had blossomed into a full-scale movement. Arguably for the first time in history, foreign archaeologists working in Egypt had the interests of that country at heart as well as their own.

Now that all of Nubia had become one vast archaeological camp, CEDAE's large boat, which served as its floating headquarters, was no longer the sole vessel moored off the banks of the Nile. "Nowadays," Desroches-Noblecourt wrote in 1961, "it's hardly possible to travel 15 to 20 miles on the river without finding a boat." Each boat, loaded with supplies, served as the base for an archaeological team from one of a wide array of countries, including Spain, Italy, Austria, the United

States, Poland, Switzerland, West Germany, the Netherlands, Czechoslovakia, Sweden, Belgium, Britain, Yugoslavia, France, and Denmark.

The expeditions, which were exploring, mapping, and recording dozens of archaeologically important sites, all worked under the direction of Desroches-Noblecourt and CEDAE, using modern methods to compile the most minute details about the architecture and decoration of each antiquity. One of the new techniques was photogrammetry, which Desroches-Noblecourt had adopted for use early in her tenure at the Cairo center. Photogrammetry involves the digital overlap of a number of two-dimensional photographs to make three-dimensional models. By comparing photos taken from at least two different locations, researchers can determine "lines of sight" that intersect to produce three-dimensional coordinates of points of interest. Geographers used the technique to produce contour lines on topographic maps. Archaeologists used it to produce 3-D models of large, complex sites. All the foreign survey teams were given photogrammetric maps of the areas and monuments on which they were working, which had been prepared by the French National Geographical Institute in collaboration with the Egyptian armed forces.

By the end of the first two years of the effort, virtually all the sites threatened with submersion had been thoroughly explored and surveyed, resulting in an archive of thousands of copied texts and complete architectural drawings kept at the Cairo center.

THE ARCHAEOLOGISTS INVOLVED IN the Nubia campaign were taking part in the largest dig in history. They seemed to be everywhere in the lower Nile Valley—measuring, surveying, and excavating temples, tombs, fortifications, rock faces, and the remains of ancient churches and mosques. As construction work on the dam progressed, shifts of archaeologists "worked frantically day and night to record and save the monuments, turning the temples into film studios of study and documentation," wrote the British journalist Tom Little. Never before had an entire region, encompassing almost two hundred square miles, been excavated on so grand a scale.

Thanks to the expeditions' work, there was a growing awareness of the immense archaeological wealth of this relatively unexplored area, in regard not only to the native peoples who had lived in Nubia but also to the various ancient civilizations that had cycled through there—Egyptians of pharaonic times, Ptolemaic Greeks, Roman legions, Christians, and finally Muslims. As André Malraux put it, "Nubia belongs to the dawn of our own history."

One of those caught up in the excitement of the finds was none other than Jacqueline Kennedy, the thirty-one-year-old wife of the newly elected American president, John F. Kennedy. The First Lady, who had been given an issue of UNESCO's magazine, *The UNESCO Courier,* that outlined some of the discoveries, wrote in a memo to her husband,

> The Sudanese think of the [Nile's] 2nd cataract as the gateway to the classic world. It is there that all knowledge of Greece filtered down the Nile from Egypt to them. They had an incredible heritage—it sounds like the Aztecs and Incas in South America—now it is all buried and forgotten, and people think of Africa as a continent of primitive tribesmen. . . .
>
> The most exciting thing to me was that I thought everything had been explored in the world—Troy, Carthage, Babylon, the Aztecs, etc. There wasn't much left for archaeologists to do but study things already in museums. But, now, if I were a young man, I would be an archaeologist and go to that region.

Jacqueline Kennedy's comment—"if I were a young man"—was psychologically telling. She seemed never to have considered the possibility that a young woman like herself might have a similar desire. And she clearly didn't know, at least at that point, that a French woman archaeologist had been working in Egypt for more than twenty years and was in fact overseeing the operation that had led to this massive breakthrough in research and understanding of ancient and medieval Nubia.

Echoing the First Lady's excitement about the explorations in Nubia, Desroches-Noblecourt later wrote, "To the layman, perhaps, these scientific results may not always seem spectacular or correspond to the fabulous treasures associated with the world of the Pharaohs. But in archaeological terms, they're just as important. It was long believed that previous explorations had completely exhausted the subject of ancient Nubia. But the dozens and dozens of discoveries we've made have provided an astonishing enrichment of our knowledge."

Among those finds was considerable evidence of Nubia's prehistoric cultures, a subject that had never before been thoroughly investigated and that revised all previous ideas of Nubia's early development in the Nile Valley. A joint expedition of the University of Geneva and the University of Chicago's Oriental Institute found a Paleolithic site near Abu Simbel, including a burial ground that had never been excavated before as well as an array of stone tools. Meanwhile, teams from France's University of Strasbourg and East Germany's Humboldt University discovered rock carvings and paintings of giraffes, elephants, hippos, and ostriches from the Neolithic period on, indicating that the arid Nubian desert had once been a fertile steppe, teeming with animal life.

The campaign's most spectacular find, however, was a huge collection of artifacts from a considerably later period in Nubian and Egyptian history—the era of Byzantine rule, from the fourth to the seventh century A.D. The emperor Constantine had established Christianity as the official religion of the Byzantine Empire, and Christian missionaries from Byzantium came to Nubia and Egypt in the sixth century to convert their people, who at that point were still fervent worshippers of Isis and other Egyptian deities. Within a century, a large part of Nubia had turned Christian.

The discovery was made by a team of Polish archaeologists in the town of Faras, on the border of Egypt and Sudan, which had been a major metropolis for much of its history of more than three thousand years. During the pharaonic era, Faras was the capital of northern Nubia, but the height of its influence and power came during the reign of Byzantium, when the city served as the center of Christian culture in the region.

In 1961, the Polish team, led by Kazimierz Michałowski, Desroches-

Noblecourt's old boss and mentor at the 1938 dig in Edfu, had begun excavating a huge mound below the walls of a seventeenth-century Islamic fortress. Michałowski thought that the tell might contain an Egyptian temple. What he and his team found instead were the well-preserved remains of a medieval Christian basilica, complete with more than 160 spectacular frescoes. During its four years of work on the project, the Polish team succeeded in bringing to light a largely unknown chapter in the history of Christian Nubia and rescuing a substantial portion of its art. No one had suspected that Faras contained such a priceless cache of Byzantine treasures.

The eighth-century basilica, built of brick and stone, had been abandoned four hundred years later when northern Nubia came completely under Muslim rule. Thanks to the sand enveloping the enormous structure, most of the vivid, delicate colors of the frescoes covering its walls seemed as fresh as the day they were applied. The finest surviving examples of Christian art in Nubia, they depict scenes from the Old and New Testaments, including the Nativity and Crucifixion. There were also portraits of the Virgin Mary, the Archangel Michael, the Apostles, and a number of saints, including a captivating painting of Saint Anne, the mother of Mary, who is pictured pressing her index finger to her lips, a gesture calling for silent prayer.

Over the four seasons that they worked on the basilica—each season lasting five to six months—the Poles succeeded in salvaging 120 frescoes, along with bronzes, ceramics, and other artifacts. Sixty-six of the paintings, including that of Saint Anne, are now on display at the National Museum in Warsaw, while the rest are at Sudan's National Museum in Khartoum.

Michałowski and his crew finished their work just in time. They had scarcely sent off the last of the cases containing the frescoes when water released by the new dam began engulfing their dig and swallowing up the ruins of the basilica.

UNQUESTIONABLY, ONE OF THE Nubian campaign's greatest accomplishments was the richness and breadth of its archaeological finds. But

KAZIMIERZ MICHAŁOWSKI IN FRONT OF THE FRESCO OF SAINT ANNE DISCOVERED BY HIS ARCHAEOLOGICAL TEAM IN NUBIA IN THE EARLY 1960S

another important achievement was the extraordinary teamwork displayed by participants from the different countries' expeditions. "From the standpoint of lasting scientific progress, the interdisciplinary collaboration and cross-fertilization that took place were probably the most important and most lasting of all the accomplishments of the Nubia campaign," wrote the American archaeologist and anthropologist William Y. Adams, who took part in the excavations. "The survey and excavation teams brought together prehistorians, cultural historians, philologists, anthropologists, and other specialists from a variety of backgrounds and with previous experience in many parts of Europe, Asia, Africa, and North and South America. From this conjunction of interests and outlooks, there arose a new perspective on Nubia, its peoples, and its history."

The Nubia campaign made yet another important contribution: providing young archaeologists throughout the world with the chance to do actual fieldwork. "In the lean years between 1930 and 1960, few of those just starting out had had the opportunity to work in the area of their specialty," John Wilson remarked. "In archaeology, book learning is a poor substitute for the laboratory of unearthing new puzzles every day."

Jacqueline Kennedy wasn't wrong in her belief that virtually all the novice archaeologists were men. But there were several notable exceptions, including a twenty-four-year-old Danish princess and a twenty-two-year-old graduate in Egyptology from the University of Cairo.

Princess Margrethe, the heir to the Danish throne, was part of a large expedition in the northernmost part of Sudan organized by four Scandinavian countries—Sweden, Denmark, Norway, and Finland. During its four years of work there, the group documented thousands of rock drawings and excavated some 4,200 tombs, as well as a number of settlements, fortresses, and churches.

Working in the field in Nubia was hardly a dilettantish endeavor for the tall, blond royal, who participated in the expedition's third season. A serious, knowledgeable archaeologist, she was treated as such by other members of the Scandinavian team, including its Swedish head, Dr. Torgny Säve-Söderbergh. "She was an active archaeologist like the rest of us," Säve-Söderbergh said, "and her work was of great value to the expedition."

Obsessed with archaeology since childhood, Princess Margrethe had followed in the footsteps of her maternal grandfather, King Gustav of Sweden, who had taken part in archaeological digs all over the world when he was younger and was now a fervent supporter of the Nubia campaign. As a teenager, Margrethe had spent several summers with her grandfather observing and working on the excavation of Etruscan settlements near Rome—a project sponsored by the Swedish Institute there. She later studied prehistoric archaeology at Girton College at the University of Cambridge, earning a diploma in the subject.

Although her royal duties prevented her from pursuing an archaeology career, Margrethe, who succeeded her father as monarch in 1972, never lost her passion for it. In 2010, the National Museum of Denmark mounted an exhibition entitled *Queen Margrethe II of Denmark and Archaeology*, detailing her lifelong love affair with the field. The audio guide prepared for exhibition visitors was written and recorded by the seventy-year-old Margrethe herself.

PRINCESS MARGRETHE OF DENMARK WORKING AT THE SCANDINAVIAN DIG IN NUBIA, 1963

Equally passionate about the work in Nubia was Fayza Haikal, a native of Cairo who had just received her Egyptology degree when the great dig began. Haikal came from a family that in many aspects resembled that of Christiane Desroches-Noblecourt. For one thing, she had an intellectual father who encouraged his daughters to follow their dreams, a distinct rarity in Egypt. "Having a daughter is not necessarily a calamity," he jokingly said—a good attitude to have, since he had five of them.

A literary scholar and lawyer, her father had earned a doctorate in law from the Sorbonne and was active in Egyptian politics and government, serving as minister of education in 1937 and later as president of the Egyptian senate. He sent his girls to the Lycée Français in Cairo because he wanted them to have an international secular education. When Fayza, who was fluent in French and English, told him she was interested in studying Egyptology, he dispatched her on a visit to several archaeological sites in Egypt before she enrolled at Cairo University.

It was at the university, she said, that "I discovered my real Egyptian roots." She was a superlative student, and when she graduated in 1960, she received a fellowship for graduate study in Britain the following year. Until she left, she worked at CEDAE in Cairo, checking the research reports of members of the survey teams to make sure there were no errors before they were published.

But Haikal was not content with office work. What she wanted to do above all was to "go to Nubia to visit the monuments with which I was dealing and contribute to their documentation. That proved to be the real challenge." At the time, it was not socially acceptable for young Egyptian women to live away from their family and mingle with male colleagues. But she "pushed and pushed" until her family and superiors at CEDAE finally agreed.

The first woman to do fieldwork for the center, Haikal joined the team working at Abu Simbel, where she was assigned to copy texts from the huge wall carvings of the Battle of Kadesh in the Great Temple. Years later, she remarked, "I can proudly say that I paved the way for women Egyptologists to work in Nubia. When I went to England, my successor was a female friend of mine, and it became normal for Egyptian women to pursue fieldwork far away from home."

Haikal continued to break ground throughout her career. After her studies at Oxford, under the tutelage of one of Desroches-Noblecourt's mentors, Jaroslav Černý, she became the first Egyptian woman to earn a PhD in Egyptology. She went on to help found the Egyptology program at the American University in Cairo. The foremost woman Egyptologist in her country, she has trained many of today's top Egyptian experts in the study of their country's ancient civilization.

CHAPTER 14

A CHAMPION IN THE WHITE HOUSE

BY 1961, THE WORK OF SALVAGING THE ENDANGERED TEMPLES WAS well under way. Egypt took the lead, moving some of the smaller monuments on its own. Those designated as future gifts to nations that were particularly generous in their donations were dismantled, their stones and columns stored on a large island in the Nile until it was determined where they would go. They included the Temple of Taffa, a Roman antiquity built during the reign of Emperor Caesar Augustus and dedicated to Isis, and the Temple of Debod, a Ptolemaic-era structure dedicated to Amun. Debod's north and south walls were adorned with paintings of Ptolemaic pharaohs making offerings to Amun and other gods and goddesses.

Another diminutive Roman-era monument, the Temple of Qertassi, was taken apart by Egyptian workers and reerected on a hill on the west bank of the Nile, less than a mile south of the new dam. It would be joined there by the Temple of Kalabsha, the first and largest of the major temples to be moved.

The rescue of the smaller antiquities was child's play compared with the challenges facing the Germans in dismantling and transporting a temple the size of a cathedral. From the beginning, there was a great sense of urgency about the effort. Located about thirty miles south of Aswan, Kalabsha lay close to the riverbank and would be one of the first temples drowned by the Nile once the dam was completed.

Also built by Caesar Augustus, Kalabsha was the greatest freestanding structure in Nubia, measuring 400 feet—longer than a football field—by 230 feet. It consisted of a gateway, a columned court, a hall of pillars, and an inner chamber. A thick outer wall surrounded the temple buildings, and on the eastern side, a stone jetty led to the Nile.

Kalabsha had been known for what one archaeologist called "its almost overwhelming richness of texts," along with reliefs in vibrant colors, carved on the temple's inner walls. One of the most notable carvings showed Augustus, dressed like an Egyptian pharaoh, presenting sacrifices to Isis, Osiris, Horus, and the Nubian god Mandulis. After the first Aswan dam was built in 1902, the Kalabsha complex, like Philae, was half submerged in water for nine months a year, causing considerable fading of its once brilliant hues.

Hanns Stock, the director of the German Archaeological Institute in Cairo, was in charge of moving the temple. In his youth, Stock had wanted to be both a priest and an archaeologist, much like Desroches-Noblecourt's mentor Father Étienne Drioton. But just before his ordination as a Jesuit, he decided against the priesthood. After working as a research assistant at the Egyptian Museum in Berlin, he was drafted into the Wehrmacht during World War II. He escaped being sent to the front because of his language skills—he spoke fluent French, Italian, and Greek—and became a military interpreter instead. Uncompromised by any connection with the Nazis, he resumed his archaeological career following the war.

After a careful study by Hochtief engineers and Stock's team of archaeologists, the decision was made to dismantle Kalabsha block by block—more than sixteen hundred sandstone blocks in all, some weighing as much as twenty tons. The immense job was complicated by the fact that only in July, August, and September would the lower half of the temple be above water level.

In August 1961, after winning the contract to move the temple, Hochtief decided to start work in November, when the structure would be half submerged, and begin removing its upper sections by means of cranes stationed on barges. But the annual flood was exceptionally high that year, and the temple was completely underwater until the following May. Having lost so much time, the operation became a breakneck effort, with a ceaseless line of barges loaded with blocks shuttling back and forth between the work site and the temple's new location, a four-hour journey each way. After being taken to the new site, thirty miles to the north, the blocks were off-loaded and transported by truck to a storage area, where they would remain until reconstruction began.

The operation involved more than 450 people, most of them Egyptian laborers. The work was done in two shifts, twenty-four hours a day, with daytime temperatures averaging between 93 and 122 degrees Fahrenheit. "It is difficult to imagine the effect of such conditions on the small group of German technicians and archaeologists and especially on the Egyptian workers who labored under the burning sun," an observer wrote. "In spite of the stifling heat, which barely abated at night, few dared to risk a swim in the Nile because of the danger of waterborne diseases." Snakes, scorpions, and spiders were other ever-present threats.

The crews faced a multitude of additional challenges, including building a new harbor and road near the new site before the first stones could be unloaded. According to Stock, the unloading effort was a particularly difficult task, which he described as "hard-hitting, dangerous labor . . . a *tour de force* under circumstances of privation and according to a strict schedule, sweating day in, day out, between the cliffs and sand dunes."

Despite all the difficulties, the reconstruction of Kalabsha began in October 1962, with the last piece of this giant jigsaw puzzle finally put into place—with millimetric precision—the following October. The overwhelming success of the first major salvage operation was greatly reassuring to Desroches-Noblecourt and the Nubian campaign's other organizers. Their sense of relief, however, was short-lived: They had just learned that the relocation of another major temple had now become a giant question mark.

WHILE WORK WAS PROCEEDING on Kalabsha, Desroches-Noblecourt attended a meeting of archaeologists, engineers, and Egyptian officials in Cairo to discuss how to go about the rescue of the Temple of Amada. The oldest temple in Nubia, Amada had been built in the mid-fourteenth century B.C. by Pharaoh Thutmose III, a warrior king who had led seventeen successful military campaigns in twenty years and created the largest empire Egypt had seen up to that time. His son and successor, Amenhotep II, completed work on the temple.

Its seven halls were decorated with an array of important hieroglyphic inscriptions. One, carved on a stela on the rear wall of the sanctuary, described a bloody military campaign by Amenhotep into Asia, which culminated in an Egyptian victory and the pharaoh's bringing back the bodies of rebel chieftains to hang on the walls of Thebes as a warning to anyone foolish enough to challenge his might.

But it was Amada's finely cut, brightly painted wall reliefs that were its crowning glory. During the Byzantine era in Nubia, the temple had been used as a Christian church, and its priests had plastered over the reliefs, which showed Thutmose and Amenhotep embracing and making offerings to various Egyptian gods. The plastering had preserved the vibrant colors of the paintings, which had first been discovered by archaeologists in the early twentieth century.

During the meeting in Cairo, most of those present seemed to favor following the method used for Kalabsha, taking Amada apart block by block. But if they did that, the exquisitely painted reliefs would be ruined. After considerable debate, there was consensus that no option was available other than consigning the temple to a watery grave. Desroches-Noblecourt adamantly disagreed. "To me," she said, "that seemed like a crime."

When she objected, one of the other participants said there was not enough money in the budget to pay the extraordinarily high costs of finding a way to preserve it intact, if that was even possible. Desroches-Noblecourt shook her head. "In a voice that seemed to replace mine," she recalled, "and with the anguish of a mother whose child was about to drown, I declared, 'France will take charge of the Temple of Amada! Immediately!'"

An Egyptian official pointed out that France had already made a substantial financial pledge for the salvage of Abu Simbel. She waved his concern aside. She would find not only the extra funds, she said, but also the engineers and other workers capable of performing what most in the room considered an impossible task. In hindsight, Desroches-Noblecourt remarked, "my intervention was a little foolish, but I thought it necessary to protect this temple from being battered or destroyed."

After she returned to Paris, two creative-minded engineers whom she and others consulted came up with an ingenious solution—detaching the entire monument from its rock foundation, then moving it hydraulically on a railway track to its new location more than 270 feet higher. The operation would be done in three stages: bracing the temple with steel bands and placing an iron plate under it; detaching it in one piece from the rocky ground, with a sufficiently thick stone footing; then transporting it by rail almost two miles up a sharp incline.

The estimated cost of the operation was as audacious as the plan itself: 32 million francs, equivalent to $650,000 ($6.2 million today). Desroches-Noblecourt, who wasn't easily frightened, later admitted, "That quote terrified me." Where could she possibly get the money? She knew that French economic officials would turn her down, citing the $1 million pledge the government had already made to save Abu Simbel. Financially, France was stretched to the limit. She finally decided she had only one recourse: a last-ditch appeal to the French president, Charles de Gaulle himself.

She made an appointment to see him, and on the designated day, she drove to the Élysée Palace. As she parked on a nearby street and got out of her car, a sudden rainstorm drenched her. She arrived at de Gaulle's office with soaked clothes and dripping hair, all of which "added to my already terrible apprehension that things were not going to go well."

At first, her worry seemed justified. De Gaulle, known for his quick temper and caustic tongue, had already been informed of her rash promise, and when she entered his office, he rose from his desk. At six feet five inches, he towered intimidatingly over the five-foot archaeologist. "How dare you engage France in this without the authorization of my government!" he thundered.

Desroches-Noblecourt paused for a moment before replying. She remembered how, on June 18, 1940, de Gaulle had broadcast to the French people from the BBC in London, urging them to resist the Germans and defy the collaborationist Vichy government of Marshal Philippe Pétain, which at the time was the legal government of France. Looking up at him, she replied, "And you—did you demand the authorization of Pétain's government on June 18, 1940? No! You judged that the circumstances required you to take a stand. Well, that's what I've done."

For a moment, he stared at her, dumbfounded. Then Charles de Gaulle did something exceedingly rare for him: He laughed. "You win!" he said. The money was approved.

On December 12, 1964, after years of planning and preparatory work, the Temple of Amada, secured with steel bands and mounted on concrete beams, was detached from the rocky soil beneath it. It was then placed on three railroad tracks and began its trip up the steep hill to safety. Powered by giant hydraulic jacks, it moved only a few feet each day, taking sixteen months to travel 1.6 miles. The temple's progress was so slow that as it inched forward on the tracks, the rails it had traversed were lifted up and placed in front of it again.

True to de Gaulle's promise, France did indeed fund the temple's move and reconstruction at its new site, on a cliff overlooking the vast new lake created by the Aswan High Dam.

IN ADDITION TO AMADA'S rescue, Desroches-Noblecourt was coping with an array of other challenges. One involved the cumbersome decision-making process of the campaign and the agonizing slowness of getting anything decided and accomplished. The delays were largely the result of the sluggish bureaucracies of UNESCO and the governments of its member countries with which she and the campaign's other leaders had to deal.

UNESCO had set up a plethora of committees to handle various aspects of the project—an international action committee; various honorary committees; consultative and control committees of engineers, archaeologists, and other experts; and national committees in the member countries, which largely focused on fundraising. Few of these bodies were regarded as efficient. In 1962, an Egyptian government report complained that "among the mass of committees and reports, the Nubian countryside would end up being submerged before the monuments themselves could be rescued." But the Egyptians themselves were afflicted with more than their own share of bureaucratic lethargy.

Adding to those difficulties were constant clashes between UNESCO and the Egyptian government over which entity was actually in charge of the Nubia campaign. In the beginning, UNESCO was supposed to play only an intermediary role between the Egyptians, the governments of its member countries, and the international array of professionals who would do the actual rescue work. But as time went on, the U.N. agency became more and more involved in the organization and implementation of the effort—an increasingly sore point for Egyptian authorities, who insisted that their country must be acknowledged and treated as its leader. At one point, the Egyptians argued that UNESCO, like its member countries, should provide a financial contribution to the campaign from its own budget—a demand that UNESCO rejected. In the middle of all this was Desroches-Noblecourt, who, throughout the campaign, was frequently called upon to smooth ruffled feathers on both sides.

IN THE MIDST OF dealing with their own internal strife, UNESCO and Egyptian officials were faced with yet another thorny issue: the reluctance of a number of member countries to commit specific amounts of money as their contributions for saving the temples. UNESCO had originally proposed that members' participation in the campaign be made mandatory, with each country donating an amount based on its annual contribution to UNESCO's operation. For example, the United States, which provided one-third of UNESCO's funding, would be asked to pay one-third of the cost of the campaign. But when the agency asked its members to agree to that plan, paying the funds in installments over an eight-year period, it met with intense opposition from several countries, including the United States.

There were also questions about the raising of money from private sources. Should the campaign focus on a promotional effort aimed at the general public or make more targeted solicitations to companies, foundations, and wealthy individuals? Skeptics of the public approach pointed out that while seeking small donations from schoolchildren and other private citizens made for good PR, it could not possibly generate the vast sums needed. On the other hand, appeals to potential large donors didn't seem to be working all that well either. The idea of arts patronage and sponsorship by the wealthy hadn't yet become popular in the 1960s. There was a simple reason for that: No tax breaks were available for cultural donations.

Making things even more difficult was the extremely tense political climate of the time. Although Desroches-Noblecourt and the campaign's other proponents insisted that saving the temples was a cultural—not a political—issue, others did not agree. In several countries, there was still fierce antagonism toward Nasser and Egypt and a disinclination to do anything that might help them, as Desroches-Noblecourt discovered early in the process.

At a dinner one night in London, she asked the chief curator of the British Museum's Egyptian department to support the UNESCO effort. "No," he retorted, "you won't get anything from me. These people have driven our troops out of Egypt. I won't do anything until they come and ask forgiveness on their knees!"

When she appeared on a BBC television program to discuss the campaign, a prominent British archaeologist asked her with more than a tinge of condescension if it was really necessary to save these Nubian shrines. Infuriated by his attitude, she brusquely asked him how he would feel about the disappearance of the castles in the Loire Valley or the inundation of Westminster Abbey. The next day, a London newspaper indignantly asked in a story: "Who is this Frenchwoman who wants to drown our national monument?"

In Paris, a delegation of Frenchmen whose businesses in Egypt had been expropriated by Nasser came to Desroches-Noblecourt's office at the Louvre to protest her participation in the drive. "How do you claim to seek help for a nation that has robbed us of our property?" the group's leader demanded. "Not only will we remain deaf to your requests but we will speak out against any financial participation of our government in this project!"

Yet as awkward as these confrontations were for her, they were nothing compared to the discomfort and anger she felt in her dealings with American officials. With the United States embroiled in Cold War politics, the Eisenhower administration, guided by its staunch anticommunist policies, adamantly opposed any help to Egypt because of Nasser's acceptance of Soviet aid in building the Aswan dam.

The U.S. ambassador to Egypt, G. Frederick Reinhardt, made his position and that of his country insultingly clear to Desroches-Noblecourt during an embassy dinner party in Cairo. In the middle of the meal, Reinhardt suddenly called out to her, "Madame Noblecourt, have you ever been told you are insanely reckless? How dare you drag UNESCO and all its member states into a fallacious enterprise that has no basis in fact?" Reinhardt insisted that the dam would never be completed, that the United States would stop it in its tracks, and that his country would never contribute money to the effort she was promoting. "He paid no attention to any of my vehement responses," Desroches-Noblecourt wrote. "I was frozen, stunned, by this extraordinary outburst. I didn't know what to say or do."

Forty years later, she was still fuming about that dinner and other clashes she had had with American authorities. "The Americans were the worst!" she told an interviewer. "They were terrible. They did everything to stop me. They branded me a madwoman and a trickster, irresponsibly dragging UNESCO into an impossible situation. John

Foster Dulles, who I hope is dead, and the U.S. ambassador, Mr. Reinhardt, said I had a perverted imagination. These cowboys treated the Egyptians and Nasser abysmally."

While the United States had joined other UNESCO members in January 1960 to support the idea of saving the Nubian temples, that did not mean it was willing to actually provide any money for the effort. The Eisenhower administration's refusal to contribute any funding was a critical problem for the campaign's organizers, who desperately needed the United States, as the largest contributor to UNESCO, to be on board with the project. Without U.S. help, there was little chance the effort could succeed.

And then something akin to a miracle occurred. In November 1960, the Democratic presidential candidate, John F. Kennedy, narrowly defeated Vice President Richard M. Nixon to become Eisenhower's successor. Although they weren't aware of it at that point, the leaders of the campaign finally had a champion in the White House—the new president's wife, Jacqueline Bouvier Kennedy.

Over the next three years, Jacqueline Kennedy would become one of the key participants in the fight to save the temples, joining Desroches-Noblecourt as the only women to have a major impact on the campaign and its outcome. On the surface, the two, who wouldn't actually meet until fourteen years later, seemed to have little in common. Ebullient and outgoing, Christiane had been raised to believe she could do anything she set her mind to, never once thinking to hide her energy, outspokenness, and intellect. By contrast, the shy, reserved Jacqueline had been brought up to believe that marriage and motherhood were the only roles to which she could—or should—aspire. To all appearances, she acquiesced to that dictum, even as inwardly she rebelled. "Jacqueline accepted the life that fate offered her and did all the things that were expected of her," recalled her cousin John Davis. "Her outward conformity to the conventions of her class, however, belied a fiercely independent inner life." Although it would take years for her to become her own person and have an impact on the world, the seeds were planted during the transformative year she spent as a college student in Desroches-Noblecourt's hometown.

WHEN JACQUELINE BOUVIER TRAVELED to Paris in 1949 to spend her junior year abroad, she was already predisposed to love France. Intensely proud of her French blood from her father's side of the family, she had been a Francophile since childhood, going so far as to name her French poodle Gaullie, after General Charles de Gaulle. Her time in Paris was everything she'd hoped for—and more. Above all, it produced an intellectual flowering on her part—an immersion in art, literature, poetry, history, and other aspects of French culture and life that would be a guiding force from that point on.

"I loved it more than any year in my life," she later wrote. "I learned not to be ashamed of a real hunger for knowledge, something I had always tried to hide." One of her biographers, Barbara Leaming, wrote, "She prized the sense she had in France that in her dealings with others, men included, she need not conceal she had a mind." She attended classes at the Sorbonne and the École du Louvre at a time when Desroches-Noblecourt was teaching there. It's unlikely, however, that they ever crossed paths. Like the French archaeologist, Jacqueline Bouvier had been fascinated by Egyptian antiquities since childhood, when she first read about the discovery of King Tutankhamun's treasures. Almost certainly she spent time in the Egyptian antiquities department at the Louvre, which she visited frequently. During that time, however, her coursework and other activities were focused almost entirely on European art history and French literature.

When she began dating John F. Kennedy in the early 1950s, one of the things that drew her to the young Massachusetts senator was their common love of books and history. Both were constantly reading—she mostly French history and classical literature, he American and British history. "She wanted to know history not just for herself but for her husband," said Letitia Baldrige, Jacqueline's social secretary in the White House. "They were almost competitive in the knowledge they consumed, [each] trying to one-up the other on historical facts." Their daughter, Caroline, later wrote that both her parents thought of history not as an academic pursuit but as "a gathering of the most fascinating people you could ever hope to meet."

In their early married life, Jacqueline's command of French, both written and spoken, proved to be of great value to her husband in his work on the Senate Foreign Relations Committee. The Algerian conflict and France's difficulties in Indochina were both major foreign policy issues in the early and mid-1950s, and she translated and summarized several French-language books on those subjects for him.

Until he married Jacqueline, John Kennedy had had little exposure to the arts, but under her tutelage, he developed a keen interest in them, particularly painting, music, and sculpture. He began frequenting the shop of an antiques dealer on New York's Madison Avenue that specialized in artifacts from ancient Rome, Greece, and Egypt. Over the course of their ten-year marriage, he presented his wife with a number of gifts from that shop. For their last anniversary, he offered her a choice of antiquities that he had selected for her approval. "I could see the present he wanted me to choose the most was this [Egyptian] bracelet," she later said. "It's terribly simple, gold, [in the form of] a snake. . . . I could just see how he loved it." It was indeed her choice.

By the time the Kennedys entered the White House, the arts, according to the historian Arthur M. Schlesinger, Jr., had become a central part of both their lives. "The President's curiosity and natural taste had been stimulated by Jackie's informed and exquisite responses," said Schlesinger, who served as a White House adviser.

From his first weeks in office, Kennedy made support for the arts an intrinsic part of his presidency. As Schlesinger put it, "He saw the arts not as a distraction in the life of a nation but something close to the heart of a nation's purpose. . . . He looked for opportunities to demonstrate his concern." His wife did the same. Almost immediately after Kennedy's inauguration, she announced her plans to make the White House a "showcase for everything that was finest in American music, poetry, and the arts." But her interests stretched far beyond the boundaries of the United States.

A few weeks after her husband became president, Jacqueline sent him a lengthy memo asking him to reconsider the U.S. position on funding the Nubia campaign. She had been reading a great deal about it, she wrote, and she put forth a list of arguments for why the Nubian treasures should be saved and why the United States had an obligation to do its part.

The president passed his wife's memo along to a young aide, Richard Goodwin, for "possible action." An assistant special counsel to Kennedy, the twenty-nine-year-old Goodwin, a graduate of Harvard Law School, was already a seasoned Washington veteran. Before joining the White House staff, he'd been a law clerk for a Supreme Court justice, a congressional investigator who helped uncover the television quiz show scandals in the 1950s, and a speechwriter on Kennedy's presidential campaign. He was known for his intensity, energy, and rough-edged personality, and for the ever-present cigar in his mouth.

Goodwin soon discovered that Jacqueline Kennedy was not the only one intent on persuading the president and his staff to back the Nubian rescue attempt. A delegation of UNESCO emissaries—including Sadruddin Aga Khan and two prominent U.S. archaeologists, John Wilson and Harvard's John O. Brew—had come to town in the spring of 1961 to make their own pitch to the White House.

In a meeting with Goodwin, they argued that the U.S. withdrawal of its promise of aid to help Nasser build the Aswan dam had had an extremely adverse effect on American prestige in developing countries, particularly those in Africa. While the loss of that goodwill could never be totally overcome, the UNESCO representatives declared, a decision to help save the Nubian temples would be a huge step in the right direction. Conversely, failure to participate would reinforce the feeling in Egypt and elsewhere on the African continent that the United States was indifferent to their welfare, resulting in serious damage to the U.S. national interest. "The rest of the world is looking to the United States for some initiative in this campaign," John Wilson said. "We should not put ourselves in the position of standing outside."

He and the others were elated when Goodwin told them he had already done some research on the issue and was sympathetic to their cause. "It became clear to me," Goodwin later wrote, "that without American help the monuments would perish—not only Abu Simbel but a large number of statues, temples, and other artifacts. I had no doubt about the merits of the project. I was less certain that JFK could be persuaded to ask Congress for an appropriation."

With the help of Kennedy's science adviser, Jerome Wiesner, Goodwin put together a large scrapbook filled with photos of Abu Simbel and the other threatened monuments, together with summaries of opinion from international experts on why they should be saved. When he presented the book to the president in the Oval Office, Kennedy flipped through it while Goodwin went on at length about how unique and priceless the antiquities were and how they belonged to all the world, not just to Egypt.

"That's all fine," Kennedy responded, "but what do you think Rooney's going to say when I ask him for millions of dollars to save a bunch of rocks in the middle of the Egyptian desert?" He was referring to Rep. John J. Rooney, a New York Democrat who was chairman of the House Appropriations subcommittee in charge of foreign aid. "I know what he'll say," Kennedy continued. "He'll say, 'Jack, you must be out of your mind. There's not one Egyptian voter in the whole country.'"

Goodwin later wrote, "I wasn't going to argue politics with the master. Naturally, Rooney wouldn't think much of the idea, but he was a Kennedy loyalist." Instead, he told the president of Egypt's offer to award some of the smaller temples to countries that had made generous donations to the Nubia campaign. "Imagine, Mr. President," Goodwin exclaimed, "Napoleon only brought an obelisk back to Paris. You can bring an entire temple to Washington!" Kennedy stared at his aide for a moment, and Goodwin thought that he'd gone too far. Then the president leaned back in his chair and smiled. "Let's give it a try," he said.

While Goodwin's description of his meeting with Kennedy makes for a good story, it doesn't give a complete picture of the reasoning behind JFK's decision to reverse America's stand on saving the Egyptian antiquities. The president's interest in doing so was spurred by much more than the offer of a trophy temple.

During the 1960 presidential campaign, Kennedy had accused the

Eisenhower administration of allowing the United States to become dangerously weak in the face of increasing Soviet military strength. Yet while promising to be tougher on Communism, he wanted to get away from relying solely on military means to do so. He was particularly interested in developing a new kind of diplomacy to deal with the countries in the Middle East, Africa, and Asia that were emerging from colonial rule.

The Eisenhower administration had viewed the national concerns of these nonaligned countries—such as the building of the Aswan dam—solely through the prism of Communism, treating the countries and their people merely as assets or weapons, without regard for their own interests. Such a focus, Kennedy believed, represented an "open invitation" to the Soviet Union to exploit discontent throughout the Third World. Like it or not, he said, an "inevitable tide of revolutionary nationalism was sweeping away the old colonial order," and unless the United States learned to live with it, the Soviets would win the Cold War.

When he took office, Kennedy placed particular emphasis on developing better ties with Egypt and Nasser. Unlike the critics of Nasser, the historian Douglas Little wrote, the new American president did not view "the Arab world's foremost nationalist as either a Kremlin stooge or Hitler on the Nile. [He] saw an energetic young leader much like himself, for whom practical considerations like neutralism or modernization were more important than ideological or religious dogma."

In his search for ways to woo Egypt and other Third World nations away from the temptation of allying themselves with the Kremlin, Kennedy and his administration employed as one of their weapons what is now called soft diplomacy—persuading others to cooperate with the United States without force or coercion, chiefly by championing the importance of self-determination and human values. Jacqueline Kennedy was a key figure in that effort.

In a lengthy 1970 article in *The New York Times*, the writer Susan Sheehan echoed the conventional wisdom about the First Lady when she wrote that Jacqueline "had never feigned an interest in world affairs" and was content "to play a comparatively frivolous role. . . . She was an esthetically inclined social butterfly." Not true, countered Letitia Baldrige, who said her boss was in fact "intensely interested in foreign affairs." Agreeing with that view, the astronaut John Glenn, who became a close friend of the Kennedys, recalled, "Whenever there was a discussion going on about the Far East or the Mideast or Russia or any other world affairs topic, she was very well informed and could hold her own in any conversation. She never made this public knowledge, and it wasn't the way most people viewed her. Behind the scenes, though, once you got past the way she had been pigeonholed, you realized it." According to the historian Whitney Walton, Jacqueline Kennedy "engaged actively in foreign affairs in her position as first lady."

Several decades after her father's presidency, Caroline Kennedy wrote, "My parents believed America should lead with her ideals, not just with economic or military power." They thought, she said, that the arts and culture were important unifying and civilizing elements that could be employed with great benefit as part of soft diplomacy. "My mother understood that the past was a source of pride for people around the world, just as it is in America, and convinced my father that the United States could build goodwill among countries like Egypt, with which we had political differences, by assisting in their historic preservation efforts."

In 2013, the architectural historian and critic Lucia Allais would liken the dueling efforts of the Soviets and Westerners in Egypt in the 1960s to "a veritable Iron Curtain neatly dividing the Nile valley between Eastern and Western blocs." Their weapons, she said, were engineering projects. Downstream, Soviet engineers were rushing to complete the Aswan dam. Upstream, Western archaeologists and engineers were desperately working to survey and salvage dozens of priceless antiquities before the flooding from the dam reached them. In 1961, the United States finally joined that battle.

On April 4 of that year, urged on by his wife, President Kennedy sent a message to Congress requesting an immediate appropriation of $4 million for the Nubia rescue project, declaring that it was "in the interests of the United States to assist in rescuing these historic remains of a former civilization from destruction." His request, he emphasized, was part of "an international effort which has captured the imagination and sympathy of people throughout the world. I recommend that we now join with other nations through UNESCO in preventing what would otherwise be an irreparable loss to science and the cultural history of mankind. By thus contributing to the preservation of past civilizations, we will strengthen and enrich our own."

The president added: "The United States, one of the newest civilizations, has long had a deep regard for the study of past cultures, and a concern for the preservation of man's great achievements of art and thought. We have also had a special interest in the civilization of ancient Egypt from which many of our own cultural traditions have sprung—and a deep friendship for the people who live in the valley of the Nile."

Kennedy made it clear that he considered the $4 million to be a down payment to the Nubia campaign—the first in a series of funding requests that he planned to make in the future. The initial appropriation would be used to help pay for the salvage of three of the smaller temples, as well as for the expenses of American archaeological expeditions performing surveys and excavations.

Later, he said, funding would be recommended for the rescue of the temples of Philae once plans for their salvage had been finalized. He added that it was too early to talk about the temples at Abu Simbel because it was not yet clear how they were going to be saved. But he intimated that when that decision was finally made, the United States would step in to help finance the work.

Kennedy proved to be correct in his prediction of John Rooney's response to his request. There was no built-in constituency in the United States for helping Egypt save some of its temples, and the overall congressional reaction was tepid, with some members, including Rooney, expressing outright hostility to the idea.

Kennedy, however, employed a secret weapon—his wife—in the campaign to woo the congressman. Many years later, Jacqueline noted that Rooney had "always been against giving money to foreigners," but her intensive lobbying effort finally turned him around on the Nubian temples. "I convinced him," she proudly said. According to Richard Goodwin, Rooney told the president, as he had predicted, "Jack, you must be out of your mind, but if that's what you want, I'll try it." He put pressure on a number of his fellow Democrats, and the legislation squeaked through, passing in the House and Senate by only a handful of votes.

With the United States now involved, there was much to celebrate at UNESCO headquarters and in Egypt. The financing for salvaging most of the temples was now assured, as was the funding for excavation and survey efforts. But one major problem remained: the lack of funds to save Abu Simbel, the centerpiece—and greatest engineering challenge—of the effort. As the months passed, that prospect was looking more and more doubtful.

CHAPTER 15

A TIME OF CRISIS

By early 1962, the ticking clock was close to becoming a time bomb. Two years had passed since the start of construction on the Aswan High Dam, but there still was no definite plan for saving the Abu Simbel temples. It was a mind-boggling challenge: how to find a way to extract their massive façades and interior chambers from the cliff enclosing them, raise them above the encroaching floodwaters, and restore them to their original appearance—all without causing serious damage. Although engineering technology had progressed considerably by the 1960s, many of the team's experts seriously doubted that the project's difficulties could be overcome.

That, however, did not stop a throng of people from trying. Engineers, architects, other experts and would-be experts from all over the world had bombarded UNESCO with futuristic Buck Rogers–style proposals. An American construction executive suggested building concrete barges under the temples and waiting for the rising water level of the reservoir to float them, while a number of scenarios advocated leaving the temples underwater. A film producer and a modernist architectural firm, both from Britain, had the most ingenious, if far-fetched, solutions in that regard. The producer recommended sealing the temples off by an underwater cement wall that would separate the reservoir's muddy water from clear, filtered water inside. Visitors could then don scuba diving gear and swim around the monuments. The architectural firm suggested creating a gigantic aquarium around them—a dam-like structure with tunnels and shafts that would allow visitors to enter at the top and descend in an elevator to three underwater levels of curved pathways offering varying views of the temples' façades. Although both proposals received considerable public attention, they were rejected by UNESCO and Egyptian officials as being totally impracticable.

Christiane Desroches-Noblecourt was immersed in an endless series of feverish discussions and disputes raging within the UNESCO committee of engineers and other specialists that was to decide on the final plan. After months of debate, its members concluded that only two proposals—one from France, the other from Italy—were technically feasible.

The first, by the French engineering firm of Coyne and Bellier, also called for construction of a dam, but in this version, the temples would remain aboveground and on their original site, with a reflecting pool placed in front of them. Coyne and Bellier, which specialized in building thin-walled concrete dams, envisioned a semicircular, 240-feet-high structure surrounding the temples to keep the reservoir waters at bay. Visitors would arrive by boat from the reservoir and disembark at the top of the dam, where they would have a bird's-eye view of the site. They then could walk down a series of paths on the inner slope of the dam's embankment to the foot of the temples.

Architectural renderings of the proposed dam complex were stunning, but they failed to show a major element of the project: an elaborate pumping station, located behind the temples, needed to continuously suction the water seeping through the dam's thin concrete shells. Citing the enormous expense of building the dam, coupled with costly permanent maintenance and the specter of a pumping malfunction that could ruin the temples, UNESCO and Egyptian authorities, after considerable debate, turned thumbs down on the proposal.

They were far more intrigued by the Italian project, whose price tag was equally heart-stopping but whose extreme audacity captured their imagination. The plan called for cutting away the summit of the cliff above the temples—more than a quarter million tons of rock. The temples would then be severed from the cliff with three extended cuts and eased away in one piece with a reinforced concrete plate under them. Once that step was taken, they would be encased in a giant concrete box and hoisted two hundred feet, one-sixteenth of an inch at a time, by a grid of several hundred hydraulic jacks and relocated on the cliff's now level top, overlooking the reservoir.

The estimated weight of the Great Temple alone was 250,000 tons, while the concrete box and small temple together weighed about 100,000 tons. Such an extraordinary test of strength had never been tried before; in fact, every element of the project was experimental. Yet despite the breathtaking riskiness of hoisting nearly 350,000 tons of rock at one time, the proposal won the approval of a majority of the members on the UNESCO committee. One member described it as "one of the bravest and smartest projects ever proposed in the archaeological sector."

Little attention was paid to the committee's few naysayers, who noted the scant detail in the proposal about how the massive grid of hydraulic jacks would actually work. They pointed out that in the dramatic architectural renderings of the temples and the concrete box enclosing them, which were circulated worldwide for fundraising purposes, the hydraulic jacks were barely visible. "Wonderful as this modern technological feat might appear, it seemed fantastical and unachievable" to its critics, Sarwat Okasha acknowledged many years later.

Concerns were also raised about whether such an ambitious venture could be completed in time. The initial work—excising the temples, building the box, installing the jacks—was scheduled to take at least three years. Meanwhile, the water level of the new Aswan High Dam reservoir was scheduled to start rising in the fall of 1964. Nonetheless, despite the objections, UNESCO announced on June 10, 1962, that it had selected the Italian proposal. A Swedish engineering firm—Vattenbyggnadsbyrån (VBB), which had served as geological consultant to the Italian project—was chosen to oversee it.

At that point, the most immediate worry was how to raise the vast amount of money needed for the Abu Simbel project, whose estimated cost was at least $80 million ($762 million today). UNESCO's executive board recommended that financing be in place for the first stage of the venture before the Egyptian government put it out for bids, to protect Egypt from financial liability. The initial funds would come from a $30.5 million loan issued by banks in Italy and Egypt.

But despite two fundraising appeals from UNESCO in 1961, insufficient money was raised to guarantee the loan. As their anxiety mounted, agency officials decided to resurrect the idea of compulsory contributions by member countries, which could be paid off in installments over twenty years. René Maheu, who was now UNESCO's director general, and his team launched an intense lobbying effort of the organization's members prior to its annual conference in October 1962. Although a number of countries, including Italy, the Netherlands, and Sweden, agreed to the plan, UNESCO's major members—the United States, Britain, France, and the Soviet Union—were adamantly against it. Declaring that making contributions compulsory would set a dangerous precedent, they also argued that it was a mistake to spend so much money on one project, especially when there might be less costly ways of saving Abu Simbel. The proposed loan failed to win the conference's approval.

To Sarwat Okasha's fury, *Al-Ahram*, Egypt's largest and most influential newspaper, published a report charging that the international campaign to save Abu Simbel was in dire straits, beset by multiple crises and mired in uncertainty. "I raced to issue a statement of denial," Okasha recalled, "but I cannot to this day construe a reason for such a destructively negative fabrication." Even decades later, he couldn't bring himself to acknowledge that *Al-Ahram*'s reporting was true.

Yet while the conference's rejection of the financing proposal was a stinging setback, it also turned out to be a crucial turning point in the temples' rescue. With the level of the Nile set to begin steadily rising, the time for endless debates about intriguing but impractical proposals was over. If Abu Simbel was to be saved, a decision based in reality had to be made immediately.

Some six months earlier, Okasha had secretly commissioned an alternative plan to preserve the temples, in case the French and Italian projects failed. The scheme was developed by VBB, the Swedish firm chosen to oversee the Italian project. With a projected price tag of $36 million, less than half of the other proposals' costs, it called for slicing the temple façades and interiors into blocks and assembling them at a higher elevation. There were deep concerns about the possibility of irreparable damage to the colossal statues and other elements of the façades, but with no other choice available, the Egyptian government and UNESCO elected to go with the plan.

Now the campaign's organizers had to try to raise the money as quickly as possible. Once again, the United States was the key, but the outlook there was increasingly dire. After the funding kick-start provided by President Kennedy in 1961, the Nubia campaign was again facing an uphill battle.

IN THE EARLY 1960S, the United States had shown little interest in the concept, let alone the practice, of historic preservation. According to *The Washington Post*, preservation at that time was "neither a public policy issue nor part of America's architectural and real estate development culture. Historic preservation laws didn't exist." In the decades immediately following World War II, the emphasis in the United States was on building the new rather than saving the old. During that era, architects and urban planners had no compunction about getting rid of old urban structures and neighborhoods, no matter how historically rich their past, to make room for highways, office buildings, stadiums, and new housing. The idea of winning over American public opinion and influencing Congress to provide money to save a foreign antiquity like Abu Simbel was viewed as an outlandish pursuit, to say the least. Even among the members of what seemed like a natural constituency—American Egyptologists and leaders of major U.S. museums—there was considerable apathy, and on the part of some, active hostility.

John Wilson, one of the few prominent U.S. Egyptologists to champion the campaign, discovered that fact for himself at a meeting of a large group of archaeologists, anthropologists, and museum curators who gathered in late 1960 to discuss their response to the launch of UNESCO's Nubia effort. Wilson himself was highly enthusiastic about the venture. "This promised to be the biggest cultural cooperation ever undertaken and a pilot project for similar crises in other countries," he wrote. "Some of us believed that if we evaded this challenge, we would not be true to the cultural heritage of ancient Egypt that had been entrusted to us for study." He was shocked to learn that many at the meeting failed to share his view. A number of participants raised doubts about whether the temples were worth saving. Others thought that rescuing them was simply impossible. Still others believed that they had been sufficiently studied by archaeologists and other scholars and hence didn't need to be preserved.

The pros and cons of the Abu Simbel rescue were also a hot topic of debate in the American press. Although the Nubian campaign received considerable positive coverage in U.S. newspapers and magazines, there was also substantial criticism of the idea of America's helping to save the temples. Some opponents declared that if the United States was going to give foreign aid to Egypt, it should be spent on raising Egyptians' standard of living, not on monuments that very few people would get to see. Others were of the view that no aid should go abroad at all.

A UNESCO report about the difficulties of raising private money in the United States noted "the complexities of getting wealthy Americans or foundations to contribute to foreign cultural problems. Grants for Versailles, the restoration of Chartres, the Parthenon, or a museum in Athens fall out of the scope of consideration quite easily." The writer of the report added that philanthropic-minded families and groups were donating money to causes closer to home. "The Mellons are concentrating on civic projects in Pittsburgh. The Rockefellers are giving large sums to the U.N. or Lincoln Center, primarily because they are New Yorkers and secondarily because they already have humanitarian or technical assistance projects under way in underdeveloped areas. Ditto for the Ford Foundation."

John Wilson, meanwhile, insisted that the issues of aid should not be seen as either/or propositions. "If the costs of the Nubian campaign are measured against the costs of feeding hungry children, the debate can be endless," he wrote. "Yet in defense, one can say that a case can be made that the value of things of the spirit—the great artistic achievements of man over the ages—go beyond mere price tags."

Also taking that view was John Canaday, the chief art critic of *The New York Times*. When the debate first began over the merits and demerits of saving Abu Simbel, Canaday was inclined to side with the argument that the temples were just "a gigantic novelty, built by a publicity-seeking, unimportant pharaoh." But, "impelled in part by a sense of duty and in part by curiosity," he and his wife decided to travel to Egypt to judge the value of the temples for themselves. They were far from alone in doing so.

Ironically, the flood of publicity about the threats to the Nubian antiquities had prompted a tourist boom in an area that had seen very few travelers in previous decades. Travel agencies and tourist bureaus joined with airlines to promote trips to Egypt and Nubia. An Italian company provided daily hydrofoil transportation to Abu Simbel, while paddle-wheel steamers made the trip at a more leisurely pace.

The steamer that took the Canadays there arrived at three o'clock in the morning, tying up directly in front of the temples. "My wife and I, awakened by the silence, went ashore," Canaday recalled. "In full moonlight, we walked across the sand to the huge sentinel figures on the façade." Awestruck by the size of the colossi and the gravity and power they conveyed, he judged them to be "among the few productions of Egyptian art that carry the full impact of their scale." For the next hour or so, the couple wandered around the dark interior of the Great Temple, shining a flashlight on the monumental columns and the extraordinary wall art, which Canaday described as possessing "a breadth, vigor and inventiveness unsurpassed in any Egyptian art we had seen."

Later, in a column he wrote for *The New York Times,* he admitted he "had fallen in love" with Abu Simbel as soon as he saw it on that moonlit night. "Every argument for the temple's preservation has been given except the one that surprised me the most and impresses me as the most valid," he remarked. "It's the fact that the temple as a whole and the bas-reliefs on its walls are aesthetically among the half dozen or so examples of Egyptian art where the presence of a creative artist is most strongly felt."

Canaday acknowledged the arguments questioning the ethics of spending vast sums of money on the preservation of an ancient monument when so much else could be accomplished in the world with those funds. But, he contended, "you just can't make this kind of comparative evaluation. The word 'priceless' does not mean 'terribly expensive' but simply without relation to price. Abu Simbel is priceless in the pure sense of the word. It happens to be, aesthetically, a paramount work of art."

It was true, he added, that "the loss of Abu Simbel would affect directly only the relatively few members of each generation who would otherwise have seen it. But it would affect indirectly the millions of people who will be part of this world as long as it exists. Our heritage is all pervasive, and if Abu Simbel goes, that heritage is lessened forever."

EARLIER IN THE U.S. DEBATE over the fate of the temples, John Wilson and several other American archaeologists active in the campaign had urged Egyptian authorities to agree to a U.S. tour of treasures from King Tutankhamun's tomb. Froelich Rainey, director of the University of Pennsylvania's Museum of Archaeology and Anthropology and the main advocate of the tour, told Sarwat Okasha that it could make all the difference in persuading the American public to support the Nubia effort, which in turn might have an impact on congressional funding.

"I confess I hesitated over this decision," Okasha recalled, "since the treasures of the young pharaoh had never left Egypt since their discovery in 1922, and many of them were quite fragile. However, extreme need overcame doubt."

With Nasser's permission, thirty-four small artifacts from Tutankhamun's tomb, some of which had been found next to his mummified body, were dispatched to the United States in November 1961 for a fifteen-city, eighteen-month tour. The objects included a gold dagger and embossed sheath, a miniature mummy case that was an exact replica of the larger sarcophagus containing the pharaoh's body, and a gold flail and crook, which were prominent items of pharaonic regalia. There were other gold articles, many of them inlaid with lapis lazuli and other gems, as well as jewelry and carved and inlaid alabaster cups, statues, and other items.

Okasha had suggested that, to raise money for the campaign, admission fees be charged at the museums mounting the exhibition. Rainey rejected the idea, however, saying that the boy king no longer had the allure he once possessed and that the number and quality of objects being displayed were insufficient to justify charging admission. He later admitted it was "one of the most spectacular mistakes in my career as a museum director."

On November 3, 1961, Jacqueline Kennedy opened the exhibition at the National Gallery of Art in Washington, with a glittering array of political and social figures from her husband's administration in attendance. "It is unbelievable to be able to see these beautiful things," she later said in a statement. "I remember as a child reading about the discovery of the tomb, and these were among the things I hoped most in the world to be able to see one day."

At the opening, Sarwat Okasha presented the First Lady with a gift from Nasser—a four-thousand-year-old limestone statue called *The Striding Man,* which stood thirty-one inches tall. Visibly moved, Mrs. Kennedy urged the cultural minister to include it in the tour so it could be viewed by the American public. He agreed. When it was returned to the White House, the president installed it on a bookshelf in the Oval Office.*

When the Tutankhamun exhibit opened to the general public the next day, the weather in Washington was windy and bitingly cold, but it failed to deter the thousands of people who queued patiently for hours before they were allowed in. "It was the most popular exhibit [up to that point] in our history," said S. Dillon Ripley, head of the Smith-

* After Kennedy's death in 1963, his wife retained possession of the statue, putting it on prominent display in her Fifth Avenue apartment in New York. It now can be seen at the Kennedy presidential library in Boston.

JACQUELINE KENNEDY AND SARWAT OKASHA ADMIRE A GOLD STATUETTE FROM TUTANKHAMUN'S TOMB AT THE NATIONAL GALLERY IN WASHINGTON, D.C., NOVEMBER 1961

sonian Institution, which operates the National Gallery. In a 1963 report to Congress, Ripley noted, "Total attendance was over 1.3 million. This is almost exactly the total attendance for all home baseball games of the New York Yankees. I do not mean in any way to discredit our national sport, being a distant cousin of Casey Stengel, but let our experience with King Tut lay to rest forever the notion that Americans are not interested in the art and history of ancient peoples."

The huge crowds that showed up in the nation's capital were repeated at the exhibit's next stop, Froelich Rainey's museum in Philadelphia. "Every day," Rainey remembered, "there were lines of people extending for several city blocks." His delight with the massive turnout was overshadowed by an acute sense of dismay. More than thirty years later, he would write in his memoirs, "I still shudder at the loss we all took because of my decision. I had never been more wrong."

Despite record crowds in every city of the tour, the exhibit produced no direct benefit for the Nubian campaign. Photographs of the threatened temples and monuments were displayed as part of the show, but there was no other mention of the fight to save them, including in the catalog describing the treasures on display. Some museums did charge admission fees, but the revenue was retained by the museums themselves.

In a memo to fellow UNESCO officials, Sadruddin Aga Khan noted that although the "tour was a huge success on the cultural level, it brought absolutely nothing to us in financial terms even though it had been designed in part to raise funds." UNESCO and the Egyptian government had gambled that it would aid in generating at least $20 million, some of that from the private sector and the rest from congressional appropriations. They soon discovered that members of Congress were not inclined to help either.

By the spring of 1962, the political climate in Washington had changed dramatically since President Kennedy had won congressional approval of aid for the temples early in 1961. Over the previous year, there had been an escalation of tensions between the United States and Soviet Union that would lead in the autumn of 1962 to the Cuban missile crisis and the threat of nuclear war. At the same time, Kennedy's quest to improve U.S. relations with Egypt had sparked strong opposition not only from Israel but also from two close U.S. allies in the Middle East—Saudi Arabia and Jordan—which regarded Nasser's calls for Arab nationalism as "mortal threats to their own traditional regimes."

Anti-Nasser feeling, already strong in Washington, was heightened by the Egyptian president's continued acceptance of Soviet aid and his strong opposition to Israel. Faced with these political headwinds, members of Congress who had supported the Nubia campaign in 1961 were now on the fence. Those seeking reelection in the 1962 congressional midterms were especially wary.

In a 1962 report, one of UNESCO's top Washington lobbyists noted that three of the campaign's most stalwart advocates in the Senate—J. William Fulbright of Arkansas, Stuart Symington of Missouri, and Mike Monroney of Oklahoma, who had authored the Senate legislation authorizing aid for the temples—were all now running scared. "Senator Fulbright is more concerned with his reelection," the lobbyist wrote, "than with the championing of a cause that might be used by his political enemies against him. . . . Senator Symington is not that willing to sponsor our cause as he was before. Monroney, who has been so helpful to us in the past, is also running for reelection. After a long conversation with members of our committee, Monroney agreed to carry the ball but on condition that this deed should be made as quietly as possible and without any publicity that might injure him in Oklahoma."

The unsettled outlook in Congress coincided with an atmosphere of increasing crisis within UNESCO and the Egyptian government. In late 1962, UNESCO issued a new appeal, its most alarming yet, about the urgent need for funds to begin work on Abu Simbel. Only twenty member countries had come up with new contributions, which weren't nearly enough to fund the first stage of the project. The time was now or never, the appeal made clear. If other member states did not respond quickly, the temples would be lost forever. The appeal never mentioned the United States by name, but it was obvious that its participation was considered especially critical.

To have any chance of succeeding in Washington, the campaign's organizers needed the White House's wholehearted support. Fortunately for them, their most important ally in the nation's capital decided to rejoin the fight. It had been almost two years since Jacqueline Kennedy's first behind-the-scenes intervention in the effort to save the temples. Since then, she had become a power to be reckoned with.

Again, Paris had played a major role in her transformation.

CHAPTER 16

THE FIRST LADY INTERVENES

In May 1961, just four months after he became president, John F. Kennedy and his wife traveled to France for their first state visit abroad. Until then, Jacqueline Kennedy had been a somewhat controversial figure in the United States. "I was," she said years later, "a liability to Jack."

Her elegance and interest in fashion, her love of all things French, and her discomfort with taking part in campaigning and other public activities were among the things that marked her as an interloper during her first days in the White House. "The trouble with me is that I'm an outsider, and that's a very hard thing to be in American life," she once told a reporter. In another interview, she acknowledged that "people take my diffidence for arrogance and my withdrawal from publicity as a sign . . . that I am looking down on the rest of mankind." Judged by some to be all style and no substance, she was a president's wife who didn't fit the traditional First Lady mold.

And then, in Paris, everything shifted. From the day she arrived, Jacqueline Kennedy enchanted the French with her beauty, grace, knowledge of their culture and history, and fluency in their language. After a grand state dinner for the Kennedys at Versailles, a French newspaper declared, "For a few hours, a queen reigned [there] again." According to Clint Hill, a Secret service agent assigned to guard the

First Lady, French president Charles de Gaulle "couldn't take his eyes off her [at the dinner], and I daresay neither could any of the other guests—men or women." Having been warned that de Gaulle could be distant and difficult to talk to, Jacqueline acted as the interpreter between him and Kennedy. The crusty French leader would later describe her as JFK's "dazzling and cultivated wife." Kenneth O'Donnell, one of Kennedy's top aides, remembered that she "drew de Gaulle into long and entertaining conversations with her husband that probably made him more relaxed with Kennedy than he had ever been with another head of a foreign country. . . . Privately [JFK] gave Jackie credit for establishing an easy and intimate understanding between himself and de Gaulle." At the end of the couple's visit to France, Kennedy himself took note of his wife's popularity when he opened a press conference with a bemused smile and this statement: "I do not think it altogether inappropriate for me to introduce myself. I am the man who accompanied Jacqueline Kennedy to Paris."

Both the French and American press extolled her performance, declaring her to be as important as the president in projecting a new and more sympathetic image of America. According to *The Washington Post,* the Kennedys had been successful in "renewing the vibrant connection between the two countries that bickering and misunderstanding had blurred in recent years." An NBC News documentary about the trip said Jacqueline Kennedy's appeal abroad had turned her into an effective weapon of the Cold War and symbol of the United States.

The First Lady, *The New York Times*'s Charlotte Curtis wrote, "stands for . . . an effort to understand foreign people in a country that tends to think it is the only country and that English is the only language. She stands for a sensitivity to art and beauty despite pragmatic politics, nuclear tests, and the Cold War. She is one of the few independent spirits left in an age of conformity."

Arthur M. Schlesinger, Jr., later declared that thanks to Jacqueline's triumphant visit to France, "the things people had once held against her—the unconventional beauty, the un-American elegance, the taste for French clothes and French food—were no longer liabilities but assets."

As it happened, Jacqueline Kennedy's success in Paris not only had a major impact on others' opinion of her, it affected her self-image as well, helping her gain greater confidence and a sense of her own power and influence, all of which she used to great effect in her future activities as First Lady. One of her most important guides in that regard was André Malraux, the French minister of culture, with whom she established a warm personal relationship during her visit to Paris.

Malraux, who was France's most renowned literary figure, had been a hero of hers since she was a teenager. It was then that she had read his first novel, *La Condition Humaine* (*Man's Fate*), which won the Goncourt Prize, France's top literary award, in 1933 and catapulted him to international attention. Five years later, he followed that book, which takes place during a failed Communist insurrection in Shanghai in 1927, with *L'Espoir* (*Man's Hope*), a novel based on Malraux's experience fighting alongside antifascist forces during the Spanish Civil War.

Caroline Kennedy once described her mother as a "true romantic. She lived her life on a dramatic scale." That was even more true of the fifty-eight-year-old Malraux, who was both an intellectual and a man of action, thriving as he did on danger and adventure. In addition to his exploits in Spain, he had dug for ancient treasure in Indochina, searched for lost cities in Saudi Arabia and Yemen, and been captured and escaped from the Gestapo while in the French resistance during World War II. Dashing and charismatic, with black hair, intense green eyes, and "a pale Napoleonic brow," Malraux was, in the words of *The New York Times*, "the romantic man of destiny."

Before Jacqueline left for Paris, she had told Nicole Alphand, the wife of the French ambassador in Washington, that the only thing she wanted to do there was meet Malraux and perhaps be seated next to him at some events. She got her wish and more: Malraux volunteered to act as her guide for an hours-long tour of Paris's cultural highlights, during which he became as smitten with her as she was with him. "He talks so fast," she exclaimed to Schlesinger a couple of years later. "It's like being taken over this incredible obstacle course at ninety miles an hour. . . . He makes your mind jump back [and] forth. He is the most fascinating man I've ever talked to."

JACQUELINE KENNEDY AND ANDRÉ MALRAUX
IN PARIS, JUNE 1961

Her conversations with Malraux focused on his views about the importance of the arts and cultural heritage to the life of a nation. According to Letitia Baldrige, Malraux became her most important cultural mentor: "She listened to him and wrote to him. Malraux was her prize." Their instant rapport led to a dialogue between the two that would last for the rest of her time in the White House. They exchanged frequent letters through diplomatic pouch, and in May 1962, she and Kennedy hosted a White House state dinner for Malraux—a highly unusual occurrence, since only heads of government or reigning monarchs normally receive that honor. But since de Gaulle had made it clear he had no plans to travel to the United States to reciprocate the Kennedys' visit, she persuaded White House officials to honor Malraux in his place, hoping, she later said, that his visit "would call attention to the importance of the arts."

During the Kennedy years, White House state dinners were glittering affairs, but by all accounts, the Malraux dinner was among the most memorable. The First Lady invited a panoply of America's top cultural figures: the abstract artists Mark Rothko and Franz Kline; the choreographers George Balanchine and Agnes de Mille; the composer Leonard Bernstein; the playwrights Tennessee Williams, Thornton Wilder, and Arthur Miller; and the writers Saul Bellow, Archibald MacLeish, Edmund Wilson, Robert Lowell, and Paddy Chayefsky. The most surprising guests were the reclusive Charles Lindbergh and his wife, Anne Morrow Lindbergh, a talented writer whose books Jacqueline greatly admired. But the guest who meant more to her than any other was Jeanne Saleil, a French-born writer and Smith College professor, who had been in charge of Jacqueline's junior year abroad program in France. "I could hardly wait to take her up to Malraux," she later told a friend, "and say, 'This is the woman who taught me to love France more than anything!'"

JACQUELINE KENNEDY CHATS WITH ANDRÉ MALRAUX AT THE WHITE HOUSE DINNER HELD IN HIS HONOR, MAY 1962

Malraux's visit to Washington and his growing friendship with the First Lady led a year later to an even greater coup on her part: the French government's agreement to send the *Mona Lisa* on a tour of the United States, the first time France's most precious painting had ever been allowed out of the country. In 1968, when Malraux's memoirs were published in the United States, he dedicated the book to Jacqueline. "There was a personal purpose to that," Malraux's stepson, Alain, remembered. "It was to show the whole world that he was her friend and admirer."

One of the several ways Malraux influenced the First Lady's thinking was through his advocacy of government support for the arts and other cultural pursuits, a view that both Kennedys shared. Unlike France and a number of other countries in the world, the U.S. government had never played a role in funding national theaters, opera houses, or other cultural institutions.

Jacqueline told Senator Claiborne Pell, a Rhode Island Democrat and an ardent supporter of the arts, that she had discussed with Malraux the idea of creating a new cabinet-level federal agency for culture, much like the ministry he headed in France. Her husband had agreed to give it serious consideration. "She was always appalled that America spends billions at the Pentagon but had no ministry of culture," said Vivian Crespi, a longtime friend. "No support of the museums on a regular basis, no educational television—all these things troubled her. She was a great influence on Jack in that regard. She did not want this known, she did not seek credit for any of it, but she discussed it with him."

Even before his election, Kennedy, thanks to the intercession of his wife, had also supported the creation of a national cultural center in Washington. "In other countries, capital cities have their theaters, opera houses and concert halls," Jacqueline Kennedy wrote. "But our capital city has lacked an adequate place. Now, at last, we will have a home for the performing arts in Washington." Although it had been authorized by Congress in 1958, the project had lain dormant until Kennedy came to office and, urged on by his wife, kick-started a massive fundraising campaign and implementation of a design plan by the architect Edward Durrell Stone. Finished in 1971, the cultural complex was named the John F. Kennedy Center for the Performing Arts, the only monument in the city honoring the martyred president.

While the proposals for a federal cultural agency and national cultural center would take considerable time to germinate, there was another issue close to Jacqueline Kennedy's heart that promised a more immediate payoff: historic preservation and restoration. Even before she moved into the White House, she had begun considering plans for the renovation of its public rooms, recasting them as a showcase for the finest examples of American furniture, paintings, sculpture, and other artifacts. In choosing objects for the restoration, she was heavily influenced by the White House's furnishings during the administrations of Thomas Jefferson and James Monroe, both former ambassadors to Paris, who had adorned the mansion with French furniture and other French-inspired items.

Jacqueline Kennedy's work in restoring the White House served as a catalyst for her leadership in the rescue and preservation of another important historic site nearby—the neighborhood surrounding Lafayette Square, directly across Pennsylvania Avenue from the White House. Called "the President's park" by Pierre L'Enfant, the original architect of Washington, Lafayette Square was bordered by elegant nineteenth-century houses, among them the small mansion in which Dolley Madison lived after her husband's death.

In the late 1950s, the Eisenhower administration drew up plans to raze these historic structures and replace them with modern government office buildings that would dwarf the White House. Also scheduled to share their fate was the Old Executive Office Building, on Pennsylvania Avenue next to the White House, which was noted for its ornate porticoes, colonnades, and mansard roof.

When John Kennedy became president, he enlisted a longtime close friend—the painter William Walton—to help him come up with a plan to save Lafayette Square. A former *Time* magazine correspondent who had covered World War II in Europe, the witty, tough-talking Walton also served as an unofficial adviser to the Kennedys on art and historic preservation. His and JFK's brainstorming to save the square proved fruitless, however: In the spring of 1962, the General Services Administration, the agency that manages federal government buildings and real estate, was set to begin tearing down the houses.

At that point, Jacqueline Kennedy took action. As she wrote to a friend, she couldn't bear to sit still while America's monuments were "ripped down and horrible things put up in their place. I simply panicked at the thought of this and decided to make a last-minute appeal." As Walton remembered it, however, her meeting with him and JFK was less of an appeal and more of a forceful intervention in the form of an unsparing scolding. "She basically told us, 'You lily-livered characters need some help, and I'm going to get involved. The wreckers haven't started yet, and until they do, these buildings can be saved.' Without her, we would never have saved the square. . . . She kept us at it and said that until the bulldozers move, we're ahead and we can't give up. . . . She really was riding us hard."

Shortly after her lecture to Walton and the president, Bernard Boutin, GSA's administrator, received a call from the White House "to stop everything." Alternative plans were then drawn up to save the houses and erect new, unobtrusive government buildings, with red brick rather than concrete exteriors, behind them. Thanks to the administration's crusade, Lafayette Square was designated a National Historic Landmark District, which included the Old Executive Office Building in its purview.

According to Boutin, Jacqueline Kennedy "was the one who really deserved the credit for the whole thing. It was her idea, her imagination, her drive, her ability to work with people. She could get you to break your arm for her." Yet she wanted no public attention for herself. Just before the press conference unveiling the new plans for the square, she insisted to Boutin that he must not mention her involvement. "Remember, it's not me," she whispered in his ear. "It's the president. It's the president, Bernie."

In the end, the only thing the First Lady cared about was that Lafayette Square had been preserved. In the middle of the crusade, she wrote to Bill Walton, "Perhaps saving old buildings and having the new ones be right isn't the most important thing in the world—if you are waiting for the bomb—but I think we are always going to be waiting for the bomb and it won't ever come, and so saving the old—and making the new beautiful—is terribly important."

Again using André Malraux's thought and work as a model, she went even further, calling for the passage of legislation to provide protection for historic buildings and places throughout the United States that were considered important examples of the country's heritage. As cultural minister, Malraux had helped engineer such a law in France in the early 1960s.

In 1966, in no small part due to her lobbying, Congress approved the National Historic Preservation Act, which has shaped the fate of many American historic and cultural sites for more than half a century. "Jacqueline Kennedy gave a voice and visibility to the historic preservation movement in this country," said Richard Moe, a former president of the National Trust for Historic Preservation. "In her position as first lady, she provided a moral authority to make a difference. She showed what a lifetime commitment could do." Few people have had a more important impact on historic preservation in the United States than she.

WHILE SHE WAS ENGAGED in these efforts at home, Jacqueline Kennedy was also keeping a close eye on what was happening in the fight to save Abu Simbel, which she had discussed in detail with André Malraux. Thanks to the interest of both Kennedys in the Nubia campaign, the State Department—specifically Lucius Battle, the assistant secretary of state for educational and cultural affairs—had been monitoring the situation very closely.

As soon as Battle had been named to the post in June 1962, he was told about the importance that the Kennedys, particularly the First Lady, placed on the effort to preserve the temples, as well as about her desire to do everything possible to help the cause. At first, he was not enthusiastic about the concept of U.S. aid for the Abu Simbel rescue. "I didn't think we had much of a chance to get it through Congress," he later said, "especially since the early ideas, like lifting it on hydraulic lifts or floating it on pontoons, were so incredibly costly as to be ludicrous." As head of the U.S. delegation, Battle helped lead the fight at the 1962 UNESCO conference against mandatory contributions by member countries and the selection of the Italian project to save Abu Simbel.

But when Battle found out about the alternate plan—cutting the temples into blocks—he thought it might have a chance. "It was far less expensive than the others," he said, "and since we would be paying about one-third of the cost, that fact was very important." It had an additional advantage over the other salvage proposals, which would have involved intricate machinery like hydraulic jacks and pumping stations and thus would have to be imported and paid for in hard currency—i.e., dollars. By contrast, cutting required considerable labor by local workers, which could be paid in local currency—and local currency was what the State Department wanted to spend in Egypt.

As it happened, the United States had accumulated a vast holding of Egyptian pounds through its Food for Peace program, which sold American surplus crops like wheat and corn at a steep discount, thus making them affordable to the Egyptian government. Under the program's regulations, the United States was to be paid in Egyptian pounds, which could be spent only on economic development projects within the country. Aside from its economic benefit, the cutting plan's reliance on Egyptian workers would also be good public relations for the United States, whose decision to help save Abu Simbel with local labor would serve as a cultural bridge between the two countries at a time when their diplomatic ties were strained.

The only problem with the idea was that under the Food for Peace plan, which had been enacted as Public Law (PL) 480, Congress still had to approve any administration proposal to use local currency for development projects, even though no dollar appropriations were being requested. "It seemed to me," Battle later said, "that we should have been given a freer hand and not been made to justify an expenditure of a foreign currency as though we were spending actual dollars."

Members of Congress, however, saw it differently. In the late 1950s and early 1960s, as tensions with the Nasser government increased, they put so many roadblocks in the way of proposed projects in Egypt that American holdings of Egyptian pounds had skyrocketed, with little chance of spending them.

Battle hoped that Congress might be persuaded to look favorably at a cultural project like Abu Simbel as a noncontroversial way to expend $12 million of the PL 480 funds. But with anti-Nasser feeling still strong in the country, he knew it would be an uphill battle.

In late 1962, UNESCO announced a final deadline—the spring of 1963—for raising enough money to launch the rescue of the Abu Simbel temples. If the funds hadn't been pledged by then, the race against the rising Nile River would be over and the temples would be doomed to drown.

With that deadline in mind, Jacqueline Kennedy sat down to write a three-page, single-spaced memo to her husband. Over the previous few months, she had been corresponding about the issue with several friends in her international social network, including Malraux and Fiat head Gianni Agnelli. She had seen Agnelli the summer before, when she, her daughter, and her sister, Lee Radziwill, had vacationed for several weeks on the Amalfi Coast of Italy. They had spent part of that time aboard a yacht owned by Agnelli and his wife, Marella, both of whom Jacqueline had known for years.

Agnelli, as it happened, had long been involved in the plan to save the temples. His interest was piqued when Fiat, as part of Italconsult, played a role in the Italian proposal to raise the temples by hydraulic jacks. If the plan had been approved by the UNESCO conference, Fiat would have helped develop the hydraulic jack system. But even after it was rejected, Agnelli kept lobbying for Abu Simbel's preservation. He provided Jacqueline with considerable reading material, including copies of the magazine *The UNESCO Courier*, which carried multiple stories about the project, and discussed with her ways to get the United States on board.

In early January 1963, President Kennedy received a telegram from Agnelli asking for his support on Abu Simbel. Simultaneously, Jacqueline sent the president her memo spelling out in great detail why she considered the rescue of the temples to be of critical importance and why the United States should participate as an international partner. "Abu Simbel is the major temple of the Nile," she wrote. "Nothing will ever be found to equal it." Allowing it to be flooded, she added, would be like destroying the Parthenon in Athens. She went on to argue that helping to finance the temples' rescue would provide a boost to America in its Cold War jousting with the Soviets and improve its image with the rest of the world.

As he had in 1961, Kennedy responded immediately, again reaching out to Richard Goodwin to research the issue. Goodwin had left the White House in 1962 to become an official with the Peace Corps, but he was reassigned to the president's staff on a temporary basis. On January 11, he sent a memo to Kennedy saying he'd "gone fairly deeply into the Abu Simbel matter" and thought the project was feasible and that the United States had enough surplus money in Egypt to cover one-third of the costs. It would take five more months to work out the details, but in June 1963, the Kennedy administration committed $12 million in Egyptian pounds for salvage of the monuments.

The U.S. pledge reinvigorated the Abu Simbel campaign. With American funds assured, Egypt and UNESCO officially adopted the plan to dissect the temples, agreeing that Egypt would pay one-third of the cost; the United States would cover another third; and the rest would come from other member countries and private donations.

To raise the hard currency needed to start the project, Egypt received a $3 million loan from the Kuwaiti government, to be used in part as a down payment to the companies that would be awarded the contract. The group of bidders that eventually won was a consortium of six engineering firms that called itself Joint Venture Abu Simbel. Its members were companies from Germany, Italy, France, Sweden, and Egypt, almost all of which had been involved in the rescue of the other Nubian temples. Hochtief, the German company that had dismantled and reassembled the Temple of Kalabsha, acted as principal spokesman for the group and would be in overall charge. With the signing of the contract, the atmosphere at UNESCO headquarters and the Egyptian culture ministry was buoyant: Finally, it seemed, everything was on the right track. Preliminary work at Abu Simbel was set to begin immediately.

Then two disasters struck, one right after the other. On November 22, President Kennedy was assassinated in Dallas. Three months later, in February 1964, a House appropriations subcommittee unexpectedly disallowed the $12 million in Egyptian pounds promised by Kennedy for Abu Simbel, and the full House refused to reconsider the subcommittee's decision. Again, the fate of the temples was thrown into question at a time when the campaign was least prepared to survive such a blow.

The administration of Kennedy's successor, President Lyndon B. Johnson, decided to battle back. Framing the proposed funding as a way of honoring the martyred JFK, the administration mobilized its forces to put pressure on Congress to restore the appropriations. It focused first on the Senate. At Lucius Battle's request, the head of the Smithsonian, S. Dillon Ripley, personally lobbied every member of the Senate appropriations subcommittee that would consider the project, telling them that the rescue of Abu Simbel was "the single most important international effort in the history of archaeology."

At a Senate subcommittee hearing in May 1964, a number of statements from prominent Americans supporting the appropriation were read into the record. In his statement, Secretary of State Dean Rusk declared that U.S. failure to join Egypt and other nations to save the temples would have a deeply adverse impact on America's foreign relations. Echoing that view, Senator William Fulbright remarked, "It would be a real calamity, resulting in a setback to the prestige and influence of our country, if the Abu Simbel monuments were lost through our unwillingness to expend $12 million in foreign currencies."

The eminent architect Edward Durrell Stone was even more blunt. "Architecture stands as the most enduring record of mankind's cultural achievements," he said. "If for a comparative pittance, we allow this great treasure to disappear under the Nile, posterity may rightly condemn our generation for gross negligence."

For his part, Joshua Logan, the Pulitzer Prize–winning Broadway director and producer, countered arguments made by anti-Nasser and pro-Israel lobbyists who opposed U.S. involvement. Logan contended that the funding of Abu Simbel was "neither aid to Nasser nor to Egypt. It is aid to us—to our children, to our knowledge, to the ultimate knowledge of the people of the world. . . . I have personally seen the temples of Abu Simbel. They are one of the greatest sights and emotional and cultural experiences of my life."

Logan's contention was reinforced by statements from several prominent Jewish organizations and individuals, including Morris Abrams, president of the American Jewish Committee, the country's most prominent Jewish advocacy group. "These archaeological monuments are, in the opinion of the Committee, a cultural treasure belonging not merely to Egypt but to the world," Abrams declared.

As the Johnson administration's main spokesman for the Abu Simbel funding, Lucius Battle offered passionate testimony in support of reversing the House's decision. The assistant secretary of state pointed out that, based on JFK's pledge, the Egyptian government had gone out on a limb to sign a contract and begin preliminary work because of the urgency of the situation. "The race with the rising water of the Aswan reservoir would have been lost except for this act of confidence on the part of Egypt," he said.

Battle also noted that the announcement of U.S. appropriations had ignited a great surge of enthusiasm and expectation in Egypt and elsewhere that Abu Simbel would in fact be saved. "If we fail to do this, we can expect deep feeling and criticism to be aroused," he contended. "Our relations with Egypt have improved considerably in the recent past, and we have been able to exert a more useful influence in the Middle East in support of policies which are of importance to us. We need to preserve and extend these gains." He added that, in the administration's view, the political importance of U.S. involvement in the temples' rescue was just as significant as the historic and cultural importance of the monuments themselves.

Reminding the subcommittee that President Kennedy and his wife had an "enormous personal interest" in saving Abu Simbel, he noted that the president himself had contacted him several times in the months before his death to inquire about the status of congressional passage of the funding.

When senators began questioning Battle, however, most made it clear they were still skeptical about the project. One of them was Senator John McClellan of Arkansas, the subcommittee's chairman, who told Battle he was "not unduly enthusiastic" about the appropriations request, adding, "I do not think that every time something should be done in the world, it is the burden of the United States to pick up the tab." Some senators said they thought the United States was already providing too much aid to Egypt, while others believed the Egyptian government should be paying even more of the cost of moving the temples than it now was.

Senator Allen Ellender, a conservative Democrat from Louisiana, was not thrilled with the idea either. Nonetheless, in his exchange with Battle, he suddenly threw the assistant secretary of state and the temples' other supporters a lifeline. There was, he said, another possible way of acquiring the Egyptian pounds sought by the administration.

Ellender told Battle about an arcane section in Public Law 480, called the Cooley provision, that allowed the U.S. government to provide money from its local currency accounts in foreign countries to private firms for business development and trade expansion in those countries. The main advantage of using this method, the senator said, is that the release of idle Cooley funds did not have to be approved by Congress if the money had been in the local currency accounts for more than three years.

Battle was nonplussed. He had never heard of the provision, and neither had his State Department colleagues. He was also surprised that Ellender, "who was not exactly a great lover of culture," was prepared to help them. When he expressed doubts about the possibility of getting the money through the Cooley provision, Ellender told him that it was his only option. "I am simply throwing out these suggestions," he said, "because I feel confident that the House will not agree to your original plan since they've already turned it down." Senator McClellan agreed, telling Battle, "I do not think the House will appropriate the dollars. If you are really interested, I think you ought to explore this further."

Battle did—and discovered that everything Ellender had said was true. Before initiating an application by the State Department for $12 million in Egyptian pounds under the provision, he paid a call on

Rep. John Rooney, the chairman of the House subcommittee that had rejected the administration's original request. "Rooney said he wasn't enthusiastic, but he wasn't going to object," Battle recalled. "I had the feeling that he knew how important this was to the Kennedys and that's what led him to accept it without fighting."

Thanks in part, then, to Allen Ellender and John Rooney, the United States finally made good on its pledge to provide one-third of the cost of rescuing Abu Simbel. When the campaign was finally over, more than fifty other countries had pitched in too. After the United States and Egypt, the largest contributions came from France ($1 million), Italy ($856,000), India ($588,000), and Sweden ($500,000). Also giving money were, among others, Yugoslavia ($226,000), Algeria ($105,000), Ghana ($46,000), Bolivia ($7,000), and Ecuador ($1,000). Britain, still angry over Suez, initially refused to contribute anything to the project, but after a considerable uproar within the country and around the world, the British government reversed its position and donated $213,000 to the cause.

During and after the long, bruising battle over Abu Simbel, few people knew of the crucial role played by Jacqueline Kennedy in that fight. Without her support and the quiet behind-the-scenes pressure she put on her husband, it's highly unlikely that he would have taken the steps he did.

She never talked in public about her work on behalf of the Nubia campaign. But according to her daughter, she took enormous pride in what she had accomplished, telling Caroline that her work to save Abu Simbel meant as much to her as her restoration of the White House.

CHAPTER 17

"GO, BABY, GO!"

AT LONG LAST—AFTER YEARS OF UNCERTAINTY AND A SEEMINGLY endless series of setbacks—the salvage of Abu Simbel appeared ready to begin. The funds had been pledged, contracts had been signed, and workers were being hired. Yet there was still a great sense of angst about the decision to carve some three thousand years of history into more than a thousand blocks of stone.

At this late stage, it clearly was the only possible solution, both economically and politically. But the nagging question remained: Could the temples be cut into pieces without suffering serious harm? Many experts believed the answer was no.

Sandstone is a very fragile, crumbly rock, and the kind found in the Nile Valley is especially so. It's made up of grains of quartz that are only tenuously cemented together, resulting in cracks and fissures that riddle the stone. As late as May 1963, a panel of UNESCO experts wrote that they were "immensely repulsed at the thought of recommending a project that leads to the cutting or fragmenting of these precious monuments in any way, even if they can be reconstituted on another site." A number of prominent archaeologists issued a statement saying they regarded the cutting of the temples as an act of wanton destruction and "a solution of despair." According to estimates, up to a third of the sandstone blocks would probably be ruined.

Even Walter Jurecka, the German construction engineer who would serve as project manager for Joint Venture Abu Simbel, believed it had been a mistake to reject the Italian proposal for saving the temples. "Each and every one of us will loyally do his best for the project," Jurecka told a journalist. "But there is such a thing as keeping faith with the spirit of engineering, and I can only say that the raising of the temples in one piece would have done justice to the broad vision of their builders."

Those involved in the cutting project had agreed that the temples should be dissected in segments as large as possible. But neither UNESCO and Egyptian authorities nor the contracting companies knew at that point exactly how this unprecedented dismantling and reassembly operation would work. They hadn't yet determined, for example, how to make the minute excisions on the temple's façades and interiors that had been promised or how to hold the sandstone together so it wouldn't crumble.

Hochtief, the company in charge of the overall work, had already successfully dismantled and relocated the Temple of Kalabsha, but that project had almost nothing in common with the challenge facing it now. Kalabsha was a free-standing temple, while the temples of Abu Simbel were part of the cliff into which which they were carved. It was one thing to take apart the walls of a building and quite another to excise the intricately sculpted faces and bodies of the colossi fronting the Great Temple.

From the outset, Carl Theodor Mackel, the German foreman in charge of the construction site, made it clear that the removal of the temples must be regarded as a hazardous experiment, no matter how careful and vigilant his workers were. "We take every possible precaution within the time available," he said. "We could perform the dismantling work virtually free of risk, but to do this, we would need more than two years. That would mean we might as well pack up right now. By August 15, 1966, we must be entirely clear of the site."

As Mackel's remarks suggest, the extremely late launch of the project meant it was now in a neck-and-neck race with the rising waters of the Nile. Only a few weeks separated the beginning of disassembly work on Abu Simbel in the spring of 1964 and the conclusion of the first stage of construction of the Aswan High Dam, when the water level of the river would begin to rise.

When the annual floodwaters arrived in the summer of 1964, the level would be significantly higher than the previous high-water mark at the old Aswan dam. By the time winter made its appearance that year, the Nile's water level would crest some 410 feet above sea level, sixteen feet higher than the base of the small temple at Abu Simbel and four feet higher than the base of the Great Temple, causing catastrophic flooding to both.

Having made the audacious rescue attempt of Abu Simbel possible, Christiane Desroches-Noblecourt and the other architects of the Nubia campaign had little or no say in how it was carried out. During their visits to the site, they could only observe as the experts made their crucial, agonizing decisions about how to proceed.

WITH FLOODING A CERTAINTY within six months, an immediate first priority for Joint Venture Abu Simbel was to build an eighty-two-foot-high temporary barrier, called a cofferdam, around the temples to hold back the encroaching river and keep the terrain dry between the dam and the work site. Construction on the enclosure began in November 1963, before all the contracts had been signed. Even with the cofferdam, it was impossible to prevent a certain amount of water from infiltrating the porous Nubian sandstone, so powerful pumping stations also had to be installed to deal with the seepage.

Work on the dam continued twenty-four hours a day, seven days a week, with three overlapping twelve-hour shifts each day. "We could not lose a minute," one engineer noted. In the autumn of 1964, just as he and his colleagues thought they had the dam finished, abnormally high floodwaters forced them to raise it several feet higher than originally planned. By late that year, the Nile was cresting just inches from its top. The water seeped through so fast that three drainage tunnels had to be dug around the temples, and twenty-five pumps sucked away three-quarters of a million gallons of water every hour. "It was a razor's edge between success and catastrophe," said Torgny Säve-Söderbergh, a Swedish archaeologist who played a major role in the project. "Happily, the dam and its drainage system stood up to the test."

As the drama over the dam was unfolding, the clock was ticking, too, for the overall project. In just a little over two years, the work of dismantling the temples and moving them to safety had to be completed. It was a mission of almost unimaginable magnitude, and to carry it out, its organizers had assembled nearly two thousand engineers, archaeologists, architects, surveyors, administrators, craftsmen, and other laborers from more than a dozen countries.

While Hochtief was in overall control, the Swedish engineering firm VBB was in charge of supervising the engineering work. The cutting and reassembly operations were handled by Impregilo, a Milan-based construction and civil engineering company, whose workers came from the Carrara marble quarries in the Italian Alps. As an Impregilo executive noted, the Italian *marmisti* were tailor-made for the job, with their "deeply engrained understanding of the mysterious language of stone and a lifetime spent hewing out stone from the mountains behind them." In addition, two international committees of engineers, archaeologists, and architects acted as advisers. The Egyptian government had its own representatives at the site—a resident engineer and his staff and several archaeologists from the Egyptian Antiquities Organization.

In the spring of 1964, an initial workforce numbering about a thousand people had begun arriving at Abu Simbel to perform a myriad of jobs. "I don't think that the management at any other construction site has ever had to coordinate so many operations," a German supervisor remarked at the time. "On some days, we have several hundred going on at the same time. And everything, of course, was complicated by the multiplicity of languages." The headaches of managing such a complex operation and diverse crew were compounded by the difficulties of working and living in such a remote, barren place, with nothing surrounding the temples but desert. For most of the year, the heat was searing, with temperatures rising as high as 120 degrees Fahrenheit and no shade available anywhere. "It was so hot," one young German engineer recalled, "I sometimes thought I was going to die."

Because of the rush to complete the cofferdam, plans to build a small modern settlement for the workers were delayed for more than a year, forcing them to live on houseboats on the Nile and in tents and huts near the temples. They were warned not to stray far from the site because of the danger posed by Bedouin tribesmen in the area, who were known to prey on unwary foreigners. In the late 1950s, Christiane Desroches-Noblecourt had visited Abu Simbel with Mustafa Amer, the head of the Cairo survey and research center, who came armed with a revolver. He told her that the region was infested with members of a Bedouin tribe known for their attacks on nearby villages and foreign tourists. "He wasn't wrong," she remembered. "One night I heard a number of gunshots. Mustafa had just gotten rid of some very formidable Bedouins who had tried to invade our little boat."

At the beginning of the project, those working at Abu Simbel were almost completely out of touch with the outside world. Radio and telephone communication was hit-or-miss, while the shipment of goods to the site was agonizingly slow. All materials and supplies—from food, drinking water, and fuel to building materials and heavy machinery—had to be transported up the Nile. Abu Simbel was about 175 miles from Aswan, the closest major city, and getting there by boat took almost thirty hours. Most of the machinery and other equipment—earth movers, compressors, pneumatic hammers and drills, hoisting gear, cranes, vehicles, and a plethora of other large items—came from Europe by sea. It took up to five months to get goods from there and four to six weeks from Cairo, which was 660 miles away.

Keeping spare parts in stock was a particular problem. "No matter how large a stock we have on hand, the part you want is always missing," a machinery foreman said. "To get its replacement from Europe takes at least three months. Just go over to the workshops and ask the men there what working at Abu Simbel means. They'll say, 'Improvisation and invention.'"

AS THEY BEGAN WORK, the newcomers to Abu Simbel had no idea that not long before they arrived, the slopes overlooking the banks of the Nile had been dotted with Nubian villages containing large whitewashed houses adorned with vividly colored geometric patterns and boasting domed roofs and stately inner courtyards. Each one was different from the others, and most were brimming with life. Behind the houses, emerald-green fields yielded bountiful harvests for their inhabitants after the yearly flood washed over the land and left behind a thick layer of rich sediment. But as the river's level crept higher and higher in the early and mid-1960s, the riverbanks, along with their villages and fields, were eventually swallowed up.

As a result of the flooding, tens of thousands of Nubians in Egypt and Sudan had been forced to leave the villages where their ancestors had lived for centuries and move more than a hundred miles inland. "Among Nubians there was a strong feeling of ethnic unity, based on common cultural traditions and languages," said Torgny Säve-Söderbergh. "So deep was the attachment of the Nubian to his homeland that to leave it for good was unthinkable."

The mass uprooting of these people from a life they loved came as a personal blow, too, to Desroches-Noblecourt, who had gotten to know a number of them during her frequent trips to the area with CEDAE survey missions. She had become particularly close to an elderly Nubian sheikh in a nearby village and went to see him every time she returned to the region. Dressed in billowing white robes and white turban, he greeted her at his front door, his arms raised in welcome. Over tea, dates, and honey cakes, they caught up on their lives since they had last seen each other, and he introduced her to members of his large family, which included a son who was a doctor in London.

During her last visit to the sheikh's home, he talked sadly about "the disappearance of his beloved Nubia and his upcoming move north, far from the calm and majesty of the river." But just before he and his family left, he said, they planned to celebrate the wedding of his youngest daughter—"our last big ceremony before we are forced to leave everything." He invited her to come, and she accepted with alacrity. An honored guest, she was taken to the bridal chamber to greet his daughter before the ceremony and took part in the traditional dancing and singing that followed.

When the exodus finally occurred, Desroches-Noblecourt felt an obligation to record for history "the tearing of the Nubian population from their cradle." She participated in the making of a French documentary film, *Nubie 64*, that showed the villagers tearfully gathering their belongings and being loaded onto barges carrying them off to their new, unwanted lives. In addition to household goods, they took with them chickens and donkeys and even brightly painted shutters and doors from their old houses, but they were forced to leave behind their dogs and other pets.

Their lives had been intertwined with the Nile, and most of them had an extremely difficult time adjusting to an existence away from it. The Nubians in Egypt were resettled on a barren, rocky, crescent-shaped strip of land some thirty miles north of Aswan, which required years of work before it was cultivated enough to produce crops. The homes the government built for them bore little resemblance to the spacious houses they had left behind. The new ones were small and cramped, barely big enough to accommodate one's immediate family, let alone the extended clans that often had lived together on the banks of their beloved river.

It was a sad fact of life that Egyptian authorities, as well as UNESCO officials, seemed far more worried about the fate of Abu Simbel than they did about the fate of the Nubians who were displaced by the Aswan High Dam.

THE EXTRAORDINARY CARE OF the two temples included several weeks of preliminary protective work before the actual cutting began. Boulders and other rubble were cleared away from the gulley separating them, and five thousand truckloads of sand were piled up against their façades to shield them from falling stones and other debris during removal of rocks from the cliff above. When the sand reached the chests of the colossi fronting the Great Temple, dump trucks atop the cliff rained more sand down on their heads and crowns. After the trucks had finished, the façade's only visible element was its uppermost frieze, depicting sacred monkeys welcoming the morning sun. A roofed wooden structure was built above the frieze to safeguard it as well. Swathed in their sandy shrouds, the temples looked much as they had when they were first discovered by the Swiss explorer Johann Burckhardt in 1813.

Engineers, meanwhile, constructed aluminum tunnels through the sand to allow laborers to enter the interior of the temples and begin their work. A dense forest of steel scaffolding was erected in all the inner chambers to prevent the walls, ceilings, and colonnades from collapsing during the extraction of rock from the cliff over them. When ripper tractors began gouging out the rock above and behind the temples, the noise inside was deafening.

THE DISMANTLING OF ABU SIMBEL'S GREAT TEMPLE BEGINS IN 1964

In all, nearly 300,000 tons of rock were removed from around the monuments. To reach the ceilings of the innermost rooms, the excavators had to burrow down nearly 190 feet from the top of the cliff. Oscillographs were mounted inside the temples to measure vibrations. When the vibrations were judged too high, the last 60,000 tons of rock had to be removed by laborers using pneumatic hammers. They continued the work until only about two and a half feet separated the outer rock from the temples' ceilings and walls. Freed of the support they had rested against for more than three thousand years, the shrines buckled slightly, but the scaffolding inside kept them intact.

Now came the hardest and most perilous part—the actual dismantling of the façades and interiors. According to the terms of the contract, the statues, interior walls, ceilings, and fronts of the monuments were to be cut up into about eleven hundred blocks, each one weighing an average of 20 to 30 tons. To ensure that the cuts on the fragile sandstone façades and interiors would be invisible once the blocks were reassembled, it was decided to limit the width of the cuts to no more than one quarter of an inch—a task that would require surgical delicacy and precision.

While the cofferdam was being built and the preliminary work completed, those in charge of the cutting operation conducted tests with all kinds of saws—chain saws, disk saws, wire saws, and handsaws—and compared various sawing processes. They decided that only small handsaws could be used on the façades and interiors. The two most commonly used were the helicoidal saw—wire coils shaped like a helix—and a Novello saw, which had a thirteen-inch blade and diamond-tipped teeth.

As the cutting tests proceeded, Egyptian technicians began reinforcing the stones to enable them to withstand the rigors of dismantling, transfer to a storage site, and reassembly. After chemists ran hundreds of tests of their own to determine the proper strengthening material, they, along with restorers and other specialists, decided on an epoxy resin, which had an adhesive power stronger than mortar. Egyptian teams spent seven months at Abu Simbel injecting the surfaces of the temples' façades and interiors with the resin, making sure to fill every surface cavity and crack to guard against crumbling.

When the initial reinforcement work was finished, the Italian quarry workers took over. Having devoted their lives to cutting and moving stone, "we know rocks like hearts," one of them said. "We know when they break." Armed with chain saws, they began by making oblique cuts about three and a half feet deep into the rock in the interior rooms where the ceilings and walls were joined, to relieve the stresses that would arise when the rock directly above the ceiling was removed.

Other *marmisti*, working in two-man teams, used handsaws to cut inch-deep grooves into the painted ceiling. Their working conditions were extraordinarily difficult. The temperature in the cramped interiors was never less than 100 degrees Fahrenheit, sometimes rising to as high as 150 degrees. The men were given goggles and masks as protection against the omnipresent thick clouds of dust, but some of them chose not to wear the gear because they couldn't see well enough with it on. They did their work crouched on scaffolding beneath the ceiling, reminding a visiting *National Geographic* writer of the excruciating working conditions Michelangelo endured while painting the ceiling of the Sistine Chapel. "The men, however, showed little concern for the extreme discomfort their work involved," the writer noted. "Their sole interest was in the width of their cuts. If they made a finer cut—by a hairline or perhaps a full millimeter—than the maximum width stipulated in the contract, they felt well rewarded."

The *marmisti* operated by instinct, sometimes deviating from the blueprint when they felt that a particular cut called for in the plans was located in a weak spot. "These men could feel the soul of stone," said an Italian engineer in charge of the cutting. "They shed tears over a single chip. They worked like demons, but with the touch of angels."

After the interior cuts were made, steel pins were inserted through specially drilled holes at the end of each cut to show workers removing rock from the other side where to make their cuts to join the inside excisions. When excavators using heavy equipment were within thirty-one inches of the interior, they stopped work and the *marmisti* took over. In cutting the rear sides of the blocks, the Italians used power saws, which made much wider excisions, but that didn't matter since the backs of the blocks would never be seen. The slabs would be worked loose when the cuts from the rear met those from the front.

Figuring out how to move the blocks once they had been separated from the rock was another critical decision. Because of the stones' fragility, the use of jacks, slings, belts, and other hoisting gear was out of the question. The decision was finally made to drill holes in the blocks and insert steel lifting bolts cemented in with resin. They then would be hooked by the tackle of a derrick and lifted to safety. Once free, the blocks would be coated with a protective substance to prevent them from splitting and fracturing during transport and storage in a temporary holding area. Blocks from decorated interior walls would be wrapped in linen strips to prevent their edges from crumbling.

About five hundred workers labored day and night for nine months to complete the cutting operation. In the words of one observer, "The human effort required to save Abu Simbel could scarcely have been less than was needed to build it 3,000 years earlier."

The first crucial test of that work came on the morning of May 21, 1965. The heat on that spring day was already blistering—at least 100 degrees—but it didn't stop hundreds of those who worked at the site from gathering in front and on the sides of the temples to witness a milestone—the initial marker of whether Joint Venture Abu Simbel would succeed or fail. One thought was on everyone's mind, a witness recalled: "Would all those calculations and experiments in lifting blocks up to 30 tons prove to be effective, or would the Cassandra-like utterances of the cutting scheme's opponents be justified?"

The project manager, Carl Theodor Mackel, stood at the edge of the excavation pit, while the head engineer, Sweden's Karl Fredrick Ward, stretched out prone on a bluff below the crest of the cliff. Pino Lucano of Italy, chief of the section directly responsible for the dismantling, walked restlessly back and forth along the rocky ridge over the Great Temple's façade as Egypt's resident archaeologist, Dr. Anwar Shoukry, looked on from the top of the cofferdam.

The four men—and everyone else at the site—had their eyes fixed on a narrow cut in the rock at the northern end of the cliff. At a sign from a member of Ward's staff, the operators of bulldozers working in the excavation pit shut off their engines, and other workmen put down their pneumatic hammers and electric drills. The silence was total, the tension palpable.

As the onlookers watched, a derrick, anchored by wires to the cliff and cofferdam, swung its tackle over to the slight cut at the top of the cliff. Suddenly the cut widened and became a gaping fissure, "as if the mountain were silently yawning," an observer wrote. A giant block of stone was eased away from the cliff, and the derrick operator attached the tackle to steel bars inserted in the stone. As those watching held their breath, the heavy load hovered almost motionless against the deep blue sky. "Go, baby, go!" a spectator whispered.

With agonizing slowness, the operator lowered the eleven-ton stone more than a hundred feet, then gently deposited it onto a low-slung, sand-cushioned trailer. Only then did a cheer erupt from the crowd. After all the months and years of excruciating doubt, the first piece of the temple had been successfully extracted from the mountain that had sheltered it for millennia. Before it was carried off at a snail's pace to the storage area, it was assigned a name: GA1AO. The letters and numbers indicated its precise location at the topmost section above the façade of the Great Temple. Little more than an hour later, a second block was lowered onto a trailer and transported to the storage yard, which was set up at the rear of the cliff, well back from the Nile's rising waters.

A journalist who was present during the first week of the dismantling operation marveled at its assembly-line precision. "Anyone visiting the construction site and seeing how the effort was proceeding like clockwork," he wrote, "must have had the impression that the firms participating in the project had never done anything else but saw up and dissect giant rock-hewn temples."

THE SMOOTHNESS OF THE dismantling operation was a reflection of the camaraderie and cooperation that had sprung up among the myriad specialists and other workers at Abu Simbel, despite their widely varied occupations and nationalities. Because of the uniqueness of the project, it required close collaboration among everyone involved, each drawing on his own area of expertise and sharing it with others.

The majority of those working at the site had known little or nothing about the history and cultural importance of the temples when they first arrived. But it didn't take long for most of them to develop a passionate commitment to accomplishing a feat that few thought was possible. "Amid the great, dusty blocks, they breathed in the fascination of an ancient past that risked being swept away," an Italian writer noted. "It was impossible for them not to respond to the urgency of the challenge facing them." That shared spirit of dedication helped weld them into a tightly knit community—an experiment in international coexistence that proved to be a remarkable success.

It helped that by 1965, they were living in a much more pleasant environment than the primitive, rough-and-ready conditions of the early days. The houseboats and tents were gone, replaced by a small town conjured out of the desert that offered most of the amenities of civilization, among them modern houses, some of them with gardens. Poignantly, the houses resembled those of the drowned Nubian villages, with interior courtyards and dome-shaped roofs to help keep out the heat.

The community also sported a cafeteria, club, movie theater, and sports facilities, including a swimming pool and tennis and bocce courts, not to mention a hospital, water purification plant, and power station. One of the few local touches was the Nubian donkey that accompanied the postman when he collected and delivered mail.

On the day the first block was removed from the cliff, more than three thousand people were living at the site. About nineteen hundred were workers; the rest were wives and children. Foreign engineers, architects, and other specialists were allowed to bring their families with them, and many did so. In addition, several babies were born during the four-year period of the project. (Reportedly, at least a couple of them bore the middle names Rameses or Nefertari.) Yet among the few institutions the town lacked was a school. One or two teachers couldn't possibly cope with the extensive array of languages spoken by the children living there, including German, Swedish, English, French, Italian, Arabic, Spanish, and Polish. During their time at Abu Simbel, school-age children were taught by correspondence.

Although the area sported eight miles of roads, the only paved thoroughfare was the one connecting the operation site and main storage yard. "It was far more important to ensure a smooth ride for the stones of Abu Simbel than for the people," one of the engineers said, only slightly tongue in cheek. In time, a makeshift airport was built, and two small planes established a daily airlift between Aswan and Abu Simbel, carrying personnel, mail, and small cargoes of spare parts and other goods that were needed as soon as possible.

Luciano Paoli, who at twenty-six was the youngest member of the Italian *marmisti* team, recalled his year at Abu Simbel as one of the happiest experiences of his life. "In the evening after work, we'd get together in the village with everyone else—Swedes, French, Germans, British, you name it," he said more than fifty years later. "We'd have a beer and a swim, or we showed them how to play bocce and they showed us how to play tennis. We also played volleyball. I had wonderful relationships with everyone there. It was a really warm community, all working for a common goal, and that's something I'll always remember."

Medhat Abdul Rahman Ibrahim, a young Egyptian engineer fresh out of college, felt much the same about his four years of work at Abu Simbel. "I would arrange trips on Fridays for foreign and Egyptian engineers to go to Lake Nasser," he said. "The social relationships we built with Germans, Swedes, French and the various other nationalities have lasted a lifetime. We still keep in touch."

There were frequent celebrations, often involving a successful end to activities on the work site. The May 1965 removal of the first blocks was one such occasion. But as joyful as the merrymaking was that night, those participating in it were acutely aware that more nail-biting challenges lay in store.

Particularly worrisome was the possibility of damage to the more intricate, decorated blocks—those belonging, for example, to the pillars, carved as huge statues of Rameses, that guarded the Great Tem-

A STATUE OF NEFERTARI IS LIFTED TO SAFETY FROM THE FAÇADE OF THE GREAT TEMPLE, 1965

ple's hall, or the bas-reliefs depicting the Battle of Kadesh. But they, too, were extracted without incident. On August 12, 1965, the first ceiling stones of the Great Temple were removed as night was falling. For the first time in their extremely long history, the statues of Rameses and the three gods seated in the sacred sanctuary could look out that night on the moon and the stars.

As the temples' interiors were being dismantled, front-loading trucks began removing the heavy veils of sand from their façades. Next to come was the most difficult and daring operation of all: extracting the giant figures of the colossi from the front of the Great Temple. Not surprisingly, the first step—removing the pharaoh's heads—caused the most anxiety. The statues, with their serene, enigmatic expressions, represented the iconic image of Abu Simbel, and it was essential that no harm come to their stone faces.

Engineers, archaeologists, and stonemasons spent countless hours discussing how to accomplish this. They all would have preferred to cut and lift the heads in one piece, but according to engineers' calculations, the weight would have far exceeded the permissible maximum of thirty tons. It was finally decided to extract the statues' crowns first and then cut the faces, detaching them from between their ears.

On October 15, the first face of the colossi was scheduled to be removed, and the two most experienced *marmisti* were assigned the task. Both understood that this was the greatest challenge their team would face during the entire project and that it would call upon every ounce of their skill and endurance. Beginning at midday under a blazing sun, they worked for seventeen hours straight, sawing continuously through the night. Covered in dust and sweat and bathed in the garish glow of floodlights, they proceeded slowly and methodically—occasionally diverging from the blue lines drawn on the face to guide their saws when they encountered a problem area.

At dawn the next day, they finally finished and clambered exhaustedly down the scaffolding. Not long afterward, the derrick operator received his long-awaited signal. As he moved the tackle toward the face, a large group of engineers and workmen, their own faces reflecting their weariness and strain, watched from the ground below. As the derrick whirred and the tackle made contact, the pharaoh's nineteen-ton face began separating from his body. Once it was clear and suspended from the hoisting rope, it slowly revolved in the air, "taking on all the fleeting expressions—from somber to benign—that the sun in its daily passage across the sky normally bestowed on its immovable features only by slow degrees," one witness remembered.

Then, like the hundreds of blocks before it, it was gently deposited on a sand-cushioned trailer and taken at a stately pace to the storage yard. There, also like the others, a series of letters and numbers was painted on its back to identify its location, and it was covered with straw mats to protect it from sandstorms and the heat of the sun. Every

THE FACE OF ONE OF THE COLOSSAL RAMESES SENTINELS IS SLOWLY LOWERED TO THE GROUND EN ROUTE TO ITS NEW LOCATION, 1965

block was continuously inspected and given more resin injections if necessary to strengthen it during the months it was in storage.

On April 16, 1966, the temples' last blocks were extracted and taken to the yard—six months after the beginning of the dismantling work and two weeks ahead of schedule. Not one piece of stone had been lost or seriously damaged. Even more important, the race against the rising Nile had been won.

In the weeks that followed, Joint Venture Abu Simbel evacuated the construction site, which now featured two enormous, gaping holes where the temples had been. The derrick was moved to the monuments' new location to begin the arduous task of reassembling them, while the top rows of steel piling were removed from the cofferdam. Some of the dam's rock and sand filling was carted away to the top of the heights above the new site, to be used later in re-creating the hills above the temples.

In late August 1966, bulldozers helped topple the rest of the cofferdam, and water from Lake Nasser, the rapidly filling reservoir created by the new Aswan dam, began flooding in. The excavation pit disappeared first, followed by the hollowed-out cliff. Soon fishermen were trolling for catfish in water covering the sacred ground that had seen scores of splendid pharaonic ceremonies and processions more than three millennia before.

EVEN BEFORE THE START of the dismantling operation, work had begun at the new site, which was located on a plateau only a tenth of a mile away from the temples' original location but more than two hundred feet higher and almost seven hundred feet back from the shore. Bulldozers and other earth-moving equipment extracted tons of rock from the plateau's crest to level the base before reinforced concrete foundations and walls were poured.

In January 1966, as workers finished dismantling the bodies of the colossi at the Great Temple, foundation stones were laid at the new site and derricks set up to begin the reassembly process, which came to resemble nothing so much as a giant Lego construction. The project's overseers had planned the operation down to the last detail, knowing exactly where every stone was to go. It was crucially important that the temples be reconstructed in an identical manner and in the exact same orientation as on their original site, so that as the sun rose on February 22 and October 22 each year, a single beam of light would flash through the Great Temple and penetrate the sanctuary at the back.

As the blocks were lowered into their preassigned places, a small army of surveyors and their assistants, using instruments with rotating telescopes to measure horizontal and vertical angles, carefully checked and rechecked their positions. Determined to guarantee the accuracy of a block's placement to within a millimeter, they often spent hours making minute adjustments.

The temples' walls and ceilings were reassembled first, followed by their interiors, with workers using the same scaffolding framework that had reinforced the inner chambers during the dismantling operation. Once the interior blocks were positioned, specialists began filling in the cuts. The wide excisions at the backs of the blocks were joined together by mortar made of cement and water, while the narrow excisions on the interior blocks and those on the façades required more skilled and precise filling in. The task was carried out by specialists from the Egyptian Antiquities Organization, who used sand paste, its color adjusted to exactly match the stones they were working on. They were so deft at concealing the excisions that it was almost impossible to detect that the stones had been cut, transported, and reset.

September 14, 1966, marked another high point of the temples' restoration. On that day, the face of the first colossus to be reassembled was slated to be reunited with the rest of its head and body. While the dismantling of the faces had been a cause of enormous stress, the ceremony surrounding the restoration of the first face was joyful and triumphant.

More than a thousand people—at least half the population of the Abu Simbel village—flocked to the site to cheer as the pharaoh's giant visage arrived, swaddled in its sand-cushioned trailer. The derrick operator carefully lifted the twenty-one-ton slab, using the same steel lifting bars that had been implanted in it before it was removed from the original site. To prevent it from toppling forward as it rejoined its body, engineers had attached a concrete counterweight to the back surface.

Rising slowly over the crowd of spectators, the face and its concrete appendage hovered briefly over the two southernmost, partially rebuilt colossi and finally came to rest on the figure immediately north of the temple entrance. There it was carefully fitted between the pharaoh's ears and above his ceremonial beard. The sight of the first rebuilt colossus was mesmerizing for everyone present, but particularly for the workers who had joined the staff while the massive statues were still covered with their protective blanket of sand. This was their first inkling of the majesty of the monument they had helped bring back to life.

Within a few weeks, all the colossi had reclaimed their faces, which once again peered out toward the eastern horizon, over the ever-rising water of Lake Nasser. By the end of 1966, the temple dedicated to Nefertari was finished, looking exactly as it had on its original site. Six months later, after restoration of its topmost frieze featuring the sacred baboons greeting the rising sun, the Great Temple was completed in all its original splendor as well.

REASSEMBLY OF THE RAMESES COLOSSI, 1966

While those working on the project felt a palpable sense of relief, they still had more than a year's worth of work ahead of them to reconstruct the rocky heights above and around the monuments. The temples, fragile as they were, could not be expected to support the weight of the artificial hills that would be built atop their ceilings. To relieve them of that burden, two huge reinforced concrete domes were constructed over them, transferring the stress to the area outside the temples and keeping enough space between the domes' tops and the temple's ceilings to allow for ventilation. Thousands of tons of rock and stone, much of it coming from the temples' original location, were then heaped over the domes, making the new site look as much as possible like the cliff that had once overlooked the antiquities.

By the early summer of 1968, the greatest archaeological rescue effort in history had come to an end. After all the high-voltage tension, the head shaking and warnings, the experts had won their race against time in a striking fashion. Rameses II's ancient temples had been installed in their new surroundings eighteen months ahead of schedule, without any significant loss or damage.

Four months earlier, on February 22, engineers and archaeologists had gathered in front of Abu Simbel at dawn to see if one final, crucial hurdle had been cleared. It had. As the sun rose in the east, a single sunbeam flashed through the great temple's entrance, lit up the interior, and stabbed deep into the sanctuary in the back. As soon as the light entered the sanctuary, it illuminated three of the figures sitting there—Rameses, Amun, and Ra-Horakhty—just as Rameses had planned 3,200 years before.

CHAPTER 18

"NO ONE WAS MORE RESOLUTE THAN SHE"

On September 22, 1968, more than five hundred dignitaries from around the world gathered on the shore of Lake Nasser to celebrate a day that many people had claimed would never come. The guests, seated under a huge multicolored party tent, were there to witness the triumphant reopening of the Abu Simbel temples.

The woman who'd sparked the campaign to save them and the other Nubian antiquities had shown up a day early to check that everything was running smoothly. For the past ten years, ever since she'd persuaded Sarwat Okasha to join her in what virtually everyone else considered an impossible rescue effort, Christiane Desroches-Noblecourt had been hell-bent on ensuring that it succeeded. "Her voice was insistent and undaunted by difficulties," remembered the University of Chicago's John Wilson. "Without her demand that the monuments of Nubia be saved, many of the rest of us might not have bestirred ourselves. No one was more resolute than she."

In nearly every aspect of the endeavor—from the planning of the project to the lobbying of government officials for aid to overseeing the archaeological surveys in Nubia—Desroches-Noblecourt had been indispensable. On this last day before the gala reopening celebration, she was determined to make sure no important details had been overlooked.

Several weeks earlier, Okasha had arranged for several large buses to travel by barge to Abu Simbel. They would collect the guests the following morning at a newly built airport nearby and transport them to the ceremony. Prominent among the dignitaries were a number of high-ranking UNESCO officials, including its director general, René Maheu, and one of its top fundraisers, Prince Sadruddin Aga Khan. Also coming were ambassadors and other key officials from the fifty countries that had contributed to the monuments' rescue; Egyptian government ministers; executives from the companies that had participated in the rescue; and an array of international artistic, literary, and intellectual figures. The event would be covered by dozens of journalists who had flown in from all corners of the globe.

As she conducted her inspection, Desroches-Noblecourt gazed up at the façades of the temples looming above her. Her mind slipped back to thirty years earlier and the first time she'd seen them, shortly after she'd finished her work at the Edfu dig. Everything looked the same as it had then—the colossi and their enigmatic smiles; the drift of golden sand between the two temples; the nearby mimosa bushes, with their delicious odor; and even the chirping of birds, which had returned to the rebuilt temples to build their nests in the deep indentations of the carved hieroglyphs on the façades.

A feeling of euphoria stole over her. It was, she later told an interviewer, "a very emotional moment. I had been talking about it, day in and day out, for so long that it had become an obsession. Now that it was here, I had to ask myself if I was dreaming. It seemed like a miracle."

Her elation, however, didn't last long. It vanished the moment she inspected a dedication plaque installed by the Egyptian government in front of the temples. It was meant to commemorate their reconstruction as a triumph of international collaboration, as well as to honor the building of the Aswan High Dam, meant "to ensure the welfare and prosperity of the Egyptian people." The wording had been agreed upon by UNESCO and Egyptian officials, but Desroches-Noblecourt noticed that one crucial line had been left out: a sentence giving credit to UNESCO for its support.

It was unclear to her whether the omission was accidental or intentional. Over the previous few years, the skirmishes between the Egyptian government and UNESCO hierarchy over which of them was in overall charge of the project had lessened in intensity; yet at the same time, Egyptian officials, including Sarwat Okasha, had grown increasingly vocal in their public declarations that Egypt had been primarily responsible for originating and overseeing the plan.

When René Maheu arrived at Abu Simbel later that day, Desroches-Noblecourt informed him of the missing sentence. UNESCO's director general was irate. "If it's not put back in place before tomorrow morning, I will leave before the inauguration," he told her. She said she would leave with him if nothing was done, but first they had to give Okasha a chance to rectify the error.

The Egyptian minister of culture, who had put in a long day of work at his ministry in Cairo, did not arrive at Abu Simbel until very late that evening. Maheu and Desroches-Noblecourt took him to the plaque to point out the missing sentence. "His reaction exceeded ours in violence," Desroches-Noblecourt recalled. "He said, 'Don't worry. I'll have it fixed.'" Okasha lived up to his word, although the line squeezed in at the bottom of the plaque—"This has been achieved through cooperation with UNESCO"—could hardly be regarded as heartfelt thanks.

With that crisis averted, the ceremony took place without a hitch. Maheu and Okasha were the main speakers, both of them underscoring the continuity between two extraordinary achievements: the original construction of the temples and their deliverance from extinction. Maheu's speech took the form of a direct address to Rameses II: "We have come, O King, to add our work to yours in preserving your quest for eternity," he declared.

> Using methods that you could not imagine but constantly having in mind your intentions and your rites, we hollowed out the mountain, cut out statues, pillars and subterranean walls. Then we rebuilt in the light what you had dug in the darkness. Your priests, your architects, your masons and your sculptors, your scribes, and your craftsmen could not have taken any more care

> in carrying out the deification of your glory than we have taken, O King, to preserve your earthly presence. Thanks to the efforts of all, you are safe, ready to resume your journey through the centuries toward the rising of the sun each day.

Okasha, for his part, acted as host, welcoming the guests on behalf of Nasser and his government. He called the rescue of the Nubian temples "a mission accomplished" and harked back to the issuing of the UNESCO appeal eight years before. "No one then could have foreseen the results," he declared. "No precedent existed to guide us. Never before had the peoples of the world been asked to work together on so grand a scale for a purely cultural purpose."

The response was phenomenal, he added—"as immediate as it was generous and heart-warming. . . . In no previous project had East and West—men of widely different races, creeds and political persuasions—cooperated from the beginning in such a task and followed it through to a successful end."

As Desroches-Noblecourt knew only too well, Okasha's statement was neither complete nor entirely accurate. She was living proof that women as well as men had been involved in the rescue from the beginning. And his claim of immediate and full-throated international cooperation, particularly in terms of donations, was stretching the truth, to say the least. The reality, as Desroches-Noblecourt told an interviewer years later, was that "we were preaching in the desert for years. Most people didn't want to do this at the beginning. We had to convince them to do it."

Okasha went on, "We owe so much to so many that it is almost unfair to single out any special names for mention. Yet our debt is of such a nature that I'm sure you will bear with me for a moment if I tell you about some of them." He proceeded to thank a long list of individuals for their contributions, foremost among them René Maheu and his predecessor as UNESCO director general, Dr. Vittorino Veronese: "Only UNESCO had the standing and authority to make the kind of international appeal that was required. Words are inadequate to express what we owe the two of them."

He then offered praise for Sadruddin Aga Khan and other UNESCO officials and committee members, followed by plaudits for the governments of the contributing countries, the international companies and their employees who carried out the work, museums and universities. Toward the end of his speech, he briefly mentioned Christiane Desroches-Noblecourt, citing her "very special gift of vision," "boundless energy, "very high standard of scholarship," and "true devotion to Egyptology." But nowhere in his address did he pay tribute to her crucial role in the effort.

When Okasha later wrote a long essay about the Nubia campaign, he failed to address Desroches-Noblecourt's seminal role as his partner in reaching out to UNESCO at the beginning of the project. In his telling of the story, he had done it all on his own. In one footnote in the essay, he included a sentence praising her work in surveying and documenting the temples and saving the Temple of Amada. But he never gave her credit for being one of the three key figures in launching the campaign and seeing it through to its completion. In sharp contrast, the other key figure, René Maheu, sent this heartfelt telegram to Desroches-Noblecourt after the triumphant conclusion of the effort: "After this extraordinary accomplishment how can I not think of you, who pulled me in, guided me, and took me on the most marvelous adventure of my life."

Years later, after Desroches-Noblecourt had become a well-known figure in France, there were numerous print and broadcast stories about her crucial role in rescuing the temples. Okasha disputed their veracity. Torgny Säve-Söderbergh in turn challenged Okasha's denial of her importance. Writing in a Swedish archaeological journal, Säve-Söderbergh, who had been part of the Nubia project from the beginning, observed that when the idea of saving the temples was first broached, the attitude of Okasha and other Egyptian authorities was one of "sad resignation. . . . The task of saving over twenty temples seemed so overwhelming, especially in the short time available, that everybody felt more or less paralyzed." Everyone, that is, but Christiane Desroches-Noblecourt. Her enthusiasm, Säve-Söderbergh said, encouraged Okasha and other authorities not to give in.

It's unclear why Okasha was so adamant about refusing to acknowledge Desroches-Noblecourt's contributions. However, one possible reason leaps to mind: that as a liberal, pro-Western official in a government whose other members tended to be conservative nationalists, he felt obliged to downplay any idea that a European—and a woman at that—had influenced his actions and thinking.

If Desroches-Noblecourt cared about his public slighting of her, she didn't show it. She never criticized him and indeed always referred to him in her memoir and other writings as a good friend and partner, whose lobbying for the temples had played a vital part in their rescue. In the end, the only thing that mattered to her was that Abu Simbel and the other monuments were now safe.

In 2009, UNESCO honored Desroches-Noblecourt at a gala ceremony that made clear how highly the organization rated her role in the Nubia campaign. "It is to you that we owe this adventure which made it possible to save these immense archaeological treasures from destruction," declared UNESCO's director general, Irina Bokova, the first woman to be appointed to the post. "UNESCO is proud to have shared in your struggle. Alongside Egyptian and Sudanese authorities, you fought tirelessly to convince politicians and decision-makers in multiple countries to embark on this adventure of unparalleled magnitude, which will be long remembered."

Throughout her extremely long career, Desroches-Noblecourt was given several nicknames by French journalists and others who knew her, including "the high priestess of Egyptology" and "Lady of the Nile." But the sobriquet she preferred was one conferred on her by her Egyptian colleagues. It was *"Umm Simbel"*—Arabic for "Mother of Simbel."

DESROCHES-NOBLECOURT'S REPUTATION WAS NOT the only one burnished by the rescue of the Nubian antiquities. The companies that participated in the salvage of Abu Simbel, which was quite rightly regarded as one of the most brilliant engineering achievements of the twentieth century, benefited greatly in terms of influence and new business. Hochtief, for example, acquired a reputation of legendary proportions in the construction industry for taking on seemingly impossible projects and bringing them to fruition.

The critical role played by Italian engineers and quarrymen at Abu Simbel, meanwhile, reinforced Italy's postwar renown as a construction and engineering powerhouse. The country was enormously proud of its achievements in saving the temples, which made headlines in Italian newspapers for years. HOW OUR BUSINESSES SAVED THE PHARAOHS was the headline of one newspaper article in 2006, which carried a half-page photo of the head of a Rameses colossus being lifted by a crane.

In 2019, Rizzoli, an Italian publishing company, brought out a sumptuously illustrated coffee table book marking the fiftieth anniversary of the Abu Simbel rescue. The book was underwritten by Salini Impregilo, the Italian construction and civil engineering conglomerate that succeeded Impregilo, the firm directly responsible for the temples' reassembly. In the book's introduction, Pietro Salini, the company's chief executive officer, noted the firm's pride "in having written a few pages of that story." The preservation of Abu Simbel, he said, showed how successful human intervention can be "in redirecting progress without slowing it down, simply by changing its course to avoid losing a piece of human history forever."

For Egypt, the antiquities' rescue was a triumph, too. It meant not only the preservation of a crucial part of the country's heritage but also a major financial boon provided by the swarms of tourists who were drawn to the Nubian region. In addition, it demonstrated Egypt's concern for saving its cultural riches and helped the country increase its visibility and influence in the world, thanks in part to an intense promotional campaign carried out by its government in parallel with the rescue of the temples.

Even more important, the international cooperation engendered by the Nubian campaign contributed to an easing of tension between Egypt and several Western countries, particularly the United States and France. Even though Britain had refrained from an active role in saving Abu Simbel, eventually it, too, saw a warming of its relationship with Nasser.

In addition, the success of the Nubia campaign paved the way for the protection of precious historic monuments on an international scale. As a direct result of its involvement in the rescue of the temples, UNESCO, capitalizing on an idea promoted by Desroches-Noblecourt and André Malraux, among others, introduced the idea of "world heritage sites," declaring that certain monuments were too important to be considered the property of individual countries and should belong to humanity as a whole.

Four years after Abu Simbel was salvaged, the United Nations introduced a convention protecting such sites. The most popular and successful program in its history, UNESCO's World Heritage Site activities have included, among many others, the protection of Venice and its lagoon; excavation of the four-thousand-year-old Mohenjo-daro ruins in Pakistan, the best-preserved ancient urban settlement in South Asia; and restoration of the Borobudur temple complex in Indonesia, built in the ninth century A.D. and considered one of the greatest Buddhist monuments in the world.

IN THE UNITED STATES, meanwhile, another major actor in the Abu Simbel campaign plunged back into the cultural preservation fray, with New York City as her new battleground. In 1975, Jacqueline Kennedy Onassis joined other historic preservation activists in a highly publicized fight to save a beloved Beaux-Arts landmark, Grand Central Terminal, from demolition by a developer who wanted to build an office tower on top of it.

After the city's Landmarks Preservation Commission denied the developer's request, he went to court and won a favorable ruling from the New York Supreme Court. That's when preservationists created an ad hoc group called the Committee to Save Grand Central Terminal.

Its star member was Onassis, who, at a press conference at Grand Central's Oyster Bar, stepped before a bank of microphones to repeat the same message she had delivered to John Kennedy and others about saving Lafayette Square and Abu Simbel: "If we don't care about our past, we can't have very much hope for our future," she said. "We've all heard that it's too late, or that it has to happen, that it's inevitable. But I don't think that's true. Because I think if there is a great effort, even if it's the eleventh hour, then you can succeed, and I know that's what we'll do."

In 1978, the U.S. Supreme Court agreed to hear the case. In June of that year, it ruled against the developer and upheld New York City's landmark preservation law, saving Grand Central Terminal and preventing the destruction of other historic buildings in the city.

It was a personal triumph for Onassis, who went on to help save other landmarks in Manhattan, including St. Bartholomew's Church on Park Avenue. But her satisfaction with those achievements was not enough to erase the sting of losing out a decade earlier on something she'd desperately wanted as a memorial to her late husband for his crucial role in rescuing Abu Simbel: the little temple promised to the United States by Egypt.

CHAPTER 19

THE BATTLE FOR DENDUR

WELL BEFORE THE REOPENING OF ABU SIMBEL, EGYPT MADE GOOD on its promise to award four of the smaller salvaged temples to the countries that had contributed the most generously to the Nubia campaign. The United States stood at the top of the list.

In August 1963, shortly after the Kennedy administration announced its intention to give $12 million for the rescue of Abu Simbel, the White House convened a group of experts to decide which temple the country should choose. John Wilson and several other prominent American Egyptologists were at the meeting, along with Dick Goodwin, representing the president, and officials from the Smithsonian Institution and the State Department.

After discussing the merits of each, the group decided on the Temple of Dendur, built by the Romans in 10 B.C., shortly after Caesar Augustus and his legions occupied Egypt. According to legend, Dendur had been erected on the west bank of the Nile, about fifty miles south of Aswan, in honor of a local Nubian ruler who had sided with the Romans during a battle against Egyptian forces. It was dedicated to his two sons, who had drowned in the river, as well as to the Egyptian goddess Isis.

Tiny, simple, and elegant, Dendur consisted of a sanctuary with bas-reliefs carved on its outer walls, a gateway, and a long stone walkway leading down to the Nile. On her trip up the river in 1873, Amelia Edwards was entranced by the little antiquity, describing it as looking like "an exquisite toy" steeped in "an atmosphere of romance."

The experts summoned by the White House agreed. In a report summarizing the committee's opinion, its members called Dendur "small, complete in itself, well preserved, a little gem. It could be exhibited beautifully and effectively, since much could be seen by spectators without going inside. Externally, it is lovely and is almost intact."

The consensus of the members was clear: They wanted Dendur, and they believed it should—and would—end up in Washington. "If reconstructed on the Potomac, the landing platform could be rebuilt to give a closer semblance of the original appearance," the report said. "Dendur would be especially appropriate for use in Washington as a permanent monument to Egyptian-American friendship."

Dick Goodwin backed the choice of Dendur with considerable enthusiasm, as did John and Jacqueline Kennedy. The president "always thought Dendur should come to Washington," his wife noted. "He wanted it along the banks of the Potomac, in a setting which would reflect as much as possible its original site in Egypt."

Unbeknownst to Goodwin and the Kennedys, however, one of the experts attending the meeting had a very different idea about where the temple should end up. He was Henry Fischer, the boyish-looking forty-year-old curator of Egyptian antiquities at the Metropolitan Museum of Art in New York. A graduate of Princeton, Fischer had earned a PhD at the University of Pennsylvania and taught Egyptology at Yale University before being hired by the Met in 1958.

Fischer was already very familiar with Dendur. During a five-day trip up the Nile in the late 1950s, he had spotted the temple and fallen in love with it. News about the looming threat to the Nubian temples from construction of the Aswan dam had broken several years before, and Fischer was undoubtedly aware that Dendur was one of the antiquities in danger. If any of them became available, he wanted this one for the Met. It was small enough to fit inside a museum, and all its decorative carvings were on its exterior walls, which meant there was no reason for museumgoers to enter it.

It's perhaps not coincidental that Fischer's trip and his discovery of Dendur took place just before James Rorimer, director of the Met, and Raymond Hare, the American ambassador to Egypt, paid their fateful call on Sarwat Okasha in late 1958. That visit, whose purpose was to negotiate the purchase of one or two of the temples under threat, was the spark that prompted Okasha to join forces with Desroches-Noblecourt in approaching UNESCO for help in salvaging the antiquities.

At the meeting with Goodwin and the others, Fischer made no mention of his previous interest in Dendur, but he did make clear he was an ardent supporter of the United States acquiring it, praising its simplicity, small size, and historical significance. After the session, the State Department informed the Egyptian government that Dendur was America's choice, and the Smithsonian began making preparations to receive it.

Soon afterward, however, the twin disasters of Kennedy's assassination and the House's reversal of the Abu Simbel appropriations occurred. Since the United States hadn't lived up to its end of the deal, Egypt imposed a temporary halt on plans to dispatch the stones of Dendur for reassembly in America. Even after a solution for supplying the aid was found and implemented the following year, Egypt waited until July 1965, when work on Abu Simbel was well under way, to notify the U.S. government it was ready to cede the temple.

Years later, Dick Goodwin described how he had urged S. Dillon Ripley to take immediate action to acquire it. Specifically, Goodwin said, he told the Smithsonian director that he should call Robert McNamara, the secretary of defense, and ask him to load and transport Dendur's stones to the nation's capital aboard a Navy ship. "Once the Smithsonian had it in Washington, there'd be time to decide what to do with it," Goodwin remarked. "But Ripley wouldn't do it."

Meanwhile, news of America's acquisition of the temple began making headlines across the country, and a number of cities clamored to claim it for themselves. Because of the burgeoning public interest, the Johnson administration, which had been expected to award Dendur to Washington, deferred action and appointed a commission to consider the various cities' applications.

The administration's decision set off what journalists called "the Dendur Derby." Philadelphia, Baltimore, and Boston sought the temple, as did Albuquerque and Phoenix. In its bid, Indio, a small town in the California desert, touted its climate and topography as being similar to that of Nubia and thus ideal for the transplanted monument. Two other candidates—Memphis in Tennessee and Cairo in Illinois—noted that they were namesakes of two storied Egyptian cities and should be given consideration based on that fact alone.

The Dendur Derby was a bonanza for newspaper feature writers, but in the end, no one gave any city or museum much of a chance to beat out Washington and the Smithsonian. After all, without John and Jacqueline Kennedy's intervention, the United States would never have provided the crucial funds for saving Abu Simbel. And furthermore, during the congressional fight over the Abu Simbel appropriations, Ripley had engaged in an extensive lobbying campaign in the Senate, which reportedly favorably influenced some of its members.

The Smithsonian also argued that Dendur was a government-to-government gift, much like the cherry trees around the Tidal Basin, presented by the Japanese government decades ago, and a carillon tower on a hill overlooking the Potomac, gifted by the Netherlands in thanks for U.S. aid after World War II. No one had ever suggested these symbols of friendship be located anywhere but the nation's capital. Why should Dendur be any different?

A particularly potent lobbyist for Washington's cause was Jacqueline Kennedy, who, still consumed by grief for her late husband, thought of Dendur as a memorial to him and fiercely fought for its transfer to the city. In a letter to the commission considering the applications, she wrote about Kennedy: "It was his thought that Washington, with all its examples of statuary and monuments and its increasing attraction for tourists, was really the only appropriate place for such a gift. . . . As

I'm sure you know, it was his message to Congress that made possible the U.S. contributions and with it the gift of Dendur."

In its own letter to the commission, the Smithsonian echoed Jacqueline's appeal, declaring that awarding the temple to Washington would be "honoring the wishes of the person who did the most to bring Dendur to the United States and to commemorate his keen interest in the Nubian campaign as a landmark in international cooperation."

IN NEW YORK, MEANWHILE, Henry Fischer refused to acknowledge the inevitability of Washington's winning the prize he had long coveted. Determined to get the Metropolitan to mount a campaign of its own, he approached Thomas Hoving, the museum's flamboyant new director, to make a passionate last-minute pitch for Dendur.

The thirty-five-year-old Hoving, known for his dynamism and flair for showmanship, had just taken control of the Met when Fischer came to see him. The son of a wealthy department store executive, with a doctorate in art history from Princeton, Hoving had been hired by James Rorimer seven years earlier as a curatorial assistant at the Cloisters, the annex of the museum specializing in medieval European art and architecture.

In 1965, he was named head curator at the Cloisters, but he was lured away just a few months later by New York's new mayor, John Lindsay, who made him the city's parks commissioner. Although he knew next to nothing about parks, Hoving swiftly became a familiar figure around town, zipping from park to park on his motorcycle. Adept at promoting both himself and the park system, he attracted considerable public attention for his successful fight to close Central Park's east and west drives to car traffic on Sundays and for launching a series of public events there, which became known as Hoving's Happenings. Less than six months after Hoving took the job, Rorimer died unexpectedly. In December 1966, the Met's board of trustees named Hoving as his replacement after he told its members that the museum was "moribund," "gray," and "dying" and promised that he would shake things up.

THOMAS HOVING, 1974

When Fischer spoke to Hoving about Dendur, he carefully framed his pitch to appeal to the new director's penchant for the bold and dramatic. "He implored me to have the courage to make the most unusual acquisition in the history of the Met, perhaps in the history of all museums," Hoving recalled. "It was an entire ancient Egyptian temple."

At first, Hoving was unimpressed. After studying the photos of Dendur that Fischer showed him, he noted that the temple actually wasn't all that ancient and asked Fischer if the Met really needed a building erected *after* the pharaonic period. "I have doubts that any other complete temple will be coming our way," Fischer dryly replied. "This is not far in overall shape from commemorative temples built thousands of years before. And it's beautiful. You have to admit that."

Hoving remained unconvinced. If the Met went after Dendur and won, it would have to pay a considerable amount to bring the stones to New York and reassemble them. "I had half a mind," he recalled, "to tell [Fischer] I wasn't interested in such a ponderous structure that would bring me, I was sure, a great deal of grief and sweat."

Nonetheless, Fischer knew his man. Whether he wanted the temple or not, Hoving's keen sense of competitiveness had been aroused. The Met, with its vast array of art treasures, was the foremost cultural institution in New York, possessing, as Hoving said, "a power that is out of proportion to its size and mission." In his memoirs, he acknowledged with startling frankness that he sought the director's job not because he "really cared about the institution" but because he "wanted to be accepted into the prestige and power of the Met."

The idea of another museum, particularly the Smithsonian, acquiring this headline-making temple quickly became anathema to him. The Met had long disdained the Smithsonian museums and for years had engaged in a contest of one-upmanship with them. When Washington's National Gallery was chosen as the first American museum to host the *Mona Lisa* in 1962, James Rorimer sent spies there to see how the museum had hung da Vinci's masterpiece and to measure the public reaction. Rorimer's informants reported back that the lighting had been abysmal and the painting had been hung too high and was barely visible, thanks to the shiny bulletproof glass protecting it. By contrast, the Met later claimed, when the *Mona Lisa* arrived in New York, it was staged to perfection.

Even though Hoving still worried about the expense of Dendur, as well as about its true aesthetic and historical worth, he became obsessed with the challenge of acquiring it. As he and Fischer prepared the Met's arguments to the Washington commission, he rejected the curator's emphasis on the importance of the museum's Egyptian collections and others like it in New York. "The idea that the temple would enhance or be enhanced by other nearby centers of Egyptology seemed irrelevant to me," he remarked.

Viewing the temple as "mere stage setting," Hoving decided that the most dramatic way of showing it off would be to enclose it in a huge glass showcase. Without consulting anyone to determine how feasible such a plan was, he ordered an architectural rendering of the glass-encased temple at night, with its golden sandstone shimmering under floodlights. The rendering, meant as "sheer theatrics," turned out beautifully, just as he'd hoped.

At the same time, he found he had made a formidable enemy. The discovery came as he tried to line up prominent New York politicians, including Senator Robert Kennedy, to lobby the Washington commission on the Met's behalf. When Hoving approached Kennedy, the late president's younger brother told him to talk to Dick Goodwin, who was now advising him. Goodwin, in turn, said Kennedy could not support the Met's bid because of Jacqueline Kennedy's determination to bring Dendur to Washington.

So Hoving decided to call JFK's widow. Any hope of sweet-talking her, however, vanished as soon as she came on the line. "I know the senator has obligations and constituents in New York, but I don't care about them," she said, her voice taut with fury. "I won't let him write a letter to stick that temple in some dusty museum in New York. Jack got that temple for the United States. If Jack had not helped out Egypt at the critical moment, the temple would never have been awarded to us. I don't want it in some museum. I don't care if you are going to put glass over it to protect it. I resent the way Johnson is shopping it around the country. . . . I want it built in the center of Washington as a memorial to Jack." In case she hadn't made herself perfectly clear, she repeated her message: "I don't care about the Met. I don't care about New York or Bobby's senatorial duties. . . . It's going to be built in Washington."

Uncharacteristically rendered speechless, Hoving recovered fast enough to sputter, "Thank you, Mrs. Kennedy, for your frank opinion." After hanging up, he recalled, he "stomped around the room, almost foaming at the mouth." Yet although taken aback by her diatribe, he was more determined than ever to snag Dendur for the Met. Not even the skepticism voiced by several members of the museum's board of trustees when he informed them of the plan was enough to deter him.

The battle lines were now clearly drawn, with the Met facing off against the Smithsonian. Hoving's main line of attack was to claim that Dendur was much too fragile to be exhibited outdoors in Washington's humid climate. Both museums performed extensive tests on samples of sandstone from the temple, and the Smithsonian reported that the stone consisted of very loosely grained quartz that soaked up water like a sponge. After testing various preservatives, the museum's department of mineralogy declared that a substance called Pencapsula hardened the sandstone substantially. If the temple stones were treated with Pencapsula, the Smithsonian said, the antiquity could be safely erected outside on the banks of the Potomac, which would much more closely resemble its native environment on the Nile.

Hoving argued otherwise. During his presentation before the commission, he insisted that installing Dendur outdoors, regardless of the preservative used, would expose it to wind and precipitation that would cause the stones to crumble and lead to the temple's destruction in as little as twenty-five years. It wasn't worth the risk, he declared, especially when compared to the safe alternative that he was offering.

He showed the group's members two huge architectural renderings in color of how Dendur would look in the Met, one during the day and the other at night. The renderings, which depicted the temple set inside a floor-to-ceiling glass display case that made it visible to strollers in nearby Central Park, were stunningly beautiful. In his presentation, Hoving didn't tell the commissioners that he had no idea yet how that display case would actually be built.

His performance in Washington that day was pure showmanship, as he himself acknowledged. "I went so far as to accuse any plan that did not completely enclose the temple as irresponsible," he wrote in his memoirs. "I concluded by throwing a sop to Henry Fischer, vowing that the study of Egyptology would be significantly enhanced by the temple's erection in New York, hinting that the discipline would stop dead in its tracks if the stones were not awarded to the Met. I closed with some appropriately snide and hypocritical remarks about those cities that wanted the grandiose structure purely for tourist reasons." Two weeks later, he received a letter from President Johnson awarding the Temple of Dendur to the Met. Having won the contest, he now had to figure out what to do with the prize.

IN THE FALL OF 1968, 661 huge crates containing the stones of Dendur were floated on barges to the port of Alexandria, then loaded on board a freighter and transported to New York. The Met housed them temporarily in a transparent, tentlike vinyl bubble in one of its parking lots. They were later moved to a steel hangar in another parking lot, where they were meticulously cleaned and repaired while awaiting construction of the new glassed-in wing that would house this monumental acquisition.

The wing's designer was a young, balding Irish-born architect named Kevin Roche, whose New Haven firm had just been recruited to draw up a master redesign plan for the entire museum. An inspired choice, Roche had spent time in the Nile Valley and had been heavily influenced by the architecture of ancient Egypt since the beginning of his career. "It actually means a lot more to me than the Greek or Roman forms," he said in an interview. "I can understand it much better. To my mind, the Egyptians invented everything the Greeks used later."

Roche was enamored with Dendur from the start. "Obviously, this little temple is just a gesture," he said. "But it's been done with a lot of skill, and you see reflected in it the high level of achievement in Egyptian architecture. You would be hard put to find a building in our culture which matches up to it." He was determined, he said, "to do the temple justice, always remembering that our responsibility is to preserve a work of art and let as many people as possible see it."

Aiming to evoke the temple's original setting on the Nile, Roche's design called for construction of a reflecting pool in front of it, complete with a wharf and landing. A sloping stone wall was to be placed behind the temple, to suggest the cliffs overlooking Dendur in Egypt. Roche had been captivated by "the extraordinary clarity of light" in the Nile Valley, and he tried to replicate that luminosity as much as possible in the wing's stippled glass ceiling and the glass north wall that looked out over Central Park.

It would take another ten years for his design to become reality. Hoving's initial challenge was to raise more than $4 million to construct the new wing. Not an easy task in the best of times, it was made much more difficult by a spike in anti-Egypt sentiment following the Six-Day War between Israel and the Arab states of Egypt, Syria, and Jordan in 1967. Eventually, though, Hoving found his savior in Arthur Sackler, an art collector and philanthropist who had made a considerable fortune by marketing pharmaceuticals and was active in an effort to bring peace to the Middle East. After Sackler pledged the money, construction began on the wing, which was named for him.* Once it was finished, stonemasons from Italy reassembled the temple, using as their guide photos and detailed drawings and plans sent by Egyptian officials.

When it finally opened in September 1978, the Temple of Dendur and the lofty, light-filled space that enclosed it were an immediate critical and popular success. "The simplicity of its setting, like a minimal frame on a painting, gives the temple a context which does not overwhelm it," one critic wrote. "When one enters the hall, one sees the

TEMPLE OF DENDUR, METROPOLITAN MUSEUM OF ART, NEW YORK CITY

* In December 2021, the Met removed Sackler's name from the wing in response to widespread public anger over charges that the company controlled by the Sackler family played a key role in creating the opioid crisis then raging in the United States.

temple, and not the building in which it was housed." Another declared, "Dendur itself is a superb work enriched by history and tradition, and architect Kevin Roche has created a 'display case' as successful in what it sets out to do as the tiny temple itself." Almost half a century after its opening, Dendur remains one of the Met's biggest tourist draws and the site of innumerable high-wattage events, from classical concerts to lavish parties like the annual Met Gala.

Although greatly distressed by the Met's acquisition of the temple, Jacqueline Kennedy eventually ended her feud with Hoving and indeed worked with him more than a decade later on several major exhibitions at the museum, among them a spectacular show on Russian fashion in the eighteenth and nineteenth centuries. It featured, among other items, Catherine the Great's wedding dress and a shimmering white ball gown and cloak adorned with swan feathers belonging to the doomed Russian czarina Alexandra that Jacqueline persuaded Soviet officials to include in the show.

Even so, losing Dendur remained a sore point for her—one she was reminded of every night. In 1964, she had bought a penthouse in a high-rise Fifth Avenue apartment building whose windows overlooked the Metropolitan Museum and, when it was added, the Sackler Wing. From those windows, she could look down and see an ever-present reminder of her loss—the tiny Temple of Dendur, lit by floodlights, glowing in the dark.

CHAPTER 20

"A CULTURAL JUGGERNAUT"

WHEN CHRISTIANE DESROCHES-NOBLECOURT FINALLY FOUND time to write her memoirs, she called the book *La Grande Nubiade*. It was an obvious title, considering the fact that, as one of her successors at the Louvre noted, "this titanic feat was the most extraordinary adventure of her career." But the Nubia campaign was hardly her only significant achievement. Indeed, even as she began working on it, she'd embarked on yet another project—one that would lead to a lavish Paris exhibition of King Tutankhamun's treasures, which in turn would spark the start of what Thomas Hoving called "the international madness for King Tut."

Her involvement began in 1960 when a British book publisher named George Rainbird sought her help in gaining permission from the Egyptian government to take color photographs of the golden masks and some of the other priceless artifacts found in Tutankhamun's tomb. There had been no further photos of the tomb's contents since their discovery by Howard Carter in the 1920s. Rainbird was betting that there would be great public interest throughout the world in seeing new photos, this time in glorious color.

At the time, Desroches-Noblecourt was doing her best to juggle her work to save the temples with her duties as acting chief curator of the

Louvre's Egyptian department and professor of archaeology at the École du Louvre. But she was intrigued by Rainbird's project and impressed by Frederick Kenett, the photographer who would take the pictures. "It seemed to me eminently fair that these objects discovered by an Englishman would be photographed by a very talented English photographer for an English publisher," she recalled. "I decided to plead their cause with the Egyptian ministry of culture."

Although Kenett had British citizenship, he was actually a German Jew whose family had sent him to London as a child when the Nazis came to power. Toward the end of World War II, he had joined the U.S. Counter Intelligence Corps and developed an interest in photography. After the war, Kenett became noted for his evocative photographs of sculpture and other artifacts, taken on assignment for museums as well as for art magazines and other publications.

When Desroches-Noblecourt approached Sarwat Okasha on Rainbird's and Kenett's behalf, Okasha told her that, in gratitude for her efforts to help rescue the temples, he would see what he could do. But he warned that even if he could persuade the government to grant permission, "there would still be great problems and barriers to overcome." Desroches-Noblecourt would soon find that his prediction was a massive understatement. As one British newspaper later put it, "Breaking into Fort Knox would have been an easier assignment than photographing the treasure of Tutankhamun."

The 1922 unearthing of the boy pharaoh's tomb had coincided with a growing sense of nationalism in Egypt and a heightened determination to break free from foreign control of its institutions. Several weeks before the discovery, the Antiquities Service had announced it was ending its long-standing practice of allowing an equal division of finds between foreign excavation teams and the Egyptian government. The Service would now claim all the antiquities found during a dig and then would decide which items would be handed over to those who discovered them.

In granting Howard Carter the concession for his excavation, the Service had stipulated that if any intact tomb were discovered, Egypt would retain everything found there. If the tomb had already been looted by vandals, Egypt would keep the objects considered the most valuable and divide the rest. After Carter unearthed Tutankhamun's resting place, the Antiquities Service duly claimed all its contents for the state, much to the explorer's outrage. His protests and subsequent lawsuits against the Egyptian government went nowhere.

Although a number of the Tutankhamun items were eventually put on display at the Egyptian Museum, curators there remained extremely protective of them. At the time Rainbird appealed for Desroches-Noblecourt's help, none of the treasures had yet been allowed to leave the country.* Direct access to them was extremely limited.

After Rainbird agreed to build a photo studio at his own expense inside the museum, Okasha, with considerable difficulty, secured permission for Kenett to photograph about a hundred of the collection's more than one thousand artifacts. For the photographer, it was a nightmarish experience from beginning to end.

To start with, the museum demanded that three senior museum officials, including its director, along with an army officer and armed guard, be present to oversee the removal of each item from its case to be photographed. During the actual photography, Kenett was under nonstop surveillance from the officer, guard, and main conservator of the collection.

"The obstacles were often unexpected—and then repeated," Desroches-Noblecourt said, recalling that she was frequently summoned to the museum to calm Kenett's "impatience and fury." At one point, he was accused of damaging an item but was able to prove his innocence by showing museum officials early black-and-white photos of the artifact, taken at the time of Carter's discovery, that revealed the damage had already been done.

When Kenett was finally finished (not a moment too soon, in his opinion), Rainbird took his negatives to Italy to be printed. The result was extraordinary, according to Desroches-Noblecourt, who described

* It wasn't until late 1961 that, at Okasha's urging, thirty-four small artifacts from the tomb were sent to the United States to help stir up interest in the Nubian campaign. Museum officials were not happy about the tour.

Kenett's richly colored photos as "remarkably executed and absolutely magnificent."

Needing someone to write the text for the book he had in mind, Rainbird pursued Desroches-Noblecourt for weeks, both in France and in Egypt, determined to persuade her to accept the assignment. She had no time, she repeatedly told him—she couldn't possibly combine writing a book with the myriad other things she had to do.

Even if she were tempted, she knew that working on the book would pose an almost impossible challenge. She would have to describe Tutankhamun's life as well as the treasures found in his tomb, but other than the fact he was a pharaoh, almost nothing was known about him. The irony was obvious: Thanks to the finding of his burial chamber, Tutankhamun had become the world's most famous embodiment of ancient Egypt, but in reality he was a mysterious, shadowy figure who, as it turned out, was really just a minor footnote in pharaonic history. There was no documentary evidence of where he was born, who his parents were, or where and how he died. According to examinations of his mummy, he was in his late teens at the time of his death, but there were few clues anywhere, including in his burial vault, that would help shed light on his personality or short-lived reign. "The objects placed in his tomb did little more than evoke in general terms the impersonal and purely theoretical existence of a king," one historian wrote. "Everything of a personal nature had been removed."

But Rainbird was persistent, and Desroches-Noblecourt began to weaken. She had already demonstrated a penchant for taking on seemingly impossible challenges when she launched the fight to save the Nubian temples. But what appealed to her most about the book was that it would give her a chance to write about a period and ruler for which she had a particular passion: the tumultuous final years of the Eighteenth Dynasty and the man who was one of Tutankhamun's immediate predecessors as pharaoh. He was Amenhotep IV, also known as Akhenaten—one of the most fascinating and controversial figures to occupy the kingship in the entire history of ancient Egypt. While many Egyptologists regarded him as a heretic and dictator, Desroches-Noblecourt thought of him as one of the most interesting, even attractive, personalities among the pharaohs. Perhaps that was because, like Desroches-Noblecourt, he was a renegade.

Akhenaten, who came to the throne around 1350 B.C., was known for his attempts to overturn many of the basic religious traditions that had governed Egypt for more than a thousand years. Specifically, he rejected the existence of the many gods worshipped by his countrymen and insisted that there was only one god—a form of the Egyptian sun god Ra, whom he called the Aten, meaning the disk of the sun. Akhenaten's father, Amenhotep III, had already begun the process of elevating the sun god. But under Akhenaten, the shift became a full-blown revolutionary movement, and its impact was staggering. As one historian put it, "For the first time in recorded history, an individual took a step toward monotheism."

As part of his effort to repudiate old religious rituals and traditions, Akhenaten founded a new Egyptian capital, which he called Amarna, in the desert above the eastern bank of the Nile. From there he sent teams of workers throughout the country to deface and destroy images of Amun, the ruler of the gods, as well as the dozens of other deities revered by Egyptians. His aim was to demolish not only the physical representation of the various gods and goddesses but also the power of the priests who controlled their temples.

Akhenaten's revolutionary ways extended to art as well as religion. Prior to his reign, pharaohs, their queens, and other prominent individuals were depicted in paintings and sculpture in an idealized form. Under Akhenaten, however, sculptors adopted a far different style, especially in depictions of the king, elongating his head and limbs and distorting his face, giving him eyes like slits, a long nose, and an exaggeratedly pointed chin. Some depictions of Queen Nefertiti, Akhenaten's favorite wife, however, were more realistic. A prime example is the famous brightly colored limestone bust of the queen, which depicts her as an elegant beauty who would have been at home on the cover of a modern fashion magazine, with her swanlike neck, high cheekbones, slender nose, red lips, and enigmatic smile. Although little is known about Nefertiti, the bust, once it was discovered in 1912, established her as one of the most famous figures in ancient Egyptian history. The sculpture itself is arguably the best-known Egyptian artifact other than the funeral mask of Tutankhamun.

Yet as transformative as Akhenaten's dramatic changes to Egyptian religion and art were, they did not long survive him. After his death, the priests serving the various gods and goddesses regained control and the deities and traditional religious practices began to be restored, notably under Tutankhamun, who was pressured to go back to the old ways. Less than a decade after he became pharaoh, the boy king died too.

Some fifteen years later, the Eighteenth Dynasty ended when Horemheb, a former chief of the Egyptian army, rebelled against the current ruling family in what is thought to be the first military coup in history. As his successor, Horemheb named another military officer, who became Rameses I, the first ruler of the Nineteenth Dynasty. The dynasty's third pharaoh was Rameses II.

One of the first missions of the new dynasty's pharaohs was to wipe out every trace of Akhenaten and his short-lived successors, among them Tutankhamun. Amarna's royal buildings and temples were torn down, and statues and other images of Akhenaten and family members who followed him on the throne were destroyed. With the restoration of orthodoxy, wrote Toby Wilkinson, "he and all his associates had been expunged from history as if they had never existed."

From her research and writing, however, Desroches-Noblecourt developed a far more sympathetic view of Akhenaten than those held by his pharaonic successors or, for that matter, by most Egyptologists. It didn't bother her that many of her colleagues vehemently disagreed with her iconoclastic stance regarding this question—or any other.

According to Guillemette Andreu-Lanoë, Desroches-Noblecourt was sometimes faulted by her peers for "trusting her instinct too much and not sufficiently demonstrating the merits of her ideas." Desroches-Noblecourt fiercely rejected such censure and urged her students at the École du Louvre not to "be afraid to take a stand when it comes to honestly substantiated suggestions. Do not fear criticism from 'dear colleagues.' . . . Feel free to disturb comfortable positions."

Explaining her view of Akhenaten, she told an interviewer, "They speak of heresy or schism, but it really wasn't that. He was a reformer. What he tried to do was to make the Egyptian religion evolve by simplifying it. Rather than speaking of gods in the plural, Akhenaten understood that all those wonderful animal-headed beings were manifestations of a single god. They are all projections of the same creator; they are in the sun, the vital force." She went on, "The experience ended badly, but that's no reason to say he was wrong. There are not thirty-six gods, and if God exists, he is not our friend with whom we shake hands every day. That was Akhenaten's message. And he was right."

When Desroches-Noblecourt finally gave in to Rainbird's pressure to write the Tutankhamun book, working on it during her frequent trips between Paris and Cairo for the Nubia campaign, she described in detail the history of Akhenaten's reign. In doing so, she brought to vivid life the revolutionary-minded monarch, his beautiful consort, and the rest of his court, along with his young royal relative, Tutankhamun, who would himself become pharaoh before he entered his teenage years.

Based on her research, Desroches-Noblecourt advanced several speculations about Tutankhamun, too, that didn't correspond with the theories of other Egyptologists. Most of her colleagues, for example, believed that Tutankhamun was Akhenaten's son, while she suggested that the two might be brothers—the offspring of Amenhotep III and his wife, Queen Tiye. Desroches-Noblecourt's "theories on Amarna and the post-Amarna period, some of them daring, helped to lift the veil that hid the person and the reign of Tutankhamun," said Christian Leblanc, a noted French Egyptologist who had been a student of Desroches-Noblecourt and later worked closely with her. "They also brought to light the significance of this young pharaoh's treasure."

When her book, illustrated with Frederick Kenett's photographs and entitled *Tutankhamen: Life and Death of a Pharaoh*, was published in 1963, it caused an immediate international sensation. "Like the treasure, the book is gorgeous, colorful, positively lush," enthused the Baltimore *Sun.* "Perusing it, modern man feels as he does in the presence of the Tutankhamun display in the museum in Cairo—small, poor, unable to comprehend the lavishness of a bygone era of splendor."

Translated into twenty-two languages, the book was a bestseller in virtually every country in which it appeared. In the United States, the October 1963 issue of *National Geographic* displayed many of its stunning color photos, including Tutankhamun's golden funeral mask, along with a long article by Desroches-Noblecourt. The book was also an alternate Book of the Month Club selection.

Many Americans, of course, had heard about Tutankhamun and his antiquities, but most had never seen photos of them, and nobody until then had viewed any in color. The effect of Kenett's photos was mesmerizing, as attested by dozens of U.S. newspaper and magazine reviews of the book. "These treasures blaze with magnificent color and richness of detail, looking even more breathtaking than the originals," said one review. Another proclaimed, "This is a magnificent book in all respects, and you should not miss it." Referring to Desroches-Noblecourt's text, yet another declared, "An Egyptologist of the first rank, she combines a wealth of personal knowledge, observations and experience with a skill in writing and a sense of excitement that makes her story come alive."

Among the readers on whom the book had a major impact was a six-year-old boy from Britain named Toby Wilkinson, who, as an adult, recalled picking it up and poring through it on a stair landing at his home. It was, Wilkinson said, "my first introduction to the exotic world of ancient Egypt." He sat there, "marveling at the jewels, the gold, the strange names of kings and gods"—all of which "planted a seed in my mind that was to grow and flourish in later years." Thanks in part to its influence, Wilkinson went on to get a degree in Egyptology at Cambridge and is now regarded as one of Britain's leading authorities on ancient Egypt.

Another reader dazzled by the book was Charles de Gaulle. In a handwritten note to Desroches-Noblecourt, the French president declared, "Your book is filled with knowledge, but also color, interest, and humanity. Thanks to you, Tutankhamen's extraordinary reappearance seems more gripping and moving than ever. Allow me to extend my strongest and most grateful compliments."

According to the Dutch historian Kees van der Spek, the 1963 publication of Desroches-Noblecourt and Kenett's volume marked the rebirth of public interest in Tutankhamun—a fascination that underpinned the astonishing success of the worldwide museum exhibitions of his treasures that followed in the late 1960s and 1970s and that continues to this day.

BY 1965, ALTHOUGH FRANCE and Egypt had not yet reestablished diplomatic relations after the Suez debacle, the unofficial relationship between the two governments had warmed up considerably, in large part because of France's enthusiastic support of the Nubia campaign. In a gesture of thanks, Egyptian president Nasser took an extraordinary step, authorizing the first-ever major exhibition of Tutankhamun's treasures outside his country. It would be staged in early 1967 at Paris's Petit Palais and would be arranged and curated by Desroches-Noblecourt.

Once the initial excitement of acquiring the exhibition had abated, she was faced with the challenge of negotiating with Egyptian Museum authorities about which antiquities they would agree to send to Paris. Desroches-Noblecourt had been on the sidelines during the initial dealings between George Rainbird and the museum about the items to be photographed by Frederick Kenett. Now that she was directly involved, it was clear that she would encounter even more recalcitrance than the publisher had. It was bad enough, in the authorities' eyes, to allow these precious artifacts to be photographed by foreigners; it was far worse to contemplate the thought of their going abroad.

Under the terms of Nasser's offer, Desroches-Noblecourt would be allowed to choose forty-five artifacts from the collection. But virtually every one she proposed, she later wrote, "was the subject of bitter discussion on the part of museum officials." Various reasons were offered for why they could not leave the museum. Some were said to be too valuable; others were too fragile and could not withstand the journey.

Still others would be misunderstood by the museumgoers who would view them and thus put Tutankhamun and ancient Egypt in a bad light. Among the latter was a walking stick, the lower part of which was adorned with images of two men—an Asian and an African, who were obviously captured prisoners—chained together.

As Desroches-Noblecourt would learn, opposition to permitting the treasures to leave the country extended far beyond the confines of the museum. With nationalist sentiment still strong in Egypt, attacks appeared in the press about the exhibition, with the Egyptian culture ministry and Sarwat Okasha bearing the brunt of the criticism. Some newspaper stories went so far as to suggest that Okasha was planning to sell the artifacts to Western museums and art dealers once he got them out of Egypt.

The haggling between Desroches-Noblecourt and museum officials continued for almost a year. She told them she was interested in items that would allow her to tell the story of Tutankhamun and his times, making it accessible to the general public but at the same time ensuring it was based on extensive scholarship and study. "I wanted to evoke the historical context in which the prince had been brought up," she said, "his crowning, the splendor of his life in the palace, his death, the preparation for his eternity, and the resurrection of a young pharaoh who was barely known."

Finally, an agreement on the items was reached, signed, and countersigned by both governments, with the French acceding to an Egyptian request to send art restorers from the Louvre to work with Egyptian restorers in inspecting the chosen artifacts and preparing them for their journey to Paris. The restorers' work was finished by July 1966, and the packing of the items was scheduled for October. It appeared that everything was on track for the exhibition's gala opening in February 1967.

When Desroches-Noblecourt arrived with the packers, however, she discovered that things were not proceeding as smoothly as she'd hoped. Earlier in the year, Sarwat Okasha had resigned from his post as cultural minister after a dispute with Nasser and was appointed president of the National Bank of Egypt. By the time Desroches-Noblecourt appeared in Cairo, he had been reinstated in his former post. Greeting her with a solemn expression, he handed her a report from the British Museum's head of conservation, who had been in Cairo that summer and, unbeknownst to Desroches-Noblecourt, had been asked to inspect the items chosen for the Paris exhibition. He had told museum officials that five of the treasures were too fragile to travel. Among them were a life-size statue of Tutankhamun, coated with black bitumen and adorned with gold ornaments; a large gilded bed in the shape of a cow; and a statuette of the boy pharaoh balanced on a papyrus basket, aiming with a harpoon at an invisible target in the water.

"Choose what you want from the other items in the collection," Okasha told Desroches-Noblecourt. "I can't oppose the findings of this man." He made clear that Egyptian authorities, who had recruited the British specialist the year before to advise on how to reinforce and strengthen the sandstone blocks of Abu Simbel before they were cut, greatly valued his expertise and were not inclined to question his warning.

Desroches-Noblecourt, for her part, didn't believe for a minute that the items the British Museum man singled out were too delicate to travel. Rather, it was his museum getting back at the Louvre for having been awarded the first major Tutankhamun exhibition. "The English weren't pleased," she said. "They had discovered the treasure in 1922 and thought it was a preserve for the sons of Albion. And now a Frenchwoman had the temerity to exhibit it in her country. But they had forgotten that England had refused to help save the Nubian temples."

Throughout their histories, there never had been any love lost between the Louvre and the British Museum, especially when it came to Egyptian artifacts. Their rivalry extended back almost two centuries, to Britain's snatching the Rosetta Stone away from the French in 1798 and installing it in its national museum. As the current chief curators of Egyptian antiquities for their respective institutions, Desroches-Noblecourt and her British counterpart, Iorwerth Eiddon Stephen Edwards, had often found themselves in a contentious relationship.

One of the most highly respected Egyptologists in Britain, the fifty-seven-year-old Edwards had earned a first-class degree in Oriental languages from Cambridge in 1933 and gone to work soon afterward as an assistant curator in the British Museum's Egyptian department. During World War II, he had served as a military intelligence officer at the British embassy in Cairo. After the conflict, he returned to the museum and became chief curator in the Egyptian department in 1955.

Edwards's service in the British army in Cairo undoubtedly influenced his strong support of his country's military incursion into Egypt during the 1956 Suez crisis. It was he who had snapped at Desroches-Noblecourt when she asked him for his assistance in the Nubian campaign: "No, you won't get anything from me!"

Five years later, they clashed again when her book on Tutankhamun was published. Amid widespread praise for the book, *The Sunday Times* of London printed two critical articles about it, one following the other by a week. Both were anonymous. While the writer—or writers—approved of the photos, they had nits to pick with several of Desroches-Noblecourt's conclusions about Tutankhamun and his life, including her theory that he and Akhenaten might have been brothers rather than father and son. The articles claimed her suppositions were clearly errors, adding that she provided no evidence to back them up.

Desroches-Noblecourt was convinced that Edwards had written the pieces. She was particularly disappointed and angry at the criticism because her theories, she later wrote, were based on her "meticulous—and extremely careful—study of the few historical records that have come to our knowledge."

She decided to write Edwards a letter asking him if he had any idea who could have written the articles. He could not be a gentleman, she wrote, because a gentleman would have attached his name to them. He also couldn't be an Egyptologist because if he "had approached the problem seriously and really studied the sources," he would have seen that what she posited might in fact be true. After a long silence, Edwards finally wrote back. It was, Desroches-Noblecourt said, "a somewhat confused" missive in which, while he did not own up to being the author, he said he didn't know why she was so upset because the criticisms were obviously meant as "banderillas"—little darts meant to sting but do no real harm.

When she learned of the maneuver to deny the Louvre the five items for the Tutankhamun exhibition, she was sure that Edwards had been involved in it. She appealed the decision, declaring that the artifacts were essential elements for the display she had planned. "I argued, I quibbled, I pleaded," she recalled. Finally, museum officials gave in on two of them, restoring the life-size statue and the cow-shaped bed. But the three others, including the exquisite statuette of the little harpooner, were still off-limits.

Conceding defeat, Desroches-Noblecourt chose replacements. At that point, the packing experts from Paris, donning white gloves, carefully prepared the forty-five items for travel. Screws, rather than nails, were used to close the covers of the crates carrying the smaller items, to avoid the shocks that a hammer or mallet would have caused. They were dispatched to Paris aboard French air force planes, while a sixteen-foot-tall quartzite statue of Tutankhamun, along with other large and heavy antiquities, were sent by ship to Marseille. There they were placed in trucks and accompanied by armed guards to Paris. The famous gold funerary mask of the pharaoh was flown by Air France to the French capital, where it was greeted by a contingent of the Republican Guard, cultural minister André Malraux, the Egyptian ambassador to France, the French foreign minister, and legions of television cameras.

The treasures were transported to a huge metal vault at the Petit Palais, where they were unpacked and inspected. Meanwhile, all the craftsmen's shops at the Louvre had been mobilized to prepare the rooms in the exhibition hall where the items would be displayed. The hall's floor was reinforced to support the extra weight of the quartzite statue and other large items, while the walls of the rooms were sheathed in flame-retardant fabric.

In her carefully planned staging of the exhibit's rooms, Desroches-Noblecourt drew on her work over the previous thirty years to interpret the meaning of the wall paintings and objects found in royal tombs. Unlike many Egyptologists, who believed that the portrayals of everyday life reflected the dead royals' earthly existence that they wanted to continue in the afterlife, Desroches-Noblecourt believed they should

CHRISTIANE DESROCHES-NOBLECOURT EXAMINES TUTANKHAMUN'S GOLD MASK DURING THE UNCRATING OF ITEMS FOR THE 1967 LOUVRE EXHIBITION

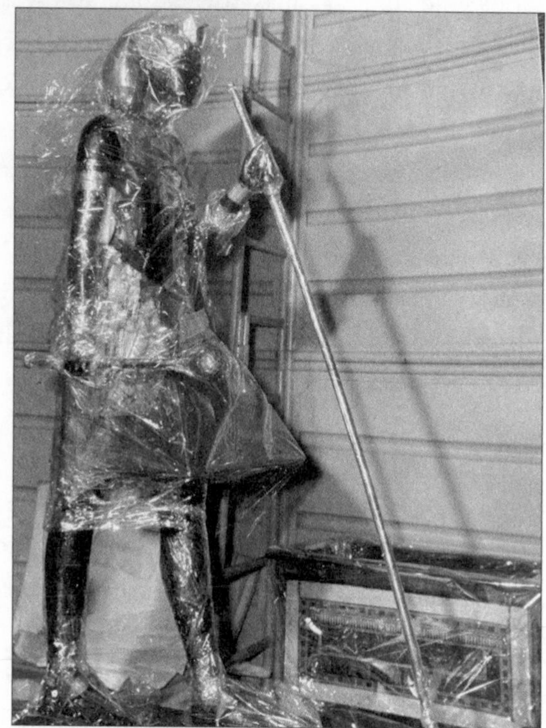

SHRINK-WRAPPED STATUE OF TUTANKHAMUN EN ROUTE TO THE 1967 PARIS EXHIBITION

be viewed as symbolic images of the challenges facing the deceased during their journeys through the underworld.

For example, as she saw it, the clumps of papyrus reeds often found in the tombs evoked the primeval marshland in which the deceased's spirit began its metamorphosis from death to new life. A wall painting showing the hunting of ducks and other wild fowl signified the spirit's attempt to destroy the demons trying to block his path to the hereafter, while the portrayal of harvesting grain and picking grapes was meant to represent the offering of bread and wine to Osiris, the god of death and resurrection.

ACCOMPANIED BY A BLAZE of publicity, the "exhibition of the century," as the Tutankhamun show was dubbed, opened at the Petit Palais on February 17, 1967. At a gala reception the night before, several hundred notable guests, including Charles de Gaulle and his wife, were given a sneak peek at the treasures.

CHRISTIANE DESROCHES-NOBLECOURT, ANDRÉ MALRAUX, AND SARWAT OKASHA AT THE 1967 LOUVRE EXHIBITION

The day before the reception, André Malraux asked Desroches-Noblecourt to guide the de Gaulles through the exhibit. Taken aback, she tried to beg off, thinking but not saying that Malraux, with his erudition and flowery rhetoric, would be a far better escort for the French president and his wife. She did make the point, though, that the twenty minutes allotted for the presidential tour was not nearly enough time to cover the exhibit's highlights. In response, Malraux asked her, "Do you like to dance?" Puzzled by the question, she said, "Yes." "In that case," the cultural minister said, "you know what it's like to be swept up in the arms of a good guide. Just let yourself go. I won't tell you more."

He was right, she later wrote. Her anxiety that night was akin to the nervousness she had felt more than thirty years earlier when, as a student at the École du Louvre, she'd been asked to deliver a public lecture on Tutankhamun and his treasures. Minutes into the talk, her passion for the subject had overridden her fear.

Her experience at the Petit Palais was the same. From the start, de Gaulle seemed caught up in her story of the boy king and the meaning of the various magnificent antiquities found in his tomb. At the beginning of the tour, she explained to him and his wife how the Egyptians used material images to explain the spiritual and abstract. Paying close attention, he "seemed interested in everything concerning pharaonic civilization, but he was particularly interested in Egyptian religion," Desroches-Noblecourt recalled. He peppered her with so many questions that after twenty minutes, they were still in the second room of the exhibit. When she told him that her twenty-minute allotment was up, de Gaulle turned to an aide standing behind him and said he would stay for another hour and a half.

In the next room, whose blue satin walls were the color of lapis lazuli, a popular semiprecious stone used in royal Egyptian jewelry, the objects on display, which dealt with Tutankhamun's short reign, prompted another torrent of questions from de Gaulle. He wanted to know a variety of details about a pharaoh's coronation and the way he conducted war: Did he go into battle himself, or did he send his generals in his stead? Desroches-Noblecourt's response was swift: "Like you, general, he was at the head of his troops."

In the dimly lit Salon Royale, swathed in midnight-blue satin to evoke Tutankhamun's death, a variety of gold objects glowed in the semidarkness: a gilded armchair trimmed with ebony and ivory, meant to carry the pharaoh on his post-death journey, along with royal scepters, an array of earrings and necklaces, and other glittering objects. But de Gaulle was most struck by a life-size statue of the king, wearing a wig cover, loincloth, and gold sandals, his skin coated with black bitumen to show that he had passed into a world without light. De Gaulle studied the statue for more than a minute, then turned to Desroches-Noblecourt and remarked, "He is truly the invisible man." She later wrote, "That was exactly what I wanted to evoke."

Moving on to the next chamber, covered in green velvet and featuring a thicket of papyrus, meant to call to mind the primordial swamp that Tutankhamun's spirit was navigating, de Gaulle was fascinated by a statuette of the pharaoh as a small naked child, also coal-black, making his way through this marshy expanse. Beside it Desroches-Noblecourt had placed a wooden rattle, adorned with gold and ivory, with which the pharaoh could beat off the wild ducks hidden behind the papyrus thicket, representing the demons attempting to stop him from leaving the purgatory of the marsh.

The exhibit's final room, swathed in coral to suggest the rising sun, contained the pièce de résistance of the treasures—Tutankhamun's magnificent funeral mask, with its blaze of gold, lapis lazuli, carnelian, and turquoise. But Desroches-Noblecourt was pleased to see that de Gaulle seemed more interested in a translucent alabaster goblet in the shape of a lotus. A small spotlight overhead shone down on the goblet to make it appear phosphorescent. She explained that the lotus, which closes its petals at dusk and opens them again at dawn, was an important Egyptian symbol for the daily rebirth of the sun after its nightly journey to the netherworld. Just like the sun, the pharaoh's spirit was proceeding from death to life.

She added that there was little difference between this Egyptian concept and the Christian Eucharist, in which the priest takes from a chalice a circular host, looking like the sun and representing Christ's body and the resurrection, and holds it high. This rite, she said, had its roots in ancient Egypt. In fact, she added, Christianity owed much more to ancient Egyptian traditions than to Hebrew practices.

De Gaulle nodded enthusiastically and said he agreed with her. But as she further explained her theory, Yvonne de Gaulle, a devout Catholic, expressed outrage at what she considered a heretical thought. According to Desroches-Noblecourt, the French president turned to his wife and "spoke, with great consideration, these words that I will always remember, 'You will have to get used to it, *ma bonne amie*!'"

Desroches-Noblecourt was later told that de Gaulle had been so taken with the exhibit and what he had learned there that for months afterward, he was still making comments to members of his cabinet about it. The French seemed as fascinated by the show as their president. For the four months of its stay in Paris, the entire city, according to *Time* magazine, was "infected with Pharaonic fever." On the day the exhibition opened, hundreds of people milled outside the entrance to the Petit Palais, pressing against its plate glass doors. Jacques Jaujard, André Malraux's deputy, asked the military governor of Paris to

A MASSIVE CROWD GATHERS OUTSIDE THE PETIT PALAIS ON THE LOUVRE EXHIBITION'S OPENING DAY, 1967

assign a contingent of Republican Guards to the museum to keep the throngs of excited visitors under control.

The following days and weeks saw mammoth crowds waiting for hours in long serpentine lines that stretched for several blocks. By the time the exhibition left, more than 1.25 million museumgoers had viewed it, making it the most popular exhibition in the Louvre's history. VIP visitors like Konrad Adenauer, the ninety-one-year-old former chancellor of West Germany, couldn't be squeezed in for private tours until late at night.

Tutankhamun, meanwhile, was the talk of the town. French newspapers and magazines were filled with articles featuring headlines like THE SHORT AND PATHETIC LIFE OF A PERSECUTED MONARCH and WAS KING TUT REALLY A WOMAN? An editorial cartoon in the magazine *L'Express* depicted de Gaulle as a pharaoh, and Alexandre, Paris's top hair stylist, offered Egyptian coiffures and makeup that, according to *Time*, featured "blue or black lines outlining lips and nostrils, plus eyeliner extending halfway round to a lady's ears."

Desroches-Noblecourt was particularly pleased that in the crush of publicity surrounding the exhibition, she was able to call attention to her old mentor Bernard Bruyère, the head of the Deir-el-Medina dig, whose role in the discovery of Tutankhamun's tomb had been almost completely forgotten. She invited the eighty-seven-year-old Bruyère to the gala opening and arranged several press interviews in which he explained how he had persuaded a disconsolate Howard Carter not to give up on his search for Tutankhamun's burial place and to keep digging in the area where the tomb was eventually found.

The overwhelming response to the Paris exhibition set off an international frenzy. Every country and major museum, it seemed, wanted to be the next to host the show. No one, however, was more determined to get it than Eiddon Edwards, who had been trying for years, to no avail, to persuade Egyptian authorities that since an English archaeologist had discovered the tomb, the British Museum should be allowed to exhibit its treasures first.

As it happened, he and his museum were chosen to be the second to display them, but only after they ended their opposition to providing aid for the Nubia campaign. Following the rescue of Abu Simbel in the late 1960s, one major rescue project remained—the salvage of the temple complex at Philae. The British Museum pledged that if it were awarded the exhibition, it would give the revenue from admission fees to the campaign to save Philae, and its request was granted.

Edwards later reported that he had had a change of heart about Egypt and its right to keep and preserve its archaeological antiquities. "I used to think at one time that perhaps we had a special claim to have this exhibition, because the tomb had been discovered by a British archaeologist, but [an Egyptian friend] disillusioned me," Edwards remarked. "He said that was not the way the average Egyptian viewed it. The British had been allowed to excavate in what had always been one of the richest sites in Egypt. They had made this marvelous discovery thanks to the generosity of the Egyptians in allowing them to excavate there, a sufficient reward in itself."

For Edwards, the Tutankhamun exhibition, to be mounted in 1972 in honor of the fiftieth anniversary of Howard Carter's discovery of the tomb, was the culmination of his career. In his obsession to make it as successful as the one in Paris—or more so—he "put his staff and the resources of his department under great strain," according to an associate. Already under tremendous stress, he came close to a breaking point not long before the exhibition was to open when the Egyptian Museum denied him the loan of one object on which he had his heart set.

Desroches-Noblecourt learned about the incident when Denis Hamilton, the editor in chief and chairman of *The Times* and *The Sunday Times* of London, paid her a call at the Louvre. Hamilton was also a member of the British Museum's board of trustees, he told her, and in that role, he had a great favor to ask. But, he added, "I would understand very well if your answer was no." He explained that Edwards was particularly anxious to obtain the loan of a statuette of Tutankhamun standing on a papyrus basket and aiming a harpoon at an invisible target. At that moment, Desroches-Noblecourt knew all too well why he was there.

The Egyptian authorities had rejected the request, noting that the object in question had been turned down for the Paris exhibition because of the objection of one of the British Museum's top conservators. "We can't let him go to London," the authorities said, "unless you speak directly to Mrs. Desroches-Noblecourt and get her permission."

With a sigh, Hamilton told her, "That is why I am here, although I realize I have come with a noose around my neck." Desroches-Noblecourt responded with a laugh. She wanted him to know, she said, that despite the objection that had been lodged by the British Museum, the statuette would have been sturdy enough to survive the Paris climate with no ill effect, and it would be strong enough to "face the damp mists of London without any problem." She promised to write to officials at the Cairo Museum to tell them that "although I was shocked at the time by the way in which the statue was removed from our original list, I will not hold it against them if they send it to England."

She was true to her word, and the little harpooner was one of fifty pieces lent to the British Museum. The London exhibition, opened by Queen Elizabeth II on March 29, 1972, was so popular that its stay was extended until December, attracting more than 1.6 million visitors and raising almost a million pounds for the salvage of the Philae temples. Eiddon Edwards, meanwhile, was named to the Order of Saint Michael and Saint George, a commendation by the British monarch for extraordinary service to foreign affairs—in his case, to the Anglo-Egyptian relationship, which was much improved thanks to the success of the exhibition and the substantial donation for the rescue of Philae.

IN THE REST OF the world, too, Tutmania showed no signs of slowing down. According to Thomas Hoving, "no exhibition of works of art has been more popular in history." The Soviet Union was awarded the third display of the treasures, and the United States was determined to be next. During a visit to Cairo, President Richard Nixon, who was anxious to improve America's relations with Egypt as well as its strategic position in the Middle East, suggested to Egyptian president Anwar Sadat that a Tutankhamun tour in America would be of great benefit to their countries' relationship. Sadat agreed.

On November 17, 1976, a six-city U.S. tour opened at Washington's National Gallery, with lines wrapped around the building. As was true of its earlier venues, it was an immediate sensation there, as it would be in Chicago, New Orleans, Seattle, Los Angeles, and New York. By the 1970s, the Tutankhamun exhibition had unquestionably established itself, the writer Meredith Hindley remarked, as "a cultural juggernaut."

For the next three years, Americans went crazy over Tut. Egyptian designs became prominent in jewelry, clothing, furniture, art, and architecture. "King Tut," a satirical song by the comedian Steve Martin about the commercial success of the boy pharaoh's tour, was a huge hit on *Saturday Night Live,* sold more than a million copies, and was one of the top U.S. pop singles of 1978.

The biggest museum blockbuster ever in the United States, *Treasures of Tutankhamun* sold out tickets and smashed attendance records in every city in which it appeared. It drew people from all ages and backgrounds, many of whom had never spent much time in a museum before but all of whom were willing to stand in line for hours, no matter how cold, rainy, snowy, or hot the weather.

In Chicago, the Field Museum raised a flag bearing an image of Tut's funeral mask over North Shore Drive each day to signal the availability of tickets during the exhibition's run there. When the flag was lowered to half-staff, which usually occurred well before noon, it meant all the tickets for that day were gone. As the *Chicago Tribune* saw it, the exhibition was "a grand slam homer for culture."

There was no question about the truth of that statement. As a result of Tutankhamun, the museum world in the United States and elsewhere had been irrevocably changed. Until the appearance of the treasures, one scholar wrote, most art museums "were as silent and dreary as mausoleums," catering only to the cultural elite. But with the astounding popularity of Tut, "they became as lively as the marketplace and so crowded that special showings had to be scheduled to insure supporting patrons a look at new exhibitions."

Every museum exhibiting the show was flooded with thousands of requests for membership as patrons; in some cases, museums had to limit the number they accepted because they couldn't handle all the applications. Having attracted so many new subscribers, they realized they had to continue to cater to this broader audience and became more proactive in reaching out to their communities in a variety of ways, initiating innovative new exhibits and other public programs, among them more learning opportunities for schoolchildren.

Tutankhamun also proved to be a financial bonanza, earning many millions of dollars in revenue not only for the museums and cities in which they were located but for Egypt as well. Thomas Hoving, who had arranged the U.S. tour, had suggested to Egyptian officials that instead of getting money from admissions fees to the exhibit, they allow the Metropolitan Museum to make reproductions of items from the show, which would then be sold in the museums' gift shops. Egypt would receive all the proceeds from their sale, as well as from sale of the official catalog.

The Egyptians agreed, which turned out to be an extremely wise decision. Sales of the items—ranging from coloring books, posters, tote bags, and postcards to an Hermès scarf with a Tutankhamun motif and a limited-edition Limoges plate featuring the falcon god, Horus—produced more than $9 million for Egypt, which was used to pay for major renovations to the Egyptian Museum.

The boy pharaoh aided Egypt in another way, giving the American public an insight into its people's ancient history and helping to improve its image at a time when negotiations were under way to end the long-standing enmity between Egypt and Israel. Indeed, as hundreds of thousands of Seattle museumgoers flocked to the Tutankhamun exhibition in September 1978, President Jimmy Carter met with Anwar Sadat and Israeli prime minister Menachem Begin to discuss a framework for Middle East peace. On September 17, Egypt and Israel agreed to the Camp David accords, a pair of agreements that ended three decades of war between the two nations and established diplomatic and commercial relations.

THREE MONTHS LATER, *Treasures of Tutankhamun* took up residence in New York City, its final stop on the U.S. tour. The anticipation and excitement of New Yorkers had been building steadily, ever since the Metropolitan Museum first made tickets available in September. To deal with the crush of calls, the Met added extra phone lines and personnel.

The city was just emerging from a severe financial crisis earlier in the decade when it had come perilously close to bankruptcy. In 1975, Mayor Abe Beame and New York's governor, Hugh Carey, had gone to Washington to plead with President Gerald Ford for federal assistance. Ford rejected their appeal, prompting the now famous New York *Daily News* headline FORD TO CITY: DROP DEAD.

Now, as New York was slowly coming back to life, it needed a pick-me-up—and Tutankhamun provided it. Despite heavy rain on the exhibition's opening day, the line of ticket holders stretched twenty-three blocks down Fifth Avenue, from the Met's entrance on Eighty-second Street to Fifty-ninth Street. As popular as the exhibition had been in previous cities, none of them, in the words of one writer, "took Tut to its bosom more dearly than New York."

Stories about New Yorkers' fierce determination to view the exhibition became daily fodder for TV news crews and other local reporters. In its "About New York" column, *The New York Times* featured a woman whose husband began to suffer chest pains as they were about to enter the exhibition. Before accompanying him in an ambulance to the hospital, she made museum officials promise that she could retake her place at the head of the line once his medical condition was stable. "Seeing Tut is the status symbol right now in this city," an unnamed Met official told a reporter. "It's even superseded sex."

According to a survey commissioned by the Met, the exhibition generated more than $110 million in revenue for New York City during its four-month stay there, including money spent by museumgoers on hotels, restaurants, shopping, and transportation. Every store in Manhattan, it seemed, was selling Tut-inspired goods, from jewelry to clothing to housewares. Among the items displayed by the upscale department store Bloomingdale's was a tote bag bearing the iconic I ♥ NY slogan spelled out in hieroglyphics.

By that time, Thomas Hoving no longer headed the museum. "Negotiating 'King Tut'—so full of adventure, challenges, and plain fun—was the high point of my Metropolitan career," he wrote in his memoirs. "Afterwards, slowly and almost imperceptibly, I became more and more bored with the museum." On June 30, 1977, he left the Met.

His tumultuous ten years there had been bookended by two of his biggest successes, both of them involving ancient Egypt—his acquisition of the Temple of Dendur and the Tutankhamun exhibition. Serendipitously, the Sackler Wing containing the temple was unveiled just a month before the King Tut exhibition opened, providing visitors to the pharaoh's treasures a glimpse of the temple from a balcony on the floor above.

Few if any of the visitors were aware that without the efforts of a French woman archaeologist and her campaign to save the Nubian temples, the Met quite likely would never have been graced with either attraction.

CHAPTER 21

"BRINGING THEM BACK TO LIFE"

SEVEN YEARS BEFORE THE TUTANKHAMUN EXHIBITION IN PARIS, a French schoolboy named Christian Leblanc sat down to write a letter to the president of Egypt. In it, he begged Gamal Abdel Nasser not to allow the temples of Nubia to drown. His parents and brothers were impressed with the eleven-year-old's initiative but cautioned him that Nasser probably would never see his appeal and that he should not get his hopes up for a reply.

Several weeks later, Christian received an official-looking envelope from Cairo. Inside was a letter bearing the seal of the office of the Egyptian president, which he triumphantly displayed to his mother and father. It was from the director of Nasser's cabinet, assuring him that the president was indeed working hard, together with UNESCO, to try to prevent the monuments' destruction. "In the end," Christian Leblanc recalled, "my daring had been rewarded."

Leblanc's interest in antiquities had begun several years earlier, when he and some friends began exploring the ruins of a twelfth-century château, one of the many medieval castles and monasteries that dotted the countryside near their village in Seine-et-Marne, east of Paris. When UNESCO announced its appeal to save the Nubian temples, Christian, whose class had just finished studying ancient Egypt, charged into action. He sponsored a fundraising drive at his school, sending the proceeds, along with most of his own savings, to UNESCO, along with a heartfelt letter declaring that the temples must be saved.

A high-ranking UNESCO official named Jan van der Haagen wrote back, saying that he "greatly appreciated the ardor with which you plead the cause of the temples of Nubia," which, he said, was "a precious encouragement to us to tirelessly pursue our task." Van der Haagen's note of thanks prompted the boy to write next to Nasser and then, over the next eight years of the campaign, to several more of its leaders, including Desroches-Noblecourt, Sarwat Okasha, and the Swedish archaeologist Torgny Säve-Söderbergh. Almost all of them wrote back.

By the time the Nubian campaign reached its triumphant conclusion, Leblanc, now in college, was hooked on Egyptology. He was hardly alone. Just as Howard Carter's discovery of Tutankhamun's tomb had sparked an explosion of interest in ancient Egypt in the 1920s, the successful fight to save the temples led by Desroches-Noblecourt, followed by the international tours of Tutankhamun's treasures, prompted a huge upsurge of popularity in archaeology in general and Egyptology in particular. In the 1960s and early 1970s, a flood of students in France signed up for archaeology and related courses at the École du Louvre, the Sorbonne, and other institutions of higher education. For many, Desroches-Noblecourt was their first Egyptology professor.

It had long been the custom for Louvre curators to serve as professors at its school—a role that Desroches-Noblecourt happily accepted for more than forty years. "I was born to be a teacher," she told one interviewer. "I always loved teaching people the history of antique objects and bringing them back to life." By all accounts, she did make ancient Egypt come alive in her classes, much as Étienne Drioton, her own mentor and professor, had done. Of Drioton, she had said that he "could have awakened a dead man and turned any idiot into a scholar." Her students made similarly enthusiastic comments about her.

When Christian Leblanc took Desroches-Noblecourt's Egyptian archaeology course, he was mesmerized by her description of how, late in the pharaonic period, Egyptian priests rescued the mummies of Rameses II and several other kings from destruction by vandals and secreted them in an unmarked tomb for what turned out to be several thousand years. "I was literally under the spell of this amazing epic, which we followed like the episodes of a soap opera," he recalled.

Among the École du Louvre's most popular classes, Desroches-Noblecourt's weekly lectures drew crowds of students and members of the public to the school's cavernous auditorium. According to Guillemette Andreu-Lanoë, Desroches-Noblecourt's analysis and explanation of Egyptian monuments, which she illustrated with color slides, "inspired listeners of all generations, who literally fell in love with what she had to say."

One of them was Anne-Marie Loyrette, a graduate of the prestigious Institut d'Études Politiques de Paris (known familiarly as Sciences Po), who had married a fellow student shortly after completing her studies and promptly had four children. Loyrette and her husband, who went on to co-found one of France's top international law firms, had an elegant, affluent lifestyle, but she wanted more. When she was in her late thirties, her interest in archaeology led her to enroll in Desroches-Noblecourt's class, which so captivated her that she eventually ended up as head of fieldwork for the school and became a close friend of Desroches-Noblecourt and an essential member of her survey team.

Loyrette's oldest son, Henri, was equally mesmerized by Desroches-Noblecourt. The Loyrettes lived directly across the Seine from the Louvre, and their children spent considerable time there when they were growing up. When Henri Loyrette started visiting the museum as a boy in the late 1950s, he found it quiet and stodgy. And then Christiane Desroches-Noblecourt appeared on the scene, with her crusade to save the Nubian temples, her staging of the blockbuster Tutankhamun exhibition, and her standing-room-only archaeology lectures.

The jolt of energy she injected into the Louvre inspired Loyrette to think about a career as a museum curator himself. She was, he said, his model. A scholar of nineteenth-century French art, with a focus on the painter and sculptor Edgar Degas, Loyrette did indeed become a curator and then the director of Paris's Musée d'Orsay. In 2001, he was named head of the Louvre, where he became known for his own determination to shake things up. Of Loyrette, *The New York Times* wrote in 2009: "With major plans for expansion, satellite franchises, and new partnerships that would have been unheard of even a decade ago, he is overseeing the most drastic rethinking of the Louvre's place and purpose in at least 20 years."

TO HER STUDENTS, CHRISTIANE Desroches-Noblecourt preached the importance of survey and excavation work as an essential part of their education, even if they were more interested in becoming a museum curator than a field archaeologist. During her tenure as the Louvre's chief curator of Egyptian antiquities, she instituted fieldwork as one of the courses at the school.

"We must not approach this country with received ideas," she liked to say, "but let it speak to us without acting as its interpreter." It was essential, she told her students, that they have as much firsthand knowledge as possible of Egypt and its people, modern as well as ancient. In particular, they must understand the importance of its geography, especially its all-important river: "The Nile gave the Egyptians everything—culture, landscapes—absolutely everything. To understand the country, you must go to Egypt, stand before the Nile, and observe. Only a landscape such as this could foster a culture like the Egyptian civilization. You don't need anyone to teach you. You can see it for yourself."

Nature was an essential part of life for the Egyptians, then as now, Desroches-Noblecourt believed. "Nature spoke to them. It was all a thing of God: a blossoming flower, a mountain. It wasn't superstition, it was physical. . . . After a lifetime of very scholarly research, I arrived at the conclusion that even though the Egyptians were simple, straightforward people, they were also very intelligent beings who listened to nature and who interpreted and understood it as well or better in their own way than we do." To her students, she said, "To deeply study Egyptian civilization, you have to be very open and try to get as close as possible to the mentality of the Egyptians. The more you try to understand the why of things, the closer you get to them. So you have to question, be sensitive to things, and never, never be negative."

Beginning in the late 1960s, Desroches-Noblecourt led yearly research expeditions to Egypt, choosing some of her most promising students as members of her teams. After several stints in Nubia, the teams shifted their attention to the ancient city of Thebes and the burial grounds and funerary temples located on the west side of the Nile.

Desroches-Noblecourt made it clear that the groups' mission was not only to dig for new finds but also to study and record the inscriptions and other features of monuments that had already been discovered. Thanks in part to her training by Bernard Bruyère, she had always stressed the importance of recording, through photographs and manual copying, every detail of excavated antiquities, many of which had never been fully examined after they were found. With a growing number of antiquities in various stages of physical deterioration, the need was becoming particularly urgent.

During the monthlong missions, several members of her teams searched for ancient graffiti carved in the rocks of the hills in the Valley of the Kings and surrounding areas. Others worked in the ruins of the Ramesseum, the name given by Champollion to Rameses II's enormous funerary temple complex on the west bank of the Nile, not far from the Valley of the Kings. The largest of the many monuments Rameses II erected to honor himself, the Ramesseum, which took twenty years and tens of thousands of workers to build, covered about eleven and a half acres of land.

But while those sites were—and are—rich treasure troves for Egyptologists studying the Eighteenth and Nineteenth dynasties, Desroches-Noblecourt's preferred work site was the Valley of the Queens, the burial ground for many of the wives and other relatives of those dynasties' pharaohs. Called Ta Set Neferu (the Place of Beauty) by the ancient Egyptians, it lies just over the hills from the Valley of the Kings. Unlike its counterpart, however, it had been largely ignored by Western archaeologists, who for more than 150 years had focused their attention on the tombs of the pharaohs, many of them undoubtedly

CHRISTIANE DESROCHES-NOBLECOURT (FAR LEFT) WITH MEMBERS OF HER EXCAVATION TEAM IN EGYPT, INCLUDING ANNE-MARIE LOYRETTE (CENTER) AND MONIQUE NELSON (FAR RIGHT)

hoping to discover riches like those eventually found by Howard Carter in Tutankhamun's tomb.

Princes and princesses from the Eighteenth Dynasty were the first royals to be buried in the Valley of the Queens. While the pharaohs of that dynasty boasted elaborate burial vaults that were extensively adorned with funerary inscriptions and carvings of kings and deities, most of those in Ta Set Neferu lacked such decoration, sometimes making it difficult to identify who had been buried there.

With the advent of the Nineteenth Dynasty, all that changed. The dynasty's early pharaohs—Rameses I, Seti I, and Rameses II—were strong rulers with equally strong wives and mothers, several of whom became close advisers and companions. From Rameses I on, the dynasty's pharaohs made the Valley of the Queens a burial ground for their highest-ranking and most favored women relatives, building multi-chambered tombs whose grandeur approached that of their own burial vaults. During his lengthy reign, Rameses II ordered the construction of at least eight tombs in the valley, including ones for his mother, Queen Tuya; his favorite wife, Nefertari; and four of his daughters, who also became his wives at various times and were crowned queen.

In both royal necropolises, most of the tombs had been plundered before the end of the pharaonic era, losing their mummies and most if not all of their treasures. But those in the Valley of the Queens suffered especially severe damage. When nineteenth-century archaeologists excavated tombs there and found nothing that would interest museums or private collections, they often provided no records of their finds, including the burial places' locations and probable occupants. Once discovered, the tombs lapsed back into obscurity.

At the beginning of the twentieth century, the Italian Egyptologist Ernesto Schiaparelli organized the first scientific expedition in the valley. In 1905, he made one of the greatest archaeological finds of the century: the burial place of Nefertari, which to this day is considered one of the most beautiful tombs in all of ancient Egypt. Nefertari's mummy and most of her funerary treasures vanished several millennia ago, but the thieves could not loot the 5,200 square feet of exquisite paintings and inscriptions that covered the walls, their colors as vibrant as the day the tomb was sealed. "It was unusual that a pharaoh expressed feelings for his wife in her tomb, but in the tomb [of Nefertari], Rameses left a wonderful statement of love to his wife," the historian Natalia Klimczak wrote. "The context of the inscriptions proves that the pharaoh was truly in love with her, and her death broke his heart."

Unfortunately, few later archaeologists followed up on Schiaparelli's work in the valley, continuing to believe that focusing on the kingly necropolis next door was a much more prestigious and potentially fruitful endeavor. Desroches-Noblecourt did not agree. One of her many interests was the remarkably high status and prominent roles of royal women in the Nineteenth Dynasty; in some cases they had helped govern the country. She was intent on conducting a thorough study of their tombs to learn more about them, an investigation that would include determining the identity of their former inhabitants.

She was particularly interested in locating the tomb of Rameses II's formidable mother, Tuya. One of the most important women of the Nineteenth Dynasty, Tuya served as an influential adviser both to her husband, Seti I, and her son, who built several monuments to her, including a small temple near the Ramesseum. The German Egyptologist Karl Lepsius had found Tuya's tomb in 1844, but nothing of value was discovered, and records of its location had been lost.

Yet, as Desroches-Noblecourt knew only too well, finding anything in the Valley of the Queens would be an incredibly daunting task. After so many decades of being treated as an afterthought, it had become a vast garbage heap, engulfed in countless tons of rubble and other detritus. Many of the tombs, with their gaping openings, served as dens for wild animals and were filled almost to the ceiling with rocks, bones, the centuries-old dust called *sebakh,* and shattered fragments of antiquities.

Nonetheless, Desroches-Noblecourt had a hunch where Tuya might be buried. Judging from earlier excavations, it appeared that the valley had been divided into sectors assigned to the different pharaohs and their families. The tombs built during the reigns of Rameses I and Seti I, for example, were grouped on the southern slope of the valley, while the burial vaults of the wives and daughters of Rameses II were found on the northern slope. Desroches-Noblecourt believed that Rameses II would have buried his beloved mother near Nefertari.

During the 1972 expedition, she selected an area that seemed promising. After several days of clearing away tons of trash and rubble, her Egyptian workers discovered what appeared to be a descending staircase. But its stones had been smashed to pieces, and it took her crew the rest of the excavation season to finally reach the bottom. In the course of their backbreaking work, they turned up some tantalizing clues, including a small funerary statuette, called an *ushabti,* meant to represent a servant who would work for the deceased in the afterlife. On the blue enameled figure were written the words "The Royal Mother, Tuya." For the sixty-year-old Desroches-Noblecourt, the discovery was both thrilling and agonizing. It appeared that she had found Tuya's tomb, but she had neither the money nor the time to do more work that season. She would have to wait until the following year to find out what more, if anything, was there.

In 1973, she included her former student Christian Leblanc on her team. Impressed by his diligence and dedication, she had become a mentor to him, as she had done with a sizable number of the latest generation of aspiring Egyptologists, some of whom would become leaders in the field themselves. Thanks to her, Leblanc had served as an intern in the Louvre's Egyptian antiquities department before winning a prize slot on the 1973 expedition. When he arrived in Luxor at the start of the mission's season, she informed him that he would be assisting her in the continued excavation of the tomb that she was sure was Tuya's.

When she and her team began to dig out the first room of the tomb, they discovered that the debris inside was ceiling-high. Frustrated, Desroches-Noblecourt wondered if time would once again run out before she could discover whether in fact her hunch was right.

Toward the end of the mission, the clearing operation finally began yielding more intriguing hints that she was on the right track. Amid the rubbish were dozens more *ushabti*, as well as vases and alabaster containers, fragments of toiletries, and pieces of pink granite that Desroches-Noblecourt concluded were from Tuya's shattered sarcophagus. Even more important was the discovery of a wine jar fragment bearing the number 22, which she took to mean the date of the last wine harvest before Tuya died. In other words, the dowager queen's death had occurred in the twenty-second year of Rameses II's reign.

But, to Desroches-Noblecourt's dismay, nothing else of note turned up in the following days. During the last week of the expedition, she had to make a brief trip to Cairo and deputized Leblanc to preside over the dig in her absence. Four days before the expedition was to end, an Egyptian worker unearthed a rounded object from the detritus at the foot of a wall in a corner of the anteroom. He informed Leblanc, who rushed to the spot. After careful cleaning of the discovery, he found before him an alabaster bust, "a little masterpiece of exquisite finesse," still bearing traces of lapis lazuli inlays. It was Tuya herself—the only well-preserved likeness of the queen to be discovered to this day.

The fragment—meant to be the cap of a canopic vase, which held the viscera of the mummified queen—depicted, as Desroches-Noblecourt described it, "a figure of almost mischievous charm, her

BUST OF QUEEN TUYA, DISCOVERED BY CHRISTIANE DESROCHES-NOBLECOURT'S EXCAVATION TEAM IN 1974 AND NOW IN THE LUXOR MUSEUM

mouth lifted in a slight smile, with a small but strong chin." The most precious treasure recovered from Tuya's tomb, the bust is now displayed at the Luxor Museum.

ALTHOUGH DESROCHES-NOBLECOURT OCCASIONALLY ADDED new faces to her research team, at its core were several young professionals who worked with her year after year. One was Christian Leblanc, who eventually became the mission's deputy leader. Another—Guy Lecuyot, also a former student of hers—credited her for kick-starting his career as an Egyptologist. "She knew how to recognize each person's qualities and when necessary, push and support them so that they could persevere in the path they had chosen," Lecuyot recalled. When he was called up for a year of service in the French army, she arranged for him to fulfill that duty by working at CEDAE as a technical adviser seconded from the army. Like Leblanc, Lecuyot worked with Desroches-Noblecourt for more than a decade, first at the Ramesseum and then in the Valley of the Queens, while continuing his studies. He later distinguished himself with his research and excavation work in Saqqara and other sites in Egypt, as well as in the Near East and Central Asia.

After collaborating for so long, those on the team considered themselves members of a large, close-knit family—a clan that also included a sizable number of Egyptian archaeologists and other professionals. That was hardly surprising. From its beginning, the French mission in the Valley of the Queens, at Desroches-Noblecourt's insistence, had been closely allied with CEDAE, which had emerged, since its founding twenty years before, as one of the world's preeminent centers in the study of ancient Egypt.

Several of Desroches-Noblecourt's Egyptian colleagues had worked with her for more than a decade, including Fathy Hassanein, a former inspector of the Egyptian Antiquities Organization, who had become a senior member of her team. A graduate in Egyptology from Cairo University, Hassanein had joined the CEDAE staff in 1962 and taken part in its surveys of Abu Simbel and other threatened temples during the Nubia campaign. After earning a doctorate in Egyptology at the University of Lyon in 1975, he had been at her side for most of her missions at the Ramesseum and in the Valley of the Queens.

The Valley of the Queens family also included the dozens of Egyptian laborers who had an equally close relationship with Desroches-Noblecourt, some of whom she had known for most of their lives. She kept up with news about them and their families, and from France, she sent presents on their birthdays. Jean-Louis Clouard, who worked as the mission's photographer, recalled watching Desroches-Noblecourt's easy interaction with the workers. She was fluent in literary Arabic, he said, but spoke to them in their dialect, "picking up new slang words, chatting with them, making them laugh."

Just as she had done on her earlier digs, she took on the job of providing medical care to members of her team who were sick or injured. Virtually every night, Clouard remembered, there were "six or seven workers standing in line to have their ailments treated." But the main reason they were there, he thought, was "for the simple pleasure of chatting with her."

CHAPTER 22

JACKIE AND ARI

In late March 1974, Christiane Desroches-Noblecourt and her team of young Egyptologists were finishing up work on that year's mission in the Valley of the Queens when she got a call from the French embassy in Cairo. She was told that Jacqueline Kennedy Onassis was touring Egypt with her husband and two children and wanted to visit her excavation site the following day.

It would be the first meeting between the only two women who had played pivotal roles in the success of the Nubia campaign. And, amazingly, there's no indication that either knew about the other's crucial part in the effort. Both had worked largely behind the scenes, and neither had received much if any public attention for what they had accomplished.

As it happened, Desroches-Noblecourt was less than pleased to hear about the visit. The latest excavation season was almost over, and she and her team still had much to do before it ended. She was not looking forward to having her work interrupted so that she could play tour guide to the former First Lady and her Greek multimillionaire second husband.

A few hours later, she received a note from Jacqueline asking if they could meet to go over the schedule for their tour. The couple and their party were staying aboard a river yacht they had chartered for a trip up the Nile, and Desroches-Noblecourt sent back word that she would meet Jacqueline there after she finished work that day at her current excavation site.

Late that afternoon, she decided to go straight to the boat without taking the time to shower and change. Hot and dusty when she arrived at its anchorage in the harbor outside Luxor, she was told that Mrs. Onassis would join her shortly. After half an hour, there was still no sign of Jacqueline, and Desroches-Noblecourt made it clear she had other things to do and couldn't wait much longer. Finally she was escorted to the dining area, where the former First Lady, whom Desroches-Noblecourt found "very kind and friendly but shy," joined her, thanking her profusely for coming. They agreed that the tour would begin at six o'clock the following morning in the Valley of the Queens.

During their conversation, Aristotle Onassis arrived, accompanied by two men. As Jacqueline began introducing her husband to Desroches-Noblecourt, she was called away for an urgent phone call. "Most likely, I think, Onassis hadn't heard my name," Desroches-Noblecourt later said. "He greeted me vaguely at the table at which I was sitting and ordered three whiskeys." When the drinks came, the men, ignoring her, took them in hand and continued to chat. After ten minutes or so, an increasingly annoyed Desroches-Noblecourt interrupted the discussion and asked Onassis "in a very pleasant way, if he wouldn't mind ordering me a drink, too, as I had just come from the desert."

He looked at her coolly and snapped, "Who are *you*?" With that, her temper boiled over, as it often did when dealing with arrogant, self-important men. She snapped back, "I'm the one you and your wife have pursued from Paris, the one who's supposed to take you and your friends to visit an excavation site. Just a few minutes ago, you saw your wife talking to me."

"Ah, is that you, Madame Desroches-Noblecourt?" Onassis replied. "Well, judging from the way you're talking to me, you must be very hard on the people you work with." She shot back, "I am very kind to my collaborators and usually very patient, because they are better brought up than you and it has never been an effort for them to be courteous."

At that point, Desroches-Noblecourt recalled, "we were in full aggression mode." Pressing his attack, Onassis said, "Of course, your team is both men and women, right? That must make for some very interesting situations." She responded, "Monsieur Onassis, I don't know in what kind of milieu you operate, but you must know that in ours, one does not confuse scientific research with a bordello." Their verbal sparring was interrupted by Jacqueline's return, and Desroches-Noblecourt quickly made her exit, convinced she would never see Aristotle Onassis again.

At precisely six o'clock the next morning, a minibus pulled up a few hundred feet from her excavation site. Several people, including Jacqueline and her children, Caroline and John Kennedy, got out and walked toward her and her team. Aristotle Onassis was in the lead. He spied their hostess and guide, waved his arm, and shouted, "Ah, Christiane! Here we are!" Still smarting from their contentious conversation the day before, she brusquely replied, "Calm down, Ari! Since when do you get to call me by my first name?"

After this second barbed exchange, she was sure she and he would be at each other's throats for the rest of the day. Deciding to exact a small measure of revenge, she suggested a tour of Queen Tuya's newly rediscovered tomb, which would be physically challenging, to say the least. There were no steps leading down into the tomb, and the rocky incline that served as its entrance was narrow, steep, and uneven. Inside, the walls were covered with soot.

Although Desroches-Noblecourt warned them of the difficulties, neither Jacqueline nor Ari, as Desroches-Noblecourt continued to call him, was dissuaded, and both climbed down into the burial vault on their own, holding on to the powdery walls and refusing the help of Desroches-Noblecourt and members of her team. The tour's next stops were Nefertari's tomb and those of several sons of Rameses III. As the morning proceeded, Desroches-Noblecourt began to change her mind about Onassis. He asked her innumerable questions and seemed intensely interested in her answers. He even had the grace to apologize for his earlier crassness. In the end, she said, "the tour was a real pleasure, both for me as the guide, and for everybody else."

Indeed, Desroches-Noblecourt enjoyed the couple's company so much that when Onassis thanked her for her time and said they were off to see the Ramesseum, she offered to come along as their guide. In the main temple's massive hypostyle hall, she pointed out that thirty-nine of the original forty-eight columns were still standing, each bearing elaborate carved reliefs showing Rameses II making offerings to various gods. Desroches-Noblecourt explained their meaning and showed them other carvings depicting Rameses II's great battle with the Hittites at Kadesh. Fascinated by the carvings, especially those in the upper levels of the hall, Onassis and his wife climbed a steep ladder to reach a rickety wooden scaffolding platform from which they could study them in closer detail.

CHRISTIANE DESROCHES-NOBLECOURT WITH ARISTOTLE AND JACQUELINE ONASSIS, MARCH 1974

Throughout the day, Desroches-Noblecourt recalled, "Onassis was the one asking the most relevant questions. During the time I was with him, I discovered a man of great culture. He was endlessly comparing ancient Greek thought and concepts with those of the Egyptians. We ended up spending lunchtime sitting in the shade of a temple colonnade and chatting like old friends. I found him very endearing."

Apparently Onassis and his wife felt the same about her. Instead of returning to their yacht for dinner, they spent the evening dining alfresco at Desroches-Noblecourt's excavation site. When Jacqueline learned that Desroches-Noblecourt was returning to Paris the following Sunday, she invited the Egyptologist and her husband to dinner at Maxim's, one of Paris's leading restaurants, the night after she got back. At the last minute, there was a scheduling problem, and the Noblecourts couldn't make it. When Onassis was informed about the snafu, he postponed a business trip so that the two couples could have dinner at Maxim's the next night. The evening was so successful that he and Jacqueline invited the Noblecourts to spend a week with them the following year on Skorpios, the Greek island he owned. A few months later, Onassis died, and the visit never took place. Jacqueline Onassis and Christiane Desroches-Noblecourt never saw each other again.

DURING HER BRIEF ENCOUNTERS with the couple, Desroches-Noblecourt was clearly more intrigued by the earthy, larger-than-life Onassis than by his reticent, reserved wife. That was a shame. If Christiane had been given more time to talk to Jacqueline, she likely would have discovered the former First Lady's own deep knowledge of ancient Egypt—an interest that had developed into a passion after her days at the White House. Even more important, she might well have learned how much she and the Nubia campaign owed to Jacqueline for what she had done to make it such an extraordinary success.

Ancient Egypt remained important to Jacqueline Kennedy Onassis for the rest of her life. Indeed, she credited it with playing a role in helping her reinvent herself after Onassis's death. She told friends how she had come across a saying from an Egyptian papyrus scroll noting the transitory nature of the tombs and chapels that housed the pharaohs' mummies and that eventually crumbled away, just like their inhabitants. "You must follow your desire while you live," the saying declared, because "no one goes away and then comes back."

The year after Onassis died, she began "following her desire," escaping the shadows cast by her two famous husbands and remaking her life. "I have always lived through men," she remarked to an acquaintance. "Now I realize I can't do that anymore."

Her reinvention of herself took place on her own terms. All her life, she'd been a loner, more comfortable with books than with people. As William Kuhn, one of her biographers, noted, "she found a way to turn being a reader into something that might offer her a workable new life in the years after her children were grown." At the age of forty-four, spurred by her lifelong love of history and literature, Jacqueline Onassis embarked on a new career as a book editor, working first at Viking, then at Doubleday.

When asked by an interviewer from *Publishers Weekly* what kind of books interested her most, she responded: "Books that are out of our regular experience. Books of other cultures and ancient history." She was particularly fascinated by projects that dealt with pharaonic Egypt, commissioning several in her eighteen years as an editor. Two were written by Jonathan Cott, a contributing editor at *Rolling Stone* magazine.

When Cott finished the initial draft of his first book with her, she asked him to come to her office, saying she had some books he might be interested in looking at. Piled high on her desk were more than twenty books about ancient Egyptian history, art, and religion, all of them from her private library. Among them was a first edition volume from *Description de l'Égypte,* the series of magnificently illustrated books published by French scholars in the early 1800s after their expedition to Egypt with Napoleon. Cott was astonished by Jacqueline's extensive knowledge of pharaonic Egypt, which she revealed in the notes she jotted on virtually every page of his manuscript.

"She talked to me with such intensity and passion about the book I was in the process of writing that it seemed as if she were dreaming it herself," Cott said. "Listening to my editor's wonderfully knowledgeable ideas about ancient Egypt and to her enthusiastic but specific comments about my manuscript, I soon began to imagine that . . . I too was entering the world of ancient Egypt, conversing with an Egyptian queen who was as beautiful as Nefertiti."

As it happened, Cott was not the only one who visualized Jacqueline as a member of Egyptian royalty. Shortly after JFK had won election in 1960, his wife asked the couturier Oleg Cassini to design much of her White House wardrobe. "Jackie reminded me of an ancient Egyptian princess—very geometric, even hieroglyphic, with the sphinx-like quality of her eyes, her long neck, slim torso, broad shoulders, narrow hips and regal carriage," Cassini later wrote. "I wanted to dress her cleanly, architecturally, in the style of Egypt."

Later in her collaboration with Cott, Jacqueline invited him to her Fifth Avenue apartment to show him the rest of her collection of Egypt-related books and artifacts. In the course of their conversation, she told him about her friendship with André Malraux, saying that the French cultural minister apparently had had a crush on her but leaving unmentioned the fact that she had felt the same way about him. She also said Malraux was the one who had told her about Christiane Desroches-Noblecourt and suggested she seek her out if and when she went to Egypt.

At one point, Jacqueline took Cott to her window overlooking the Metropolitan Museum and pointed out the Temple of Dendur, clearly visible through its glass casing. "Do you want to know how it got there?" she asked. When Cott said yes, "she told me this incredible story about how she was personally responsible for getting it," he remembered. "She had gotten Jack Kennedy to give money to Egypt."

Cott's second book with Jacqueline touched on the legend of the Egyptian deities Isis and Osiris. "She was really enamored with the Isis and Osiris myth," Cott said. "We used to talk about it a lot. . . . Jackie was very, very attached to that story. It's about the dead husband who is restored and remembered, so to speak, by his wife and given eternal, immortal life by her. She didn't say that to me, but I assume she maybe had an identification with that story."

Jacqueline's fascination with Egypt extended to the modern era as well. After the Egyptian writer Naguib Mahfouz won the Nobel Prize in Literature in 1988, she read a French translation of his best-known work—a trilogy of novels about a family living in Cairo from World War I to the end of World War II. Originally published in Arabic in the

1950s, the three books are regarded as an epic portrait of Egypt and its people during that period, particularly their struggle for independence from foreign influence and control.

Although Mahfouz's publisher, the American University Press of Cairo, had arranged a small printing of an English-language edition, the trilogy and its author were virtually unknown to American readers. Jacqueline was determined to correct that situation. She successfully lobbied Alberto Vitale, Doubleday's publisher, to buy the rights for the trilogy—*Palace Walk*, *Palace of Desire*, and *Sugar Street*—as well as more than a dozen of Mahfouz's other novels. "We ended up selling those rights everywhere in the world," Vitale recalled.

In her dealings with Jonathan Cott and some of her other authors, Jacqueline was fond of repeating to them a famous Egyptian saying: "To speak of the dead is to make them live again." They were doing so in their books, she said. She didn't mention the fact that she had done the same, not only in the books she commissioned and published but in her passionate fight to save the temples of Abu Simbel and keep alive the astonishing achievement of the ancient Egyptians who had built them.

CHAPTER 23

OPERATION RAMESES

On a sunny autumn afternoon in 1976, some sixty years after Christiane Desroches-Noblecourt first saw the Obelisk of Luxor, she viewed it again—this time from a motorcade that, at her instruction, slowly circled the pink granite monolith in the center of the Place de la Concorde. Inside one of the motorcade's vans, flanked by a motorcycle police escort, was the mummy of the pharaoh who had ordered the obelisk built more than three thousand years before. Having accompanied Rameses II from Cairo to Paris earlier that day, Desroches-Noblecourt could not resist the idea of reuniting the man who had dominated so much of her life with the monument that had sparked her lifelong passion for ancient Egypt.

The story of Rameses's visit to Paris began two years earlier when Michel Guy, France's then minister of culture, summoned Desroches-Noblecourt to his office. Still basking in the triumph of the Tutankhamun exhibition, he wanted her to host another major show at the Louvre, this time focusing on Akhenaten, the heretic pharaoh.

Desroches-Noblecourt had little enthusiasm for the idea. The reigns of Akhenaten and Tutankhamun were only a few years apart, and she had already covered that period—the end of the Eighteenth Dynasty—in the earlier exhibition. Even more problematic was the lack of funerary treasures to display: Akhenaten's tomb, like those of virtually every other pharaoh but Tutankhamun, had been looted of all the riches buried with him. The relatively few superior artifacts associated with him and his reign would be difficult to acquire, scattered as they were in various Egyptian museums. Remembering her difficulties with the Cairo curators, she didn't want to endure that kind of haggling with officials from multiple institutions.

Michel Guy accepted her arguments but told her she had to come up with an alternative. She immediately suggested Rameses II. As a child, she had been fascinated by Tutankhamun, but as an adult, her passion lay with the creator of Abu Simbel. She also chose him because of Rameses's extremely long reign and predilection for building monuments to himself, which meant there was a plethora of antiquities from which to choose. In addition, an exhibition devoted to him would give her the chance to explore the origins of the Nineteenth Dynasty. There was a multitude of subjects to examine: Rameses's parents and earlier ancestors; his wives and children; his empire-building; Abu Simbel and his many other monuments; religion, education, and culture during his reign; and even the lives of those who worked for him, including his scribes, architects, and the sculptors and other artisans who lived at Deir-el-Medina.

Along with her team at the Louvre, Desroches-Noblecourt began planning the show, spending long hours negotiating with Egyptian officials in Cairo over which items they would be willing to lend her. Christian Leblanc—who was now based permanently in the Egyptian capital as CEDAE's French liaison—assisted her with the planning. There would be seventy-two objects in all, almost twice as many as those displayed in the Tutankhamun exhibition.

Although she never acknowledged the fact in her memoirs, Desroches-Noblecourt broached the possibility with French officials of including the mummy of Rameses II as the centerpiece of the exhibition. During a state visit to Egypt, French President Valéry Giscard d'Estaing raised the issue with Egyptian President Anwar Sadat, promising that the mummy would be displayed in "an appropriate and respectful setting." Word of the request, however, was leaked to the Egyptian press, resulting in an eruption of outrage. "We ask the friendly French people: would they allow the remains of Napoleon to be displayed in Egypt?" the newspaper *Al-Ahram* thundered.

Sadat said no, and Giscard d'Estaing backed down, assuring his Egyptian counterpart that France had no intention of "offending the sensitivities of some of your compatriots." But then, at the behest of Desroches-Noblecourt, he offered an alternative plan, stemming from an assertion by a French doctor living in Cairo that Rameses's mummy was no longer fit to be exposed to public view anywhere, including in the Egyptian Museum, where it was now on display. Dr. Maurice Bucaille, who had been researching the cause of Rameses II's death, had received permission from the museum to examine his mummy. After removing the bandages encasing the ruler's remains, he found that parts of it had been eaten away—by what, it was not immediately clear.

It wasn't the first time that the mummy of this celebrated pharaoh had been in dire straits. Thousands of years before, it had been torn from its tomb by vandals, who had removed everything of value, including the jewels adorning Rameses's body, and then abandoned it. It had been reburied more than a century later, but that grave was also violated. In roughly the tenth century B.C., Theban priests collected Rameses's remains, along with those of some thirty-five other pharaohs whose tombs had suffered the same fate, and hid them away for safekeeping in an empty burial vault in the Valley of the Kings. There the royal mummies remained, wrapped in coarse linen shrouds and ignominiously stacked like firewood, for nearly three thousand years.

They were discovered in 1881 and ended up at the Egyptian Museum, where they were initially stored in a first-floor room that was kept off-limits to the public. Several decades later, however, they were put on display in sarcophagi with removable glass covers. According to Bucaille, the mummies had survived for millennia in the desert not only because they had been embalmed but also because they had been hidden in a dry, airless underground space. In the museum, they were exposed to extreme heat and humidity—conditions made worse by the occasional removal of the glass lids to allow medical experts like him to examine the mummies.

After being told of Rameses's deteriorating state, Desroches-Noblecourt had consulted with Bucaille and several Egyptian medical authorities, then met with Gamal Mokhtar, the director of the Egyptian Antiquities Organization, to explain the situation and underscore the urgent need to address it. She had been advised, she said, that Egyptian medical facilities did not have the means to tend to the mummy, and she suggested that it be transported to Paris for examination and treatment.

Mokhtar shook his head. While sympathetic to her appeal, he considered such an action impossible; it was far too politically fraught, as the outraged reaction to reports of the mummy's possible inclusion in the Paris exhibition had already made clear. Never, he said, would government officials agree to allow such a trip for one of the greatest figureheads in Egyptian history. "We cannot expatriate the remains of such an illustrious hero, even temporarily," he went on. "Some of our people, especially those who are religious, would be up in arms over it."

When Desroches-Noblecourt continued to press her case, Mokhtar said her only chance for success was to gain the approval of the countries' two heads of state, Giscard d'Estaing and Sadat. An old hand at persuading French presidents to do her bidding, Desroches-Noblecourt convinced Giscard d'Estaing to contact Sadat and offer this new plan to save the mummy. At the same time, she approached Lionel Balout, the director of the Musée de l'Homme, which, thirty-five years before, had served as the headquarters for the wartime resistance organization to which she had belonged. One of the most renowned anthropology museums in the world, it was known for, among other things, its forensic examinations of ancient human remains.

Balout agreed to authorize and preside over an examination of Rameses's mummy. Now all Desroches-Noblecourt had to do, in addition to getting the approval of Sadat, was to arrange for the venture's financing. Knowing that the French government would never agree to pay for it, she contacted a former student of hers from the École du Louvre who was now the president of a French oil company with a drilling concession in Egypt. He gave her an immediate thumbs-up.

In his letter to Sadat requesting permission to treat the mummy, Giscard d'Estaing assured him that France was eager "to do anything it could to contribute to the preservation of the testimonies of your glorious past." In an interview years later, the former French president said he made it clear to Sadat that if "he agreed to the proposal, we would treat the mummy of Rameses II as if it were the body of a reigning head of state." According to Christian Leblanc, Sadat was keenly aware of "the significance of this deferential proposal which would glorify an ancient ancestor and allow him to be treated in the best laboratories then existing in Europe." The Egyptian leader finally agreed.

It was then that Operation Rameses was launched. Desroches-Noblecourt began preparing for the pharaoh's journey, which would take place several months after the opening of the exhibition in his honor in early May.

MUCH LARGER IN SCALE than the Tutankhamun show, *Rameses le Grand,* with its seventy-two antiquities and many oversized photographs of Abu Simbel, Nefertari's tomb, and other monuments, occupied eight rooms on three floors of the Grand Palais, a sprawling exhibition hall and museum near the Louvre. At the exhibition's entrance stood a stunning black granite statue of Rameses as a naked child sitting between the legs of a protective giant hawk representing the Canaanite god Horun and the Egyptian god Horus. The child holds the index finger of his right hand to his mouth, while a long sidelock of hair falls to his shoulder—both symbols of a young male royal.

The overall effect of the statue is one of childish innocence—a state that the real Rameses apparently abandoned very early in his life. According to one scribe who served him, he was supplied with the services of a harem while "still a child on his father's knee." By the time he was twenty, he had two official wives—Nefertari and Isisnofret—and four children by them, not to mention an unknown number of offspring whom he had fathered by concubines.

The exhibition's other antiquities ranged from the colossal—an eight-foot-tall rose granite statue of Rameses and the elaborately painted wooden sarcophagus in which priests first reburied his mummy more than a century after his tomb was looted—to small items such as the instruments used by his surveyors and architects to design and build monuments like Abu Simbel.

In planning the exhibition, Desroches-Noblecourt knew she would have to deal with one particularly ticklish issue: the question of Rameses II's putative role in the exodus of Jews from Egypt, as described in the Old Testament's Book of Exodus. Although the Bible does not specifically name the pharaoh who was the contemporary of Moses, Rameses was commonly believed to be the ruler, as seen in depictions of the event in popular culture, such as Cecil B. DeMille's 1956 film *The Ten Commandments*, starring Yul Brynner as Rameses.

However, there's a problem with that idea: No allusion exists in contemporaneous Egyptian texts to any such episode. There are no records of Moses, Israelites in bondage, or mass expulsions or departures of any foreigners from the country. Desroches-Noblecourt nonetheless believed it would be "unscientific to dodge the problem." She resolved it by devoting a display to the life of Semitic tribes in Egypt during Rameses's time, pointing out the parallels between historical reality and the story of Moses and his people.

According to the display, it was not unusual for promising young Semites like Moses to grow up in the pharaoh's court and later occupy senior positions. "Among the Semitic colonies that settled in Egypt, it was common that a certain number of their members would have been chosen on the basis of their aptitudes and trained in schools," Desroches-Noblecourt wrote. "Once assimilated, they would be put in positions of responsibility in the Egyptian administration." Meanwhile, their fellow tribesmen, who she emphasized were not treated as slaves, worked alongside Egyptian laborers to build the pharaoh's monuments. Even though she and other Egyptologists could not definitively say one way or another that the Exodus actually occurred at all, the display indicated that for the most part, "a peaceful understanding reigned between these peoples."

IN MAY 1976, GISCARD d'Estaing presided over the opening of the exhibition, the first museum-related event he had attended since taking office two years before. Also attending the gala pre-opening reception was a throng of top French officials, including Prime Minister Jacques Chirac, the foreign minister Jean Sauvagnargues, and of course Michel Guy, the minister of culture whose request to Desroches-Noblecourt had sparked the whole affair.

A major success, the exhibition came close to rivaling its blockbuster predecessor, attracting more than one million visitors during its Paris stay. An average of ten thousand people a day waited in lines that stretched several blocks for their turn to enter the Grand Palais. One particularly popular display was Desroches-Noblecourt's reconstruction of a temple garden in Thebes, complete with a carp-filled pool and lush vegetation including papyrus, lotuses, blueberries, poppies, and mandrake. Heard in the background were the croaking of frogs and chirping of birds. The birdsong, which had been recorded near Rameses's funerary temple near Luxor, was so lifelike, Desroches-Noblecourt recalled, that a number of visitors reproached the museum for keeping birds trapped and forcing them to sing without stopping.

The garden's beauty, however, was not the sole reason for its popularity. It also happened to be air-conditioned—a potent lure for visitors during a prolonged heat wave that baked Paris that summer.

IN EARLY SEPTEMBER 1976, with the exhibition still attracting crowds of visitors, Desroches-Noblecourt left Paris aboard a French air force plane to collect the body of the show's honoree. All the arrangements for receiving Rameses's mummy had been completed. After preparing a sterilized room for it, the Musée de l'Homme had dispatched several of its specialists to Cairo to help ready it for travel.

Desroches-Noblecourt supervised Rameses's departure from the Egyptian Museum. His mummy, encased in a specially made wooden crate covered with burlap, was placed under tarpaulins on the bed of a truck, which was surrounded by an honor guard commanded by the museum's police chief. At the Cairo airport, the French ambassador, on behalf of his government, signed a document accepting full responsibility for the safekeeping of one of Egypt's most precious treasures.

Before the plane took off, Desroches-Noblecourt approached the pilot about the possibility of flying over the pyramids of Giza as a mark of respect and honor for the pharaoh. He agreed. "So it was," she later said, "that 3,190 years after his death, Rameses passed above the only one of the Seven Wonders of the Ancient World that was still standing."

In Paris, the plane was greeted with lavish ceremony. A band played the Egyptian national anthem, and a contingent of the Republican Guard, wearing their ornate nineteenth-century cavalry helmets with red rooster plumes, presented arms as the crate containing the mummy was carefully removed from the aircraft. Also present were the Egyptian ambassador to France, several French government officials and high-ranking air force officers, and a member of Giscard d'Estaing's cabinet—Alice Saunier-Seïté, the minister for higher education. In a brief speech, Saunier-Seïté saluted "the mortal remains of one of the greatest chiefs of state in the ancient world." A large press contingent, meanwhile, was at the airport to cover the mummy's arrival.

While some Egyptians, including a number of authorities at the Egyptian Museum, remained unhappy about the trip, others were thrilled by the kingly welcome given to Rameses by the French. Among them was six-year-old Khaled el-Anani, a student at a French-language school in Cairo. El-Anani, who went on to earn a doctorate in Egyptology and become the government minister in charge of antiquities, recalled being transfixed by a film about Rameses's visit to France that was shown in his class. "I was amazed to see the crowd of reporters and television cameras at the Paris airport who welcomed Rameses as a president or a king," he remarked.

Rameses's mummy spent seven months at the Musée de L'Homme, attended by more than one hundred scientists, mostly French and Egyptian, who had volunteered for the lengthy project to detect the agents attacking the remains and devise a way to get rid of them. Since the Egyptian government had forbidden performing experiments on the mummy, the researchers were restricted in their methods of analysis, relying heavily on multiple X-rays and the extraction of samples from the mummy that were intensively studied.

The X-rays determined that the pharaoh had been five feet nine inches tall, was white-skinned and red-haired, suffered from arteriosclerosis, and had been about eighty-five years old when he died. X-rays revealed that his heart, which had been removed from his body during embalming, had been reinserted very high in his chest, with a gold ring attached. They also detected peppercorns in his nose, which apparently were inserted to maintain the shape of the nose's cartilage.

However, the researchers' main focus—pinpointing the organisms that had been attacking the remains—was a mystery that took several months to solve. According to the scientists' final findings, Rameses's body had been ravaged by two kinds of insects, sixty types of fungi, and an undisclosed number of bacteria. Once the problem was diagnosed, the next challenge was to find a way to get rid of all the destructive agents.

The Egyptian government had stipulated that no form of liquid or gas could be used on the mummy. After considerable discussion, Lionel Balout and his team decided on radiation. At France's Center for Nuclear Studies in Grenoble, experiments were carried out on Egyptian mummies from the Musée de l'Homme to make sure that the nails and hair would withstand radiation treatment. The results were positive, and arrangements were made to irradiate Rameses's mummy at the Nuclear Research Center in Saclay, the heart of French nuclear research since its founding by the Nobel Prize–winning nuclear physicist Frédéric Joliot-Curie after World War II.

Once the treatment was finished, the mummy would be returned immediately to the Egyptian Museum with a royal send-off orchestrated by Desroches-Noblecourt. At her instruction, Rameses was to be placed in the elaborately decorated wooden sarcophagus in which he had been reburied after his tomb's first looting and that had been on display in the exhibition. It would also undergo radiation at Saclay.

The day before Rameses's radiation, President Giscard d'Estaing paid a call to the museum to inspect the mummy and thank the dozens of scientists who had worked on the project. After the radiation procedure was completed, the body was placed on a linen cloth dating from Rameses's time that had been stored in the Louvre's Egyptian reserves.

It covered a mattress filled with compacted cedar shavings, which were impermeable to attacks by vermin.

As a covering for the sarcophagus, Desroches-Noblecourt had commissioned the Louvre's upholstery workshop to sew a large funeral sheet of lapis-lazuli-blue velvet lined with gold taffeta. Embroidered in gold thread at the top and bottom of the cloth were the heraldic plants of ancient Egypt—the papyrus and the lily—copied from their representations on pillars at the Temple of Karnak.

On May 10, 1977, France bade farewell to Rameses's mummy with the same pageantry that had welcomed the ruler seven months before. Again, French government dignitaries and a Republican Guard contingent gathered at the airport to pay their respects, and again, Desroches-Noblecourt escorted her royal charge, keeping watch over him aboard the French air force plane to Cairo and accompanying him back to the museum there.

FORTY-FOUR YEARS LATER, ON April 2, 2021, Rameses II embarked on another journey, this one just across town. His mummy, along with those of twenty-two other pharaohs and members of ancient Egyptian royal families, traveled through the streets of Cairo from the Egyptian Museum to their new home in the recently built National Museum of Egyptian Civilization.

The parade, reminiscent of a Hollywood extravaganza, involved months of preparation that included building special shock-absorbent vehicles as well as repaving the roads along the route to ensure the smoothest possible ride. Each mummy—enclosed in a hermetically sealed, climate-controlled case—was transported in its own gold-and-blue vehicle, designed to look like the pharaonic boats used to carry the mummies of ancient royals to their tombs. Also in the procession were horse-drawn chariots and hundreds of singers and dancers in ancient Egyptian garb. When the mummies arrived at the new museum, they were greeted by the president of Egypt, Abdel Fattah el-Sisi, and a twenty-one-gun salute.

The spare-no-expense pageant, which attracted extensive international news coverage, was the brainchild of the antiquities minister Khaled el-Anani, whose inspiration was the impressive French welcome to the mummy of Rameses II that he had viewed as a child. Determined to do something just as grand or even more so, he said, he set out to "organize an unrivaled parade to show our respect for our ancestors, who are so much a part of mankind's cultural heritage."

CHAPTER 24

SAVING PHILAE

ON MARCH 10, 1980, THE MOST NOTABLE CHAPTER OF CHRISTIANE Desroches-Noblecourt's lengthy career came to an end. Before dawn that morning, she and more than five hundred other guests were ferried down the Nile to the new home of the temple complex of Philae. They were there to celebrate Philae's resurrection but also to mark the completion of the entire Nubia campaign. Twenty years after UNESCO's international appeal to save the temples, the venture had finally accomplished everything it had set out to do.

As she listened to the Cairo Symphony performing in the shadow of Philae's Temple of Isis, with the sun rising behind it, Desroches-Noblecourt's mood was both joyful and melancholy. With a rush of emotion, she thought back to the tumultuous days before the campaign's beginning, when she, Sarwat Okasha, and René Maheu had banded together to save Egypt's threatened antiquities. Of the trio, she was the only one there for the final act. Maheu had died in 1975, and Okasha, who had never gotten along with the then current Egyptian president, Anwar Sadat, had been dismissed from the government.

Desroches-Noblecourt deeply missed both of them. Their absence on this triumphant day was "the only regret I had about the whole exhilarating period that I call the Grande Nubiade," she later wrote. "The struggles we experienced had been disconcerting, often very harsh, sometimes cruel. But my memory of [those struggles] faded when I thought about the almost miraculous presence of the treasures we had saved."

Even as she lamented their absence, Desroches-Noblecourt had one consolation. Sitting beside her at the Philae ceremony was a more recent ally and partner, none other than her onetime nemesis, Eiddon Edwards.

BEFORE SHE AND EDWARDS finally joined forces on Philae, however, one more episode of their contentious relationship would play out. In 1972, as the British Museum was basking in its triumphant staging of the Tutankhamun treasures, the Louvre was preparing to mount a new show marking the 150th anniversary of the greatest achievement in Egyptology: Jean-François Champollion's deciphering of hieroglyphs in 1822. A gala week of festivities was planned—speeches and concerts at the Institut de France, the unveiling of Champollion's restored tomb at Père Lachaise cemetery, and a new display of Egyptian antiquities at the Louvre, including a stunning bust of Akhenaten, the museum's most recent and prized acquisition.

When Egyptian authorities had begun distributing gifts to the most generous donor countries in the Nubia campaign, France was high on the list. The United States and most of the others wanted a temple. But Desroches-Noblecourt, who had a major say in France's request, had her eye on a much smaller treasure—a bust from one of four colossal statues of Akhenaten found at a temple near Karnak. "Of all the monuments on offer, this masterpiece was perfectly suited for our museum," she later wrote. "We could certainly never acquire, by any other means, such a striking witness of this exceptional period."

Yet, as proud as she was of the bust's inclusion in the Champollion exhibition, there was one antiquity that she and other Louvre officials yearned to display above all others: the Rosetta Stone, whose hieroglyphic inscriptions Champollion had deciphered, thus making ancient Egypt's written language intelligible. Champollion had never actually seen the stone, which, after being spirited away by the British in 1798, had been exhibited at the British Museum. The young French scholar had to make do with a lithographic copy of the inscriptions.

"It seemed to me that the Rosetta Stone, the starting point of his prodigious discovery, should appear in Paris as an exceptional tribute to this brilliant scientist," Desroches-Noblecourt said. Aware that the stone had never been allowed to leave Britain's borders, she wrote several letters to the British Museum's top officials asking them to make an exception for the Champollion exhibition. Each time, the answer was no.

Finally, in desperation, she decided to contact Edwards. To her surprise, he sent back a warm response, saying he would do everything possible to help her acquire the stone but that the final decision would be made by the museum's board of trustees. After hearing nothing for several weeks, she finally received a regretful letter from him saying that the trustees had unanimously voted to refuse her request. "What were they afraid of—that we would keep the stone or give it back to the Egyptians?" she asked herself. "I couldn't understand or resign myself to their decision."

Not long afterward, she received an invitation to the March 1972 opening of the Tutankhamun exhibition in London. During a pre-opening reception at the British Museum, she encountered Denis Hamilton, at whose urging she had persuaded Egyptian Museum authorities to lend the harpooner statuette to the British. Reminding him of her help, she expressed her "deep disappointment about the trustees' refusal to grant our loan request." Taken aback, Hamilton replied, "Madam, we were never asked about the stone." He asked another guest—former British prime minister Alec Douglas-Home, who was also a museum trustee—to confirm to Desroches-Noblecourt what Hamilton had just told her.

When Douglas-Home did so, she said to both men, "So if you want to repay us for the little king in his boat, which despite so many obstacles came to float on the banks of the Thames, and if you want to correct this prevarication, you must help me." Specifically, she asked them to urge Queen Elizabeth II to authorize the loan of the Rosetta Stone to the Louvre for one month.

Seven months later, the priceless artifact made its first—and only—journey outside Britain. After arriving in Paris, it was placed on display in the Louvre's department of Egyptian antiquities. "Thanks to Tutankhamun the harpooner," Desroches-Noblecourt wrote, "the Rosetta Stone finally came to the shores of the Seine to pay homage to Champollion, its decryptor."

She never publicly said whether she confronted Edwards about what she considered his "prevarication." In any event, it no longer mattered; she had received what she wanted. Not long afterward, she and her old rival finally put their past disputes behind them to join in saving the temples of Philae.

IT'S NOT DIFFICULT TO understand the two Egyptologists' mutual passion for this enchanting complex just south of the old Aswan dam and some five hundred miles from Cairo. For more than two millennia, countless visitors to the tiny island of Philae had felt the same. According to Robert Curzon, a British aristocrat who visited Philae in 1834, "Every part of Egypt is interesting and curious, but the only place to which the epithet 'beautiful' can be correctly applied is the island of Philae."

Also succumbing to Philae's charms was Amelia Edwards, who recalled approaching it in a small boat and watching

> the island, with its palms, its colonnades, its pylons, seeming to rise out of the river like a mirage. Piled rocks frame it on either side, and purple mountains in the background close up the distance. As the boat glides nearer between glistening boulders, those sculptured towers [of the pylons] rise higher and ever higher against the sky. They show no sign of ruin or of age. . . . If a sound of antique chanting were to be borne along the quiet air—if a procession of white-robed priests bearing aloft the veiled ark of the God, were to come sweeping round between the palms and the pylons—we should not think it strange.

Compared to the gigantism of Abu Simbel and most other Egyptian monuments, Philae and its antiquities were like jewels on display in an exquisitely decorated box. Covered as it was with lush vegetation, including palm trees and flowering shrubs, the island was, as Eiddon Edwards noted, "in effect an oasis—entirely unlike any other ancient site in Egypt."

But Philae was known for much more than its beauty: It was regarded as one of the most sacred places in Egypt. Its graceful main temple, dedicated to the goddess Isis, had become the center of a worldwide cult soon after it was built by a Ptolemaic pharaoh in the third century B.C. "No one could have foreseen how prominently the island and its priesthood would figure in Egyptian political and religious history for the next thousand years," Edwards wrote.

From the outset of their 275-year rule, the Ptolemies, who were of Greek origin, adopted the Egyptian religion and in particular the cult of Isis and her husband, the god Osiris, which focused on the myth of Osiris's death and rebirth. According to legend, after Osiris's brother Seth, the god of violence and destruction, killed and dismembered him, Osiris's grieving wife, Isis, in the form of a bird, tracked the pieces down and reassembled them. Still in the shape of a bird, she infused her husband with new life, performing one of the first acts of resurrection. Osiris became not only the god of the underworld but also the power that granted new life in nature every year, from the regrowth of vegetation in the spring to the annual flooding of the Nile.

Osiris had supposedly been buried on Biga, an island neighboring Philae. But because Biga was considered sacred ground, no one was allowed there except priests who tended his reputed burial place. So worshippers flocked instead to Philae, appealing to Isis to use her regenerative powers on their behalf. By the first century B.C., "the cult of Isis was the most powerful in Egypt and her island sanctuary regarded as the holiest place in the whole country," Toby Wilkinson noted.

The cult of Isis, however, was not confined solely to Egypt. Many Greeks—fellow countrymen of the Ptolemaic pharaohs—had traveled to or settled in Egypt. When they returned to their homeland, they brought the cult back with them. By the year 30 B.C., after the Roman Empire had taken control of Egypt and much of the rest of the Mediterranean region, the cult of Isis had established itself throughout the empire.

Caesar Augustus, who had conquered Egypt, was reluctant at first to acknowledge the goddess, primarily because she had been the favorite deity of his foe, Cleopatra, whose troops he had defeated. But finally, bowing to the strength of the cult, he built a temple in Isis's honor at the northern end of Philae in 9 B.C. Later Roman emperors added their own monuments. An imposing ceremonial gateway—in honor of Trajan, who ruled from A.D. 98 to 117—served as the main entrance to the complex from the Nile. Called Trajan's Kiosk, it featured fourteen massive columns, along with carvings in its interior that depicted Trajan in Egyptian dress presenting offerings to Isis, Osiris, and their son, Horus. During annual festivals at Philae, boats would dock outside the Kiosk, bringing worshippers who had come to take part in the festivals' rituals that were staged by the powerful priesthood of Isis and focused on symbolic death and rebirth.

The legend of Isis and Osiris bore striking parallels to some of the beliefs and rituals of the new Christian religion taking hold in the Mediterranean region during the first and second centuries A.D. Indeed, many scholars believe that the Isis cult was a key influence on Christianity's development. The figure of the Virgin Mary, for example, is similar to that of Isis, who, like the mother of Jesus, was known as the Queen of Heaven. Osiris's resurrection prefigures that of Christ, who, like Horus, was considered a divine child.

With the decline of the Roman Empire and the emergence of the Byzantine Empire, Christianity became the state religion of all Byzantine-ruled lands, including Egypt and Nubia. Other religions were deemed pagan and banned, with their monuments ordered destroyed or converted to another use, usually as churches. But although Christianity took firm hold in Egypt and Nubia in the third and fourth centuries A.D., many of their citizens continued to cling to the rituals of the Isis cult and to come to Philae for its annual festivals. Byzantine authorities did little to stop them, fearing that the temple's closure would spark fierce resistance by Nubian tribes who were staunch Isis believers.

Not until the sixth century was Philae, the last pagan outpost in the Byzantine Empire, finally shut down. In 536, Emperor Justinian sent troops to close the Temple of Isis, disband its priesthood, imprison those who resisted, and transport its statues to Constantinople. Soon afterward, the temple was turned into a church, and many of the figures of the gods carved in relief on its walls were defaced. But the temple itself suffered little structural damage. When Amelia Edwards saw it in 1873, it still retained its original beauty—although not for long.

In 1902, when the first Aswan dam was built downstream from Philae, the temple complex was swallowed up in water for nine months of the year, with only the top few feet of the temple pylons and gateway

PHILAE PARTIALLY SUBMERGED, C. 1910

visible above the waves. In his book *The Death of Philae*, the French writer Pierre Loti joined other scholars in appealing to Egyptians to rally to the defense of their cultural heritage. Their protests went unheeded.

After the dam's completion, when its valves were opened in the summer to allow floodwaters to cover the land of the lower Nile valley, the temple emerged for three months from the water, "its reliefs intact but now deprived of their shimmering color," Desroches-Noblecourt wrote. "Before long the palm trees and bushes, one of the charms of the island, had also disappeared, and only the buildings, bespeckled with silt and aquatic incubations, survived as sad reminders of a magic island."

Battered as it was, however, the complex was still mostly intact. But that would change forever once construction of the Aswan High Dam was completed. Philae, which was located between the old and new dams on the Nile, lay in a subsidiary reservoir, whose fluctuating water level, if nothing was done, would not only end up totally submerging the island within a few years but also result in the complete collapse of its temples.

AFTER THE RESCUE OF Abu Simbel, Egyptian authorities and UNESCO turned their attention to Philae—the last and next to Abu Simbel, the most important of the antiquities to be rescued. On May 8, 1968, René Maheu launched a new appeal for contributions to preserve the monuments that were dubbed "the Pearl of the Nile." But unlike Abu Simbel, there would be no controversy surrounding its salvage, thanks to the stunning success of the dismantling and reassembly of the earlier project. Indeed, the work at Abu Simbel would serve as a model for Philae's rescue, which would involve cutting the Temple of Isis, along with several smaller temples and shrines, into blocks and rebuilding them in the same relative positions on the island of Agilkia, which resembled Philae geographically and lay only about a quarter of a mile away. In the end, twenty-two nations, including the United States, provided more than $15 million toward the $30 million cost, with Egypt picking up much of the rest of the tab. The Tutankhamun exhibition in London brought in an additional $1.6 million.

In 1972, just as the Tutankhamun display was being unveiled at the

British Museum, work began on Philae and the rocky terrain of Agilkia, which is situated about forty feet higher than the original site of the temple complex. Several of the archaeological advisers on the project, among them Desroches-Noblecourt and Eiddon Edwards, not only insisted that the various buildings be located in roughly the same relative positions on Agilkia as they had been on Philae, but that the surrounding geographic features should resemble the original environment as closely as possible. That meant that the new site had to be flanked on its western shore by another island, where, according to legend, Osiris's burial place lay, watched over by the faithful Isis. Fortunately, a nearby island called Saliba, separated from Agilkia by a narrow channel, was considered suitable.

According to Desroches-Noblecourt, the contours of Philae resembled the shape of a bird, mirroring Isis's transformation, and she argued that the contours of Agilkia must also be given an avian appearance. However, several of her colleagues on the committee had trouble accepting her conclusion.

To prove her point, she asked the committee members to accompany her to a cliff on the heights of Biga, which looked out over Philae. From that elevation, one could indeed make out on the smaller island the form of a bird. According to Desroches-Noblecourt, the main structures—the Temple of Isis, Hadrian's Kiosk, and the immense double colonnade connecting the two—followed the curve of the island and represented the entrails of the bird. She pointed out areas that resembled the head and beak, which pointed toward Nubia, and a long protrusion of land in the north that could be the tail. She even noted a large protruding rock, which was where the bird's eye would be.

Her colleagues surrendered, and, over the next five years, Agilkia was leveled off and reshaped to assume the birdlike appearance of Philae. A monumental job, it involved reducing the summit of the island by one hundred feet and using the countless tons of granite that were removed to widen Agilkia on each side.

While that effort was under way, work began on Philae itself. The first step was to build a cofferdam around much of the island and pump out the water enveloping the monuments—also a slow, painstaking process. When the flood finally retreated, it left behind a huge amount of glutinous silt, sludge, and encrusted algae, forming deposits more than six feet high in some places on the floors of the colonnade and temples. That, too, had to be cleared. Once that job was finished, the surfaces of all the structures had to be cleaned to remove the stains.

The actual work of dismantling the stones began on May 21, 1974. In charge was an Italian engineering firm called Condotte Mazzi, which modeled its cutting operation on that of Abu Simbel. As each structure was taken apart, the stones were lifted by giant cranes and placed on barges, which hauled them to a storage area on the mainland. There they were laid out in long rows, each stone meticulously measured and numbered. On Agilkia, meanwhile, concrete foundations for the structures were poured.

Reassembly of the temples and shrines began in March 1977. To cement the stones, the workmen used the same mixture of sand and gypsum employed by the structures' original builders. Only a few changes were made, including the replacement of several broken stones and restoration of some of the temples' and colonnade's flooring, which had been badly damaged. Toward the end of the process, Agilkia was blanketed with rich new vegetation—palm trees, acacia bushes, henna, papyrus, and lotus, among other plants—to make it look as much as possible like the original landscape of Philae.

The project's final major task was to recover several submerged Roman structures, including a triumphal arch built by the emperor Diocletian and a stone quay, at the other end of Philae from the main temple complex. The costs of extending the cofferdam all the way around the island would have been exorbitant, so a decision had been made to allow the Roman artifacts to be swallowed by the floodwater.

Thanks to a request from Eiddon Edwards, the British government authorized the loan of thirty-nine experienced Royal Navy divers to come to Philae and work with an equally skilled group of Egyptian divers to dismantle the structures underwater and help bring their stones to the surface. For this binational team, the six-month mission was a monumental challenge, requiring "every ounce of their extraordinary tenacity and skill," said the British divers' commander.

PHILAE RESTORED, 2006

Before they could disassemble the antiquities, the divers had to clear away an estimated 1,700 cubic tons of mud that had collected around the antiquities' bases. The decades-old mud, once stirred up, made the water almost completely opaque, which severely limited the divers' vision. After completing that thoroughly unpleasant task, they used hammers and chisels to dismantle the monuments. Once the huge stones were cut away, heavy straps were hooked to them, and they were raised hydraulically to the surface. Cranes then lifted the blocks—450 in all—and deposited them on barges, which transported them to the storage area. According to one British diver, the work had been onerous but well worth it. "To think that these ancient things will stand for thousands more years and to know we helped make that possible . . . well, it gives you a thrill," he said.

Desroches-Noblecourt was equally jubilant, a feeling that stemmed not only from the successful relocation of the Philae complex but also from a conversation she had had with Eiddon Edwards at the end of the effort. "I had the great satisfaction," she wrote, "of hearing this old friend and stubborn adversary tell me that, as it turned out, I had been right about the whole Nubian adventure."

CHAPTER 25

VALLEY OF THE QUEENS

FOR ALMOST ALL OF CHRISTIANE DESROCHES-NOBLECOURT'S LIFE, the Louvre had been a second home. She had haunted its galleries as a child, attended its school, and worked there for fifty years, ending up as one of its top curators. In 1983, however, she turned seventy—and her remarkable tenure there came to an end.

Yet even after her departure from the museum, she did not consider herself retired. She was still an Egyptologist, after all, and was determined to remain in the field. As a journalist friend put it, she was "galloping like a gazelle over the sands of the Egyptian deserts at an age when others had long since put on their slippers." Those colleagues included John Wilson, her old friend and ally from the University of Chicago, who wrote that "archaeology is a young man's game. Scrambling in and out of pits, crouching over some new find or bracing oneself against a driving sandstorm are all part of what an archaeologist does, but only if one is young and vigorous." After straining his back on a dig at the age of sixty-eight, Wilson realized he could no longer play the game.

Not so Desroches-Noblecourt. She had major plans for her work in the Valley of the Queens, including a massive cleanup of the rubble still hiding many of the tombs, followed by archaeological and architectural surveys mapping the valley's topography and documentation of as many burial places as possible. "Nothing prevented me from dreaming," she later said. "I wanted to give back to this lost valley its ancient appearance and to understand its message. I was searching for anything that would allow us to reconstruct the history of the site and its region."

Her dream included the possibility of finding the missing mummies of the royal women and children once buried in the necropolis. It seemed unlikely that they had all been destroyed by the tombs' pillagers. Could they in fact have been spirited away by priests, like the mummies of Rameses II and other pharaohs in the Valley of the Kings, and deposited in a secret hiding place that had not yet been found? If so, she wanted to be the one to discover them.

The challenge was to raise enough money to turn her ambitious plans into reality. Desroches-Noblecourt's retirement from the Louvre meant a severe reduction in the subsidies from various government institutions, particularly France's National Center for Scientific Research (NCRS), that had helped finance her yearly survey missions. The allowances had been fairly small, to be sure, just enough to fund fieldwork for one month a year, but now she was unable to afford even that. At the many conferences, symposia, and other meetings she attended before and after her retirement, she let it be known that she was seeking private money for her venture.

One day, during a cultural symposium in Cannes, a dark-haired woman who was about Desroches-Noblecourt's age approached her and introduced herself as Germaine Ford de Maria. The elegantly dressed Ford de Maria was a wealthy philanthropist who lived in Cannes and was noted for her generous donations to a variety of environmental and cultural causes. She had provided money to restore a twelfth-century chapel in Cannes and to purchase paintings for one of the city's museums. She also helped fund a television series on plant biology and ecology by Jean-Marie Pelt, a noted French ecologist and urban planner.

Another major interest of hers was promoting peace in the Middle East. She gave a large donation to fund the Israeli Film Institute and was intent on finding a way to honor the late Egyptian president Anwar

Sadat, whose efforts to create peace between Israel and its Arab neighbors had led to his assassination in 1981.

Ford de Maria had learned about Desroches-Noblecourt's restoration project from a mutual acquaintance, a photographer and writer living in Cannes who specialized in the art and religion of ancient Egypt. It seemed a perfect fit for the philanthropist, combining her interests in environmental and cultural protection with a project in the homeland of her hero, Sadat.

She told Desroches-Noblecourt she was interested in investing in her venture and asked her to provide a report outlining her goals and needs for the next four years, along with an estimate of costs. Desroches-Noblecourt did so, describing an expansive operation requiring an army of tractors and other clearing equipment, as well as at least fifteen researchers and the purchase of a house near the Valley of the Queens where her team could both work and live.

As she added up the money needed for all this, she was aghast at how high the figure turned out to be. So she decided to present Ford de Maria with a second plan as well—one that would cut back on the project's operations and be considerably less expensive. Her would-be patron considered both proposals, then asked her two sons what they thought she should do. They replied, "Mother, if you want to act effectively, do it right." She agreed, telling Desroches-Noblecourt that she would fund the more expensive proposal—at a cost estimated to be more than a million dollars.

As a result of this enormous windfall, Desroches-Noblecourt was able to end her archaeological career with a consequential final act, thanks to a woman whose life story was, in its own way, as colorful and dramatic as her own.

FEW PEOPLE MEETING GERMAINE Ford de Maria for the first time would ever have associated the dignified, even regal matron with her earlier self—a beautiful, spirited young woman who acquired her wealth through a liaison with an Indian maharajah and marriage to a

British movie mogul. After her husband died, she became involved with a flamboyant French avant-garde artist.

Germaine Pellegrino's complicated romantic life began in 1930, when, at the age of seventeen, she met the fifty-eight-year-old Maharajah of Kapurthala in Cannes. Of all the rulers of the various Indian states, Jagatjit Singh, whose kingdom was located in the province of Punjab, was arguably the most cultured and cosmopolitan. He had ascended to the throne of Kapurthala at the age of five, and as a young man he became a great favorite of Queen Victoria, who, as the proclaimed empress of India, took a great interest in Britain's most important colony and some of its potentates. The queen exchanged frequent letters with the maharajah, who would go on to represent India at the League of Nations in the late 1920s. Victoria also commissioned a painting of him, which was displayed prominently at Osborne House, her summer home on the Isle of Wight.

But although he was intensely loyal to Britain, Singh's real passion was for France. He loved everything about the country, prominently including its language, culture, social life, and food. A fluent French speaker from an early age, the maharajah owned a mansion in Paris's Bois de Boulogne, where he staged lavish dinners and garden parties for members of international royalty and France's high society. Back in Kapurthala, he set out to make his capital "the Paris of the East" and modeled his palace there after Versailles.

His cosmopolitanism was also reflected in his many dalliances with a succession of young European women. Like other Indian princes, he had multiple wives—in his case, six —as well as a harem. But unlike most of his princely colleagues, two of his marriages were to Europeans—a Spanish dancer and a Czech countess. "He enjoyed the pleasures and high society of the West," his grandson recalled. "He also enjoyed the company of interesting and attractive young ladies and he brought back many from Europe to stay in Kapurthala as his guests and personal friends, some of them the most beautiful women I have ever seen."

British authorities were less than pleased with his unorthodox lifestyle, but according to the British historian Charles Allen, who wrote a book about Indian maharajahs, "it was equally true that the Maharajah always behaved with the utmost discretion in public. He treated all his guests with great charm and courtesy and retained the friendship of his lady friends even after they had ceased to enjoy the comforts of the palace."

One of Singh's favorite holiday spots was Cannes, a playground for the rich and famous on the French Riviera. That's where he met Germaine Pellegrino, the daughter of an Italian stonemason, who was employed as an occasional model by the House of Worth, the famed Paris couturier, which had a branch in Cannes. Spying her at a fashion show one day in 1928, the maharajah was instantly smitten.

He asked Germaine to tea at the Hotel Negresco, where he was staying, then invited her to dinner. After several encounters, he asked if she would like to visit India, where he would host her at his palace. According to Jarmani Dass, one of Singh's top aides, she agreed, albeit with the stipulation that he not treat her *"comme un petit jouet"* ("like a little toy"). He concurred.

When she arrived in Kapurthala, troops lined the road leading to the main gate of the palace, and a band played "La Marseillaise." Waiting in front of the Versailles-like residence to greet her were the maharajah, his royal offspring, and Kapurthala's prime minister and other top officials. That night, Singh staged a dinner in her honor in the ornate state dining room, which featured Gobelins-style tapestries on the walls.

For the duration of Germaine's long stay, she was lodged in a luxurious apartment in the west wing of the palace, overlooking its vast parks and gardens. While the maharajah's wives and concubines, housed in a smaller palace, were seldom seen, Germaine, according to Jarmani Dass, attended all official functions and was included in dinners with Indian politicians and officials. "She began to understand the politics of India and the kingdom and the intrigues of the palace," Dass said. The maharajah, he added, respected her political acumen.

Germaine returned to Paris in 1932. According to Dass, the maharajah followed her there and asked her to marry him, promising to make her his chief maharani. She declined. But she had much to remember him by, including a king's ransom in jewelry, from priceless pearl necklaces to diamond and emerald bracelets and earrings.

Soon after her return to France, she married Reginald Ford, a wealthy British film entrepreneur in his early forties who'd been involved in the production and distribution of silent movies since the industry's earliest days. In the early 1920s, Ford founded a company in New York to import French films to the United States. He then established a business in Paris to distribute American movies in Europe, including the Harold Lloyd classic *Safety Last!*, which boasts one of the most famous scenes from the silent film era: Lloyd dangling from the hands of a large clock high on a skyscraper above moving traffic.

In the late 1920s, Ford, inspired by a similar operation in the United States, founded a chain of theaters in France and other Western European countries devoted exclusively to newsreels and other short subjects like cartoons and travelogues. First created by the French company Pathé in 1908, newsreels, featuring filmed coverage of major events, were popular staples in movie theaters around the globe from the silent era until the 1950s, when television news supplanted them.

In 1937, Ford died suddenly at the age of forty-seven. His twenty-five-year-old widow inherited his businesses and continued to run them, which included the opening of new theaters throughout Europe. Two years later, she met Pierre de Maria, an artist who had been involved in the French modernist movement in Paris in the 1920s. A former architect and decorator, Maria was linked with the leading figures of surrealism, who sought to portray the workings of the unconscious mind through the use of fantastic, irrational images. He later became known for his fanciful paintings of machinery.

In 1940, Maria and Germaine married, and the couple had two sons in rapid succession. The younger son was barely a year old when Maria, a well-known ladies' man, left his family in Geneva, where they had settled, and returned to Paris. Germaine and her sons eventually ended up in the south of France. Although she was only in her thirties, her days of romantic adventures were over. It was time to reinvent herself—this time as a patron of worthy causes.

—

THANKS TO FORD DE MARIA's largesse, Desroches-Noblecourt's project was able to follow in the footsteps of major institutions like New York's Metropolitan Museum of Art and the University of Chicago's Oriental Institute in establishing a comfortable, modern base camp near where her team would be working. Ford de Maria provided the funds to buy a dilapidated mud brick house on the edge of the Valley of the Queens near the ruins of Malgatta, an ancient palace built by Amenhotep III, the father of the notorious Akhenaten and (according to Desroches-Noblecourt) perhaps also Tutankhamun. Occupied by an American archaeological team working on the Malgatta site in the 1970s, it had been abandoned once their work was done.

Within months of its purchase, the building had been totally renovated, with several bedrooms, bathrooms, a kitchen, workrooms, a large photo laboratory, and abundant storage space for technical equipment. A power line was installed, along with a water tower, which enabled the creation of a garden filled with trees and plants—a small flowery oasis in the middle of the desert. Germaine Ford de Maria was so taken with the place, the work, and the people at Malgatta House, as the camp was called, that she had a small studio apartment built on the terrace for her use during her frequent visits to the valley.

With such abundant financial and human resources invested in their venture, "these two ladies weren't doing things by halves," Guillemette Andreu-Lanoë observed. She speculated that Desroches-Noblecourt and Ford de Maria had in mind becoming the female equivalents of Howard Carter and Lord Carnarvon, the archaeologist-patron team responsible for the discovery of Tutankhamun's tomb. They cherished the hope that they might make a significant find in the Valley of the Queens, much as Carter and Carnarvon had done in the Valley of the Kings six decades earlier.

With the establishment of the Malgatta operation, the Valley of the Queens, that once desolate area with a largely forgotten past, came truly alive. Instead of just one survey and excavation mission a year, lasting only a month, there were now two expeditions, lasting two months each, in the spring and autumn.

For a time, it was the largest excavation operation in the area, involving more than 350 people in its workforce, some twenty of them professionals and most of the rest Egyptian laborers. While the professionals included a number of archaeologists, there were representatives of other disciplines as well, among them architects, anthropologists, botanists, and conservation experts.

Over the next several years, the appearance of the valley was transformed. Bulldozers, tractors, and other earth-moving equipment lowered the level of rubble and other garbage by some six to nine feet, allowing clear access to a growing number of tombs, which in turn were cleared of rubbish and inventoried. Steps leading down to the burial vaults were reconstructed. Unsightly huts selling souvenirs were moved out of the valley proper, as was a parking lot filled with tour buses that kept their motors running and thus posed an environmental danger to the tombs' fragile contents. They were relocated around a bend in the road leading to the area, restoring a sense of serenity and dignity to the necropolis.

With its access to an expanding number of tombs, Desroches-Noblecourt's team, which came to be known as the French Archaeological Mission of West Thebes (MAFTO), was able to get a much clearer picture of the burial sites and their functions. "We couldn't understand the cemetery before, because we were working tomb by tomb," Christian Leblanc said in 1989. "Today we've uncovered the major tombs and have returned the valley to the way it would have looked when burials began. For the first time, we can write its history."

When the expedition began its work in the 1970s, seventy-eight burial vaults had been identified in the necropolis. By the 1990s, the total had risen to more than a hundred. The ones that had already been found were further explored and studied. Thanks to this large-scale operation, the mission made a surprising discovery: There were far more burials of pharaohs' sons and daughters than formerly thought. Indeed, Leblanc, whom Desroches-Noblecourt had chosen to succeed her as head of the mission, came to the conclusion that the valley had been misnamed. "We should be calling it the Valley of the Royal Children," he said. "They were here first, but the valley became tied only to the queens and named by tradition rather than history."

Among the graves cleared and excavated were those of three of Rameses II's daughters, all of whom had gone on to become his wives as well. Their mummies, like all the others throughout the Valley of the Queens, were gone, but the digs produced a profusion of artifacts, including painted breastplates, canopic vases, beer jars, royal scepters, and pottery from a variety of periods.

Although Leblanc took day-to-day control of the mission in 1983, Desroches-Noblecourt continued working alongside the team in the valley until her late seventies. According to Jean-Louis Clouard, she never seemed to slow down. "At Malgatta House," he recalled, "there was a light in her room all night. And in the morning, she was present for breakfast at 5 A.M. with her impeccable perm. We wondered if she ever slept at all."

Desroches-Noblecourt had devoted much of her time in the 1980s to an intensive search for the tomb of Isisnofret, Rameses II's other favored wife and the mother of Merneptah, Rameses's eventual successor as pharaoh. But to her lasting regret, she failed to find any trace of the tomb, even though workers at Deir-el-Medina had left behind ostraca indicating they had been working on a burial vault for her in the valley. The missing mummies of Nefertari and other queens had not turned up either.

She wanted to continue the hunt, but in the late 1980s, Leblanc decided to shut down most of the team's work in the Valley of the Queens and switch its focus to exploration of the Ramesseum, Rameses II's funerary temple near Luxor. While Desroches-Noblecourt was unhappy with his decision, it's unlikely that she could have carried on in any case. As indefatigable as she seemed, old age had finally caught up with her. She had developed severe arthritis in her knees, making it more and more difficult for her to climb in and out of excavation sites. She finally stopped going to Egypt in 1992.

The French Archaeological Mission of West Thebes, meanwhile, lives on to this day, still working in collaboration with CEDAE. Over the past several decades, MAFTO's focus, in addition to new excavations, has been on the conservation and restoration of tombs and other antiquities that have already been discovered. In the late 1980s and early 1990s, it was involved in a major international effort to preserve the remnants of the extraordinary wall paintings in Nefertari's tomb, which were deteriorating at an alarming rate, as were those in other royal burial places in the valley. Half the paintings depicting the elaborately dressed and coiffed wife of Rameses II had already been lost by the time the Egyptian Antiquities Organization (EAO) enlisted the help of the Getty Conservation Institute, based at the Getty Center in Los Angeles, which in turn brought in experts from all over the world. "This project has established a new level of conservation in Egypt, which will serve as a model for other sites in Egypt and throughout the world," said Gamal Mokhtar, head of the EAO (now called the Supreme Council of Antiquities) and a former close associate of Desroches-Noblecourt.

During the restoration work on Nefertari's tomb, a number of the specialists, who came from Italy, the United States, and various other countries, lived at Malgatta House. The fruits of their four years of labor were remarkable: The paintings now glowed and shimmered as if the original artists had just laid down their brushes. "Our basic principle guiding every aspect of the conservation effort was that of minimum intervention," said Miguel Angel Corzo, the Getty Conservation Institute's director. "Because the colors of the tomb seem so exceptionally brilliant, it may be hard to believe that they are original. But this is unequivocal: not one drop of new paint was added to any of the surfaces. Instead, after conservation and cleaning, the wall paintings have recaptured their original magnificence."

Corzo called the collaboration between the Getty Conservation Institute, the Egyptian government, and the other organizations involved in the project "a true milestone in international cooperation." After the restoration of Nefertari's tomb was completed, the collaboration continued, with the Getty, Egypt's Supreme Council of Antiquities, CEDAE, and the French Archaeological Mission of West Thebes working as partners to develop and implement a comprehensive plan for the conservation and management of the Valley of the Queens. At the same time, MAFTO and Leblanc joined forces with the Egyptians in working to restore and preserve the Ramesseum.

This kind of archaeological cooperation between the West and Egypt, which Christiane Desroches-Noblecourt espoused from the beginning of her career, is still relatively rare. For many if not most Western archaeologists, as *The New Yorker*'s Peter Hessler noted, "there's been a divide between the pharaonic past and the Arabic present." Matthew Adams, a New York University archaeologist based in Egypt, told Hessler in 2011 that "Egyptologists as a group have not been too interested in dealing with the Egypt of today. The Egypt of today is sometimes seen as an impediment to the Egypt of the past." Desroches-Noblecourt was a striking exception to that dictum. Her insistence on getting to know and forming partnerships with Egyptians, whether government officials or laborers, continued to reverberate among those with whom she worked long after she was gone.

In 2002, a French friend of Desroches-Noblecourt's was visiting the Valley of the Kings near Deir-el-Medina when an old Egyptian, wearing black robes and a white turban, approached her and, speaking French, offered to sell her a small antiquity. After she responded in French, he asked her, "So do you know Madame Desroches-Noblecourt?" When she said yes, he identified himself as Gamal Mokhtar and told her he had worked on Desroches-Noblecourt's digs for more than twenty years. Then he asked her to pass on a message: "Tell her how much we love her here—and how much we miss her." He added, "You know, she didn't just order us around. She explained things to us." After pausing a moment, he said, "It's not the same anymore."

When the friend returned to Paris and delivered Gamal's message to Desroches-Noblecourt, the doyenne of Egyptologists replied, "It's true. Every evening, after making them work hard, I told them about our discoveries, what they meant, and how important they were. . . . Dear Gamal! I loved him, too."

CHAPTER 26

"THE MOST PRESTIGIOUS LIVING EGYPTOLOGIST IN THE WORLD"

ON A SUNNY SPRING AFTERNOON IN 2004, JACINTO ANTÓN, A cultural reporter for one of Spain's leading newspapers, knocked on the door of an apartment in Paris's 16th arrondissement. He was there, he later told his *El País* readers, to interview "the most prestigious living Egyptologist in the world." A woman opened the door and led him into an elegant sitting room, where Christiane Desroches-Noblecourt stood waiting.

At first glance, Antón wrote, the ninety-year-old archaeologist, with her curly white hair and sparkling eyes, reminded him of "an endearing grandmother." But within seconds, that impression was replaced by another: the sense of a "personality so overwhelming that it seems to absorb all the space around her, to the point that it is difficult to perceive the details of the room."

Only later did Antón take note of the surroundings: a large screen in the sitting room; a garden on an outside terrace featuring the figurine of an ibis; a work table strewn with books and photographs of archaeological excavations; framed photographs of Desroches-Noblecourt's brother, a French Navy vice admiral, and her late husband, André Noblecourt, who had died five years earlier.

After retiring from fieldwork, Desroches-Noblecourt had devoted the next decade to writing books about various aspects of what she considered the most fascinating civilization in world history. The French shared her ardor for ancient Egypt: Of the eleven works of nonfiction she produced over that period, several, including her memoir, were bestsellers. "No one has been able to make readers dream like Mme. Desroches-Noblecourt," commented the French magazine *L'Express*. "Her passion infected thousands."

Jacinto Antón had come to interview her about her latest book, *The Fabulous Heritage of Egypt*, which detailed the vast and varied contributions of ancient Egypt to Western civilization. To the delight of her publishing house, a small firm called Éditions Télémaque, it would turn out to be her biggest seller yet.

In the book, she contended that "the ideas that still form the basis of our thinking"—including theological concepts like original sin, an underworld rife with dangers and demons, resurrection after death, and a final judgment before an almighty god—were first devised in pharaonic Egypt. The country also came up with the concepts of a nation-state and an all-powerful monarchy, she added, along with the earliest versions of, among other things, an alphabet, a calendar, pregnancy tests, and treatments for such ailments as migraine headaches and cataracts.

Jacinto Antón was hardly the only journalist to seek out Desroches-Noblecourt during this final phase of her life, which turned out to be as richly productive in its own way as earlier periods. Thanks to her stewardship of the attention-getting Tutankhamun and Rameses II exhibitions, not to mention the rescue of Rameses's mummy, she was already well known to the French public. The success of her books, which were published internationally, only added to her fame, which she seemed to enjoy immensely. Writers from French newspapers and magazines trooped to her apartment on the rue Docteur Blanche, as did correspondents from publications in other parts of the world. She was also frequently interviewed by French radio and television and was even the subject of a ten-episode podcast.

During her conversation with Antón, Desroches-Noblecourt sat, a cane by her side, in an upholstered armchair of lapis lazuli blue, which, as Antón pointed out in his article, was "the favorite color of the pharaohs." Explaining the cane, she said, "I have had my knee operated on," but quickly added, "It's osteoarthritis, not old age." Yet as they talked, Antón noted that when she got up to look for a book, "she was carried along by her considerable energy and crossed the room without needing any support."

After a few minutes of discussion about her new work, the conversation turned to another subject about which she was passionate: the lives of women in ancient Egypt. In an earlier book, *La Femme au Temps des Pharaons,* Desroches-Noblecourt noted that unlike women in classical Greece and Rome, those in Egypt were regarded as the equals of men under the law. They could own land, inherit and manage their own property, marry whomever they wanted, and get a divorce if they chose. Some learned to read and write, and a select few were given advanced instruction before taking positions in government administration, commerce, and scientific professions.

In a number of cases, pharaohs' wives were named high priestesses, which gave them considerable wealth and political influence of their own. It was not unusual for a queen to assume temporary power over the country when the pharaoh went off to fight or when he died and his successor, usually his son, was too young to take his place. On at least three occasions, queens actually became rulers themselves, each coming to the throne when no male successor was immediately available. In 2002, Desroches-Noblecourt wrote a biography of one of them—the mysterious Queen Hatshepsut, who ruled from around 1479 to 1458 B.C. Acting as regent to her stepson, who was also her nephew, she did something no earlier female regent had ever dared: She proclaimed herself pharaoh, a scion of the gods like her male predecessors, and ruled the country for some twenty years.

Arguably Desroches-Noblecourt's most provocative book, *La Reine Mysterieuse Hatshepsut* set out to resuscitate the reputation of a female ruler who had long been vilified by male Egyptologists as a wily, unscrupulous woman who had wrested away and unlawfully occupied a throne meant only for men. That image had first been crafted by Egyptologists from New York's Metropolitan Museum of Art who in the 1920s had been involved in excavations at Deir-el-Bahri, Hatshepsut's magnificent funerary temple in the male-only necropolis, the Valley of the Kings. In the words of the Met's William Hayes, Hatshepsut must be regarded as "the vilest type of usurper."

When assessing that judgment, however, one must keep in mind an important fact about the Egyptian pharaohs: Not much is known about any of them. As the American archaeologist Michael Jones has noted, "The ancient Egyptians have been dead for thousands of years. Nobody alive knows what they were thinking. We create an image of them, and it's based on our own ideas. It's a bit like looking in a mirror. . . . We can only ever access the past through our own frame of reference." In the case of ancient Egypt, the frame of reference governing how we view these long-dead figures has, for the most part, been male.

Desroches-Noblecourt challenged that masculine view of Hatshepsut. According to her, Hatshepsut was neither an intriguer nor a usurper, and "her reign, if you study it carefully, was a great one." For Egypt, it was a time of peace and prosperity, to which the sharp-witted, astute female pharaoh contributed by emphasizing, among other things, the importance of foreign trade. She was noted for sending an ambitious trade expedition to the distant and fabled land of Punt, on the Red Sea coast in northeast Africa, which was, in the words of one historian, "the first great commercial, scientific, and peaceful operation of which we have news." More recent scholarship has generally supported Desroches-Noblecourt's conclusions that not only has Hatshepsut been woefully underestimated as a ruler, but her self-declaration as pharaoh was more likely the result of a political crisis threatening the country's stability than a naked power grab.

As the interview proceeded, Desroches-Noblecourt's regal bearing and imperious manner reminded Antón more and more of Hatshepsut herself. Clearly growing tired after an hour or so of questioning, she impatiently ordered the photographer who had accompanied the journalist to stop circling her to snap pictures. When the photographer asked if she had any Egyptian antiquities with which she could pose, she retorted, "No, no, no! I have never taken any item home with me during my entire career. I'm an archaeologist, sir!" To another journalist who had previously broached the same question, she said she made it a point never to acquire or display any ancient Egyptian object: "Everybody would think I'd stolen it from some tomb."

FROM THE BEGINNING OF her career, Christiane Desroches-Noblecourt had been a controversial figure among her French archaeological colleagues. Amandine Marshall, a young Egyptologist who worked for several years with Christian Leblanc's French Archaeological Mission of West Thebes, observed that she was "admired and appreciated" by some but "detested and regarded with jealousy" by others. Another French Egyptologist, Guillemette Andreu-Lanoë, remarked, "She was disruptive. . . . Her spontaneity and outspokenness, her aplomb, her oratorical talent deeply irritated a large number of her colleagues. They didn't like that kind of behavior."

As Desroches-Noblecourt grew older, her queenly airs and high-profile media presence made her even more a locus of controversy. "She became more difficult," observed Henri Loyrette. "It was hard for her to share sometimes with the younger generation." Anick Coudart, a former director of research at the French National Center for Scientific Research, was more blunt, describing Desroches-Noblecourt as "domineering to the point of crushing those around her." Amandine Marshall made a similar point, contending that Desroches-Noblecourt's dominance in the spotlight meant that significant work by other archaeologists went unnoticed.

More troubling, in Marshall's view, was what she saw as Desroches-Noblecourt's failure in some of her works to provide adequate scientific support to justify her theories and conclusions about various aspects of ancient Egypt, a number of which Marshall claimed were erroneous. "In her books, there are many statements but no footnotes," she said. "A scientist remains a scientist, even if she is at the top of the pyramid, and she must not exempt herself from supporting her work with arguments and references. . . . Having to blindly believe what is written because it is the great Christiane Desroches-Noblecourt who wrote it, without being able to question, reassemble or verify the reasoning or the theory, that is what bothers me in her works, because it is not the way that research should function."

Yet it's also important to remember that most of Desroches-Noblecourt's later books were not meant to be scholarly tomes backed up by extensive documentation but popular works aimed at bringing ancient Egypt alive for a much broader audience. In the view of Henri Loyrette, any perceived flaws in Desroches-Noblecourt's research methods should not, in any case, obscure her extraordinary contributions to the Louvre, Egyptology, and international cultural preservation and cooperation. In addition to saving the temples of Nubia, he said, "she gave the Louvre and Egyptology a totally new image by bringing in the media and public to see the exhibitions and collections. . . . We like to say that Egypt is a French passion, and it's true, you can see it everywhere. She was the one who really developed this passion."

IN THEIR RELATIVELY BRIEF sessions with Desroches-Noblecourt, Jacinto Antón and her other interviewers managed to elicit a scattering of colorful quotes and sound bites from her, but in general, their questions and her answers merely skimmed the surface of her remarkable career. That, however, was not the case in her interaction with Olga Prud'homme Farges, a French documentary filmmaker who in 2007 embarked on a much more thorough excavation of the famed Egyptologist's life for a film entitled *Une Passion Égyptienne.*

Ninety-three years old at the time, Desroches-Noblecourt was living in a retirement home in Sézanne, a town in northeastern France, near a manor house owned by her father's family in the village of Mondement-Montgivroux. She had agreed to participate in eight hours of interviews, spaced out over a month, to be conducted at her family's ancestral home.

Keenly aware of the advanced age of her subject, Prud'homme

Farges, who was then in her late thirties, had no idea what to expect. At their initial meeting, her first reaction was one of amazement—and relief. Although physically frail, Desroches-Noblecourt was full of fire and life—articulate, forceful, and able to recall the most minute details about events that had occurred decades before. "I remember how reassuring her energy and passion was to me," Prud'homme Farges later said, "to realize that it was possible to get to her age and be all there mentally."

During her conversations with the filmmaker, Desroches-Noblecourt revealed more personal details about her early life and career than she had done in other interviews or even in her own memoir. She remembered, as if it were yesterday, being carried on the shoulders of her grandfather to see the Obelisk of Luxor in the Place de la Concorde. She recalled the sheer fun of dancing the Charleston with her brother and his friends and then gathering around her family's dining room table to play ping-pong.

Above all, she talked about the great debt she owed her parents for encouraging her to do what she wanted and for providing her with the unstinting support, not to mention the stellar education, that enabled her to enter a male-only field and overcome the daunting challenges put in her way. In the book *Sous le Regard des Dieux*—a collection of interviews with Desroches-Noblecourt—one of its editors observed in the introduction that she "has served the cause of women better than an army of suffragettes." Nonetheless, despite the fact that her own success as an archaeologist, not to mention her encouragement of younger women to follow in her footsteps, helped broaden the field for women, she never considered herself a feminist.

"When I asked her, 'Were you a feminist at the time?'" Prud'homme Farges recalled, "she said, 'No, why? I'm just myself. It happens I'm a woman, and I had to fight for what I wanted to do. But not as a woman, just as a human being.'" The filmmaker continued, "She never felt inferior being a woman. She had an unshakable belief that she was as good as any man, and she never believed otherwise." At the same time, though, it's obvious from her remarks that the ferocious work ethic she displayed throughout her career was prompted, at least in part, by the belief that she had to work harder than any man to prove herself in the field.

When others told her she couldn't do something, she refused to accept their verdict. "People often didn't take her seriously," Prud'homme Farges said. "Here was this little woman, small in stature, who wanted to save these temples. Nobody thought for a second it was possible. But she had so much power and energy and she worked so hard, talking to people—discussing and arguing and convincing. She had to prove her authority, and sometimes she was a bit tyrannical, but it was only a strategy to accomplish what she wanted. And, of course, she did it."

Throughout their conversations, Desroches-Noblecourt made it clear that her work as an Egyptologist had always been the most important thing in her life, with everything else, including her family, taking a distinct second place. "I think she could not have achieved what she did if work had not been her top priority," Prud'homme Farges said. "The moment she opened her eyes in the morning, that's all she thought of. . . . Egypt was her whole world. She was addicted to it, and she wanted to go back again and again. It was her religion."

When the filmmaker probed Desroches-Noblecourt about her private life, she generally shied away from answering. But Prud'homme Farges did manage to elicit one of the few public remarks Desroches-Noblecourt ever made about her husband. Talking about their courtship, she recalled that she had agreed to marry André Noblecourt only after he promised that he would never stand in the way of her career. "She had such a strong character that the only thing he could do was to support her," Prud'homme Farges observed. "He had no choice. She didn't let him have a choice. She said to him, 'I'm doing this. You can follow or not. But I'm doing it.'"

It seemed, at least from outward appearances, that the couple were devoted to each other. They appeared together frequently at social gatherings in Paris, and her husband accompanied her on some of her trips. He was one of six people to whom she dedicated her memoir, which was published in 1999, the same year as his death. "For André," the dedication said, "who supported, encouraged, and sustained fifty years of Egyptology and without whom I could not have carried out the Grande Nubiade."

The couple's son, Alain, was among the five others to whom the book was dedicated—one of the rare times she ever mentioned him. Another of those occasions was in *La Grande Nubiade*, when she wrote about her reluctance in 1954 to leave eight-year-old Alain to go to Egypt and orchestrate the creation of CEDAE. But as her memoir makes clear, such hesitation was short-lived. "I tried to ask her questions about him, but she never really answered them," Prud'homme Farges said. "She didn't want to talk about him. When she was saving the Abu Simbel temples, she didn't have time to take care of him. She was much more dedicated to Egyptology."

As Prud'homme Farges saw it, Desroches-Noblecourt directed most of her maternal feelings toward her Egyptian laborers: "I remember her telling me that her workers were like her children. She took care of them, sent them presents for their birthdays. They were her second family."

Even as she formed close relationships with Egyptian archaeologists and other professionals throughout her career, she felt most at home with the fellahin, peasants who worked the land or engaged in other manual labor, like the workers on her digs. To her, their beliefs and ways of living were reminiscent of those of their ancestors from the pharaonic age. "She believed that the pulse of the country and the pulse of history and antiquity could be found in their blood today," Prud'homme Farges said. "She had a passion for these simple people."

To another interviewer, Desroches-Noblecourt remarked that Egypt's fellahin "have not changed in thousands of years. They offer the same lessons in humanity, serenity, justice, and patience as their ancient forbears—lessons that are particularly useful for me, since I'm very temperamental, you know."

In the later years of her life, Desroches-Noblecourt tried to shut out the modern world as much as possible. She confessed to a friend that she could no longer bring herself to go to ancient sites in Egypt that were overrun with tourists. "I don't feel anything when I'm there," she said. "Their soul has been taken away." When her friend asked if there were any sites that spoke to her more than others, she replied, "Those that are not visited by tourists, where you are alone with the monuments. Mostly the sites I like are behind the cliff in the Valley of the Kings, where no tourists ever go. When I'm on the path that connects the two valleys, I'm in ancient Egypt, eternal Egypt. There, I am at home."

ON NOVEMBER 26, 2009, UNESCO hosted the first showing of Prud'homme Farges's film at a gala celebration in honor of Desroches-Noblecourt at its Paris headquarters. Before the screening began, Irina Bokova, the new director general of UNESCO, stood at a lectern in front of an audience of several hundred people and addressed her remarks to the elderly woman sitting before her. "Tonight," Bokova said to Desroches-Noblecourt, "allow us to pay tribute to you, a woman whose life is a model of learning, sharing, and courage. Thanks to your passion for ancient Egypt, you have been able to . . . bring the past to life, making it intelligible and fascinating. You fought tirelessly to convince politicians and decision makers in multiple countries to embark on an adventure of unparalleled magnitude. You were the origin of the concept of the world heritage of humanity which, more than ever, matters in our time. . . . With the Tutankhamun exhibit in 1967, you truly gave birth to a new popular fervor for art and museums."

After enumerating several more of Desroches-Noblecourt's achievements, Bokova concluded her remarks with this statement: "I am proud that one of my first acts as the first woman director general of UNESCO is to pay homage to a great lady of knowledge, action and commitment—a humanist." For Desroches-Noblecourt, Bokova's calling her a humanist was the highest compliment she could have been paid. Her parents had been humanists, she'd proudly told Prud'homme Farges, who inculcated in her the values by which she tried to live her life—"respect for one another, for your neighbors, for people in general, for civilization."

Prud'homme Farges had escorted Desroches-Noblecourt to the screening and sat next to her as the film was being shown. The honoree

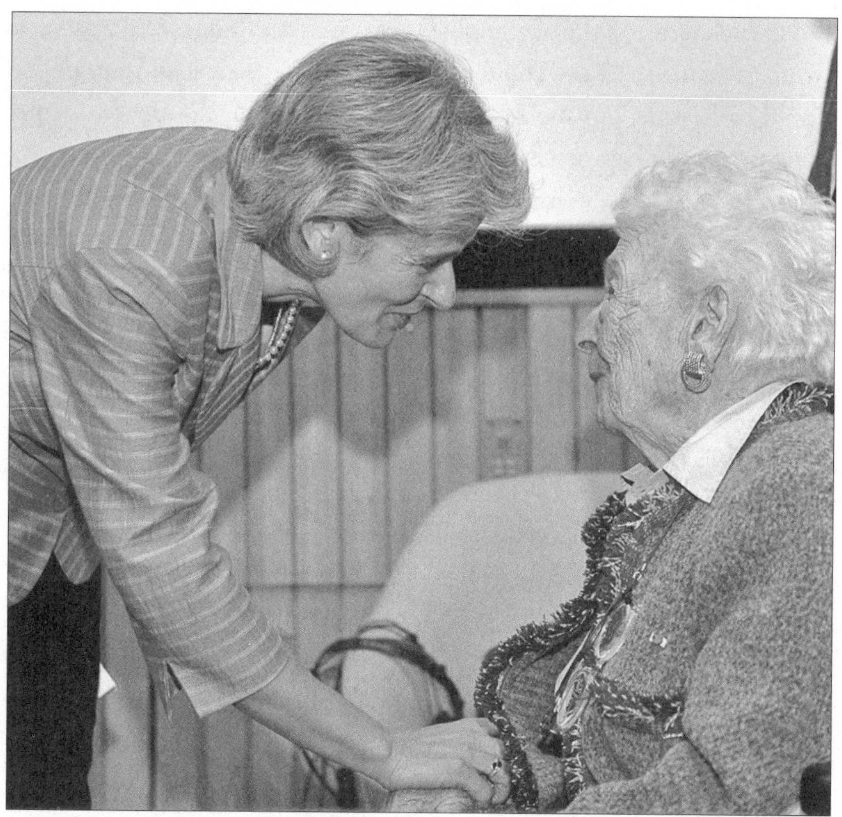

UNESCO DIRECTOR GENERAL IRINA BOKOVA GREETS CHRISTIANE DESROCHES-NOBLECOURT AT A PARIS CEREMONY IN 2009 HONORING THE NINETY-SIX-YEAR-OLD EGYPTOLOGIST

wore a stylish black-and-white tweed suit with a tiny scarlet-and-white pin attached to her jacket. That emblem signified that she had been awarded the highest level of France's most prestigious order of merit, the Grand Cross of the Legion of Honor—one of only six women to receive it in the order's 220-year history. As Desroches-Noblecourt watched the film, Prud'homme Farges remembered, "sometimes she laughed; sometimes she said, 'Did I really say that?' She seemed very moved, very touched by it. It was quite a lovely moment."

The UNESCO tribute marked her last public appearance. "She was content, I think," Prud'homme Farges observed. "She was not the type of person who had regrets. She had a wonderful life, full of experience and knowledge and the accomplishment of great things. She was very proud of that. . . . If she could have physically gone back to Egypt she would have gone, but she accepted that she was old and physically not able to. She was happy with what she had done."

On June 23, 2011, Christiane Desroches-Noblecourt died at the age of ninety-seven. Among the flood of tributes that followed her death was one from then French president Nicolas Sarkozy, who called her "the grande dame of the Nile" and compared her to the great Jean-Francois Champollion, the founding father of Egyptology. Henri Loyrette, who headed the Louvre at the time, credited Desroches-Noblecourt's "energy and passion" with making "Egyptology truly popular, in the best sense of the word." Years later, he described her as "a very special person, one who was very dear to my heart."

In the final few months of her life, Desroches-Noblecourt made it clear she intended to go on working—and living—until the last possible moment. On the bookshelves in her room, she left behind voluminous notes for possible future writing projects. "As long as there's life, there's hope," she had told Prud'homme Farges. "Never give up. Never abandon what you set out to do. That's my philosophy."

ACKNOWLEDGMENTS

When I finished my last book and began thinking about my next project, my first impulse was to find another subject dealing with World War II. That's no surprise, really, since the war has been the backdrop for all but one of my eight previous books. With that in mind, I began to research possible subjects, among them the first resistance network to be organized in Paris following the 1940 German occupation of France.

What interested me most about the Musée de l'Homme network was that it was an unlikely collection of rebels. Most of its members were scholars, among them anthropologists, archaeologists, art historians, museum curators and directors, linguists, writers, and librarians. Equally intriguing was the fact that women played key roles in creating and running it, a highly unusual phenomenon in the overall resistance movement in France, which was heavily androcentric.

But as I read more about the group, I became particularly absorbed by the story of one of its women members—a young archaeologist named Christiane Desroches-Noblecourt. The acting chief curator of Egyptian antiquities at the Louvre, she led a double life during the war, working at the museum during the week while enmeshed in the secret world of the resistance at night and on weekends.

As I learned more about her, I realized what a bold, trailblazing, history-making woman she had been—a natural-born rebel who defied society's strictures about the proper role of women and refused to allow men to tell her what to do. Yet even though she had done amazing things during and after the war, her life and achievements remained largely unknown outside France.

Finding out about Desroches-Noblecourt was the first of two lightbulb moments for me. I was captivated by her as a person and equally enthralled by her seemingly hopeless campaign in the 1960s to save several ancient temples in Egypt from drowning—a crusade that morphed into the greatest example of international cultural cooperation the world has ever known. In leading that charge, she went toe to toe with some of the most daunting government leaders of the mid-twentieth century, among them Egyptian president Gamal Abdel Nasser and French president Charles de Gaulle.

The second lightbulb moment was my discovery that one of the most famous women in American history—Jacqueline Kennedy, the country's new First Lady—had also played a crucial role in the rescue of the temples. Jackie Kennedy insisted, however, that her activism not be publicized, and as a result, her role is also largely uncelebrated today.

Astonishingly, there is no biography of Desroches-Noblecourt in either French or English. But I found a wealth of other material to draw on, including her French-language memoir and a series of interviews with her conducted by two journalists and published in book form. Another key resource was an excellent French TV documentary about her life and times by the filmmaker Olga Prud'homme Farges. Also immensely helpful were interviews with, among others, Prud'homme Farges and Henri Loyrette, a celebrated former director of the Louvre, whose memories of and insights into Desroches-Noblecourt were of crucial importance in bringing her to life on the page.

My colleague and friend Dorie Denbigh-Laurent, who took part in those interviews, also spent a week at the National Archives of France (Archives Nationales de France) near Paris, examining Desroches-Noblecourt's extensive papers there as well as translating and analyzing numerous broadcast and print interviews with her. As is true of my previous book, *Madame Fourcade's Secret War*, I could not have written *Empress of the Nile* without Dorie's immeasurable contribution.

Also helpful was the memoir of Christian Leblanc, Desroches-Noblecourt's trusted deputy during her later field missions in Egypt, who succeeded her as director after she retired. Thanks, too, to other noted Egyptologists whose writings and research I drew on, among them Toby Wilkinson, John Wilson, Torgny Säve-Söderbergh, Donald Malcolm Reid, and Jason Thompson.

I owe a special debt of gratitude to my brilliant editor, Susanna Porter, as well as to the rest of the Random House team. This is my fifth collaboration with Susanna, whose enthusiasm for the subject, support and encouragement throughout my research and writing, and skilled and perceptive editing helped make *Empress of the Nile* a joy to work on and a much better book. Huge thanks as well to the incomparable Gail Ross, my agent and friend for almost thirty years.

And, finally, to the two most important people in my life—my husband, Stan Cloud, and our daughter, Carly—whom I love beyond measure.

NOTES

INTRODUCTION

xiii **"Not only do I not speak it"**: Christiane Desroches-Noblecourt, *Sous le Regard des Dieux* (Paris: Albin Michel, 2016), 153.

xiv **"I had encountered"**: Daniel Bermond, "Christiane Desroches-Noblecourt: 'I Had to Face a Certain Misogyny,'" *L'Express,* July 1, 2002.

xiv **"share the library"**: Ibid.

xiv **"I can't believe"**: Desroches-Noblecourt, *Sous le Regard des Dieux,* 154.

xv **"You don't get anywhere"**: Anne-Marie Romero, "The Death of Christiane Desroches-Noblecourt," *Le Figaro,* June 24, 2011.

xvi **"The pharaonic state"**: Toby Wilkinson, *The Rise and Fall of Ancient Egypt* (New York: Random House, 2011), 36.

xvii **"Those images spoke to me"**: Desroches-Noblecourt, *Sous le Regard des Dieux,* 20.

xvii **"these funny men"**: Ibid., 14.

xvii **"Look at her eyes"**: Ibid.

xvii **"Every time I walk"**: Ibid.

xviii **"their paradise would be like"**: John Wilson, *Thousands of Years: An Archaeologist's Search for Ancient Egypt* (New York: Scribners, 1972), 140.

xx **"For me it was like"**: Desroches-Noblecourt, *Sous le Regard des Dieux,* 14.

CHAPTER 1: A CHILDHOOD PASSION

4 **"I am listening to an opera"**: Desroches-Noblecourt, *Sous le Regard des Dieux,* 15.

4 **"living proof"**: Ibid., 17.

4 **"already a feminist"**: Ibid.

4 **"My parents were humanists"**: Olga Prud'homme Farges (director), *Christiane Desroches-Noblecourt: Une Passion Égyptienne,* TV film documentary, CDP Productions and *France Télévisions,* aired on France 5, December 11, 2009.

4 **"we were considered"**: Desroches-Noblecourt, *Sous le Regard des Dieux*, 16.

4 **"It was a sacred ritual"**: Ibid., 14.

5 **not to take literally**: Ibid., 18.

5 **"a nursery for our aspirations"**: *Centenary of the Lycée Molière Memorial 1888–1988*.

6 **"embraced the culture"**: William Grimes, "Jacqueline de Romilly, Who Studied Greek Culture, Dies at 97," *New York Times*, December 20, 2010.

6 **"At the time"**: Desroches-Noblecourt, *Sous le Regard des Dieux*, 21.

6 **"bored me stiff"**: "Christiane Desroches-Noblecourt," *Telegraph*, July 1, 2011.

8 **"listed all the possibilities"**: Desroches-Noblecourt, *Sous le Regard des Dieux*, 23.

8 **"a very interesting abbot"**: Bermond, "Christiane Desroches-Noblecourt: 'I Had to Face a Certain Misogyny.'"

CHAPTER 2: COMING OF AGE AT THE LOUVRE

10 **"From its very inception"**: Toby Wilkinson, *A World Beneath the Sands: The Golden Age of Egyptology* (New York: W. W. Norton, 2020), 13.

10 **"For over forty generations"**: Ibid., 57.

10 **"[Champollion's] achievement allowed"**: Ibid., 357.

11 **"Antiquity is a garden"**: Ibid., 122.

13 **"Every time you stop"**: Desroches-Noblecourt, *Sous le Regard des Dieux*, 96.

14 **"was even more talkative than me"**: Ibid., 28.

14 **"could have awakened a dead man"**: Ibid., 27.

15 **"a museum within a museum"**: Ibid., 32

15 **"we never risked being dazzled"**: Christiane Desroches-Noblecourt, *La Grande Nubiade: Le Parcours d'une Égyptologue* (Paris: Stock/Pernoud, 1992), 15.

15 **"There were no manuals"**: Ibid., 34.

16 **"On the contrary"**: Ibid., 16.

16 **"If you don't have good transitions"**: Desroches-Noblecourt, *Sous le Regard des Dieux*, 29.

16 **"I sweated blood and water"**: Ibid.

17 **"Over the course"**: Amanda Adams, *Ladies of the Field: Early Women Archaeologists and Their Search for Adventure* (Vancouver, B.C.: Greystone Books, 2010), 9.

19 **"A unique, intoxicating blend"**: Wilkinson, *World Beneath the Sands*, 207.

19 **"The beauty of sand"**: Amelia B. Edwards, *A Thousand Miles up the Nile* (London: George Routledge and Sons, 1891), 287.

19 **"The worst enemy"**: Andrew H. Bellisari, "Raiders of the Lost Past: Nineteenth-Century Archaeology and French Imperialism in the Near East, 1798–1914," Master of Arts thesis, Rutgers University, 2010.

20 **"Almost singlehandedly"**: Wilkinson, *World Beneath the Sands*, 233.

21 **"a very restricted community"**: Robert Solé, *La Grande Aventure de l'Égyptologie* (Paris: Perrin, 2019), 326.

21 **"the fear of intellectual domination"**: "Christiane Desroches-Noblecourt: Première Égyptologue Française," *Égypte Ancienne*, October 2016–January 2017.

22 **"I would spend every Sunday"**: *Christiane Desroches-Noblecourt: Une Passion Égyptienne*.

22 **"were trying to destroy me"**: "The Career of an Egyptologist," podcast, *France Culture*, December 26, 2017.

22 **"They thought the fact"**: Desroches-Noblecourt, *Sous le Regard des Dieux*, 68.

23 **"Can you imagine"**: Ibid., 92.

23 **"I got to handle"**: *Christiane Desroches-Noblecourt: Une Passion Égyptienne.*

CHAPTER 3: "A DANGEROUS BLACK SHEEP"

24 **"We were emerging from"**: Jean Cassou, *Une Vie pour la Liberté* (Paris: Éditions Robert Laffont), Loc. 656 (Kindle edition).

25 **"people's ineradicable love of political"**: Stacy Schiff, *Saint-Exupéry: A Biography* (New York: Knopf, 1995), Loc. 4875 (Kindle edition).

27 **"had a hard time"**: Interview with Henri Loyrette.

27 **"this invasion by the public"**: Desroches-Noblecourt, *Grande Nubiade*, 106.

27 **"a wave of panic"**: Ibid., 107.

28 **"obviously considered me"**: Desroches-Noblecourt, *Sous le Regard des Dieux*, 124.

28 **"dangerous black sheep"**: Desroches-Noblecourt, *Grande Nubiade*, 108.

28 **"Mademoiselle," he said**: Desroches-Noblecourt, *Sous le Regard des Dieux*, 124.

28 **"Although the minister"**: Ibid., 124–25.

CHAPTER 4: A SPLENDID ADVENTURE

30 **"wrong kind of men"**: Desroches-Noblecourt, *Grande Nubiade*, 40.

31 **"the most delectable dishes"**: Desroches-Noblecourt, *Sous le Regard des Dieux*, 60.

31 **"She was absolutely right"**: Ibid., 61.

32 **"No ancient site"**: Wilkinson, *World Beneath the Sands*, 339.

35 **"Your duty is not to overlook"**: Desroches-Noblecourt, *Grande Nubiade*, 56.

35 **"His find was"**: Desroches-Noblecourt, *Sous le Regard des Dieux*, 24.

35 **"When we compare his files"**: Ibid., 25.

36 **"his memory almost disappeared"**: Desroches-Noblecourt, *Grande Nubiade*, 53.

36 **"Czech by birth but French at heart"**: Ibid., 42.

38 **"It is these ostraca"**: David O'Connor, "Jaroslav Cerny, 1898–1970," *Expedition Magazine* 12, no. 4 (1970).

38 **"He learned to sift"**: John Romer, *Ancient Lives: The Story of the Pharaohs' Tombmakers* (London: Weidenfeld and Nicolson, 1984).

40 **"looking like great wolves"**: Desroches-Noblecourt, *Grande Nubiade*, 49.

40 **"shaped Egypt's geography"**: Toby Wilkinson, *The Nile: A Journey Downriver Through Egypt's Past and Present* (New York: Knopf, 2014), 12.

41 **"The Egyptians have always"**: Ibid., 20.

42 **"If we put together"**: Desroches-Noblecourt, *Sous le Regard des Dieux*, 89.

44 **"Every morning . . . this boy"**: Ibid., 90.

47 **"Nothing frightened her"**: Claudine Le Tourneur d'Ison, *Une Passion Égyptienne: Jean-Philippe et Marguerite Lauer* (Paris: Plon, 1996), Loc. 2395 (Kindle edition).

48 **"You are sacred"**: Desroches-Noblecourt, *Grande Nubiade*, 53.

49 **"Get up here"**: Desroches-Noblecourt, *Sous le Regard des Dieux*, 66.

CHAPTER 5: UPHEAVAL IN CAIRO

52 **"These were not unpleasant smells"**: Penelope Lively, *Oleander, Jacaranda: A Childhood Perceived* (New York: HarperCollins, 1994), 9.

53 **"whole towns and villages"**: Wilkinson, *The Nile*, 166.

55 **"with all the racial baggage"**: Alan Allport, *Browned Off and Bloody-Minded: The British Soldier Goes to War, 1939–1945* (New Haven: Yale University Press, 2015), 149.

57 **"To be French-speaking"**: Artemis Cooper, *Cairo in the War 1939–1945* (London: John Murray, 2015), 38.

58 **"Ah, Monsieur Lacau"**: Reid, *Contesting Antiquity in Egypt*, 117.

59 **"jealously closed environment"**: Desroches-Noblecourt, *Grande Nubiade*, 61.

59 **"caused a huge scandal"**: Ibid.

59 **"a woman could never be"**: Desroches-Noblecourt, *Sous le Regard des Dieux*, 63.

60 **"What are you so afraid of"**: Ibid., 64.

60 **"I immediately declared"**: Ibid.

60 **"Of course," she said**: Ibid.

CHAPTER 6: "LUCK SMILED ON ME AGAIN"

64 ***"grand seigneur"***: Desroches-Noblecourt, *Sous le Regard des Dieux*, 71.

64 **"They accepted me"**: Ibid.

65 **"I kept begging him"**: Ibid., 70.

65 **"a real Chinese puzzle"**: Ibid.

66 **"acting," she recalled**: Desroches-Noblecourt, *Grande Nubiade*, 68.

67 **"as if by a miracle"**: Ibid.

67 **"At first they treated me"**: Desroches-Noblecourt, *Sous le Regard des Dieux*, 71.

67 **"treat my male comrades"**: Desroches-Nobelcourt, *Grande Nubiade*, 66.

68 **"Unlike some Egyptologists"**: Desroches-Noblecourt, *Sous le Regard des Dieux*, 71.

69 **"behaved in the most odious way"**: Ibid., 68.

69 **"had completely lost his mind"**: Desroches-Noblecourt, *Grande Nubiade*, 66.

69 **"Ah," said the foreman**: Ibid.

69 **"The Egyptian people are deeply generous"**: Desroches-Noblecourt, *Sous le Regard des Dieux*, 78.

70 **"helped them keep a rhythm"**: Desroches-Noblecourt, *Grande Nubiade*, 67.

70 **"These same gestures"**: Christiane Desroches-Noblecourt, *Le Secret des Découvertes* (Paris: Télémaque, 2006).

71 **"so that these gentlemen could have"**: Desroches-Noblecourt, *Sous le Regard des Dieux*, 72.

71 **"Christiane, have some pity"**: Ibid., 74.

72 **"I'll never forget that moment"**: Desroches-Noblecourt, *Grande Nubiade*, 70.

72 **"I watched the workers"**: Desroches-Noblecourt, *Sous le Regard des Dieux*, 75.

73 **"Sire, Your Majesty must come"**: Ibid., 76.

CHAPTER 7: SAVING THE TREASURES OF THE LOUVRE

83 **"still capable of overshadowing"**: "Karnak Temple," *Discovering Egypt*, discoveringegypt.com/karnak-temple/.

84 **"We want work!"**: Desroches-Noblecourt, *Grande Nubiade,* 83.
84 **"I could not conceive"**: Desroches-Noblecourt, *Sous le Regard des Dieux,* 137.
86 **"Madame," Desroches replied**: Ibid., 141.
86 **"Do you honestly believe"**: Ibid., 142.
87 **"My reputation with the Gontaut-Birons"**: Ibid.
87 **"an anthill that had been knocked over"**: Lynne Olson, *Madame Fourcade's Secret War: The Daring Young Woman Who Led France's Largest Spy Network Against Hitler* (New York: Random House, 2019), 19.
87 **"one of the most beautiful"**: en.wikipedia.org/wiki/Château_de_Valençay.
88 **"Why are we involved"**: Desroches-Noblecourt, *Grande Nubiade,* 86.
88 **"If the sound of cannons"**: Desroches-Noblecourt, *Sous le Regard des Dieux,* 139.
89 **"Of course," she later said**: Ibid., 143.
89 **"by some inexplicable luck"**: Desroches-Noblecourt, *Grande Nubiade,* 87.
90 **"I wasn't going to stay there"**: Desroches-Noblecourt, *Sous le Regard des Dieux,* 145.

CHAPTER 8: RESISTING THE NAZIS

92 **"I was a leader without an army"**: Desroches-Noblecourt, *Sous le Regard des Dieux,* 145.
92 **"We all had tears"**: Ibid., 146.
93 **"My poor young friend"**: Ibid., 147.
93 **"This was a decision"**: Ibid., 148.
93 **"I will go mad, literally"**: Agnès Humbert, *Résistance: Memoirs of Occupied France* (London: Bloomsbury, 2008), 38.
95 **"It was," a British historian remarked**: Barbara Mellor, "Bold Defiance in Nazi Paris," *Today,* BBC Radio, September 26, 2008.
95 **"transformed itself into a veritable"**: Laura Spinney, "The Museum Director Who Defied the Nazis," *Smithsonian,* June 2020.
96 **"Resistance! That's the cry"**: Matthew Cobb, *The Resistance: The French Fight Against the Nazis* (London: Pocket Books, 2010), 52.
97 **"For me, there is one word"**: Humbert, *Résistance,* 331.
97 **"Although [the network's members]"**: David Schoenbrun, *Soldiers of the Night: The Story of the French Resistance* (Lexington, Mass.: Plunkett Lake Press, 2016), Loc. 2584 (Kindle edition).
97 **"We did not slink about"**: Ibid.
98 **"Every day, we heard"**: *Hitler's Museum: The Secret History of Art Theft During World War II,* film documentary, 2006.
99 **"take into custody the French"**: Gerri Chanel, *Saving Mona Lisa: The Battle to Protect the Louvre and Its Treasures from the Nazis* (London: Icon Books, 2018), 143.
99 **"Sir, you are the first"**: Françoise Cachin, ed., *Pillages et Restitutions: Le Destin des Oeuvres d'Art Sorties de France Pendant la Seconde Guerre Mondiale* (Paris: Éditions Adam Biro, 1997), 29.
102 **"You're right, mademoiselle"**: Desroches-Noblecourt, *Sous le Regard des Dieux,* 150.
104 **"That's why I was released"**: Ibid., 170.

105 **"At a time when most of the French"**: Alan Riding, *And the Show Went On: Cultural Life in Nazi-Occupied Paris* (New York: Knopf, 2010), 143.
105 **"fed and watered the Resistance"**: Spinney, "The Museum Director Who Defied the Nazis."
109 **"He knew I had been arrested"**: Desroches-Noblecourt, *Sous le Regard des Dieux*, 177.
109 **"a veritable miracle"**: Cachin, *Pillages et Restitutions*, 28.
110 **"the time has come to restore"**: Ibid.
110 **"I can't tell you how emotional"**: Ibid.
111 **"Our two groups, face-to-face"**: Marie de Thézy and Thomas Michael Gunther, eds., *Images de la Libération de Paris* (Paris: Paris Musées, 1994), 143.
112 **"I just want to go back"**: Desroches-Noblecourt, *Sous le Regard des Dieux*, 161.
112 **"I look like I'm seventy"**: Humbert, *Résistance*, 212.
113 **"I suppose that gentleman's"**: Antoine Sabbagh, "Sir, You Will No Longer Consider Yourself My Son," *Guardian*, July 10, 2009.

CHAPTER 9: SHOCK WAVES IN EGYPT

115 **"He had repeatedly fought"**: Chanel, *Saving Mona Lisa*, 389.
116 **"The first ambition"**: Desroches-Noblecourt, *Sous le Regard des Dieux*, 36.
116 **"I repeated what the masters"**: Ibid.
116 **"He was too intelligent"**: Prud'homme Farges, *Christiane Desroches-Noblecourt: Une Passion Égyptienne*.
116 **"I was still in the resistance"**: Ibid.
117 **"I told him"**: Ibid.
117 **"He demonstrated a feminism"**: Guillemette Andreu-Lanoë, "Christiane Desroches Noblecourt (1913–2011)," newsletter of the French Institute of Oriental Archaeology, 2011.
117 **"prince consort"**: Interview with Henri Loyrette.
118 **"the military capital"**: Allport, *Browned Off*, 139.
119 **"one of the last acts"**: James Morris, *Farewell the Trumpets: An Imperial Retreat* (New York: Harcourt Brace Jovanovich, 1978), 440.
119 **"Your Majesty is no longer fit"**: Ibid.
119 **"So much for the events"**: Ibid.
120 **"an incubator of intense Egyptian nationalism"**: Gershon Gorenberg, *War of Shadows: Codebreakers, Spies, and the Secret Struggle to Drive the Nazis from the Middle East* (New York: PublicAffairs, 2021), 69.
120 **"Oppose them with all the force"**: Saïd K. Aburish, *Nasser: The Last Arab* (New York: Thomas Dunne Books, 2013), 245.
122 **"The ascent every day"**: Desroches-Noblecourt, *Grande Nubiade*, 82.
123 **"One can imagine"**: Desroches-Noblecourt, *Sous le Regard des Dieux*, 136.
123 **"I was getting ready"**: Desroches-Noblecourt, *Grande Nubiade*, 82.
123 **"You might have fallen"**: Ibid.
123 **"This kind of gesture"**: Desroches-Noblecourt, *Sous le Regard des Dieux*, 136.
125 **"the liquidation of colonialism"**: Aburish, *Nasser*, 51.
126 **"the spiritual father"**: Omnia El Shakry, *The Great Social Laboratory: Subjects of*

Knowledge in Colonial and Postcolonial Egypt (Palo Alto: Stanford University Press, 2014), 50.

128 **"promoting collaboration"**: Lynn Meskell, *A Future in Ruins: UNESCO World Heritage and the Dream of Peace* (Oxford: Oxford University Press, 2018), 13.

128 **"books, works of art"**: Ibid., 126.

129 **"You were full of enthusiasm"**: Desroches-Noblecourt, *Grande Nubiade*, 121.

CHAPTER 10: "OZYMANDIAS, KING OF KINGS"

130 **"You can't possibly"**: Desroches-Noblecourt, *Sous le Regard des Dieux*, 446.

130 **"At the time, a woman"**: Ibid., 447.

132 **"One morning we woke up"**: Milton Viorst, "Man of Gamaliya," *New Yorker*, June 24, 1990.

133 **"this symbolic death"**: Sarwat Okasha, "Ramses Recrowned: The International Campaign to Preserve the Monuments of Nubia, 1959–68," IJBF Online, 224.

133 **"What else is left to us"**: Georg Gerster, "Threatened Treasures of the Nile," *National Geographic*, October 1963, 587.

135 **"We made him accept"**: Desroches-Noblecourt, *Grande Nubiade*, 126.

135 **"It obviously seemed monstrous"**: Ibid., 130.

137 **"We know now"**: Edwards, *Thousand Miles*, 316.

140 **"looking like the rising"**: Museo Egizio and Salini Impregilo, *Nubiana: The Great Undertaking That Saved the Temples of Abu Simbel* (Milan: Rizzoli, 2019), 82.

141 **"Although he was the incarnation of god"**: Christiane Desroches-Noblecourt and Georg Gerster, *The World Saves Abu Simbel* (Vienna: Verlag A. F. Koska, 1968), 43.

141 **"there is an indefinable charm"**: Ibid., 34–35.

141 **"coupled and inseparable"**: Edwards, *Thousand Miles*, 347.

143 **"I found that my heart"**: Emma Slattery Williams, "Was Rameses II Really That Great?" historyextra.com/period/ancient-egypt/was-ramesses-ii-pharaoh-great-brilliant-why/.

144 **"They took a mountain"**: Edwards, *Thousand Miles*, 339.

144 **"the daily miracle"**: Ibid., 334.

145 **"They will live"**: Rahul Jacob, "The Art of the Day Trip," *Financial Times*, August 22, 2008.

145 **"not to resign themselves"**: Desroches-Noblecourt, *Grande Nubiade*, 130.

146 **"Mr. Minister, you have not"**: Ibid., 132.

147 **"was in the grip of these shrines"**: Ibid., 136.

147 **"I had not yet realized"**: Ibid., 131.

CHAPTER 11: DISASTER AT SUEZ

149 **"What use are the grand words"**: Desroches-Noblecourt, *Grande Nubiade*, 140.

149 **"She's the one"**: Ibid.

149 **"someone I know"**: Ibid., 141.

149 **"rather awkward grace"**: Hazel Rowley, *Tête-à-Tête: The Tumultuous Lives and Loves of Simone de Beauvoir and Jean-Paul Sartre* (New York: HarperCollins, 2015), Loc. 344 (Kindle edition).

150 **"My greatest happiness"**: Ibid., Loc. 347.
150 **"I need Sartre"**: Ibid., Loc. 547.
150 **"He was a very exciting teacher"**: Ibid., Loc. 6767.
151 **"Tell me your story"**: Desroches-Noblecourt, *Grande Nubiade,* 141.
151 **"At the time"**: Ibid., 140.
152 **"His work was flawless"**: Ibid., 144.
154 **"Nasser never closed the door"**: Aburish, *Nasser,* 82.
154 **"had developed almost"**: Alex von Tunzelmann, *Blood and Sand: Suez, Hungary, and Eisenhower's Campaign for Peace* (New York: HarperCollins, 2016), 43.
155 **"a thumb on our windpipe"**: Ibid., 29.
155 **"painted a haunting picture"**: Ibid., 31.
156 **"I want him destroyed!"**: Ibid., 361.
156 **"But I don't want an alternative!"**: Ibid., 12.
156 **"Ben-Gurion could not"**: Ibid., 51.
157 **"an atrocity by anyone's"**: Ibid., 82.
159 **"The Americans . . . could have"**: Aburish, *Nasser,* 100.
159 **"the Israelis dealt him"**: Ibid., 85.
160 **"jeopardizing its ability"**: Tunzelmann, *Blood and Sand,* 32.
161 **"For Dulles"**: Ibid., 33.
161 **"weakness in the Egyptian economy"**: Aburish, *Nasser,* 139.
162 **"He regarded it as"**: Tunzelmann, *Blood and Sand,* 36.
162 **"in the name of the people"**: Ibid., 37.
163 **"For the first time in the twentieth century"**: Aburish, *Nasser,* 141.
163 **"that an upstart like him"**: Tunzelmann, *Blood and Sand,* 52.
163 **"We all know"**: Ibid., 61.
165 **"In the eyes of the whole world"**: Ibid., 286.
166 **"Port Said, shattered"**: Morris, *Farewell the Trumpets,* 528–29.

CHAPTER 12: "THESE MONUMENTS BELONG TO ALL OF US"

168 **"This futile aggression"**: Desroches-Noblecourt, *Grande Nubiade,* 168.
169 **a poignant farewell**: Ibid., 159.
169 **"I told people"**: Ibid., 163.
170 **"Don't hesitate"**: Ibid., 165.
170 **"The country appeared"**: Ibid., 179.
171 **"I went two nights"**: Stephane Foucart, "Christiane Desroches-Noblecourt," *Le Monde,* June 23, 2011.
172 **"his surprise to see"**: Desroches-Noblecourt, *Grande Nubiade,* 177.
172 **"It was like preaching"**: Jacinto Antón, "Entrevista a Christiane Desroches-Noblecourt," *El País,* July 11, 2004.
173 **"Nothing," he told her**: Desroches-Noblecourt, *Grande Nubiade,* 181.
175 **"a bulldog"**: Robert M. Edsel, *The Monuments Men: Allied Heroes, Nazi Thieves, and the Greatest Treasure Hunt in History* (New York: Center Street, 2009), 78.
175 **"Think, Christiane, of the insult"**: Desroches-Noblecourt, *Grande Nubiade,* 182.
175 **"These monuments belong"**: Ibid.
175 **"With UNESCO"**: Ibid., 183.

175 **"haunted by the threat"**: Okasha, "Ramses Recrowned," 227.

175 **"very dynamic"**: Associated Press obituary of Christiane Desroches-Noblecourt, June 27, 2011.

176 **"When he made a decision"**: Desroches-Noblecourt, *Grande Nubiade,* 183.

176 **"Egyptians note with a mixture"**: Viorst, "Man of Gamaliya."

176 **"convinced that I had found"**: Okasha, "Ramses Recrowned," 227.

179 **"I'll do it"**: Desroches-Noblecourt, *Grande Nubiade,* 183.

180 **"I hope you don't mind"**: Ibid., 184.

181 **"a magnificent sense of popularization"**: "French Egyptologist, Saviour of Nubian Temples, Dies," AFP, June 25, 2011.

182 **"the stunning virtuosity"**: Desroches-Noblecourt, *Grande Nubiade,* 206.

182 **"springing out of the twilight"**: Ibid., 200.

183 **"an irreparable loss for the world"**: Chloé Maurel, "Le Sauvetage des Monuments de Nubie par l'UNESCO (1955–1968)," *Égypte / Monde Arabe,* 2013.

184 **"dubious" about the effort**: "Death by Drowning," *Time,* November 23, 1959.

184 **"although we would never"**: Wilson, *Thousands of Years,* 160.

CHAPTER 13: THE GREATEST DIG IN HISTORY

185 **"For the first time"**: Desroches-Noblecourt, *Grande Nubiade,* 228.

186 **"a plan of magnificent"**: Ibid., 229.

186 **"We know deep in our hearts"**: Ibid., 226.

187 **"I have made sacrifices"**: Torgny Säve-Söderbergh, ed., *Temples and Tombs of Ancient Nubia: The International Rescue Campaign at Abu Simbel, Philae and Other Sites* (London: Thames and Hudson, 1987), 124.

187 **"so that the beautiful temples"**: Desroches-Noblecourt, *Grande Nubiade,* 214.

189 **"having a foot"**: "Interview with Sadruddin Aga Khan," *UNESCO Courier,* May 1991.

192 **"Never before had such generous"**: John Wilson, "The Nubian Campaign: An Exercise in International Archaeology," American Philosophical Society, October 16, 1967.

192 **"Nowadays," Desroches-Noblecourt wrote**: Christiane Desroches-Noblecourt, "Floating Laboratories of the Nile," *UNESCO Courier,* October 1961.

193 **"worked frantically day and night"**: Paul Betts, "The Warden of World Heritage: UNESCO and the Rescue of the Nubian Monuments," *Past and Present,* 2015.

194 **"Nubia belongs to the dawn"**: "Now or Never," *UNESCO Courier,* October 1961.

194 **"The Sudanese think"**: Undated memo, Jacqueline Kennedy to John F. Kennedy, Jacqueline Bouvier Kennedy Onassis personal papers, John F. Kennedy Presidential Library.

194 **"To the layman, perhaps"**: Christiane Desroches-Noblecourt, "Nubia's Sands Reveal Their Last Secrets," *UNESCO Courier,* December 1964.

197 **"From the standpoint"**: Säve-Söderbergh, *Temples and Tombs,* 202.

197 **"In the lean years"**: Wilson, *Thousands of Years,* 160.

198 **"She was an active archaeologist"**: Säve-Söderbergh, *Temples and Tombs,* 206.

199 **"Having a daughter"**: Samia Spencer, *Daughters of the Nile: Egyptian Women*

Changing Their World (Newcastle upon Tyne: Cambridge Scholars Publishing, 2016), 171.

200 **"I discovered my real"**: Ibid., 173.

200 **"go to Nubia"**: Ibid., 174.

200 **"I can proudly say"**: Ibid.

CHAPTER 14: A CHAMPION IN THE WHITE HOUSE

202 **"its almost overwhelming richness"**: Säve-Söderbergh, *Temples and Tombs*, 127.

203 **"It is difficult to imagine"**: Facebook page, Deutsches Archaeologiches Institut, Cairo, April 23, 2020.

203 **"hard-hitting, dangerous labor"**: Suzanne Voss, "A New Beginning: Cairo Department of German Archaeological Institute After World War II," *Archaeology in Egypt*, November 2019.

204 **"To me," she said**: Desroches-Noblecourt, *Grande Nubiade*, 238.

204 **"In a voice that seemed"**: Ibid.

205 **"my intervention was a little foolish"**: Ibid.

205 **"That quote terrified me"**: Ibid.

205 **"added to my already"**: Ibid.

206 **"How dare you engage France"**: Prud'homme Farges, *Christiane Desroches-Noblecourt: Une Passion Égyptienne.*

206 **"And you—did you demand"**: Ibid.

206 **"You win!"**: Ibid.

207 **"among the mass of committees"**: Maurel, "Sauvetage des Monuments," 17.

208 **"No," he retorted**: Desroches-Noblecourt, *Grande Nubiade*, 215.

209 **"Who is this Frenchwoman"**: Ibid.

209 **"How do you claim"**: Ibid., 216.

209 **"Madame Noblecourt, have you"**: Ibid., 221.

209 **"The Americans were the worst"**: Antón, "Entrevista."

210 **"Jacqueline accepted the life"**: Carl Sferrazza Anthony, *As We Remember Her: Jacqueline Kennedy Onassis in the Words of Her Friends and Family* (New York: HarperCollins, 1997), 18.

211 **"I loved it"**: Ibid., 41.

211 **"I learned not to be ashamed"**: Elizabeth J. Natalle, *Jacqueline Kennedy and the Architecture of First Lady Diplomacy* (New York: Peter Lang, 2018), 24.

211 **"She prized the sense"**: Barbara Leaming, *Jacqueline Bouvier Kennedy Onassis: The Untold Story* (New York: Thomas Dunne Books, 2014), 24.

211 **"She wanted to know history"**: Anthony, *As We Remember Her*, 88.

212 **"a gathering of the most"**: Jacqueline Kennedy, *Historic Conversations on Life with John F. Kennedy* (New York: Hyperion, 2011), xii.

212 **"I could see the present"**: Ibid., 144.

212 **"The President's curiosity"**: Natalle, *Jacqueline Kennedy and the Architecture*, 27.

212 **"He saw the arts"**: Ibid.

212 **"showcase for everything"**: Ibid., 169–70.

213 **"The rest of the world"**: Undated memo, John Wilson to White House, Nubian Monuments file, John F. Kennedy papers, John F. Kennedy Presidential Library.

213 **"It became clear to me"**: Richard N. Goodwin, *Remembering America: A Voice from the Sixties* (New York: Open Road Media, 2014), 255.

214 **"That's all fine"**: Ibid.

214 **"I wasn't going to"**: Ibid.

215 **"open invitation"**: Douglas Little, "The New Frontier on the Nile: JFK, Nasser, and Arab Nationalism," *Journal of American History*, September 1988.

215 **"the Arab world's foremost"**: Ibid.

215 **"had never feigned an interest"**: Susan Sheehan, "The Happy Jackie, the Sad Jackie, the Bad Jackie, the Good Jackie," *New York Times*, May 31, 1970.

216 **"intensely interested"**: Anthony, *As We Remember Her*, 148.

216 **"Whenever there was"**: Ibid., 170.

216 **"engaged actively in foreign affairs"**: Whitney Walton, "Jacqueline Kennedy, Frenchness, and French-American Relations in the 1950s and Early 1960s," *French Politics, Culture and Society*, Summer 2013.

216 **"My parents believed"**: Kennedy, *Historic Conversations*, xiv.

216 **"My mother understood"**: Ibid., xvii.

216 **"a veritable Iron Curtain"**: Lucia Allais, "Integrities: The Salvage of Abu Simbel," *Grey Room*, MIT Press Journals, January 1, 2013.

216 **"in the interests of the United States"**: JFK message to Congress, April 4, 1961, John F. Kennedy Presidential Library.

217 **"always been against giving money to foreigners"**: Anthony, *As We Remember Her*, 148.

218 **"Jack, you must be out of your mind"**: Goodwin, *Remembering America*, 255.

CHAPTER 15: A TIME OF CRISIS

221 **"Wonderful as this modern technological feat"**: Okasha, "Ramses Recrowned," 232.

222 **"I raced to issue a statement"**: Ibid., 235.

223 **"neither a public policy issue"**: Roger K. Lewis, "Historic Preservation Doesn't Have a Long History in U.S.," *Washington Post*, September 11, 2015.

224 **"This promised to be the biggest"**: Wilson, *Thousands of Years*, 149.

224 **"the complexities of getting wealthy Americans"**: Memo from Edmundo Lassalle to Dr. J. O. Brewer, April 10, 1961, Jacqueline Kennedy Onassis Private Papers, John F. Kennedy Presidential Library.

224 **"If the costs of the Nubian campaign"**: Wilson, *Thousands of Years*, 160.

225 **"a gigantic novelty"**: John Canaday, "Temple in Extremis," *New York Times*, April 4, 1963.

225 **"My wife and I"**: Ibid.

225 **"had fallen in love"**: Ibid.

226 **"I confess I hesitated"**: Okasha, "Ramses Recrowned," 233.

227 **"one of the most spectacular mistakes"**: Froelich Rainey, *Reflections of a Digger* (Philadelphia: University of Pennsylvania Museum of Archaeology and Anthropology, 1992), 165.

227 **"It is unbelievable to be able"**: Natalle, *Jacqueline Kennedy and the Architecture*, 184.

227 **"It was the most popular"**: Hearings before Senate Appropriations Subcommittee,

Departments of State, Justice, and Commerce, Appropriations, June 23, 1964, Government Printing Office.

228 **"Every day," Rainey remembered**: Rainey, *Reflections of a Digger*, 165.

229 **"tour was a huge success"**: Maurel, "Sauvetage des Monuments," 22.

229 **"mortal threats to their own"**: Douglas Little, "The New Frontier on the Nile: JFK, Nasser, and Arab Nationalism," *Journal of American History*, September 1988.

229 **"Senator Fulbright is"**: Memo from Edmundo Lassalle to Dr. J. O. Brewer, April 10, 1961, Jacqueline Bouvier Kennedy Onassis Private Papers, John F. Kennedy Presidential Library.

CHAPTER 16: THE FIRST LADY INTERVENES

231 **"I was," she said**: Kennedy, *Historic Conversations*, 141.

231 **"The trouble with me"**: Anthony, *As We Remember Her*, 251.

231 **"people take my diffidence"**: Ibid., 260.

231 **"For a few hours"**: Walton, "Jacqueline Kennedy, Frenchness, and French-American Relations in the 1950s and Early 1960s."

232 **"couldn't take his eyes"**: Clint Hill, *Mrs. Kennedy and Me: An Intimate Memoir* (New York: Gallery Books, 2012), 70.

232 **"dazzling and cultivated wife"**: Natalle, *Jacqueline Kennedy and the Architecture*, 67.

232 **"drew de Gaulle into"**: Anthony, *As We Remember Her*, 150.

232 **"I do not think it"**: Leaming, *Jacqueline Bouvier Kennedy Onassis*, 120.

232 **"renewing the vibrant"**: Natalle, *Jacqueline Kennedy and the Architecture*, 69.

232 **"stands for . . . an effort"**: Anthony, *As We Remember Her*, 156.

232 **"the things people had once"**: Margaret Leslie Davis, *Mona Lisa in Camelot: How Jacqueline Kennedy and Da Vinci's Masterpiece Charmed and Captivated a Nation* (Washington, D.C.: White House Historical Association, 2008), 174.

233 **"true romantic"**: Natalle, *Jacqueline Kennedy and the Architecture*, 68.

233 **"a pale Napoleonic brow"**: Davis, *Mona Lisa in Camelot*, 38.

233 **"He talks so fast"**: Kennedy, *Historic Conversations*, 227.

234 **"She listened to him"**: Davis, *Mona Lisa in Camelot*, 16.

234 **"would call attention"**: Anthony, *As We Remember Her*, 168.

235 **"I could hardly wait"**: Walton, "Jacqueline Kennedy, Frenchness, and French-American Relations."

236 **"There was a personal purpose"**: K. L. Kelleher, *Jackie: Beyond the Myth of Camelot* (Xlibris, 2000), 92.

236 **"She was always appalled"**: Anthony, *As We Remember Her*, 164.

236 **"In other countries"**: Natalle, *Jacqueline Kennedy and the Architecture*, 175.

238 **"ripped down"**: Kennedy, *Historic Conversations*, xxvii.

238 **"She basically told us"**: Anthony, *As We Remember Her*, 145.

238 **"to stop everything"**: Ibid.

238 **"was the one who really deserved"**: Ibid., 146.

238 **"Perhaps saving old buildings"**: Natalle, *Jacqueline Kennedy and the Architecture*, 207.

239 **"Jacqueline Kennedy gave a voice"**: Anthony, *As We Remember Her*, 144.

239 **"I didn't think we had"**: Lucius Battle oral history, John F. Kennedy Presidential Library.

240 **"It was far less expensive"**: Ibid.

240 **"It seemed to me," Battle later said**: Ibid.

241 **"Abu Simbel is the major temple"**: Undated memo, Jacqueline Kennedy to John F. Kennedy, Jacqueline Bouvier Kennedy Onassis personal papers, John F. Kennedy Presidential Library.

242 **"gone fairly deeply"**: Goodwin memo to JFK, January 13, 1963, Jacqueline Bouvier Kennedy Onassis personal papers, John F. Kennedy Presidential Library.

243 **"the single most important"**: Lucius Battle oral history, John F. Kennedy Presidential Library.

243 **"It would be a real calamity"**: Hearings before Senate Appropriations Subcommittee, Departments of State, Justice, and Commerce Appropriations, June 23, 1964, Government Printing Office.

243 **"Architecture stands as the most enduring"**: Ibid.

243 **"neither aid to Nasser"**: Ibid.

244 **"These archaeological monuments"**: Ibid.

244 **"The race with the rising water"**: Ibid.

244 **"If we fail to do this"**: Ibid.

244 **"enormous personal interest"**: Ibid.

245 **"not unduly enthusiastic"**: Ibid.

245 **"who was not exactly a great lover"**: Lucius Battle oral history, John F. Kennedy Presidential Library.

245 **"I am simply throwing out these suggestions"**: Hearings before Senate Appropriations Subcommittee, Departments of State, Justice, and Commerce Appropriations, June 23, 1964, Government Printing Office.

246 **"Rooney said he wasn't"**: Lucius Battle oral history, John F. Kennedy Presidential Library.

CHAPTER 17: "GO, BABY, GO!"

247 **"immensely repulsed"**: Lucia Allais, "Integrities: The Salvage of Abu Simbel," *Grey Room*, MIT Press Journals, January 1, 2013.

247 **"a solution of despair"**: Desroches-Noblecourt and Gerster, *The World Saves Abu Simbel*, 94.

248 **"Each and every one"**: Georg Gerster, "Saving the Temples of Abu Simbel," *National Geographic*, May 1966, 708.

248 **"We take every possible precaution"**: Ibid., 742.

249 **"We could not lose a minute"**: George de Carvalho, "Abu Simbel—A Race Is Won," *Life*, December 2, 1966.

250 **"It was a razor's edge"**: Säve-Söderbergh, *Temples and Tombs*, 112.

250 **"deeply engrained understanding"**: Museo Egizio and Salini Impregilo, *Nubiana*, 242.

250 **"I don't think that the management"**: Gerster, "Saving the Temples," 734.

251 **"He wasn't wrong"**: Desroches-Noblecourt, *Grande Nubiade*, 265.

251 **"No matter how large"**: Gerster, "Saving the Temples," 736.

252 **"Among Nubians there was a strong"**: Säve-Söderbergh, *Temples and Tombs*, 57–58.

252 **"the disappearance of his beloved"**: Desroches-Noblecourt, *Grande Nubiade*, 267.

253 **"our last big ceremony"**: Ibid.

253 **"the tearing of the Nubian population"**: Ibid., 307.

256 **"we know rocks like hearts"**: Gerster, "Saving the Temples," 737.

256 **"The men, however"**: Ibid.

256 **"These men could feel"**: Carvalho, "Abu Simbel."

257 **"The human effort required"**: "A Salvage Operation That Inspired the World," *Sarat: Safeguarding the Archaeological Assets of Turkey* (report), January 10, 2018.

257 **"Would all those calculations"**: Säve-Söderbergh, *Temples and Tombs*, 121.

258 **"as if the mountain"**: Desroches-Noblecourt and Gerster, *The World Saves Abu Simbel*, 89.

258 **"Go, baby, go!"**: Ibid.

258 **"Anyone visiting the construction site"**: Ibid., 104.

259 **"Amid the great"**: Museo Egizio and Salini Impregilo, *Nubiana*, 245.

260 **"In the evening"**: Ibid., 251.

260 **"I would arrange trips"**: Medhat Abudul Rahman Ibrahim, "Saving Abu Simbel: Fifty Years On," *Egypt Today*, February 22, 2018.

262 **"taking on all the fleeting expressions"**: Gerster, "Saving the Temples," 696.

CHAPTER 18: "NO ONE WAS MORE RESOLUTE THAN SHE"

268 **"Her voice was insistent"**: Wilson, *Thousands of Years*, 147.

269 **"a very emotional moment"**: Episode 1, "Le Sauvetage des Temples de Nubie," *Radio France Culture* podcast, December 17, 2007, franceculture.fr/emissions/a-voix-nue/christiane-desroches-noblecourt-110-le-sauvetage-des-temples-de-nubie.

270 **"If it's not put back"**: Desroches-Noblecourt, *Grande Nubiade*, 48.

270 **"His reaction exceeded ours"**: Ibid.

270 **"We have come"**: Ibid., 48.

271 **"a mission accomplished"**: Museo Egizio and Salini Impregilo, *Nubiana*, 251.

271 **"as immediate as it was generous"**: Ibid.

271 **"we were preaching"**: Antón, "Entrevista."

271 **"We owe so much"**: Museo Egizio and Salini Impregilo, *Nubiana*, 251.

272 **"very special gift of vision"**: Ibid.

272 **"After this extraordinary"**: Telegram from René Maheu to Christiane Desroches-Noblecourt, May 16, 1967, National Archives of France.

272 **"sad resignation"**: Torgny Säve-Söderbergh, "International Salvage Archaeology," *Annals of the Royal Academy of Science*, Uppsala, 1971–72.

273 **"It is to you"**: Irina Bokova speech, UNESCO, November 26, 2009.

274 **"in having written a few pages"**: Museo Egizio and Salini Impregilo, *Nubiana*, 19.

274 **"in redirecting progress"**: Ibid.

275 **"If we don't care"**: Tina Cassidy, "The Surprising Role Jackie Kennedy Onassis Played in Saving Grand Central," Bloomberg City Lab, February 5, 2013.

CHAPTER 19: THE BATTLE FOR DENDUR

278 **"an exquisite toy"**: Edwards, *Thousand Miles*, 431.

278 **"small, complete in itself"**: Advisory Group Meeting Report on Dendur, August 9, 1963, Jacqueline Bouvier Kennedy Onassis Papers, John F. Kennedy Presidential Library.

278 **"always thought Dendur"**: Undated letter from Jacqueline Kennedy Onassis to Barnaby Keeney, chairman of the National Endowment for the Humanities, Jacqueline Bouvier Kennedy Onassis Papers, John F. Kennedy Presidential Library.

279 **"Once the Smithsonian"**: Sophy Burnham, "A Little Bit of Egypt on Fifth Avenue," *New York*, November 18, 1968.

280 **"It was his thought"**: Undated letter from Jacqueline Kennedy Onassis to Barnaby Keeney, chairman of the National Endowment for the Humanities, Jacqueline Bouvier Kennedy Onassis Papers, John F. Kennedy Library.

281 **"honoring the wishes"**: Smithsonian Institution Proposal for Locating the Temple of Dendur in the National Capital Area, Jacqueline Bouvier Kennedy Onassis Papers, John F. Kennedy Presidential Library.

281 **"moribund," "gray," and "dying"**: Thomas Hoving, *Making the Mummies Dance: Inside the Metropolitan Museum of Art* (New York: Touchstone, 1993), 32.

282 **"He implored me"**: Ibid., 51.

282 **"I have doubts"**: Ibid., 52.

282 **"I had half a mind"**: Ibid.

283 **"a power that is out"**: Ibid., 14.

283 **"really cared about"**: Ibid., 35.

283 **"The idea that the temple"**: Ibid., 58.

283 **"mere stage setting"**: Ibid.

283 **"sheer theatrics"**: Ibid., 59.

284 **"I know the senator"**: Ibid., 60.

285 **"I went so far"**: Ibid., 62.

286 **"It actually means"**: William H. Rockett, "A Temple at the Met," *Aramco World*, May/June 1980.

286 **"the extraordinary clarity"**: Ibid.

287 **"The simplicity of its setting"**: Ibid.

288 **"Dendur itself"**: Ibid.

CHAPTER 20: "A CULTURAL JUGGERNAUT"

289 **"this titanic feat"**: Andreu-Lanoë, "Christiane Desroches Noblecourt."

289 **"the international madness for King Tut"**: Thomas Hoving, *Tutankhamun: The Untold Story* (New York: Cooper Square Press, 2002), 12.

290 **"It seemed to me eminently fair"**: Desroches-Noblecourt, *Grande Nubiade*, 18.

290 **"there would still be great"**: Ibid.

291 **"The obstacles were often"**: Desroches-Noblecourt, *Grande Nubiade*, 18.

292 **"remarkably executed"**: Ibid.

292 **"The objects placed"**: Christiane Desroches-Noblecourt, *Tutankhamun* (London: Penguin, 1965), 71.

293 **"For the first time in recorded"**: Peter Hessler, *The Buried: An Archaeology of the Egyptian Revolution* (New York: Penguin, 2019), 242.

294 **"he and all his associates"**: Wilkinson, *World Beneath the Sands*, 328.

294 **"trusting her instinct"**: Andreu-Lanoë, "Christiane Desroches Noblecourt."

294 **"be afraid to take a stand"**: Desroches-Noblecourt, *Sous le Regard des Dieux*, 407.

295 **"They speak of heresy or schism"**: Antón, "Entrevista."

295 **"theories on Amarna"**: Christian Leblanc, "Christiane Desroches-Noblecourt, the Lady of the Nile 1913–2011," *Égyptophile*, June 22, 2011.

295 **"Like the treasure"**: "Gorgeous Book on King Tut," Baltimore *Sun*, October 13, 1963.

296 **"These treasures blaze"**: Binghamton *Press and Sun Bulletin*, December 22, 1963.

296 **"This is a magnificent"**: *Sacramento Bee*, December 1, 1963.

296 **"An Egyptologist of the first rank"**: *Calgary Herald*, March 7, 1964.

296 **"my first introduction"**: Wilkinson, *Rise and Fall*, 33.

296 **"Your book is filled"**: Letter from Charles de Gaulle to Christiane Desroches-Noblecourt, Desroches-Noblecourt papers, National Archives of France.

297 **"was the subject"**: Desroches-Noblecourt, *Grande Nubiade*, 22.

298 **"I wanted to evoke"**: Ibid.

299 **"Choose what you want"**: Ibid., 24.

299 **"The English weren't pleased"**: Bermond, "Christiane Desroches-Noblecourt: 'I Had to Face a Certain Misogyny.'"

300 **"meticulous—and extremely careful"**: Desroches-Noblecourt, *Grande Nubiade*, 19.

300 **"had approached the problem"**: Ibid., 20.

301 **"I argued, I quibbled"**: Ibid., 24.

304 **"Do you like to dance?"**: Ibid., 29.

304 **"seemed interested in everything"**: Antón, "Entrevista."

304 **"Like you, general"**: Desroches-Noblecourt, *Grande Nubiade*, 30.

305 **"He is truly"**: Ibid.

306 **"spoke, with great consideration"**: Ibid., 32.

306 **"infected with Pharaonic fever"**: "Exhibitions: Tutankhamen Mania," *Time*, March 17, 1967.

307 **"blue or black lines"**: Ibid.

308 **"I used to think"**: Tonisha Bell, "The Western Perception of Ancient Egypt: The Discovery, Spectacle, and Exposition of King Tutankhamun," master's thesis, Wichita State University, 2017.

308 **"put his staff"**: "I.E.S. Edwards," *Journal of Egyptian Archaeology*, 1998.

308 **"I would understand"**: Desroches-Noblecourt, *Grande Nubiade*, 8.

309 **"We can't let him go"**: Ibid.

309 **"That is why"**: Ibid.

309 **"no exhibition of works of art"**: Hoving, *Tutankhamun*, 12.

310 **"a cultural juggernaut"**: Meredith Hindley, "King Tut Comes to America," National Endowment for the Humanities, September 2015.

310 **"grand slam homer"**: Ibid.

310 **"were as silent"**: Bell, "Western Perception of Ancient Egypt."

312 **"took Tut to its bosom"**: "NYC Loves King Tut," tutnyc.com/nyc-loves-king-tut, November 21, 2015.
312 **"Seeing Tut is the status symbol"**: Ibid.
312 **"Negotiating 'King Tut'"**: Hoving, *Making the Mummies Dance*, 414.

CHAPTER 21: "BRINGING THEM BACK TO LIFE"

314 **"In the end"**: Christian Leblanc, *La Mémoire de Thèbes: Fragments d'Égypte d'Hier et d'Aujourd'hui* (Paris: L'Harmattan, 2015), 20.
315 **"greatly appreciated the ardor"**: Ibid.
315 **"I was born"**: *Christiane Desroches-Noblecourt: Une Passion Égyptienne*.
316 **"I was literally under the spell"**: Leblanc, *Mémoire de Thèbes*, 27.
316 **"inspired listeners"**: Andreu-Lanoë, "Christiane Desroches Noblecourt."
317 **"With major plans"**: "On a Mission to Loosen Up the Louvre," *New York Times*, October 9, 2009.
317 **"We must not approach this country"**: Prud'homme Farges, *Christiane Desroches-Noblecourt: Une Passion Égyptienne*.
317 **"Nature spoke to them"**: Desroches-Noblecourt, *Le Secret des Découvertes*, 295.
317 **"To deeply study"**: Ibid., 297.
320 **"It was unusual"**: Natalia Klimczak, "Ta Set Neferu: A Valley Where Beauties Sleep," *Ancient Origins*, May 16, 2016.
322 **"a little masterpiece"**: Leblanc, *Mémoire de Thèbes*, 56.
322 **"a figure of almost"**: Desroches-Noblecourt, *Grande Nubiade*, 475.
324 **"She knew how to recognize"**: Email interview with Guy Lecuyot, June 19, 2021.
325 **"picking up new slang words"**: Jean-Louis Clouard, "Dans l'Intimité de Christiane Desroches-Noblecourt," *Égyptophile*, June 22, 2015, egyptophile.blogspot.com/2015/06/dans-lintimite-de-christiane-desroches.html.
325 **"six or seven workers"**: Ibid.

CHAPTER 22: JACKIE AND ARI

327 **"very kind and friendly"**: Desroches-Noblecourt, *Grande Nubiade*, 382.
327 **"Most likely, I think"**: Ibid., 383.
328 **"Ah, Christiane!"**: Ibid., 384.
329 **"the tour was a real"**: Ibid.
329 **"Onassis was the one"**: Ibid., 386.
330 **"You must follow your desire"**: William Kuhn, *Reading Jackie: Her Autobiography in Books* (New York: Anchor, 2010), Loc. 647 (Kindle edition).
331 **"I have always lived"**: Ibid., Loc. 779.
331 **"she found a way"**: Ibid., Loc. 433.
331 **"She talked to me"**: Greg Lawrence, *Jackie as Editor: The Literary Life of Jacqueline Kennedy Onassis* (New York: Thomas Dunne Books, 2011), 190.
332 **"Jackie reminded me"**: Oleg Cassini, *A Thousand Days of Magic: Dressing Jacqueline Kennedy for the White House* (New York: Rizzoli, 2015), 15.
332 **"Do you want to know"**: Lawrence, *Jackie as Editor*, 191.

332 **"She was really enamored"**: Kuhn, *Reading Jackie,* Loc. 4677.
333 **"We ended up"**: Lawrence, *Jackie as Editor,* 202.
333 **"To speak of the dead"**: Ibid., 191.

CHAPTER 23: OPERATION RAMESES

335 **"an appropriate and respectful"**: Letter from Giscard d'Estaing to Anwar Sadat, April 30, 1976, National Archives of France.
335 **"We ask the friendly French people"**: Leblanc, *Mémoire de Thèbes,* 101.
337 **"We cannot expatriate"**: Desroches-Noblecourt, *Grande Nubiade,* 435.
337 **"to do anything it could"**: Letter from Giscard d'Estaing to Anwar Sadat.
338 **"he agreed to the proposal"**: *Ramesses II: The Great Journey,* television documentary, YouTube, October 11, 2014.
338 **"the significance of this deferential"**: Leblanc, *Mémoire de Thèbes,* 108.
339 **"unscientific to dodge the problem"**: Desroches-Noblecourt, *Grande Nubiade,* 432.
339 **"Among the Semitic colonies"**: Ibid.
341 **"So it was," she later said:** Antón, "Entrevista."
341 **"the mortal remains"**: *Ramesses II: The Great Journey.*
341 **"I was amazed"**: Tom Mueller, "Egypt's Royal Mummies Are on the Move," *National Geographic,* April 2, 2021.
344 **"organize an unrivaled parade"**: Ibid.

CHAPTER 24: SAVING PHILAE

345 **"the only regret"**: Desroches-Noblecourt, *Grande Nubiade,* 426.
346 **"Of all the monuments on offer"**: Ibid., 336.
347 **"It seemed to me"**: Ibid., 36.
347 **"What were they afraid of"**: Ibid.
347 **"deep disappointment"**: Ibid.
347 **"So if you want to repay"**: Ibid., 37.
348 **"Thanks to Tutankhamun"**: Ibid.
348 **"Every part of Egypt"**: Robert Curzon, *Visits to the Monasteries of the Levant,* 1834.
348 **"the island, with its palms"**: Edwards, *Thousand Miles,* 260.
349 **"in effect an oasis"**: Desroches-Noblecourt and Gerster, *The World Saves Abu Simbel,* 239.
349 **"the cult of Isis"**: Wilkinson, *The Nile,* 84.
352 **"its reliefs intact"**: Desroches-Noblecourt, *Grande Nubiade,* 22.
354 **"every ounce of their extraordinary"**: Peter Howard, "The Gate They Took from the Nile," *Navy News,* April 1977.
355 **"To think that these ancient"**: Ibid.
355 **"I had the great satisfaction"**: Desroches-Noblecourt, *Grande Nubiade,* 422.

CHAPTER 25: VALLEY OF THE QUEENS

356 **"galloping like a gazelle"**: Romero, "The Death of Christiane Desroches-Noblecourt."

356 **"archaeology is a young man's game"**: Wilson, *Thousands of Years*, 182–83.

357 **"Nothing prevented me"**: Desroches-Noblecourt, *Grande Nubiade*, 73.

358 **"Mother, if you want"**: Ibid.

359 **"He enjoyed the pleasures"**: Charles Allen and Sharada Dwivedi, *Lives of the Indian Princes* (Mumbai: Eshwar, 1998), 227.

360 ***"comme un petit jouet"***: Jarmani Dass, *Maharajah* (New Delhi: Hind Pocket Books, 2008), 207.

360 **"She began to understand"**: Ibid., 208.

362 **"these two ladies"**: Andreu-Lanoë, "Christiane Desroches Noblecourt."

363 **"We couldn't understand"**: Mimi Mann, "Ancient Egyptian Burial Ground Misunderstood and Misnamed," Associated Press, July 11, 1989.

364 **"We should be calling it"**: Ibid.

364 **"At Malgatta House"**: Clouard, "Dans l'Intimité de Christiane Desroches-Noblecourt."

365 **"This project has established"**: "Gamal Mokhtar: A Life Devoted to Egypt's Cultural Heritage," Getty Conservation Institute newsletter (undated), getty.edu/conservation/publications_resources/newsletters/7_3/mokhtar.html.

365 **"Our basic principle"**: Miguel Angel Corzo, ed., *Art and Eternity: The Nefertari Project Wall Paintings Conservation Project, 1986–1992* (Los Angeles: Getty Conservation Institute, 1993), 4.

366 **"there's been a divide"**: Hessler, *Buried*, 127.

366 **"Egyptologists as a group"**: Ibid.

366 **"So do you know"**: Romero, "The Death of Christiane Desroches-Noblecourt."

CHAPTER 26: "THE MOST PRESTIGIOUS LIVING EGYPTOLOGIST IN THE WORLD"

367 **"the most prestigious"**: Antón, "Entrevista."

367 **"an endearing grandmother"**: Ibid.

367 **"personality so overwhelming"**: Ibid.

368 **"No one has been able"**: Bermond, "Christiane Desroches-Noblecourt: 'I Had to Face a Certain Misogyny.'"

368 **"the ideas that still form"**: Antón, "Entrevista."

369 **"the favorite color"**: Ibid.

369 **"I have had my knee"**: Ibid.

370 **"the vilest type"**: Elizabeth B. Wilson, "The Queen Who Would Be King," *Smithsonian*, September 2006.

370 **"The ancient Egyptians"**: Hessler, *Buried*, 205.

370 **"her reign, if you study it"**: Antón, "Entrevista."

371 **"No, no, no!"**: Ibid.

371 **"Everybody would think"**: "Christiane Desroches-Noblecourt," *Telegraph* (London), July 1, 2011.

371 **"admired and appreciated"**: "Christiane Desroches-Noblecourt: Première Égyptologue Française," *Égypte Ancienne*, October 2016–January 2017.

371 **"She was disruptive"**: Andreu-Lanoë, "Christiane Desroches Noblecourt."

371 **"She became more difficult"**: Interview with Henri Loyrette.

371 **"domineering to the point"**: Margarita Díaz-Andreu and Marie Louise Stig Sørensen, eds., *Excavating Women: A History of Women in European Archaeology* (New York: Routledge, 1998), 74.

371 **"In her books"**: "Christiane Desroches-Noblecourt: Première Égyptologue Française."

372 **"she gave the Louvre"**: Interview with Henri Loyrette.

373 **"I remember how"**: Interview with Olga Prud'homme Farges.

373 **"has served the cause"**: Desroches-Noblecourt, *Sous le Regard des Dieux*, 9.

373 **"When I asked her"**: Interview with Olga Prud'homme Farges.

374 **"People often didn't take her seriously"**: Ibid.

374 **"I think she could not have achieved"**: Ibid.

374 **"She had such a strong character"**: Ibid.

374 **"For André"**: Desroches-Noblecourt, *Grande Nubiade,* dedication page.

375 **"I tried to ask her questions"**: Interview with Olga Prud'homme Farges.

375 **"I remember her telling me"**: Ibid.

375 **"She believed that the pulse"**: Ibid.

375 **"have not changed in thousands"**: Antón, "Entrevista."

375 **"I don't feel anything"**: Desroches-Noblecourt, *Le Secret des Découvertes,* 289.

376 **"Tonight," Bokova said**: Irina Bokova speech, UNESCO, November 26, 2009.

377 **"sometimes she laughed"**: Interview with Olga Prud'homme Farges.

378 **"the grande dame of the Nile"**: "Christiane Desroches-Noblecourt, Pioneering Egyptologist, Dies at 97," *Washington Post,* June 28, 2011.

378 **"As long as there's life"**: Prud'homme Farges, *Christiane Desroches-Noblecourt: Une Passion Égyptienne.*

BIBLIOGRAPHY

ARCHIVAL MATERIAL

John F. Kennedy Presidential Library, Boston. Jacqueline Bouvier Kennedy Onassis Personal Papers.

National Archives of France (Archives Nationales de France), Paris. Gestion du Département des Antiquités Égyptiennes du Musée du Louvre sous la direction de Christiane Desroches-Noblecourt.

PUBLISHED MATERIAL

BOOKS

Aburish, Saïd K. *Nasser: The Last Arab*. New York: Thomas Dunne Books, 2013.

Adams, Amanda. *Ladies of the Field: Early Women Archaeologists and Their Search for Adventure*. Vancouver, B.C.: Greystone Books, 2010.

Allen, Charles, and Sharada Dwivedi. *Lives of the Indian Princes*. Mumbai: Eshwar, 1998.

Allport, Alan. *Browned Off and Bloody-Minded: The British Soldier Goes to War, 1939–1945*. New Haven: Yale University Press, 2015.

Anthony, Carl Sferrazza. *As We Remember Her: Jacqueline Kennedy Onassis in the Words of Her Friends and Family*. New York: HarperCollins, 1997.

Blanc, Julien. *Au Commencement de la Résistance: Du Côte du Musée de l'Homme 1940–1941*. Paris: Éditions du Seuil, 2010.

Blumenson, Martin. *The Vildé Affair: Beginnings of the French Resistance*. Boston: Houghton Mifflin, 1977.

Cachin, Françoise, ed. *Pillages et Restitutions: Le Destin des Oeuvres d'Art Sorties de France Pendant la Seconde Guerre Mondiale*. Paris: Éditions Adam Biro, 1997.

Cassini, Oleg. *A Thousand Days of Magic: Dressing Jacqueline Kennedy for the White House*. New York: Rizzoli, 2015.

Cassou, Jean. *Une Vie pour la Liberté*. Paris: Éditions Robert Laffont, 1981.

Chanel, Gerri. *Saving Mona Lisa: The Battle to Protect the Louvre and Its Treasures from the Nazis*. London: Icon Books, 2018.

Cobb, Matthew. *The Resistance: The French Fight Against the Nazis*. London: Pocket Books, 2010.

Cooney, Kara. *When Women Ruled the World: Six Queens of Egypt*. Washington, D.C.: National Geographic, 2018.

Cooper, Artemis. *Cairo in the War 1939–1945*. London: John Murray, 2015.

Corzo, Miguel Angel, ed. *Art and Eternity: The Nefertari Project Wall Paintings Conservation Project, 1986–1992*. Los Angeles: Getty Conservation Institute, 1993.

Dass, Jarmani. *Maharajah*. New Delhi: Hind Pocket Books, 2008.

Davis, Margaret Leslie. *Mona Lisa in Camelot: How Jacqueline Kennedy and Da Vinci's Masterpiece Charmed and Captivated a Nation*. Washington, D.C.: White House Historical Association, 2008.

Desroches-Noblecourt, Christiane. *La Femme au Temps des Pharaons*. Paris: Stock/Pernoud, 1986.

———. *Gifts from the Pharaohs: How Ancient Egyptian Civilization Shaped the Modern World*. Paris: Flammarion, 2007.

———. *La Grande Nubiade: le Parcours d'une Égyptologue*. Paris: Stock/Pernoud, 1992.

———. *Ramses II: An Illustrated Biography*. Paris: Flammarion, 2007.

———. *Le Secret des Découvertes*. Paris: Télémaque, 2006.

———. *Sous le Regard des Dieux*. Paris: Albin Michel, 2016.

———. *Tutankhamen*. London: Penguin, 1965.

Desroches-Noblecourt, Christiane, and Georg Gerster. *The World Saves Abu Simbel*. Vienna: Verlag A. F. Koska, 1968.

Díaz-Andreu, Margarita, and Marie Louise Stig Sørensen, eds. *Excavating Women: A History of Women in European Archaeology*. New York: Routledge, 1998.

Edsel, Robert M. *The Monuments Men: Allied Heroes, Nazi Thieves, and the Greatest Treasure Hunt in History*. New York: Center Street, 2009.

Edwards, Amelia B. *A Thousand Miles up the Nile*. London: George Routledge and Sons, 1891.

El Shakry, Omnia. *The Great Social Laboratory: Subjects of Knowledge in Colonial and Postcolonial Egypt*. Palo Alto: Stanford University Press, 2014.

Fagan, Brian M. *The Rape of the Nile: Tomb Robbers, Tourists, and Archaeologists in Egypt*. Boulder, Colo.: Westview Press, 2004.

Flanner, Janet. *Men and Monuments: Profiles of Picasso, Matisse, Braque, and Malraux*. New York: DaCapo Press, 1990.

Fletcher-Jones, Nigel. *Abu Simbel and the Nubian Temples*. Cairo: American University in Cairo Press, 2020.

Gardner, James. *The Louvre: The Many Lives of the World's Most Famous Museum*. New York: Atlantic Monthly Press, 2020.

Goodwin, Richard N. *Remembering America: A Voice from the Sixties*. New York: Open Road Media, 2014.

Gorenberg, Gershom. *War of Shadows: Codebreakers, Spies, and the Secret Struggle to Drive the Nazis from the Middle East*. New York: PublicAffairs, 2021.

Hessler, Peter. *The Buried: An Archaeology of the Egyptian Revolution*. New York: Penguin, 2019.

Hill, Clint. *Mrs. Kennedy and Me: An Intimate Memoir*. New York: Gallery Books, 2012.

Hours, Magdeleine. *Une Vie au Louvre*. Paris: Robert Laffont, 1987.

Hoving, Thomas. *Making the Mummies Dance: Inside the Metropolitan Museum of Art*. New York: Touchstone, 1993.

———. *Tutankhamun: The Untold Story*. New York: Cooper Square Press, 2002.

Humbert, Agnès. *Résistance: Memoirs of Occupied France*. London: Bloomsbury, 2008.

Kelleher, K. L. *Jackie: Beyond the Myth of Camelot*. XLibris, 2000.

Kennedy, Jacqueline. *Jacqueline Kennedy: Historic Conversations on Life with John F. Kennedy*. New York: Hyperion, 2011.

Kuhn, William. *Reading Jackie: Her Autobiography in Books*. New York: Anchor, 2010.

Lawrence, Greg. *Jackie as Editor: The Literary Life of Jacqueline Kennedy Onassis*. New York: Thomas Dunne Books, 2011.

Leaming, Barbara. *Jacqueline Bouvier Kennedy Onassis: The Untold Story*. New York: Thomas Dunne Books, 2014.

Leblanc, Christian. *La Mémoire de Thèbes: Fragments d'Égypte d'Hier et d'Aujourd'hui*. Paris: Harmattan, 2015.

Le Tourneur d'Ison, Claudine. *Une Passion Égyptienne: Jean-Philippe et Marguerite Lauer*. Paris: Plon, 1996.

Lively, Penelope. *Moon Tiger*. New York: Grove Press, 1987.

———. *Oleander, Jacaranda: A Childhood Perceived*. New York: HarperCollins, 1994.

Mann, Carol. *Paris Between the Wars*. London: Vendome Press, 1996.

Mertz, Barbara. *Red Land, Black Land: Daily Life in Ancient Egypt*. New York: Morrow, 2009.

———. *Temples, Tombs, and Hieroglyphs: A Popular History of Ancient Egypt*. New York: Morrow, 2009.

Meskell, Lynn. *A Future in Ruins: UNESCO World Heritage and the Dream of Peace*. Oxford: Oxford University Press, 2018.

Morris, James. *Farewell the Trumpets: An Imperial Retreat*. New York: Harcourt Brace Jovanovich, 1978.

Museo Egizio and Salini Impregilo, *Nubiana: The Great Undertaking That Saved the Temples of Abu Simbel*. Milan: Rizzoli, 2019.

Natalle, Elizabeth J. *Jacqueline Kennedy and the Architecture of First Lady Diplomacy*. New York: Peter Lang, 2018.

Nicholas, Lynn. *The Rape of Europa: The Fate of Europe's Treasures in the Third Reich and the Second World War*. New York: Vintage, 1995.

Olson, Lynne. *Madame Fourcade's Secret War: The Daring Young Woman Who Led France's Largest Spy Network Against Hitler*. New York: Random House, 2019.

Rainey, Froelich. *Reflections of a Digger*. Philadelphia: University of Pennsylvania Museum of Archaeology and Anthropology, 1992.

Reid, Donald Malcolm. *Contesting Antiquity in Egypt: Archaeologies, Museums, and the Struggle for Identities from World War I to Nasser*. Cairo: American University in Cairo, 2015.

Riding, Alan. *And the Show Went On: Cultural Life in Nazi-Occupied Paris*. New York: Knopf, 2010.

Romer, John. *Ancient Lives: The Story of the Pharaohs' Tombmakers*. London: Weidenfeld and Nicolson, 1984.

Rowley, Hazel. *Tête-à-Tête: The Tumultuous Lives and Loves of Simone de Beauvoir and Jean-Paul Sartre*. New York: HarperCollins, 2015.

Säve-Söderbergh, Torgny. *Temples and Tombs of Ancient Nubia: The International Rescue Campaign at Abu Simbel, Philae and Other Sites*. London: Thames and Hudson, 1987.

Schiff, Stacy. *Saint-Exupéry: A Biography*. New York: Knopf, 1995.

Schoenbrun, David. *Soldiers of the Night: The Story of the French Resistance*. Lexington, Mass.: Plunkett Lake Press, 2016.

Shirer, William L. *The Collapse of the Third Republic: An Inquiry into the Fall of France in 1940*. New York: Simon and Schuster, 1969.

Singh, Brigadier H. H. Sikhjit, and Cynthia Meera Frederick. *Prince, Patron and Patriarch*. New Delhi: Roli Books, 2019.

Solé, Robert. *La Grande Aventure de l'Egyptologie*. Paris: Perrin, 2019.

Spencer, Samia. *Daughters of the Nile: Egyptian Women Changing Their World*. Newcastle upon Tyne: Cambridge Scholars Publishing, 2016.

Thézy, Marie de, and Thomas Michael Gunther, eds. *Images de la libération de Paris*. Paris: Paris Musées, 1994.

Thompson, Jason. *Wonderful Things: A History of Egyptology*, vol. 3: *From 1914 to the Twenty-first Century*. Cairo: American University in Cairo Press, 2018.

Tunzelmann, Alex von. *Blood and Sand: Suez, Hungary, and Eisenhower's Campaign for Peace*. New York: HarperCollins, 2016.

Waxman, Sharon. *Loot: The Battle over the Stolen Treasures of the Ancient World*. New York: Henry Holt, 2008.

Wilkinson, Toby. *The Nile: A Journey Downriver Through Egypt's Past and Present*. New York: Knopf, 2014.

———. *The Rise and Fall of Ancient Egypt*. New York: Random House, 2011.

———. *A World Beneath the Sands: The Golden Age of Egyptology*. New York: W. W. Norton, 2020.

Wilson, John A. *Signs and Wonders upon Pharaoh: A History of American Egyptology*. Chicago: University of Chicago Press, 1964.

———. *Thousands of Years: An Archaeologist's Search for Ancient Egypt*. New York: Charles Scribner's Sons, 1972.

FILM AND VIDEO

Prud'homme Farges, Olga. *Christiane Desroches-Noblecourt: Une Passion Égyptienne*. television documentary, CDP Productions and *France Télévisions*, aired on France 5, December 11, 2009.

PERIODICAL ARTICLES

Andreu-Lanoë, Guillemette. "Christiane Desroches Noblecourt (1913–2011)." Newsletter of the French Institute of Oriental Archaeology, 2011.

Antón, Jacinto. "Entrevista a Christiane Desroches-Noblecourt." *El País*, July 11, 2004.

Carvalho, George de. "Abu Simbel—A Race Is Won." *Life*, December 2, 1966.

Gerster, Georg. "Saving the Temples of Abu Simbel." *National Geographic*, May 1966, 708.

Maurel, Chloé. "Le Sauvetage des Monuments de Nubie par l'UNESCO (1955–1968)." *Égypte / Monde Arabe*, 2013.

Okasha, Sarwat. "Ramses Recrowned: The International Campaign to Preserve the Monuments of Nubia, 1959–68," IJBF Online, 232.

Viorst, Milton. "Man of Gamaliya." *New Yorker*, June 24, 1990.

PHOTO CREDITS

xvi	Dreamstime
xviii	Creative Commons—Attribution: Rama
8	Library of Congress
33	Alamy
36	Archives Nationales de France
37	agefotostock
39	Archives Nationales de France
53	Alamy
74	Archives Nationales de France
78	Archives Nationales de France
81	Archives Nationales de France
100	Creative Commons—Attribution: Bundesarchiv (German National Archives)
121	Alamy
138–39	Creative Commons—Attribution: Than217
141	Creative Commons—Attribution: Cecioka
142	Creative Commons—Attribution: Brooklyn Museum
174	Archives Nationales de France
177	Creative Commons—Attribution: UNESCO (Connected Open Heritage Project)
197	Creative Commons—Attribution: Henry Weinberg
199	Library of Congress
228	John F. Kennedy Presidential Library
234	Shutterstock
235	John F. Kennedy Presidential Library

254 Creative Commons—Attribution: UNESCO (Connected Open Heritage Project)
261 Archives Nationales de France
263 Creative Commons—Attribution: UNESCO (Connected Open Heritage Project)
266 Creative Commons—Attribution: UNESCO (Connected Open Heritage Project)
282 Alamy
287 Creative Commons—Attribution: Mary Harrsch
302 Archives Nationales de France
303 Rue des Archives / GRANGER
306 Archives Nationales de France
319 Sophie Loyrette
323 Creative Commons—Attribution: Jon Bodsworth
329 Archives Nationales de France
351 Library of Congress
355 Creative Commons—Attribution: Jerome Bon
377 Archives Nationales de France

INDEX

Page numbers of photographs appear in italics.

KEY TO ABBREVIATIONS:

CEDAE = Documentation and Study Center for the History of the Art and Civilization of Ancient Egypt;
Desroches = Christiane Desroches-Noblecourt;
IFAO = French Institute of Oriental Archaeology;
JFK = John F. Kennedy;
King Tut = Tutankhamun

ABOUT THE AUTHOR

LYNNE OLSON is the *New York Times* bestselling author of *Madame Fourcade's Secret War*, *Last Hope Island*, *Those Angry Days*, and *Citizens of London*. She has been a consultant for the National World War II Museum in New Orleans and the United States Holocaust Memorial Museum in Washington, D.C.

lynneolson.com

Facebook.com/lynneolsonbooks

W9-BIR-381

QUALITY IN AMERICA

How To Implement A Competitive Quality Program

QUALITY IN AMERICA

How To Implement A Competitive Quality Program

V. DANIEL HUNT
President
Technology Research Corporation

BUSINESS ONE IRWIN
Homewood, Illinois 60430

The views, opinions and conclusions in this book are those of the author and do not represent those of the United States Government.

Public domain information and those documents abstracted or used in full, edited or otherwise used are noted in the acknowledgements or on specific pages or illustrations.

This publication is designed to provide accurate and authoritative information in regard to the subject matter covered. It is sold with the understanding that neither the author nor the publisher is engaged in rendering legal, accounting, or other professional service. If legal advice or other expert assistance is required, the services of a competent professional person should be sought.

From a Declaration of Principles jointly adopted by a Committee of the American Bar Association and a Committee of Publishers.

Sponsoring editor: Jeffrey A. Krames
Project editor: Jean Roberts
Production manager: Irene H. Sotiroff
Designer: Larry J. Cope
Jacket designer: Tim Kaage
Compositor: Carlisle Communications, Ltd.
Typeface: 11/13 Palatino
Printer: R. R. Donnelley & Sons Company

Library of Congress Cataloging-in-Publication Data

Hunt, V. Daniel.
Quality in America : how to implement a competitive quality program / V. Daniel Hunt.
p. cm.
Includes bibliographical references.
ISBN 1-55623-536-4
1. Total quality management—United States. 2. Quality control—United States. I. Title.
HD62.15.H86 1992
658.5′62′0973—dc20 91–25971

Printed in the United States of America

1 2 3 4 5 6 7 8 9 0 DOC 8 7 6 5 4 3 2 1

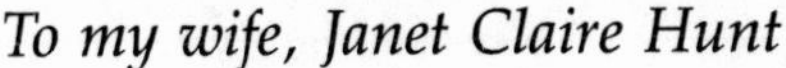

To my wife, Janet Claire Hunt

Preface

Producing quality goods and services is crucial not only to the continued economic growth of the United States, but also to our national security and the well-being and the standard of living of each American family. America has been recognized for its leadership in producing quality products. However, in recent years, the position of America as quality leader has been challenged by foreign competition in domestic and overseas markets.

Reasserting our leadership position will require a firm commitment to quality and the "Quality First"[1] principle of continuous quality improvement. America can, and must, excel in this area, setting new standards for world-class quality and competing vigorously in international markets.

Improving quality takes time and resources and can only be achieved through a combination of factors. It takes a long-term commitment by top management that involves working with suppliers to improve performance; educating, training, and motivating workers; developing accurate and responsive management systems; and establishing targets for quality improvement.

Quality improvement principles apply to small companies as well as large corporations, to service industries as well as manufacturing, and to the public sector as well as private enterprise. Improving the quality of goods and services goes hand in hand with improving productivity and lowering costs. It is also essential to enhancing worker fulfillment and customer satisfaction.

Private sector organizations and government institutions across the country are joining forces to promote a national commitment to "Quality First." Business executives are working again together to develop the skills and techniques needed to produce quality goods and services in America.

V. DANIEL HUNT
Fairfax Station, Virginia

[1]"Quality First" is a trademark of Technology Research Corporation.

Acknowledgements

Quality in America has been developed based on information from a wide variety of authorities who are specialists in their respective fields.

The following publications were used as the basic resources for this book. Portions of these publications may have been used in the book. Those definitions or artwork that have been used are reproduced with the permission to reprint of the respective publisher.

AT&T Quality Improvement Process Guidebook, AT&T, Baskin Ridge, New Jersey, 1988.

Deming Management at Work, Mary Walton, G.P. Putnam, New York, 1990.

The Deming Route to Quality and Productivity, William W. Scherkenbach, CEE Press, Washington, D.C., 1988.

Diffusion of Innovations, Everett M. Rogers, Free Press, New York, 1983.

Excellence in Government: Total Quality Mangement in the 1990s, David K. Carr, and Ian D. Littman, Coopers and Lybrand, Washington, D.C., 1990.

Federal Total Quality Management Handbook, U.S. Government Printing Office, Washington, D.C., 1990.

A Guide to Benchmarking in Xerox, NTIS Publication PB91-780106, Washington, D.C., 1990.

State-of-the-art report, *A Guide for Implementing Total Quality Management*, Reliability Analysis Center, Rome, New York, Report SOAR-7, 1990.

In Search of Excellence, Thomas J. Peters and Robert H. Waterman, Jr., Harper and Row, 1982.

An Introduction to the Continuous Improvement Process, Principles and Practices, Brian E. Mansir and Nicholas R. Schacht, Logistics Management Institute, Bethesda, MD, August, 1989.

Juran on Planning for Quality, J.M. Juran, The Free Press, New York, 1988.

Juran's Quality Control Handbook, J.M. Juran, Editor in Chief and Frank M. Gryna, Associate Editor, McGraw-Hill, New York, 1988, 4th Edition.

Made in America: Regaining the Productive Edge, Michael L. Dertouzos, Richard K. Lester, Robert M. Solow, The MIT Commission on Industrial Productivity, The MIT Press, 1989.

Out of the Crisis, W. Edwards Deming, MIT Center for Advanced Engineering Study, Boston, MA, 1986.

A Passion for Excellence, Tom Peters and Nancy Austin, Random House, New York, 1985.

Quality is Free, Philip B. Crosby, McGraw-Hill, New York, 1979.

Quality and Productivity Self-Assessment Guide for Defense Organizations, Department of Defense, Washington, D.C., 1990.

Quality Without Tears, Philip B. Crosby, New American Library, New York, 1985.

Total Quality Management Guide, Volumes 1 and 2, Office of the Deputy Assistant Secretary of Defense for Total Quality Management, DoD 5000.51-G, February 15, 1990. Washington, D.C.

USMG Partnership: The Way We Work, Xerox, USMG Printing Office, Rochester, New York, 1988.

This book was conceived during a series of discussions with Mr. G. Raymond Fox of Andersen Consulting and the author. I appreciate Ray's interest in seeing this book come to fruition.

The preparation of a book of this type is dependent upon an excellent staff, and I have been fortunate in this regard. Special thanks to Donald Keehan, Ronald Fraser, Charles Wolfgang Zschock, and Chuck Doe, for research assistance of the material for this book. I appreciate the careful and conscientious editing of Lori Ackerman. The technical graphic art was prepared by Karl J. Samuels.

I appreciate the careful and accurate preparation of the manuscript by Anne Pond.

Many individuals provided material, interview comments, and their insights regarding how to improve quality in America. I appreciate their input and help in defining this book. Special recognition is noted for: Peter Angiola, TQM Manager, Office of the Under Secretary of Defense for Acquisition, Total Quality Management; Dr. Laurie A. Broedling, Deputy Under Secretary of Defense for Total Quality Management; Richard Bueton, Senior Vice President and Director of Quality, Motorola Inc.; David K. Carr, Partner, Coopers & Lybrand; Jeffrey M. Clark, Cadillac Motor Car Division; James C. Cline, Corporate Quality Manager, Globe Metallurgical Inc.; Karen A. Collard, Xerox Corporation; John F. Cooney, Manager, National Quality Award Office, Xerox Business Products and Systems; Dr. Robert Costello, Hudson Institute; Dr. Mary A. Hartz, Total Quality Management Section Leader, IIT Research Institute; Robert H. Hayes, Professor of Management of Technology, Harvard Business School; Newt Hardie, Vice President, Quality, Milliken & Company; Sandi

Janssen, International Business Machines Corporation; Bob King, GOAL; Ian D. Littman, Director, Total Quality Management, Coopers & Lybrand; Paul A. Noakes, Vice President and Director, External Quality Programs, Motorola, Inc.; William Smith, Vice President and Senior Quality Assurance Manager, Communications Sector, Motorola Inc.; Mike Spiess, Executive Vice President, Wallace Co., Inc; Frank Voehl, Vice President of QualTec; Chuck Vogel, Manager-Total Quality, Westinghouse Electric Corporation, Commercial Nuclear Fuel Division; John R. West, Manager, Corporate Quality Improvement, Federal Express.

Table of Contents

Chapter One

Quality in America Today

"The improvement of quality in products and the improvement of quality in service—these are national priorities as never before."

George Bush

QUALITY IS GOOD BUSINESS

Quality pays. Quality gets results. Quality sells. Quality increases profit. The first question CEOs ask when they evaluate whether they need to improve their quality program is, "What's in it for the company?"

All too often, companies ask this question in times of crisis. Their markets are changing, global competitors have sneaked up on them, and then they are forced to change the way they do business to survive.

Listen to why American quality leaders improved their quality, and what they got in return.

William Smith, Vice President and Senior Quality Assurance Manager at Motorola, Inc., tells us: "We put Motorola's quality process in place to satisfy customers. The real payoff from our quality improvement program is that it has certainly been instrumental in helping us to increase market share, to increase sales, to increase profitability. The corporate goal that we stated was to improve quality 10 times by 1989, and 100 times by 1991. Our sales per employee in 1985 was $60,500; by 1990 it has increased to $113,200."

Globe Metallurgical, Inc., also demonstrates that any firm, large or small, can develop an excellent quality program, and one that pays off. James C. Cline, Corporate Quality Manager for Globe Metallurgical Inc., gives this account of his company's renewed commitment to quality begun in 1984. "That was our turning point from what we call the detection mode to the prevention mode. The benefits, we found, are both measurable and unmeasurable, and in many ways the unmeasurable ones are the most significant. We have been able to increase our market share tremendously. . . . Before 1984 we shipped virtually no products overseas, less than a truckload a year. Today one of our biggest customers is in Europe, and we also ship to Australia, Korea, and Taiwan.

"We have a much more stable work force because of employee satisfaction and have not laid off a single employee in seven years. Absenteeism has been virtually eliminated, and workers leaving Globe to go to work somewhere else are virtually unheard of. The climate in our company is no longer 'us and them.' It's not workers and management. It's just us."

Chuck Vogel, quality manager for Westinghouse, CNFD Division, reiterated that "total quality is people." You should not look at quality improvement as a marketing tool, but as a management tool. Lots of American companies are shortsighted. They concentrate too much on near-term profits and fail to see the long-term impact of quality improvement on their global markets. Westinghouse recognized the changing global market and made quality a priority in its business.

If you don't care where American industry and your firm are headed in the 1990s, if you think your quality performance can not be improved, or if you're still in a state of "global marketplace denial," this book won't help you.

On the other hand, if you are not so sure business as usual is the wave of the future, read on. This book can help you. Because the 1990s are shaping up as a change-filled period full of opportunities—and risks—this book is designed to help make sure you and your firm are well positioned not only to cope in the increasingly competitive global marketplace of the 1990s, but to prosper in it.

Unlike the overly optimistic quality rhetoric of the 1980s, this down-to-earth book seeks a middle ground. It recognizes that in the 1990s American business leaders must strike a balance between the quick-fix approach of the past and the fact that widespread ignorance concerning the real level of quality performance in American business is still found in many parts of the manufacturing and service sectors. Improved quality is not a cure-all for all American business ills, but it is an essential first step in the right direction.

A very few American companies are counted among the world-class leaders in quality improvement. But, thousands upon thousands of other companies have yet to take that all-important first step to ensure their products and services deliver to each customer a dependable high level of quality. Drawing in part on the lessons learned by the early quality leaders in America, this book is a no nonsense guide for the next wave of American firms—some large, some small—that must adopt quality management practices in the next 5 to 10 years if they are to survive.

QUALITY DRIVEN BY GLOBAL COMPETITION

Since World War II, the world has been "shrinking." Advances in telecommunications have linked all parts of the world electronically and, to a lesser extent, politically. Over the years a new economic infrastructure has also replaced the old one. As national companies serving primarily domestic markets expanded into the international marketplace, a "global web," as Robert Reich calls it, of economic interconnectedness formed and is today a dominant economic force shaping the American economic scene.

That the coming decade will see a further extension of these trends and become an economic turning point for America and the rest of the world is beyond question. During the 1980s, two significant events—in addition to the coming of age of the global economy—have set the stage for the 1990s. First, under growing pressure from foreign competition, American corporations rediscovered "quality." After decades of indifference to, and neglect of, what was happening in Japan and elsewhere in the world, the American business community began its turnaround in the mid-1980s when a few large corporations became convinced that quality products and services were their ticket to the future. By the late-1980s, talk about quality became the "in" topic.

The end of the 40-year Cold War and the collapse of the Soviet economy in 1990-1991 is the second fundamental sea change that will make the coming decade unique. With the "evil empire" preoccupied with its own internal economic turmoil, both America and Europe could redirect their energies from military confrontation to worldwide commercial competition. A new Germany serving as the economic core of a unified European Community will soon become the world's third regional economic super-force. In addition to the United States and the Pacific Rim, including Japan, these three regions will dominate the international economy of the 1990s.

American manufacturing and service companies cannot afford to remain passive in the coming years. The American economy will either fully integrate itself into new and evolving global markets, or large parts of it are likely to be left behind as foreign competitors absorb greater and greater shares of the only market that really matters anymore: the global market. Economic isolationism means stagnation and slow economic death. The time is ripe for virtually all American businesses to adopt a new world view built on proven quality improvement practices.

A better understanding of the nature of global competition, and what it means for American companies, is found in the work of Robert Reich of Harvard University. Reich is very much interested in the changing independent national economies that dominated the world economic order prior to World War II, and in the rise of the interconnected global economy. The old American national economy was characterized by the popular "Built by Americans for Americans" slogan often heard in the 1950s. Now it is very difficult to tell what "Made in America" means. The new global economy is described by Reich, in his new book entitled *The Work of Nations,* in the following terms: "When an American buys a Pontiac Le Mans from General Motors, for example, he or she engages unwittingly in an international transaction. Of the $20,000 paid to GM, about $6,000 goes to South Korea for routine labor and assembly operations, $3,500 to Japan for advanced components (engines, transaxles, and electronics), $1,500 to West Germany for styling and design engineering, $800 to Taiwan, Singapore, and Japan for small components, $500 to Britain for advertising and marketing services, and about $100 to Ireland and Barbados for data processing. The rest—less than $8,000—goes to strategists in Detroit, lawyers and bankers in New York, lobbyists in Washington, insurance and healthcare workers all over the country, and General Motors shareholders.

"The proud new owner of the Pontiac is not aware of having bought so much from overseas, of course. General Motors did the trading, within its global web. This is typical. By the 1990s, most 'trade' no longer occurred in arm's-length transactions between buyers in one nation and sellers in another, but between people within the same web who are likely to deal repeatedly with each other across borders."

Reich paints an entirely new picture of how American companies go about building a car. The very same picture, however, is equally valid for thousands of other products and services. It is becoming more and more difficult for an American company to isolate itself from what is going on in other nations. Consequently, when the rest of the world, or important parts of it, shifts to a new method for organizing work, it is almost impossible for American firms to ignore this change.

Figure 1–1 captures the scope of this remarkable shift described by Reich. The message it delivers loud and clear is this: Because of these intricate global webs in which American companies are now full-fledged partners, they have little or no choice but to keep up with the other global competitors in the web if they want to remain competitive. Whether or not to adopt improved quality practices is no longer a real option for most American companies. The only option, really, is when to

FIGURE 1–1
Shift to Global Integration

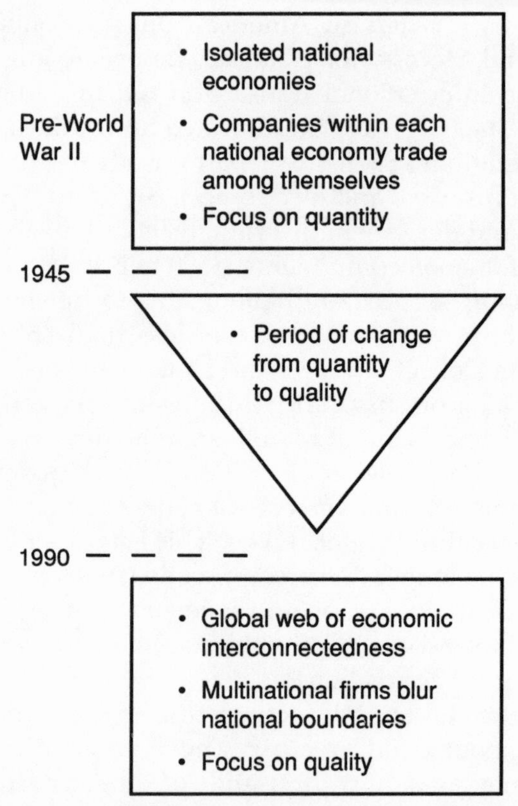

shift and whether your company will do it soon enough to remain competitive.

But still, the United States has been slow to accept and adapt to the realities of a highly competitive global marketplace, and slow to regard the industrial development of competing countries as a challenge to, as well as an opportunity for, our own economic growth. Consequences of this national failure to adapt are measured in terms of loss of market share, unnecessary plant closings, high unemployment, and noticeable deterioration in the quality of jobs available to American workers. Most observers of this condition have long since concluded that

FIGURE 1–2
Level of Quality Adoption in Japan and America

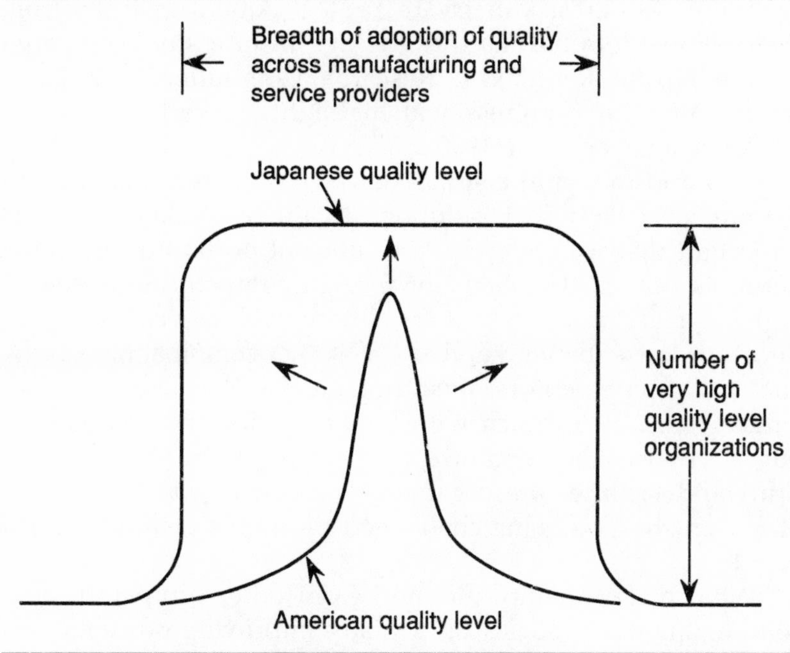

any successful challenge to these problems entails the need for the United States to acknowledge the erosion of the comparative advantage of many of its manufacturing and service industries in such important activities as quality, technology, innovation, investment, and productivity, and to take the needed corrective actions.

Figure 1–2 graphically shows that the number of companies in America that have aggressively adopted quality management practices lags far behind their global competitors, such as Japan. Japanese firms, on average, have also attained a higher level of quality in their products and services. As quality improvement spreads throughout America in the 1990s, the U.S. spike shown in Figure 1–2 should swell both outward and upward.

It is important that business executives fully appreciate that Washington cannot solve the global competition problems facing American firms in the years ahead. The role traditionally played by the federal government with regard to international trade is largely obsolete in the emerging global market economy. Congress can try to protect American firms from their competitors but, as this passage from a study prepared by the House Republican Research Committee Task Force for members of Congress will highlight, protection is not a workable answer in the 1990s. "For the U.S. to remain strong, to grow and to regain lost markets, we must recognize where we are weak and seek solutions to those weaknesses. It is important that we recognize a significant portion of our trade deficit is due to the ability of foreign competitors to deliver higher-quality products that are either novel, less costly to produce, promise better service, or some combination of the above. Our competitors, most notably the Japanese, are challenging us, not so much with better science and technology, but in the way they organize their work . . . in the way their firms and factories are organized and managed. The United States, in short, is being challenged through a commitment to quality.

"What makes quality different from other competitiveness solutions is its emphasis on actually improving our ability to compete. Most competitiveness solutions seek to relieve competitive pressures rather than working to strengthen the competitor. While streamlining regulations, ensuring foreign market access, providing market information, and other such efforts are laudable, they will all be for naught if 'Made in America' is viewed as a euphemism for costly, inferior products and services. No amount of playing field 'leveling' will obtain U.S. market share in fields that are on the technological cutting edge without a commitment to quality. That goes for computers, cars, machinery, chemicals or whatever."

Experts all have a slightly different view of the global business in the 1990s. The common thread, however, is strong. Nearly every American manufacturing and service sector will be increasingly vulnerable to imports in the foreseeable future. Automation isn't the answer, for it would only quicken the production of poor-quality products. Import barriers and protection are not the answer, either. Americans can no longer hide from foreign competition or survive by selling only to

Americans. The only way out is through the door marked "Quality."

HOW ARE WE DOING?

America's global competitors create and produce items of high quality because it pays! Continual improvement in quality leads to reduced costs because of less rework, fewer mistakes, fewer delays, and better use of time and materials. In America, 20 to 25 percent of production costs is spent in finding and correcting mistakes. Add the additional costs incurred in repairing or replacing faulty products in the field and the total cost of poor quality may approach 30 percent. In Japan it is about 3 percent. The cost of ignoring quality is enormous. American companies all too often achieve quality by setting acceptable quality levels and using "tailgate" inspection to measure compliance. With this passive-reactive approach, improving quality results in increased scrap and rework, and in increased costs. Our competitors do not do it that way. First, they do not subscribe to the notion of an acceptable quality level because it assumes that some defects are acceptable. Their goal is one of no defects, that is, through a process of continuous improvement. Second, they have adopted a proactive or preventive approach to quality. They consider quality to be an integral part of product and process design, not something that is achieved through management oversight or inspection. To achieve designed-in quality, global competitors use systematic product and process techniques based on statistical analyses to identify sources of process or material variation, to decide when it is economical to reduce these sources of variation, and to ensure the product is robust in light of remaining variability. They then closely monitor process performance.

World-class, quality-focused companies declare that quality is the concern and responsibility of every employee, "from the president to the janitor," and that quality concerns are pervasive from product inception through customer support. Top management is directly involved in quality, as contrasted with just supporting quality or committing the company to it. Managers in quality-focused companies accept responsibility for quality, direct and participate in quality education, establish quality goals, and take management action required to help realize these goals. Managers direct and participate in quality policy, self-assessments, direct allocation of resources for quality efforts, and spend substantial time with workers on the projects. Quality teams provide the principal mechanism for workers to meet frequently with their colleagues on improvement projects and for periodic and frequent meetings with management, so that management can find concrete ways to help.

While global competitors believe that quality is a design and process issue, they still recognize the need for inspection as part of an overall process control strategy. The responsibility for in-process inspection and analysis is primarily assigned to individual production workers, not to quality assurance personnel. There are quality assurance personnel in the competitors' companies, but their role generally is limited to participating in the concurrent design teams and carrying out quality planning and higher level analyses. The workers carry out the elementary statistical analyses to detect unacceptable process variability and in most cases are authorized to take corrective action when indicated by the analyses. Only if the worker can not solve the problem does it get referred to a higher level.

By placing so much quality emphasis on the individual worker, our competitors generate individual pride in workmanship and quality with a resulting major gain in employee motivation. They have also achieved a closed-loop operation in which variations in process quality are determined very early and corrected at the lowest level of the organization at which such a correction can be made.

Coopers and Lybrand have developed a set of "World-Class Metrics" for manufacturing companies, as shown in Table 1–1. In terms of quality, you can see the disparity between the quality performance of American companies and of our competitors.

Closing the Competitive Gaps: The International Report of the Manufacturing Futures Project, published by Boston University, states, "Each part of the world (Europe, Japan, and America) believes that it has an advantage over its competitors in a different dimension. The Europeans believe they are ahead in

TABLE 1–1
World-Class Metrics

Attribute	World-Class Standard	US Average
Setup time	System < 30 minutes	2-4 hrs
Quality	Cell < 1 minute	
	1500 PPM captured	3-5% captured
	300 PPM escapes	2-5% in warranty
	cost of quality 3-5%	15-25% cost of quality
Ratio of manufacturing space to total space	> 50%	25-35%
Work as a function of time	20%	1.75-5%
Material velocity	> 100 turns	2-4 turns
Material residence time	3 days	3 months
Flexibility	270 parts/machine tool	25 parts/machine tool
Distance	300 ft	> 1 mile
Uptime	95%	65-75%

Source: Ronald R. Barris, National Director of Industrial Automation, Coopers and Lybrand.

product performance, the Japanese in flexibility, and the Americans (to their surprise) in price." As these competitors approach parity on the fundamentals of quality in the 1990s, performance, price, and especially flexibility, will become more important elements of business strategies.

Global competitors have made significant changes in their strategic plans over the past decade. European and American manufacturers have improved their manufacturing capabilities in order to hold or attempt to regain a viable market share position depending on type of products. Their strategy often has been based on a return to the fundamentals of effective product and process development integration, with a special focus on quality improvement and organizational restructuring. In contrast, the Japanese, feeling confident that they produce the best quality products in the world, have emphasized flexibility through the use of automation (CAD—computer added design, robots, CIM—computer integrated manufacturing) and price reduction of their products.

Figure 1–3 shows the relative importance of the generic strat-

FIGURE 1–3
Importance of World-Class Competitive Strategies

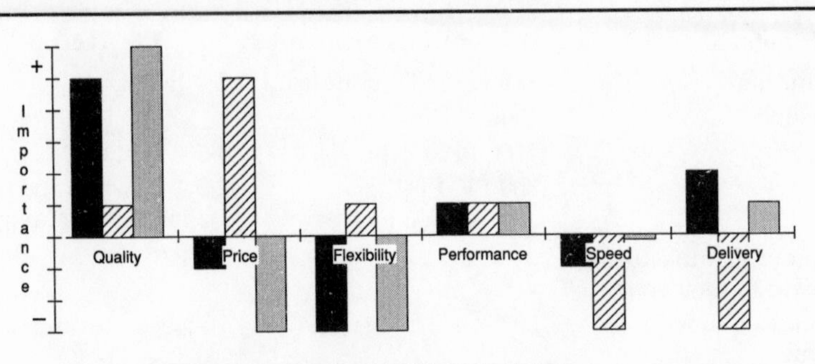

Source: Reproduced with permission of Manufacturing Roundtable, Boston University.

egies used in American, European, and Japanese companies. These generic strategic elements help distinguish the direction of international competitive strategies for the 1990s. The strategic elements are:

- Quality manufacturing—The ability to provide consistent high-quality products.
- Flexible manufacturing—The ability to make rapid design changes and/or introduce new products very quickly.
- Competitive pricing—The ability to compete worldwide on price.
- Product performance—The ability to design and produce high-performance products.
- Speed of product introduction—The ability to deliver products quickly.
- Reliable delivery—On-time delivery (as promised).

Figure 1–3 illustrates the differences between American, Japanese, and European manufacturing strategic priorities. Compared with Japan, the Americans and Europeans still place the least emphasis on quality; the Japanese are emphasizing price. Next most important for the Americans and Europeans is on-time delivery, but to the Japanese the critical strategic issue is flexible manufacturing. The Japanese emphasis on flexibility allows them to introduce new products and incorporate changes quickly.

Global competitive strategies in the typical European approach are to exploit a perceived lead in delivering quality products while avoiding head-on price competition. The Japanese strategy seeks to gain advantage by offering a wide variety of new products while redressing their price disadvantage. The American strategy focuses on improving quality, maintaining on-time delivery capability, and enhancing product performance.

Table 1–2 lists, in rank order, the importance of programs that companies in America, Japan, and Europe stress as their near-term priorities. The Americans and Europeans are focused on quality improvement programs such as statistical process control, zero defects, and supplier quality enhancement efforts. The Japanese appear to be aggressively advancing their lead in flexible production by their emphasis on computer-aided flexible systems (CAD, Computer Automated Manufacturing, CIM), and creating new production processes for new products.

NO QUICK FIX

What to do? The key to American competitiveness in the 1990s is to avoid emulating the German or Japanese companies, and to keep an honest set of American priorities firmly fixed in our corporate minds to guide our actions. We should not be drawn into playing another nation's game. We will be far better off if we follow an American-made blueprint to our quality future.

Perhaps the most daunting part of the challenge facing the American business community is the nature of the change that is required in the years ahead. If the problem was just slow pro-

TABLE 1–2
Enhancement Priorities in America, Japan, and Europe

America	Japan	Europe
Supplier quality	Lead time reduction	Zero defects
Statistical process control	Computer-aided design	New product introduction
Systems integration	Value analysis	Supplier quality
Lead time reduction	New process/product development	Systems integration
Worker safety	Systems integration	Team motivation
Zero defects	New product introduction	Lead time reduction
Defining strategy	Job enlargement	Supervisor training
Supervisor training	Supplier lead time reductions	Just-in-time
New product introduction	FMS/CIM/EIS*	Statistical quality control

*Flexible Manufacturing Systems, Computer Integrated Manufacturing, Enterprise Integration Systems

Source: Reproduced with permission of Manufacturing Roundtable, Boston University.

duction, we could design faster machines. If the problem was simply one of poorly trained workers, we could redesign the education system to accommodate the needs of the modern worker. As we will see in the pages that follow, American organizations are facing the prospect of massive changes in the basic culture that underlies how we do business.

Unlike mechanical fixes, cultural change takes time and is hard work. When it comes to building quality into a company where it does not now exist, there is simply no quick fix. Interviews with business leaders have repeatedly confirmed how difficult it is for a company to shift from a culture that condones poor quality to one that insists on high-quality processes, products, and services. Many firms simply don't have sufficient energy and leadership to make the change, and for them the future is bleak. Change may be difficult, but what's the alternative? In the 1990s, as you shall see repeatedly in this book, the *quick fix* mentality is the problem, not the cure.

When confronting a new crisis or problem, individuals and organizations characteristically react in a similar way: They deny that a problem exists. The denial period may last a brief moment or it may never end. Nonetheless, until the individual or organization overcomes this initial stage in the problem-solving process and faces reality, the crisis will remain unsolved. Those firms entering the 1990s with a business-as-usual attitude are unwilling to acknowledge reality and are stuck—for a moment or forever—in denial. Until they get over or go around this barrier, they are setting themselves up for failure in the coming years.

"QUALITY FIRST"

The concept of "Quality First" is used in this book as a shorthand way of stressing two fundamental tenets:

- Quality must become the company's *number one* business strategy priority. Quality is not a sprint; it is a long-distance event that takes top management attention and persistence, and lots of it. If you have world-class quality products, services, and people, you will also generate world-class profits.
- A company's quality program must address its own unique needs. Off-the-shelf, "just add water" canned quality solutions cannot generate the level of human commitment within the organization needed to succeed. In fact, you may substitute your company's quality initiative name in place of the term "Quality First" when thinking about the concepts presented in this book.

"Quality First" is both a philosophy and a set of guiding concepts, principles, and practices that represent the foundation of a continuously improving organization. It applies human resources and quantitative methods to improve the materials and services supplied to your company; to improve all of the processes within the company; and to improve the company's ability to meet the needs of the customer now and in the future. It integrates fundamental management techniques, existing improvement efforts, and technical tools in a disciplined, focused, and continuous improvement process.

"Quality First" addresses the quality of management as well as the management of quality. It involves everyone in an organization in a systematic, long-term endeavor to develop processes that are customer oriented, flexible and responsive, and constantly improving in quality. Quality includes all aspects of every product or service of value to a customer. Ultimately, "Quality First" is a means through which an organization creates and sustains a culture committed to continuous improvement.

Thousands of American firms are still employing the tools, management techniques, and paradigms of the Machine Age as we begin to deal with the problems and complexities of the 21st century. The management methods that still predominate are based on the theories of Taylor, Skinner, and other pioneers of scientific management. Those approaches were reductionist in nature and were patterned on the very machines that shaped the age. They were appropriate for their time, but they are excess baggage today.

Russell Ackoff illustrates the point with the following example: Suppose you were to acquire all the makes of automobiles produced in the world and then systematically select from the set the best carburetor, transmission, brakes, and so forth. When you attempt to assemble the world's best possible automobile from the collection of the best parts, you would not even be able to produce an automobile, because the parts would not fit together. The performance of the whole—its quality—is not the sum of the performance of the parts; it is a consequence of the relationship between the performance of the parts.

Under "Quality First," your organization will deliberately seek to create a positive and dynamic working environment, foster teamwork, apply quantitative methods and analytical techniques, and tap the creativity and ingenuity of all of your people. You will focus on collective efforts to better understand and meet internal and external customer needs and to continuously increase customer satisfaction.

The "Quality First" philosophy provides a comprehensive way to improve total organization performance and quality by examining each process through which work gets done in a systematic, integrated, consistent, organization-wide manner. It includes understanding the concept of variation and its implications for process improvement. "Quality First" addresses all forms of work and applies equally to every person in the organization, including top management, marketeers, service providers, designers, production workers, white-collar workers, and laborers.

Whoever you are, it is often easy to fall into the trap of thinking that your company is too big to be affected by individual actions. That perception is common and frustrating, and fortunately, it is a false one. Only through the collective efforts of their individual members do companies change; companies are incapable of changing themselves.

Whatever your position in your company, your efforts to perform a job and to improve your performance directly affect the influence you will have in the company, the control you will have over your personal situation, and your ability to manage and lead. Combined with the efforts of others, your effectiveness directly influences the company's overall ability to meet its mission and ultimately affects the performance of the United States as a nation. Furthermore, how you perform today will also affect future generations.

"Quality First" is a means for improving personal effectiveness and performance and for aligning and focusing all individual efforts throughout an organization. It provides a framework within which you may continuously improve everything you do and affect. It is a way of leveraging your individual effort and extending its effect and its importance throughout an organization and beyond.

"Quality First" is not a destination but a journey toward improvement. The rest of this book will help you get started on that journey. It will help you understand the benefits of continuous improvement and your role and responsibilities in leading the improvement effort in your company. In it, you will explore why continuous improvement is important to each of us. This book will serve as a frame of reference for the ongoing dialogue about "Quality First," and it will help you set the direction for your own journey of improvement. As you read these words, your journey has begun.

If you care about where American industry in general, and your company in particular, are headed in the 1990s, now is the time to act. Companies that procrastinate and delay taking the first step toward the "Quality First" concept, or stay in a state of denial too long, risk failure in the competitive years ahead.

The choice is yours. You can pick a smooth, planned transition to your competitive future, or you can wait for the coming crisis to force your company into the quality arena. The choice is yours. Read on!

Chapter Two

An Executive's Guide to Quality

"Neither a wise man nor a brave man lies down on the tracks of history to wait for the train of the future to run over him."

Dwight D. Eisenhower, 1952

WHAT IS QUALITY?

Why All the Fuss about Quality?

During the 1980s, America rediscovered quality. Suddenly, the word seemed to appear everywhere, here as an adjective, there as a noun. Parents were expected to spend quality time with their children, kids were going to receive quality educations, and everyone was concerned about the declining quality of life in America. In the business community, management by objective was out. Total Quality Control and Total Quality Management were suddenly in. Even President Bush got into the act, declaring that if American business was to be a world-class player it would have to "look at quality first."

The purpose of this chapter is threefold. First, it will acquaint you with the language and key concepts of "Quality First" management. Second, it will serve as a primer, raising your awareness of quality to a level sufficient to ensure you will benefit fully from the book. Finally, it is hoped this chapter will develop in you a personal desire to assume a leadership role in your company's "Quality First" efforts.

Definitions Galore

Table 2–1 is a good place to start your search for the meaning of quality. Notice that businessmen do not have a monopoly on the term. The quotes from Robert Pirsig, a novelist, and Barbara Tuchman, a historian, indicate how far the quality idea has infiltrated other parts of society. The so-called quality movement in America has become a society-wide issue.

The table also shows how broadly and subtly the term is being defined within the business community. Quality is not just a product-based term or a service-based term or a manufacturing-based term. As you read over this array of definitions, ask yourself this question:

> Is quality resident only in a firm's product or service, or is quality also found in the process that produces the product or service?

The answer to this question will bring you to a new level of awareness concerning the real meaning of quality, and a realization that quality *is* actually present in, or missing from, every aspect of a firm's operation from top to bottom and side to side. And remember, there is no one "right" definition of quality. The definition adopted by your firm will be "right" only if it fits the firm's unique managerial conditions and competitive requirements.

For the "Quality First" concept we define quality as the extent to which products and services produced conform to customer requirements. Customers can be internal as well as external to the organizational system (e.g., products or services may flow to the person at the next desk or work area rather than to people outside of the immediate organization).

The days of limiting the definition of quality to the "soundness" of the product—its hardness or durability, for example—

TABLE 2–1
Definitions of Quality

1. **Customer-based**

   "Quality is fitness for use."

   J. M. Juran

   "Total Quality is performance leadership in meeting customer requirements by doing the right things right the first time."

   Westinghouse

   "Quality is meeting customer expectations. The Quality Improvement Process is a set of principles, policies, support structures, and practices designed to continually improve the efficiency and effectiveness of our way of life."

   AT&T

2. **Manufacturing-based**

   "Quality [means] conformance to requirements."

   Philip B. Crosby

   "Quality is the degree to which a specific product conforms to a design or specification."

   Harold L. Gilmore

3. **Product-based**

   "Differences in quality amount to differences in the quantity of some desired ingredient or attribute."

   Lawrence Abbott

   "Quality refers to the amount of the unpriced attribute contained in each unit of the priced attribute."

   Keith B. Leffler

4. **Value-based**

   "Quality is the degree of excellence at an acceptable price and the control of variability at an acceptable cost."

   Robert A. Broh

   "Quality means best for certain customer conditions. These conditions are (a) the actual use and (b) the selling price of the product."

   Armand V. Feigenbaum

5. **Transcendent**

   "Quality is neither mind nor matter, but a third entity independent of the other two . . . even though Quality cannot be defined, you know what it is . . . "

   Robert Pirsig

   ". . . a condition of excellence implying fine quality as distinct from poor quality . . . Quality is achieving or reaching the highest standard as against being satisfied with the sloppy or fraudulent."

   Barbara W. Tuchman

are gone. The new kind of quality American firms rediscovered in the 1980s is far more cultural than physical, far more the way things are done than the nature of the things themselves.

THE LANGUAGE OF QUALITY

Like any other field of study, "Quality First" brings with it a new set of ideas and a new vocabulary to express these ideas. But be careful. While the quality management literature is full of familiar sounding business terms, many take on a somewhat different meaning when used in a "Quality First" context. The language of quality vocabulary includes the following terms.

Process. The familiar definition of process is simply an agreed-upon set of steps. But, in the "Quality First" context the word *process* also means "the logical way things are done," in an organization. "Quality First" is based on a "continuous process improvement" approach, meaning it is a never-ending, cyclical search for ways to do things better.

Customer. In traditional management lore, attention is usually given only to the external customers. In "Quality First," however, a second, equally important customer is the internal customer. End users of a firm's product or service located inside the firm are the internal customers.

Patrick Townsend, in his book *Commit to Quality*, provides a simple model which splits quality into two halves. In Table 2–2, "Quality in Fact" represents the view of quality from the perspective of a supplier, while "Quality in Perception" examines how a customer looks at quality. A firm is located between its suppliers and its customers and, if the company is to serve as a world-class organization linking the two, it must also adopt a quality-focused—a "Quality First"—approach as its principal business objective.

But this seemingly simple supplier-customer model is complicated by the fact that the company is *both* a customer of its suppliers (internal and external) and a supplier to its customers (both internal and external). A "Quality First" approach is the means to bring the views of the suppliers and the views of the

TABLE 2–2.
Quality: Fact and Perception

Quality in fact

Doing the right thing
Doing it the right way
Doing it right the first time
Doing it on time

Quality in perception

Delivering the right product
Satisfying your customer's needs
Meeting your customer's expectations
Treating every customer with integrity, courtesy, and respect

customers into harmony with each other. In graphic form, this relationship of the company to its many suppliers and customers is shown in Figure 2–1.

Customer requirements. The needs of the customers—both internal and external users—constitute a company's customer requirements. The ultimate aim of the company is to satisfy these requirements, as shown in Figure 2–1, and thereby satisfy its customers.

Supplier specifications. Once customer requirements are known, you can then determine supplier specifications. "Quality First" companies reject the idea that their suppliers should be picked mainly on the basis of price. Far more emphasis is placed on whether a supplier can meet the company's customer-driven specifications on a continuous basis, thus avoiding the introduction of defects into the company's production process.

Conformance. This term is closely linked to customer requirements. In the "Quality First" context, conformance demands that products and services be measured against known and reliable customer requirements to ensure that they will, in fact, meet the customer's needs. Guesswork is not allowed. Dependence only on historical data is rejected. Conformance must be based on continuously updated data that reflect current, objective measures of customer needs.

Data. "Quality First" is a data-driven approach to qual-

FIGURE 2–1
"Quality First" Customer/Supplier Relationships

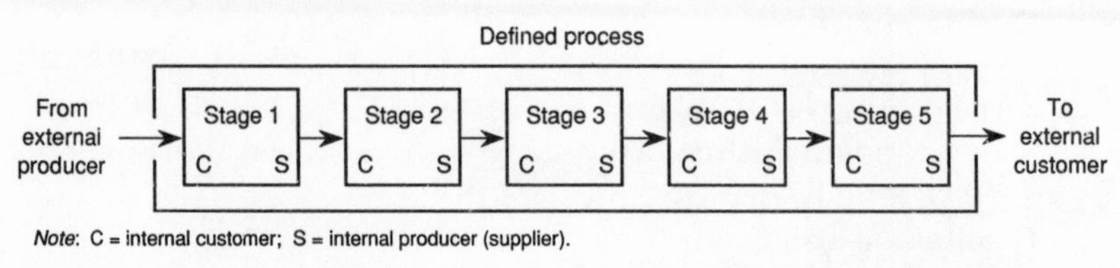

Note: C = internal customer; S = internal producer (supplier).

Source: *Continuous Improvement Process: Principles and Practices*, Logistics Management Institute, Bethesda, MD, August 1989.

ity improvement. Information or a set of facts are presented in descriptive form. There are two basic kinds of data: measured (variable data) and counted (known as attribute data).

Statistical process control. Statistical Process Control (SPC) is a disciplined way of identifying and solving problems in order to improve performance. It involves use of fishbone diagrams (see Chapter Ten) to identify causes and effects of problems. Data are then collected and organized in various ways (graphs, Pareto charts, and/or histograms) to further examine problems. The data may be tracked over time (control charts) to determine variation in the process. The process is then enhanced in some way and new data are collected and analyzed to determine whether the process has been improved.

Cross-functional teams. These teams are similar to quality teams but the members are from several work units that interface with one another. These teams are particularly useful when work units are dependent upon one another for systems integration, materials, information, and so forth.

Employee empowerment. In many companies, employees, by design, are doers, not thinkers. They are expected only to perform to minimum standards. In "Quality First" companies, on the other hand, all employees are expected to solve problems, participate in team-building efforts and, generally, expand the scope of their role in the organization. The goal of employee empowerment is to stop trying to motivate workers with extrinsic incentives, as is the case in traditional practices, and build a work environment in which all employees take pride in their work accomplishments and begin motivating themselves from within.

This enhanced role of the worker draws on the work of Douglas McGregor during the 1950s and his familiar Theory X and Theory Y assumptions about the nature of the worker. He argues that the Theory X view is fundamentally flawed. His Theory Y assumptions, on the other hand, many of which underlie the "Quality First" approach, invite a wider and more responsible role for the worker in an organization. A review of McGregor's two sets of assumptions, shown in Table 2–3, will facilitate a better understanding of the expanded role of the worker in "Quality First" firms in the 1990s.

Culture. Culture does not mean going to the opera. Rather, culture is the prevailing pattern of activities, interactions, norms, sentiments, beliefs, attitudes, values, and products in your company. Many executives want to ignore "culture." It is too nebulous, too difficult to "fix." Some believe "all is well," or "if it's not broke, don't fix it."

Recently a vice president for a large American company became a born-again quality advocate. He met late Friday with the CEO to outline his plan to improve the organization's quality by changing the corporate culture and adopt the "Quality First" concepts. All was well until the CEO jumped up, full of enthusiasm, and said he wanted the corporate culture changed by close of business Monday!

One of the most difficult tasks for top management is to understand the impact of culture modification on their near-term and long-term business strategy. Changing your corporate culture takes years, not days.

FUNDAMENTAL CONCEPTS OF QUALITY

The fundamental concepts and principles of "Quality First" include (1) need for a single interdependent system, (2) adoption of the "Quality First" paradigm, (3) enhanced leadership for management's new role, (4) constancy of purpose, (5) commitment to quality, (6) customer focus, (7) benchmarking, (8)

TABLE 2–3
McGregor's Theory X and Y

Theory X Assumptions of the Worker

1. The average human being has an inherent dislike of work and will avoid it if he can.
2. Because of this human characteristic of dislike of work, most people must be coerced, directed, threatened with punishment to get them to put forth adequate effort toward the achievement of organizational objectives.
3. The average human being prefers to be directed, wishes to avoid responsibility, has relatively little ambition, wants security above all.

Theory Y Assumptions of the Worker

1. The expenditure of physical and mental effort in work is as natural as play or rest.
2. External control and the threat of punishment are not the only means for bringing about effort toward organizational objectives. Man will exercise self-direction and self-control in the service of objectives to which he is committed.
3. Commitment to objectives is a function of the rewards associated with their achievement.
4. The average human being learns, under proper conditions, not only to accept but to seek responsibility.
5. The capacity to exercise a relatively high degree of imagination, ingenuity, and creativity in the solution of organizational problems is widely, not narrowly, distributed in the population.
6. Under the conditions of modern industrial life, the intellectual potentialities of the average human being are only partially utilized.

Source: Douglas McGregor, *The Human Side of Organizations* (New York: McGraw-Hill, 1960) pp. 33–34; pp. 47–48.

process orientation, (9) continuous process improvement, (10) system-centered management, (11) investment in knowledge, (12) teamwork, (13) total involvement, and (14) long-term commitment. These synergistic concepts and principles of "Quality First" are described below.

These "Quality First" concepts and principles work together in a logical and holistic manner to give substance and vitality to the continuously improving corporate culture. Figure 2–2 illustrates this holistic view.

FIGURE 2–2
Holistic View of "Quality First" Integration

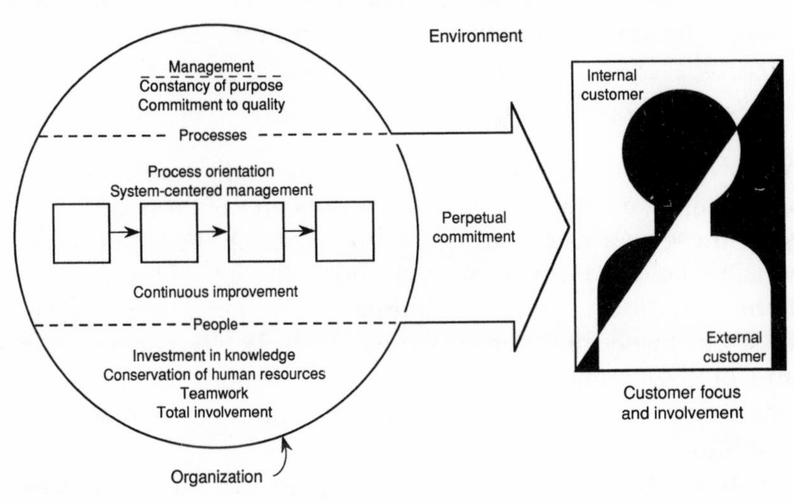

Source: *An Introduction to the CIP Principles and Practices,* Logistics Management Institute, Bethesda, MD, 1989.

A Single Interdependent System

In traditional management, a company's product or service—its output—is the focal point of attention. Typically, the company's goal was to make sure its output was error-free before it left the plant. This was usually accomplished with an in-house inspection department designed to spot defective products. In other words, because each work unit was treated separately, the mistakes of one department could easily become the input for another department. Mistakes were not avoided, but detected and corrected.

In a "Quality First"–focused company, all work units, suppliers, and customers are viewed as part of a single, interdependent system. From a quality perspective, either the whole system is working well, or the whole system is not working well. "Quality First" rejects the notion that one unit's defects can be passed along to another unit and become its inputs. "Quality First" insists that each work unit does its job correctly, the first time around, every time around. When the total process is designed to perform its tasks correctly, the system is said to be healthy, the customer is satisfied, and the cost of maintaining the system is reduced to its minimum level.

A New Business Paradigm

A few of the characteristics associated with the traditional way of managing a company have already been mentioned. Underlying these characteristics is a set of generally held but largely invisible beliefs and values, including "the job of top management is to find answers to company problems, and workers must be closely monitored if they are to be productive." The sum of the common beliefs held by a majority of managers today comprises what is called the traditional management paradigm.

A different set of beliefs and assumptions about the nature of life in the business organization underlies the "Quality First" practices described throughout this book. "Quality First" is a paradigm shift. A paradigm, according to futurist Joel Barker, is a set of values and regulations that first establishes boundaries and then establishes how to be successful in solving problems within those boundaries. In the individual, a paradigm shift requires a profound change in one's thinking. In your company, it requires cultural change. And, as you know, cultural change does not come easily. For example, it is assumed in a quality management company that workers are capable of managing themselves (once given the tools to do so) and that solutions to most problems faced in the work place can be found within the work force itself, not in the CEO's office. Clearly, the belief systems of traditional management and "Quality First" are not compatible. That is, a company operating under the traditional paradigm cannot fully adopt "Quality First" practices without first replacing the old belief system with a new one. A company shifting its belief system is said to be undergoing a change in its internal culture.

As the number of American business firms shifting from the old to the new "Quality First" paradigm grows in the 1990s, as shown in Figure 2–3, there will come a point—some-

FIGURE 2–3
American Business Adopts "Quality First" Principles by the Year 2000

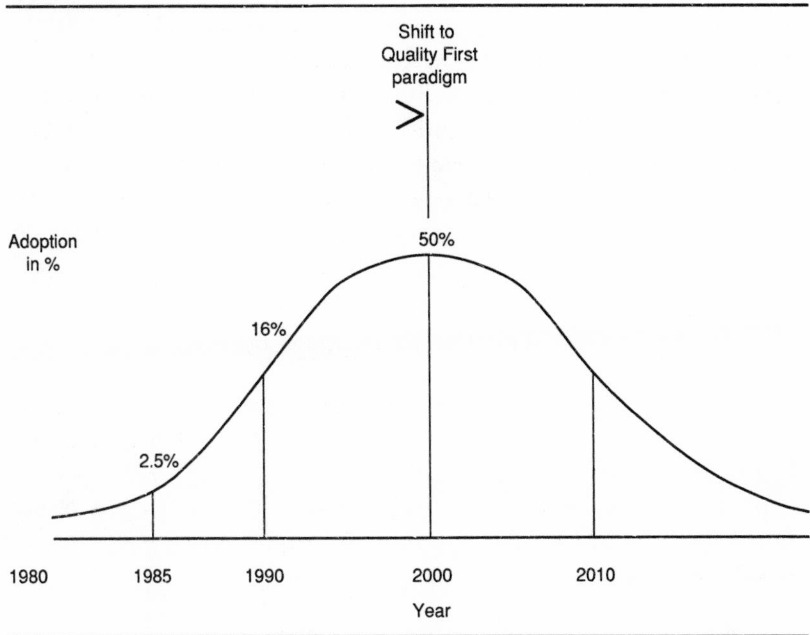

where around the 50 percent mark—when the entire competitive American business community will have made the paradigm shift. After that point any laggard firms wishing to remain competitive will, of necessity, have to shift to the new paradigm or retire their business. My estimate is that the turning point from the old to the new "Quality First" paradigm in the American business community will take place around the year 2000. After that point, the pros and cons of "Quality First" will no longer be debated, as they are today. After 2000, "Quality First" will become the operative belief system of the entire American business community, and the shift from only a bottom-line mentality to a customer-first way of corporate life will be complete.

Unfortunately, it is our view that the "Quality First" concept is all too frequently advocated without sufficient substance or understanding. It is much easier to jump on particular aspects of the concept—such as statistical process control, employee involvement, structured problem solving, and other tools and techniques—than it is to understand and embrace the concept in its holistic sense. If the number of government and industry organizations that claim to be doing quality improvement in its fundamental sense were really doing it, world-class competitors of the United States would be begging for mercy. We cannot afford to settle for the easy way. We cannot take shortcuts. And we cannot pretend that buzzwords, slogans, rhetoric, and posturing are enough to meet the competitive challenges American business faces.

Leadership and Management's New Role

"Quality First" is destined to alter both the definition of leadership in an organization as well as the role of top management. Read what *A Guide for Implementing Total Quality Management*, by the ITT Reliability Analysis Center (RAC), has to say about the role of top management in implementing a "Quality First" process:

> RAC recommends the top-down model because it has the highest probability for success, although it doesn't guarantee success. The top-down model fosters management commitment, the single most important requirement for . . . success. . . . Top-down implementation requires management leadership as well as commitment. Management must lead the effort, providing . . . vision and philosophy for the organization. Management must lead the cultural change required.
>
> The top-down approach assures the availability of the resource support that is crucial for success. Time, money, and people are going to be required. . . . The bottom-up approach sends the message that quality management is something for the employees, but not necessarily for management.

Vision and Philosophy

Leadership is the key role for top managers. In more traditional management cultures, the meaning given to the term *leadership* is somewhat amorphous. In a "Quality First" culture, however, leadership takes on a more precise definition. A quality leader must first establish a common vision of what the company is all about, its purpose. He or she must also put into place that vision through his or her unique "Quality First" philosophy—a set of guiding principles and practices—that will form a top-to-bottom, organization-wide belief system of the way in which the company will go about its business.

Management's New Role

Traditional management methods—the accepted norm today in America—are in conflict with "Quality First" practices. For example, traditional management practices require managers to hold employees accountable; yet in a firm practicing "Quality First" the customer, not top management, controls the actions of the workers. In traditionally managed firms, fighting daily fires consumes management's energies, and competition among work groups is encouraged. In "Quality First" organizations, however, these practices are replaced with a managerial focus on teamwork and continuous process improvement to permanently put out brush fires.

W. Edwards Deming describes the new role for top management in *Out of Crisis*:

> The job of management is not supervision, but leadership. Management must work on sources of improvement, the intent of quality of product and of service, and on the translation of the intent into design and actual product. The required transformation of Western style of management requires that managers be leaders. The focus on outcome (management by numbers, MBO, work standards, meeting specifications . . .) must be abolished, and leadership put in place.

Changing the Corporate Culture

Table 2–4 gives you a realistic idea of the magnitude of change often required when your company moves from a traditional to a "Quality First" culture. Don't underestimate the initial resistance to change that is likely to be generated in an organization once it is clear to its employees how deeply the proposed changes will alter the old way of doing things.

Constancy of Purpose

The constancy of purpose principle is a core "Quality First" concept. For the "Quality First" organization, constancy of purpose is generally articulated by management through a broad statement of corporate purpose.

Such a statement provides individuals with a steady and consistent vision of where they are going, what is expected of them, and what they expect of themselves. Likewise, a constancy of purpose demonstrated consistently by management's behavior enables each individual to construct a reliable mental road map on which to base decisions and actions.

Top management is responsible for providing constancy of purpose. It must be provided from the highest possible level so that it can be infused throughout all parts of an organization. It is conveyed by a clear statement of a vision for the company with a set of consistent goals and objectives, and it is supported by strategic and tactical plans. This constancy of purpose is reinforced by an ongoing stream of management

TABLE 2–4
Culture Change from Traditional to "Quality First" Implementation

"Quality First" is . . .	"Quality First" is not . . .
• demonstrating executive leadership and commitment.	• assigning responsibility for quality to others.
• listening to customers to determine their requirements.	• assuming you know your customer's requirements.
• doing the right thing right the first time.	• doing it over to make it right.
• identifying cost of quality and focusing on prevention.	• overlooking the hidden costs of poor quality.
• continuous process improvement.	• one-time fix.
• taking ownership at all levels of the organization.	• assigning responsibility for quality to one department.

signals and actions that nurture and support the realization of the vision.

Commitment to Quality

Commitment to quality is a cornerstone of the "Quality First" concept. The concept of quality improvement must encompass both measurability and the customer's perceptions of usefulness. Improvement implies a comparison with past performance. Quality improvement implies increasing degrees of excellence with reference to specific and accepted points of reference. Those points of reference include specifications, cost, performance, schedule, responsiveness, and product or service improvement based on competitive benchmarks.

A commitment to quality must begin with top management. Consistent with its constancy of purpose, working within the corporate philosophy, top management must identify the external customers for the organization's products and services. Top management must understand the customer's needs and expectations and assure that those needs are translated into the attributes and characteristics of the products or services. Top management must direct the resources of the organization toward continuously improving the product or service with respect to the customer-relevant attributes.

Customer Focus and Involvement

Without customer focus and involvement, both constancy of purpose and commitment to quality become meaningless. Attracting, serving, and retaining customers is the ultimate purpose of any company, and those customers help the organization frame its quality consciousness and guide its improvement effort. A process, product, or service has no relevance without customers; everything done in an organization is done for the customer. The quality of a product or service is defined by customer behavior and response. Process improvement must be guided by a clear understanding of customer needs and expectations.

Increased customer satisfaction is the ultimate result of customer focus and involvement. The responsibility for assuring customer focus and involvement starts with a top-management focus on the organization's external customer and extends down through every level of activity to involve all customers in the improvement process. "Quality First" emphasizes satisfying all customers, internal and external.

Just as your company is dynamic, so are its customers. Customer requirements change for a variety of reasons, often uncontrollable and unpredictable. To serve its customers adequately, therefore, the organization must continually reassess its customers' needs and requirements and factor them into its improvement efforts. Failure to consider customers and to actively involve them in the improvement effort is a fatal flaw in a company's quality philosophy.

Benchmarking

A benchmark is a standard of excellence or achievement against which other similar things must be measured or judged. Simply speaking, benchmarking is the process of:

- Figuring out what to benchmark.
- Finding out what the benchmark is.
- Determining how it's achieved.
- Deciding to make changes or improvements in one's own business practices to meet or exceed the benchmark.

These four questions—while sounding fairly simple—require thinking and analysis. They require that you know your own business processes and practices down to the smallest detail. Benchmarking is a process of comparing—comparing results, outputs, methods, processes or practices in a systematic way. One of the purposes of this book is to help you through the process of self-assessment.

Process Orientation

The most effective means for an organization to address customer needs and improve itself is to focus improvement efforts on its processes. Process orientation requires a significant change in thinking for many American managers. American management practices, particularly quality functions, have traditionally focused on the postproduction identification and rejection of defective products.

While that approach may be reasonably successful in preventing most unsatisfactory products from reaching customers, it does little to change the processes that create defects.

"Quality First" forces management to think in terms of process rather than in terms of finished product. Everything that is done in an organization is accomplished through a process comprised of definable stages, steps, or activities. Each step of a process involves both producer and customer. The customer is always the step subsequent to the producer. Hence, the principle of customer focus and involvement provides a precise means for defining the purpose (and often the means) of the process.

Continuous Process Improvement

The central, unifying concept in the "Quality First" approach is the idea that everything a firm does is part of a continuous improvement process. Here is how Brian E. Mansir and Nicholas R. Schacht, both of the Logistics Management Institute, describe this key concept in their report entitled *An Introduction to the Continuous Improvement Process: Principles and Practices.*

Continuous process improvement is the fundamental principle around which quality is centered. It complements and animates the principles of process orientation and customer focus and involvement with the certain recognition that no process, product, or service ever attains perfection and that neither the customer's expectations nor the quality of the competition remains static. A deliberate positive change (improvement) is required to win and hold a customer base or to remain economically competitive. Devotion to continuous improvement is a demonstration of constant, purposeful commitment to quality.

Continuous improvement depends on both innovative and small incremental changes. Innovation is characterized by large dramatic changes (see Figure 2–4) resulting from new technologies or new ways of thinking and is often the product of research and development.

FIGURE 2–4
The Large-Step Innovation-Driven Improvement Process

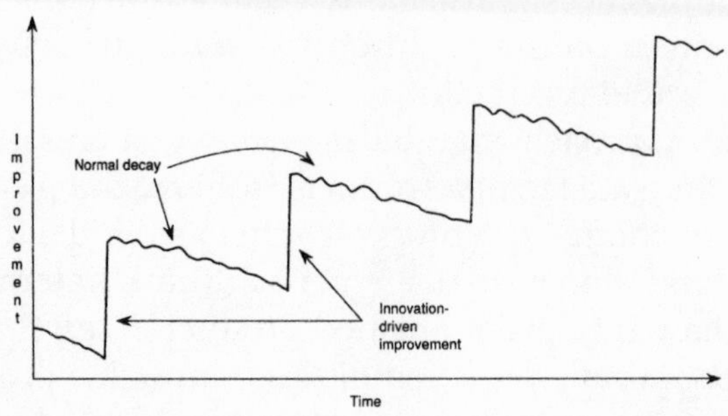

FIGURE 2–5
The Small-Step Improvements Process

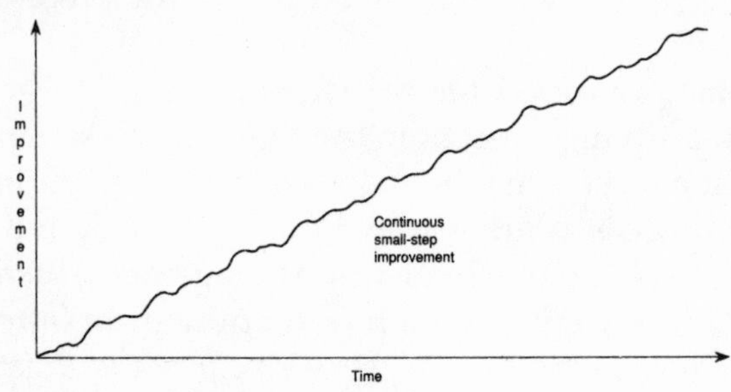

FIGURE 2–6
Balance between Innovation and Incremental Improvement

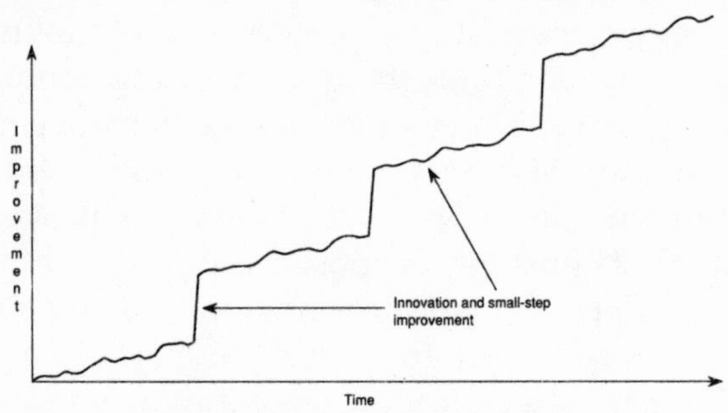

Source: *Continuous Improvement Process: Principles and Practices,* Logistics Management Institute, Bethesda, MD, 1989.

American management has traditionally focused on innovation as the primary engine of improvement. The "Quality First" organization also recognizes the importance of innovation for developing new processes, products, and services. It also recognizes small incremental improvements (see Figure 2–5) as essential for maintaining and building on the new performance standards achieved through innovation. "Quality First" organizations seek a better balance between innovation and small incremental improvement.

Eventually the opportunities from small incremental process improvements reach a point of diminishing returns. Before that occurs, the company should be prepared to introduce the next level of innovation and to begin again the incremental improvement cycle. The balance between innovation and incremental improvement is key and is illustrated by the growth curves in Figure 2–6.

System-Centered Management

System-centered management requires managers to actively improve the system within which they work. Management's new job is to study and reform the processes by which work is accomplished. This concept is anathema to many American managers. Many managers come to their positions with the idea that their job is to assure that work is accomplished in accordance with the established processes. They tend to see their role as keeping people busy and processing the paper that constitutes their deliverable products. True, a substantial part of their job is motivating the work force, providing better discipline, hiring better people, or performing administrative tasks. However, when managers assume that the fundamental structure and processes of the system are fixed and correct, they fail to address their most important job: system improvement.

The traditional attitude about management's role leads managers to deal with a continuous stream of momentary demands for attention. The demands of the "in-basket" never cease, squeaky wheels constantly need oiling, and most managers get bogged down in detail and are unable to step back and deal with the entire process or system. The manager becomes a mechanic, so busy tinkering with the sources of noise that he cannot see that the machine—the organizational system—is becoming obsolete and incapable of performing to modern standards.

Investment in Knowledge

Personal knowledge, teamwork, security, and personal involvement are among the key factors that govern how individuals function and interact within the company. Expanding knowledge is both a personal and a company responsibility. Both the individual and the company must commit to investing in knowledge.

Investment in knowledge is aimed at maximizing human potential and capital. All planned improvement comes from growth in understanding. Improvement is achieved through questioning why things are done and the ways they are done, by trying new ways of doing things, and by learning. Increased education and knowledge should be a lifelong opportunity and experience. In the workplace, every employee should be challenged to grow in value to the organization and in self-worth. An organization that practices "Quality First" makes this growth happen!

Teamwork

Although knowledgeable, skilled employees are crucial to the "Quality First" improvement process, the individual skills they provide may be substantially leveraged when employed in the context of teamwork. Teamwork is essential to the success of the "Quality First" culture in an organization. One universal goal is ultimately to involve every member of the organization in process-improvement team activity.

Teamwork does not necessarily imply that new organizational entities must be created. Rather, in most applications it means that existing groups will begin working as teams, using the techniques that take advantage of interpersonal dynamics.

Most process-improvement teams mirror the natural function or work group structures and thus overlay the existing organizational hierarchy. Additional teams are created to ensure cross-functional process improvement and attention to processes of special interest or broad application such as reward and recognition or quality-of-work-life issues.

For the most part, creation of the team network flows from the top down. Training team members within the team setting is an integral part of the deployment process to produce what H. James Harrington, author of *The Improvement Process*, calls a "waterfall effect" that systematically washes out the counterproductive ideas and signals as the culture is deployed down into the organization.

Each team, once created, engages in an ongoing process-improvement activity that is appropriate to its level and area of responsibility. These activities include customer recognition, process definition, performance requirements definition, performance measurement and assessment, and process-improvement cycle activity. Statistical information provides a common language for the examination of process performance and for the assessment of improvement efforts.

Conservation of Human Resources

Consistent with and embedded in its constancy of purpose, the organization must recognize that its people are its most important asset. This recognition is rooted in the principle of conservation of human resources. Often management behavior does not reflect an appreciation of this principle. Work force reduction is frequently the first avenue of cost reduction. Rank-and-file employees are too frequently perceived as pairs of hands or strong backs with too little regard for the available mind.

An enlightened and consistent approach to leadership is a cornerstone of every successful "Quality First" application. All of the leaders in the field, including Deming, Juran, Drucker, and Crosby, stress the importance of creating a stimulating, secure, and supportive environment in which teamwork, creativity, and pride of workmanship can thrive. Without this environment none of the other elements of "Quality First" can be totally successful.

A key message of the principle of human resource conservation is, "We expect the best from our people and we give them our best in return." The creation and maintenance of a work environment that is compatible with a "Quality First" culture is absolutely a top management responsibility.

Total Involvement

Ultimately, all the "Quality First" principles will guide the actions of every person in the organization. The principle of total involvement (participation and empowerment) addresses this universal involvement in "Quality First." It is concerned with ensuring continuity of appropriate signals throughout the organization and realizing process-improvement benefits in every area of activity. Total participation means that every individual gets involved and has a responsibility to seek continuous improvement at both the individual and team levels. Total empowerment means that individuals are given the necessary authority to make decisions and initiate improvement actions within their own work areas and expertise. Employees are encouraged through respect and trust to exercise self-direction and self-discipline. Empowerment is a source of pride, a wellspring of creativity, and an engine for improvement action.

This empowerment is essential if the principle of total involvement is to be followed. Participation and empowerment are stimulated, nurtured, and guided by management involvement, teamwork, clear objectives, and vigorous open communication.

Perpetual Commitment

Perpetual commitment makes it clear that "Quality First" is not a program that has starting and finishing points; rather, it is a process that, once begun, will be used by the company to conduct all future business. Commitment is a management action that implies a management responsibility to encourage and facilitate positive change even when such change is difficult or time-consuming, or lacks immediate return on the investment. Commitment is measured by behavior: It means holding a steady, long-term course in the face of short-term pressure; making improvement the top agenda item in communications and decisions; being willing to invest for the long-term benefit; supporting the creative improvement initiatives of the work force; structuring the recognition system to reward initiative and improvement; providing for extensive education and training, including everyone in the process; and becoming personally involved in improvement activity. In sum, it means making "Quality First" the company way of life.

Initial deployment of "Quality First" into an organization requires a considerable amount of time and effort. Many changes must occur—ways of thinking, individual and group behavior, methods of accomplishing tasks, attitudes, priorities, relationships, signals, and knowledge levels. These changes will not, and indeed cannot, happen overnight. Experience indicates that three to 10 years, depending on your current state of practice for quality, may be required for an organization to reach "Quality First" maturity. It may take that long before the "Quality First" process is fully in place and considered to be the standard way of doing business.

The length of time required to reach maturity should not be perceived as a reason for you not to begin the transition process to "Quality First." Experience shows that positive results and significant returns on investment start very early in the process. "Quality First," when managed correctly, should essentially pay for itself even in the first year. Companies that are only two or three years into the process report return on their investments of $4 or $5 for every $1 invested.

Top management in an organization is responsible for ensuring that "Quality First" is a perpetual commitment. Every member of the organization should know with certainty that "Quality First" is not just another fad that management will soon forget. Everyone should understand that getting on board is mandatory and that it is not possible to "wait until this 'Quality First' thing blows over." The responsibility for knowing what is going on and for providing the leadership to shape and guide the change process cannot be delegated. Each manager and each individual must recognize a personal role and responsibility and must be given a personal, intrinsic incentive in the "Quality First" effort.

THE COST OF QUALITY

One of the more compelling reasons prompting early quality leaders to trade in traditional practices for "Quality First" practices was the projected cost of poor quality if they did business as usual. Once CEOs realize how costly their old way of doing business is, mainly because it actually builds poor quality and unnecessary costs into the process, shifting to a new, defect-free process becomes very attractive cost wise. According to *A Guide for Implementing Total Quality Management*, of the ITT Reliability Analysis Center:

> The cost of poor quality has been quoted by various sources as being between 15 percent to 50 percent of the cost of doing business. . . . One of the most effective actions management can take to improve productivity in any organization is to improve the quality of its processes. Quality saves, it does not cost. . . . Reducing the cost of poor quality directly affects the bottom line. Improving quality is the most direct way for an organization to increase profit.

More specifically, in *Quality Is Free*, Crosby zeros in on the cost of quality, stating:

> Quality is free. It's not a gift, but it is free. What costs money are the unquality things—all the actions that involve not doing jobs right the first time.
>
> Quality is not only free, it is an honest-to-everything profit maker. Every penny you don't spend on doing things wrong, over, or instead becomes half a penny right on the bottom line. In these days of "who knows what is going to happen to our business tomorrow" there aren't many ways left to make a profit improvement. If you concentrate on making quality certain, you can probably increase your profit by an amount equal to 5 to 10 percent of your sales. That is a lot of money for free.

The key event then in a company's journey toward "Quality First" is an awareness among top management that their finan-

FIGURE 2–7
The Cost of Quality: Before and After "Quality First"

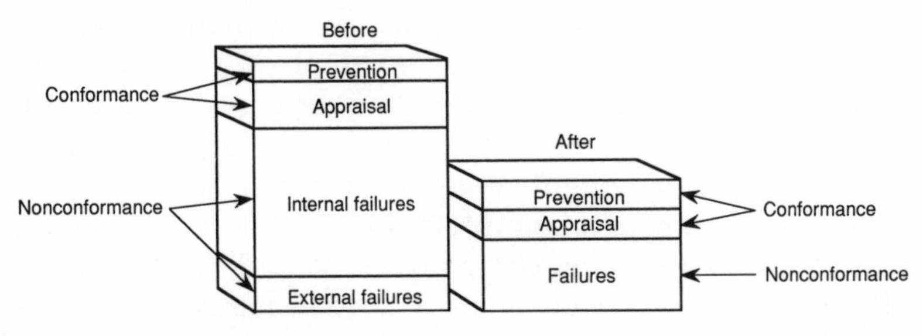

cial statements already reflect the costs of not doing things right the first time around, that they must change their definition of quality, and that to be successful, the "Quality First" program must be organization-wide and involve everyone at all levels.

Let's look at how Xerox Corporation learned to deal with the cost of quality. Simply stated, the cost of quality aims at spending capital wisely and avoiding wasting it. At Xerox Corporation, the Cost of Quality is defined as the measurement of what your division, department, teamwork group or family group is spending for its overall Quality. There are three kinds of measurements in Cost of Quality:

Conformance. Spending that is in conformance with customer requirements. Conformance means that work outputs are being measured against known customer requirements . . .

Cost of nonconformance. Spending that is not in conformance with customer requirements . . . and measured in time needed to go back and do a job over . . . *and* nonconformance can also cost money by exceeding your customer requirements . . .

Lost opportunities. A profit not earned because a customer is lost due to lack of quality.

Figure 2–7 will help you visualize the cost shifts that can be expected before and after a company adopts a "Quality First" approach to management.

Implicit in this Cost of Quality diagram is the notion that the firm will continuously set and achieve higher and higher quality standards.

THE CORPORATE QUALITY CHAMPION

Earlier in this chapter we discussed the anticipation of the coming paradigm shift from traditional management to "Quality First" practices. Once this shift takes place, "Quality First" practices will quickly displace existing practices—that is, they will become standard operating procedures—in most American firms. Until that paradigm shift takes place, however, the process of introducing and institutionalizing a set of new management ideas in an existing company is a very difficult task.

Each new procedure introduced into a firm is certain to upset an existing status quo. Workers who identify personally with the existing status quo will, in turn, feel vulnerable and insecure. Their response is likely to be resistance to the new ideas and the changes in behavior required to implement them. For this reason, if a new idea is to pass from simply a new concept to actual practice in an organization it needs a boost from a champion.

A full-time champion is needed to overcome the resistance the change process will generate and to settle the myriad of problems and barriers that will crop up from day to day. In the absence of a dedicated champion, the initiation of a new idea will soon falter before it is routinized. A "Quality First" champion—an individual that leads by his or her own participation—is needed to inspire others to participate fully in the change process. A successful "Quality First" champion will:

- Visibly support the company's "Quality First" strategy.
- Insist on the team approach.
- Measure his or her success by customer satisfaction.
- Build feedback loops within the firm and to suppliers and customers.
- Meet goals.

Figure 2–8 describes the four stages through which a new

idea such as "Quality First" must pass before it is institutionalized in your company.

> Stage 1: The source of the new ideas such as the "Quality First" concept are located *outside* of the target organization. The "Quality First" concept captures the interest of an organizational *insider,* such as the CEO or quality manager.

FIGURE 2–8
The "Quality First" Idea—Adoption–Implementation Process

Stage 1: New idea originates outside of the organization, and captures the interest of a leader inside an organization

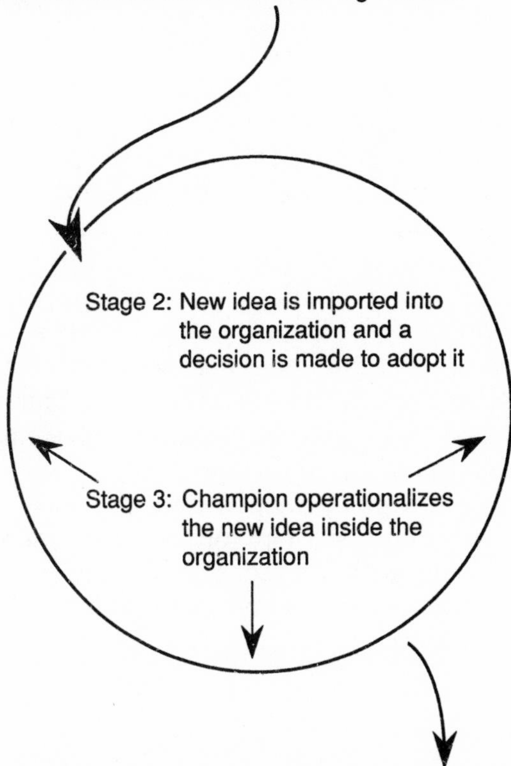

Stage 4: The new idea becomes routinized and becomes the "way business is done" in the organization

Stage 2: An *insider* (or group of insiders) makes the decision to adopt the new idea.

Stage 3: Once the decision to adopt the idea is made, an internal change process must then be set in motion to make the new idea operate. Characteristically, a champion—a person with strong personal convictions concerning quality management, sufficient formal or informal authority, expertise, or some other mix of desired qualities—is given responsibility for the day-to-day implementation process.

Step 4: Only when the new idea is finally internalized and accepted as the "way things are done" in an organization is the champion's job complete.

In their book, *In Search of Excellence,* Thomas Peters and Robert Waterman, Jr., identified the "fired-up champion" as an indispensable part of all of the best-run companies. They define the champion's role like this: "The champion is not a blue-sky dreamer, nor an intellectual giant. The champion might even be an idea thief. But, above all, he's the pragmatic one who grabs onto someone else's theoretical construct if necessary and bullheadedly pushes it to fruition. . . . Champions are pioneers, and pioneers get shot at. The companies that get the most from champions, therefore, are those that have rich support networks so their pioneers will flourish. This point is so important it's hard to overstress. No support system, no champions. No champions, no innovation."

The question now is does your company have a "Quality First" champion? If not, why not you? The next chapters of this book will arm you with the concepts, principles, practices, tools, and techniques that will begin to help you become the "Quality First" champion in your company.

Chapter Three

Different Drummers

"There is nothing more difficult to plan, more doubtful of success, nor more dangerous to manage than the creation of a new order of things. . . . Whenever his enemies have occasion to attack the innovator they do so with the passion of partisans, while the others defend him sluggishly so that the innovator and his party alike are vulnerable."

Niccolo Machiavelli
The Prince, 1513

MORE THAN ONE WAY

The Innovators

At the turn of the century, most Americans believed that leaders were born, not made. The idea that anyone could develop leadership traits was gradually accepted. Today, however, the study of leadership is a part of most business school curriculums. The diffusion of "Quality First" practices throughout American manufacturing and service industries has followed a similar path as managers cautiously redefine how they view, and perform, their work.

Like innovators before them, Philip Crosby, W. Edwards Deming, Joseph M. Juran, and Robert Costello are change agents,

FIGURE 3–1
Distribution of Adopters of Innovations

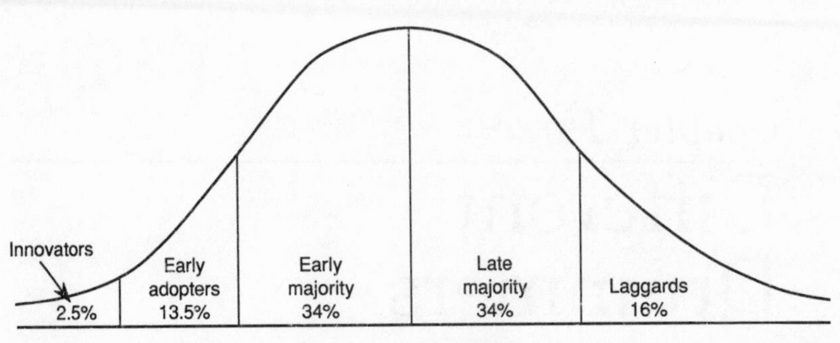

Source: Everett M. Rogers, *Diffusion of Innovations* (New York: Free Press, 1983).

spreading the notion that business and government leaders can, and must, learn to build quality performance into their enterprises; that quality is neither a matter of chance nor an act of magic. But since change involves risks for individuals and organizations alike, with each new idea also comes resistance to change. Familiar habits and beliefs are traded in slowly for new ones. Research has shown that the diffusion of new ideas and successful change processes—whether occurring society-wide or within individual companies—pass through predictable stages. Figure 3–1 is based on Professor Everett M. Rogers's grouping of innovation adopters into five categories, from "innovators" to "laggards."

Professor Rogers's classification scheme helps us better appreciate the process of quality-management change in several ways. First, it places the quality movement in America into a long-range historical context, and suggests that Crosby, Costello, Deming, and Juran—the "innovators" of new ideas—were the starting points of a society-wide change process. Second, we also learn from Rogers that the "early adopters," the risk-taking companies (such as the Malcolm Baldrige Award winners) that first embraced the new ideas, represent only a fraction of the potential adopters.

Finally, as quality management ideas spread into the business population at large, dependence on the guru-dominated diffusion process used by the relatively few early adopting firms will probably be complemented by customized, mix-and-match approaches to better accommodate the needs of thousands upon thousands of adopting companies in the years ahead.

Toward Customized Adoption

In Japan in the 1950s, quality management innovators achieved a charismatic appeal. Only in the early 1980s, as these innovators spread their ideas among American clients who were also feeling the impact of global competition, did quality management begin to gain a similar appeal in the United States. Under the influence of a single innovator, firms tended to adopt a more or less pure approach—á la Deming, Juran, or some other guru. Not until the middle and late 1980s were the ideas of these innovators popularized and their various approaches adopted.

Today, business and government organizations throughout America are on the verge of mass adoption of "Quality First" practices. In this emerging era, the one-on-one, guru-dominated approach will become less and less able to keep up with the demand as the number of adopters skyrockets. Now that both the experiences of the early adopters, and the wide variations in methodology promoted by the gurus, have percolated through the business community, it seems only natural that mix-and-match, customized approaches to "Quality First" will replace the original, guru-dominated approach.

Is There One Best Approach?

The remainder of this chapter introduces the basic ideas and concepts of a few leading quality management experts. These experts, it should be stressed, are just a sampling of a still larger community of quality management thinkers, including Armand V. Feigenbaum, Kaoru Ishikawa, and Rosabeth Moss-Kanter. The four quality management experts highlighted here do, nonetheless, offer the reader a wide range of approaches to better understand quality in America today.

Deming's approach is selected because of his well-known role in the reconstruction of Japan's industrial base following World

War II and his broad, philosophical approach to change with an emphasis on a statistically based implementation process. Juran's contribution, on the other hand, contains a distinct product-development flavor and a systematic, three-step methodology to help managers zero in on quality management.

Because Crosby stresses a well-structured, stage-by-stage development of an organization's culture, his model may have greater appeal for those executives interested in a more incremental road-map approach. Costello's work, leading to the adaptation by the federal government of a total quality management program predominantly based on Deming, is included here to round out our survey of the state of quality management in America in the early 1990s.

Caution: Don't assume that a single best method should, or does, exist. Maybe it does, maybe it doesn't. Only you can decide. If, after comparing the Crosby approach to those of Deming and Juran, for example, you conclude that Crosby's model fits exactly the needs of your firm, you might consider adopting it wholesale. On the other hand, after a careful comparison of the strengths and weaknesses of each approach, you may decide that a pick-and-choose approach is the way to go. For example, you might use a version of Crosby's maturity grid at the organization-wide level, and a version of Deming's control chart approach at the sub-unit level. The latter chapters in this book provide a description of the "Quality First" methodology that can be used as an aid in developing your own unique "Quality First" program.

The challenge facing America's business executives in the 1990s is not simply to decide whether to adopt any quality management program, but to adopt one that best fits their specific competitive business environment.

THE CROSBY SCHOOL

Like Chester Barnard, a 40-year veteran of AT&T and author of the 1938 classic study of management, *The Functions of the Executive,* Philip Crosby's quality management ideas also followed a long corporate career. Rising through managerial ranks, Crosby was a vice president of ITT for 14 years. Crosby's insider corporate perspective is reflected in a down-to-earth approach to quality management. He believes an organization can "learn" and that top management should adopt a quality-management style, not because it is the right thing to do, but because it is "free" and good for the bottom line.

The problem organization. Crosby believes "the problem organization" will benefit most from his quality-management program. In his book, *Quality Without Tears*, Crosby identifies a problem organization by the presence of five symptoms:

- The outgoing product or service normally contains deviations from the published, announced, or agreed-upon requirements.
- The company has an extensive field service or dealer network skilled in rework and resourceful corrective action to keep the customers satisfied.
- Management does not provide a clear performance standard or definition of quality, so the employees each develop their own.
- Management does not know the price of nonconformance. Product companies spend 20 percent or more of their sales dollars doing things wrong and doing them over. Service companies spend 35 percent or more of their operating costs doing things wrong and doing them over.
- Management denies that it is the cause of the problem.

In other words, virtually every business firm is, by Crosby's definition, a "problem organization." Why? Because, managers traditionally attack problems as they crop up in the organization and seek random improvements. Top management, according to Crosby, is too quick to " . . . send everyone else to school, set up programs for the lowest levels of the organization, and make speeches with impressive-sounding words. It is not until all the problems are pulled together, particularly the financial ones, that the seriousness of the situation is exposed."

Crosby's View of Quality

The real meaning of quality, Crosby asserts in *Quality Is Free*, suffers from several erroneous assumptions. Quality is not:

- Goodness, or luxury, or shininess.
- Intangible, therefore not measurable.
- Unaffordable.
- Originated by the workers.
- Something that originates in the quality department.

Quality is:

- Conformance to requirements; nonquality is nonconformance.

To put this definition into practice, Crosby assumes that quality either is or is not present in the whole organization; that quality is the responsibility of everyone in the organization; and that quality is measurable. In addition, he cautions the quality-bound executive, "The process of instilling quality improvement is a journey that never ends. Changing a culture so that it never slips back is not something that is accomplished quickly."

Crosby's Quality Management Maturity Grid

The first step for an organization moving toward a quality management profile is to determine its current level of "management maturity." Table 3–1, Crosby's Quality Management Maturity Grid, is used for this purpose. Along the left-hand margin are six measures of the sophistication of an organization's management style, including how the organization handles problems, the attitude of top management, and the cost of quality to the firm. Across the top are five levels, or stages, of quality management

TABLE 3–1
Crosby's Quality Management Maturity Grid

Measurement Categories	Stage I: Uncertainty	State II: Awakening	Stage III: Enlightenment	Stage IV: Wisdom	Stage V: Certainty
Management understanding and attitude	Fails to see quality as a management tool.	Supports quality management in theory but is unwilling to provide the necessary money or time.	Learns about quality management and becomes supportive.	Participates personally in quality activities.	Regards quality management as essential to the company's success.
Quality organization status	Quality activities are limited to the manufacturing or engineering department and are largely appraisal and sorting.	A strong quality leader has been appointed, but quality activities remain focused on appraisal and sorting and are still limited to manufacturing and engineering.	Quality department reports to top management, and its leader is active in company management.	Quality manager is an officer of the company. Prevention activities have become important.	Quality manager is on the board of directors. Prevention is the main quality activity.
Problem handling	Problems are fought as they occur and are seldom fully resolved; "fire-fighting" dominates.	Teams are established to attack major problems, but the approach remains short term.	Problems are resolved in an orderly fashion, and corrective action is a regular event.	Problems are identified early in their development.	Except in the most unusual cases, problems are prevented.
Cost of quality as percentage of sales	Reported: unknown Actual: 20%	Reported: 5% Actual: 18%	Reported: 8% Actual: 12%	Reported: 6.5% Actual: 8%	Reported: 2.5% Actual: 2.5%
Quality improvement actions	No organized activities.	Activities are motivational and short term.	Implements the 14-step program with full understanding.	Continues the 14-step program and starts Make Certain.	Quality improvement is a regular and continuing activity.
Summation of company quality posture	"We don't know why we have quality problems."	"Must we always have quality problems?"	"Because of management commitment and quality improvement programs, we are identifying and resolving our quality problems."	"We routinely prevent defects from occurring."	"We know why we don't have quality problems."

Source: Adapted from Philip B. Crosby *Quality is Free*, (New York: McGraw-Hill, 1979).

maturity. These range from Stage I, "Uncertainty," in which an organization is characterized by the statement, "We don't know why we have quality problems," to Stage V, "Certainty," reserved for organizations in which top management can proclaim, "We know why we don't have quality problems."

Once a firm has located its current maturity stage on the grid, it then implements a quality improvement program based on Crosby's Fourteen (14) Steps of Quality Improvement (delineated in Table 3–2). Each step is designed as a building block to move the organization's management style toward the right-hand side of the management grid, passing through progressively higher level maturity stages—titled "Awakening," "Enlightenment," and "Wisdom"—and ultimately, to Stage V. Only at this final stage is conformance to the firm's stated quality requirements assured. A zero-defects culture—a set of beliefs held throughout the organization that says, in effect, "Do it right the first time"—is established and the cost of quality is reduced to its lowest possible level.

The Crosby Quality College

A mood of intellectual progress established by the labels Crosby has given to each stage on his management maturity grid—"awakening," "enlightenment," and "wisdom"—reinforces the role of organizational learning in his "do it right the first time" approach to quality management. Wishful thinking won't work. Only constant, top-level effort will move an organization toward the right-hand side of the grid. To make sure this happens, the Crosby Quality College offers a no-nonsense environment that reinforces again and again one basic theme: zero-defect management is possible.

In *Quality Without Tears*, Crosby says,

> The main problem of quality as a management concern, is that it is not taught in management schools. It is not considered to be a management function, but rather a technical one. . . . However, with the pressure on quality erupting worldwide and the difficulty in getting senior management to do something about it, it becomes apparent that a new measurement is needed for quality. The best measurement for this subject is the same as for any other—money.

TABLE 3–2
Crosby's Fourteen-Step Program

Step 1. Management Commitment
Top management must become convinced of the need for quality improvement and must make its commitment clear to the entire company. This should be accompanied by a written quality policy, stating that each person is expected to "perform exactly like the requirement, or cause the requirement to be officially changed to what we and the customers really need."

Step 2. Quality Improvement Team
Management must form a team of department heads (or those who can speak for their departments) to oversee quality improvement. The team's role is to see that needed actions take place in its departments and in the company as a whole.

Step 3. Quality Measurement
Quality measures that are appropriate to every activity must be established to identify areas needing improvement. In accounting, for example, one measure might be the percentage of late reports; in engineering, the accuracy of drawings; in purchasing, rejections due to incomplete descriptions; and in plant engineering, time lost because of equipment failures.

Step 4. Cost of Quality Evaluation
The controller's office should make an estimate of the costs of quality to identify areas where quality improvements would be profitable.

Step 5. Quality Awareness
Quality awareness must be raised among employees. They must understand the importance of product conformance and the costs of nonconformance. These messages should be carried by supervisors (after they have been trained) and through such media as films, booklets, and posters.

Step 6. Corrective Action
Opportunities for correction are generated by Steps 3 and 4, as well as by discussions among employees. These ideas should be brought to the supervisory level and resolved there, if possible. They should be pushed up further if that is necessary to get action.

Step 7. Zero-Defects Planning
An ad hoc defects committee should be formed from members of the quality improvement team. This committee should start planning a zero defects program appropriate to the company and its culture.

Step 8. Supervisory Training
Early in the process, all levels of management must be trained to implement their part of the quality improvement program.

TABLE 3–2 *(continued)*

Step 9.	**Zero-Defects Day** A Zero-Defects Day should be scheduled to signal to employees that the company has a new performance standard.
Step 10.	**Goal Setting** To turn commitments into action, individuals must establish improvement goals for themselves and their groups. Supervisors should meet with their people and ask them to set goals that are specific and measurable. Goal lines should be posted in each area and meetings held to discuss progress.
Step 11.	**Error Cause Removal** Employees should be encouraged to inform management of any problems that prevent them from performing error-free work. Employees need not do anything about these problems themselves; they should simply report them. Reported problems must then be acknowledged by management within 24 hours.
Step 12.	**Recognition** Public, nonfinancial appreciation must be given to those who meet their quality goals or perform outstandingly.
Step 13.	**Quality Councils** Quality professionals and team chairpersons should meet regularly to share experiences, problems, and ideas.
Step 14.	**Do It All Over Again** To emphasize the never-ending process of quality improvement, the program (Steps 1–13) must be repeated. This renews the commitment of old employees and brings new ones into the process.

The Crosby Quality College does not educate individuals per se. According to Crosby, "The college deals with whole companies, not with individuals." While at this college, every action taken by the student, from the manner in which he or she registers at the hotel upon arrival to ownership of problems in class, is designed to reinforce *the* central message: Conformance to requirements—the definition of quality—is both beyond compromise and financially wise.

THE DEMING PHILOSOPHY

Born in 1900, and recipient of a Ph.D. in mathematics and physics from Yale University, W. Edwards Deming was first introduced to the basic tenets of traditional management principles in the late 1920s, as a summer employee at Western Electric's famous Hawthorne plant in Chicago. Here the revolutionary human relations studies of Harvard University Professor Elton Mayo began to raise a fundamental question: How can firms best motivate workers? Deming found the traditional motivation system in use at that time to be degrading and economically unproductive. Under that system, worker incentives were linked to piecework to maximize worker output, followed by an inspection process in which defective items were subtracted from the worker's piecework credits. The virtues of an equalitarian work place is an enduring theme found throughout Deming's philosophy.

During the 1930s, Deming's collaboration with Walter A. Shewhart, a statistician working at Bell Telephone Laboratories, led to his conviction that traditional management methods should be replaced with statistical control techniques. Deming recognized that a statistically controlled management process gave the manager a newfound capacity to systematically determine when to intervene and, equally important, when to leave an industrial process alone. During World War II, Deming got his first opportunity to demonstrate to government managers how Shewhart's statistical-quality-control methods could be taught to engineers and workers and put into practice in busy war production plants.

Following the war, Deming left government service and set up a private consulting practice. The State Department, one of his early clients, sent him to Japan in 1947 to help prepare a national census in that devastated country. While American managers soon forgot their wartime quality-control lessons—and continued their prewar love affair with traditional management practices, which prized production over quality—Deming's evolving quality-control methods received a warm reception in Japan.

In fact, the Japanese now credit much of their postwar industrial renaissance to Deming's statistical process control (SPC), based philosophy of quality. Each year in his name, the Union of Japanese Scientists and Engineers awards the Deming Prize to companies that have demonstrated outstanding contributions to product quality and dependability. In addition, in 1960 the Japanese emperor awarded Deming with Japan's Second Order Medal of the Sacred Treasure, a tribute rarely paid to a foreigner.

The Quality Crisis

In his book *Out of the Crisis*, Deming holds American managers responsible for causing a society-wide quality crisis.

> Western style of management must change to halt the decline of Western industry, and to turn it upward. . . . There must be an awakening to the crisis, followed by action, management's job. . . . The transformation can only be accomplished by man, not by hardware (computers, gadgets, automation, or new machinery). A company cannot buy its way into quality.

Deming's philosophy is prone to put quality in human terms. When a firm's work force is committed to doing a good job, and has a solid managerial process in which to act, quality will flow naturally. A more practical, composite definition of quality might read: Quality is a predictable degree of uniformity and dependability at low cost, and suited to the market.

Since Japan adopted statistical-based control techniques in the early 1950s, it has had a 30-year head start on the United States. Deming estimates it will take American managers another 30 years to achieve the advanced level of statistical control now in wide practice in Japan. While Western managers have focused on outcome and practiced "retroactive management," such as management by objective, the Japanese have perfected quality. In 1985, as quoted in *The Deming Management Method*, by Mary Walton, Deming summed up his indictment this way: "Failure to understand people is the devastation of Western management." The American quality crisis is being prolonged by what Deming calls the Seven Deadly Diseases (see Table 3–3) associated with traditional management practices.

TABLE 3–3
The Seven Deadly Diseases

1. Lack of constancy of purpose. A company that is without constancy of purpose has no long-range plans for staying in business. Management is insecure, and so are employees.
2. Emphasis on short-term profits. Looking to increase the quarterly dividend undermines quality and productivity.
3. Evaluation by performance, merit rating, or annual review of performance. The effects of these are devastating—teamwork is destroyed, rivalry is nurtured. Performance ratings build fear and leave people bitter, despondent, beaten. They also encourage defections in the ranks of management.
4. Mobility of management. Job-hopping managers never understand the companies they work for and are never there long enough to follow through on long-term changes that are necessary for quality and productivity.
5. Running a company on visible figures alone. The most important figures are unknown and unknowable—the "multiplier" effect of a happy customer, for example.
6. Excessive medical costs for employee health care, which increase the final costs of goods and services.
7. Excessive costs of warranty, fueled by lawyers who work on the basis of contingency fees.

Deming's Fourteen Points

To eliminate these underlying managerial diseases, Deming prescribes his fourteen-point cure, found in Table 3–4 on pages 61 and 62. Both the philosophical foundation for Deming's managerial transformation, and the role assigned to statistical quality control in the execution of that philosophy, are present in his fourteen-point program of quality management. These points are so central to his approach that Deming will not accept a new company client until its president has promised to faithfully implement *all* fourteen points. Halfway measures will not do. If a company is unwilling to change its management philosophy 100 percent to the Deming way, Deming passes that client by. Why? Because Deming is convinced that about 85 percent of all quality problems are caused by harmful management practices. Consequently, a CEO intent on changing the way production workers perform—without changing the obsolete management system—will, at best, only address 15 percent of the problems.

FIGURE 3–2
A Typical Deming Control Chart

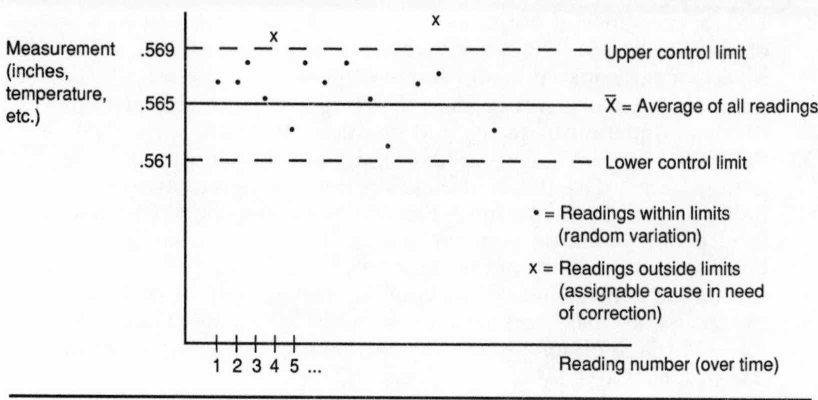

Statistical Process Control

Identifying the Problem

The methodological core of Deming's quality management approach is the use of simple statistical techniques to continuously improve a firm's management process. Only through statistical verification, according to Deming, can the manager (1) know that he or she has a problem, and (2) find the cause of the problem. Deming uses quality-control charts, like the one shown in Figure 3–2, to identify the absence or presence of a quality problem. Since all human activity will contain unavoidable variations—that is, every product or service is slightly different from all the others—an acceptable range of "random variations" must be established for every product or service.

Once measurable upper and lower control limits have been set for a product or service, and a control chart prepared to reflect these limits, the workers performing the activity periodically plot actual measurements on the chart. When these measurements fall outside of the acceptable, "random variation" range, the worker immediately knows a "non-random" quality problem exists.

TABLE 3–4
Deming's Fourteen Points

1. Create constancy of purpose for improvement of product and service. Deming suggests a radical new definition of a company's role: Rather than to make money, it is to stay in business and provide jobs through innovation, research, constant improvement, and maintenance.
2. Adopt the new philosophy. Americans are too tolerant of poor workmanship and sullen service. We need a new religion in which mistakes and negativism are unacceptable.
3. Cease dependence on mass inspection. American firms typically inspect a product as it comes off the assembly line or at major stages along the way; defective products are either thrown out or reworked. Both practices are unnecessarily expensive. In effect, a company is paying workers to make defects and then to correct them. Quality comes not from inspection but from improvement of the process. With instruction, workers can be enlisted in this improvement.
4. End the practice of awarding business on the price tag alone. Purchasing departments customarily operate on orders to seek the lowest price vendor. Frequently, this leads to supplies of low quality. Instead, buyers should seek the best quality in a long-term relationship with a single supplier for any one item.
5. Improve constantly and forever the system of production and service. Improvement is not a one-time effort. Management is obligated to continually look for ways to reduce waste and improve quality.
6. Institute training. Too often, workers have learned their job from another worker who was never trained properly. They are forced to follow unintelligible instructions. They can't do their jobs well because no one tells them how to do so.
7. Institute leadership. The job of a supervisor is not to tell people what to do, nor to punish them, but to lead. Leading consists of helping people do a better job and of learning by objective methods who is in need of individual help.
8. Drive out fear. Many employees are afraid to ask questions or to take a position, even when they do not understand what their job is or what is right or wrong. They will continue to do things the wrong way, or not do them at all. The economic losses from fear are appalling. To ensure better quality and productivity, it is necessary that people feel secure.
9. Break down barriers between staff areas. Often a company's departments or units are competing with each other, or have goals that conflict. They do not work as a team so they cannot solve or foresee problems. Worse, one department's goals may cause trouble for another.

TABLE 3–4
Deming's Fourteen Points *(continued)*

10. Eliminate slogans, exhortations, and targets for the work force. These never helped anybody do a good job. Let workers formulate their own slogans.
11. Eliminate numerical quotas. Quotas take into account only numbers, not quality or methods. They are usually a guarantee of inefficiency and high cost. A person, to hold a job, meets a quota at any cost, without regard to damage to the company.
12. Remove barriers to pride of workmanship. People are eager to do a good job and distressed when they cannot. Too often, misguided supervisors, faulty equipment, and defective materials stand in the way of good performance. These barriers must be removed.
13. Institute a vigorous program of education and retraining. Both management and the work force will have to be educated in the new methods, including teamwork and statistical techniques.
14. Take action to accomplish the transformation. It will require a special top management team with a plan of action to carry out the quality mission. Workers cannot do it on their own, nor can managers. A critical mass of people in the company must understand the Fourteen Points, [and] the Seven Deadly Diseases.

Classifying the Problem's Cause

The next step is to identify the cause behind the problem. Two possibilities exist. The cause could be a "common cause"—one rooted in the basic management system in use and, therefore, a problem that is potentially company-wide in scope. Fundamental design errors or the use of imprecise machinery are examples of common causes. Alternatively, the problem could be the result of a "special cause," or one stemming from a more isolated source—a few poorly trained workers in one department, for example.

Deming recommends using several additional charting methods to learn more about the factors causing the quality problems exposed in a control chart. Mary Walton, in *Deming Management at Work*, sums up the crucial role of statistics this way: "American managers pride themselves on hunches and intuition. When they succeed, they take credit. When they fail, they find someone to blame. But a quality transformation rests on a different set of assumptions: decisions must be based on facts . . . [and] . . . it is helpful to display information graphically." Figure 3–3 summa-

FIGURE 3–3
Doing It with Data—Seven Helpful Charts

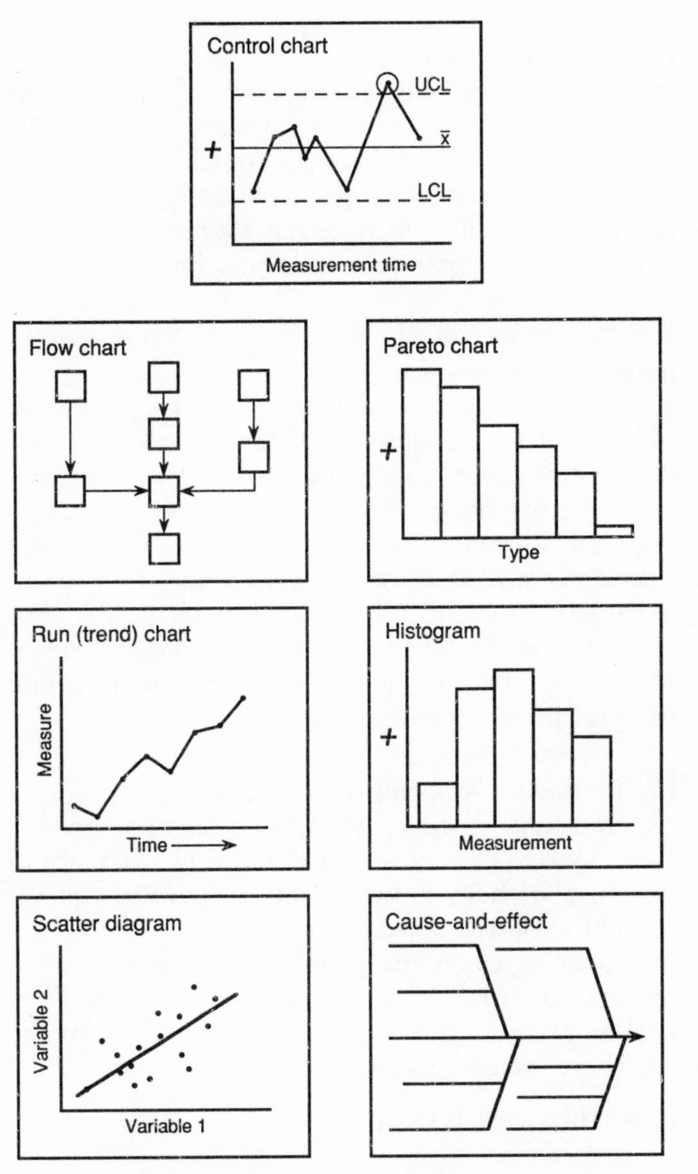

Source: Mary Walton, *Deming Management at Work*, (New York: Putnam, 1990).

rizes the full array of Deming's charting techniques. More is said concerning the specific uses of these charting methods in Chapter 10, Quality First Tools and Techniques.

Correcting the Problem

The final step in the quality-management cycle is for the manager and the workers to eliminate the cause of the quality problem by taking the necessary actions contained in the fourteen points. These actions may range from redesign of a faulty manufacturing assembly line, to a one-day training course for workers to learn how to operate a new machine or how to better serve a new type of customer.

Boosting Performance

While finding and curing quality problems keep a firm's activities within *established* quality limits, there is another way Deming uses control charts to actually boost a firm's performance. By narrowing the established range between the upper and lower random variation limits for an activity, a firm will, in effect, artificially and deliberately create and then solve self-inflicted quality problems. The result is an increase in the firm's attainable level of quality. In this way, managers can plan for and implement a long-range quality-improvement program to stay ahead of the competition.

The Plan-Do-Check-Act (PDCA) Cycle

Deming envisions a never-ending, circular management process. The Plan-Do-Check-Act (PDCA) Cycle, an adaptation of the work of Shewhart, links the seven diseases, the fourteen points, and the statistical techniques into a continuous process, without a starting or ending point. Only through the ongoing application of the four-stage cycle shown in Figure 3–4 can an organization attain and retain a superior quality-management process. There are no shortcuts.

THE JURAN TRILOGY

Joseph M. Juran was educated during the first quarter of this century in engineering and law. His outlook, in general,

FIGURE 3–4
The Shrewhart/Deming PDCA Cycle

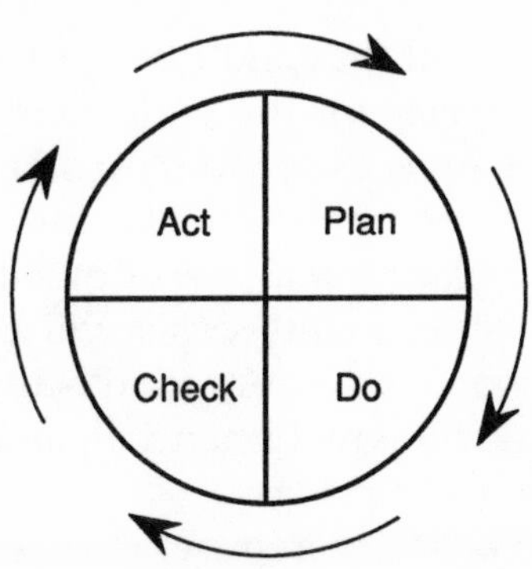

reflects a rational, matter-of-fact approach to business organization and one heavily dependent on sophisticated "shop floor" planning and quality-control processes. The focal point of Juran's quality management philosophy is the firm's individual product or service, not the organization per se. By making sure the building blocks—each individual product or service—meet the customers' requirements, a company-wide quality program will emerge.

Like Deming, Juran also played a significant role in rebuilding Japan after World War II, and he also received the Second Class of the Order of the Sacred Treasure for "the development of Quality Control in Japan and the facilitation of U.S. and Japanese friendship." His search for underlying principles of the management process led to his focus on quality as the ultimate goal. Before becoming a quality management consultant and lecturer, Juran worked in both government and business organizations.

A National Quality Crisis

The basic society-wide problem, according to Juran, is that American industry is caught up in a quality crisis. And while many U.S. managers agree with him on the existence of the crisis, too few understand how to end it. Juran identifies two widely held but wrong assumptions that are preventing American managers from finding solutions to their problems.

The first error in thinking is that many managers have not yet accepted the fact that they, not the workers, must shoulder most of the responsibility for the performance of their companies. Juran's conclusion is that, until top management redirects its energies toward planning quality into their products—rather than actually planning a lack of quality into them, as is presently the case—the quality crisis will continue. Complementing the first erroneous assumption is the fact that managers also fail to realize the great financial gains to be made once quality becomes their top priority.

The result of this obsolete mindset is summarized in Juran's book, *Juran on Planning for Quality*:

> Many companies are facing serious losses and wastes that have their main origin in deficiencies in the quality planning process:
>
> - Loss of sales due to competition in quality.
> - Costs of poor quality, including customer complaints, product liability lawsuits, redoing defective work, products scrapped, and so on.
> - The threats to society . . . [since the ability of] the products of an industrial society . . . to lengthen the human life span; relieve people of drudgery; provide opportunities for educational, cultural, and entertainment . . . depend absolutely on the continuing and proper performance of those products, that is, on their quality.

Juran's Quality Trilogy

The challenge facing American managers, according to Juran, is to abandon the traditional approach to product planning, which carelessly introduces quality flaws into the product's original design. The traditional approach depends on an inspection-and-rejection process to find and correct quality problems in individual products, without ever redesigning the planning process itself.

Adoption of Juran's quality trilogy requires that a firm, once and for all, redesign its product and service planning and control systems and then, through an ongoing improvement program, ensure that the basic causes of quality flaws are permanently eliminated. This means a firm's planning system should contain a single, *universal* thought process that supersedes the *particular* processes used in the production of an individual product. It also requires the adoption of Juran's definitions of quality presented in *Juran on Planning for Quality*:

> Quality is (1) product performance that results in customer satisfaction, (2) freedom from product deficiencies, which avoids customer dissatisfaction. A shorthand expression that conveys both meanings is "fitness for use."

Trilogy Parts

Conceptually, Juran divides quality management into three parts:

- Quality planning
- Quality control
- Quality improvements

While planning, controlling, and improving managerial processes have long been considered fundamental executive functions, Juran asserts they are seldom combined in a structured way—as they are in the quality trilogy—for managing product quality. Figure 3–5 describes the way in which Juran's three-part approach is designed to reduce the cost of quality over time.

Quality Planning

In Juran's approach to quality management, the central task is "the activity of developing the products and processes required to meet customers' needs." To accomplish this task, he recommends the road map shown in Figure 3–6. During the quality planning stage, a firm *prepares* to meet established quality goals. The result of the planning stage is *a dependable process* that can be trusted to perform as planned under operating conditions.

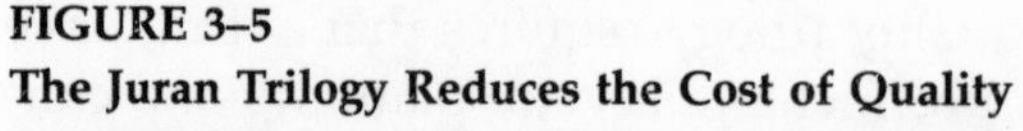

FIGURE 3–5
The Juran Trilogy Reduces the Cost of Quality

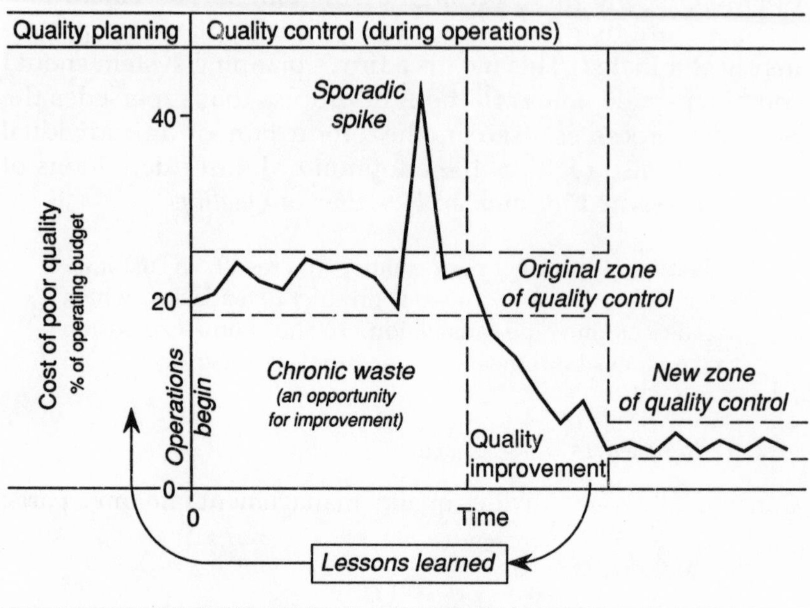

Source: J. M. Juran, *Juran on Planning for Quality* (New York: The Free Press, 1988).

Quality Control

Control processes are designed to ensure that the quality goals set in the planning stage are, in fact, being met during the actual production or rendering of the firm's products and services. Figure 3–7 illustrates Juran's quality-control process.

Quality Improvement

Unlike quality planning and quality-control processes that logically fit together to form a step-by-step, product idea-to-quality-product continuum, quality improvement is the means by which a firm selectively identifies and implements change on a subsystem level. Quality planning and quality control establish a stabilized product quality "culture," or foundation, throughout an organization. The third part of the trilogy, however, known both as quality improvement and Juran's "breakthrough sequence," provides managers the means to find and

FIGURE 3–6
The Quality Planning Road Map

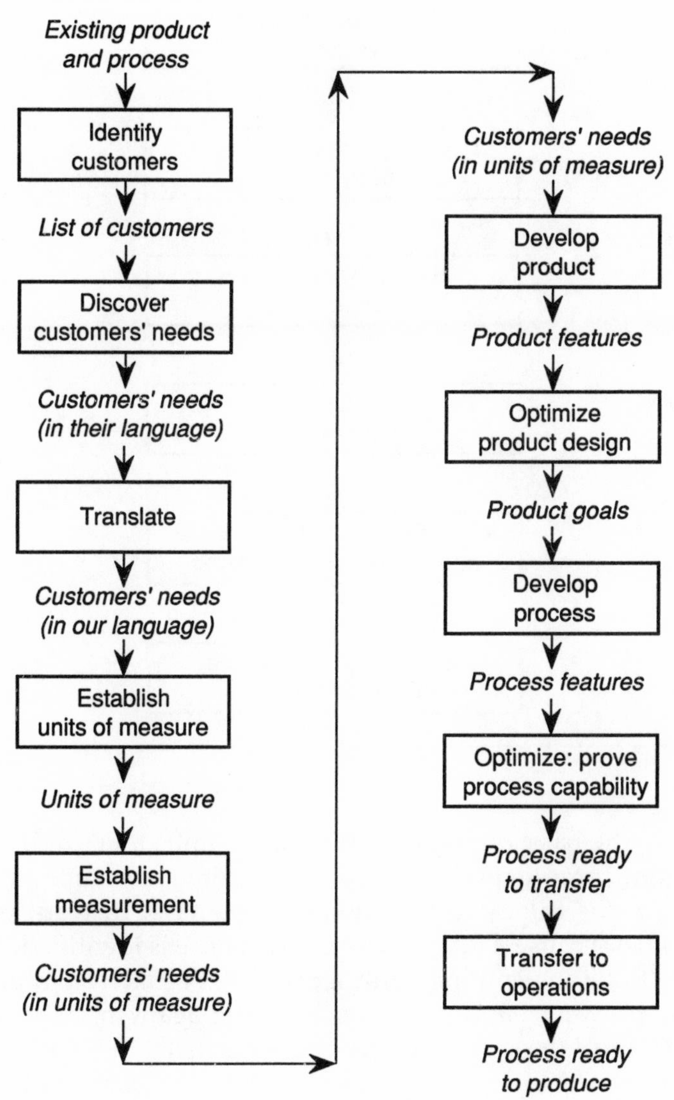

Source: J. M. Juran, *Planning for Quality* (New York: The Free Press, 1988).

FIGURE 3–7
Juran's Quality Improvement Process

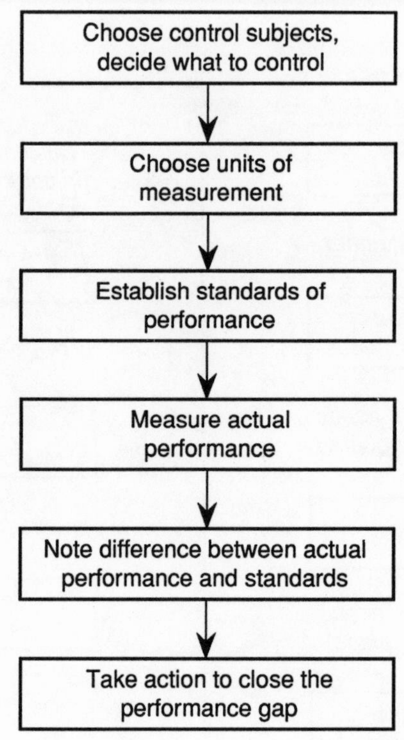

remedy the basic quality-limiting causes imbedded in the organization. Juran expressly does not consider the improvement phase of his trilogy to be a quick-fix exercise. Instead, whenever a basic cause leading to a quality failure is identified, Juran insists that the planning-control processes be altered to permanently prevent that cause from occurring again in the future.

The "breakthrough" process described in Table 3–5 is used in conjunction with Juran's planning and control processes while the trilogy is first being installed in an organization, and as a trouble-shooting tool to keep the planning-control sequence running smoothly after it is established in the organization. Juran uses the term *breakthrough* to emphasize that this part of the

TABLE 3–5
Juran's Breakthrough Sequence

1. Breakthrough in attitudes. Managers must first prove that a breakthrough is needed and then create a climate conducive to change. To demonstrate need, data must be collected to show the extent of the problem; the data most convincing to top management are usually cost-of-quality figures. To get the resources required for improvement, expected benefits must be presented in terms of cost and return on investment.
2. Identify the vital few projects. Pareto chart analysis is used to distinguish the vital few projects from the trivial many and to set priorities based on problem frequency.
3. Organize for breakthrough in knowledge. Two organizational entities should be established: a steering group and a diagnostic group. The steering group, composed of people from several departments, defines the program, suggests possible problem causes, gives the authority to experiment, helps overcome resistance to change, and implements the solution. The diagnostic group, composed of quality professionals and sometimes line managers, is responsible for analyzing the problem.
4. Conduct the analysis. The diagnostic group studies symptoms, develops hypotheses, and experiments to find the problem's true causes. It also tries to determine whether defects are primarily operator-controllable or management-controllable. (A defect is operator-controllable only if it meets three criteria: operators know what they are supposed to do, have the data to understand what they are actually doing, and are able to regulate their own performance.) Theories can be tested by using past data and current production data and by conducting experiments. With this information, the diagnostic group then proposes solutions to the problem.
5. Determine how to overcome resistance to change. The need for change must be established in terms that are important to the key people involved. Logical arguments alone are insufficient. Participation is therefore required in both the technical and social aspects of change.
6. Institute the change. Departments that must take corrective action must be convinced to cooperate. Presentations to these departments should include the size of the problem, alternative solutions, the cost of recommended changes, expected benefits, and efforts taken to anticipate the change's impact on employees. Time for reflection may be needed, and adequate training is essential.
7. Institute controls. Controls must be set up to monitor the solution, see that it works, and keep abreast of unforeseen developments. Formal follow-up is provided by the control sequence used to monitor and correct sporadic problems.

trilogy is the means to achieve unprecedented levels of quality performance in an organization. Juran estimates that approximately 80 percent of the problems identified with breakthrough analysis, including defect rates, are correctable only by improving the management control system. The remaining 20 percent are attributable to the actions of the operating work force.

Cost of Quality Accounting System

To keep top management interested in, and supportive of, the department-level quality-planning process, Juran uses a cost of quality (COQ) accounting system to demonstrate how cost-effective it really is to shift to a quality management process. Here is how it works.

By comparing the rising costs of implementing Juran's appraisal and prevention process to the decreasing costs of detecting internal and external product failures, an executive can determine his optimal level of effort. Figure 3–8, for example, indicates that, in the early stages of implementing a quality management process, every dollar invested in appraisal and prevention activities cuts the firm's external and internal failure costs by far more than one dollar. As the defect rate and failure costs drop in response to the widespread adoption of quality management processes, the firm's level of investment will be optimal whenever a dollar spent on appraisal and prevention equals one dollar reduction in detecting and fixing failures. Since the costs of finding and preventing the last few defects in a production system are extremely high—higher than the costs saved if these defects were eliminated—the optimal quality level is somewhat less than a 100 percent, defect-free system.

ROBERT COSTELLO AND TOTAL QUALITY MANAGEMENT

Long before his appointment as the Under Secretary of Defense for Acquisitions on January 15, 1988, Robert Costello, an engineer by training, was quite familiar with corporate buyer-seller relations. Before going to Washington, Costello was the executive director, purchasing activities, for General Motors Corp.

FIGURE 3–8
Minimal Cost of Quality Curve

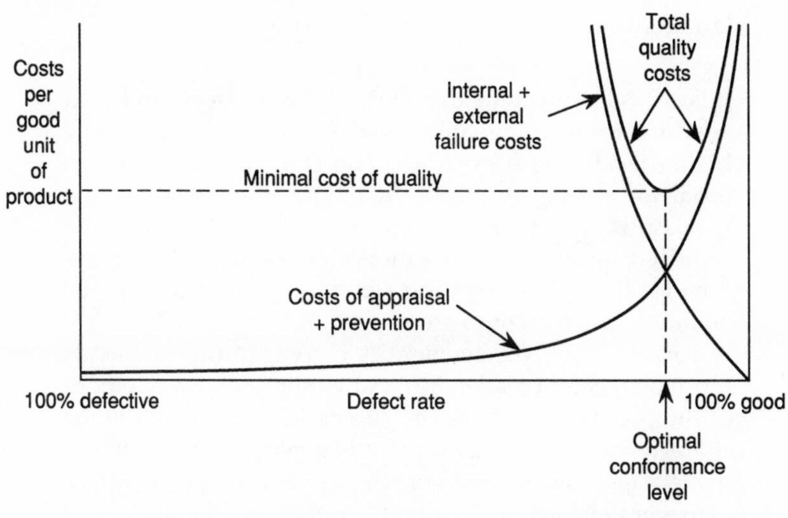

Source: J. M. Juran, *Planning for Quality* (New York: The Free Press, 1988).

(GM) and in charge of acquiring parts and materials from worldwide suppliers in excess of $50 billion per year. This experience would, of course, be useful at the Department of Defense (DoD), where about one-third of the agency's budget goes for the acquisition of weapons, supplies, and military research services. While at GM, Costello also became familiar with, and applied, statistical methods in his quality management process.

By coincidence, Costello arrived at DoD just as the federal government in general, and the DoD's acquisition bureaus in particular, were about to adopt their first large-scale quality management program. In 1986, President Reagan set the stage by issuing Executive Order 12552, which calls for all of the federal government to improve its productivity by 20 percent by 1992. While Costello is not the intellectual source of the ideas that were ultimately put into practice in DoD's Total Quality Management (TQM) program, his hand was very much on the tiller during the crucial formative period and, for this reason, his name is linked with TQM at DoD.

Total Quality Management: A Synthesis Approach

Costello set the tone for the development of DoD's Total Quality Management Master Plan by declaring:

> It is critical at this time that DoD, its contractors, and their vendors focus on quality as the vehicle for achieving higher levels of performance. The DoD budget leaves no room for solving problems that flow from poor quality. Quality is synonymous with excellence. It cannot be achieved by slogans and exhortation alone, but by planning for the right things and setting in place a continuous quality improvement process.
>
> Total Quality Management is a concept that demands top management leadership and continuous involvement in the process activities. The successful TQM operation is characterized by an organization of quality trained and motivated employees, working in an environment where managers encourage creativity, initiative, and trust, and where each individual's contributions are actively sought to upgrade quality. . . . The ultimate goal is the satisfied, quality-equipped, quality-supported soldier, sailor, airman, and Marine.

DoD's Total Quality Management Master Plan, issued in August 1988, defined TQM as:

> . . . a strategy for continuously improving performance at every level, and in all areas of responsibility. It combines fundamental management techniques, existing improvement efforts, and specialized technical tools under a disciplined structure [or model, as shown in Figure 3–9] focused on continuously improving all processes. Improved performance is directed at satisfying such broad goals as cost, quality, schedule, and mission need and suitability. Increasing user satisfaction is the overriding objective. The TQM effort builds on the pioneering work of Dr. W. Edwards Deming, Dr. Joseph H. Juran, and others, and benefits from both private and public sector experience with continuous process improvement.

FIGURE 3–9
A TQM Model

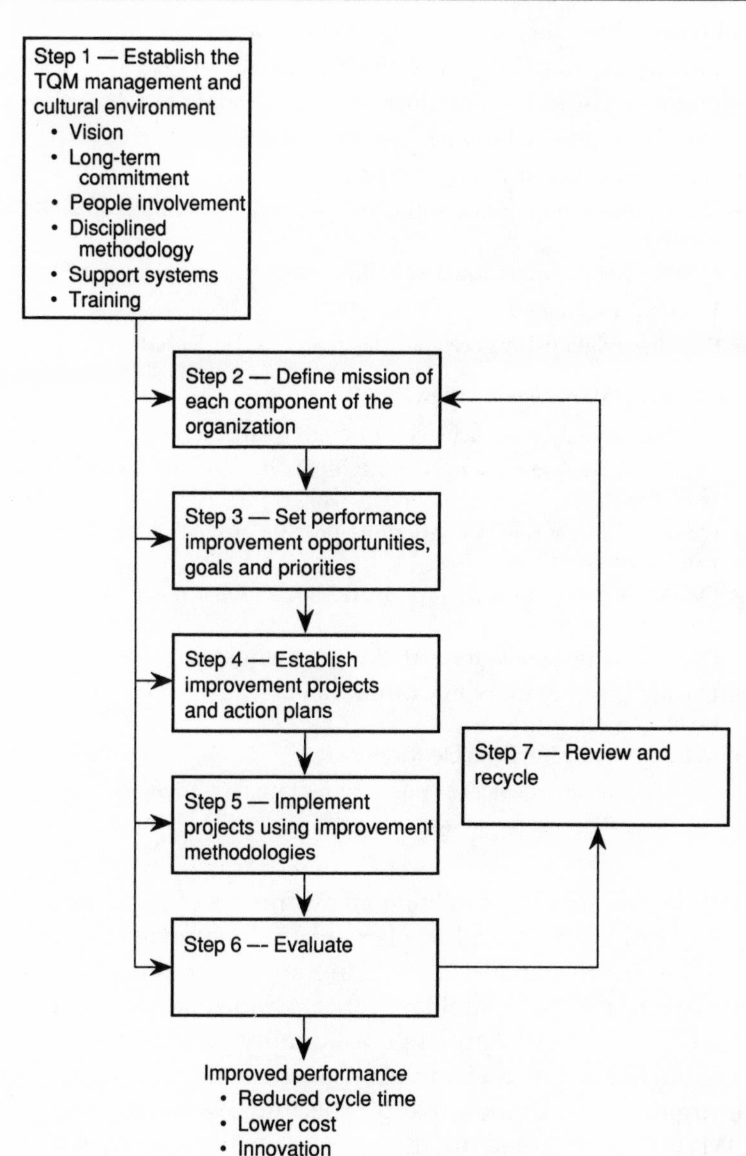

Source: Department of Defense, *Quality and Productivity Self-Assessment Guide for Defense Organizations.* (Washington, D.C.: Department of Defense, 1990).

TABLE 3–6
Two Views of Quality

Traditional View

- Productivity and quality are conflicting goals.
- Quality is defined as conformance to specifications or standards.
- Quality is measured by degree of nonconformance.
- Quality is achieved through inspection.
- Some defects are allowed if the product meets minimum quality standards.
- Quality is a separate function and focused on evaluating production.
- Workers are blamed for poor quality.
- Supplier relationships are short-term and cost-oriented.

Total Quality Management View

- Productivity gains are achieved through quality improvements.
- Quality is conformance to correctly defined requirements satisfying user needs.
- Quality is measured by continuous process/product improvement and user satisfaction.
- Quality is determined by product design and is achieved by effective process controls.
- Defects are prevented through process-control techniques.
- Quality is part of every function in all phases of the product life cycle.
- Management is responsible for quality.
- Supplier relationships are long-term and quality-oriented.

Among his first steps to build an awareness of TQM among the top DoD executives, and implement the new plan, Costello invited Deming to stand by his side in the presentation of Deming's approach to DoD's top military officers and senior managers.

DoD's synthesis approach to quality management is reflected in Table 3–6, a vision of what the DoD leadership wants the organization to look like by the mid-1990s. The eight-part TQM View contained in this table functions as the guiding "principles" for the DoD's quality management program. Note that these "principles" reflect a mixture of the quality improvement ideas of Crosby, Deming, and Juran.

TABLE 3–7
DoD's Total Quality Management Master Plan

Mid-Range (Three-Year) Goals:

- Harmonize DoD regulations with TQM goals.
- Eliminate attitudinal and policy barriers to TQM.
- Cultivate TQM champions in Congress.
- Promote TQM programs in top defense contracting firms.

Long-Range (Seven-Year) Goals:

- Establish TQM as a way of life.
- Have all DoD personnel directly participating in continuous process improvement.
- Gain Congressional understanding and support for TQM.

The Key: Cultural Change

Costello was well aware that the fate of TQM within a federal agency the size of DoD depended largely on the ability of its managers to gain outside support from congress, and to control cultural changes within its 3-million-person work force. Culture is a set of beliefs, values, and attitudes that guides how members of an organization perceive and interpret events. Consequently, DoD's TQM Master Plan stresses a three-stage strategy of cultural change both within DoD and within the organization's environment.

Since Costello launched the DoD quality management effort, a number of government-wide TQM support and recognition systems have been put into place. These include a 1987 Presidential Executive Order setting out agency productivity and implementation guidelines, formation of the Federal Quality Institute in 1988 to serve as a clearinghouse for TQM techniques and methods, and the President's Award for Quality and Productivity Improvement. Because public-sector quality management programs face institutional barriers not normally found in private firms—unsteady commitment for TQM among elected leaders, for example—federal TQM support systems will take on an extra measure of importance.

COMPARATIVE ASSESSMENT

Before comparing the specific quality management approaches of Crosby, Deming, and Juran, let's first place the ideas of these innovators into their larger, societal framework. As a group, they are all advocates of the need for a greater commitment to quality in the work place. But each holds a somewhat different view of what causes the quality vacuum. Table 3–8 attempts to identify the genesis, or the root causes, of the quality challenge facing America. Of the three, Crosby tends to locate the roots of the problem within the firm itself. Juran and Deming, on the other hand, seem to trace company-based quality problems back to the values found in the general, post-World War II American society.

The Early Adopters

A measure of the adoption of "Quality First" principles and practices in America in the last 10 years is shown in Table 3–9. The table provides a partial listing of some of the growing number of well-known companies that have adopted the ideas of Crosby, Deming, Juran, and other gurus.

Common Ground

The various "Quality First" approaches explored here build on a solid base of commonly held expectations and assumptions. In many respects they are far more alike than they are different from one another. Each approach:

- Requires a very strong top-management commitment.
- Shows that quality management practices will save, not cost, money.
- Places the responsibility for achieving quality primarily on the managers and the systems they control, not on the workers.
- Stresses that "Quality First" is a never-ending, continuous improvement process.

TABLE 3–8
The Genesis of the Quality Management Movement

	Nature of the Crisis	Cause of the Crisis	The Solution	Their Definition of Quality
Crosby	Communication of failure within the firm	Lack of commitment to quality	Company culture committed to quality	Conformance to company's own quality requirements
Deming	Loss of international competitiveness	Society and company acceptance of low quality	Society and company committed to quality	Dependable, customer-satisfying product or service at a low cost
Juran	Loss of international competitiveness	Company acceptance of low quality	Company committed to quality	Product or service that is fit for use
Costello	Unresponsive management process	Rule-based standards	Total Quality Management—a synthesis approach	Meeting customer's expectations

TABLE 3–9
Some of the Early "Quality First" Adopters*

	Crosby	Deming	Juran	TQM
AT&T		X		
Bechtel	X			
Burroughs	X			
Campbell Soup		X		
DoD Contractors				
Hewlett-Packard				X
McDonnell Douglas				X
Westinghouse				X
Boeing				X
Chrysler	X			
Dow Chemical		X		
Du Pont			X	
Federal Agencies				
Defense				X
IRS				X
Social Security				X
Veterans Administration				X
Postal Service				X
Ford		X		
GM	X	X		
Hughes Aircraft		X		
IBM	X			
Johnson & Johnson	X			
Mobil			X	
Monsanto			X	
Texas Instruments			X	
Xerox			X	

*Note: Reflects primary initial quality philosophy

- Is customer-oriented.
- Assumes a shift from an old to a new organizational culture.
- Is founded on building a strong management/worker problem-solving team.

But, the differences do matter. The differences among the approaches, then, will most influence a manager's decision to adopt portions of one over the other. Let's compare and contrast Crosby, Deming, and Juran on a number of key issues in terms of balancing the strengths and weaknesses of each approach.

What Is the Nature of the Organization?

Crosby

More so than the others, Crosby's approach has an unmistakable, organization-wide, team-building flavor. The organization is treated almost as if it were a whole, living organism that evolves through time toward higher and higher levels of self-awareness.

Deming

Resident in Deming's view of the business organization is a deep current of social responsibility. The purpose of the organization is to stay in business. But why? Not to make a lot of money, but to lend stability to the community it serves and to treat workers throughout the organization with the respect naturally due every human being. There is a moral tone to the Deming approach that is absent in the others.

Juran

Of the three, Juran's outlook focuses more on the parts rather than the whole organization. The whole does matter, but the path to a healthy organization is to make sure each part is finely tuned. Juran seems to invite the use of his trilogy on an isolated, troubled department.

Is a Step-by-Step Implementation Process Readily Apparent?

Crosby and Juran

In both of these approaches, we have a feeling that a starting point and an end point is visible. Crosby's maturity grid and Juran's trilogy might be called "user-friendly."

Deming

With Deming, there is a feeling that a road map does not exist, that without a tutor's guiding hand one would not readily know where to start on the journey.

Can the Approach Be Implemented Piecemeal?

Crosby and Deming

Both of these approaches are holistic and do not invite a piecemeal implementation strategy. That said, however, the Crosby model does lend itself more to prudent modifications to suit the host organization. Deming, on the other hand, calls for an almost instantaneous belief and total adoption of a new way of organizational life—one filled with radical value shifts.

Juran

A danger, perhaps, in the Juran model is the apparent ease with which his methodology could be targeted at parts of the organization only. A manager attempting a piecemeal implementation of Juran's methods might forget that, in the end, the entire organization must subscribe to the same deep commitment to quality. While Juran selectively picks his sub-units for application of the quality improvement process, he still requires an organization-wide commitment.

How Well Does Each Approach Handle Resistance?

Crosby and Juran

Resistance to change is inevitable, but it need not be a barrier. Crosby's learning-based model is perhaps best suited to accommodating resistance by allowing the individual to acknowledge his or her doubts and, then, to satisfy them through education and training. Juran also accommodates resistance by insisting that changes be justified through analysis and team-building processes.

Deming

On the surface, one can easily conclude that Deming's approach is dogmatic and uncompromising, and in many respects Deming himself cultivates this image. Yet his statistical methods are, in effect, learning tools that not only objectively structure problems in ways that make them easily understood, but also objectively disarm critics of change by depending on facts, not gospel.

WHERE TO FROM HERE?

Adopting a "Quality First" program is a big decision and one that should be made with care and after consultation with others in your organization. Consider the advice given to Alice by the Cheshire Cat when, during her adventures in Wonderland, she could not decide which of two paths to take:

> "Cheshire Puss," Alice began, rather timidly . . . "Would you tell me please, which way ought I go from here?"
>
> "That depends a good deal on where you want to get to," said the Cat.
>
> "I don't much care where—" said Alice.
>
> "Then it doesn't matter which way you go," said the Cat.
>
> "—so long as I get somewhere," Alice added as an explanation.
>
> "Oh, you're sure to do that," said the Cat, "if you only walk long enough."*

If, like Alice, you really don't care where you and your company are going, then it really doesn't matter what you do regarding quality management. But if you do care, then which way you go will make all the difference in the world.

JUST PICK ONE

As Tom Peters notes in his book, *Thriving on Chaos*:

> You should have a system. There's a lot of controversy here: Should you follow W. Edwards Deming, father of the Japanese quality revolution via statistical process control?

---

*From *Alice's Adventures in Wonderland* by Lewis Carroll, 1865.

> Or Phil Crosby, author of *Quality is Free*, and so prominent that GM bought a 10 percent stake in his firm? . . . Or Joseph Juran? Or invent a system of your own? Eventually you will develop your own scheme if you are successful.

During the mid-1980s, when quality management was first gaining some acceptance in America, it really didn't matter which approach—Crosby, Deming, or Juran—was adopted. Simply by being among the leaders, the early adopting firms were easily well ahead of competitors still operating under traditional management practices. Those days are over. In the 1990s, as more and more firms turn to "Quality First" strategies out of necessity—just to maintain their competitive positions nationally and internationally—there will be a growing need to carefully compare approaches and to adopt the quality initiatives that best fit a company's situation.

The Situational Approach

Perhaps the single most crucial step for a CEO preparing to adopt and implement a "Quality First" program is an honest and frank appraisal of the current status of the organization. For starters, the following questions should be carefully answered:

- How will the organization react to change?
- Who are the potential champions of the change?
- What are realistic expectations for the organization?
- How much time is available to make changes?
- Will it be an organization-wide effort, or will you target a single sub-unit?
- How will you measure results?

During your situational assessment, keep good notes. It will be to your advantage to construct your own version of an "As-Is/To-Be" table that summarizes and compares your organization's current quality situation to your vision of it in the future. Table 3–10 can be used as a prototype.

TABLE 3–10
Where to from Here?

"As-Is" State	"To-Be" State
From an environment that . . .	**To one that . . .**
has many different and often conflicting goals among its divisions and departments.	has a common vision shared by everyone.
punishes mistakes, and hides or rationalizes problems.	openly discusses problems and sees defects as opportunities for improvement.
rewards following established policies.	rewards risk-taking and creative thinking.
lets short-term problems drive and dominate work activity.	focuses on long-term continuous process improvement.
relies on inspection to catch mistakes before the customer receives the product.	improves work processes to prevent mistakes from occurring.
gives management full authority for top-down decisions for change.	trusts and empowers employees to contribute to decision making.
tolerates turf battles as inevitable.	facilitates and rewards cross-functional cooperation.
makes decisions arbitrarily.	bases all decisions on objective data.
has a negative or indifferent self-image.	feels like a winner, with achievements creating good morale.

Source: David Carr and Ian Littman, *Excellence in Government* (Coopers and Lybrand, 1990).

Picking a Strategy

In Chapters 8 and 9, you will find a step-by-step methodology for putting together your own "Quality First" program. In anticipation of that more detailed involvement, this chapter has been designed to first introduce you to, and then compare, the ideas of a few of the leading quality gurus. Once you have a feel for your organization's current needs and the depth of your initial step toward "Quality First" management, you can begin to consider how the strategies of Crosby, Deming, and Juran apply specifically to your situation.

As discussed earlier, each approach has a number of common elements. The decision to adopt elements of one approach over another, therefore, will probably hinge on the appeal you find in a unique aspect present in one approach but absent in the others. For example, a highly technical firm employing many engineers may find Juran far more appealing than the idealistic approach favored by Deming. A firm with a history of organizational development may find Crosby's organizational stage model culturally more comfortable.

Table 3–11 is a comparison of Crosby's fourteen steps, Deming's fourteen points, and Juran's seven-point breakthrough sequence. Each of the steps and/or points was allotted to one of eight generic "Quality First" implementation tasks. Four of the task categories deal with people-oriented tasks, and four are more technical in nature. The resulting table will help you compare the relative weight given by the quality gurus to each of the eight "Quality First" categories. With an idea of the strengths and weaknesses of your current organization in mind, try to decide which of the eight categories will be your greatest challenge to begin your "Quality First" program.

If, for example, you anticipate that building an awareness of quality in your organization will be a particularly difficult challenge, you may want to take a closer look at Crosby and Deming since their approaches have a strong awareness-building focus.

QUALITY DEMYSTIFIED

This chapter has been both a historical and an intellectual introduction to the central ideas behind the American "Quality First" movement. As with all innovations that challenge a long-held set of beliefs and practices, "Quality First" has not been quickly accepted in the American business community. While the ideas of Deming are as American as apple pie, they were first exported in the 1950s to Japan, where they ripened, and only recently have they been imported back into the United States.

Having surveyed a range of definitions of quality, and a variety of well-known approaches to implanting "Quality First" in an organization, you are ready to seriously consider the development of a specific "Quality First" methodology for your

TABLE 3–11
Comparative Assessment Matrix: Quality Management Tasks

	Crosby's 14 steps (Table 3–2)*	**Deming's 14 points** (Table 3–4)*	**Juran's 7 points** (Table 3–5)†
People oriented tasks			
Build top management commitment	1	1	1
Teamwork	2,10,13	9,4	3,5,6
Improve quality awareness	5,7,9,12	2,3,8,10,11,12	5
Expand training	8	6,7,13	5
Technically oriented tasks			
Measure quality	3	3,4	4
Quality of cost recognition	4	4,3	2†
Take corrective action	6,11	14	6,7
Continuous improvement process	14	5	7

*Refer to table noted for detailed description of each step/point delineated in quality leaders philosophy.
†Also see Juran's Cost of Quality Curve.

firm. The background you have gained here will help you better appreciate the step-by-step guidelines contained in Chapters six through ten. While there are risks whenever an organizational status-quo is upset, I hope you have gained a solid appreciation for the enormous benefits that the introduction of "Quality First" offers American industry.

It is hoped that this chapter has also helped "demystify" the aura that often surrounds the quality management gurus. Crosby, Deming, and Juran do, indeed, offer new insights into a leader's role in the management process. But there is no magic hidden behind their ideas. With determination, every American executive can learn to achieve a higher level of quality. What the gurus cannot do, however, is supply that precious ingredient—the will to act. That comes from within, and is developed bit by bit. By the time you have finished this book, you should have acquired both the tools and the desire to put "Quality First" into practice.

The final message contained in this chapter is this: There is no one best way. A situational approach, where business leaders must carefully match their unique organizational environment to a customized "Quality First" program, is the recommended route to achieving world-class quality products and services in the 1990s.

Chapter Four The American Quality Awards

"The process of applying for the Malcolm Baldrige National Quality Award gives us an opportunity to look at our company as our customers see us, which in the end is the only thing that counts. If we get out of this process what we really have to, we will identify our frailties, our shortcomings. The benefits go way beyond winning the award; winning will be only 10 percent of the real impact."

David T. Kearns, Chairman and CEO
Xerox Corporation, February 10, 1989

THE MALCOLM BALDRIGE NATIONAL QUALITY AWARD

The quality of U.S. goods and services is central to the nation's trade balance, competitiveness improvement, and standard of living. Some American firms are rising to the challenge of the quality imperative. They are working hard to meet the ever-increasing requirements of customers who now have broader market choices. More businesses must join in quality improvement efforts to help themselves—and the nation—in the quest for excellence.

On August 20, 1987, President Reagan signed the Malcolm Baldrige National Quality Improvement Act, establishing an annual National Quality Award, shown in Figure 4–1. The purposes of the award are to promote quality awareness, recognize quality achievements of U.S. companies, and publicize successful quality strategies.

The award program is managed by the National Institute of Standards and Technology, United States Department of Commerce. It is administered by the Malcolm Baldrige National Quality Award Consortium, a joint effort of the American Society for Quality Control and the American Productivity and Quality Center. All funding for the program is from private contributions.

The Malcolm Baldrige National Quality Award recognizes American companies that excel in quality achievement and quality management. The award promotes:

- Awareness of quality as an increasingly important element in competitiveness.
- Understanding of the requirements for quality excellence.
- Sharing of information on successful quality strategies and on the benefits derived from implementation of these strategies.

There are three eligibility categories of the award:

- Manufacturing companies.
- Service companies.
- Small businesses.

Up to two awards may be given in each category each year. In addition to publicizing the receipt of the award, recipients are expected to share information with other U.S. organizations about their successful quality strategies.

Companies participating in the award process submit applications that include completion of the award examination. The award examination is based upon quality-excellence criteria created through the public/private partnership. In responding

FIGURE 4–1
The Malcolm Baldrige National Quality Award

to these criteria, applicants are expected to provide information and data on their quality processes and quality improvement. Information and data submitted must be adequate to demonstrate that the applicant's approaches could be replicated or adapted by other companies.

The award examination is designed not only to serve as a reliable basis for making awards but also to permit a diagnosis of the applicant's overall quality management. All award applicants receive feedback reports prepared by teams of U.S. quality experts.

SHOULD YOU APPLY?

The question is often asked of Malcolm Baldrige National Quality Award winning companies if one should apply for the award. Newt Hardie, vice president of quality for Milliken & Company, said he is often asked if companies "should go for the Baldrige" award. He responded "What is your objective? If your objective is to win an award--don't do it. But if you want to improve your company, you cannot afford not to apply." From the, perspective of a small business, Mike Spiess, executive vice president of the Wallace Company, one of the 1990 Malcolm Baldrige Award winners, said that he believed that applying for the award is the "best investment you will ever make." The major benefits described by Spiess are:

1. The award changed Wallace Co. forever. The winning of the award made a significant difference in the company's level of visability and in its "credibility for a small business to compete in world markets." Wallace Co. gained new business in America, Canada, and Australia as a result of its enhanced reputation.
2. He believes that the small business investment in the award filing fee of $1,000 is the best bargain in quality in America, because small businesses normally could not buy the level of consulting analytical support that is provided in the feedback reports provided by the award examiners. Many small companies just couldn't

afford to spend the thousands of dollars for the advice provided by the award examiners for the $1,000 filing fee.

3. By going through the preparation of the requirements of the examination application, your company will learn more about itself than you thought possible. The self-examination of your company causes you to improve and take a new look at how you are operating your business.

In summary, after dozens of interviews I could not find a company that was not enhanced by participation in the Malcolm Baldrige Award process. Make the investment now. See how good you really are!

THE XEROX QUALITY AWARD STRATEGY

In order to present a case study of the typical process used to apply for the Malcolm Baldrige National Quality Award, Xerox Corporation's strategy in winning the award is briefly described here.

The award process enabled Xerox to look at itself through the eyes of the customer, and every aspect of the business came under this scrutiny. The company was able to assess its strengths and identify areas that needed improvement against the strict and demanding total-quality-control criteria of the award.

The decision for Xerox to apply in 1989 was made by David Kearns and Paul Allaire in the fourth quarter of 1988. On December 8, 1988, Wayland R. Hicks, executive vice president of the Business Products and Systems Group (later renamed Development and Manufacturing), and A. Barry Rand, president, United States Marketing Group, announced that Xerox was making a major commitment to achieve the Malcolm Baldrige National Quality Award. Although it was felt that the award would be a symbol of their dedication to customer satisfaction, there was a stronger feeling that through the process of competing for the award, substantial opportunities for improvement in the company's business effectiveness would be identified.

A National Quality Award Office was established to lead the two organizations in the achievement of this award. James E. Sierk was appointed to head the effort, with team members drawn from both organizations to provide support.

The number of core Xerox National Quality Award (NQA) team members varied as the team entered various stages of the process. The core team comprised approximately 20 full-time employees and 8 part-time employees.

Xerox had multiple objectives, according to Norman E. Rickard, corporate vice president of quality, for the application process: to intensify the focus on leadership through quality; to build teamwork; and to involve all employees, including corporate officers and senior managers, in the process. This was accomplished through meetings consisting of senior managers, the NQA-team steering committees, category-sponsoring executives, and specific site teams, as well as through a concentrated company-wide communications effort. Throughout the various stages of the process, a large percentage of the 50,200 employees of the Business Products and Systems Organization in the United States became actively involved and supported the effort.

The National Quality Award team had its first meeting January 3, 1989, to determine the approach and strategy for developing the Xerox application by the May 5, 1989, deadline. The team identified three deliverables:

1. An application for the National Quality Award.
2. Development, implementation, and coordination of site-visit logistics.
3. An assessment report to senior management on Xerox's quality efforts to date, based on insights gained by the team during the application process.

Figure 4–2 represents the team's assessment of the allocation of their time for the three outputs identified.

The team researched and subsequently wrote the first draft of the Xerox application, which was completed February 22. The initial draft was 175 pages, more than double the number permitted.

FIGURE 4–2
Xerox National Quality Award Team Time Allocation

Team Outputs	January 3–May 1	May 1–August	August
1. Application	90%		
2. Site Examination	5%	70%	
3. Assessment	5%	30%	100%

The application was subsequently refined and edited through three additional drafts before submission on May 1.

Senior management was actively involved, providing valuable input and direction, throughout the application and site-visit process.

Xerox was one of 40 companies submitting an application in 1989. On May 25, Xerox received notification that its application had been judged and was one of 23 in the manufacturing category to undergo a preliminary screening. The preliminary screening evaluation, conducted by a team of examiners, was based on an evaluation of 16 of the 44 questions responded to in the application.

Xerox was notified on July 10 that its application had been selected to move forward to the second stage of the review process, which entailed a complete evaluation of the entire application.

On August 17, 1989, Xerox was notified that it had been selected to receive a site visit a month later.

A team of five members of the board of examiners conducted the site visit on Monday, Tuesday, and Wednesday of that week. In addition, two observers representing the National Institute of Standards and Technology accompanied the examiners. The examiners spent three days at Xerox Corporation facilities, including Xerox Square in Rochester, New York; Joseph C. Wilson Center for Technology in Webster, New York; the Denver, Colorado, District Office; and Development and Manufacturing facilities in El Segundo, California.

The team of examiners talked with more than 400 employees during their three-day visit in order to clarify issues and verify the contents of the application submitted by Xerox. Examiners were also checking the extent to which the company's quality efforts were deployed across the breadth of the Business Products and Systems organization. To accomplish this, examiners talked to three different groups of employees:

- Category teams: Groups of five to eight employees were formed and met with examiners to answer specific questions on each of the seven categories contained in the application.
- Teams: Examiners, during the course of their visit, requested to meet with many employee-involvement and quality improvement teams to discuss their project, process, and results.
- Individual employees: During walk-arounds and in cafeterias, examiners met at random with employees to discuss quality within Xerox.

Following their visit to Xerox, the examiners submitted their site-visit report to the nine-member panel of judges. During the first week in October, the judges met to review all the site-visit reports and select the award recipients.

The 1989 awards were presented at the Department of Commerce on November 2, 1989, to the following companies:

- Milliken & Co.
- Xerox Corporation.

BENCHMARK YOUR QUALITY PERFORMANCE

The purpose of the balance this chapter is twofold. First, it is designed as a guide for award applicants. It includes a description of award processes and requirements, and the award examination. Second, it provides an evaluation framework for use by all American organizations that are pursuing quality excellence.

Reliable evaluation of the examination criteria requires experience with quality improvement systems. Nevertheless, the examination may also be used as a self-assessment tool. Thousands of organizations—businesses, government, healthcare, and education—they are currently eligible for or plan to apply for the award, are using the examination for a variety of purposes. These purposes include training, self-assessment, quality-system development, quality improvement, and strategic planning.

DESCRIPTION OF THE EXAMINATION[1]

The award examination is based on criteria designed to be a quality-excellence standard for organizations seeking the highest levels of overall performance and competitiveness. The examination addresses all key requirements to achieve quality excellence as well as the important interrelationships among these key requirements. By focusing not only on results but also on the conditions and processes that lead to results, the examination offers a framework that can be used by organizations to tailor their systems and processes toward ever-improving quality performance. Moreover, the mechanisms for tailoring are themselves included in the examination.

Key Concepts in the Award Examination Criteria

The award examination is built on a number of key concepts. Together, these concepts are the basis for all requirements in the examination, including the following:

- Quality is defined by the customer.
- The senior leadership of businesses needs to create clear quality values and build the values into the way the company operates.
- Quality excellence derives from well-designed and well-executed systems and processes.
- Continuous improvement must be part of the management of all systems and processes.

[1]This section is based on the 1991 Application Guidelines for the Malcolm Baldrige National Quality Award.

- Companies need to develop goals as well as strategic and operational plans to achieve quality leadership.
- Shortening the response time of all operations and processes of the company needs to be part of the quality improvement effort.
- Operations and decisions of the company need to be based on facts and data.
- All employees must be suitably trained and developed and involved in quality activities.
- Enhanced design quality and defect prevention should be major elements of the quality system.
- Companies need to communicate quality requirements to suppliers and work to improve supplier quality performance.

Several of these concepts are described in greater detail below.

Customer-Driven Quality

Quality is judged by the customer. All product and service attributes that contribute to value to the customer, lead to customer satisfaction, and affect customer purchase preferences must be addressed appropriately in quality systems. Value, satisfaction, and preference may be influenced by many factors throughout the overall purchase, ownership, and service experiences of customers. This includes the relationship between the company and customers—the trust and confidence in products and services—that leads to loyalty and preference. This concept of quality includes not only the product and service attributes that meet basic requirements. It also includes those that enhance them and differentiate them from competing offerings. Such enhancement and differentiation may include unique product-product, service-service, or product-service combinations. "Quality First" customer-driven quality is thus a strategic concept. It demands constant sensitivity to customer and market information and rapid response to requirements. These requirements extend well beyond defect and error reduction, merely meeting specifications, or reducing complaints. Nevertheless, defect and error reduction and elimination of causes of dissatisfaction contribute significantly to the customers' view of quality and therefore are important parts of customer-driven quality.

Leadership

A company's senior leaders must create clear quality values, specific goals, and well-defined systems and methods for achieving the goals. The systems and methods need to guide all activities of the company and encourage participation by all employees. Through their regular personal involvement in visible activities such as goal setting, planning, review of company quality performance, and recognizing employees for quality achievement, the senior leaders reinforce the values and encourage leadership in all levels of management.

Continuous Improvement

Achieving the highest levels of quality and competitiveness requires a well-defined and well-executed approach to continuous improvement of all operations and of all work unit activities of a company. Improvements may be of several types: (1) enhancing value to the customer through improved product and service attributes, (2) reducing errors and defects, (3) improving responsiveness and cycle-time performance, and (4) improving efficiency and effectiveness in use of all resources. Therefore, improvement is driven not only by the objective to provide superior quality but also by the need to be responsive and efficient. Both provide additional marketplace advantages. To meet all of these requirements, the process of continuous improvement must contain regular cycles of planning, execution, and evaluation. It must be accompanied by a basis—preferably a quantitative basis—for assessing progress, and for deriving information for the next cycle of improvement.

Fast Response

Meeting customer requirements and expectations and achieving success in competitive markets increasingly demand ever-shorter product and service introduction cycles and more rapid response to customers. Indeed, fast response itself is often a major quality attribute. Reduction in cycle times and lead times and rapid response to customers can occur only when quality systems and processes are designed to meet both quality and response goals, and when response time is included as a major focus of quality improvement processes. This requires that all designs, objectives, and work-unit activities include measurement and monitoring of cycle time and responsiveness to seek opportunities for improvement. Major gains in response may occur when work processes and paths are simplified and shortened. Such improvements are often accompanied by simultaneous improvements in quality. Therefore, it is highly beneficial to consider response time and quality together.

Actions Based on Facts, Data, and Analysis

Meeting quality improvement goals of the company requires that actions in setting, controlling, and changing systems and processes be based on reliable information, data, and analysis. Facts and data needed for quality assessment and quality improvement are of many types—including customer, product and service performance, operations, market, competitive comparisons, supplier, and employee-related concerns. Analysis refers to the process of extracting larger meaning from data to support evaluation and decision making at various levels within the company. Such analysis may entail using data individually or in combination to reveal information—such as trends, projections, and cause and effect—that might not be evident without analysis. Facts, data, and analysis support a variety of company purposes, such as planning, reviewing company performance, improving operations, and comparing quality performance with that of competitors.

The creation and use of performance indicators are a major consideration of data analysis in connection with quality system development, competitive performance, and continuous improvement. Performance indicators are measurable characteristics of products, services, processes, and operations that the company uses to evaluate performance and to track progress. The indicators should be selected to best represent the attributes that link customer requirements to customer satisfaction and competitive performance, as well as to operational effectiveness and efficiency. A system of indicators represents a clear and objective basis for aligning all activities of the company toward well-defined goals and for tracking progress toward those goals. Through the analysis of data obtained in the tracking process, the indicators themselves may be evaluated and changed. For example, indicators selected to measure product and service quality may be judged by how well they correlate with customer satisfaction.

Participation by All Employees

Meeting the company's quality objectives requires a fully committed, well-trained work force that is encouraged to participate in the company's continuous-improvement activities. Reward and recognition systems need to reinforce participation and emphasize achievement of quality objectives. Factors bearing on the safety, health, well-being, and morale of employees need to be part of the continuous-improvement objectives and activities of the company. Employees need to receive training in basic quality skills in performing their work and understanding and solving quality-related problems.

Key Characteristics of the Award Examination

1. The examination is nonprescriptive.

The examination is based on the set of values embodied in the key concepts outlined above. However, the examination does not prescribe approaches to implementation. This means that there are no specific tools, techniques, technologies, or types of organizations required to demonstrate excellence. These may vary greatly among businesses, depending on business size and type.

2. The examination is part of a diagnostic system.

The examination and the scoring system make up a two-part diagnostic system. The examination items represent *what* is to be evaluated. The scoring system represents *how* evaluations are made.

3. The examination stresses quality-system integration.

The examination criteria represent a system of requirements. Integration is achieved through numerous direct and indirect relationships among examination items. Many items link directly to others. Also, information is requested on company-level and unit-level quality performance. This information allows an assessment of how well the overall system is coordinated.

FRAMEWORK OF THE MALCOLM BALDRIGE NATIONAL QUALITY AWARD EXAMINATION

The Malcolm Baldrige National Quality Award examination consists of a framework designed for reliable evaluation and diagnosis. Applicants are required to provide information on their quality management systems, methods, and results using this framework.

THE EXAMINATION

The examination comprises seven categories that represent the major components of a quality management system. The categories are:

1.0 Leadership—senior management's success in creating and sustaining a quality culture.

2.0 Information and analysis—the effectiveness of the company's collection and analysis of information for quality improvement and planning.

3.0 Strategic quality planning—the effectiveness of the integration of quality requirements into the company's business plans.

4.0 Human resource utilization—the success of the company's efforts to utilize the full potential of the work force for quality.

5.0 Quality assurance of products and services—the effectiveness of the company's systems for assuring quality control in all operations.

6.0 Quality results—the company's results in quality achievement and quality improvement.

7.0 Customer satisfaction—the effectiveness of the company's systems to determine customer requirements and its demonstrated success in meeting them.

Each examination item, such as 1.0 Leadership, includes a set of areas to address as shown in Table 4–1. The areas serve to illustrate and clarify the intent of the items to place limits on the types and amounts of information the applicant should provide. Areas are not assigned individual point values, because their relative importance depends on factors such as the applicant's type and size of business and quality system.

The following text describes the basic examination based on the 1991 requirements. This text is keyed to the paragraph numbers used in the examination.

1.0 Leadership (100 pts.)

The leadership category examines how senior executives create and sustain clear and visible quality values along with a management system to guide all activities of the company toward quality excellence. Also examined are the senior executives' and the company's quality leadership in the external community and how the company integrates its public responsibilities with its quality values and practices.

1.1 Senior executive leadership (40 pts.)

Describe the senior executives' leadership, personal involvement, and visibility in developing and maintaining an environment for quality excellence.

1.2 Quality values (15 pts.)

Describe the company's quality values, how they are projected in a consistent manner, and how adoption of the values throughout the company is determined and reinforced.

TABLE 4–1
Examination Categories and Items

Examination Categories/Items		Maximum Points
1.0 Leadership		100
1.1 Senior executive leadership	40	
1.2 Quality values	15	
1.3 Management for quality	25	
1.4 Public responsibility	20	
2.0 Information and Analysis		70
2.1 Scope and management of quality data and information	20	
2.2 Competitive comparisons and benchmarks	30	
2.3 Analysis of quality data and information	20	
3.0 Strategic Quality Planning		60
3.1 Strategic quality planning process	35	
3.2 Quality goals and plans	25	
4.0 Human Resource Utilization		150
4.1 Human resource management	20	
4.2 Employee involvement	40	
4.3 Quality education and training	40	
4.4 Employee recognition and performance management	25	
4.5 Employee well-being and morale	25	
5.0 Quality Assurance of Products and Services		140
5.1 Design and introduction of quality products and services	35	
5.2 Process quality control	20	
5.3 Continuous improvement of processes	20	
5.4 Quality assessment	15	
5.5 Documentation	10	
5.6 Business process and support service quality	20	
5.7 Supplier quality	20	
6.0 Quality Results		180
6.1 Product and service quality results	90	
6.2 Business process, operational, and support service quality results	50	
6.3 Supplier quality results	40	
7.0 Customer Satisfaction		300
7.1 Determining customer requirements and expectations	30	
7.2 Customer relationship management	50	
7.3 Customer service standards	20	
7.4 Commitment to customers	15	
7.5 Complaint resolution for quality improvement	25	
7.6 Determining customer satisfaction	20	
7.7 Customer satisfaction results	70	
7.8 Customer satisfaction comparison	70	
Total Points		**1,000**

1.3 Management for quality (25 pts.)

Describe how quality values are integrated into day-to-day leadership, management, and supervision of all company units.

1.4 Public responsibility (20 pts.)

Describe how the company extends its quality leadership to the external community and includes its responsibilities to the public for health, safety, environmental protection, and ethical business practices in its quality policies and improvement activities.

2.0 Information and Analysis (70 pts.)

The information and analysis category examines the scope, validity, use, and management of data and information that underlie the company's overall quality-management system. Also examined is the adequacy of the data, information, and analysis to support a responsive, prevention-based approach to quality and customer satisfaction built on "management by fact."

2.1 Scope and management of quality data and information (20 pts.)

Describe the company's base of data and information used for planning, day-to-day management, and evaluation of quality, and how data and information reliability, timeliness, and access are ensured.

2.2 Competitive comparisons and benchmarks (30 pts.)

Describe the company's approach to selecting quality-related competitive comparisons and world-class benchmarks to support quality planning, evaluation, and improvement.

2.3 Analysis of quality data and information (20 pts.)

Describe how data and information are analyzed to support the company's overall quality objectives.

3.0 Strategic Quality Planning (60 pts.)

The strategic quality planning category examines the company's planning process for achieving or retaining quality leadership and how the company integrates quality improvement planning into overall business planning. Also examined are the company's short-term and longer-term plans to achieve and/or sustain a quality leadership position.

3.1 Strategic quality planning process (35 pts.)

Describe the company's strategic quality planning process for short-term (one to two years) and longer term (three years or more) quality leadership and customer satisfaction.

3.2 Quality goals and plans (25 pts.)

Summarize the company's goals and strategies. Outline principal quality plans for the short term (one to two years) and longer term (three years or more).

4.0 Human Resource Utilization (150 pts.)

The human resource utilization category examines the effectiveness of the company's efforts to develop and realize the full potential of the work force, including management, and to maintain an environment conducive to full participation, quality leadership, and personal and organizational growth.

4.1 Human resource management (20 pts.)

Describe how the company's overall human resource management effort supports its quality objectives.

4.2 Employee involvement (40 pts.)

Describe the means available for all employees to contribute effectively to meeting the company's quality objectives; summarize trends and current levels of involvement.

4.3 Quality education and training (40 pts.)

Describe how the company decides what quality education and training is needed by employees and how it uses the knowledge and skills acquired; summarize the types of quality education and training received by employees in all employee categories.

4.4 Employee recognition and performance measurement (25 pts.)

Describe how the company's recognition and performance-measurement processes support quality objectives; summarize trends in recognition.

4.5 Employee well-being and morale (25 pts.)

Describe how the company maintains a work environment conducive to the well-being and growth of all employees; summarize trends and levels in key indicators of well-being and morale.

5.0 Quality Assurance of Products and Services (140 pts.)

The quality assurance of products and services category examines the systematic approaches used by the company for assuring quality of goods and services based primarily on process design and control, including control of procured materials, parts, and services. Also examined is the integration of process control with continuous quality improvement.

5.1 Design and introduction of quality products and services (35 pts.)

Describe how new and/or improved products and services are designed and introduced and how processes are designed to meet key product and service quality requirements.

5.2 Process quality control (20 pts.)

Describe how the processes used to produce the company's products and services are controlled.

5.3 Continuous improvement of processes (20 pts.)

Describe how processes used to produce products and services are continuously improved.

5.4 Quality assessment (15 pts.)

Describe how the company assesses the quality of its systems, processes, practices, products, and services.

5.5 Documentation (10 pts.)

Describe documentation and other modes of knowledge preservation and knowledge transfer to support quality assurance, quality assessment, and quality improvement.

5.6 Business process and support service quality (20 pts.)

Summarize process quality, quality assessment, and quality improvement activities for business processes and support services.

5.7 Supplier quality (20 pts.)

Describe how the quality of materials, components, and services furnished by other businesses is assured, assessed, and improved.

6.0 Quality Results (180 pts.)

The quality results category examines quality levels and quality improvement based on objective measures derived from analysis of customer requirements and expectations and from analysis of business operations. Also examined are current quality levels in relation to those of competing firms.

6.1 Product and service quality results (90 pts.)

Summarize trends in quality improvement and current quality levels for key product and service features; compare the company's current quality levels with those of competitors and world leaders.

6.2 Business process, operational, and support service quality results (50 pts.)

Summarize trends in quality improvement and current quality levels for business processes, operations, and support services.

6.3 Supplier quality results (40 pts.)

Summarize trends and levels in quality of suppliers and services furnished by other companies; compare the company's supplier quality with that of competitors and with key benchmarks.

7.0 Customer Satisfaction (300 pts.)

The customer satisfaction category examines the company's knowledge of the customer, overall customer-service systems, responsiveness, and its ability to meet requirements and expectations. Also examined are current levels and trends in customer satisfaction.

7.1 Determining customer requirements and expectations (30 pts.)

Describe how the company determines current and future customer requirements and expectations.

7.2 Customer relationship management (50 pts.)

Describe how the company provides effective management of its relationships with its customers and uses information gained from customers to improve products and services as well as its customer relationship management practices.

7.3 Customer service standards (20 pts.)

Describe the company's standards governing the direct contact between its employees and customers and how these standards are set and modified.

7.4 Commitment to customers (15 pts.)

Describe the company's commitment to customers

on its explicit and implicit promises underlying its products and services.

7.5 Complaint resolution for quality improvement (25 pts.)

Describe how the company handles complaints, resolves them, and uses complaint information for quality improvement and for prevention of recurrence of problems.

7.6 Determining customer satisfaction (20 pts.)

Describe the company's methods for determining customer satisfaction, how satisfaction information is used in quality improvement, and how methods for determining customer satisfaction are improved.

7.7 Customer satisfaction results (70 pts.)

Summarize trends in the company's customer satisfaction and in indicators of adverse customer response.

7.8 Customer satisfaction comparison (70 pts.)

Compare the company's customer satisfaction results and recognition with those of competitors that provide similar products and services.

HOW IT'S SCORED

The system for scoring examination items is based on three evaluation dimensions: approach, deployment, and results. All examination items require applicants to furnish information relating to one or more of these dimensions. Specific criteria associated with the evaluation dimensions are described in the following text. Scoring guidelines are outlined in Table 4–2.

Approach

"Approach" refers to the methods the company uses to achieve the purposes addressed in the examination items. The scoring criteria used to evaluate approaches include one or more of the following:

TABLE 4–2
Scoring Guidelines

Score	Approach	Deployment	Results
0%	• Anecdotal, no system evident	• Anecdotal	• Anecdotal
10-40%	• Beginnings of systematic prevention basis	• Some to many major areas of business	• Some positive trends in the areas deployed
50%	• Sound, systematic prevention basis that includes evaluation/ improvement cycles	• Most major areas of business	• Positive trends in most major areas
	• Some evidence of integration	• Some support areas	• Some evidence that results are caused by approach
60-90%	• Sound systematic prevention basis with evidence of refinement through evaluation/ improvement cycles	• Major areas of business	• Good to excellent in major areas
	• Good integration	• From some to many support areas	• Positive trends—from some to many support areas • Evidence that results are caused by approach
100%	• Sound, systematic prevention basis refined through evaluation/ improvement cycles	• Major areas and support areas	• Excellent (world-class) results in major areas
	• Excellent integration	• All operations	• Good to excellent in support areas • Sustained results • Results clearly caused by approach

- The degree to which the approach is prevention-based.
- The appropriateness of the tools, techniques, and methods to the requirements.
- The effectiveness of the use of tools, techniques, and methods.
- The degree to which the approach is systematic, integrated, and consistently applied.
- The degree to which the approach embodies effective evaluation and improvement cycles.
- The degree to which the approach is based on quantitative information that is objective and reliable.
- The indicators of unique and innovative approaches, including significant and effective new adaptations of tools and techniques used in other applications or types of businesses.

Deployment

"Deployment" refers to the extent to which the approaches are applied to all relevant areas and activities addressed and implied in the examination items. The scoring criteria used to evaluate deployment include one or more of the following:

- The appropriate and effective application to all product and service characteristics.
- The appropriate and effective application to all transactions and interactions with customers, suppliers of goods and services, and the public.
- The appropriate and effective application to all internal processes, activities, facilities, and employees.

Results

"Results" refer to outcomes and effects in achieving the purposes addressed and implied in the examination items. The scoring criteria used to evaluate results include one or more of the following:

- The quality levels demonstrated.
- The contributions of the outcomes and effects to quality improvement.
- The rate of improvement.
- The breadth of quality improvement.
- The demonstration of sustained improvement.
- The significance of improvements to the company's business.
- The comparison with industry and world leaders.
- The company's ability to show that improvements derive from their quality practices and actions.

Business Factors Considered in the Evaluation of Applications

The award examination is designed to permit evaluation of the widest range of quality systems for manufacturing and service companies of any size, type of business, or scope of market. The 32 items and 99 areas to address have been selected because of their importance to virtually all businesses. Nevertheless, the importance of the items and areas to address may not be equally applicable to all businesses, even to businesses of comparable size in the same industry. Specific business factors that may bear on the evaluation are considered at every stage of preparation for evaluations as well as in the evaluations themselves. Below is an outline of the key business factors and how they are considered in the award examination.

Key Business Factors

The key business factors include:

- Size and resources of the applicant.

- Number and type of employees.
- Nature of the applicant's business: products, services, and technologies.
- Special requirements of customers or markets.
- Scope of the applicant's market: local, regional, national, or international.
- Regulatory environment within which the applicant operates.
- Importance of suppliers, dealers, and other external businesses to the applicant, and the degree of influence the applicant has over its suppliers.

DOES YOUR COMPANY RANK AMONG THE BEST?

You can obtain a copy of the latest application guidelines for the Malcolm Baldrige National Quality Award by contacting:

Malcolm Baldrige National Quality Award
National Institute of Standards and Technology
Route 270 and Quince Orchard Road
Administration Building, Room A537
Gaithersburg, MD 20899
Telephone: (301) 975-2036
Telefax: (301) 948-3716

Since 1988, more than nine American companies have won the Malcolm Baldrige National Quality Award. Their approach to "Quality First" principles and practices is described for each of these world-class, quality-driven organizations in Chapter 5, which follows. You can tell how you rank by reviewing the award requirements described in this chapter and evaluating your organization's quality status. You may wish to apply for the award, but if you decide not to, consider reviewing these award requirements, ask your staff to review them, and determine by self-examination the areas in which you can improve your business.

Chapter Five

American Quality Leaders

"The winners of the Malcolm Baldrige National Quality Award have made quality improvement a way of life. Quality is their bottom line, and that kind of can-do attitude makes for world-class products and services."

Robert A. Mosbacher, Secretary of Commerce,
1990 Award Announcement

The Malcolm Baldrige National Quality Award, as described in Chapter 4, has been awarded to Cadillac Motor Car Division of General Motors Corporation (1990 winner), Federal Express Corporation (1990), Globe Metallurgical, Inc. (1988), IBM Rochester (1990), Milliken & Co. (1989), Motorola, Inc. (1988), Wallace Co. Inc. (1990), Westinghouse Commercial Nuclear Fuel Division (1988), and Xerox Business Products and Systems (1989). Several of these American quality leaders are described briefly in this chapter. The corporate mission, objectives, and unique approach to quality are described to provide a reference point in determining how your organization's quality efforts can be enhanced.

FEDERAL EXPRESS CORPORATION

The Federal Express Corporation was the Malcolm Baldrige National Quality Award's first winner in the service category. Federal Express Corporation launched the air-express delivery industry 18 years ago. By constantly adhering to a management philosophy emphasizing people, service, and profit, in that order, the company achieved high levels of customer satisfaction and experienced rapid sales growth. Annual revenues topped $1 billion within 10 years of the company's founding, an exceptional achievement.

But past accomplishments do not ensure future success. That's why the management of Federal Express is setting ever-higher goals for quality performance and customer satisfaction, enhancing and expanding service, investing heavily in advanced technology, and building on its reputation as an excellent employer. Company leaders are increasingly stressing management by fact, analysis, and improvement.

Through a quality improvement process focusing on 12 Service Quality Indicators (SQIs), all tied to customer expectations and articulated at all levels of its international service business, the Memphis-based firm continues to set higher standards for service and customer satisfaction. Measuring themselves against a 100 percent service standard, managers and employees strive to continuously improve all aspects of the way Federal Express does business.

Federal Express at a Glance

Conceived by Chairman and Chief Executive Officer Frederick W. Smith, Federal Express began operations in 1973. At that time, a fleet of eight small aircraft was sufficient to handle demand. Five years later, the company employed 10,000 people, who handled a daily volume of 35,000 shipments. Today, approximately 90,000 Federal Express employees at more than 1,650 sites process 1.5 million shipments daily, all of which must be tracked through a central information system, sorted in a short time at facilities in Memphis, Indianapolis, Newark, Oakland, Los Angeles, Anchorage, and Brussels, and delivered by a highly decentralized distribution network. Federal Express's air cargo fleet is now the world's largest.

Federal Express revenues totaled $7 billion in fiscal year

1990. Domestic overnight and second-day deliveries accounted for nearly three-forths of the total, with the remainder being international deliveries. The company's share of the domestic market in 1989 was 43 percent, compared with 26 percent for its nearest competitor.

People-Service-Profit

Federal Express Corporation's "people-service-profit" philosophy guides management policies and actions. The company has a well-developed and thoroughly deployed management evaluation system called Survey/Feedback/Action (SFA), which involves a survey of employees, analysis of each work group's results by the work group's manager, and a discussion between the manager and the work group to develop written action plans for the manager to improve and become more effective. Data from the SFA process are aggregated at all levels of the organization for use in policy making.

Training of frontline personnel is a responsibility of managers, and "recurrency training" is a widely used instrument for improvement. Teams regularly assess training needs, and a worldwide staff of training professionals devises programs to address those needs. To aid these efforts, Federal Express has developed an interactive video system for employee instruction. An internal television network, accessible throughout the company, also serves as an important avenue for employee education.

Consistently included in listings of the best U.S. companies to work for, Federal Express has a "no layoff" philosophy, and its "guaranteed fair treatment procedure" for handling employee grievances is used as a model by firms in many industries. Employees can participate in a program to qualify frontline workers for management positions. In addition, Federal Express has a well-developed recognition program for team and individual contributions to company performance. Over the last five years, at least 91 percent of employees responded that they were "proud to work for Federal Express."

Service Quality Indicators (SQI)

To spur progress toward its ultimate target of 100 percent customer satisfaction, Federal Express replaced its old measure of quality performance—percent of on-time deliveries—with an index that comprehensively describes how its performance is viewed by customers. Federal Express established the service quality indicators (SQI) to determine what the main areas of the customers' perception of service are and how they are meeting them. *The purpose of the SQI is to identify and eliminate causes, not place blame.*

The SQI has 12 components weighted to reflect the customers' view of the company's performance by placing greater weight on SQI categories that have the greatest impact on the customers' perception of service received. The number of average daily failure points for each component is calculated by multiplying the number of daily occurrences for that component by its assigned importance weight. Factors such as abandoned calls are included in order to measure internal performance that can significantly affect external customer service. SQI categories are expanded and adjusted as necessary.

The SQI is the sum of the average daily failure points for all 12 components and is tracked and reported on a weekly basis, with monthly summaries.

The service goal will always be 100 percent failure-free performance, with the emphasis on finding the root causes of failure and implementing solutions that *prevent* the failures rather than simply fix the consequences of failures. For example, if courier-mislabeled packages are a major cause of wrong day/late failures, the SQI team would focus on creating effective new solutions to prevent courier-miscoding at the source, rather than perfecting the expensive expediting system. Effective quality improvement programs and teamwork such as this are essential to achieving the SQI goal. Knowing what makes a customer unhappy is important, but it is even more important to understand it and solve it through a concerted effort by several areas. Goal congruence, improved methods, contingency plans, and teamwork are vital parts of the total commitment to service.

To reach its aggressive quality goals, Federal Express has set up one cross-functional team for each service component in the SQI. A senior executive heads each team and assures the involvement of frontline employees, support personnel, and managers from all parts of the corporation when needed. Two of these corporate-wide teams have a network of more than 1,000 employees working on improvements.

The SQI measurements are directly linked to the corporate-planning process, which begins with the CEO and COO and an executive planning committee. SQIs form the basis on which corporative executives are evaluated. Individual performance objectives are established and monitored. Executive bonuses rest on the performance of the whole corporation in meeting performance improvement goals. And, in the annual employee survey, if employees do not rate management leadership at least as high as they rated them the year before, no executive receives a year-end bonus.

Quality Improvement at Federal Express

Although Federal Express is an acknowledged leader in the air freight industry, a formal Quality Improvement Process (QIP) has been implemented throughout the entire corporation to continue meeting the needs of its customers. The objectives of the QIP are to:

- Achieve a 100 percent service level.
- Increase profits.
- Make Federal Express a better place to work by focusing everyone's attention on the corporate policy of "Doing Right Things Right" and catching and fixing problems when they happen.

The corporate mission supports the philosophy that quality must be a part of the way it does business. Themes such as "Do it right the first time," "Make the first time you do it the only time anyone has to," "Fedexcellence" and "Q=P" (Quality=Productivity) have always been a part of the Federal Express culture. Even the people/service/profit philosophy is an expression of their commitment to quality. Now, in light of intense competition and expansion into global markets, quality becomes more than a slogan at Federal Express—it is the normal way of life.

Experts say that in an organization committed to quality as a way of life, three things happen:

- The level of customer satisfaction increases and satisfied customers bring more business, which ensures the financial health of the corporation and continued job security.
- Profits increase because employees don't waste time and money correcting mistakes.
- The quality of work-life is improved because they have fewer customer complaints, less hassle, and less rework to deal with.

Quality improvement means the company meets the needs of its internal and external customers. While it is easy to recognize the ultimate customer, the company also must recognize that it has many customer-supplier relationships with other Federal Express employees. Quality improvement activities are critical to the continued success of Federal Express. Constantly striving to improve the system and finding better ways of doing things will make it possible for the company to keep its leadership position in the industry as it expands into the global marketplace. The competition will continue to get tougher and customers will continue to demand the best quality of service available for the price they pay. Federal Express must meet all of these challenges, and do so better than anyone else can.

Continuous Improvement

Quality improvement requires you to continuously develop ways to do better work. Continuous improvement means "Fix it now!" and "Prevent problems before they happen" and "Look for new ways to meet customer needs." The theory of

"If it ain't broke, don't fix it," has no place in a quality organization. Instead, the approach needs to be, "If it ain't broke, improve it."

Satisfying Internal and External Customers

Quality begins and ends with the customer. The customer tells what the right thing to do is, and then the company has to find the right way to do it. As the supplier of a service, Federal Express is famous for doing whatever it takes to satisfy the customer. Federal Express's team recognizes who the ultimate customer is and knows how important it is to meet their customer needs. However, team members also need to recognize and meet the needs of their internal customers—other Federal Express employees with whom they exchange information, products, and services every day. All of you have people who depend on you for products or services to do their jobs and each of you depends on services or products from others in order to do your job.

To make the work process flow smoothly and deliver a quality product to external customers, Federal Express builds positive working relationships with its internal customers. This can be accomplished by asking three questions:

- What do you need from me?
- What do you do with what I give you?
- Are there any gaps between what I give you and what you need?

The answers to these questions are the key to "Doing Right Things Right."

Quality Action Teams

In a quality organization, everyone, not just management, must be committed to improving both quality and productivity. Everyone must share responsibility for achieving corporate goals. Quality Action Teams (QATs) get employees involved in designing the work process for maximum quality at minimum cost. Teams are generally more effective than individuals in solving problems or improving the way things get done. When you start your quality improvement actions, employees often ask "What's in it for me?" Federal Express's experience has shown that:

- Doing right things the first time makes your job easier.
- Quality of work-life is improved because you have fewer customer complaints, less hassle, and less rework to deal with.
- Profits increase because time and money aren't wasted correcting mistakes.
- Quality work keeps Federal Express financially healthy and ensures job security.
- You have the opportunity to actively participate in problem solving.
- You are eligible to receive awards and recognition through various corporate programs.

Quality improvement activities are critical to the continued success of Federal Express. The competition will continue to get tougher and customers will continue to demand the best quality of service available for the prices they pay. Federal Express must meet all of these challenges and do so better than anyone else can. Constantly striving to improve the system and finding better ways of doing things will make it possible for Federal Express to keep its leadership position in the industry as it moves aggressively into the global marketplace.

GLOBE METALLURGICAL, INC.

Globe Metallurgical, Inc., a small business, is a major producer of silicon-metal and ferrosilicon products, with plants located in Beverly, Ohio, and Selma, Alabama. The company was founded in 1873 as the Globe Iron Company in Jackson, Ohio, and subsequently built the Beverly plant in 1955 and acquired the Selma plant in the mid-1960s. At the Beverly plant, Globe operates five submerged-arc electric furnaces, and has the capability to produce silicon metal and a full range of ferrosilicon products. The furnaces range in size from 10 to 20 megawatts. Once a specialist in the production of ferrochromium products, Globe abandoned the environmentally hazardous ferrochromium lines in 1985 to concentrate its ferrosilicon effort in the production of magnesium ferrosilicon products to serve the foundry industry. Magnesium ferrosilicon is used to convert gray iron to ductile iron in foundries, and ductile iron represents a growing segment of the iron castings market. The Selma plant contains two submerged-arc electric furnaces, and the plant specializes in the production of high-grade, low-impurity silicon metal. The furnaces at Selma are both in the 15 to 16 megawatt range. The silicon metal produced at Selma is devoted primarily to the chemical silicones industry and to applications requiring extremely low iron levels in silicon metal, such as the electronics and solar cell industries.

Development of the Globe Quality System

In 1985, the Ford Motor Co. approached its suppliers with its quality certification program, called Q-1. Since Globe supplied Ford with a number of alloys for its foundries, Globe management recognized that the criteria specified in the Q-1 program would have to be satisfied to sustain a long-term relationship with Ford. The first step to obtaining Q-1 certification was to undergo an extensive audit of the quality system by Ford personnel, called the Q-101 audit. If the supplier passes, with a score of 140 or more out of 200, the supplier becomes eligible for an internal review of its performance history at all Ford locations using its products. If all the locations approve the supplier, the Q-1 Award is forthcoming. Since the criteria are demanding, the Q-1 Award is recognized as a significant quality achievement in the U.S. auto industry.

The Ford Q-1 program has had the greatest initial impact on the development of the quality system at Globe. A self-assessment of the Q-101 criteria indicated to Globe management that the quality system in place was inadequate to satisfy the criteria, so a new quality system was built around the criteria. The primary inadequacies of the system were that it was detection-based as opposed to prevention-based, and lacked implementation of statistical process control techniques, quality planning, and employee participation in the improvement process.

Since Globe was deficient in so many areas, the building of the quality system was begun simultaneously in three areas: (1) training the entire work force in Statistical Process Control (SPC), (2) establishing a quality manual and the mechanics of the quality system, and (3) educating and training Globe's suppliers in the necessity for implementing statistical process control and a quality system.

Quality-Efficiency-Cost Committee

To establish the mechanics of a workable quality system, a Quality-Efficiency-Cost (QEC) committee was established at each plant, with a QEC steering committee overseeing the activities of the plant committees. The committees provide ideas for improvement in all three areas: quality, efficiency, and cost. The QEC steering committee comprises the top management of the company and is chaired by the president and chief executive officer. It meets monthly and discusses the broader issues of development and maintenance of the quality system, such as allocation of significant resources and planning. The plant QEC committees meet daily and are chaired by the plant manager. All department heads attend the meetings, and the discussion is much narrower in scope than the steering committee meetings, concentrating on specific projects and implementation techniques. Since the plant manager serves on the steering committee with upper management, he acts as the conduit for bringing plant issues up to the steering-committee level, and for bringing steering committee issues down to the plant level for implementation. Initially, the Beverly plant QEC committee was given the task of identifying the critical process variables within each of the plant's processes which must be controlled through SPC or other techniques. This was done to assure that the final product will always be consistent with the customers' requirements without the need for 100 percent inspection of the final product. Thus, the emphasis was to build a quality system based on prevention techniques as opposed to the historical protection methodologies.

Globe Project Teams

Project teams are called on an ad hoc basis to address a particular problem or project. Unlike the other teams, salaried employees with particular expertise are invited onto project teams. This expertise includes Taguchi design of experiments, storyboarding, brainstorming techniques, and other statistical tools and techniques. Since all the salaried employees utilize personal computers, the computers are frequently used to facilitate the team's activities. Historically, the activities now undertaken by project teams were done solely by salaried employees, and the implementation of their ideas was dictated by management within a given department. In many instances, the hourly employees, whose ideas were not solicited in the development of the project, resented the implementation technique, or felt that they knew of more effective techniques. Now that input is actively solicited from hourly employees, the hourly employees take pride of ownership in the decision process, and are much more likely to assist in implementation. Typically, there are seven departmental teams, three interdepartmental teams, two project teams, and two interplant teams in operation at any given time. More than 60 percent of the work force of both plants is involved in quality circle teams. An average of 70 ideas per week are generated to improve the quality, efficiency, and/or cost of the operation.

Quality Planning

Prior to 1986, quality was not given consideration in the planning process. Today, the Continuous Improvement Plan is a vital document that is updated annually and distributed widely both internally and outside of the company. The current plan is 20 pages, with 96 items for improvement identified. Each item in the plan fully supports items found in the company's Strategic Plan. Both plans cover a period of five years.

The structure of the Continuous Improvement Plan includes the goal of the improvement, the objective of the improvement item, individual projects that support the objectives, and assigned responsibilities and target dates. The QEC steering committee is responsible for developing the goals that are found in the plan, but the plant QEC committees are responsible for the much more specific activities of project determination and assignment of responsibilities. To ensure that the hourly employees have input and the ability to comment on the plan, copies are distributed, and hourly employees are invited to attend planning meetings. Many quality circle ideas that require large capital expenditures are incorporated into the plan each year. To track the progress of individual projects, an audit system has been established that requires the persons responsible to file update reports quarterly. The update reports are distributed by the quality manager, to whom they are returned. To assist the responsible parties in remembering their assignments, the projects have all been translated into a calendar format, which each employee receives, to hang on the wall. As project deadlines approach, employees can readily be aware of their responsibilities by looking at the calendar. On due dates, the employee's name, project number, and a brief description of the specific project are printed on the calendar.

Quality Pays!

Since QEC emphasizes quality, efficiency, and cost, many productivity improvements have been realized through the implementation of both quality-enhancing and productivity-enhancing techniques. In 1986, management became interested in the works of Shigeo Shingo, and began to apply many Shingo methods, such as Just In Time (JIT), to the manufacturing process. It has been found that the Shingo techniques work in harmony with the techniques of Deming, Taguchi, and others. Using the formula

(Net Sales-Total Cost) + (Total Cost EQ)

the index for productivity has improved 36 percent company-wide in the period 1986 through 1988. Documented savings of $10.3 million per year have been realized through the implementation of quality-related techniques.

MOTOROLA, INC.

Motorola, Inc., is one of the world's leading manufacturers of electronic equipment, systems, and components produced for both United States and international markets. Motorola products include two-way radios, pagers, and cellular radiotelephones, other forms of electronic communications systems, integrated circuits and discrete semiconductors, defense and aerospace electronics, data communications, and information processing and handling equipment.

Ranked among the United States' 100 largest industrial companies, Motorola has about 102,000 employees worldwide.

As a leader in its high-technology markets, Motorola is one of the few end-equipment manufacturers that can draw on expertise in both semiconductor technology and government electronics.

The company was founded in Chicago by Paul V. Galvin in 1928 as the Galvin Manufacturing Corporation. Its first product was a "battery eliminator," allowing customers to operate radios directly from household current instead of from the batteries supplied with early models. In the 1930s, the company successfully commercialized car radios under the brand name "Motorola," a new word suggesting sound in motion. During this period, Motorola also established home radio and police radio departments; instituted pioneering personnel programs; and began national advertising. The name of the company was changed to Motorola, Inc., in 1947—during a decade that also saw the company enter government work and open a research laboratory in Phoenix, Arizona, to explore solid-state electronics.

Motorola's attention to quality also has shown up on the bottom line, according to Richard Buetow, vice president and director of quality, who says that defects have been cut by 80 percent during the past few years, and the company has saved about $962 million in inspection and rework costs.

It wasn't always that way. Ten years ago, admits Motorola President Gary L. Tooker, the company faced the grim fact that many of its products and operations simply weren't making the grade. Top executives had a choice: Motorola could either continue losing its customers to Japan (as it had in consumer electronics during the late 1970s) or it could go back to basics.

Robert W. Galvin (then Motorola's chairman and head of the company's executive committee) chose the latter by personally visiting key customers around the world, then calling for a tenfold improvement in quality within five years. But even that wasn't tough enough, says Tooker; Galvin's goal eventually became one of "total customer satisfaction." Motorola now aims for a condition of six sigma—3.4 defects per million opportunities—not just in manufacturing, but within every one of the company's operations by 1992. Buetow puts it another way: "We're striving for absolute perfection."

At Motorola, the quality culture is pervasive. Motorola top management formally restated their company objectives, beliefs, goals, and key initiatives in 1987, and quality remained as a central theme. Total customer satisfaction is Motorola's fundamental objective. It is the overriding responsibility of everyone in the company, and the focus of all of their efforts.

Motorola top management also reaffirmed two key beliefs that have been part of the Motorola culture since the company began in 1928: uncompromising integrity, and constant respect for people. The CEO has identified the following key goals for Motorola:

1. Increased global market share.
2. Best in class in terms of people, technology, marketing product, manufacturing, and service.
3. Superior financial results.

Quality and Productivity at Motorola

In an era of intense international competition, Motorola has maintained a position of leadership in the electronics industry through a combination of aggressive product innovation, strategic long-range planning, and a unique philosophy that allows each employee to contribute insights to the achievement of quality standards. This philosophy is translated into action through the teams to openly and effectively communicate ideas to help improve processes and products. The Participative Management Program (PMP) assumes that under the right conditions, employees will suggest better ways to do their jobs. For many years, Motorola has sought the ideas of its employees. For about 10 years, a process of participatory management has been in place. Each U.S. employee of the company who is not part of the Motorola Executive Incentive Program (MEIP) is a member of a PMP team. Teams are usually organized by function within an organization. Their purpose is to continually assess the process of performing their work, and to change it in ways that will reduce defects and reduce cycle time. The problem-solving efforts of these teams are directly analogous to quality circles. The quality and cycle-time improvement rates for these teams are the same as the corporate goal, thereby providing incentives that directly support the quality improvement process.

The Motorola Quality Improvement Process

Management of the quality improvement process is based on Motorola's practice of Management by Measurement. This style of management says that by establishing measurements that are correlated to the desired end result, and regularly reviewing the actual measurements, the organization will focus on those actions necessary to achieve the required improvement.

In 1986, the communications sector adopted a uniform metric, called "total defects per unit." In addition, because all operations were using the same measurement, the goal for defect reduction was uniformly applied to all operations. The required percent reduction was the same, regardless of the absolute level. The improvement rate achieved by the communications sector was much greater than had been achieved in the five-year Ten Times program, and so the measurement was adopted by the entire corporation.

In January 1987, Motorola restated its corporate quality goals to be:

1. Improve 10 times by 1989.
2. Improve 100 times by 1991.
3. Achieve six-sigma capability by 1992.

This goal is applied to all areas of the business, not just product quality.

Motorola's Quality Initiatives

The first of these initiatives is the achievement of six-sigma quality. Motorola intends that all products and services are to be at the six-sigma quality level (3.4 defects/million products) by 1992. This means designing products that will accept reasonable variation in component parts, and developing manufacturing processes that will produce minimum variation in the final output product. It also means analyzing all the services provided, breaking them down into their component parts, and designing systems that will achieve six-sigma performance. Motorola, Inc., is taking statistical technologies and making them a part of each and every employee's job, regardless of assignment. Measuring this begins by recording the defects found in every function of their business, then relating these defects to a product or process by the number of opportunities to fabricate the product or carry out the process. Motorola has converted their yield language to parts per million (ppm), and the six-sigma goal is 3.4 ppm defect levels across the company. Despite the wide variety of products and services, the corporate goal is the same six-sigma quality level by 1992.

The company's second key initiative, total cycle-time reduction, is closely related to six-sigma quality. Motorola defines cycle time as the elapsed time from the moment a customer places an order for an existing product to the time the company delivers it. In the case of a new product, it is from the time the company conceives of the product to the time it ships. Motorola examines the total system, including design, manufacturing, marketing, and administration.

The third initiative, product and manufacturing leadership, also emphasizes the need for product development and manufacturing disciplines to work together in an integrated world, applying principles of teamwork and simultaneous engineering.

Motorola's fourth initiative, profit improvement, is a long-term, customer-driven approach that shows the company where to commit its resources to give customers what they need, thus improving long-term profits. It recognizes that investing in quality today will produce growth in the future.

The final initiative is participatory management within, and cooperation among organizations. This team-work approach is designed to achieve more synergy and greater efficiency, and to improve quality.

WALLACE COMPANY, INC.

Wallace Company, Inc., a Houston-based industrial distribution company, bucked the conventional business wisdom during the mid-1980s. With the Texas Gulf Coast economy in the doldrums and new construction activity—its primary source of revenues—at a standstill, Wallace avoided short-term remedies, and pursued a long-term strategy of continuous quality improvement.

In only a few years, Wallace has distinguished itself from its competitors by setting new standards for service. It has emerged as a stronger firm with a rapidly growing sales volume, steadily increasing market share, and better profit performance.

Now entering the final stage of the three-phase quality program it initiated in 1985, Wallace has effectively merged business and quality goals, built new partnerships with customers and suppliers, and instilled associates with a commitment to one overriding aim: total customer satisfaction.

Wallace at a Glance

Founded in 1942, Wallace is a family-owned distribution company primarily serving the chemical and petroleum industries.

Its 10 offices, located in Texas, Louisiana, and Alabama, distribute pipe, valves, and fittings, as well as value-added specialty products such as actuated valves and plastic-lined pipe. Wallace distributes directly in the Texas Gulf Coast area but serves international markets as well.

In tandem with its move to continuous quality improvement, Wallace shifted its marketing focus from engineering and construction activities to maintenance and repair operations, now the source of 70 percent of its sales. In 1989, sales totaled $79 million. The company employs 280 associates, all of whom have been trained in quality improvement concepts and methods.

Continuous Quality Improvement

The seeds of the Wallace quality process were sown and cultivated by the company's five top leaders, directed by John W. Wallace, chief executive officer, and C.S. Wallace, Jr., president. Comprising the quality-management steering committee, each of the five top leaders has undergone more than 200 hours of intensive training on the methods and philosophy of continuous quality improvement. Their hands-on involvement is typified by the participation of at least one senior leader in all quality activities, including on-the-job training for associates.

Leadership drafted the company's quality mission statement, which was circulated throughout the company. Embodying input from all associates, the final document serves as Wallace's public commitment to continuous quality improvement. It is distributed to all associates, customers, and suppliers. Furthermore, Wallace developed 16 quality strategic objectives—nine of which focus on improving customer satisfaction—to guide business decision making. In fact, business and quality aims are one and the same, formulated in Wallace's quality business plan.

Associates are responsible for devising and carrying out plans to accomplish objectives under the company's cooperative, yet centralized, approach to quality improvement. Since 1985, participation on teams, whose membership is voluntary and cuts across department and district-office boundaries, has increased sixfold. Team planning and decision making are greatly aided by an extensive set of customer-focused databases, accessible to all associates through the company's computer system. Teams are assisted by 12 statistical process control (SPC) coordinators, who chart trends, conduct failure-mode effects analysis to isolate real and potential problems, and evaluate progress in accomplishing quality objectives. Each district office has at least one SPC coordinator on staff, and at all sites, one day a week is devoted to evaluating and planning quality improvements.

Wallace has fixed its sights on providing the products and services that best meet the needs of its regional market, but the scope of its quality improvement efforts is truly worldwide. Measurable quality benchmarks are identified in global searches for the top-performing companies in each category of service or business operation, from on-time delivery to safety performance.

Not only does Wallace comprehensively monitor its activity—it has identified and now measures 72 discrete processes that contribute to on-time delivery and accurate invoicing—but it also invites the scrutiny of customers. Customers receive computer-generated reports that document how well the company has been servicing its accounts. Customer feedback is ensured through four types of surveys, "partner building" meetings, frequent contacts by sales representatives, and a total customer-response network that must respond to all inquiries and complaints within 60 minutes.

Moreover, customers have access to some of Wallace's databases. Wallace also has led the way in converting customers to electronic data interchange. Both Wallace and its customers reap the advantages of better inventory management, time savings, error reduction, and more accurate data. About 40 percent of Wallace's sales orders are now handled electronically, compared with less than five percent in 1988.

Wallace holds suppliers to its same high standards, requiring firms to provide statistical evidence of the quality of their shipments and to guarantee their products for a minimum of 12 months. Based on its quality surveillance measures, the distributor has trimmed the number of its suppliers to 325, down from more than 2,000 in 1987. To ensure that suppliers consistently provide products meeting the expectations of customers, Wallace provides training in continuous quality improvement to its suppliers, a first in the industry. Last year, 15 suppliers initiated processes based on the Wallace model. In another pioneering initiative spawned by a committee of Wallace customer and supplier representatives, the company has implemented a vendor-certification process, in which Wallace and its major customers will jointly assess the quality processes of suppliers.

Because associates drive quality improvement, Wallace has invested about $2 million in formal training between 1987 and the end of 1990. Teams of associates closest to a specific area targeted for improvement are charged with identifying the steps necessary to accomplish a quality objective, with standardizing the methods to ensure consistent performance, and with conducting the necessary training at all departments and offices.

"Quality wins" are reported in the company's monthly newsletter, acknowledged in congratulatory letters from the CEO, and rewarded with dinners for the responsible associates and their families, or with team picnics.

Simultaneous with management's efforts to increase associate involvement in continuous quality improvement, rates of absenteeism, turnover, and work-related injuries have dropped sharply. New associate-led projects are intended to foster greater dedication and higher levels of job satisfaction. For example, teams are studying ways to enhance career development opportunities. In a newly begun program, each associate will visit at least one customer site to discuss service performance.

These and other initiatives have paid numerous dividends. Since 1987, Wallace's market share has increased from 10.4 percent to 18 percent. Its record of on-time deliveries has jumped from 75 percent in 1987 to 92 percent in 1990. By July 1991, the distributor has committed to guarantee all customers an on-time delivery rate of 98 percent. Its customer base has grown, while existing clients have increased their business. As a result, sales volume has grown 69 percent and, because of greater efficiency, operating profits through 1989 have increased 7.4 times.

WESTINGHOUSE COMMERCIAL NUCLEAR FUEL DIVISION

Westinghouse Electric Corporation is involved in many aspects of nuclear power plant design, manufacturing, and operation. The Commercial Nuclear Fuel Division (CNFD) is responsible for the engineering, manufacturing, and supply of Pressurized Water Reactor (PWR) fuel assemblies for commercial nuclear power reactors. The fuel contained in these assemblies generates heat (through nuclear fission), which is converted to electricity.

CNFD is a division within the Energy Systems Business Unit of Westinghouse. It is a fully integrated fabricator of commercial PWR fuel comprised of the Western Zirconium Plant, near Ogden, Utah (which became part of CNFD in 1988), where zircalloy extrusions and other components are produced from zircon sands; the Specialty Metals Plant (SMP) in Blairsville, Pennsylvania, where nuclear-grade tubing is produced from the extrusions; the Fuel Manufacturing Plant in Columbia, South Carolina, where enriched uranium is converted into ceramic pellets and loaded into the fuel-rod assemblies; and nuclear engineering, marketing, and administrative activities in Monroeville, Pennsylvania.

CNFD currently supplies 40 percent of the U.S. light-water reactor fuel market and 20 percent of the free-world market. This market leadership can be directly attributed to the quality of the division's products and services. Fuel produced at the Columbia plant is responsible for more than 7 percent of the electricity produced in the United States.

Value Creation at Westinghouse

In the early 1980s, dramatic changes in the global marketplace caused Westinghouse corporate leadership to create a new management vision for the corporation. The corporation was becoming concerned about maturing market conditions and international competition. The new vision of Westinghouse was based on a management strategy independent of changes in technology or market conditions. It was based on the principle of "value creation."

As Westinghouse CEO John Marous has stated, the primary mission of both corporate- and division-level managers is to create value for the people who have a stake in the corporation—primarily its customers, stockholders, employees, and the community. Westinghouse believes that managing all of its businesses around the concept of "Quality First" is the fundamental strategy for value creation.

The Westinghouse model for "Quality First" is built on four imperatives: management leadership, product and process leadership, human resource excellence, and customer orientation. These imperatives, in turn, are broken down into conditions of excellence. Under the imperative of management leadership, there are four conditions required of management in a "Quality First" environment. The first task of management is to create the right culture. The next task is planning, followed by communications, and, last, accountability.

Strategic Quality Planning

Westinghouse has discovered that the "Quality First" concept must be viewed as an all pervasive operating strategy for managing a business every day.

"Quality First" begins with a strategic decision—a decision that can only be made by top management—and that decision, simply put, is the decision to compete as a world-class company. "Quality First" concentrates on quality performance—in every facet of a business—as the primary strategy to achieve and maintain competitive advantage. It requires taking a systematic view of an organization—looking at how each part interrelates to the whole process. In addition, it demands continuous improvement as a "way of life."

The Westinghouse "Quality First" model is built on four imperatives. These imperatives simply state that an organization must have quality management systems, quality products and technology, and quality people—and that the combined energies of its management, products, and people must be focused on customer satisfaction.

Today, CNFD has programs in place to improve quality on a continuous basis in every segment of the organization. Management has discovered that "Quality First" is not merely the sum of a lot of individual quality improvement programs. The power of "Quality First" is much greater than that. "Quality First" results from the synergy of all components of an organization working together.

Results Count

"Quality First" has been the single most important factor in the division's overall business strategy. It has helped to reinforce CNFD's position as a world leader in the marketplace. But more importantly, it has given division personnel a totally new perspective and a new way of thinking. CNFD people constantly come up with new ideas for making things better.

The division is also living up to its commitment to deliver software—proposals, reports, documentation, and the like—to its customers on time and devoid of errors. Accurate and timely data is crucial to customers, and the division rating is 98 percent on both scores.

In 1988, CNFD completed a record of 42 consecutive months of 100 percent on-time delivery of finished assemblies and related hardware.

"Quality First" costs, which include internal and external failure costs as well as prevention and appraisal costs, have been reduced by 30 percent in four years, due mainly to reduced rework and scrap costs. CNFD has been able to increase its customer satisfaction rating, a relatively new measure, by about 6 percent in less than one year. That means customers are attaching greater value to the division's products and services than they did a year ago.

Lessons Learned

From its experience in quality improvement, Westinghouse CNFD has learned a number of lessons, which it believes can be applied with reasonable success to any business.

First, an organization must have a common vision, and all people in that organization must embrace a common mission.

Next, a framework for "Quality First" is absolutely critical.

This is the model or blueprint that keeps everyone focused on continuous improvement in all aspects of the business.

The third lesson can be summarized as: measure, measure, and measure. In addition, CNFD discovered that no quality improvement program can be successful unless both employees and customers are intimately involved in the process.

And finally, "Quality First" requires a long-term commitment to continuous quality improvement. A "Quality First" culture cannot be built overnight. "Quality First" is not a short-term proposition. But neither are the rewards. The benefits of Quality First are long-term for a company willing to make the commitment.

Long-term customer satisfaction and long-term industry leadership are what "Quality First" is all about.

XEROX BUSINESS PRODUCTS AND SYSTEMS

For its first 15 years, Xerox was without equal, best in an industry whose products were synonymous with its name. But challenges came in the mid-1970s from foreign and U.S. competitors that surpassed Xerox reprographic products in both cost and quality.

Not even second best in some product categories, Xerox launched an ambitious quality improvement program in 1984 to arrest its decline in the world market it created. Today, the company can once again claim the title as the industry's best in nearly all copier product markets. As a result, Xerox has not only halted loss of world market share, but also reversed it.

Xerox Business Products and Systems (BP&S), headquartered in Stamford, Connecticut, attributes the turnaround to its strategy of Leadership Through Quality. The company defines quality through the eyes of the customer. Xerox BP&S knows what customers want in products and services.

Analyses of a wide variety of data, gathered with exhaustive collection efforts that include monthly surveys of 55,000 Xerox equipment owners, enable the company to identify customer requirements. The company uses this information to develop concrete business plans with measurable targets for achieving the quality improvements necessary to meet customers' needs.

Xerox at a Glance

One of two Xerox Corporation businesses, Business Products and Systems employs 50,200 people at 83 U.S. locations. BP&S makes more than 250 types of document-processing equipment, generating $6 billion in 1988 U.S. sales, or 54 percent of the company's domestic revenues. Copiers and other duplicating equipment account for nearly 70 percent of BP&S revenues. The remainder is divided among sales of electronic printers and typing equipment, networks, work stations, and software products.

Leadership through Quality

Customer satisfaction is the number one priority at Xerox. The corporation's strategy for achieving that priority is Leadership Through Quality, the Xerox total quality initiative that pervades the entire organization. Personally driven by CEO David T. Kearns and his senior management team, Leadership Through Quality, initiated in 1983, is guided by the simple but powerful Xerox Quality Policy:

> Xerox is a quality company. Quality is the basic business principle for Xerox. Quality means providing our external and internal customers with innovative products and services that fully satisfy their requirements. Quality improvement is the job of every Xerox employee.

At Xerox, quality is defined as "fully meeting customer requirements." To do this, Leadership Through Quality encompasses a wide range of initiatives. Key initiatives are the *benchmarking* of Xerox's performance against its competitors and industry leaders; *employee involvement* to fully realize all of their people's talents and capabilities to satisfy customers; and the use of *quality tools and processes* developed specifically for Xerox to achieve continuous quality improvement. Among these processes are a six-step problem-solving process and a nine-step quality-improvement process. The thrust of Leadership Through Quality is prevention; both processes are used at all levels of the organization to identify and correct potential difficulties, as well as to act on quality opportunities.

Leadership Through Quality has transformed the way Xerox does business. Establishing objectives with individual units, planning for future products, delivering current products, reviewing progress—all of these activities start with a focus on customer requirements, proceed through work processes built around quality, and are reviewed and evaluated against the original set of customer requirements. Decisions at every point are guided by Leadership Through Quality processes and based on factual data. Data for decision making in all these activities comes from over 375 major information systems—of which 175 relate specifically to the management, evaluation, and planning of quality.

To support this massive quality effort, Xerox created an extensive training program. All Xerox employees have received at least the basic 28-hour Leadership Through Quality training; many have been trained in advanced quality techniques. Over the last four years, Xerox has invested four million man-hours and $125 million in Leadership Through Quality training.

Training and empowerment have furthered the basic Xerox strategy of employee involvement. Xerox estimates that at any given time, 75 percent of its employees are actively working on one or more of 7,000 quality improvement teams. The empowerment of field managers has been greatly enhanced by the creation of district partnerships, in which employees involved with sales, service, and administration functions work closely to make customer-oriented decisions once made at higher organization levels. And on the front lines, the service organization's work-group strategy empowers customer service engineers to manage their work loads in ways that deliver better service to customers.

An important factor in Xerox's quality initiative is the Amalgamated Clothing and Textile Workers Union. Xerox and the union jointly encourage participation by union members in quality improvement processes, with such success that the partnership, unique in American industry, is considered a role model by other corporations. The recently ratified contract states that "every employee shall support the concept of continuous quality improvement while reducing quality costs through teamwork and the tools and processes of Leadership Through Quality." Union/management study teams have found ways to retain work inside the corporation—with resulting savings of $7 million annually and 250 jobs.

Xerox is proud of the results realized by Leadership Through Quality. Among those results achieved over the last 5 years are:

- A 78 percent improvement in the quality of Xerox machines.
- Year after year, Xerox copiers and printers continuously set new benchmarks for copy quality.
- More than 40 percent improvement in product reliability.
- The introduction of the industry's first three-year warranty, now offered on five Xerox copiers.
- A 73 percent reduction in production-line defective parts.

Xerox suppliers are made full partners with Xerox through continuous supplier involvement. Xerox supplier parts are process-qualified, which means a step-by-step procedure is in place to analyze and qualify suppliers' production and control processes. Xerox provides training and follow-up in such areas as statistical process control, just-in-time, and total quality techniques.

But Xerox's proudest achievement is the response of their customers to Xerox's efforts to improve quality. They are actively soliciting their customers' requirements and reactions, surveying 55,000 of them monthly about performance in equipment, sales, service, and administrative support. Results have shown a 38 percent improvement in their customers' perceptions of Xerox's performance. Customers also show their satisfaction with Xerox in other ways: Their purchases of Xerox products enabled Xerox to reverse the erosion of their market share by Japanese firms—one of the very few American companies to have accomplished this. Customers also respond to Xerox quality through formal ratings.

In Xerox's continuous drive for quality improvement, the corporation has set very demanding future targets. For example, their targets for 1993 include:

- Benchmark performance in the corporation's product development cycle schedule.
- A 50 percent reduction in unit manufacturing cost.
- A fourfold improvement in reliability.

Xerox is committed to continuous quality improvement because it is committed to customer satisfaction. Using Leadership Through Quality, the corporation is determined to constantly upgrade those processes and decisions that deliver world-class products to the most important members of Team Xerox: its customers.

Xerox Benchmarking System

In its quest to elevate its products and services to world-class status, Xerox BP&S devised a benchmarking system that has, in itself, become a model. The company measures its performance in about 240 key areas of product, service, and business performance. Derived from international studies, the ultimate target for each attribute is the level of performance achieved by the world leader, regardless of industry.

Returns from the company's strategy for continuous quality improvement have materialized quickly as noted below:

Customer Processes

- Highly satisfied customers have increased 38 percent and 39 percent for copier/duplicator and printing systems, respectively.
- Customer satisfaction within Xerox sales processes have improved 40 percent; service processes, 18 percent; and administrative processes, 21 percent.
- Billing quality has improved 35 percent.

- Service response time has improved 27 percent.
- Supply order returns have improved 38 percent.

Productivity

- Service visits per day have been increasing 4 percent a year.
- Product performance during the first 30 days of installation has increased 40 percent.
- Manufacturing lead times have been reduced 50 percent.
- Manufacturing labor and material overhead rates have been improved by 31 percent and 46 percent, respectively.
- Customer retention rate is 20 percent better than U.S. industry average and Xerox is gaining customers at a rate of more than four new customers for every three customers lost.

People

- 75 percent of all Xerox employees are actively involved with quality-improvement or problem-solving projects.
- 94 percent of Xerox employees acknowledge that customer satisfaction is their top priority.
- Employee turnover is 17 percent better than the average reported by the Bureau of National Affairs.

Safety

- Product safety has improved 70 percent with an associated 90 percent decrease in claims. Xerox has not had a product liability judgment in the last five years.
- Xerox employees are three times safer on the job than around the home. There has never been an industrial fatality or a major OSHA citation in Xerox.

These improvements have enabled Xerox BP&S to take additional steps to distinguish itself from the competition; for instance, it was the first in the industry to offer a three-year product warranty.

The thrust of Leadership Through Quality is ongoing with Xerox BP&S. The process of continuous quality improvement, directed toward greater customer satisfaction and enhanced business performance, is currently targeting a 50 percent reduction in unit manufacturing cost and fourfold improvement in reliability by 1993. Such goals illustrate the commitment concentrated in the Xerox quality policy, which states that "quality is the basic business principle at Xerox."

FOLLOW BY EXAMPLE!

This chapter has presented the approaches taken by some of America's quality leaders who are world-class providers of products and/or services—from very large to small companies involved in diverse business, from Federal Express overnight package delivery to Xerox's turnaround of its copier business. Each of these companies has developed its own customized approach at improving quality. Each has recognized that "Quality First" is not a buzzword but a bedrock upon which these American quality leaders are now prospering.

After examination of these American quality leaders' efforts to improve their business by adopting "Quality First" principles, you may wish to assess your own organization's quality climate, implementation processes, management tools, and accomplishments by completing the "Quality First" self-assessment provided in the next chapter.

Chapter Six

Quality First Self-Assessment

"Look for the ways you trip yourself up—how you get in your own way without meaning to. It will help you anticipate where problems and setbacks will likely occur."

Tom Peters and Nancy Austin
A Passion for Excellence

SELF-ASSESSMENT APPROACH

This chapter provides a method to assess the current practices, policies, procedures, and attitudes throughout your own organization as they relate to quality enhancement, and provides the opportunity to assess the effects of any changes as they relate to quality enhancement. It also provides an opportunity to check your progress by occasionally re-evaluating your performance.

This self-assessment asks questions concerning:

- Climate—People's perceptions about their organization and/or work units.
- Processes—The organization's or work unit's policies, practices, and procedures.

- Management tools—The specific techniques used to promote quality improvements throughout the organization or work units.
- Outcomes—Mission accomplishment.

The self-assessment questions are divided into four groups: climate, processes, tools, and outcomes. Some of the questions ask you to consider the entire organization in your response, and others ask you to think only about your immediate work unit. The definitions of these two terms need to be clear in your mind prior to the use of this self-assessment so that you are referring to the organization and work unit in the same way as the self-assessment.

Decide which organization and work unit you wish to examine and enter the names below. For example, you may be in charge of a corporation. The corporation may contain three divisions. The divisions, in turn, may be composed of several departments. Depending on your interest, the corporation may be designated as the organization, and one of the three divisions as the work unit.

Name of organization = ______________________________

Work unit = ______________________________

Another term you will encounter is "customer," defined as anyone who receives the work that your work unit(s), or your organization, performs. Note that customers can be another organization, another work unit, or any organization member. The traditional notion of customer as someone outside your immediate organization or work unit that uses or buys your product or service can also apply. In all cases, consider that your customer relies on and judges the quality of the work that you do.

The source of this evaluation structure is the "Quality and Productivity Self-Assessment Guide," a public-domain federal report. You may reproduce this chapter to aid in your use of this self-assessment tool.

To conduct the "Quality First" self-assessment, complete the following worksheets for each self-assessment element (climate, processes, tools, outcomes). There are 215 self-assessment questions, which can be answered in approximately 15 minutes. The scoring rationale follows the questions.

ASSESSMENT OF ORGANIZATION CLIMATE

The following list of statements is presented for your evaluation and ranking. There are no wrong answers. Circle the number 1, 2, 3, 4, 5, or 6 that you feel best indicates the extent of your agreement with the statement. The legend for the questionnaire is: (1) strongly disagree, (2) disagree, (3) somewhat disagree, (4) somewhat agree, (5) agree, and (6) strongly agree.

	Strongly Disagree					*Strongly Agree*
1. People in this organization are aware of its overall mission.	1	2	3	4	5	6
2. In general, this organization's customers believe that we care about what they think.	1	2	3	4	5	6
3. People in this organization are aware of how their jobs contribute to the organization's mission.	1	2	3	4	5	6
4. It's in everyone's best interests that this organization be successful.	1	2	3	4	5	6
5. People in this organization are aware of how the organization's mission contributes to higher-level missions and objectives.	1	2	3	4	5	6
6. In general, this organization's customers would not go elsewhere even if it were possible.	1	2	3	4	5	6

Legend: (1) strongly disagree, (2) disagree, (3) somewhat disagree, (4) somewhat agree, (5) agree, and (6) strongly agree.

	Strongly Disagree					*Strongly Agree*
People in this organization:						
7. try to plan ahead for changes (such as in policy) that might impact our mission performance.	1	2	3	4	5	6
8. try to plan ahead for technological changes (such as new development in computer software) that might impact our mission performance.	1	2	3	4	5	6
9. regularly work together to plan for the future.	1	2	3	4	5	6
10. see continuing improvement as essential.	1	2	3	4	5	6
11. care about what will happen to the organization after they are reassigned.	1	2	3	4	5	6
12. Creativity is actively encouraged in this organization.	1	2	3	4	5	6
13. Innovators are the people who get ahead in this organization.	1	2	3	4	5	6
14. The quality of our work is second only to mission accomplishment as the overriding focus of this organization.	1	2	3	4	5	6
15. Every member of this organization is concerned with the need for quality.	1	2	3	4	5	6

Legend: (1) strongly disagree, (2) disagree, (3) somewhat disagree, (4) somewhat agree, (5) agree, and (6) strongly agree.

	Strongly Disagree					*Strongly Agree*
16. Continuous quality improvements within this organization can lead to more productive use of our resources.	1	2	3	4	5	6
17. People in this organization know how to define the quality of what they do.	1	2	3	4	5	6
18. Every member of this organization needs to contribute to quality improvement.	1	2	3	4	5	6

People in this organization:

19. live up to high ethical standards.	1	2	3	4	5	6
20. like to do a good job.	1	2	3	4	5	6
21. emphasize doing things right the first time.	1	2	3	4	5	6

The leader(s) in this organization (people at the highest level):

22. are committed to providing top-quality services/products/work.	1	2	3	4	5	6
23. regularly review the quality of work produced.	1	2	3	4	5	6
24. ask people about ways to improve the work produced.	1	2	3	4	5	6
25. follow up suggestions for improvement.	1	2	3	4	5	6

The leader(s) in this organization (people at the highest level):

26. set examples of quality performance in their day to day activities.	1	2	3	4	5	6

Legend: (1) strongly disagree, (2) disagree, (3) somewhat disagree, (4) somewhat agree, (5) agree, and (6) strongly agree.

	Strongly Disagree					*Strongly Agree*
27. regularly review the organization's progress toward meeting its goals and objectives.	1	2	3	4	5	6
28. attempt to find out why the organization may not be meeting a particular goal/objective.	1	2	3	4	5	6
People in my work unit:						
29. turn to their supervisors for advice about how to improve their work.	1	2	3	4	5	6
30. know how their supervisors will help them find answers to problems they may be having.	1	2	3	4	5	6
31. are challenged by their supervisors to find ways to improve the system.	1	2	3	4	5	6
The supervisors in my work unit:						
32. make the continuous improvement of our work top priority.	1	2	3	4	5	6
33. regularly ask our customers about the quality of work they receive.	1	2	3	4	5	6
34. The structure of our organization makes it easy to focus on quality.	1	2	3	4	5	6
35. The way we do things in this organization is consistent with quality.	1	2	3	4	5	6

Legend: (1) strongly disagree, (2) disagree, (3) somewhat disagree, (4) somewhat agree, (5) agree, and (6) strongly agree.

	Strongly Disagree					*Strongly Agree*
36. People in my work unit understand how a quality emphasis leads to more productive use of resources.	1	2	3	4	5	6
37. People in my work unit can describe the organization's quality and productivity policy.	1	2	3	4	5	6
38. People in my work unit believe that quality and productivity improvement is their responsibility.	1	2	3	4	5	6
39. People in my work unit take pride in their work.	1	2	3	4	5	6
40. People in my work unit share responsibility for the success or failure of our services/products.	1	2	3	4	5	6
41. People in my work unit believe that their work is important to the success of the overall organization.	1	2	3	4	5	6
42. We have good relationships between departments in this organization.	1	2	3	4	5	6
43. Co-workers in this organization cooperate with each other to get the job done.	1	2	3	4	5	6
44. A spirit of cooperation and teamwork exists in this organization.	1	2	3	4	5	6
45. We have good relationships with other organizations that we work with.	1	2	3	4	5	6

Legend: (1) strongly disagree, (2) disagree, (3) somewhat disagree, (4) somewhat agree, (5) agree, and (6) strongly agree.

	Strongly Disagree					*Strongly Agree*
46. Supervisors in my work unit request employee opinions and data.	1	2	3	4	5	6
47. People in my work unit are involved in improving our services/products/work.	1	2	3	4	5	6
48. We have the appropriate personnel in my work unit to get the job done properly.	1	2	3	4	5	6
49. The work goals or standards in my work unit are generally fair.	1	2	3	4	5	6
50. The supervisors in my work unit do a good job of setting work expectations.	1	2	3	4	5	6
51. People in my work unit are friendly with one another.	1	2	3	4	5	6
52. People in my work unit enjoy their co-workers.	1	2	3	4	5	6
53. We have the right tools, equipment, and materials in my work unit to get the job done.	1	2	3	4	5	6
54. The materials and supplies we need in my work unit are delivered on time as ordered.	1	2	3	4	5	6
55. The distribution of work among the people in my work unit is well-balanced.	1	2	3	4	5	6

Legend: (1) strongly disagree, (2) disagree, (3) somewhat disagree, (4) somewhat agree, (5) agree, and (6) strongly agree.

	Strongly Disagree					*Strongly Agree*
56. In my work unit, we have enough time to perform our jobs in a professional manner.	1	2	3	4	5	6
57. My work unit is structured properly to get the job done.	1	2	3	4	5	6
58. People in my work unit are rewarded for good work.	1	2	3	4	5	6
59. People in my work unit are paid fairly for the work that they do.	1	2	3	4	5	6
60. Attempts are made to promote the people in my work unit who do good work.	1	2	3	4	5	6
61. People in my work unit receive promotions because they have earned them.	1	2	3	4	5	6
62. Supervisors in my work unit give credit to people when they do a good job.	1	2	3	4	5	6
63. There are penalties for people in my work unit.	1	2	3	4	5	6
64. There is quick recognition for people in my work unit for outstanding performance by an individual or team.	1	2	3	4	5	6
65. People in my work unit know who their customers are.	1	2	3	4	5	6
66. People in my work unit care about our customers.	1	2	3	4	5	6

Legend: (1) strongly disagree, (2) disagree, (3) somewhat disagree, (4) somewhat agree, (5) agree, and (6) strongly agree.

	Strongly Disagree					*Strongly Agree*
67. There are effective communication channels between departments in this organization.	1	2	3	4	5	6
68. People in my work unit do not have to rely on "the grapevine" or rumors for information.	1	2	3	4	5	6
69. People in my work unit have ample opportunity to exchange information with their supervisors.	1	2	3	4	5	6
70. People in my work unit get the facts and the information they need to do a good job.	1	2	3	4	5	6

ASSESSMENT OF PROCESSES

The statements in the following sections are varied in format. In each case, circle the response number to the right of each statement that most closely represents the extent of your perception about your organization.

	Yes	*No*	*Not Sure*
This organization has:			
71. used surveys of some/all of its members in order to determine whether improvements in quality are needed.	2	1	1
72. used formal interviews with some/all of its members in order to determine whether improvements in quality are needed.	2	1	1

	Yes	No	Not Sure
73. informally asked some/all of its members for their opinions about whether improvements in quality are needed.	2	1	1
74. asked senior management people for their opinions about whether improvements in quality are needed.	2	1	1
75. analyzed data concerning goal/objective accomplishments in order to determine whether improvements in quality are needed.	2	1	1
76. relied on "higher order" directives in order to determine whether improvements in quality are needed.	2	1	1
77. asked established team members to report periodically.	2	1	1

This organization is (or might become) committed to quality improvement because:

78. we are mandated to do so by a higher authority.	2	1	1
79. the people at the top level of this organization are/were dissatisfied with the quality being achieved.	2	1	1
80. we want to improve an already acceptable quality record.	2	1	1
81. we want to maintain a specified level of service in the face of budget reductions.	2	1	1

	Yes	*No*	*Not Sure*
82. the people we serve deserve our best efforts.	2	1	1

	Yes	*No*	*Don't Have Policy*
This organization has a quality improvement policy that:			
83. is written.	2	1	1
84. has specific goals and objectives.	2	1	1
85. everyone in the organization has seen.	2	1	1
86. is taken seriously by people.	2	1	1
87. holds people accountable for success/failure.	2	1	1

	Yes	*No*	*Does Not Apply*
Responsibility for quality performance improvement:			
88. is accepted by senior management.	2	1	1
89. is accepted by middle management.	2	1	1
90. is accepted by almost all organizational members.	2	1	1
91. This organization has a separately identified office that oversees its quality improvement efforts.	2	1	1

	Yes	No	Does Not Apply
92. Quality improvement concerns are discussed/monitored at least on a quarterly basis.	2	1	1
93. Managers at all levels have clearly defined roles in our quality improvement process.	2	1	1
94. This organization uses teams to monitor quality improvement projects.	2	1	1
95. Managers at all levels are responsible for the success or failure of our quality improvement efforts.	2	1	1
96. This organization has a database or tracking system for relevant quality information.	2	1	1

	Yes	No	Not Sure
In order to determine what our customers think about our products/services work, we:			
97. conduct surveys on a regular basis.	2	1	1
98. ask them informally.	2	1	1
99. monitor complaints.	2	1	1
100. ask our employees who have contact with our customers.	2	1	1
The leaders at the top level in this organization:			
101. have agreed upon a definition of quality improvement.	2	1	1

	Yes	No	Not Sure
102. have set long-term goals concerning quality improvement.	2	1	1
103. have set short-term objectives concerning quality improvement.	2	1	1
104. have defined performance measures to monitor progress toward reaching objectives and goals.	2	1	1

	Almost None					Almost All
How many work units within this organization:						
105. know how the organization defines quality improvement?	1	2	3	4	5	6
106. have set long-term goals concerning quality improvement?	1	2	3	4	5	6
107. have set short-term objectives concerning quality improvement?	1	2	3	4	5	6
108. have defined performance measures to monitor progress toward reaching their objectives and goals?	1	2	3	4	5	6
How many organizational members:						
109. can specify, if asked, what goals or objectives they are working toward?	1	2	3	4	5	6
110. were invited to participate in setting goals or objectives related to their work?	1	2	3	4	5	6

Legend: (1) almost none, (2) very few, (3) some, (4) quite a few, (5) most, and (6) almost all.

	Almost None					*Almost All*
111. know how the goals/objectives they are working toward relate to their work unit's mission?	1	2	3	4	5	6
112. know how performance measures relate to monitoring their accomplishment of goals and objectives?	1	2	3	4	5	6

Legend: (1) almost none, (2) very few, (3) some, (4) quite a few, (5) most, and (6) almost all.

	Yes	*No*	*Not Sure*
Long-range planning in this organization includes:			
113. integration of quality improvement planning into general business planning.	2	1	1
114. prioritizing quality improvement issues.	2	1	1
115. customer input.	2	1	1
116. employee input.	2	1	1
117. quality improvement implementation strategies for all work units.	2	1	1
118. a means for monitoring quality improvement effectiveness over time.	2	1	1

In terms of setting organizational improvement priorities, we have considered or evaluated:

119. changing our business strategy.	2	1	1
120. improving our work methods or procedures.	2	1	1
121. bettering our employee utilization.	2	1	1

	Yes	*No*	*Not Sure*
122. revising or instituting training programs.	2	1	1
123. acquiring recent technological improvements (equipment, materials).	2	1	1

	Strongly Disagree					*Strongly Agree*
124. The structure of this organization supports its efforts to carry out its mission.	1	2	3	4	5	6
125. Organizational members have the information they need to do their work.	1	2	3	4	5	6
126. This organization has a realistic schedule for replacing outdated equipment.	1	2	3	4	5	6
127. Organizational members have been adequately trained to use the equipment they have.	1	2	3	4	5	6
128. Before equipment is bought by or issued to this organization, plans have been made concerning how it will be used and who will use it.	1	2	3	4	5	6
129. Efforts are made to update work methods in this organization (e.g., the way work is organized and the tools or materials used to accomplish it).	1	2	3	4	5	6

Legend: (1) strongly disagree, (2) disagree, (3) somewhat disagree, (4) somewhat agree, (5) agree, and (6) strongly agree.

	Strongly Disagree					*Strongly Agree*
130. People in charge of similar work units frequently share information about their work methods and practices.	1	2	3	4	5	6
131. Updating work methods can be the key to quality improvement.	1	2	3	4	5	6

Organization members with good ideas are likely to:

132. formally submit them through a suggestion system.	1	2	3	4	5	6
133. tell their supervisors.	1	2	3	4	5	6
134. be asked periodically what they think.	1	2	3	4	5	6

	Yes	*No*	*Not Sure*
135. This organization has a suggestion program.	2	1	1
136. This organization has conducted "brainstorming" sessions that included lower-level organizational members.	2	1	1
137. This organization has used teams to gather information or solve problems.	2	1	1

	Strongly Disagree					*Strongly Agree*
138. Creative thinking is rewarded in this organization.	1	2	3	4	5	6

Legend: (1) strongly disagree, (2) disagree, (3) somewhat disagree, (4) somewhat agree, (5) agree, and (6) strongly agree.

	Strongly Disagree					*Strongly Agree*
139. Taking risks is rewarded in this organization.	1	2	3	4	5	6
140. Managers at all levels have the authority to try a promising new approach.	1	2	3	4	5	6
141. A promising new approach is likely to be approved quickly for a trial.	1	2	3	4	5	6
142. The future strength of this organization is dependent on the continuing growth of its members through appropriate training.	1	2	3	4	5	6

Legend: (1) strongly disagree, (2) disagree, (3) somewhat disagree, (4) somewhat agree, (5) agree, and (6) strongly agree.

143. Circle the response number next to the *one* statement that best represents your organization.

Most nonsupervisory members have direct input in setting goals or expectations for their work. 6

Most nonsupervisory members have indirect input through representatives in setting goals or expectations for their work. 4

Most nonsupervisory members can negotiate with management after they are assigned goals or expectations for their work. 3

Most nonsupervisory members have no input about goals or expectations for their work. 1

144. Circle the response number next to the *one* statement that best represents your organization.

Most organizational members attend mandatory in-house training programs to learn about quality improvement techniques. 6

Most organizational members attend in-house training programs on a voluntary basis to learn about quality improvement techniques. 5

Most organizational members attend outside seminars to learn about quality improvement techniques.	4
Most organizational members review resources (books, tapes) that are available in-house to learn about quality improvement techniques.	3
None of the above.	1

	Yes	*No*	*Not Sure*
In order to tell how well we are doing as an organization, we monitor data about:			
145. our efficiency.	2	1	1
146. our effectiveness.	2	1	1
147. our productivity.	2	1	1
148. the quality of our services/products/work.	2	1	1
149. the timeliness of our work.	2	1	1
150. our innovativeness.	2	1	1
151. the quality of working life for our members.	2	1	1
152. our finances.	2	1	1

	Yes	*No*	*Don't Collect Data*
The performance data that this organization collects:			
153. are tracked over time.	2	1	1
154. are compared with goals, standards, or objectives.	2	1	1
155. are compared with other similar organizations.	2	1	1

	Yes	No	Don't Collect Data
The performance data that this organization collects:			
156. are evaluated at least quarterly.	2	1	1
157. are used to identify problems/ barriers.	2	1	1
158. are evaluated by a team or task force.	2	1	1
159. are used to identify opportunities for quality improvement.	2	1	1

	Yes	No	Not Sure
160. Organizational members are informed about how this work unit stands in relation to goals, objectives, or standards.	2	1	1
Top-performing managers at all levels in this organization:			
161. can expect a monetary bonus or award.	2	1	1
162. can expect an award.	2	1	1
163. can expect to be recognized by leaders at the top level.	2	1	1
164. can expect to be told they are doing a great job.	2	1	1
165. can expect increased responsibility.	2	1	1
Top-performing organizational members:			
166. can expect a monetary bonus or award.	2	1	1

	Yes	*No*	*Not Sure*
167. can expect an award.	2	1	1
168. can expect to be recognized by leaders at the top level.	2	1	1
169. can expect to be told they are doing a great job.	2	1	1
170. can expect increased responsibility.	2	1	1
171. The performance appraisals (non-Deming organizations) of managers at all levels include quality improvement criteria.	2	1	1
172. The performance appraisals (non-Deming organizations) of organizational members include quality improvement criteria.	2	1	1

MANAGEMENT TOOLS ASSESSMENT

	Yes	*No*	*Not Sure*
This organization has:			
173. used surveys to assess employee opinion about the organization's practices or policies.	2	1	1
174. used surveys to gather information about what in the organization needs improving.	2	1	1
175. used surveys to assess the outcomes of its work.	2	1	1

	Yes	*No*	*Not Sure*
176. used surveys to assess the quality of its work.	2	1	1
177. used surveys to assess employee opinions about the goals/objectives they are working toward.	2	1	1
178. called groups of individuals together to define or clarify the organization's mission and/or work.	2	1	1
179. called groups of individuals together to define long-term organizational-level goals and/or long-term work unit-level goals.	2	1	1
180. called groups of individuals together to define short-term organizational objectives and/or short-term work unit objectives.	2	1	1
181. called groups of individuals together to identify obstacles to goal/objective accomplishment.	2	1	1
182. called groups of individuals together to define performance measures to track progress toward goal attainment.	2	1	1
183. The organization uses statistical process-control charts or graphs to track data over time.	2	1	1
184. This organization uses diagrams or flow charts to highlight potential causes of problems.	2	1	1

	Yes	No	Not Sure
185. This organization has evaluated its office and work space design.	2	1	1
186. This organization has a high-quality information resource library.	2	1	1
187. This organization has arranged workshops to promote quality awareness among its members.	2	1	1
188. This organization has published newsletters containing quality improvement information.	2	1	1
189. This organization has posted information on bulletin boards about quality improvement.	2	1	1
190. This organization has held contests to reward the "most improved" work units.	2	1	1
191. This organization has attempted to inform and involve everyone in quality improvement.	2	1	1
192. This organization has used team building (techniques to improve group member relationships).	2	1	1
193. This organization has established improvement teams (groups of individuals who come together to solve quality-related problems).	2	1	1

ORGANIZATIONAL ASSESSMENT

	Strongly Disagree					*Strongly Agree*
194. Work delays are uncommon in this organization.	1	2	3	4	5	6
195. Once a job or project gets started, it's usually finished without undue delay.	1	2	3	4	5	6
196. There is little wastage of materials and supplies.	1	2	3	4	5	6
197. People make efforts to reuse or salvage excess materials and supplies whenever possible.	1	2	3	4	5	6
198. Tools and/or equipment are maintained and operated at peak efficiency.	1	2	3	4	5	6
199. Our tools and/or equipment rarely require repair.	1	2	3	4	5	6
200. This organization has sufficient personnel to accomplish its mission.	1	2	3	4	5	6
201. The personnel turnover rate is low.	1	2	3	4	5	6
202. Working conditions (noise, heat, light, dirt) in this organization are excellent.	1	2	3	4	5	6
203. Work facilities (bathrooms, cafeterias, conference rooms, etc.) are excellent.	1	2	3	4	5	6

Legend: (1) strongly disagree, (2) disagree, (3) somewhat disagree, (4) somewhat agree, (5) agree, and (6) strongly agree.

	Strongly Disagree					*Strongly Agree*
204. Organizational members are well trained.	1	2	3	4	5	6
205. Organizational members receive the guidance and assistance they need to accomplish their work.	1	2	3	4	5	6
206. This organization's materials and supplies are well accounted for without unexplained losses.	1	2	3	4	5	6
207. This organization's materials and supplies meet quality specifications.	1	2	3	4	5	6
Organizational members rarely need to:						
208. shift work priorities in order to get jobs done.	1	2	3	4	5	6
209. rework a job or task.	1	2	3	4	5	6
The organization's customers:						
210. are satisfied with the quality of our work.	1	2	3	4	5	6
211. seldom complain.	1	2	3	4	5	6
The organization's customers:						
212. are satisfied with the quantity of our work.	1	2	3	4	5	6
213. are satisfied with the timeliness of our work.	1	2	3	4	5	6

Legend: (1) strongly disagree, (2) disagree, (3) somewhat disagree, (4) somewhat agree, (5) agree, and (6) strongly agree.

	Strongly Disagree					*Strongly Agree*
The organization's customers:						
214. find minimal errors in our work.	1	2	3	4	5	6
215. find our work consistent.	1	2	3	4	5	6

Legend: (1) strongly disagree, (2) disagree, (3) somewhat disagree, (4) somewhat agree, (5) agree, and (6) strongly agree.

SCORING SELF-ASSESSMENT

The following scoring worksheets provide a way to evaluate your self-assessment. Transfer the value of your responses to the questions or sets of questions, as indicated by the worksheet groupings, then divide the number shown on the form. Carry out the division to two decimal points. For example, say you responded "6," "5," "4," "3," "2," and "1" to Climate questions 1 through 6, respectively. On the Climate Scoring Worksheet you would write "21" in the blank for Awareness of Strategic Challenge, divide 21 by 6 (the value indicated), then write "3.50" in the blank in the Your Score column. A scoring summary table, which shows the target score for each category, follows each worksheet. Transfer the worksheet scores to the corresponding category in the table. In our example, you would write "3.50" in the Your Score column next to the Awareness of Strategic Challenge category.

By comparing your scores with the target scores, you can evaluate how you and your organization perceive quality. If your score is equal to or lower than a target score, you need to improve your approach to quality in that area. Review the "Quality First" principles and practices described in Chapter 7 to discover ways you can significantly improve your quality.

Climate Scoring Worksheet

		Your Score
Awareness of Strategic Challenge	Add response numbers from questions 1–6 and place total in space at right.	___ ÷ 6 = ___
Vision for the Future	Add response numbers from questions 7–11 and place total in space at right.	___ ÷ 5 = ___
Innovation	Add response numbers from questions 12–13 and place total in space at right.	___ ÷ 2 = ___
Quality Policy/ Philosophy	Add response numbers from questions 14–18 and place total in space at right.	___ ÷ 5 = ___
Value Systems/ Ethics	Add response numbers from questions 19–21 and place total in space at right.	___ ÷ 3 = ___
Strategic Focus =	Total of scores (questions 1–21)	___ ÷ 21 = ___
Top Management Involvement	Add response numbers from questions 22–25 and place total in space at right.	___ ÷ 4 = ___
Visible Commitment to Goals	Add response numbers from questions 26–28 and place total in space at right.	___ ÷ 3 = ___

		Your Score
Role in Quality Improvement Process	Add response numbers from questions 29–31 and place total in space at right.	___ ÷ 3 = ___
Concern for Improvement	Add response numbers from questions 32–33 and place total in spaces at right.	___ ÷ 2 = ___
Systems/ Structure for Quality Improvement	Add response numbers from questions 34–35 and place total in space at right.	___ ÷ 2 = ___
Leadership and Management =	Total of scores (questions 22–35)	___ ÷ 14 = ___
Awareness of Quality Issues	Add response numbers from questions 36–37 and place total in space at right.	___ ÷ 2 = ___
Attitudes/ Morale	Add response numbers from questions 38–41 and place total in space at right.	___ ÷ 4 = ___
Cooperation	Add response numbers from questions 42–45 and place total in space at right.	___ ÷ 4 = ___
Involvement	Add response numbers from questions 46–47 and place total in space at right.	___ ÷ 2 = ___

		Your Score
Perceptions of Work Environment	Add response numbers from questions 48–50 and place total in space at right.	___ ÷ 3 = ___
Social Interactions	Add response numbers from questions 51–52 and place total in space at right.	___ ÷ 2 = ___
Task Characteristics	Add response numbers from questions 53–57 and place total in space at right.	___ ÷ 5 = ___
Consequential Constraints	Add response numbers from questions 58–64 and place total in space at right.	___ ÷ 7 = ___
Work Force =	Total of scores (questions 36–64)	___ ÷ 29 = ___
Customer Orientation	Add response numbers from questions 65–66 and place total in space at right.	___ ÷ 2 = ___
Communi-cations	Add response numbers from questions 67–70 and place total in space at right.	___ ÷ 4 = ___

Copy the result for each category to the corresponding space in Table 6–1, 6–2, 6–3 or 6–4, respectively. If any score is *lower* than the target score it means that some practices typically considered helpful for quality may be absent in your organization.

TABLE 6–1
Summary of Climate Scores

Category	Your Score*	Target Score
Awareness of Strategic Challenge	______	3.50
Vision for the Future	______	3.50
Innovation	______	3.50
Quality Policy/Philosophy	______	3.50
Value System/Ethics	______	3.50
Top Management Involvement	______	3.50
Visible Commitment to Goals	______	3.50
Role in Quality Improvement Process	______	3.50
Concern for Improvement	______	3.50
Systems/Structure for Quality Improvement	______	3.50
Awareness of Productivity/Quality Issues	______	3.50
Attitudes/Morale	______	3.50
Cooperation	______	3.50
Involvement	______	3.50
Perceptions of Work Environment	______	3.50
Social Interactions	______	3.50
Task Characteristics	______	3.50
Consequential Constraints	______	3.50
Customer Orientation	______	3.50
Communications	______	3.50
TOTAL (average your score by adding the values in this column and dividing by 20)	______	3.50

* From the Climate Scoring Worksheet

Process Scoring Worksheet

Your Score

Job Analysis — Add response numbers from questions 71–77 and place total in space at right. ___ ÷ 7 = ___

		Your Score
Higher Authority	Add response numbers from questions 78–82 and place total in space at right.	___ ÷ 5 = ___
Quality Emphasis	Add response numbers from questions 83–87 and place total in space at right.	___ ÷ 5 = ___
Top Management Leadership	Add response numbers from questions 88–96 and place total in space at right.	___ ÷ 9 = ___
Customer/ Service Activities	Add response numbers from questions 97–100 and place total in space at right.	___ ÷ 4 = ___
Define Improvement	Add response numbers from questions 101–104 and place total in space at right.	___ ÷ 4 = ___
Unit Goals	Add response numbers from questions 105–108 and place total in space at right.	___ ÷ 4 = ___
Organization Goals	Add response numbers from questions 109–112 and place total in space at right.	___ ÷ 4 = ___
Quality Planning	Add response numbers from questions 113–118 and place total in space at right.	___ ÷ 6 = ___

		Your Score
Planning Strategy	Add response numbers from questions 119–123 and place total in space at right.	___ ÷ 5 = ___
Organizational Streamlining	Add response numbers from questions 124–125 and place total in space at right.	___ ÷ 2 = ___
Investment/ Appropriate Technology	Add response numbers from questions 126–128 and place total in space at right.	___ ÷ 3 = ___
Methods/ Process Improvement	Add response numbers from questions 129–131 and place total in space at right.	___ ÷ 3 = ___
New Ideas	Add response numbers from questions 132–134 and place total in space at right.	___ ÷ 3 = ___
People-Oriented Input	Add response numbers from questions 135–137 and place total in space at right.	___ ÷ 3 = ___
Track Progress	Add response numbers from questions 138–144 and place total in space at right.	___ ÷ 7 = ___
Measurement	Add response numbers from questions 145–152 and place total in space at right.	___ ÷ 8 = ___

		Your Score
Feedback	Add response numbers from questions 153–155 and place total in space at right.	___ ÷ 3 = ___
Evaluation	Add response numbers from questions 156–159 and place total in space at right.	___ ÷ 4 = ___
Results	Place response number from question 160 in space at right.	___ = ___
Awards	Add response numbers from questions 161–170 and place total in space at right.	___ ÷ 10 = ___
Personnel Evaluations	Add response numbers from questions 171–172 and place total in space at right.	___ ÷ 2 = ___

Copy the result for each process category to the corresponding space in Table 6–2. After you have placed your scores in the appropriate spaces, please refer to the adjacent column for score interpretation. Next to each category, if your score is *lower* than or equal to the target score, you need to review your quality program.

Management Tools Scoring Worksheet

		Your Score
Assessments	Add response numbers from questions 173–177 and place total in space at right.	___ ÷ 5 = ___

TABLE 6–2
Summary of Process Scores

Category	Your Score*	Target Score
Job Analysis	______	1.50
Higher Authority	______	1.50
Quality Emphasis	______	1.70
Top Management Leadership	______	1.55
Customer/Service Activities	______	1.60
Define Improvement	______	1.60
Unit Goals	______	3.50
Organization Goals	______	3.50
Quality Planning	______	1.50
Planning Strategy	______	1.50
Organizational Streamlining	______	3.50
Investment/Appropriate Technology	______	3.50
Methods/Process Improvement	______	3.50
New Ideas	______	3.50
People-Oriented Input	______	1.40
Track Progress	______	3.50
Measurement	______	1.50
Feedback	______	1.40
Evaluation	______	1.50
Results	______	1.00
Awards	______	1.50
Personnel Evaluations	______	1.50
TOTAL (average your score by adding the values in this column and dividing by 22)	______	2.12

*From the Process Scoring Worksheet

		Your Score
Definition of Tools	Add response numbers from questions 178–182 and place total in space at right.	___ ÷ 5 = ___

		Your Score
Measurement/ Process Analysis	Add response numbers from questions 183–185 and place total in space at right.	___ ÷ 3 = ___
Awareness/ Communi-cation	Add response numbers from questions 186–190 and place total in space at right.	___ ÷ 5 = ___
Organizational Development	Add response numbers from questions 191–193 and place total in space at right.	___ ÷ 3 = ___

Copy the result for each management tools category to the corresponding space in Table 6–3. After you have placed your scores in the appropriate spaces, please refer to the adjacent column for score interpretation. Next to each category, if your score is *lower* than or equal to the target score, you may want to review your quality program.

TABLE 6–3
Summary of Management Tools Scores

Category	Your Score*	Target Score
Assessments	______	1.30
Definition of Tools	______	1.50
Measurement/Process Analysis	______	1.50
Awareness/Communication	______	1.50
Organizational Development	______	1.50
TOTAL (average your score by adding the values in this column and dividing by 5)	______	1.46

*From the Management Tools Scoring Worksheet

Organizational Outcomes Scoring Worksheet

		Your Score
Work Flow/ Delays	Add response numbers from questions 194–195 and place total in space at right.	___ ÷ 2 = ___
Waste	Add response numbers from questions 196–197 and place total in space at right.	___ ÷ 2 = ___
Tools/ Equipment	Add response numbers from questions 198–199 and place total in space at right.	___ ÷ 2 = ___
Staffing	Add response numbers from questions 200–201 and place total in space at right.	___ ÷ 2 = ___
Facilities	Add response numbers from questions 202–203 and place total in space at right.	___ ÷ 2 = ___
Training	Add response numbers from questions 204–205 and place total in space at right.	___ ÷ 2 = ___
Supplies/Parts	Add response numbers from questions 206–207 and place total in space at right.	___ ÷ 2 = ___
Organization/ Group Structure	Add response numbers from questions 208–209 and place total in space at right.	___ ÷ 2 = ___

		Your Score
Customer Quality Survey	Add response numbers from questions 210–211 and place total in space at right.	___ ÷ 2 = ___
Quantity	Add response numbers from questions 212–213 and place total in space at right.	___ ÷ 2 = ___
Reliability	Add response numbers from questions 214–215 and place total in space at right.	___ ÷ 2 = ___

Copy the result for each organizational outcome category to the corresponding space in Table 6–4. If any score is *lower* than or equal to 3.50; you need to review your quality approach.

COMPUTERIZED ANALYSIS

This chapter is an edited version of the "Quality and Productivity Self-Assessment Guide." If you want to have more members of your company conduct this type of self-examination and compare your impressions of your perceived level of quality, consider purchasing an automated version of the analysis, available for use on IBM PC-compatible equipment. The software can be obtained from DPPO, Two Skyline Place, Room 1404, 5203 Leesburg Pike, Falls Church, Virginia 22041, (703) 756-3246. Contact Jack Denslow for the price and availability of the latest version of the software.

ASSESSMENT LEADS TO ACTION

This chapter has presented an "arm-chair" approach for self-assessment of your organization's perceived level of quality. It has provided a scoring methodology that alerts you to the

TABLE 6–4
Summary of Organization Outcomes Scores

Category	Your Score*	Target Score
Work Flow/Delays	______	3.50
Waste	______	3.50
Tools/Equipment	______	3.50
Staffing	______	3.50
Facilities	______	3.50
Training	______	3.50
Supplies/Parts	______	3.50
Organzation/Group Structure	______	3.50
Customer Quality Survey	______	3.50
Quantity	______	3.50
Reliability	______	3.50
TOTAL (average your score by adding the values in this column and dividing by 11)	______	3.50

* From the Organizational Outcomes Scoring Worksheet

strengths and weaknesses in your quality efforts. The total scores are really not important. But how you responded to each category and the impression you now have about the potential to improve your quality, your service, and your profitability is very important.

The next chapter provides the key "Quality First" principles and practices that you can apply to your business to significantly improve your quality.

Chapter Seven

How to Significantly Improve Your Quality

"A journey of a thousand miles must begin with a single step."

The Way of Lao Tzu

ADOPT "QUALITY FIRST" STRATEGY

"Quality First" means that you are meeting your customer requirements by doing the right things right the first time. To provide high-quality products and services, management must believe that an obsession for quality and excellence must pervade all facets of a business, from customer input to product design and engineering, production, service support, and human resource management. The driving force behind "Quality First" is customer satisfaction.

"Quality First" begins with a strategic decision—a decision that must be made and fully supported by top management. That decision, simply put, is the decision to compete as a world-class company. "Quality First" concentrates on quality performance—in every facet of a business—as the primary strategy to achieve and maintain competitive advantage. It requires taking a systematic view of an organization and looking at how each part interrelates to the whole process. In addition, it demands continuous improvement as a way of life.

The "Quality First" methodology is built on four imperatives. These imperatives simply state that an organization must have quality management systems; quality products, services, and technology; quality people; and that the combined energies of its management, products, and people must be focused on customer satisfaction.

"Quality First" provides a framework for your application of its concepts, principles, and practices in terms of your specific needs. "Quality First" is the integration and synergy of leading quality initiatives developed by Crosby, Deming, and Juran, which have also been presented in the Total Quality Management programs promoted by the U.S. government.

"QUALITY FIRST" CONCEPTS AND PRINCIPLES

Getting started with improvement would be easy if you didn't have so much work to do! But you have so much work to do precisely because you have not recognized the importance of "Quality First" and the benefits of continuously improving every system and process. You must get your systems under control and eliminate the sources of unnecessary and unproductive work.

Getting started and sustaining the early quality-improvement initiative is the most difficult task in "Quality First." It requires you to make time in your already tight schedule to do something that you perceive to be an additional task. You must modify many of your long-held notions about what good management is all about in exchange for the promise of improvement. It is surprising that anyone is willing to take these first steps; however, many have already done so and are being richly rewarded. By ultimately gaining real control over your work processes instead of permitting them to control you, you will make large gains.

Those who have blazed the trail toward continuous improvement have left a legacy of many lessons learned. Many have had false starts, traveled down dead-end roads, and had to start over. If there is one consistent lesson from those who have led this effort, it is that there is no universal strategy for success. The road to continuous improvement is and must be an appropriately tailored, optimized, and personal one. A general behavior and set of actions, however, characterize most successful efforts. That behavior and those actions are presented here as a suggested general strategy for starting your "Quality First" journey.

While this section speaks directly to you, most behavior and many actions apply equally to your organization as a whole. The elements of this general strategy are listed roughly in order of recommended implementation. The experience of many organizations is that focused application of specific improvement techniques and tools promotes continuous improvement. In this chapter, the earlier elements provide a foundation that is essential to making successful process-improvement efforts and to creating a culture of continuous improvement that will have long-term success and ultimately be self-sustaining. Some elements are necessary only during the initial phases, but most are periodic or continuous activities that should become routine, ongoing behavior by the organization or individual.

The basic elements of "Quality First" fall into 12 areas of activity: (1) demonstrate leadership, (2) build awareness, (3) improve communication, (4) continue to present your vision, (5) focus on the customer, (6) demonstrate success, (7) develop teamwork, (8) provide support, training, and education, (9) build trust and respect, (10) create a "Quality First" environment in which continuous improvement is a way of life, (11) continuously improve all processes, and (12) apply your quality improvement process to your suppliers. Each of these areas encompasses a number of actions.

Demonstrate Leadership

"Quality First" depends on people more than anything else, and people lead or are led—they are not managed. "Quality First" depends on effective leadership, and you must provide that leadership. By taking the initiative, providing an example, and showing the way, you can lead your subordinates and inspire your peers to follow your example. Top leadership is essential, but "Quality First" leaders are needed at all organizational levels. Effective "Quality First" leadership does not necessarily depend on your place in the organization but rather on your enthusiasm and your visible commitment to the process of continuous improvement.

Build Awareness

Building awareness—understanding what "Quality First" is and why it is important to you and your organization—is one of the first and perhaps most important steps in implementing "Quality First." Every person in the organization must become aware of the need to improve, of the promise offered by "Quality First," of the various "Quality First" methodologies, and of the tools and techniques available for improvement efforts. Awareness is the key that opens the door to the potential of "Quality First."

Improve Communication

As you work on building awareness throughout your organization, begin to establish lines of communication both horizontally and vertically. Honest, open communication is probably the single most important factor in successfully creating a "Quality First" environment. It will take time, but it can lead to trust and mutual respect, and can sometimes be the only thing that keeps the effort alive. If people keep talking to one another, they can work through problems, overcome barriers, and find encouragement and support from others involved in quality efforts.

Continue to Present Your Vision

Constancy of purpose establishes a common direction for all organizational elements and ensures that efforts at all levels contribute to achieving broad objectives relevant to the entire organization. Communicating your vision of the organization's goals and objectives throughout the organization is essential to focusing improvement efforts for the common benefit. Your behavior and attitudes must reinforce this constancy of purpose, and you must be conscious of the unspoken signals you send to your subordinates.

Focus on the Customer

Every process in your organization has a customer, and without a customer a process has no purpose. The customer is the recipient of the process's products or services and defines the quality of those products and services. It is only through focusing on your customers that you can truly optimize your processes, because it is only through your customers that you may effectively define your goals and objectives for improvement. You must focus on both your organization's external customers and your internal customers, who are other members of your organization that depend on your products or services for their own processes.

Demonstrate Success

The success or failure of your initial "Quality First" efforts and projects can greatly affect how easily you can get your organization to adopt "Quality First" ideas. It pays to choose these early efforts carefully, looking for opportunities that (1) have a good chance of success, (2) are visible throughout the company, and preferably, to important external customers, and (3) can significantly improve the lives of workers and managers alike. The trick is to find something that is neither so large that you are doomed to failure nor so small that no one will notice if improvements are made.

Develop Teamwork

Teamwork is the engine that drives many improvement efforts. Creating teams allows you to apply diverse skills and experience to your processes and problem solving. Teams provide an underlying basis of experience and history for your improvement effort and are a vehicle through which you allow all individuals to participate in that effort. Not only must individuals cooperate within teams, the teams must cooperate together throughout the organization. An atmosphere of teamwork should permeate your organization, affecting not only formal team efforts but also each individual's interaction in the organization.

Often, encouraging teamwork involves teaching people who already work together to consciously act as a team. These natural work groups exist as permanent teams whose objective is the continuous improvement of the processes they own.

Provide Support, Training, and Education

If you expect to implement "Quality First" yourself and expect your subordinates to follow suit, you must ensure adequate time and training resources are available to support your effort. "Quality First" does not depend on additional people or money; rather, it relies on the availability of time for individuals and groups to pursue improvement efforts, and on the availability of training and education to develop needed skills and experience in "Quality First" improvement tools and techniques. You must make those time and training resources available for yourself and your people; doing so is one way for you to demonstrate your commitment to the improvement effort.

While awareness is the way you get your "Quality First" effort moving, education and training help accelerate it dramatically. Provided in the right place at the right time, education and training allow you and your subordinates to develop skills and experience in the techniques necessary to implement "Quality First." That experience is the first step to making "Quality First" a part of your day-to-day work life. And, of course, technical training and education are essential to improving each employee's specific job skills. Education and training are comprehensive, intensive, and unending. Quality improvement efforts begin and continue with lifelong education and training.

Build Trust and Respect

Employees who trust their managers and who are trusted and respected in turn can provide the edge that organizations need to provide superior services or products. Workers have the best, most up-to-date knowledge about how well processes are working, what problems have arisen, and how things could be better. If their opinions are respected, they will share their knowledge and creativity with management—the only way to ensure continuous improvement.

Trust and respect are essential for individual participation. Without such an atmosphere, people will not take actions or make recommendations they perceive to be risky to themselves. "Quality First" is a process that depends on every person being unafraid to take chances and not worried about risking self-esteem. You must be open and honest with your people and establish channels of communication that are reliable and accessible to everyone in the organization. If people broach ideas, they should be praised; if they identify problems in the process or system, they should be thanked; when they contribute, they should be recognized; when they fail, they should be supported; and when they succeed, they should be rewarded. As their leader, you are responsible for creating an atmosphere of trust and support, and you are responsible for maintaining each individual's sense of self-worth and self-esteem.

Create a "Quality First" Environment in Which Continuous Improvement Is a Way of Life

By making continuous improvement a part of your daily routine, you will integrate it into all aspects of your work. Continuous improvement only approaches maturity when it is applied routinely to all of your organization's work. Routine application entails using the process-improvement cycle in all areas, collecting data and using those data to assess process suitability, removing roadblocks to your improvement efforts and those of others, and continuously improving your knowledge and expertise in process improvement. Ideally, continuous improvement should be your normal approach to doing your work; it must become your way of life.

Continuously Improve All Processes

Continuous process improvement, as the basis of "Quality First," is a never-ending effort. Perfection is an ultimate, unattainable goal, but its ideal is the basis for continuous improvement efforts. You must view everything your organization does in terms of interrelated processes. Process improvement should become your organization's way of life. Goals and objectives are realized through process improvement. Your own focus should be to improve all the processes you own and remove all those barriers under your control that hinder others from improving their own processes. The only true measure of your performance over time is the degree of process improvement you effect.

Process standardization is a means of defining a process and ensuring that everyone understands and employs it in a consistent manner. It is difficult to improve something that is not well-defined. Process standards communicate the current, best-known way of performing a process and ensure consistent process performance by a variety of individuals. With a standard, people have a way to know that they are doing their jobs correctly and you have a means of assessing their performance objectively. Process standards provide the baseline from which to continuously improve the process. The people doing the work should maintain and update standards as they improve their processes so that the standards always reflect the current, best-known means of doing the work.

Apply Your Quality Improvement Process to Your Suppliers

Your organization's ability to improve its processes depends in part on the inputs to those processes. To the extent that you procure materials and services from other organizations, your continuous improvement effort depends on those suppliers. Expanding your improvement culture to all your suppliers will help ensure that the quality of your process inputs is sufficient to meet your own improvement objectives. You can expand your culture of continuous improvement by working more closely with your suppliers, helping them get their own improvement efforts underway, building mutual trust and respect, and generally by becoming a better customer yourself.

QUALITY IS NOT ENOUGH

A firm's competitiveness with the company down the street, down the coast or on the other side of the world, is a composite of many factors. The quality of a firm's products or services is but one of these factors. Nonetheless there is a tendency, when trying to stress a point—such as quality—to focus one's attention on a limited number of factors. During the 1980s this is exactly what happened when the nation rediscovered quality. Business leaders tended to forget about the rest of the competitiveness equation.

Most business analysts, for example, have concentrated their attention in recent years on the benefits accruing to the American firms that adopted quality management methods in the early and mid-1980s. In particular, areas that have most benefited—quality control, delivery, and inventory turnover—were widely covered in the trade journals.

At least one major and ongoing study, however, has sounded an alarm as well. Boston University's "Beyond the Quality Revolution"* acknowledges that quality is a very important component of competitiveness in the 1990s. But, the report also raises fears that the excessive attention being given to advances in organizational and infrastructure processes in quality-managed firms may be distracting executives away from other equally important, but largely neglected, components of the competitiveness equation. These areas include teamwork, cost reduction, product development speed, and the integration of business and manufacturing strategies.

As American firms concentrate on quality, however, they are setting a low priority on other factors. These areas of neglect, if not given sufficient top-management attention, could result in self-inflicted competitive disadvantages in the future. If, while boosting our ability to compete worldwide in terms of quality we allow our standing in other areas—such as research and development—to wither, we will not have advanced our over-

*"Beyond the Quality Revolution," Jeffrey G. Miller and Jay S. Kim, Boston University, School of Management, Manufacturing Rountable, 1990.

all competitive standing in the coming years. Trading one weakness for another is hardly the way to go.

IMPROVE YOUR QUALITY

This chapter has described the concepts and principles involved in implementing the "Quality First" methodology. By tailoring these concepts and principles to your unique operation, you can significantly improve your quality, increase productivity, improve your world-class competitive position, and make more money than by doing business as usual.

The following two chapters provide an elementary road map for the planning and implementation of a "Quality First" program.

Chapter Eight

"Quality First" Planning

"Every great president in our history had a policy of his own, which eventually won the people's support."

Harry S. Truman
Memoirs—Years of Trial and Hope

TEN STEPS TO IMPLEMENTATION

American companies all too often have jumped to implement "hot" new solutions to their problems. They tend to spend too little time, thought, and energy on developing the corporate policy and planning needs to implement their actions. The Japanese, for example, spend two-thirds of their effort on building consensus, developing understanding of the clients' needs, and reviewing options for implementation. Then they think through all the steps needed to implement this change or process. In America companies tend to spend one-third of their efforts on planning, then jump into the implementation phase and continue to "fight fires" to resolve the errors and inconsistencies that with proper planning they could have avoided. The concept of doing things right the first time depends on realistic, thorough planning.

This chapter on planning, and Chapter 9 on implementation of your "Quality First" effort, form a unit. Described in these two chapters are a total of 17 planning and implementation steps for your review, modification, and adoption in your own unique "Quality First" program.

This chapter describes the 10 planning steps (see Figure 8–1) needed to help you identify your policy and plans for implementing a "Quality First" program in your company.

Step 1. Top Management Commitment to "Quality First"

Simply put, "Quality First" is a new way for companies to do business. Since the methods by which a company conducts its business are clearly the prerogative of top management, it is, therefore, top management that must be convinced of the merits of "Quality First." Top management's recognition of the need for improvement and its willingness to learn more are the first steps toward implementation.

It is probably not possible to overstate the importance of the role of top management. Leadership is essential during every phase in the development of your company's "Quality First" program, and is particularly vital at the initial stages of planning. In fact, indifference and lack of involvement by top management are frequently cited as the principal reasons for the failure of quality improvement efforts.

To be successfully implemented, "Quality First" requires not only the vision, planning, and active, involved leadership of top management, it also requires such practical support as providing the resources for implementation—the time, money, and personnel needed. Delegation and rhetoric are insufficient.

John A. Betti, former Ford Motor Co. executive and former Under Secretary of Defense for Acquisition, said "commitment to quality must start at the top. But as we at Ford learned, commitment in itself is not enough. Along with commitment must be dedication and involvement. Actions, not words, produce results."

To obtain top management commitment, you need to begin to educate senior managers regarding the impact of global quality-

FIGURE 8–1
"Quality First" Planning Steps

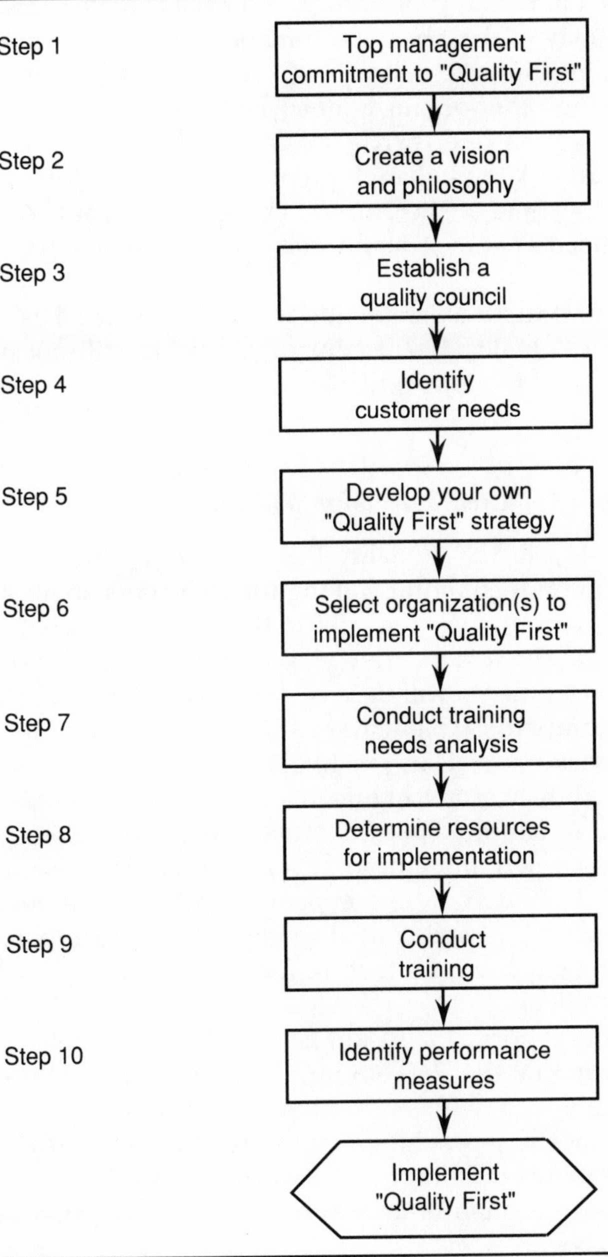

driven competitiveness; you need to encourage them to learn the basic philosophy, principles, and practices (Chapters 1, 2, and 3) involved in making your company policy "Quality First."

You may wish to host a command-performance presentation describing how "Quality First" has been successfully implemented in other organizations (see Chapter 5).

The bottom line is that top management must enthusiastically participate in changing your corporate culture. Table 8–1 identifies some of the cultural changes that your top management needs to understand and address to achieve improved quality.

Without top management's active participation as the champions of "Quality First" your organization will not obtain the full scope of benefits possible.

Step 2. Create a Vision and Philosophy

A key step in the "Quality First" process is the creation of a common understanding among top managers about what they want the company to look like in the future and what principles will guide the actions they take to achieve the desired future. These agreements will become the basis for formal statements of the company's vision and values.

The vision is a clear, positive, forceful statement of what the organization wants to be in five, and even 10 years. It is expressed in simple, specific terms. The vision allows the company to stretch and aim for a high target. The vision must be powerful enough to excite people and show them the way things can be. A well-crafted vision statement supported by action can be a powerful tool for focusing the company toward a common goal.

Whatever form the vision and guiding principles take, it is important that they be communicated throughout the company frequently and with conviction. The timing and method of communication provide an opportunity for creativity by top management. It is important that the vision be followed soon by a concrete plan of action to avoid its being dismissed as a hollow slogan.

TABLE 8–1
Examples of "Quality First" Cultural Changes

Category	Previous State	New Culture
Mission	Maximum return on investment/management by objectives (ROI/MBO)	Ethical behavior and customer satisfaction; climate for continuous improvement; ROI a performance measure
Customer Requirements	Incomplete or ambiguous understanding of customer requirements	Use of a systematic approach to seek out, understand, and satisfy both internal and external customer requirements
Suppliers	Unidirectional relationship	Partnership
Objectives	Orientation to short-term objectives and actions with limited long-term perspective	Deliberate balance of long-term goals with successive short-term objectives
Improvement	Acceptance of process variability and subsequent corrective action assigning blame as the norm	Understanding and continually improving the process
Problem Solving	Unstructured individualistic problem solving and decision making	Predominantly participative and interdisciplinary problem solving and decision making based on substantive data
Jobs and People	Functional, narrow scope; management-controlled	Management and employee involvement; work teams; integrated functions
Management Style	Management style with uncertain objectives, which instills fear of failure	Open style with clear and consistent objectives, which encourages group-derived continuous improvement
Role of Manager	Plan, organize, assign, control, and enforce	Communicate, consult, delegate, coach, mentor, remove barriers, and establish trust
Rewards and Recognition	Pay by job; few team incentives	Individual and group recognition and rewards, negotiated criteria
Measurement	Orientation toward data-gathering for problem identification	Data used to understand and continuously improve processes

Source: Department of Defense

Step 3. Establish Quality Council

Developing an organizational structure that will institute, sustain, and facilitate expansion of your "Quality First" improvement effort is an essential element for success. The structure is the vehicle for focusing the energy and resources of the company toward one common goal—continuous improvement of the products and services it provides to your customer. Successful companies tailor the structure so that it maximizes strong points and accommodates their unique mission, culture, and approach for improving quality. This accounts for some of the differences in the way organizational charts are drawn and for variations in the nomenclature used to describe the "Quality First" organization. In spite of these differences, several common practices emerge and merit examination.

Virtually every company that has successfully introduced the "Quality First" approach has formed a quality council of top managers during the early stages of implementation. This team is also sometimes called the Executive Steering Committee (ESC), Executive Steering Group (ESG), or Executive Quality Council (EQC).

By establishing your Quality Council, top management provides identity, structure, and legitimacy to the "Quality First" improvement effort. It is the first concrete indication that top management has recognized the need to improve and has begun to change the way the organization conducts business. The direction this change will take becomes clear when the council publishes its vision, guiding principles, and mission statement.

The council is chaired by the organization head or deputy and includes membership of the top management team. The council is responsible for launching, coordinating, and overseeing the "Quality First" improvement effort.

The "AT&T Quality Improvement Process Guidebook" describes a typical Quality Council Structure, shown in Figure 8–2, that consists of:

- A Leadership Structure of Linked Councils
  The leadership structure is comprised of an Executive Quality Council, Vice President Quality Councils, and

FIGURE 8–2
Quality Council Structure

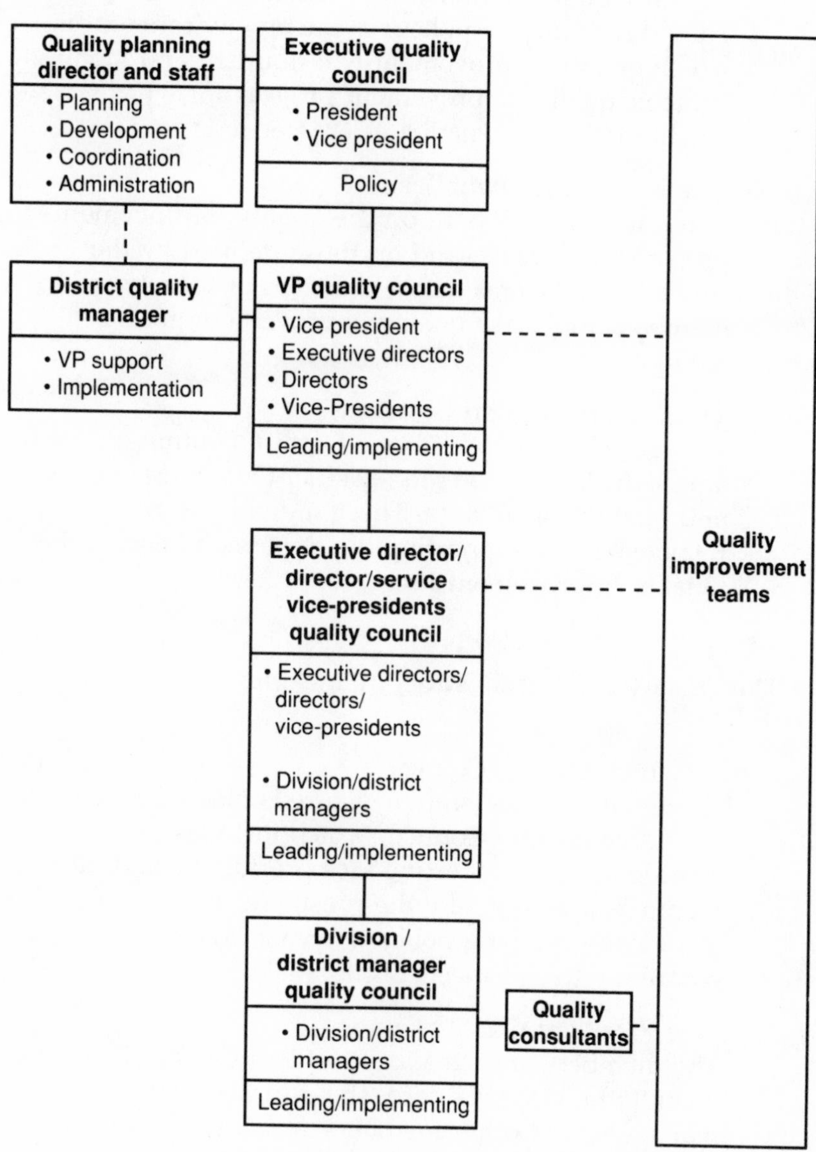

Source: Based on *AT&T, Quality Improvement Process Guidebook,* February 1988.

Quality Councils within each Vice President's unit. These interlocking councils perform the overall "Quality First" planning and management function. They direct and set policy, create an environment in which quality improvement will flourish, and identify strategic quality-improvement projects for which Quality Improvement Teams are needed.

- Quality Improvement Teams
  These teams work both on the quality improvement projects they create, and on those defined by the councils. The teams define the roles of their team members and make quality improvement goals a reality.

- The Quality Support Structure
  This group is comprised of a Quality Planning Director and staff, Vice Presidents, District Quality Managers, and quality consultants. These individuals are responsible for supporting the implementation of the Quality Improvement Process.

The Quality Leadership structure includes:

- Executive Quality Council
  The Quality Leadership Structure is headed by the Executive Quality Council, which includes the president, direct-reporting vice presidents, and other members appointed by the president. Its charter includes developing policy to create, foster, and contribute to all aspects of the quality program.

- Vice President Quality Council
  The members of each Vice President Quality Council include the vice president, the direct-reporting managers, and other members appointed by the vice president. Their charter includes ensuring the application of the "Quality First" principles throughout the vice president's area of responsibility.

- Quality Councils
  The members of the Quality Councils for organizations within a vice president's unit include the formal head of the organization (e.g., executive director, director, division, district manager), the direct-reporting managers/supervisors, and other members appointed by the organization head. Their charter includes implementing a "Quality First" concept throughout the organization and creating an environment in which quality improvement can flourish.
- All Councils are charged with establishing an environment in which quality will be improved and sustained, providing the leadership and personal involvement to guide quality management in its organization, and developing its own Quality Improvement Plan that will enable it to carry out its specific charge.

Quality Councils also can be used to link your "Quality First" company together. Vertical linkage is accomplished by having a member of a top-level Quality Council serve as chairperson of a lower-level (second tier) council. A member of that council, in turn, chairs a lower-level (third tier) council or leads a subordinate-level team. Horizontal linkage is accomplished by having members of different functional departments (e.g., manufacturing, personnel, administration, service, finance) serve together on cross-functional teams. These teams are sometimes called Quality Management Boards.

This type of Quality Council structural linkage offers a number of benefits to your company:

- It helps the organization stay focused on pursuing the same goals rather than having functional departments working at cross purposes.
- It fosters better teamwork and less internal competition.
- It improves communication throughout the

organization and better understanding of how all the pieces fit together.

- It improves the ability to replicate ideas and standardize solutions that have applicability to processes in other departments of the organization.

Step 4. Identify Customer Needs

"Quality First" means that your company is meeting your customers' expectations. Customers can be co-workers (internal customers) or end users (external customers) of your products or services.

Expectations are your customers' needs and wants. Meeting customer expectations through application of "Quality First" principles is the key to your competitive future.

The Customer/Supplier Model described in Chapter 10 is an excellent technique for determining what your customers want, need, or expect. Only by interaction between the supplier (you) and the customer can this be answered.

The Customer/Supplier Model, which was designed to analyze and help improve your customer needs analysis, involves four key steps:

- Define your process or task.
- Define your value-added contribution to that process.
- Define your customer's expectations—i.e., negotiate specific requirements and define appropriate feedback of measurements.
- Communicate with your supplier and negotiate your requirements and feedback mechanisms just as you did with your customer.

To define "requirements" and "feedback," consider:

- Requirements are the most critical key characteristics of your output as defined by your customer.
- Feedback from your customer communicates the

degree to which your output conforms to the requirements negotiated with your customer.

Taking these simple steps will significantly improve the quality of your work as it is defined by the most important person in the process: your customer.

Step 5. Develop Your Own "Quality First" Strategy

There is no *one* right way to implement "Quality First" successfully in your company, no guaranteed recipe for success. The process proposed in this book is a synthesis of approaches used successfully by companies in manufacturing and service businesses. It is offered only as a guide in developing strategies and associated plans to carry out these strategies. The intent of a flexible approach is to capitalize on a company's strong points to allow energy to be focused on key improvement opportunities.

Because the missions, cultures, and management styles of companies vary so greatly, it would be inadvisable to attempt to develop one "ideal" plan or organizational structure for implementing "Quality First." Furthermore, it would be useless to graft the experience of one organization wholesale onto another, without tailoring it to meet the unique needs of that second organization.

The best plans are those that result in action—action that improves the processes of the company and results in better services and products for the customer. A simple plan that generates action and gets results is better than an elaborate plan that collects dust. Some initial "Quality First" strategic actions might consist of specific projects designed to address system-wide problems—projects that have potential for expanding to other processes of the company; or, there might be efforts to implement "Quality First" in one organization or across the board. Examples of such efforts might include:

- Creating a team to review the "Quality First" concept and define a unique strategy for your company.
- Conducting customer surveys and feedback efforts to be reflected in quality indicators.

- Creating quality teams to address specific known operating problems.
- Defining your own quality problem-solving process.
- Defining your own "Quality First" Improvement Plan.

It is a good idea for your company to have at least begun in some key areas the process of identifying customers and their requirements, and reviewing quality indicators for products and services. This might occur in organizational components where "Quality First" will be implemented initially, or on a more wide-scale basis in anticipation of future "Quality First" implementation.

Step 6. Select Organization(s) to Implement "Quality First"

At the outset of the quality improvement effort, organizations usually choose to implement "Quality First" either organization-wide or with one or more pilots. It is also possible to tailor a combination of the two approaches to fit particular circumstances. In any case, the decision is one that each company must make after realistically assessing a number of factors, including:

- The size and complexity of the company.
- The resources (time, money, and people) that can be allocated to introduce and sustain the effort.
- The amount of resistance that can be anticipated.
- The level and intensity of support for "Quality First" throughout the organization.

Implementing "Quality First" on a broad scale across a large organization is a major undertaking. It requires significant allocations of time, money, and people, and for most companies, requires substantive operational and cultural changes. The larger the company, the more massive the change.

Some advantages to broad-scale implementation are as follows:

- It promotes consistent implementation. Each organizational element uses the same "Quality First" philosophy, language, and training, and is guided by the same vision and core principles.
- The decision to implement "Quality First" company-wide demonstrates strong commitment at the very top level of the organization. This can facilitate the removal of barriers *between* organizations.
- The "Quality First" organization structure can be cascaded throughout a company, providing linkage between the corporate headquarters and operating units for improved communications.
- It provides for economies of scale (such as when procuring consultant services, or developing in-house training support). For example, a large training contract is generally less expensive per person than a series of smaller contracts.
- It allows the company to capitalize on its staff offices to support implementation. For example, statistical specialists located at the corporate level can be used to provide technical assistance to operating units.

You would be well advised to study closely your peers' efforts (refer to Chapter 5) before undertaking a similar venture.

Some companies have found advantages to starting pilot efforts including:

- Initial expenditures of resources are less.
- Development of wholly new product/service/venture allows company to start from "green field" and create new quality culture from the start. An excellent major example is GM (General Motors Corp.) in the development, production, and marketing of their Saturn car.

- Resistance is minimized by targeting locations where local "champions" reside. Alternatively, the effort can be engineered for success by targeting locations that have demonstrated adaptability to change by participating successfully in previous pilot efforts.
- Early successes can be used to galvanize support in other parts of the organization. Skeptics can be converted by seeing that it can work in their organization.
- Early failures can be turned into lessons learned, without major disruptions throughout the parent company.
- The pilot effort can be used as a model for broad-scale implementation.
- Pilot efforts are consistent with the Plan-Do-Check-Act (PDCA) approach to improvement.
- Develop unique plan of attack for adoption of quality initiative and showcase success.

Step 7. Conduct Training Needs Analysis

Chapter 6 provides a self-assessment methodology that encourages the analysis of your perceptions of your company's quality status. This self-assessment provides a baseline analysis that can be used to identify when and where you need additional quality training.

If you examined the Malcolm Baldrige Quality Award criteria (Chapter 4) either through in-depth self-assessment or application for the award, the ongoing learning about your company's needs will also be an extremely valuable tool in improving your training.

Step 8. Determine Resources for Implementation

Your "Quality First" plan must disclose how the effort will be funded, where the required time will come from and how it is to be accounted for, who will provide what personnel, and what facilities will be used for "Quality First." Obviously, these resource decisions must be coordinated with all those affected by the decisions. This part of the plan may be the hardest to develop because "Quality First" will now be competing with other requirements for corporate resources. One must keep in mind that "Quality First" is to become a way of life in the organization, in fact, the new way of managing. In reality, "Quality First" is not competing for mission resources because it will be an integral part of the future corporate mission. This part of the plan may be the first big test of management's commitment to "Quality First." Milestones for providing the identified resources should also be included in the plan.

Step 9. Conduct Training

Training is essential to the success of your "Quality First" initiative. It is important to note that during the early stages of implementation of your "Quality First" effort, attention should be given to developing a detailed plan for training.

Ted Cocheu, writing in the January 1989 issue of *Training and Development Journal*, says:

> Quality experts . . . all agree that a comprehensive training curriculum is critical to providing everyone in the organization with the knowledge and skills to fulfill his or her quality-improvement responsibilities. Training must include:
>
> - Explaining the need for improvement as well as its individual and collective benefits.
> - Communicating the organization's quality goals.
> - Developing a common language to talk about quality-related issues.
> - Defining the structure and process through which quality improvement will take place.
> - Clarifying everyone's responsibilities.
> - Providing people with tools and techniques to manage the quality of their work.

In addition to specific "Quality First" principles and practices such as statistical quality control, continuous process improvement, benchmarking, use of data, and process analysis, most companies will also find it advisable to conduct training in such related areas as participative management, group dynamics and team development. The ideal training program will target the specific needs of each group—top management, middle managers, supervisors, and employees in various team groups—and will deliver training just at the time it is needed for smooth transition to the next step in your "Quality First" program.

All employees must understand their jobs and their roles in the company, and how their jobs will change. Such understanding goes beyond the instruction given in manuals or job descriptions. Employees need to know where their work fits into the larger context: how their work is influenced by workers who precede them and how their work influences workers who follow.

The organization's training plan should be an outgrowth of your unique "Quality First" implementation strategy, and should be directed to the organizational units or projects where top management has focused the implementation effort in the first year.

To prevent surprises and delays in implementation, the training plan must include reasonably accurate estimates of the schedule and required resources.

Step 10. Identifying Performance Measures

Earlier this book discussed measuring the success of your quality improvement efforts operationally—in terms of how your customers view you, employee satisfaction, and profitability. These measure the success of your business.

These key business-performance indicators are also critical to measuring the success of all "Quality First" activities. They are measurements that reflect the success of the quality improvement process. The objective of every "Quality First" program must be to identify performance measures for your business, then continue to improve the key measures of success.

It is also important to measure the success of the "Quality

First" process itself, and of the progress and implementation of each organization's "Quality First" Improvement Plan.

DOCUMENT YOUR "QUALITY FIRST" PLAN

Document your plan for "Quality First" adoption in your company. Create a living plan that reflects the continuous improvement of your operations and "Quality First" management efforts. Make this plan available to your managers and personnel to assure that your goals and approach are communicated throughout your company.

Chapter 9, Implementation of Quality, describes the process for implementing "Quality First" in your company.

Chapter Nine

Implementation of "Quality First"

"Practice is the best of all instructors."

Publilus Syrus
Maxim 439

IMPLEMENT YOUR "QUALITY FIRST" PLAN

This chapter delineates the seven steps to improve your quality by implementing a "Quality First" program in your company. To begin the process, the initial decision to change your emphasis to one of "Quality First" must be made and the initial planning completed as described in Chapter 8. Then, as depicted in Figure 9–1, you need to understand how your products and/or services compare with your competitors. Step 12 describes the Xerox Corporation's approach to benchmarking. Then your company must embed the continuous improvement concepts (Step 13) throughout your company. This is a major change in how your company will operate in the 1990s. Step 14 describes the need to monitor and evaluate your progress in improving your quality performance. Tell the world of your success, but more importantly let your people know

FIGURE 9–1
"Quality First" Implementation Steps

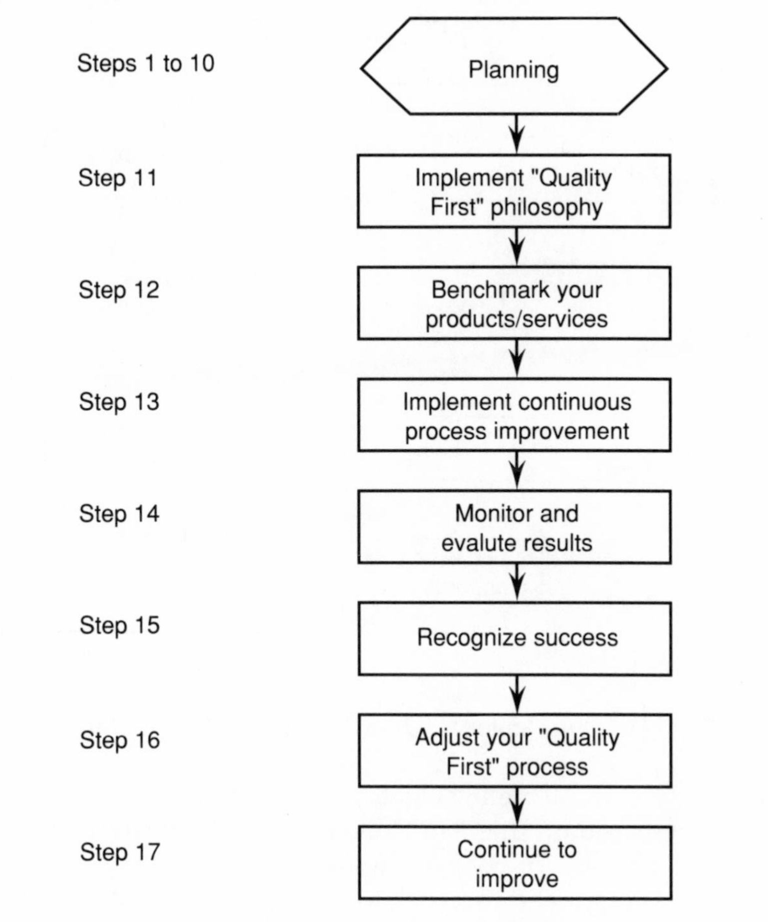

how they have contributed (Step 15) to the improved operation of your company. Recognize success! As you begin to demonstrate success and convince the doubters, you must continue to learn from feedback as to how you can do better. You must revise or adjust your "Quality First" program to meet the changing needs of your company as noted in Step 16. And finally, you must continue to improve.

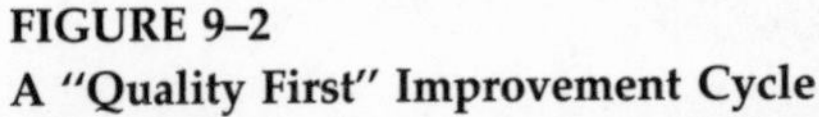

FIGURE 9–2
A "Quality First" Improvement Cycle

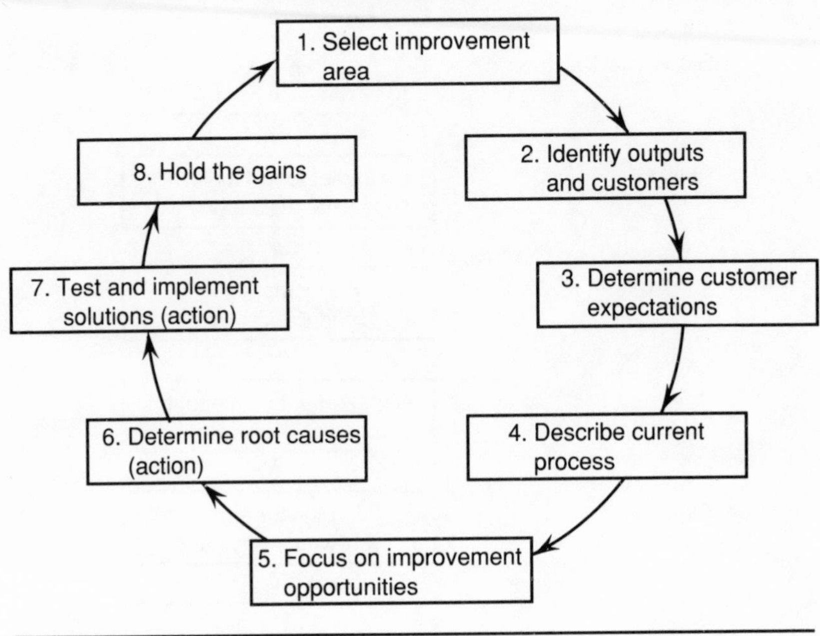

Step 11. Implement "Quality First" Philosophy

To help you implement "Quality First" in your company, an approach based on the Plan-Do-Check-Act cycle should be applied to each area of your quality improvement areas. A structured and systematic approach to identify quality improvement opportunities and resolve business-process problems is shown in Figure 9–2.

The "Quality First" Improvement Cycle offers a common language and a problem-solving methodology for use throughout your organization. It facilitates communication about work underway among groups with similar interests. It also supports the basic quality value of "managing by fact" by offering individuals and teams a disciplined, problem-solving approach. Finally, the "Quality First" Improvement Cycle increases the credibility of solutions that are developed in one part of the organization, allowing them to be readily replicated in other areas of your business.

This cycle embodies several basic quality-management theories and principles. These linkages to quality theory further assure that "managing by fact" is accomplished through the use of the cycle.

The cycle is also important as a tool for managers who are responsible for quality improvement efforts in their organizations. It provides a framework for reviewing the status of quality improvement projects underway and for preparing presentations on completed projects. Finally, it can assist in tracking the effectiveness of solutions in permanently eliminating root causes of quality problems.

The objectives of each step of the "Quality First" Improvement Cycle and recommended tools and techniques are shown in Table 9–1, and the key activities to achieve each step are outlined for use as a reference by individuals and teams as you proceed in your "Quality First" improvement efforts.

Step 12. Benchmark Your Products/Services

In 1979, Xerox initiated a process called competitive benchmarking. At first, only a few of the operating units used this process, but by 1981 it was adopted as a corporation-wide effort. Today, benchmarking practices are used throughout Xerox. Other companies look to Xerox as a benchmarking model.

In fact, Xerox's recent strong performance in regaining its competitive edge in the marketplace can be attributed largely to its benchmarking program. According to a 1987 *DataQuest* research newsletter quoted in *A Guide to Benchmarking in Xerox*:

> "Xerox's benchmarking program deserves the lion's share of the credit for the company's turnaround in recent years. A whole new way of doing business was inaugurated with the start of this program. Every group, product, and system was dissected as Xerox searched for ways to become more competitive. Although this discussion has focused on Xerox's product development system, other organizations and systems at Xerox have also been dramatically changed."

TABLE 9–1
"Quality First" Use of Tools and Techniques

Objectives	Key Activities	Tools and Techniques	Outputs
Identify a problem area and the reason for working on it.	• List possible problem areas. • Collect data. • Select problem area for improvement. • Schedule activities.	Brainstorming Multivoting Interviewing Checksheet, Graph Problem Selection Matrix	• Problem area and rationale • Team project planning schedule
Identify outputs and customers.	• Identify outputs. • Identify customers.	Customer/Supplier Model	• List of outputs • List of customers
Understand customer requirements and degree of satisfaction.	• Identify characteristics, customer requirements, and priorities. • Establish measures and collect data. • Assess conformance to requirements and describe the gap.	Customer Needs Analysis, Survey Checksheet Graph	• Description of the gap • Customer requirements and satisfaction level
Understand how things actually work and the performance necessary to meet customer requirements.	• Identify inputs and suppliers. • Flow chart the process. • Collect data. • Assess process performance and establish targets.	Customer/Supplier Model Flow Chart Checksheet Graph	• List of inputs and suppliers • Flowchart of process in question • Targets for overall process performance and outputs
Select opportunities to pursue.	• Identify contributing factors. • Select opportunities to pursue. • Write the problem statement.	Pareto Diagram Multivoting Problem Selection Matrix Problem Statement Matrix	• Prioritized list of potential problem areas • Clear, concise problem statement • Clear, concise objective statement

TABLE 9–1 *(continued)*

Objectives	Key Activities	Tools and Techniques	Outputs
Identify root causes of the problem.	• Perform cause-and-effect analysis on the problem to the level of root cause. • Select actionable root causes. • Support potential root causes with data. • Select root causes with greatest probable impact.	Fishbone Diagram Checksheet Pareto Diagram Histogram Graph	• List of root causes to be addressed
Develop, test, evaluate, and implement solutions.	• Develop and select potential solutions. • Develop an action plan. • Test, evaluate, and revise solutions. • Implement and monitor solutions.	Barriers and Aids Solutions Selection Matrix Action Plan Cost Estimation	• Implemented solution and data on impact
Sustain improvement, consider replication, evaluate implementation, and plan future actions.	• Recommend required education and revised methods and procedures. • Establish tracking system to monitor results. • Recommend areas for replication. • Plan further actions, if necessary. • Evaluate implementation.	Graph Control Chart Action Plan	• Control at new performance level • Replication recommendations • Celebration • Plans for next project

One of the first and most successful steps Xerox took to regain its competitive edge was to institute a benchmarking program. After studying the Japanese product-development system (with the help of Xerox's partner, Fuji Xerox), Xerox began to completely revamp the way its products were designed. Xerox has established benchmarks for each class of copier and for some functional business areas as well. For example, L.L. Bean served as a benchmark for shipping operations and Sears, Roebuck and Co. provided a model for management of field distribution.

In this book we have defined "benchmark" as a standard of excellence or achievement against which other similar things must be measured or judged.

Simply speaking, benchmarking is the process of:

- Figuring out what to benchmark.
- Finding out what the benchmark is.
- Determining how it's achieved.
- Deciding to make changes or improvements in one's own business practices to meet or exceed the benchmark.

These four questions—while sounding fairly simple—require thinking and analysis. They require that you know your own business processes and practices down to the smallest detail.

The Xerox benchmarking template, shown in Figure 9–3, is a guide, a mold, or a pattern for accomplishing the various analyses required for benchmarking. Unlike a process model, the template is not strictly "sequence-sensitive," nor does it focus on "actions to take." Rather, it poses four questions that might be answered in different sequences (even though the four quadrants are numbered for reference).

Notice the two vertical axes of the template—"Us and Them." The two quadrants to the left pose questions about your results or processes (US); the two quadrants to the right refer to whom or to what you are making the comparisons (THEM). The "them" may represent an outside company or another division within your company.

FIGURE 9–3
Xerox Benchmarking Template

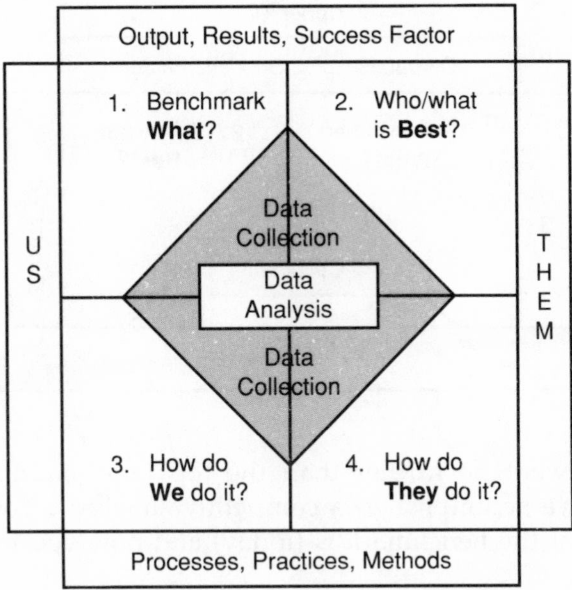

In the first comparison (tier one), when you cut the template in half horizontally (see Figure 9–4), the top two quadrants suggest comparing outputs or results. To begin a comparison, you must answer the questions, "Benchmark what?" and "Who or what is best?" In other words, what will you choose to compare yourself against? We will refer to this first comparison as the "upper tier" comparison.

At the heart of the template are data collection and analysis. "Data" is just another name for information. You will need to have a plan for collecting information both about yourself and about the object of your benchmark study. Naturally, you will need the information to be in a form that allows comparison. So, much of what you find in Chapter 10 will guide you through the process of collecting good, usable information, and some basic discussions about how to analyze and display your information.

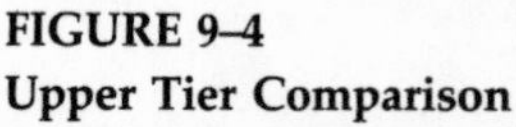

FIGURE 9–4
Upper Tier Comparison

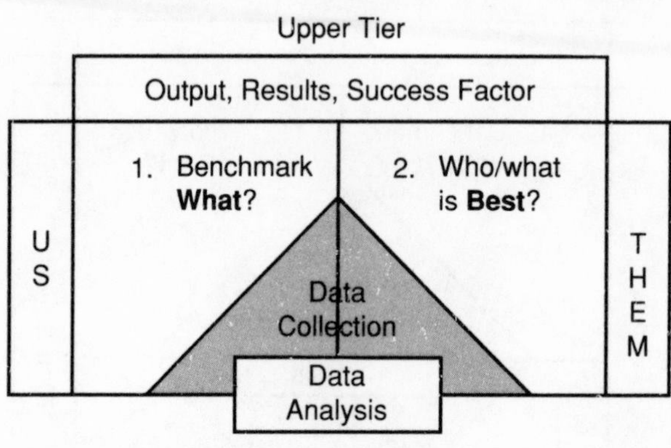

If you went no further than the top two quadrants, you would have accomplished a competitive analysis. You would know what the benchmark is (today) and how you measured against it.

The "lower tier" comparison is the comparison of the bottom two quadrants (see Figure 9–5) that constitutes true benchmarking—understanding the reasons for the differences and understanding what changes in processes, practices, or methods must be undertaken to meet or exceed the benchmark.

For example, assume that your training department averages a 3.6 (out of a possible 5.0) participant satisfaction rating on a particular course. You ask other divisions or departments that offer the same course for their participant satisfaction rating and find that one division achieves a 4.2. You have completed the upper tier study—establishing the benchmark and who has achieved it. Moreover, the gap between you and the benchmark is 0.6.

But only the lower tier study results will allow you to make changes toward improvement. Lower tier questions—"*Why* are their results better than ours?" and "*How* do they achieve that better score?"—are the questions that lead to change or improvement.

The objective of benchmarking is change leading to improvement. Without change in processes, practices, and ultimately,

FIGURE 9–5
Lower Tier Comparison

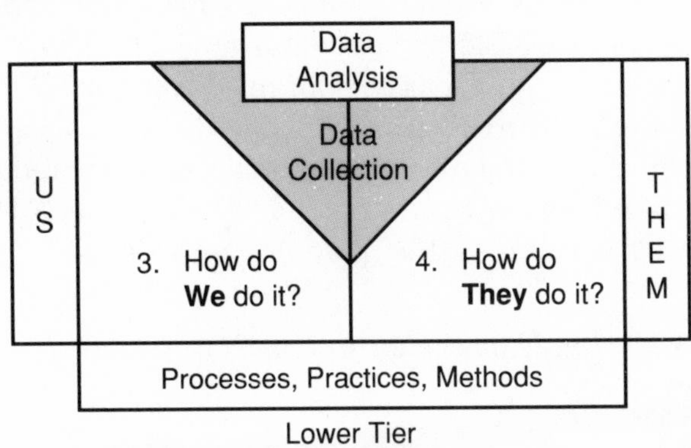

results, benchmarking is an incomplete, academic exercise. You must increase your rating by 0.6 or more in order to achieve the benchmark status prescribed above.

If your work processes are documented and measured, you will find benchmarking to be an extremely valuable (and not terribly difficult) activity. On the other hand, if you wander into a benchmark project without understanding your own process, you will find your lack of knowledge to be a barrier to your successful benchmarking attempts.

Determined to proceed anyway? Then be prepared for some hard work in the two "Us" quadrants of the template.

Competitive benchmarking helps formulate real-world guides as to whether or not you are meeting your customers' needs. If the results of a competitive benchmarking activity show that some other company is meeting customer requirements better than yours—then change in your quality efforts is clearly called for. In other words, competitive benchmarking tells you how you have met customer requirements.

Competitive benchmarking is the continuous process of measuring your products, services, and practices against your toughest competitors or those companies renowned as industry leaders. The process provides a better awareness of what competitors are doing, how they are doing it, and how well it is working.

I would encourage you to learn more about benchmarking. Xerox, as part of its technology transfer commitment under the Malcolm Baldrige Award Program, has made available to the public its corporate bible on benchmarking. The report is called "Leadership Through Quality Training Programs: A Guide to Benchmarking in Xerox." It is available through a partnership with the U.S. Department of Commerce, National Technical Information Services, in Springfield, Virginia. The NTIS document number is PB91-780106. (See Appendix C.)

Step 13. Implement Continuous Improvement Process

Continuous process improvement addresses the creation of positive change in the way work is done. It includes the definition of work flows, strengthening of supplier-customer relationships, elimination of non-value-added effort, reduction of variation, and control of processes.

The continuous process-improvement model shown in Figure 9–6 is a seven-step process that begins with the activities needed to create an environment conducive to "Quality First." It then continues through selecting and improving a process to finally assessing the level of performance improvement, where the model cycles turn around to focus on the next process-improvement effort. Even this chapter of the "Quality First" book is modeled after the process.

1. Set the stage for process improvement.

At the organizational level, setting the stage for process improvement involves everything the company does to become aware of the need for improvement and to establish a commitment to the continuous improvement process. It includes basic education and training, goal setting, barrier reduction, and leadership. Setting the stage means the company must create an environment in which continuous process improvement is encouraged and nourished. Management must have a clear vision of what it wants to accomplish and where it wants to go, and it must lay in place support systems to help the improvement effort.

FIGURE 9–6
Flow Chart of Continuous Improvement Strategy

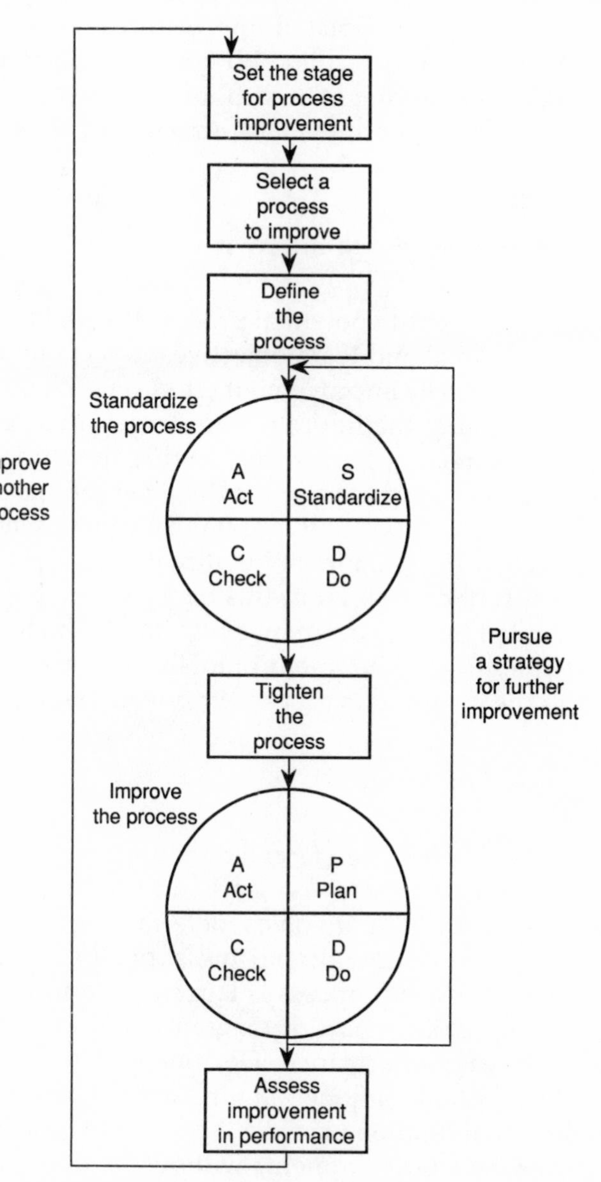

Source: ITT Reliability Analysis Center Report, SOAR-7, 1990.

At the team and individual levels, setting the stage involves selecting and educating the team or the individuals and training them in the specific concepts, tools, and techniques they will need for the contemplated improvement effort. The team or individual should determine how to function in the overall organizational environment and should ensure that all individuals involved are determined to accomplish their perceived mission.

2. Select a process to improve.

A team must identify potential processes and, in conjunction with organizational and team objectives, select one process on which it will focus its improvement effort on each pass through the cycle. Selecting the improvement target involves identifying all the potential opportunities, setting their priorities, and choosing the process that presents the most serious problem or offers the greatest opportunity for improvement. Once the process is selected, the team must identify its major problems and isolate their root causes. From this background, the team may modify its plan for improvement according to the team's objectives. Identifying measurement points is also necessary before beginning the continuous process-improvement effort.

3. Define the process.

Once a process has been targeted for improvement, the team should define that process as clearly and completely as possible. Process definition involves determining the customers (both internal and external) and the suppliers of the process, documenting how the process is currently performed (usually through using a flow chart or diagram), and identifying measures of process performance. Documentation should be formal and consistent among all organizational processes. A sound process definition provides a consistent base from which to begin process improvement; without knowing where you are at a given moment, it is hard to determine how to get to your destination.

4. Standardize the process.

By standardizing a process, the team institutionalizes the current best way to perform that process. Standardization creates a means for instructing people in their jobs within a consistent performance definition, provides a means for evaluating performance consistently, and provides a basis for evaluating the success of the improvement efforts. The team accomplishes all this by following the Standardize-Do-Check-Act cycle, which initially requires the team to bring its measurement system under control, to identify and document the current method of performing the process (which becomes the process standard), and to communicate and promote use of the standard. Management ensures that individuals are trained to the standard, and facilitates and enforces that standard's use. Once the standard is in force, teams measure all process performance against that standard and respond appropriately to deviations from it. Reducing performance variation by assessing the causes of deviation and eliminating those causes allows the teams to prevent recurrent deviation. The standard should always reflect the best current way of performing the process.

5. Tighten the process.

Once a team has defined a process standard, it should tighten the process before actually attempting to improve it. Tightening is the maintenance work that makes process-improvement efforts as effective as possible. This means ensuring that the process meets its stated and perceived requirements; cleaning and straightening the process work areas; eliminating unnecessary equipment; instituting total productive maintenance; and establishing reliable, adequate data-collection systems.

6. Improve the process.

Efforts to improve the process should follow the classic Plan-Do-Check-Act (PDCA) cycle in which an improvement plan is available and teams implement solutions, check for improvement, and act to institutionalize the improvements. The team's effort involves developing solutions that address stated requirements and conform to theories on problem causes. Data collection and measurement methodologies must support the envisioned solution. The team must be trained in the techniques necessary to carry out the plan. After it carries out its planned improvement, it should assess the data to determine how well actual performance matches planned improvements. Successful improvement should be institutionalized; less-than-successful efforts require another pass through the improvement cycle.

7. Assess improvement performance.

After an improvement has been implemented, a team should document the improved performance and the successful improvement effort thoroughly. That documentation allows others to benefit from the lessons the team has learned and brings recognition for the team's efforts. It also provides a road map for replicating successful improvement techniques. Documenting the improved process also requires the team to update its process definition and flow diagrams, and requires that process standards be rewritten to reflect the new standard of performance. Teams should set in place a means of continuously measuring performance level if this system does not already exist. Recommending follow-up actions or subsequent improvement efforts is also appropriate.

The principles at the heart of the continuous improvement process include:

- A constancy of purpose that provides a steady and consistent vision of where your organization is going.
- A commitment to quality that drives productive change in all the products and services you produce.
- A customer focus and customer involvement that ensures your improvement efforts are driven by meaningful purposes.
- Process orientation that addresses the means of work accomplishment and not just the outcomes.

- Continuous improvement that ensures dynamic and adaptive processes over time.
- System-centered management that ensures improvement of the whole and not just the parts.
- Investment in knowledge that leverages the effectiveness of the improvement process.
- Teamwork that leverages the knowledge and provides essential synergy.
- Conservation of human resources that preserves your organization's most valuable assets.
- Total involvement that brings the entire intellectual power of your organization to bear on improvement.
- Perpetual commitment that precludes giving up when the road gets a little rough.

You apply these principles together in a logical and holistic manner to give substance and vitality to the continuously improving organizational culture. A number of the suggested readings at the end of this book examine in depth these principles and their supporting practices.

No single correct formula can be used to achieve continuous improvement in all situations or all organizations. A core set of ingredients, however, is evident in most successful continuous improvement efforts and can be applied to your own effort.

Your "Quality First" effort will be unique in its details, but in general it should move your organization toward satisfying the six criteria listed below:

- Exceeding your customer's requirements and expectations and being a high-quality supplier.
- Believing in people, working to eliminate barriers that prevent people from taking joy and pride in their work, and involving everyone.
- Tapping the power of individuals, multiplying that

power through training and teamwork, and focusing on understanding and process improvement.

- Recognizing that most problems are in your systems and are not due to particular individuals or circumstances, and providing leadership to continuously improve the systems.
- Making decisions based on data rather than on opinions or emotions; stimulating creative thinking; and seeking innovation in products, processes, and services.
- Focusing more on defect prevention than on defect detection.

Step 14. Monitor and Evaluate Results

As part of their strategy for improvement, many organizations that have introduced "Quality First" have conducted more in-depth assessments aimed at identifying the existing culture and management style of the organization. An assessment helps to identify those vital processes to be targeted for change and provides a baseline measurement for judging progress. Assessments can take a variety of forms and frequently involve identifying and surveying the organization's internal and external customers, managers, and employees. The following key considerations are often probed:

- What is the mission of the company? What products and services are provided?
- Who are the internal and external customers?
- What measurement systems are presently in place?
- Does the company measure its success in terms of meeting customer requirements and expectations?
- How well does the company communicate with its customers and its suppliers?
- How much emphasis is placed on planning as opposed to fire fighting?

- How does the company generate ideas for improvement? Improvement in general or quality improvement specifically?
- What type of suggestion system is in place? How effective is it?
- What does the company reward? Improvement in general or quality improvement specifically?
- To what extent is teamwork used, encouraged, and recognized?
- What is the nature of management's relationship with employees' unions?
- How well do functional units cooperate? Are "turf" battles endemic?
- Does the executive leadership have credibility in the eyes of middle and line managers? Frontline workers?
- What type of management style is employed? Is it directive or participative?
- How much discretion do employees have in making decisions? Is authority delegated to the lowest levels possible?
- What is the attitude toward training?
- What is the attitude toward quality work? Is the focus on quality of the end product or quality of the process?
- Are the company values, goals, objectives, policies, and procedures clearly stated and widely known?
- Does the company have an abundance of priorities or have a vital few been identified and articulated?

Step 15. Recognize Success

The success of "Quality First" is determined, in large part, by the degree of importance the organization places on it. Recognition is one of the most important ways to reinforce a proactive, positive change in behavior as it relates to quality improvement. Recognition is given for the successful application of the "Quality First" principles and practices.

Your goal is to create an environment in which change in the customer's interest is encouraged and then celebrated when it does occur.

Recognition is a means to demonstrate respect and appreciation for all employees and the value they add to your business.

Traditionally, business rewards have been based on the "most" numbers: most revenue brought in, most profitable new product. "Quality First" of course also rewards bottom-line numbers; profit is a significant reason why your company is in business. But since continuous quality improvement is a process, "Quality First" also provides for recognition and reward for those who demonstrate success with the processes and behaviors of quality—in measurable or nonmeasurable ways.

Recognition and reward are not the same things. Recognition means noticing (recognizing) a person or group doing a good job. A manager may notice the good job at any point along its progress—not only when it is completed. Recognition usually takes the form of praise, either spoken or written. It may be as simple as a word of approval about the way an employee ran a team meeting, or as formal as a letter of commendation with copies sent to his or her management.

Recognition provides both motivation and support for employees; people work better when they feel their efforts are valued. Research has shown that such reinforcement can have a real and measurable impact on productivity.

To provide effective reinforcement, recognition should:

- Be specific. If someone is told, "Good job on that report, Hunt!" Hunt is left not knowing which part of the report succeeded so well. Was it the succinct executive summary, the fact that it was turned in two days early, the thoroughness of the research, the potential value of the recommendations, or the nice printing job? Managers stand a better chance of having desirable actions repeated if the actions are clearly specified.

- Be directed at the right person. If the report came from a team, and Hunt has been out of town in Springfield while it was being written, Hunt is not the person to recognize even if he is the team leader. Who wrote the report?
- Be genuine.
- Be timely. Reinforcement is most effective when given as close to when "Quality First" behavior occurs as possible.
- Recognize process, not just results. The results will be unique to any given situation. The "Quality First" processes, on the other hand, are versatile enough to handle a wide variety of situations. It is the internalization of the processes you wish to encourage; therefore, that is what you should reinforce with praise.

Reward is given at the completion of a job. It is tangible: usually cash, mementos, or merchandise. Rewards range from a simple plaque to a profit-sharing program. Rewards say, "You deserve to share in the tangible assets of your work," and as such can be powerful motivators.

"Quality First" is bolstered by effective use of recognition and reward. All managers, at all levels, should continually identify those people doing a good job—and then devise ways to tell them so.

On a corporate level, your company should bestow rewards and sponsor many recognition events. Two examples used by Xerox Corporation include Teamwork Days and the Team Excellence Awards.

Teamwork Days are recognition events designed to honor the achievements of quality teams. Teamwork Days can be held on district, regional, or functional levels. In addition, the corporation can sponsor annual Teamwork Days, at which everyone in the corporation is welcome to celebrate progress.

A teamwork event is like a cross between a professional conference, a trade fair, and a revival meeting. Teams create display booths, often with much ingenuity and exuberance, which showcase their accomplishments. Speakers discuss company progress in becoming a "Quality First" company. People learn from each other, and the total "Quality First" transformation grows.

The Team Excellence Award is a cash award given to several teams each year as a reward for using "Quality First" tools to achieve outstanding results. There are always more excellent teams than it is possible to reward. Recipients are chosen by senior staff after successfully competing at regional and district levels within their function. All teams reaching the status of "excellent" are recognized by a certificate.

What makes an "excellent team"? There are three criteria:

- Teamwork. How well does the team work together? Team members on an excellent team (1) all understand their purpose as a team, (2) start with a clear problem statement and/or desired output, (3) organize for maximum effectiveness, and (4) use interactive skills well and consistently.
- Use of quality tools and processes. Effective teams (1) use applicable analytical tools, (2) identify several possible alternatives to solving their problem, and (3) evaluate the results of their actions.
- Results. The team project should (1) produce tangible business results, (2) impact the external customer or those who support the external customer, (3) demonstrate an innovative approach, and (4) effectively maximize the Cost of Quality opportunities.

Recognition and reward must be woven into the very fabric of "Quality First." People who assume responsibility for continuous growth in meeting customer requirements are in turn motivated to further growth by honest recognition of the large role their efforts play.

Step 16. Adjust Your "Quality First" Process

Your "Quality First" planning and implementation efforts must not be locked in concrete. As you learn more about your company strengths and weaknesses, change your "Quality First" efforts to reflect the feedback.

If the results are not as expected, then a new approach for improvement, based on what was learned, must be developed.

Step 17. Continue to Improve

Don't stop now! Continue to improve (see Figure 9–7) every facet of your company's operation.

FIGURE 9–7
PDCA Cycle for "Quality First" Continuous Improvement

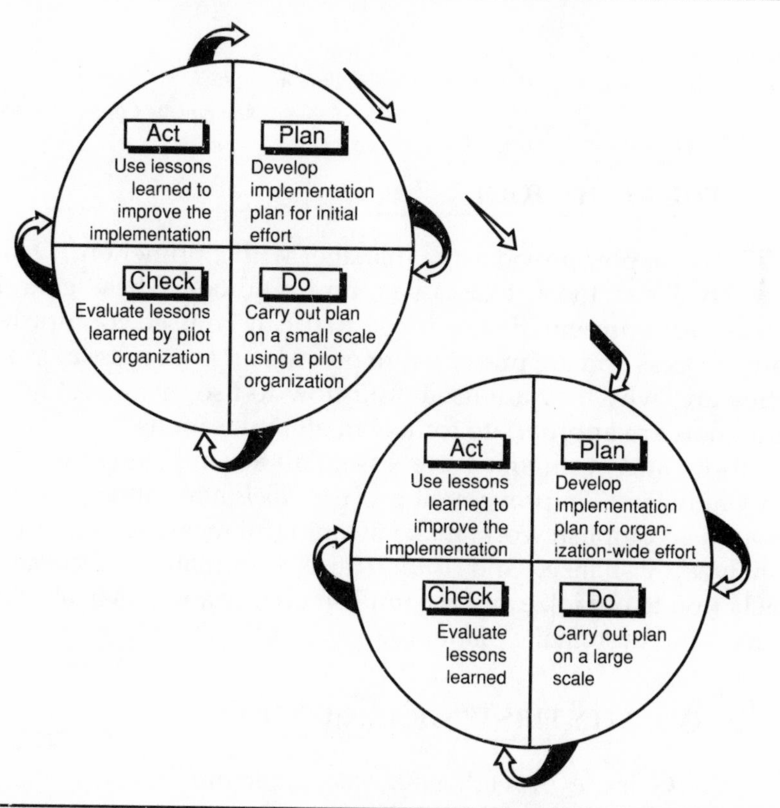

Chapter Ten

"Quality First" Tools and Techniques

"One picture is worth more than ten thousand words."

Anonymous Chinese Proverb

THE RIGHT TOOL

This chapter provides the manager with a primer on "Quality First" tools, techniques, and methods. These generic tools are representative of those that can be used to improve any process and are presented to provide an awareness of what they are, why they are used, and how to use them. Not all of the tools are appropriate for use in all applications.

Tools and techniques are essential for implementing the "Quality First" improvement process. *Tools* make it possible for you to accomplish work; make meaningful measurements; and analyze, visualize, and understand information. *Techniques* help you to organize and accomplish quality analysis in a structured and systematic manner.

"QUALITY FIRST" GRAPHIC TOOLS

As the Chinese proverb suggests, a picture is worth many words *and* numbers. Graphic displays allow you to create a logical storyboard that most people can understand at a glance.

A number of factors can lead to the decision for using a particular graphic tool, including the unique application and an individual's or team's experience and preferences. Most graphic tools are oriented toward a certain type of activity, and each tool has its strengths and weaknesses. This section summarizes some of the common graphic tools used to implement the "Quality First" methodology. Table 10–1 shows when you need to use particular graphic tools.

Each of these graphic tools is briefly described to enhance the manager's understanding of its use under the "Quality First" methodology.

TABLE 10–1
Use of Graphic Tools

Graphic Tool	Use when you need to . . .
Bar Chart	Compare quantity of data among different categories to help visualize differences.
Cause-and-Effect (Fishbone) Diagram	Systematically analyze cause-and-effect relationships and identify potential root causes of a problem.
Checksheet	Gather a variety of data in a systematic fashion for a clear and objective picture of the facts.
Control Chart	Monitor the performance of a process with frequent outputs to determine if its performance is meeting customer requirements or if it can be improved to meet or exceed them.
Flow Chart	Describe an existing process, develop modifications, or design an entirely new process.
Histogram	Display the dispersion or spread of the data under consideration.
Pareto Chart	Identify major factors in a subject being analyzed and highlight "the vital few" in contrast to "the trivial many."
Scatter Diagram	Show the relationship between two variables.
Time Line Chart	Visually display complex and quantifiable data; often shows changes in quantity over time.

Bar Chart

Bar charts show a comparison of quantities by the length of the bars that represent them (such as frequencies of events in different locations, cost of different types of breakdowns, and so on). Bars may be horizontal or vertical.

Along with time line charts, bar charts are among the most common types of data displays. There are two differences between them that are worth noting. The obvious difference is that a bar chart uses height columns, while the time line chart connects data points with a line. Visually, then, the bar chart emphasizes differences (or similarities) between and among the columns of various heights. The time line chart emphasizes the direction of change over time. The second difference is that the divisions along the horizontal line of the time line are time (quantitative) intervals. The divisions along the horizontal axis of the bar chart are nominal categories.

Figure 10–1 is an example of a bar chart. It shows the number of household appliances with some measured group (such as "within households with annual earnings of more than $50,000 per year"). Then we are led to conclude that TVs continue to be the item most frequently purchased, microwaves are increasing in popularity, but ranges and refrigerators are purchased relatively infrequently.

The bar chart (Figure 10–1) is really two bar charts superimposed: one for 1980 and one for 1990.

As with all graphic displays of data, the bar chart tells its story at a glance. The more data you have to analyze, the more important the use of graphics becomes. Bar charts make graphic comparisons of quantity easy to see.

To construct a bar chart proceed as follows:

- Collect the raw data on a checksheet, if necessary.
- List the categories (usually words rather than numbers) across the horizontal scale at the bottom. You may set them in any sequence, such as in descending order or any other way that makes sense. Label all categories.
- To set the vertical scale to the left, find both the

FIGURE 10–1
Example of Bar Chart

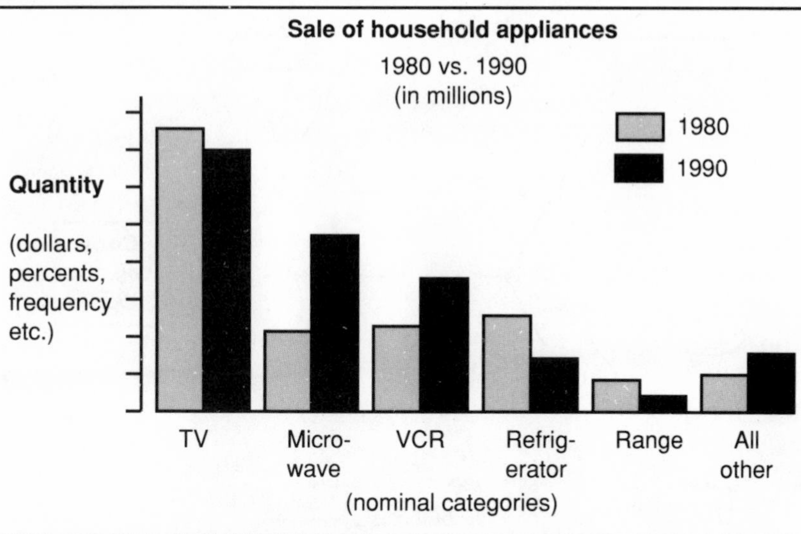

Source: A Guide to Benchmarking in Xerox

largest and smallest value from the data and make sure the scale is broad enough to include both. Label both the scale and the intervals.

- Determine the quantity of each category and draw the bar accordingly. Generally speaking, bars should not touch or overlap.
- Bar charts can show and compare double or triple bars for different years or different populations (for example, households with earnings under $50,000).
- Give your bar chart a descriptive title. Include any legends that show what different patterns or colors represent.

Cause-and-Effect (Fishbone) Diagram

The cause-and-effect diagram (Figure 10–2) is a graphic representation of the relationships between an effect (problem) and

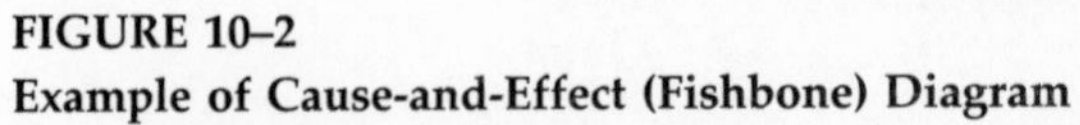

FIGURE 10–2
Example of Cause-and-Effect (Fishbone) Diagram

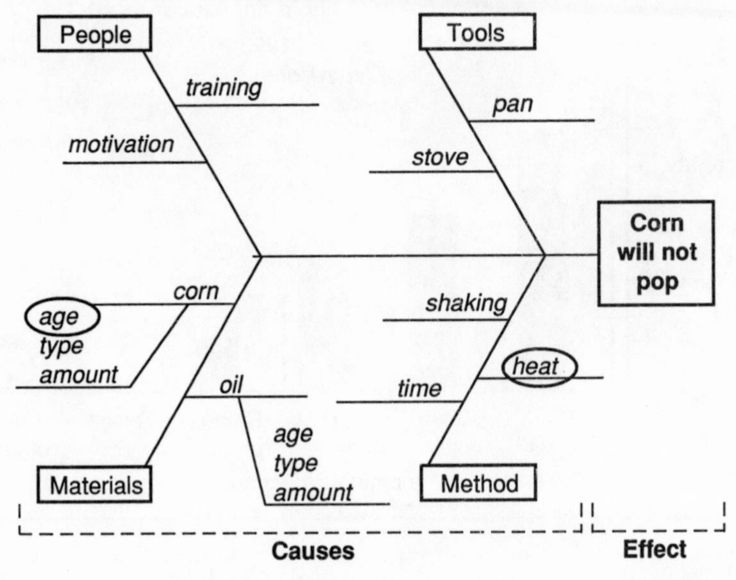

its potential causes. It is a useful tool in brainstorming, examining processes, and planning activities. The process of constructing a cause-and-effect diagram helps stimulate thinking about an issue, helps organize thoughts into a rational whole, and generates discussion and the airing of viewpoints. The cause-and-effect diagram documents the level of understanding about an issue and provides a framework from which to begin expanding that understanding.

Cause-and-effect diagrams can be used to explore a wide variety of topics, including the relationships between an existing problem and the factors that might bear on it; a desired future outcome and the factors that relate to it; or any event past, present, or future, and its causal factors.

Cause-and-effect diagrams go by several names: fishbone diagram, which describes how it looks; and Ishikawa diagram, for its inventor, Kaoru Ishikawa, a Japanese quality leader.

The problem—or effect—appears in a box to the right (the

head of the fish) as shown in Figure 10–2. To the left are the "bones" of the fish on which causes are organized and displayed as categories. The entries are words or nominal data.

In this example, the problem or effect is that the corn will not pop. The four factors that may be causing this are people, tools for popping corn, materials, and the method or process used. These are the four main bones for this example, but a different problem would suggest different major bones. For example, if our problem were "poor sales of the X3 portable," we might select salespeople, product, price, promotion, and/or environment as the major bones of the diagram.

The fishbone diagram ensures that quality analysis groups thoroughly examine all possible causes or categories. More importantly, it provides a process for groups to follow. And because the fishbone is a graphic display, it serves to focus the attention of the group on something more concrete that everyone sees and interprets in a more or less consistent manner.

To develop a cause-and-effect diagram:

- Define the effect or current situation as clearly as possible. You can always go back and refine it later as you collect new data. Write the effect in the "head of the fish."
- Many groups prefer to begin by brainstorming causes, and listing them on a flip chart in no particular order. When the group runs dry of ideas, they look for categories and similarities suggested by the list. These major categories or themes become the big bones.
- To encourage lots of ideas, ask, "Why? Why? Why?" When the answers begin to sound silly, you can stop.
- Draw the major bones and label them. You may decides on three, four, or more major themes. Use generic branches (people, methods, materials, machines) if helpful.
- Place the causes from the brainstorm list as small bones under the appropriate big bone.
- The organization of the brainstormed causes will no

doubt stimulate other ideas for causes. The group should be encouraged to add as many potential causes as they can think of. For each cause identified, ask, "What caused this?"

- The group can then highlight the cause(s) it believes to be contributing to the effect. In the popcorn example (Figure 10–2), the group has circled "age of corn" and "amount of heat" as the most likely causes.
- To verify causes, you will need to collect information to either accept or reject the cause(s).
- Work on most important causes (e.g., use design of experiments).
- Desensitize, eliminate, or control causes.

Checksheet

A checksheet provides a list of checkoff items that permit data to be collected quickly and easily in a simple standardized format that lends itself to quantitative analysis. Checksheets are frequently used to collect data on numbers of defective items, defect locations, and defect causes. Figure 10–3 is a simple example of a checksheet.

Make a checksheet by laying out the categories of information and data about the items onto a standardized form or grid. Determine the categories by asking such fact-finding questions as:

- What happens?
- Who does it, receives it, is responsible for it?
- Where—place?
- When—time of day, month, how often?
- How does it happen, how much, how long, etc.?

Do not ask, "Why?" This will lead you to search for causes while still trying to determine if a problem exists. The checksheet should be designed to facilitate the collection of as many

FIGURE 10–3
Simple Example of a Checksheet

Product: TRC Receiver unit

Date: 9/09/91

Name: Hunt

Lot: 51

Total examined: 200

Defect type	Defect count	Subtotal
Chipped	~~||||~~ ~~||||~~ ~~||||~~	15
Off-color	~~||||~~ ~~||||~~ ~~||||~~ ~~||||~~ ||	22
Bent	~~||||~~	5
	Grand total:	42

different kinds of data as are useful. The team can brainstorm items and then refine the list through multivoting. It is also helpful to gather a little data before designing your checksheet. You may determine the appropriate categories from this smaller sample. The checksheet should also clearly indicate who collected the data and where, when, and how the data was collected. In a sample, the total population from which the data were gathered should also be indicated.

Control Chart

A control chart is used to monitor the performance of a process with frequent outputs. It provides a pictorial representation of an ongoing process and is based on four concepts:

- All processes fluctuate with time.
- Individual points are unpredictable.

- A stable process fluctuates randomly, and groups of points from a stable process tend to fall within predictable bounds.
- An unstable process does not fluctuate randomly, and these fluctuations are generally out of the range of normal operations.

The control chart, shown in Figure 10–4, is a graph that displays data taken over time and also shows computed variations of those data. Control charts are used to show the variation on a variety of variables including average ($\overline{X}$) and range (R) and also the number of defects (PN), percent defective (P), defects per variable unit (U), and defects per fixed unit (C). *A Guide to Quality Control* by Ishikawa provides excellent guidance on using control charts. The control chart allows you to distinguish between measurements that are predictably within the inherent capability of the process (common causes of variation) and measurements that are unpredictable and produced by special causes.

The upper and lower control limits (UCL and LCL, respectively) must not be confused with specification limits. Control limits describe the natural variation of the process such that points within the limits are generally indicative of normal and expected variation. Points outside the limits signal that something has occurred that requires special attention because it is outside of the built-in systematic cause of variation in the process. Note that the circled point on the $\overline{X}$-bar chart, while outside the control limits, does not mean the process is out of control. A series of points outside control limits would be necessary for that determination. Each individual point out of the limits should be explained, however.

These charts help you understand the inherent capability of your processes, bring your processes under control by eliminating the special causes of variation, reduce tampering with processes that are under statistical control, and monitor the effects of process changes aimed at improvement.

To construct a control chart, follow these basic steps:

- Determine control limits to describe the expected variation of a process.

FIGURE 10–4
Example of Control Chart

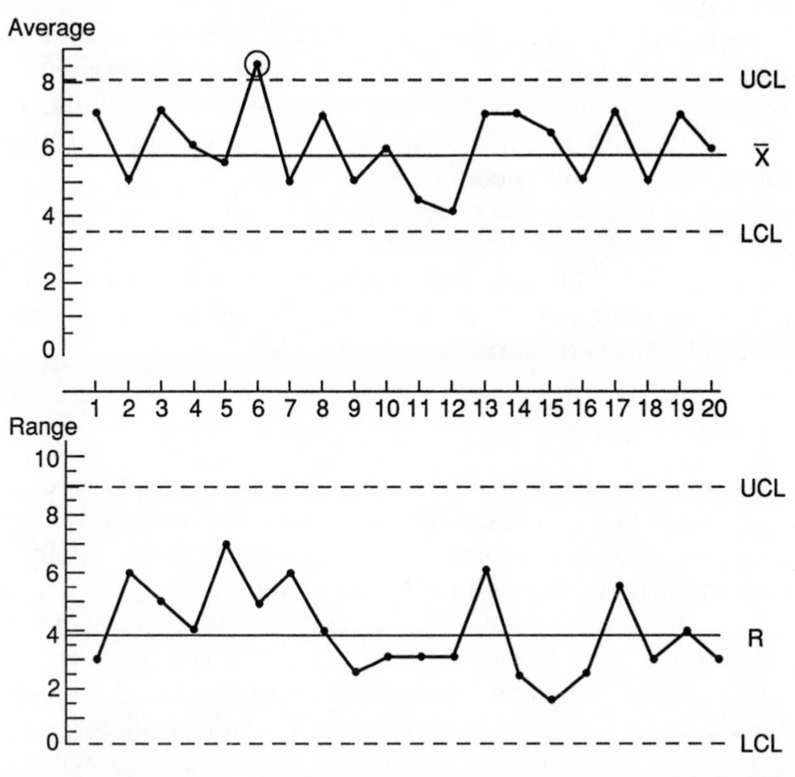

- Collect data.
- Plot data on the control chart to assess performance and identify points outside established control limits.
- Determine causes of points outside control limits.
- Identify ways to eliminate special causes, reduce normal variation, and improve the mean.

After constructing your control chart, examine it to see where the data points are located. If your process is fairly consistent and stable, most of the data points should fall within the established limits. Control charts illustrate fluctuations within the process that occur in a non-random pattern. Points that fall outside one of the control limits should be reported or investigated.

Once you've created your control chart, you can continue to use it to determine whether your operations are staying within the operating limits you've established. As you add points, examine the chart for favorable or unfavorable out-of-control points, and look for special or assignable causes.

There are many types of control charts. The one you use depends on the type of data collected. Since choosing and developing control charts are rather complex processes, it is suggested that your quality specialist be asked for assistance when a control chart is deemed necessary.

Flow Chart

A flow chart is a pictorial representation of the steps in a process. It is a useful tool for determining how a process really works. By examining how various steps in a process relate to one another, you can often uncover potential sources of trouble.

Flow charts can be applied to anything from the flow of materials to the steps in making a sale or servicing a product.

Flow charts permit you to examine and understand relationships in a process or project. They provide a step-by-step schema or picture that serves to create a common language, ensures common understanding about sequence, and focuses collective attention on shared concerns.

Several different types of flow charts are particularly useful in the continuous improvement process. Three frequently used charts are the top-down flow chart, the detailed flow chart, and the work-flow diagram. The top-down flow chart (Figure 10–5) presents only the major or most fundamental steps in a process or project. It helps you and your team to easily visualize the process in a single, simple flow diagram. Key value-added actions associated with each major activity are listed below their respective flow diagram steps. You can construct a top-down flow chart fairly quickly and easily. You generally do so before attempting to produce detailed flow charts for a process. By limiting the top-down flow chart to significant value-added ac-

FIGURE 10–5
Example of Top-Down Flow Chart

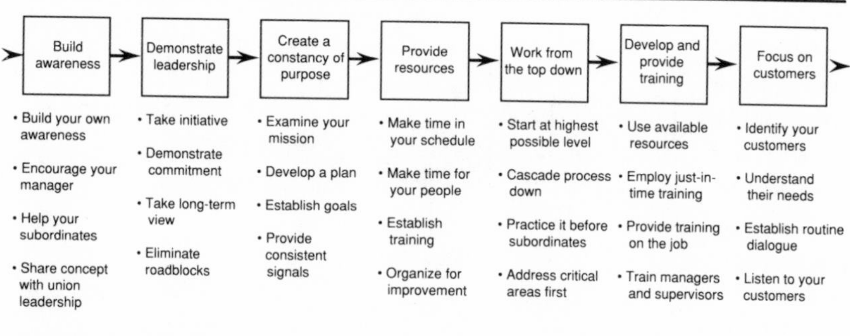

tivity, you reduce the likelihood of becoming bogged down in the detail.

The detailed flow chart (Figure 10–6) provides very specific information about process flow. At its most detailed level, every decision point, feedback loop, and process step is represented. Detailed flow charts should be used only when the level of detail provided by the top-down or other simpler flow charts is insufficient to support understanding, analysis, and improvement activity. The detailed flow chart may also be useful and appropriate for critical processes, where precisely following a specific procedure is essential. The work-flow diagram is a graphic representation or picture of how work actually flows through a physical space or facility. It is very useful for analyzing flow processes, illustrating flow inefficiency, and planning process-flow improvement.

Histogram

A histogram is a visual representation of the spread or dispersion of variable data (e.g., the number of defects per lot). In histograms of natural data, there is a tendency for many items to fall toward the center of the distribution (central tendency), with progressively fewer items as you move from the center.

This information is represented by a series of rectangles or bars proportional in height to the frequency of the group or class represented, as shown in Figure 10–7. Since class intervals

FIGURE 10–6
Sample Detailed Flow Chart

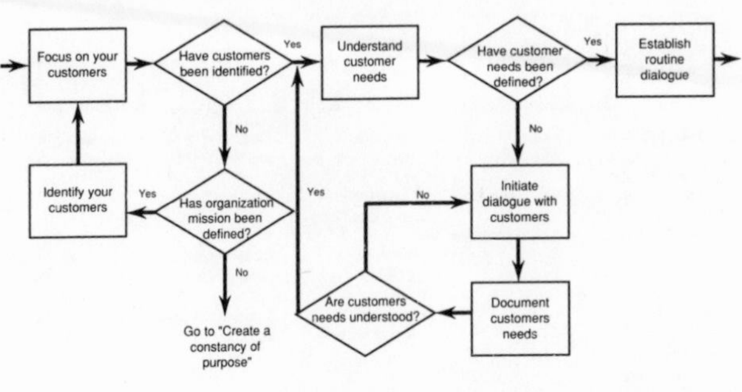

FIGURE 10–7
Example of a Histogram

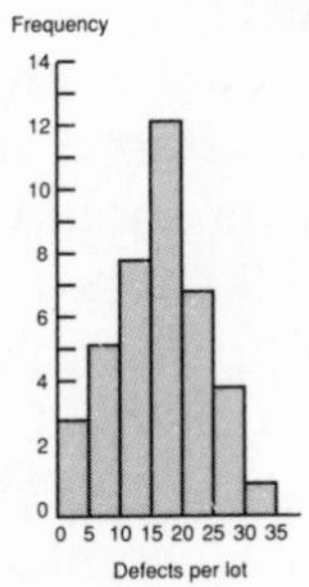

(but not numbers) will be equal in size, the rectangles are of equal width. The heights of the rectangles relative to one another indicate the proportion of data points in each class.

A histogram helps to identify changes or shifts in processes as changes are made. It shows how variable measurements of a process or product can be, and it helps in the establishment of standards. Once standards have been set, measurements can be compared to these standards.

To construct a histogram proceed as follows:

- Collect the data you plan to chart and count the total number of data points.

- Determine the range of your data by subtracting the smallest data point from the largest.
- Keep the number of data bars in your graph between six and twelve. To determine the width of each class interval (bar), divide the range (above) by the desired number of bars.
- Place your class intervals (groupings of data) on the horizontal axis.
- Place your frequency or number scale on the vertical axis.
- Arrange the data points in ascending order.
- Draw the height of each bar to represent the number or frequency of its class interval using the scale on the vertical axis; each bar should be the same width with all data points included.

Pareto Chart

A Pareto chart is used when you need to discover or display the relative importance of data or variables (problems, causes, or conditions). It helps highlight the *vital few* in contrast to the *trivial many*. It may be used to examine the "how," "what," "when," "where," and "why" of a suspected problem cause. It also helps teams identify which problems, causes, or conditions are the most significant or frequent so they can work on these first.

Like most charts and graphs, the Pareto chart is an illustration of your data as of a specific time and date. Once your team has addressed the most significant problem, cause, or condition in your Pareto chart, you can redraw it with new data and pick another area to improve.

In the late 1800s, Vilfredo Pareto, an Italian economist, found that typically 80 percent of the wealth in a region was concentrated in less than 20 percent of the population. Later, Joseph Juran formulated what he called the Pareto Principle of problems: Only a vital few elements (20 percent) account for the majority (80 percent) of the problems. For example, only 20 percent of your equipment problems account for 80 percent of your

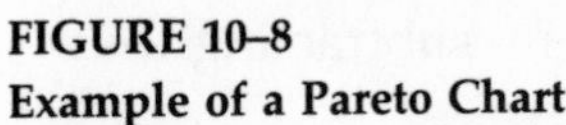

FIGURE 10–8
Example of a Pareto Chart

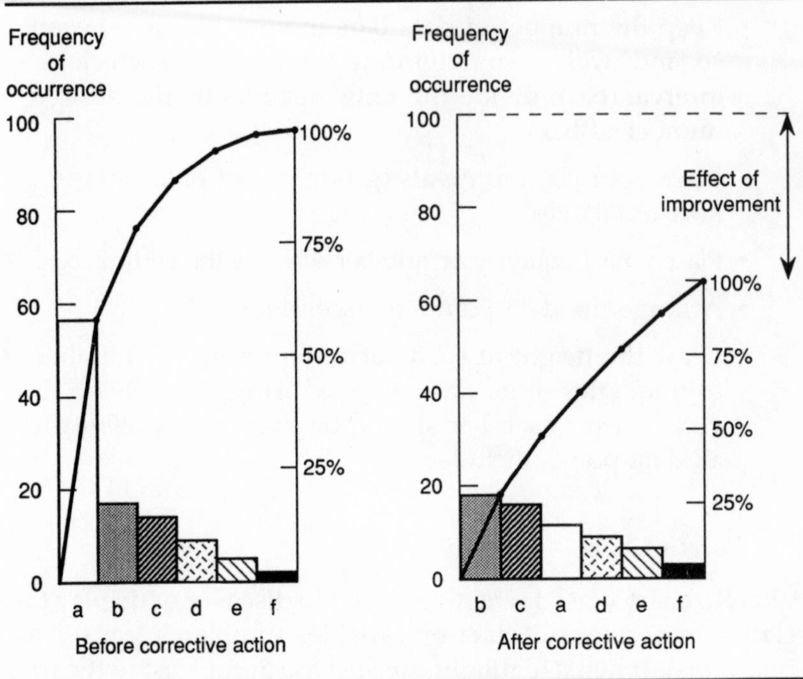

down time. Because this Pareto principle has proven to be valid in numerous situations, it is useful to examine your data carefully to identify the vital few items that most deserve attention.

The Pareto chart shown in Figure 10–8 is a bar chart in which the data are arranged in descending order of their importance, generally by magnitude of frequency, cost, time, or a similar parameter. The chart is really two charts in one. It's part bar chart and part pie chart. The bars are easy to see, but the ascending line that plots the cumulative height of the bars is really a pie chart "unrolled."

To create a Pareto chart proceed as follows:

- Select the most likely causes of a problem (from the cause/effect diagram).
- Collect the data on causes (using a checksheet, perhaps).

- Summarize the numbers of observations and calculate the percentages of each cause.
- The right vertical scale is always set from zero to 100 percent.
- The left vertical scale is the same height as the right scale; it begins with zero at the bottom and ends with the number of observations at the top, directly across from 100 percent.
- Draw the columns using the left scale.
- Plot the first point at the upper right corner of the first column.
- Calculate and add together the percentages of cause 1 and cause 2. Place the second point, corresponding to the sum, across from the right scale, directly over the second column or bar. For the third point, add the percentage of cause 3 to the total of 1 and 2 and plot accordingly. The total of all the columns added together should be 100 percent, and the last point will be at the 100 percent point.
- Join the dots with a line.

Scatter Diagram

Scatter diagrams (Figure 10–9) and their related correlation analysis permit you to examine two factors at one time and to determine the relationship that may exist between them. The graphic display can help lead you to the possible causes of problems, even when the linkage between the factors is surprising. The pattern or distribution of data points in a scatter diagram describes the strength of the relationship between the factors being examined. However, even a strong correlation does not imply a cause-and-effect relationship between the factors. Additional work may be required to uncover the nature of the indicated relationship.

The scatter diagram shows plotted points against two measures: one displayed on the vertical (y) axis, the other on the

FIGURE 10–9
Examples of Scatter Diagram Correlation

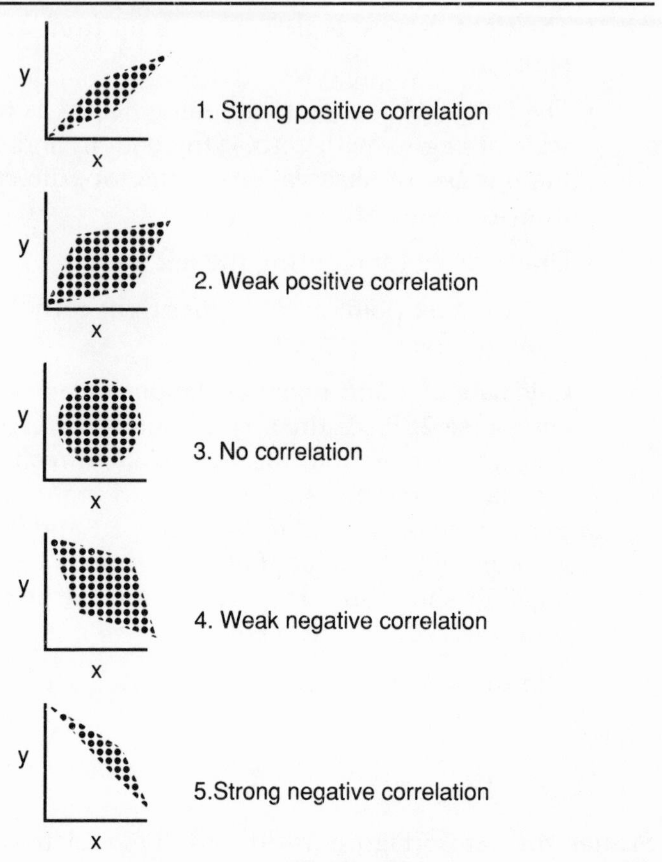

horizontal (x) axis. The visual pattern of the plotted points gives quick information about the presence of a relationship or correlation.

If there is a correlation (either positive or negative) between two measures, you can assume that if you can change the incidence of one measure, the other will move as well. For example, if telephone call duration is positively correlated to customer satisfaction, then changing telephone call duration will produce a change in customer satisfaction.

To prepare a scatter diagram proceed as follows:

- Collect the two selected measures for each occurrence.
- Draw the horizontal and vertical scales of equal lengths.
- Assign the horizontal (x) axis to the dependent variable. The dependent variable is the one you can have an effect on, such as call duration. The independent variable is the other variable that depends on the first. The independent variable is assigned to the vertical (y) axis. Establish the interval scales for both and label.
- Plot each data point on the grid.
- To interpret the relationship, you can "eyeball" it, but a statistician can perform some quantitative tests on the data to give you a more accurate numeric indication of correlation.

Time Line Chart

The time line chart as shown in Figure 10–10 is a graphic display of changes over some period of time. The left scale is a quantity: percentages or simple counts of frequency. The horizontal line is divided into time intervals such as "days of the week," "months," or even an ordinal sequence such as "first job," "second job," and so on.

The line that joins the plot marks gives a visual "moving picture" of the fluctuations over time. Defect rates are reported on time lines in order to spot trends.

To prepare a time line chart proceed as follows:

- Collect the raw data on a checksheet, if necessary.
- Develop time intervals (usually hour, day, week, etc.) across the horizontal axis at the bottom. The intervals should be evenly spaced. Label each interval.
- Draw a line to connect the quantities observed on each successive interval.
- Connect the points with a line.

- Add horizontal and vertical grid lines if the points are difficult to read, as shown in the figure.
- Title the chart to define the period of time over which the data were collected.

Use of "Quality First" Tools

There are a number of factors that may lead to the decision to use a particular tool or set of tools, including an individual's or team's experience and preference. Table 10–2 summarizes some of the tools used in implementing "Quality First" practices.

"QUALITY FIRST" TECHNIQUES

This section summarizes some of the basic techniques used to implement the "Quality First" methodology. Table 10–3 shows when you need to use particular techniques.

FIGURE 10–10
Example of Time Line Chart

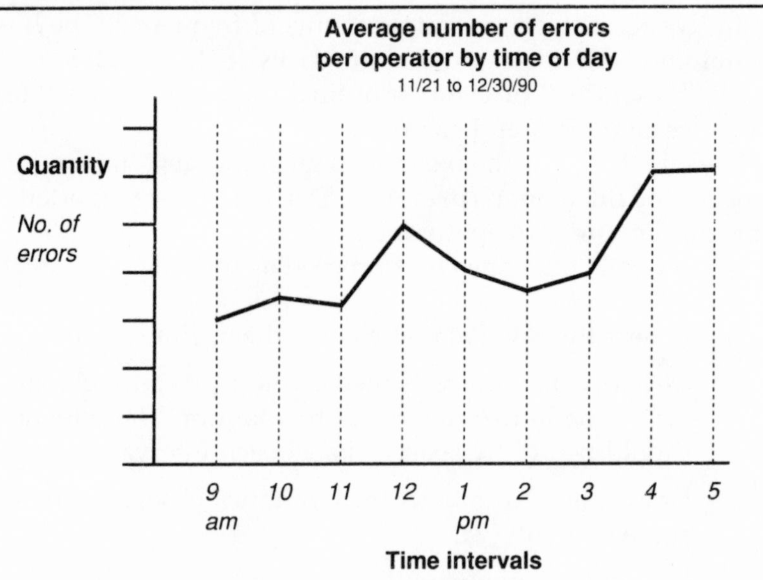

TABLE 10–2
Matrix of "Quality First" Tool Applications

Tools and Techniques (Listed without regard to priority)	*Problem-Solving Activities*					
	1. Bounds and Prioritize Problems	2. Compile Information	3. Analysis	4. General Alternatives	5. Evaluate	6. Plan and Implement
Benchmarking	✓	✓	✓		✓	
Cause-and-Effect Diagrams	✓		✓			
Nominal Group Technique	✓	✓		✓	✓	✓
Quality Function Deployment	✓		✓		✓	
Pareto Charts	✓	✓	✓			
Statistical Process Control		✓	✓			
Histograms		✓	✓			
Checksheets		✓	✓			
Input/Output Analysis			✓			
Scatter Diagrams			✓			
Concurrent Engineering			✓	✓		
Design of Experiments			✓	✓	✓	
Cost of Quality			✓		✓	
Control Charts			✓		✓	
Work Flow Analysis Flow Charts			✓			✓
Team Building						✓
Time Management	✓					✓
Shewhart Cycle	✓	✓	✓	✓	✓	✓

TABLE 10–3
Use of "Quality First" Techniques

Technique	Use when you need to . . .
Action Plan	Explain implementation plans to management and workers, and ensure an organized, objective implementation.
Barriers and Aids	Analyze a situation and make use of available aids and/or overcome barriers that prevent implementation of a solution.
Benchmarking	Measure your processes/performance against your competitors.
Brainstorming	Generate, clarify, and evaluate a sizable list of ideas, problems, or issues.
Concurrent Engineering	Shorten the design-to-development life cycle of a product.
Cost Estimation	Determine the dollar impact when prioritizing and selecting improvement opportunities.
Cost of Quality	Understand the hidden costs of a product or service.
Customer Needs Analysis	Identify what customer expectations and requirements are, and what you have jointly agreed to provide.
Customer/Supplier Model	Identify the total customer/supplier relationship and analyze and/or improve your work process.
Customer/Supplier Questionnaire	Assess your relations with your customers and suppliers.
Deming/Shewhart Cycle	Implement a continuous improvement process.
Design of Experiments	Reduce costs, stabilize production processes, and desensitize production variables.
Interviewing	Broaden the team's foundation of knowledge and identify other people who are not on the team but who are sources of needed information.
Multivoting	Accomplish list reduction and prioritization quickly and with a high degree of group agreement.
Nominal Group Technique (NGT)	Reach consensus within a structured situation.
Problem Selection Matrix	Prioritize improvement opportunities.
Problem Statement Matrix	State specifically the improvement opportunity that the team is addressing.
Quality Function Deployment (QFD)	Transform customer wants and needs into quantitative terms.
Solutions Selection Matrix	Select those potential solutions that best address the root causes of the problem.
Statistical Process Control (SPC)	Improve process performance.

FIGURE 10–11
Typical Example of an Action Plan

TASK ASSIGNMENT RECORD

Prepared By ________ Date ________ Page ___ of ___

Loc'n/Proj. ________ Period ________

NO.	TASK/PROJECT	PRIORITY/ DUE DATE	ASSIGNED TO	DATE ASSIGNED	STATUS/REMARKS

Source: *AT&T Quality Improvement Process Guidebook,* Florida Power and Light.

Each of these techniques is briefly described to enhance the manager's understanding of their use under the "Quality First" methodology.

Action Plan

The "Quality First" team's action plan is a catalog of things that must be done to ensure a smooth and objective trial and implementation of the solution. Although the action plan may have different formats, it should answer who, what, when, where, and how, and consider the barriers and aids for success. Figure 10–11 is a typical example of an action plan.

To develop an action plan proceed as follows:

- Have the team analyze the proposed improvement or solution.
- Break it down into steps.
- Consider the materials and numbers of people involved at each level.
- Brainstorm, if necessary, for other items of possible significance.
- Add items to the list until you think the list is complete.

FIGURE 10–12
Example of Elements of a Barriers-and-Aids Analysis

Forces Pushing Against Quality Improvement	Forces Pushing For Quality Improvement
• Lack of dollars	• Team
• People shortage	• Personal commitment
• Vested interest/old attitude	• Management support
• Would the team stay together?	• Support of line manager
• Other priorities:	• Communications:
Time	Within team
Maintain work flow	Outside team
Complicated techniques	• New techniques
	• Increasing cost of failure
	• Good planning
	• Specific goals

Barriers and Aids

Barriers-and-aids analysis is a technique for pinpointing and analyzing elements that resist change (barriers) or push for change (aids). This focused brainstorming technique helps a team to meet its objectives by planning to overcome barriers and making maximum use of available aids. Factors to consider are:

- people.
- environment.
- hardware.
- dollars.

Figure 10–12 is an example of a barriers-and-aids analysis. To construct a barriers-and-aids analysis proceed as follows:*

- Identify the solution, task, change, or concern.
- Brainstorm a list of barriers (forces pushing against change).

*It is not necessary to come up with an aid for every barrier.

FIGURE 10–13
Illustration of Comparative Benchmarking

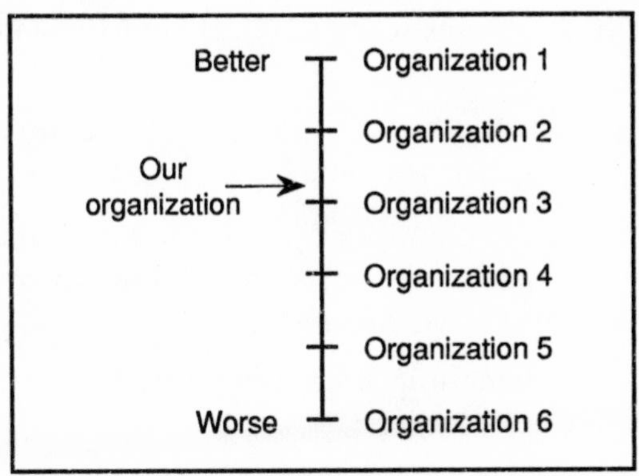

- Brainstorm a list of aids (forces pushing for change).
- Rank listed items by level of significance: high, medium, or low.
- Match aids that balance or overcome barriers.
- List matching barriers and aids on a chart.
- List nonmatching barriers and aids and brainstorm any offsetting factors.
- Using your rankings, identify items needing team action.
- Develop an action plan.

Benchmarking

Benchmarking, as described in greater detail in Chapter 8, is a principal element of the "Quality First" methodology. Benchmarking (Figure 10–13) provides a method of measuring your processes against those of recognized leaders. It helps you to establish priorities and targets leading to process improvement. Benchmarking is conducted when you want to know where you stand with respect to your local competitors or other world-class competitors.

Refer to Chapter 8 for details on conducting benchmark evaluations. The basic elements of benchmarking include the following:

- Identify processes to benchmark and their key characteristics.
- Determine what to benchmark: companies, organizations, or processes.
- Determine benchmarks by collecting and analyzing data from direct contact, surveys, interviews, technical journals, and advertisements.
- From each benchmark item identified, determine the "best of class" target.
- Evaluate your process in terms of the benchmarks and set improvement goals.

Brainstorming

Brainstorming is a way of using a group of people to quickly generate, clarify, and evaluate a sizable list of ideas, problems, issues, and so on. In this case, the emphasis is on *quantity* of ideas, not quality. It can be an excellent technique for tapping the creative thinking of a team. There are three phases of brainstorming:

- During the *generation phase,* the leader reviews the rules for brainstorming and the team members generate a list of items.
- During the *clarification phase,* the team goes over the list to make sure that everyone understands all the items. Discussion will take place later.
- Finally, during the *evaluation phase,* the team reviews the list to eliminate duplications, irrelevancies, or issues that are off-limits.

To conduct a brainstorming session, proceed as follows:*

*Brainstorming is a subjective technique that must later be substantiated by data.

- State purpose clearly.
- Each person takes a turn in sequence, or ideas may be expressed spontaneously.
- Offer one thought at a time.
- Don't criticize ideas.
- Don't discuss ideas.
- Build on others' ideas.
- Record ideas where visible to team members.

Techniques such as multivoting or Nominal Group Techniques (NGT) will generally be used next to select those items that the team should pursue.

Simultaneous (Concurrent) Engineering

Simultaneous (concurrent) engineering is an approach where design alternatives, manufacturing process alternatives, and manufacturing technology alternatives are dealt with in parallel and interactively beginning with the initial design trade-off studies.

Traditionally, quality and producibility have been an after-the-fact review of designs to assess the impact of proposed design features on manufacturing cost and to identify alternatives for the major production cost drivers. With simultaneous (concurrent) engineering, the focus is on both product and process definition simultaneously.

This approach can be used to shorten the design-to-development life cycle and reduce costs by examining the interaction of functional disciplines from the perspective of a cross-functional process.

The basic elements involved in applying simultaneous (concurrent) engineering include the following:

- Use cross-functional teams, including design, quality, marketing, manufacturing, and support.

- Carefully select design parameters to identify and reduce variability in production and use.
- Extend traditional design approach to include such techniques as enterprise integration, design for assembly, robust design, computer-aided design, design for manufacture, group technology, electronic data interchange, and value analysis.
- See also the description of the following tools: design of experiments; quality function deployment (QFD); and team building.

Cost Estimation

Cost estimation aids in selecting improvement opportunities. "Quality First" teams can determine problems with the largest dollar impact by estimating costs using the bottom-up approach and top-down approach. Use these two approaches as follows:

Bottom-Up Approach

- Estimate how many times the problem occurs per unit (example: three times per week).
- Estimate time and cost per unit to fix (example: two people × three hours × $17 per hour equals $102).
- Calculate annual cost (without overhead expenses) by multiplying above factors by weeks worked (example: three people per week × $102 × 50 weeks per year equals $15,300 per year).

Top-Down Approach

- Estimate percent of total labor or other expenditure.
- Multiply estimate by budgeted annual cost to calculate amount spent on the problem (example: 13 percent × $18,000 per year budgeted equals $2,340 per year).

Cost of Quality

Cost of quality consists of all the costs associated with maintaining acceptable quality plus the costs incurred as a result of

FIGURE 10–14
Example of Cost of Quality Impact on Nonconformance

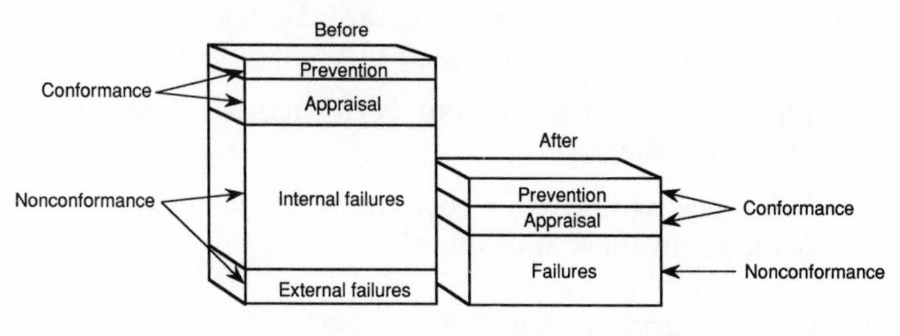

failure to achieve this quality. The cost of quality technique provides managers with cost details often hidden from them. Cost of quality analysis should be performed to highlight costs savings by doing the job right the first time.

To conduct a cost of quality review proceed as follows:

- Identify quality costs. These are cost of nonconformance and cost of conformance, as shown in Figure 10–14.
- Develop a method for collecting data and reporting on cost of quality.
- Identify the most significant costs.
- Identify the cause of these major costs.
- Identify the solutions to reduce or eliminate causes.
- Implement solutions.

Customer Needs Analysis

Customer needs analysis is a technique for determining the key measurable characteristics that are important to your customer. Customer needs analysis is a "Quality First" team effort between you and your customers to answer the following questions:

- What are the *major outputs* of your process?

- Who are the *customers* (both immediate and downstream) for each of these outputs?
- What do your customers say are the *key quality characteristics* that they need in your outputs?
- How can you *measure* your performance on these key characteristics?
- What *goal* would your customers like to see you achieve on these measures?

Possible key quality characteristics are:

- accuracy
- timeliness
- relevance
- completeness
- uniformity
- consistency
- flexibility
- understandability
- reliability

Potential measurements are:

- physical parameters
- time
- cost
- customer satisfaction
- defects and rework
- work output

Customer/Supplier Model

The customer/supplier model is a representation of the customer/supplier relationship depicted by three triangles, shown

FIGURE 10–15
Illustration of Customer/Supplier Model

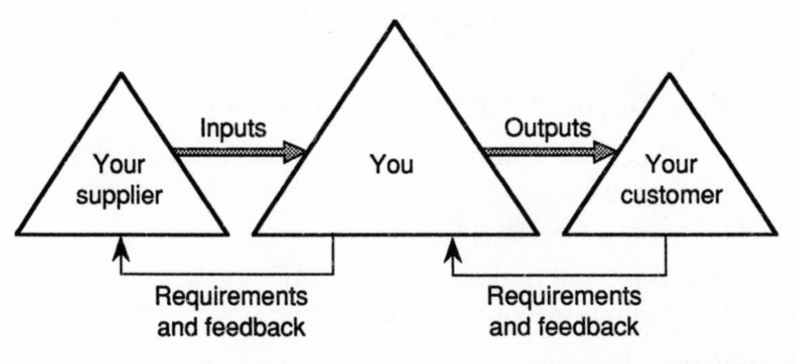

in Figure 10–15, in which the center triangle represents the work you do (i.e., your value-added tasks).

The left triangle represents your supplier(s)—the people or organizations who provide you with the input(s) you need to perform your job.

The right triangle represents your customer(s)—the people or organization(s) who receive your output or the result of your work.

Additional components of the customer/supplier model are requirements and feedback. Requirements are the most critical characteristics of your outputs as defined by your customer. Feedback from your customers communicates the degree to which your output conforms to the negotiated requirements.

Analysis of your organization's customer/supplier model is an effective technique to appraise the total impact of quality.

Customer/Supplier Questionnaire

Use this questionnaire as a technique to assess your relations with your customers and suppliers.

The following are questions you need to ask about your relationship with your customers:

- What are your primary outputs as a supplier: information, products, and/or services?

- Who are your customers—the primary, direct users or recipients of your outputs?
- What are your customers' requirements for your outputs?
- How do you determine their requirements?
- What are the characteristics of your outputs that can be measured to determine whether your customers' requirements are met?
- What are the major quality problems that prevent you from meeting your customers' requirements?
- What obstacles stand in your way of resolving these problems?
- What would it take to resolve these problems?

These are questions you need to ask about your relationship with your suppliers:

- Who are your suppliers? Who do you depend on for input—information, products, and/or services—to fulfill your requirements as one who adds value to their inputs?
- What primary inputs do you receive from them?
- What are your requirements for those inputs?
- How do you communicate your requirements to your suppliers?
- How do you provide feedback to suppliers regarding how they are performing?

Deming/Shewhart (PDCA) Cycle

The Shewhart Cycle [also known as the Deming or Plan-Do-Check-Act (PDCA) cycle] shown in Figure 10–16, represents a cyclic continuous-improvement process for planning and testing improvement activities. When an improvement idea is identified, it is often wise to validate its benefit by testing it on

FIGURE 10–16
Illustration of PDCA Shewhart Cycle

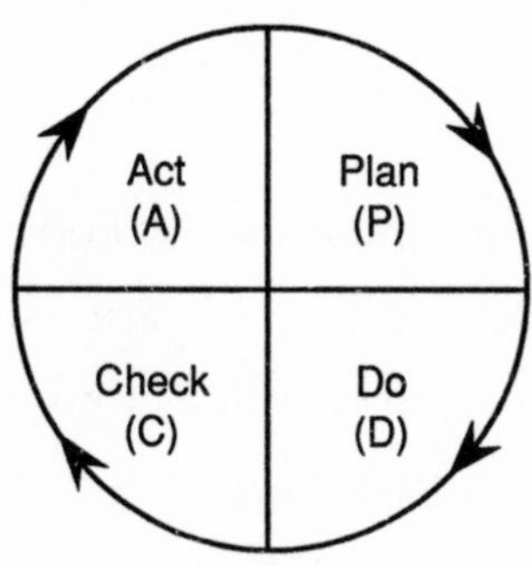

a small scale prior to full implementation. Additionally, by introducing a change on a small scale, employees have time to accept it and are more likely to support it.

The basic elements of the Deming/Shewhart cycle are the Plan (P), Do (D), Check (C), and Act (A) steps often referred to as the PDCA cycle. To implement this technique, proceed as noted below:

- Plan (P) a change or test.
- Do (D) the change or test, preferably on a small scale.
- Check (C) the effects of the change or test.
- Act (A) on what was learned.
- Repeat the Plan step, with new knowledge.
- Repeat the Do step, and continue onward with continuous process improvement.

Design of Experiments

Design-of-experiments analysis is a technique where the analyst chooses factors for study, deliberately varies those factors in a predetermined way, and then studies the effect of these actions.

Design of experiments improves the design-to-production

transition by quickly optimizing product and process design, reduces costs, stabilizes production processes, and desensitizes production variables.

The following are among the many applications for the design-of-experiments analysis:

- Compare two machines or methods.
- Study the relative effects of various process variables.
- Determine the optimal values for process variables.
- Evaluate measurement system error.
- Determine design tolerances.

To implement the design-of-experiments technique:

- Identify the important variables, whether they are product or process parameters, material or components from suppliers, or environmental or measuring equipment factors.
- Separate these important variables—generally no more than one to four.
- Reduce the variation on the important variables (including the tight control of interaction effects) through redesign, close tolerancing design, supplier process improvement, etc.
- Open up the tolerances on the unimportant variables to reduce costs.

Interviewing

Interviewing is a data-gathering process to help "Quality First" teams gain the benefit of others' experience and specialized knowledge.

Things to do:

Before the Interview

- Gather background information on topic and interviewee.

- Outline areas to be covered and major questions to be asked.
- Tell interviewee the purpose and proposed length of the interview.
- Meet in a comfortable setting.

During the Interview

- Help interviewee feel comfortable.
- Remain analytical and objective.
- Take notes.
- Ask open-ended questions to encourage ideas.
- Ask who, what, where, when, why, and how.
- Summarize what you learned.

After the Interview

- Thank the interviewee.
- Review and interpret data as soon as possible (while still fresh in your mind).

Multivoting

Multivoting is a structured series of votes by a "Quality First" team used to help reduce and prioritize a list containing a large number of items to a manageable few (usually three to five).

Multivoting may be used throughout the process after a team discusses the various items on a brainstorm list that is too lengthy for the items to be addressed at once.

Multivoting steps are as follows:

- First vote: Each person votes for as many items as desired, but only once per item. Circle the items receiving a relatively higher number of votes than the other items. (Example: For a team with 10 members, items receiving five or more votes are circled.)

- Second and subsequent votes: Each person votes the number of times equal to one-half the number of circled items. (Example: If six items received five or more votes during the first vote, then each person gets to vote three times during the second vote.)
- Continue multivoting until the list is reduced to three to five items, which can be further analyzed. Never multivote down to only one.

Nominal Group Technique (NGT)

(Nominal Group Technique NGT) is another method used for reaching consensus. It is a group decision-making process used when priority or rank order must be established. NGT is similar to brainstorming; however, it is a structured approach to generate ideas and survey the opinions of a small (10 to fifteen persons) group. NGT is very effective in producing many new ideas/solutions in a short time. It is structured to focus on problems, not people; to open lines of communication; to ensure participation; and to tolerate conflicting ideas. NGT helps build consensus and commitment to the final result.

The basic steps in using NGT are noted below:

- Present issue, instructions.
- Generate ideas during five to 10 minutes of quiet time (no discussion).
- Gather ideas round-robin, one idea at a time, written on a flip chart without discussing them.
- Process/clarify ideas by eliminating duplicates and combining like ideas. Discuss the ideas as a group, but only to clarify their meaning, not to argue about them.
- Set priorities silently.
- Vote to establish the priority or rank of each item.
- Tabulate votes.
- Develop an action plan.

FIGURE 10–17
Example of a Problem Selection Matrix

Problem Areas	Impact On Customer	Can Team Implement	Overall
Are those 3 or 4 remaining after the team has multivoted. Teams should only consider problem areas within their responsibility and control.	A rating based on the team present knowledge and judgement of the direct effect this problem area has on consumer satisfaction. Higher ratings are given to problem areas which have a more direct effect on customers.	A rating based on the team present knowledge and judgement of the difference between the present performance and what is needed to meet the customer's requirements. Higher ratings are given to problem areas with greater need to improve.	The product of impact on customers X need to improve. The problem area receiving the highest ranking should be investigated setting an indicator and actually measuring the present level and comparing it to the requirements. If there is a difference then the team should proceed. If not they should investigate the next.

Scale: 1 None 2 Somewhat 3 Moderate 4 Very 5 Extreme

Source: *AT&T Quality Improvement Process Guidebook,* Florida Power and Light.

Problem Selection Matrix

The problem selection matrix helps the "Quality First" team to select a problem area on which to begin gathering data. If a problem area can be shown to impact both the customer and business objectives, then the analysis should proceed.

Figure 10–17 is an example of a Problem Selection Matrix. The analysis team may come up with more categories to aid in the selection of a problem than are shown in the figure. For example, each column may be "rated" using a five-point scale and, thus, the problem areas are "rank ordered."

Problem Statement Matrix

A good problem statement is one of the keys to using the "Quality First" methodology. A well-stated problem is half solved. A good problem statement describes what is wrong in concrete terms, avoids hidden solutions, and meets the following requirements:

- Specific: State where and when the problem is occurring. It should locate the "pain" of the problem.
- Declarative: Clearly and definitively state the problem. It should not be a question or an incomplete statement.
- Quantified: State the difference between "what is" and "what should be." If the problem statement cannot be stated in quantified (measurable) terms, then it is not a good problem statement. While some problems may be more difficult to quantify than others, it is possible to quantify any problem. If it is not possible to quantify the problem, it is not possible to state the problem in measurable terms. The "problem" then should be reexamined.
- Should not imply cause or solution: Do not imply a solution or assume a cause. Any problem statement using "lack of" or "due to" (or similar phasing) is implying a cause or solution.

The problem statement matrix, shown in Figure 10–18, is a tool for "Quality First" teams to use in developing a good problem statement.

Quality Function Deployment (QFD)

Quality Function Deployment (QFD) is a conceptual map that provides the means for cross-functional planning and communications. It is a method for transforming customer wants and needs into quantitative terms.

Quality Function Deployment, developed in Japan, is a process for ensuring that quality is designed into products and services in an efficient and effective manner. QFD helps organizations design more competitive, higher-quality, lower-cost products more easily and quickly and is aimed primarily at the development of new products. It starts early in new product design efforts and translates customer requirements into design and product characteristics, communicating them in a

FIGURE 10–18
Example of a Problem Statement Matrix

Problem Statement (Who, What When, Where– But Not Why)	States the Effects, Not the Cause	Focuses on the Gap Between "What Is And "What Should Be"	Is It Measurable	Is It Specific (Avoids Broad Categories)	Is It Positive (Avoids "Lack Of" Statements)	Does It Focus on the Pain (How Things Are Affected)
# 1						
# 2						
# 3						

Source: *AT&T Quality Improvement Process Guidebook,* Florida Power and Light.

structured way to influence upstream design decisions and actions. Traditional design organizations have focused more on meeting specifications or technical requirements than on satisfying customer expectations. QFD links customer expectations to the technical considerations of the designer and manufacturer, and to the concept of value in a manner that connections and relationships can be understood and addressed.

Quality Function Deployment helps ensure quality products and processes by detecting and solving problems early. Downstream problems may occur and product quality may suffer when those who work on components and parts have little knowledge of customer requirements or the specifics of the final product and manufacturing processes. The QFD process forces management to analyze broad customer needs and expectations (such as ease of use or comfort) and relate them directly to product characteristics such as weight, strength, speed, and temperature. Those characteristics in turn are related to the processes involved in achieving the technical requirements. Specific techniques and tools are employed in the course of quality function deployment. One of the principal quality-function deployment tools is the "house of quality" matrix shown in Figure 10–19.

FIGURE 10–19
House of Quality Matrix

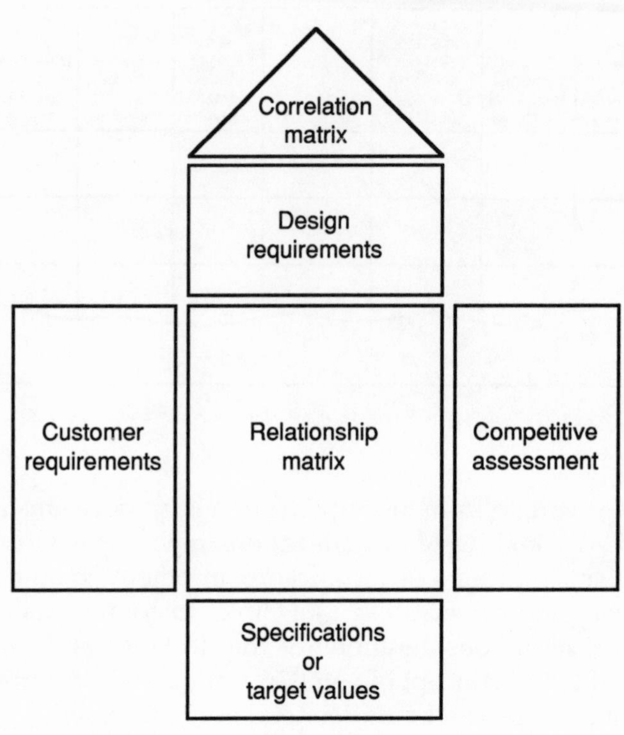

The matrix identifies specific customer-required characteristics, assigns priorities to them, and converts them to product attributes and design characteristics through cross-functional team activity. The matrix relates customer needs and expectations to specific product characteristics and links those characteristics to the product-related functional area processes. It communicates product-specific requirements, standards, and specifications in a coordinated and consistent way across all the functions that have responsibilities affecting the product. The generation and distribution of quality matrixes force early identification of conflicting objectives and potential bottlenecks. Early cross-functional communication should be centered on quality, resolving many potential problems before major investments of time and money have been made.

Products should be designed to meet customer wants and needs so that customers will buy products and services and continue to buy them. Marketing people, design engineers, manufacturing engineers, and procurement specialists work closely together from the time a product/service is first conceived to be able to meet customer requirements. Quality Function Deployment provides a framework within which the cross-functional teams can work.

To begin the QFD process, ask these questions:

- What do customers want (attributes)?
- Are all preferences equally important?
- Will responding to perceived needs yield a competitive advantage?
- What are the characteristics that match customers' attributes?
- How does each characteristic affect each customer attribute?
- How does one change affect other characteristics?

Solutions Selection Matrix

A solutions selection matrix is an illustration of factors affecting possible improvement actions or problem solutions. To help choose the best solution, the matrix could use headings similar to those in Figure 10–20 or you can develop your own headings. Be creative. Develop a matrix suitable to your situation. It is a proven technique for organizing information. It aids in comparing possible solutions and identifying voids in known information.

This matrix can help the "Quality First" team members to analyze the most significant factors affecting the solution. They can do this through analyzing the data collected during their investigation and choosing the factors of greatest significance. The team can also brainstorm to discover other, as yet hidden,

FIGURE 10–20
Example of Solutions Selection Matrix

Possible Solution	Dollar Cost to Implement	Are Involved Departments/ Areas Committed	Percentage of Problem Solved	Can Team Implement	Other
# 1					
# 2					
# 3					

Source: *AT&T Quality Improvement Process Guidebook* and Florida Power and Light.

factors. These should be reduced to a usable number of significant categories (usually five to seven) and entered in the matrix.

Then simply fill in the matrix according to data collected or data-based estimations. Remember: we want to speak with facts. Guesses and opinions are permissible but they must be educated ones—and immediately researched.

Statistical Process Control (SPC)

Statistical Process Control (SPC) is an effective tool for improving performance of any process. It helps identify problems quickly and accurately. It also provides quantifiable data for analysis, provides a reference baseline, and promotes participation and decision making by people doing the job.

Statistical Process Control is an excellent technique for determining the cause of variation based on a statistical analysis of the problem. SPC uses probability theory to control and improve processes.

Statistical Process Control is a major technique used to implement the "Quality First" methodology. Refer to one of the fundamental statistical publications noted in Appendix A—Executive Reading for substantial "how-to" information. The basic steps involved in SPC include:

- Identify problems or performance improvement areas. Identify common and special causes. Common causes are random in nature, often minor. Special causes result from an abnormality in the system that prevents the process from becoming stable.
- Do a cause-and-effect analysis.
- Collect data.
- Apply statistical techniques (may need a quality statistical specialist).
- Analyze variations.
- Take corrective action.

THE OPTIONS

This chapter has briefly described the "Quality First" tools and techniques that you may use to improve your quality. It has provided a basic vocabulary and delineation of the application options for each of the "Quality First" tools and techniques.

The past several chapters have described the principles, practices, tools, and techniques that can help you begin your "Quality First" improvement program. It's up to you to act now!

Chapter Eleven
Act Now!

"It is time for a new generation of leadership, to cope with new problems and new opportunities. For there is a new world to be won."

John Fitzgerald Kennedy
July 4, 1960

LEAD YOUR "QUALITY FIRST" TEAM

Whoever you are, it is often easy to fall into the trap of thinking that your company is too big to be affected by your individual actions. That perception is common and frustrating, and fortunately, it is a false one. Only through the collective efforts of their individual members do companies change; companies are incapable of changing themselves.

Whatever your position in your company, your efforts to perform a job and to improve that performance directly affect the influence you will have in the organization, the control you will have over your personal situation, and your ability to manage and lead. Combined with the efforts of others, your effectiveness directly influences the company's overall ability to meet its mission and ultimately affects our performance as a nation. Furthermore, how we perform today will also affect future generations.

"Quality First" is a means for improving personal effectiveness and performance and for aligning and focusing all individual quality efforts throughout your company. It provides a framework within which you may continuously improve everything you do and affect. It is a way of leveraging your individual effort and extending its effect and its importance throughout your organization and beyond.

MAKE THE DECISION TODAY

You have examined in this book the need to adopt the "Quality First" strategy to improve your competitiveness. A guide to the costs and benefits has been presented, showing that you can't afford *not* to act now in improving your level of quality performance. You have read about the different philosophies of quality improvement from Crosby, Deming, and Juran, and found that an amalgam of these principles and practices needs to be created to meet your specific needs. The Malcolm Baldrige National Quality Award has set the scene for self-assessment; and the companies that have won the award have described their experiences and the lessons they have learned in improving the quality of their products or services. A series of approximately 200 questions were raised for you to perform an armchair assessment of how your company/organization is doing in terms of quality. The "Quality First" methodology has laid out the basic planning and implementation steps needed for you to aggressively and continuously improve your operations. And the tools and techniques you and your staff need to use to understand your level of quality and show areas for improvement have also been presented.

Table 11–1 provides the basic "Quality First" action items you need to implement to improve your quality.

It is now up to you. Do it!

TABLE 11–1
"Quality First" Action Items

Planning

Step 1 Top Management Commitment to "Quality First"
- Bring executive team up to speed on quality principles.
  - Recognize importance of management commitment.
  - Review "Quality First" principles.
  - Review your competitive position.
  - Take team approach to quality improvement.

Step 2 Create a Vision and Philosophy
- Formulate your vision and philosophy to implement "Quality First," which will guide the company's quality efforts.
- Issue policy statement on the principles of quality.

Step 3 Establish Quality Council
- Include executives from headquarters office and field offices.
- Include the head of the company as an active member of the Quality Council.

Step 4 Identify Customer Needs
- Identify customers.
- Determine customer needs.
- Determine level of customer satisfaction.
- Translate needs into requirements.

Step 5 Develop Your Own "Quality First" Strategy
- Determine approach to enhance quality in the company.
- Incorporate "Quality First" activities into the strategic and business planning process.
- Establish a system for each unit to set quality improvement goals.
- Encourage early participation by the employee union in implementation of "Quality First."
- Use existing management systems, wherever appropriate, in implementing "Quality First."

Step 6 Select Organization to Implement "Quality First"
- Determine readiness of the organization.
- Decide on the scope of implementation (across the company or within a unit).

TABLE 11–1 *(continued)*

Step 7 Conduct Training Needs Analysis
- Analyze training needs of executives, managers, and employees.
- Determine what types of courses need to be developed (awareness, problem-solving, group dynamics, statistics, etc.) for each group.

Step 8 Determine Resources for Implementation
- Determine time frames and costs for developing and conducting training.
- Identify the sources of funding for training and award systems.
- Determine whether in-house staff can develop and conduct training.

Step 9 Conduct Training
- Identify individual(s) with quality expertise to help train staff.
- Identify suppliers of training.
- Develop and conduct training.

Step 10 Identify Performance Measures
- Ensure that organizational units develop standards for measuring whether products and services meet customer requirements.
- Adjust existing measurement and management systems to measure whether customer requirements are being met.

Implementation

Step 11 Implement "Quality First" Philosophy
- Implement continuous process-improvement principles.
- Implement systems for training, involving, rewarding, and recognizing employees.
- Implement strategies, goal-setting, and measurement of improvements in quality.
- Implement process analysis and structured problem-solving approaches.

TABLE 11–1 *(continued)*

Step 12	Benchmark Your Products and Services • Identify worldwide competitor products/services. • Assess who is the "best of class." • Develop product/services improvement goals.
Step 13	Implement Continuous Improvement Process • Set the stage for process improvement. • Select a process to improve. • Define the process. • Standardize the process. • Tighten the process. • Improve the process. • Assess improved performance.
Step 14	Monitor and Evaluate Results • Monitor the progress of teams on quality improvement projects. • Track quality improvements against goals.
Step 15	Recognize Success • Publicize successes. • Reward and recognize quality improvement. • Promote "Quality First" throughout the company.
Step 16	Adjust Your "Quality First" Process • Use feedback to modify and improve the process. • Expand to other segments of the company.
Step 17	Continue to Improve • Select new processes to improve. • Continue to improve all processes to remove defects. • Don't stop.

Appendix A
Executive Reading

INTRODUCTORY MATERIALS

Crosby, Philip B. *Quality is Free: The Art of Making Quality Certain*. New York: McGraw-Hill, 1979.

Ishikawa, Kaoru. *What Is Total Quality Control? The Japanese Way*. Englewood Cliffs, N.J.: Prentice-Hall, 1985.

Juran, Joseph M. *Juran on Leadership for Quality: An Executive Handbook*. New York: Free Press, 1989.

Scherkenbach, William W. *The Deming Route to Quality and Productivity*. Rockville, Md.: Mercury Press, 1988.

Walton, Mary. *Deming Management at Work*. New York: Putnam, 1990.

ADDITIONAL READINGS

Albrecht, Karl. *At America's Service: How Corporations Can Revolutionize the Way They Treat Their Customers*. Homewood, Ill.: Dow Jones-Irwin, 1988.

Albrecht, Karl, and Ron Zemke. *Service America: Doing Business in the New Economy*. Homewood, Ill.: Dow Jones-Irwin, 1985.

Aubrey II, Charles A., and Patricia K. Felkins. *Teamwork: Involving People in Quality and Productivity Improvement*. Milwaukee, Wis.: Quality Press, 1988.

Bennis, Warren, and Burt Nanus. *Leaders: The Strategies for Taking Charge*. New York: Harper & Row, 1985.

Crosby, Philip B. *Quality Without Tears: The Art of Hassle-Free Management*. New York: McGraw-Hill, 1984.

Deming, W. Edwards. *Out of the Crisis*. Cambridge, Mass.: MIT Center for Advanced Engineering Study, 1982.

Ealey, Lance A. *Quality By Design: Taguchi Methods and U.S. Industry*. Dearborn, Mich.: ASI Press, 1988.

Ernst & Young Quality Improvement Consulting Group. *Total Quality: An Executive's Guide for the 1990's*. Homewood, Ill.: The Dow Jones-Irwin/APICS Series in Production Management, 1990.

Garvin, David A. *Managing Quality: The Strategic and Competitive Edge*. New York: Free Press, 1988.

Harrington, H. James. *Excellence – The IBM Way*. Milwaukee, Wis.: Publisher's Quality Press, 1988.

Harrington, H. James. *The Improvement Process – How America's Leading Companies Improve Quality*. New York: McGraw-Hill, 1987.

Hickman, Craig R., and Michael A. Silva. *Creating Excellence*. New York: New American Library, 1984.

Imai, Masaki. *Kaizen: The Key to Japan's Competitive Success*. New York: Random House, 1986.

Ishikawa, Kaoru. *Guide to Quality Control*. White Plains, N.Y.: Kraus International Publications, 1982.

Juran, Joseph M. *Juran on Planning for Quality*. New York: Free Press, 1988.

Juran, Joseph M. *Juran's Quality Control Handbook*. New York: McGraw-Hill, 1988.

McGregor, Douglas. *The Human Side of Enterprise*. New York: McGraw-Hill, 1985.

Michalak, Donald F., and Edwin G. Yager. *Making the Training Process Work*. New York: Harper & Row, 1979.

Peters, Tom. *Thriving on Chaos*. New York: Alfred A. Knopf, 1987.

Scholtes, Peter R., et. al. *The Team Handbook – How to Use Teams to Improve Quality*. Madison, Wis.: Joiner Associates Inc., 1988.

Zemke, Ron, and Dick Schaaf. *The Service Edge: 101 Companies that Profit from Customer Care*. New York: New American Library, 1989.

Walton, Mary. *The Deming Management Method*. New York: Dodd, Mead, 1986.

Appendix B
Definitions

appraisal costs The costs associated with inspecting the product to ensure that it meets the customer's (either internal or external) needs and requirements.

best of class When overall performance, in terms of effectiveness, efficiency, and adaptability, is superior to all comparables.

brainstorming A technique used by a group of people for thought generation. The aim is to elicit as many ideas as possible within a given time frame.

cause An established reason for the existence of a defect.

common cause A source of variation in the process output that is inherent to the process and will affect all the individual results or values of process output.

control The set of activities employed to detect and correct deviation in order to maintain or restore a desired state. A historically oriented approach to quality management.

correction The totality of actions to minimize or remove variations and their causes.

cost of quality The sum of the cost of prevention, appraisal, and failure. The key financial measurement tool that ties process control and process optimization into a total process-management effort. It can be used both as an indicator and a signal for variation (more often, for patterns of variation), as well as a measure of productivity and efficiency.

corrective action The implementation of effective solutions that result in the elimination of identified product, service, and process problems.

cross-functional teams Teams similar to quality teams but whose members are from several work units that interface with one another. These teams are particularly useful when work units are dependent upon one another for materials, information, etc.

culture A prevailing pattern of activities, interactions, norms, sentiments, beliefs, attitudes, values, and products in an organization.

customer The recipient or beneficiary of the outputs of your work efforts or the purchaser of your products and services. May be either internal or external to the organization, and must be satisfied with the output of your work efforts.

data Information or a set of facts presented in descriptive form. There are two basic kinds of data: measured (also known as variable data) and counted (also known as attribute data).

defect Any state of nonconformance to requirements.

Deming Prize In 1950, W. Edwards Deming was invited to Japan by the Union of Japanese Scientists and Engineers (JUSE) to lecture on the applicability of using quality control in manufacturing companies. The impact of Deming's teaching was widespread and swift to take root. In 1951, JUSE instituted the Deming Prize to honor Deming for his friendship and achievements in industrial quality control. Today, Japanese companies wishing to improve the level of quality within their organization compete for the Deming Prize, not only to achieve the honor and prestige of winning, but also for the improvements that come from implementing his quality principles.

effectiveness How closely an organization's output meets its goal and/or meets the customer's requirement.

efficiency Production of required output at a perceived minimum cost. It is measured by the ratio of the quantity of resources expected or planned to be consumed in meeting customer requirements to the resources actually consumed.

external failure costs The costs incurred when an external customer receives a defective product.

fishbone diagrams A diagram that depicts the characteristics of a problem or process and the factors or root causes that contribute to them.

force field analysis A technique involving the identification of forces "for" and "against" a certain course of action. The nominal group technique could be used in conjunction with force field analysis. The group might prioritize the forces for and against by assessing their magnitude and probability of occurrence. The group might then develop an action plan to minimize the forces against and maximize the forces for.

frequency distribution Of a discrete variable is the count of the number of occurrences of individual values over a given range.

Of a continuous variable is the count of cases that lie between certain predetermined limits over the range of values the variable may assume.

functional administrative control technique A tool designed to improve performance through a process combining time management and value engineering. The process involves breaking activities down into functions and establishing action teams to target and solve problems in each function.

functional organization An organization responsible for one of the major organizational functions such as marketing, sales, design, manufacturing, and distribution.

gainsharing A reward system that shares productivity gains between owners and employees. Gainsharing is generally used to provide incentive for group efforts toward improvement.

goal A statement of attainment/achievement that one proposes to accomplish or attain with an implication of sustained effort and energy directed to it over a long term.

guideline A suggested practice that is not mandatory in programs intended to comply with a standard.

hypothesis An assertion made about the value of some parameter of a population.

input Materials, energy, or information required to complete the activities necessary to produce a specified output (work product).

internal failure costs The costs generated by defects found within the enterprise prior to the product reaching the external customer.

mean time between failures (MTBF) The average time between successive failures of a given product.

measurement The act or process of measuring to compare results to requirements. A quantitative estimate of performance.

need A lack of something requisite, desired, or useful; a condition requiring provision or relief. Usually expressed by users or customers.

nominal group technique A tool for idea generation, problem solving, mission, and key result area definition, performance measure definition, goals/objectives definition.

normative performance measurement technique Incorporates structured group processes so that work groups can design measurement systems suited for their own needs. This approach considers behavioral consequences of measurement to foster acceptance of measurement effort.

objective A statement of the desired result to be achieved within a specified time. By definition, an objective always has an associated schedule.

output The specified end result. Required by the recipient.

outputs Materials or information provided to others (internal or external customers).

Pareto charts Are used to classify problems or causes by priority. It helps highlight the vital few as opposed to the trivial many. It also helps to identify which cause or problem is the most significant.

performance A term used both as an attribute of the work product itself and as a general process characteristic. The broad performance characteristics that are of interest to management are quality (effectiveness), cost (efficiency), and schedule. Performance is the highly effective common measurement that links the quality of the work product to efficiency and productivity.

plan A specified course of action designed to attain a stated objective.

policy A statement of principles and beliefs, or a settled course, adopted to guide the overall management of affairs in support of a stated aim or goal. It is mostly related to fundamental conduct and usually defines a general framework within which other business and management actions are carried out.

population A large collection of items (product observations, data) about certain characteristics of which conclusions and decisions are to be made for purposes of process assessment and quality improvement.

prevention A future-oriented approach to quality management that achieves quality improvement through curative action on the process.

prevention costs The costs associated with actions taken to plan the product or process to ensure that defects do not occur.

problem A question or situation proposed for solution. The result of not conforming to requirements, which can create a potential task resulting from the existence of defects.

process A system in operation to produce an output of higher value than that of the sum of its inputs. A process is also defined as the logical organization of people, materials, energy, equipment, and procedures into work activities designed to produce a specified end result (work product).

process capability Long-term performance level after the process has been brought under control.

process control The set of activities employed to detect and remove special causes of variation in order to maintain or restore stability (statistical control).

process flow analysis A technique for identification and analysis of key processes, and for areas and methods of possible improvement. It is particularly useful for roadblock removal.

process improvement The set of activities employed to detect and remove common causes of variation in order to improve process capability. Process improvement leads to quality improvement.

process management Management approach comprising quality management and process optimization.

process optimization The major aspect of process management that concerns itself with the efficiency and productivity of the process; that is, with economic factors.

process owner A designated person within the process, who has authority to manage the process and responsibility for its overall performance.

process performance A measure of how effectively and efficiently a process satisfies customer requirements.

process review An objective assessment of how well the methodology has been applied to your process. Emphasizes the potential for long-term process results rather than the actual results achieved.

productivity Ratio of outputs produced (or service transactions) to inputs required for production/completion. Productivity is an expected outcome of quality and a necessary companion to improving service.

quality The extent to which products and services produced conform to customer requirements. Customers can be internal as well as external to the organizational system (e.g., products or services may flow to the person at the next desk or work area rather than to people outside of the immediate organization). The Federal Quality Institute defines quality as meeting the customer requirements the first time and every time. The Department of Defense (DoD) defines quality as conformance to a set of customer requirements that, if met, result in a product that is fit for its intended use.

quality circles A group of workers and their supervisors who voluntarily meet to identify and solve job-related problems. Structured processes are used by the group to accomplish their task.

quality function deployment (QFD) A disciplined approach to solving quality problems before the design phase of a product. The foundation of QFD is the belief that products should be designed to reflect customer desires; therefore, marketers, design engineers, and manufacturing personnel must work closely together from the beginning to ensure a successful product. The approach involves finding out what features are important to customers, ranking them in importance, identifying conflicts, and translating them into engineering specifications.

quality of working life The extent to which the organizational culture provides employees with information, knowledge, authority, and rewards to enable them to perform safely and effectively, be compensated equitably, and maintain a sense of human dignity.

quality teams Also referred to as Performance Action Teams or Quality Improvement Teams. They might be composed of volunteers who meet regularly to review progress toward goal attainment, plan for changes, decide upon corrective actions, etc. Members are usually from the same work unit.

range The difference between the maximum and the minimum value of data in a sample.

reliability The probability that a product entity will perform its specified function under specified conditions, without failure, for a specified period of time.

requirement A formal statement of a need, and the expected manner in which it is to be met.

requirements What is expected in providing a product or service. The "it" in "do it right the first time." Specific and measurable customer needs with an associated performance standard.

roadblock identification analysis A tool that focuses upon identifying roadblocks to performance improvement and/or problems that are causing the group to be less productive than it could be. This tool utilizes the nominal group technique to identify and prioritize performance roadblocks. Action teams are formed to analyze barriers and develop proposals to remove roadblocks. The proposals are implemented, tracked, and evaluated.

root cause analysis The bottom line of a problem. Often, problems present themselves only as symptoms. Symptoms do not explain problems, they point to them. A root cause is the reason for the problem or symptom. Root cause analysis, then, is a method used to identify potential root causes of problems, narrow those down to the most significant causes, and analyze them using other "Quality First" tools.

sample A finite number of items taken from a population.

Scanlon committees Committees comprised of managers, supervisors, and employees who work together to implement a philosophy of management/labor cooperation that is believed to enhance productivity. There are a number of principles and techniques involved, with employee participation being a major component.

simulation The technique of observing and manipulating an artificial mechanism (model) that represents a real world process that, for technical or economical reasons, is not suitable or available for direct experimentation.

special cause A source of variation in the process output that is unpredictable, unstable, or intermittent. Also called assignable cause.

specification A document containing a detailed description or enumeration of particulars. Formal description of a work product and the intended manner of providing it (the provider's view of the work product).

standard deviation A parameter describing the spread of the process output, denoted by the Greek letter sigma, σ. The positive square root of the variance.

statistic Any parameter that can be determined on the basis of the quantitative characteristics of a sample.

A descriptive statistic is a computed measure of some property of a set of values, making possible a definitive statement about the meaning of the collected data.

An inferential statistic indicates the confidence that can be placed in any statement regarding its expected accuracy, the range of its applicability, and the probability of its being true. Consequently, decisions can be based on inferential statistics.

statistics The branch of applied mathematics that describes and analyzes empirical observations for the purpose of predicting certain events in order to make decisions in the face of uncertainty. Statistics, in turn, are based on the theory of probability. The two together provide the abstraction for the mathematical model underlying the study of problems involving uncertainty.

statistical control The status of a process from which all special causes of variation have been removed and only common causes remain. Such a process is also said to be stable.

statistical estimation The analysis of a sample parameter in order to predict the values of the corresponding population parameter.

statistical methods The application of the theory of probability to problems of variation. There are two groups of statistical methods.

Basic statistical methods are relatively simple problem-solving tools and techniques, such as control charts, capability analysis, data summarization and analysis, and statistical inference.

Advanced statistical methods are more sophisticated specialized techniques of statistical analysis, such as the design of experiments, regression and correlation analysis, and the analyses of variance.

statistical process control A disciplined way of identifying and solving problems in order to improve performance. It involves use of fishbone diagrams to identify causes and effects of problems. Data are then collected and organized in various ways (graphs, fishbone diagrams, Pareto charts, and/or histograms) to further examine problems. The data may be tracked over time (control charts) to determine variation in the process. The process is then changed in some way and new data are collected and analyzed to determine whether the process has been improved.

strategy A broad course of action, chosen from a number of alternatives, to accomplish a stated goal in the face of uncertainty.

subprocesses The internal processes that make up a process.

suppliers Individuals, organizations, or firms that provide inputs to you. Suppliers can be internal or external to a company, firm, or organization.

team building A process of developing and maintaining a group of people who are working toward a common goal. Team building usually focuses on one or more of the following objectives:

(1) clarifying role expectations and obligations of team members, (2) improving superior-subordinate or peer relationships, (3) improving problem solving, decision making, resource utilization, or planning activities, (4) reducing conflict, and (5) improving organizational climate.

timeliness The promptness with which quality products and services are delivered, relative to customer expectations.

transactional analysis A process that helps people change to be more effective on the job and can also help organizations to change. The process involves several exercises that help identify organizational scripts and games that people may be playing. The results help point the way toward change.

variable A data item that takes on values within some range with a certain frequency or pattern. Variables may be discrete, that is, limited in value to integer quantities (for example, the number of bolts produced in a manufacturing process). Discrete variables relate to attribute data. Variables may also be continuous, that is, measured to any desired degree of accuracy (for example, the diameter of a shaft). Continuous variables relate to variables data.

variance In quality management terminology, any nonconformance to specifications. In statistics, it is the square of the standard deviation.

Appendix C

Information Resources

NATIONAL ASSOCIATIONS AND CENTERS

American Production and Inventory Control Society
500 W. Annandale Road
Falls Church, VA 22046
(703) 237-8344

Focus on just-in-time, capacity management, materials requirements, production activity, and master planning. Annual conference, seminars/ workshops, exhibitions, *Production Inventory Management Journal*, technical publications, professional certification, local chapters.

Quality and Productivity Management Association
300 Martingale Road
Schaumburg, IL 60173
(708) 619-2909

Network of North American quality and productivity coordinators, operating managers, and staff managers. Conferences, workshops, journal, newsletter, resources guide, local chapters.

American Productivity & Quality Center
123 North Post Oak Lane
Houston, TX 77024
(713) 681-4020

Educational advisory services to organizations in the private and public sectors. Courses, research publications, case studies, the *Letter* newsletter, resource guide, library, consulting.

American Society for Quality Control
310 West Wisconsin Avenue
Milwaukee, WI 53203
(414) 272-8575
The nation's largest professional society that is dedicated to the advancement of quality. Conferences, educational courses, seminars, *The Quality Review* magazine, journal, book service, professional certification, technical divisions and committees, local chapters.

American Society for Training and Development
1630 Duke Street
Alexandria, VA 22313
(703) 683-8100
Leader in the development of training programs.

Association for Quality and Participation
801-B West 8th Street
Suite 501
Cincinnati, OH 45023
(513) 381-1959
Focus on quality circles, self-managing teams, union-management committees, sociotechnical analysis, and other aspects of employee involvement. Conferences, library and research service, *Quality and Participation* journal, newsletter, resource guide, local chapters.

Work in America Institute
700 White Plains Road
Scarsdale, NY 10583
(914) 472-9600
Research and member advisory services focusing on productivity and quality through employee involvement, labor-management relations, and quality of working life. Member forum and seminars, site visits, policy studies, *Work in America* newsletter, library, research service, technical publications, speakers, and consultants bureau.

REGIONAL AND UNIVERSITY-BASED CENTERS

Linked through the National Productivity Network, the following centers provide a variety of productivity related services, including technical assistance, planning studies, technology transfer, continuing education, productivity audits, management development, contractual assistance, publications, seminars/workshops, and research and development.

Community Quality Coalition
c/o Transformation of America Industry Project
Jackson Community College
2111 Emmons Road
Jackson, MI 49201
(517) 789-1627

Georgia Productivity Center
Georgia Institute of Technology
219 O'Keeffe Building
Atlanta, GA 30332
(404) 894-6101

Manufacturing Productivity Center
10 West 35th Street
Chicago, IL 60616
(312) 567-4800

Center for Quality and Productivity
University of Maryland
College Park, MD 20742-7215
(301) 403-4535

Center for the Productive Use of Technology
George Mason University
Metro Campus
3401 North Fairfax, #322
Arlington, VA 22201
(703) 841-2675

Pennsylvania Technical Assistance Program (PENNTAP)
Pennsylvania State University
University Park, PA 16802
(814) 865-0427

University of Wisconsin-Madison
Center for Quality and Productivity Improvement
620 Walnut Street
Madison, WI 53705
(608) 263-2520

OTHER ORGANIZATIONAL RESOURCES

American Center for the Quality of Work Life
37 Tip Top Way
Berkeley Heights, NJ 07922
(201) 464-4609

Information, training, and consulting focused on creating and implementing organizational change and renewal.

American Supplier Institute
6 Parklane Boulevard, Suite 411
Dearborn, MI 48126
(313) 336-8877

Focus on Taguchi methods, quality function deployment, total quality management. Training, consulting, special conferences, books, videotapes, journal.

Canadian Supplier Institute
Skyline Complex
644 Dixon Road
Rexdale, Ontario M9W 1J4
(416) 235-1777

Focus on Taguchi methods, quality function deployment, total quality management. Training, consulting, books and videotapes, special conferences.

QCI International
P.O. Box 1503
Red Bluff, CA 96080
(916) 527-6970

Focus on employee involvement, total quality, and statistical process control. Seminars, in-house training, books, videotapes, *Quality Digest* magazine.

QUALITY CONSULTANTS

American Productivity & Quality Center
123 North Post Oak Lane
Houston, TX 77024
Contact: Jackie Comola
(713) 681-4020

American Supplier Institute
15041 Commerce Drive, South
Dearborn, MI 48126
Contact: John McHugh
(313) 336-8877

Coopers & Lybrand
1525 Wilson Boulevard, Suite 800
Arlington, VA 22209
Contact: Ian Littman
(703) 875-2102

Philip Crosby Associates, Inc.
807 West Morse Boulevard
P.O. Box 2369
Winter Park, FL 32790
(305) 645-1733

Dr. W. Edwards Deming
4924 Butterworth Place
Washington, DC 20016
(202) 363-8552

Ernst & Young
1225 Connecticut Avenue Northwest
Washington, DC 20036
Contact: Renee Jakubiak
(202) 862-6000

General Systems Company, Inc.
Berkshire Common, South Street
Pittsfield, MA 01201
Contact: Armand Fiegenbaum
(413) 499-2880

Goal/QPC
13 Branch Street
Methuen, MA 01844
Contact: Stan Marsh
(508) 685-3900

IIT Research Institute
Beeches Technical Campus
Route 26 North
Rome, NY 13440-8200
Contact: Steve Flint
(315) 337-0900

Juran Institute, Inc.
88 Danbury Road
Wilton, CT 06897
(203) 834-1700

Technology Research Corporation
5716 Jonathan Mitchell Road
Fairfax Station, VA 22039
(703) 451-8830 and (703) 250-5136
Contact: V. Daniel Hunt

FEDERAL GOVERNMENT

Federal Quality Institute
441 F Street Northwest
Washington, DC 20001
Contacts: John Franke, Director
(202) 376-3747
Jeff Manthos, Information Network Office
(202) 376-3753

The Federal Quality Institute (FQI) provides a start-up service in Total Quality Management for top-level federal government management teams. The FQI serves as a government-wide focal point for information about Total Quality Management through the FQI Information Network, which lends to the "federal" sector materials such as videotapes, books, and case studies at no cost.

Navy Personnel Research and Development Center
Quality Support Center
San Diego, CA 92152-6800
(619) 553-7956 (619) 553-7956 (AV)

U.S. Army Management Engineering College
Rock Island, IL 61299-7040
(309) 782-0470 (309) 793-0470 (AV)

QUALITY AWARDS

Deming Prize
Information concerning the Deming Prize application can be obtained by contacting:
Junji Noguchi
Executive Director
Union of Japanese Scientists and Engineers
5-10-11 Sendagaya
Shibuya-Ku
Tokyo 151, Japan
FAX: 9-011-813-225-1813

Malcolm Baldrige National Quality Award
Malcolm Baldrige National Quality Award
National Institute of Standards and Technology
Route 270 and Quince Orchard Road
Administration Building, Room A537
Gaithersburg, MD 20899
(301) 975-2036
FAX: (301) 948-3716

MAGAZINES AND NEWSLETTERS

PRIDE Publications
P.O. Box 695
Arlington Heights, IL 60004
(708) 398-0430

Commitment-Plus newsletter, monthly, $95/yr.

American Productivity & Quality Center
123 North Post Oak Lane
Houston, TX 77024
(713) 681-4020

The **Letter** newsletter, monthly, $125/yr.

Manufacturing Productivity Center, IIT Center
10 West 35th Street
Chicago, IL 60616
(312) 567-4808

Manufacturing Competitiveness Frontiers magazine, monthly, $100/yr.

Society of Manufacturing Engineers
P.O. Box 930
Dearborn, MI 48121
(313) 271-1500

Manufacturing Engineering magazine, monthly, $60/yr.

American Production and Inventory Control Society
500 West Annandale Road
Falls Church, VA 22046
(703) 237-8344

Production Inventory Management Journal, quarterly, $110/yr.

Productivity, Inc.
101 Merritt 7
Norwalk, CT 06851
(203) 846-3777

Productivity newsletter, monthly, $167/yr.

Hitchcock Publishing Co.
191 South Gary Avenue
Carol Stream, IL 60188
(708) 665-1000

Quality magazine, monthly, $65/yr.

QCI International
P.O. Box 882
Red Bluff, CA 96080

Quality Digest magazine, monthly, $75/yr.

Association for Quality and Participation
801-B West 8th Street
Cincinnati, OH 45023
(513) 381-1959

Quality and Participation journal, quarterly, $35/yr.

American Society for Quality Control (ASQC)
310 West Wisconsin Avenue
Milwaukee, WI 53203
(414) 272-8575

Quality Progress, 12 issues/$40, monthly publication

American Society for Quality Control
310 West Wisconsin Avenue
Milwaukee, WI 53203
(414) 272-8575

Journal of Quality Technology, 12 issues/$13, monthly publication

American Society for Quality Control
310 West Wisconsin Avenue
Milwaukee, WI 53203
(414) 272-8575

The Quality Review magazine, quarterly, $36/yr.

Buraff Publications
2445 M Street Northwest, Suite 275
Washington, DC 20037
(202) 452-7889

Work in America newsletter, monthly, $247/yr.

VIDEOTAPES

The Deming Library (16 videotapes). Contact Joyce Leon, at Films, Inc., 5547 Ravenswood Avenue, Chicago, Illinois 60640-1199, (800) 323-4222, extension 381. No preview fee for government agencies. Videotapes may be purchased for $595 each, two or more at $495 each, or the complete set of 16 volumes for $7,920. The Deming Library is a video training seminar that covers all aspects of W. Edwards Deming's philosophy.

Volume 1: The New Economic Age (33 minutes)

Volume 2: The 14 Points (40 minutes, two parts)

Volume 3: Corporate Leadership (25 minutes)

Volume 4: Adoption of the New Philosophy (21 minutes)

Volume 5: Communication of the New Philosophy (22 minutes)

Volume 6: Application of the New Philosophy (24 minutes)

Britannica Films
780 Lapeer Road
Lake Orion, MI 48035
(800) 554-6970
(313) 693-4232

The Change Masters and Change Master Companies, with Rosabeth Moss Kanter

AMA Film/Video
9 Galen Street
Watertown, MA 02172
(800) 225-3215
(617) 926-4600

Customer Service, Innovation, and Productivity Through People, with Robert Waterman

If Japan Can, Why Can't We? 77 minutes, NBC White Paper

Japan vs. U.S.A.—High Tech Shootout, 52 minutes, Films Incorporated for NBC Reports

Journey to the Future, Joel Arthur Barker, Chart House Learning Corp.

Juran On Quality Improvement, 16-tape series including workbook and leader's manual, and visual aids, Juran Institute

Juran On Quality Planning, 15-tape series including workbook, leader's manual, and visual aids, Juran Institute

Managing the Journey, Ken Blanchard, Films Inc.

Nashua Corporation Seminar—William Conway, 160 minutes, Nashua Corp. (Process Control)

On the Line, 37 minutes, King Arthur Productions for National Semiconductor (Productivity Improvement)

The Power of Vision, Joel Arthur Barker, Chart House Learning Corp.

Quality is Free, 23 minutes, Phil Crosby

Type Z: An Alternative Management Style, 105 minutes (film), Professor William Ouchi

Index

Q

R

S